Contents

The Battle with the Sea
colour section following
p.168

The Dutch Golden Age
colour section following
p.280

◀◀ Kinderdijk windmills ◀ Seven Bridges, Amsterdam

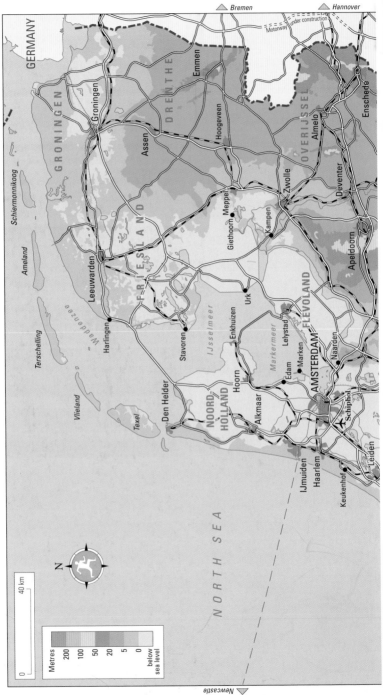

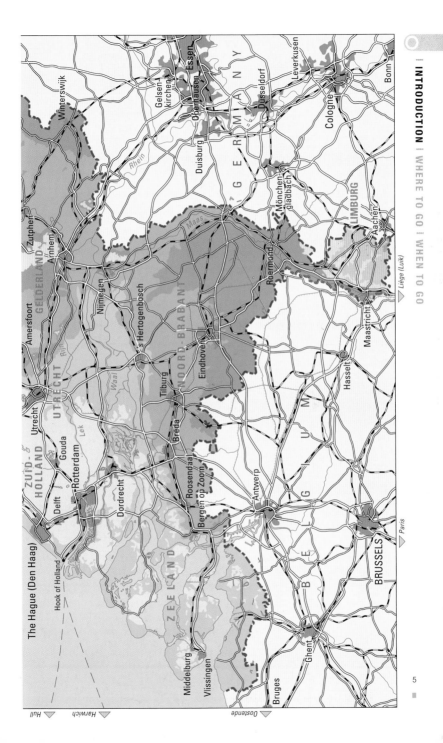

Introduction to

The Netherlands

The Netherlands is a country in part reclaimed from the blue-black waters of the North Sea, an artificially created land, around half of which lies at or below sea level. It's a country of unique and resonant images – the fertile, pancake-flat landscapes gridded with canals and interrupted by windmills and church spires, all beneath huge, open skies. Every city in the country has its ornately gabled town houses, the greatest and most noble in Amsterdam, while the bulbfields provide bold splashes of colour in springtime; in the west the long coastline is marked by mile upon mile of protective dune, backing onto wide stretches of pristine, sandy beach.

A major colonial power, the Dutch mercantile fleet once challenged the English for world naval supremacy, and throughout its seventeenth-century Golden Age, the standard of living (for the majority at least) was second to none. There have been a few economic ups and downs since then, but today the Netherlands is one of the most developed countries in the world, small and urban, with the highest population density in Europe, its sixteen million inhabitants concentrated into an area about the size of the US state of Maine. It's an international, well-integrated place too: many people speak English, at least in the heavily populated west of the country; and most of the country is easy to reach on a public transport system of trains and buses, whose efficiency may make British and American visitors weep with envy.

Successive Dutch governments have steered towards political consensus – indeed, this has been the drift since the Reformation, when the competing pillars of Dutch society (originally the Calvinists and the Catholics) learnt to live with – or ignore – each other, aided by the fact that trading wealth was lubricating the whole social structure. Almost by accident, therefore, Dutch society became tolerant and, in its enthusiasm to blunt

▲ Delft

conflict, progressive. These days, many insiders opine that the motive behind liberal Dutch attitudes towards drug use and prostitution isn't freewheeling permissiveness so much as apathy, and the country's avowed multiculturalism has been severely tested of late, with the shooting of Theo Van Gogh, as well as various racially motivated attacks, persuading many to reassess the success of the Netherlands' consensual politics.

Where to go

Mention you're going to the Netherlands and everyone will immediately assume you're going to **Amsterdam**. Indeed for such a small and accessible

Jan Vermeer

Little is known for certain about the artist Jan Vermeer (1632–75), though it is likely he lived all his life in Delft, where he was a prominent member of the painters' guild. Neither is it clear quite why his surviving oeuvre is so limited – only around 35 paintings are now attributed to him – though it's likely his paintings proved hard to sell and that he therefore had to work as an innkeeper and picture dealer to feed his large family (he had eleven children). Vermeer's painting career divides into three distinct phases and it's from the middle period that his most celebrated works come, when he adopted the compositional simplicity that was to prove so extraordinarily popular a couple of hundred years after his death: smooth and finely detailed canvases on which the predominant colours are yellow, blue and grey. Look out for examples of his work at the Rijksmuseum in Amsterdam (see p.98), including *The Kitchen Maid*, pictured, and the Mauritshuis in Den Haag (see p.176).

country, the Netherlands is, apart from Amsterdam, relatively unknown territory. Some people may confess to a brief visit to Rotterdam or Den Haag (The Hague), but for most visitors Amsterdam *is* the Netherlands,

the assumption being that there's nothing remotely worth seeing elsewhere – a prejudice shared, incidentally, by many Amsterdammers. To accept this is to miss much, but there's no doubt that the capital has more cosmopolitan dash than any other Dutch city, both in its restaurant and bar scene and in the pre-eminence of its three great attractions. These are the Anne Frank Huis, where the young Jewish diarist hid away during the World War II Nazi occupation; the Rijksmuseum, with its wonderful collection of Dutch paintings, including several of Rembrandt's finest works; and the peerless Van Gogh Museum, with the world's largest collection of the artist's work.

In the west of the country, beyond Amsterdam, the provinces of **Noord-** and **Zuid-Holland** are for the most part unrelentingly flat, reflecting centuries of careful reclamation work as the Dutch have slowly pushed back the sea. These provinces are predominantly urban, especially Zuid-Holland, which is home to a grouping of towns known collectively as the Randstad (literally "rim town"), an urban sprawl that holds all the country's largest cities and the majority of its population. Travelling in this part of the country is easy, with trains and buses that are fast, inexpensive and efficient; highlights

include amenable **Haarlem**, with its fine Frans Hals Museum – and pleasant coast around **Bloemendaal**; the old university town of **Leiden**; **Delft**, with its attractive medieval buildings and diminutive, canal-girded centre; and the gritty port city of **Rotterdam**, reborn, revitalized and festooned with prestigious modern architecture. **Den Haag (The Hague)**, is well worth a visit, too, a laidback and relaxing city, seat of the Dutch government and home to several fine museums, most memorably the Mauritshuis with

▼ Utrecht

Dutch herring

The Dutch love their herring, eaten every which way, but usually raw, on a bread roll and garnished with onions. Best of all, however, is to catch sight of occasional intrepid herring-eaters, tilting their head back and lowering a whole fish into their mouth from on high with considerable skill. The herring season starts in late May and there's a fair old frenzy to get hold of the new season's fish. The Dutch herring fleet is a shadow of its former self, numbering just 25 large ships, but the first vessel back to port with the May catch gives a barrel of herring to Queen Beatrix and receives a prize of €1500 – which the captain donates to Greenpeace.

▲ Texel island

its wonderful collection of Golden Age paintings. Neither should you miss the **Keukenhof gardens**, with the finest and most extensive bulbfields in the country. To the north of Amsterdam, the old Zuider Zee ports of **Enkhuizen** and **Hoorn** are very enticing, as is the small town of **Alkmaar**, with its touristy cheese market, and the small villages and unspoilt dunescapes of the **coast** – themes that are continued on the lovely island of **Texel**, further north.

Beyond lies a quieter, more rural country, especially in the far north where a chain of low-lying islands – the **Frisian Islands** – separates the open North Sea from the coast-hugging Waddenzee. Prime resort territory, the islands possess a blustery, bucolic charm all of their own, and thousands of Dutch families come here every summer for their holidays. Apart from Texel, the

islands lie offshore from the coast of the province of **Friesland**, named after the Germanic Frisians who first settled the region and whose language is still spoken by some of the locals. Friesland's capital, **Leeuwarden**, is a likeable, eminently visitable city, and neighbouring **Groningen** is one of the country's busiest cultural centres, given verve by its large student population. To the south, the provinces of Overijssel and Gelderland are dotted with charming old towns, most notably **Deventer** and **Zutphen**, while their eastern portions herald the Netherlands' first few geophysical bumps as the landscape rolls up towards the German frontier. Here also are two diverting towns – **Arnhem**, much rebuilt after its notorious World War II battle,

▲ Breda cathedral

but a hop and a skip from the open heaths of the **Hoge Veluwe National Park**, and the lively college town of **Nijmegen**. Further south still are the predominantly Catholic provinces of Limburg, Noord-Brabant and Zeeland. The last of these is well named (literally "Sealand"), made up of a series of low-lying islands connected by road and protected from the encroaching waters of the North Sea by one of the country's most ambitious engineering plans, the **Delta Project**. Heading east from here, you reach Noord-Brabant, gently rolling scrub and farmland which centres on the historic cities of **Breda** and **'s Hertogenbosch**, the latter with a famous cathedral,

and, not least, the modern manufacturing hub of **Eindhoven**, home to the electronics giant Philips. The province of Limburg occupies the slim scythe of land that reaches down between the Belgian and German borders. Its landscape, in the south at least, is truly hilly, and it has in its cosmopolitan capital, **Maastricht**, one of the Netherlands' most convivial cities.

When to go

The Netherlands enjoys a temperate **climate**, with relatively mild summers and moderately cold winters. Generally speaking, temperatures rise the further south you go, with the south of the country perhaps a couple of degrees warmer than the

◄ Amsterdam

CHRISTOPHE

north and east for much of the year. This is offset by the prevailing westerlies that sweep in from the North Sea, making the wetter coastal provinces both warmer in winter and colder in summer than the eastern provinces, where the more severe climate of continental Europe has an influence. As far as rain is concerned, be prepared for it at any time of year.

Average daily temperatures and rainfall

	Jan	Feb	Mar	Apr	May	Jun	July	Aug	Sep	Oct	Nov	Dec
Amsterdam												
Av min °C	1	0	2	4	8	10	13	12	10	7	4	2
Av max °C	5	6	9	12	17	19	21	22	18	14	9	7
Rainfall, mm	62	43	59	41	48	68	66	61	82	85	89	75
Sun, hrs/day	2	3	4	6	7	7	7	7	4	3	2	1
Enschede												
Av min °C	-1	-1	2	3	7	10	12	11	9	6	3	1
Av max °C	4	5	9	13	17	20	22	22	18	14	8	6
Rainfall, mm	71	43	66	46	56	74	69	60	66	64	67	77
Sun, hrs/day	2	3	3	5	6	6	6	6	4	3	2	1
Leeuwarden												
Av min °C	0	0	2	3	7	10	12	12	10	7	3	1
Av max °C	5	5	8	11	16	18	20	21	18	13	9	6
Rainfall, mm	66	42	59	39	51	69	64	60	82	78	84	73
Sun, hrs/day	2	3	4	6	7	7	7	6	4	3	2	1
Maastricht												
Av min °C	0	0	2	4	8	11	13	13	10	7	3	1
Av max °C	5	6	10	13	18	20	23	23	19	14	9	6
Rainfall, mm	61	51	61	46	64	74	67	58	60	63	66	70
Sun, hrs/day	2	3	4	5	6	6	6	6	4	4	2	1
Rotterdam												
Av min °C	1	0	2	4	7	10	13	12	10	7	4	2
Av max °C	6	6	10	13	17	19	22	22	19	14	9	7
Rainfall, mm	67	47	65	41	52	72	68	66	82	90	86	80
Sun, hrs/day	2	3	4	5	7	6	7	6	4	3	2	1

things not to miss

It's not possible to see everything that the Netherlands has to offer in one trip – and we don't suggest you try. What follows is a selective and subjective taste of the country's highlights, in no particular order: cosmopolitan cities, peaceful villages, memorable landscapes and outstanding museums. They're arranged in five colour-coded categories to help you find the very best things to see, do and experience. All entries have a page reference to take you straight into the guide, where you can find out more.

01 Amsterdam Page **57** • There's plenty to see in the Netherlands apart from Amsterdam, but it would be a strange trip that missed out this picturesque capital altogether.

02 **St Janskerk, Gouda** Page **200** • Gouda is an archetypal country town of canals and fancy gables, whose church has a wonderful set of stained-glass windows.

04 **Dutch cheeses** Page **39** • Balls of Edam and huge wheels of Gouda are the mainstays of the Dutch cheese industry, on sale everywhere at different grades of maturity and quite unlike the bland, rubbery creations sold abroad.

03 **Cannabis coffeeshops** Page **47** • Every Dutch city – and a fair few smaller towns as well – has a choice of "coffeeshops", where you can buy and smoke marijuana and hash. Many are tourist-oriented dives, but there are plenty of congenial, attractive places to sit back and enjoy a spliff or two.

05 **The Elfstedentocht** Page **42** • Watch, or even better join in with, the speed-skaters of Friesland as they tear round the province's canals in this infrequently staged open-air race.

06 **Delft** Page **184** • Eulogized by Vermeer, Delft's centre is particularly handsome, and its market square is one of the country's best.

07 Queen's Day Page **42** • Every April 30, the whole country, especially Amsterdam, goes nuts, ostensibly to celebrate the birthday of Queen Juliana, the current monarch's mother: there's live music, street-partying, parades and unregulated trading, as everyone empties out their attic to sell their accumulated junk on the streets.

08 Anne Frank Huis, Amsterdam Page **83** • A poignant and personal evocation of the Nazi persecution of the Jews. The photo shows the bookcase behind which the Frank family hid for two years.

10 's Hertogenbosch Page **328** • This lively market town features an intricate old quarter of canals and picturesque bridges, plus a stunning cathedral.

09 Cycling Page **35** • No country in Europe is so kindly disposed towards the bicycle than the pancake-flat Netherlands: you'll find bike paths in and around all towns, plus long-distance touring routes taking you deep into the countryside.

12 Kröller-Müller Museum
Page **296** • This superb art museum and sculpture garden is set in the heart of the Hoge Veluwe National Park.

11 Indonesian food Page **40** •
Thanks to the Netherlands' colonial adventures in Southeast Asia, restaurants around the country prepare some of the finest Indonesian cuisine outside Indonesia.

13 Delta Project and Expo Page **318** • The series of huge dykes and flood-barriers in the far-flung western province of Zeeland, which bear witness to the country's long battle to hold the sea at bay, are celebrated in an adjacent exhibition hall.

14 **Hoge Veluwe National Park** Page **295** • A richly forested swathe of dunes and woodland in the middle of the country. Cycle your way around thanks to a fleet of free-to-use white bicycles.

15 **Rijksmuseum, Amsterdam** Page **98** • Grand museum with a superb collection of seventeenth-century Dutch paintings, including several of Rembrandt's key works.

16 **Maastricht** Page **341** • This atmospheric, laidback city in the far south, squeezed between the porous Belgian and German borders, offers a worldly outlook and a superb old quarter.

17 **Coastal dunes** Page **153** • The Dutch have protected long stretches of their coast from the developers, one result being great tracts of pristine dune, ideal for a day's stroll and picnic.

18 Keukenhof gardens Page **169** • Some seven million flowers are on show here in these extensive gardens, which specialize in daffodils, narcissi, hyacinths and – of course – tulips.

19 IJsselmeer Page **142** • This beautiful inland lake, formerly the Zuider Zee, lies at the heart of the Netherlands and is the country at its watery best, with charming old ports like Hoorn and Enkhuizen and former islands like Urk to explore.

20 **The Biesbosch** Page **207** • As an escape from Dutch urban life, the reedy marshes and lagoons of the Biesbosch are hard to beat.

21 **Den Haag (The Hague)** Page **171** • Den Haag has a reputation for dourness that is completely undeserved, boasting a first-rate restaurant scene, smart hotels and enough prime museums to exhaust even the most energetic sightseer.

22 **Frisian Islands** Page **232** • Of the string of wild and windswept holiday islands off the northern Dutch coast, Terschelling is the most popular, a fine spot for walks and bike-rides amid the dunes.

23 **Van Gogh Museum, Amsterdam** Page **98** • Quite simply the best and most comprehensive collection of Van Gogh's work anywhere.

24 **Wadlopen** Page **256** • One novel way of getting to the Frisian Islands is to try guided *wadlopen* or "mud-walking" from the mainland at high tide.

26 **Bars** Page **40** • Drinking your way around the Netherlands isn't such a bad way of passing the time, with everything from stylish bars to cosy and relaxing brown cafés – so named for their tobacco-stained walls – to choose from. *Proost!*

25 **Frans Hals Museum, Haarlem** Page **129** • Often neglected, Hals was one of the finest of the Golden Age painters, his later canvases acutely dark and broody.

Basics

Basics

Getting there

Amsterdam is a major international air travel hub, served by dozens of short- and long-haul airlines, and there are smaller airports at Maastricht, Eindhoven and Rotterdam. However, travelling by train through the Channel Tunnel, is just as easy; it's not much cheaper than flying but is perhaps better if you're heading for the south of the country. Bus travel is probably the most affordable option of all and deals for drivers on ferry routes into Dutch and Belgian ports are particularly competitive.

Flights from the UK and Ireland

Flights to any of the major airports in the Netherlands – Amsterdam Schiphol (pronounced skip-oll), Rotterdam, Eindhoven or Maastricht – take roughly an hour from London, or ninety minutes from Scotland and the north of England. **Amsterdam** is one of the UK's most popular short-haul destinations, and you'll find loads of choice – in carriers, flight times and departure airports. Aside from the major full-service carriers (KLM, British Airways and BMI), there are plenty of no-frills airlines operating to Amsterdam, including easyJet, BMIbaby and Thomsonfly, as well as a few business-oriented small carriers such as VLM. You'll find plenty of choice of daily flights out of London – Heathrow, Gatwick, Stansted, Luton and London City – plus nonstop flights from loads of other airports, including Birmingham, Bournemouth, East Midlands, Cardiff, Coventry, Southampton, Norwich, Liverpool, Manchester, Leeds–Bradford, Doncaster–Sheffield, Humberside, Newcastle, Teesside, Edinburgh, Glasgow and Aberdeen.

To **Rotterdam**, you've a choice of KLM from Heathrow, the Belgian airline VLM from London City and Manchester, and BA from Gatwick or Birmingham. **Eindhoven** is well connected, with flights from Heathrow (on KLM, via Amsterdam) and Stansted (on KLM and Ryanair). **Maastricht** is served daily from Stansted by KLM and Ryanair. Since these flights to Eindhoven, Rotterdam and Maastricht are targeted at business travellers, expect early-morning departure times and higher flight frequency during the week.

Whichever route you choose, it's hard to say precisely what you'll **pay** at any given time: it depends so much on when you book and when you fly, what offers are available, and how lucky you get. However, flying to any Dutch city with one of the low-cost airlines between April and September you'll pay around £100 return travelling at convenient times at the weekend, including taxes, £150 with one of the full-service carriers. Weekday travel will cost £50–60 with a budget carrier, and maybe £100 or so with a full-service airline. Of course if you want more flexibility with your ticket you'll pay more, as you will if you book at the last minute – economy return tickets from London to Amsterdam can cost anything up to £400. All carriers offer their lowest prices online, rather than with phone booking.

Flying to the Netherlands from **Northern Ireland**, the easiest option is with easyJet out of Belfast International to Amsterdam. From the **Republic of Ireland**, Aer Lingus flies six times daily to Amsterdam out of Dublin and twice daily from Cork, for a minimum €175–200 return, depending on the season, up to €450 or more.

Flights from the US and Canada

Amsterdam's Schiphol airport is among the most popular and least expensive gateways to Europe from North America, and getting a convenient and good-value flight is rarely a problem. Virtually every region of the US and Canada is well served by the major airlines: KLM/Northwest, Continental, Singapore Airways and Delta all offer nonstop flights. Many more fly via London and other European centres – and are nearly always cheaper because of it.

KLM and Northwest, which operate a joint service, offer the widest range of flights, with direct or one-stop flights to Amsterdam from eleven US cities, and connections from dozens more. From elsewhere in the US, the Dutch charter firm Martinair flies year round from Miami and Orlando direct to Amsterdam. Singapore Airlines and United also fly direct to Amsterdam from Chicago, while Delta operates from Atlanta and Continental from Houston. Booking far enough in advance, you should be able to find a **fare** between April and September for $600–800 return from New York (flight time 8hr 10min), $800 from Atlanta (10hr), and around $1000 from Chicago or LA, though booking less than a couple of weeks in advance can push these prices up to well over $1000.

From Canada, KLM flies year-round direct to Amsterdam from Vancouver (9hr 45min) and from Toronto (7hr 10min). Between April and October, Martinair flies from Toronto, Vancouver, Edmonton and Calgary. There are also plenty of one-stop options via Frankfurt, London and Paris. Fares from Toronto go for around Can$1200, from Vancouver around Can$1500.

Flights from Australia and New Zealand

There's no shortage of flights to the Netherlands from Australia and New Zealand, though all of them involve at least one stop. Singapore Airways and Malaysian offer the most direct routes out of Sydney (stopping in Singapore and Kuala Lumpur respectively). Thai, Austrian and Qantas all have two stops (Bangkok/Frankfurt, Kuala Lumpur/Vienna and Singapore/Frankfurt). One further option is to pick up a cheap ticket to London, and then continue your journey to Amsterdam with one of the no-frills budget airlines. For a discounted ticket to Amsterdam from Sydney, Melbourne or Auckland, you can expect to pay A$2000/ NZ$ 2500.

Airlines and agents

Online booking

ⓦ www.expedia.co.uk (UK), ⓦ www.expedia.com (US), ⓦ www.expedia.ca (Canada)
ⓦ www.lastminute.com (UK)
ⓦ www.opodo.co.uk (UK)
ⓦ www.orbitz.com (US)
ⓦ www.travelocity.co.uk (UK), ⓦ www.travelocity.com (US), ⓦ www.travelocity.ca (Canada) ⓦ www.zuji.com.au (Australia), ⓦ www.zuji.co.nz (New Zealand)

Airlines

Aer Lingus Republic of Ireland ☏ 0818/365 000, ⓦ www.aerlingus.ie
Air Canada ☏ 1-888/247-2262, ⓦ www.aircanada.ca
Air France US ☏ 1-800/237-2747, ⓦ www.airfrance.com; Canada ☏ 1-800/667-2747, ⓦ www.airfrance.ca
Air New Zealand Australia ☏ 132 476, New Zealand ☏ 0800/737 000, ⓦ www.airnz.co.nz
American Airlines ☏ 1-800-433-7300, ⓦ www.aa.com
BMI UK ☏ 0870/607 0555 or ☏ 0870/607 0222, Ireland ☏ 01/407 3036, US ☏ 1-800/788-0555, ⓦ www.flybmi.com
bmibaby UK ☏ 0871/224 0224, Republic of Ireland ☏ 1890/340 122, ⓦ www.bmibaby.com
British Airways UK ☏ 0870/850 9850, Republic of Ireland ☏ 1890/626 747, US & Canada ☏ 1-800/AIRWAYS, Australia ☏ 1300/767 177, New Zealand ☏ 09/966 9777, ⓦ www.ba.com
Cathay Pacific Australia ☏ 131 747, New Zealand ☏ 09/379 0861, ⓦ www.cathaypacific.com
Continental Airlines US & Canada ☏ 1-800/523-3273, ⓦ www.continental.com
Delta US & Canada ☏ 1-800/221-1212, ⓦ www.delta.com
easyJet UK ☏ 0905/821 0905, Republic of Ireland ☏ 0870/600 0000, ⓦ www.easyjet.com
KLM (Royal Dutch Airlines) / Northwest/KLM UK ☏ 0870/507 4074, Republic of Ireland ☏ 1850/747 400, Australia ☏ 1300/303 747, New Zealand ☏ 09/921 6040, SA ☏ 11/961 6767, ⓦ www.klm.com; US ☏ 1-800/225-2525, ⓦ www.nwa.com
Malaysia Airlines Australia ☏ 132 627, New Zealand ☏ 0800/777 747, ⓦ www.malaysia-airlines.com
Martinair US ☏ 1-800/627-8462, Canada ☏ 1-416/364-3672, ⓦ www.martinair.com
Qantas Australia ☏ 131 313, ⓦ www.qantas.com; New Zealand ☏ 0800/808 767 or 09/357 8900, ⓦ www.qantas.co.nz

Ryanair UK ☎ 0871/246 0000, Republic of Ireland ☎ 0818/303 030, Ⓦ www.ryanair.com
Scot Airways UK ☎ 0870/606 0707, Ⓦ www .scotairways.com
Singapore Airlines US ☎ 1-800/742-3333, Canada ☎ 1-800/663 3046, Australia ☎ 13 10 11, New Zealand ☎ 0800/808 909, Ⓦ www .singaporeair.com
Thai Airways Australia ☎ 1300/651 960, New Zealand ☎ 09/377 3886, Ⓦ www.thaiair.com
Thomsonfly UK ☎ 0870/1900 737, Ⓦ www .thomsonfly.com
United Airlines US ☎ 1-800/UNITED-1, Ⓦ www .united.com
VLM Airlines UK ☎ 020/7646 0757, Ⓦ www .flyvlm.com

By train from the UK

The simplest and quickest way to go by train is to take the **Eurostar** service from London nonstop to Brussels (2hr 15–30min), from where there are numerous services to many points in the Netherlands. The encyclopedic Dutch Railways website Ⓦ www.ns.nl can give full timetable details (in English) of trains from a variety of stations in the UK to any station in the Netherlands, including ferry times.

Eurostar trains arrive at Bruxelles–Midi station (Brussel-Zuid in Dutch), from where plenty of fast trains – including Thalys high-speed services (Ⓦ www.thalys.com) – head on to Rotterdam (1hr 45min), the Hague (2hr) and Amsterdam (around 2hr 45min). The total journey time from London is six hours, give or take fifteen minutes, and Eurostar can arrange a through ticket from any point in the UK to any point in the Netherlands. A standard return fare to Amsterdam, with some flexibility, costs around £150. But special deals and bargains are commonplace, especially in the low season; and you can also sometimes reduce costs by accepting certain ticketing restrictions.

A longer, cheaper rail-and-ferry route, the **Dutchflyer**, is available through Stena Line in conjunction with Anglia Railways. The journey operates twice daily (morning and late afternoon) from London's Liverpool Street station to Harwich (1hr 40min) and connects with the rapid ferry crossing to the Hook of Holland, or Hoek van Holland (3hr 40min), from where fast trains head on to Rotterdam (35min), The Hague (50min) and Amsterdam (1hr 35min). Total journey time from London is around eight hours. Prices from London start at £50 return for an Apex fare, which must be booked at least a week in advance, with the return journey being made within one month. A standard open return costs £90, or £72 with a young person's railcard. Tickets are available from Anglia Railways and larger mainline stations, or you can book online with Dutchflyer direct.

If you're visiting the Netherlands as part of a longer European trip, it may be worth considering a **pan-European rail pass**. There are lots to choose from and **Rail Europe** (Ⓦ www.raileurope.com), the umbrella company for all national and international passes, operates a comprehensive website detailing all the options, with prices. Note in particular that some passes have to be bought before leaving home, others can only be bought in specific countries. For train travel within the Netherlands, see p.31.

Train contacts

Dutchflyer UK ☎ 08705/455 455, Ⓦ www .dutchflyer.co.uk
Eurostar UK ☎ 0870/518 6186, Ⓦ www.eurostar .com
European Rail UK ☎ 020/7387 0444, Ⓦ www .europeanrail.com
International Rail ☎ 0870/084 1414, Ⓦ www .international-rail.com
Rail Europe ☎ 0870/837 1371, Ⓦ www .raileurope.co.uk
Trainseurope ☎ 0900/195 0101, Ⓦ www .trainseurope.co.uk

Driving from the UK

To reach the Netherlands by **car** or **motorbike**, you can either use the ferries or – preferable for its simplicity and hassle-free crossing – Eurotunnel's shuttle-train through the Channel Tunnel. Note that Eurotunnel only carries cars (including occupants) and motorbikes; cyclists and foot passengers must travel by ferry instead.

Eurotunnel

Amsterdam is roughly 370km from the Eurotunnel exit in Calais, Rotterdam 200km, Arnhem 260km. There are up to four shuttle trains per hour (only 1 per hour midnight–6am), taking 35min (45min for some night

Fly less – stay longer! Travel and climate change

Climate change is the single biggest issue facing our planet. It is caused by a build-up in the atmosphere of carbon dioxide and other greenhouse gases, which are emitted by many sources – including planes. Already, flights account for around 3–4 per cent of human-induced global warming: that figure may sound small, but it is rising year on year and threatens to counteract the progress made by reducing greenhouse emissions in other areas.

Rough Guides regard travel, overall, as a global benefit, and feel strongly that the advantages to developing economies are important, as are the opportunities for greater contact and awareness among peoples. But we all have a responsibility to limit our personal "carbon footprint". That means giving thought to how often we fly and what we can do to redress the harm that our trips create.

Flying and climate change

Pretty much every form of motorized travel generates CO_2, but planes are particularly bad offenders, releasing large volumes of greenhouse gases at altitudes where their impact is far more harmful. Flying also allows us to travel much further than we would contemplate doing by road or rail, so the emissions attributable to each passenger become truly shocking. For example, one person taking a return flight between Europe and California produces the equivalent impact of 2.5 tonnes of CO_2 – similar to the yearly output of the average UK car.

Less harmful planes may evolve but it will be decades before they replace the current fleet – which could be too late for avoiding climate chaos. In the meantime, there are limited options for concerned travellers: to reduce the amount we travel by air (take fewer trips, stay longer!), to avoid night flights (when plane contrails trap heat from Earth but can't reflect sunlight back to space), and to make the trips we do take "climate neutral" via a carbon offset scheme.

Carbon offset schemes

Offset schemes run by **climatecare.org**, **carbonneutral.com** and others allow you to "neutralize" the greenhouse gases that you are responsible for releasing. Their websites have simple calculators that let you work out the impact of any flight. Once that's done, you can pay to fund projects that will reduce future carbon emissions by an equivalent amount (such as the distribution of low-energy lightbulbs and cooking stoves in developing countries). Please take the time to visit our website and make your trip climate neutral.

www.roughguides.com/climatechange

departure times); you must check in at Folkstone at least 30min before departure. It's possible to turn up and buy your ticket at the toll booths (exit the M20 at junction 11a), though at busy times booking is advisable. Fares depend on the time of year, time of day and length of stay (the cheapest ticket is for a day-trip, followed by a five-day return); it's cheaper to travel between 10pm and 6am, while the highest fares are reserved for weekend departures and returns in July and August. Prices are charged per vehicle: short-stay savers between April and October for a car start at around £110. If you wish to stay more than five days, a standard return

costs from around £130, while a more flexible "Flexiplus" fare, which entitles you to change your plans at the last minute, costs more still. Some special offers are usually also available.

Ferries

Three operators run ferries from the UK direct to ports in the Netherlands, and all offer year-round services. Tariffs vary enormously, depending on when you leave, how long you stay, if you're taking a car, what size it is and how many passengers are in it. There are discounts for students and under-26s, though these will involve some travel restrictions. The fastest route is with **Stena Line**, which sails from Harwich in Essex to the Hook of Holland; journey times are 6 hours 15 minutes, but you can take a super-fast daytime service which does the journey in just 3hr 40min; travelling at night always takes longer and you have to book a cabin. **P&O North Sea Ferries** operates from Hull to Rotterdam (11hr). **DFDS Seaways** sails once daily from Newcastle (North Shields) to IJmuiden near Amsterdam (14hr).

Aside from these options direct to Dutch ports, you might want to consider the ferry routes to Belgium and France. P&O sails once a day from Hull to Zeebrugge in Belgium (14hr 30min), while Norfolkline operates a year-round service from Dover to the French border town of Dunkerque (2hr).

Ferry companies

DFDS Seaways UK ☎0870/252 0524, ⊛www .dfdsseaways.co.uk
Eurotunnel UK ☎0870/535 3535, ⊛www .eurotunnel.com
Norfolkline UK ☎0870/870 1020, ⊛www .norfolkline.com

P&O Ferries UK ☎0870/598 0333, ⊛www .poferries.com
Stena Line UK ☎0870/570 7070, Northern Ireland ☎0870/520 4204, Republic of Ireland ☎021/427 2965, ⊛www.stenaline.co.uk

By bus from the UK

Travelling by long-distance bus is generally the cheapest way of reaching the Netherlands from the UK, but it is very time-consuming: the main route, London to Amsterdam, takes twelve hours or more. **Eurolines** (☎0870/580 8080, ⊛www.nationalexpress .com/eurolines) operates three services daily (8am, 8pm & 10pm) from London to Amsterdam, all using Eurotunnel. A standard fare is £52 return (under-26s and over-60s pay £49), though promotional return fares can be snapped up for much less. The lesser-known **Anglia Lines** (☎0870/608 8806, ⊛www .anglia-lines.co.uk) operates a daily coach service between London Victoria and central Amsterdam, via Brussels, which leaves once daily at 2.30pm and costs just £38 return (£34 if you're under 26) if booked seven days in advance. It takes around nine hours.

Getting around

Getting around is never a problem in the Netherlands: it's a small country, and the longest journey you'll ever make – say from Amsterdam to Maastricht – takes under three hours by train or car. Furthermore, the public transport system is exemplary, a fully integrated network of trains and buses that brings even the smallest of villages within easy reach, and at very reasonable prices too. Train and bus stations are almost always next door to each other, and several of the larger cities also have a tram network.

By train

The best way of travelling around the Netherlands is to take the **train**. The system, run by **Nederlandse Spoorwegen** (NS – Dutch Railways; ☎0900 9292, premium line from within the Netherlands; ⊛www.ns.nl), is one of the best in Europe: trains are fast, modern, frequent and very punctual; fares

are relatively low; and the network of lines comprehensive. Domestic services come in three main types: the speedy **Intercity** for city-to-city connections; the normal **Sneltrein**, which stops at main towns; and the snail-like **Stoptrein**, which stops at every station. Ordinary **fares** are calculated by the kilometre, diminishing proportionally the further you travel: reckon on spending about

€4 to travel 25km or so. For a one-way ticket, ask for an *enkele reis*; a return trip is a *retour*. Same-day return tickets (*dagretour*) knock about ten percent off the price of one-way tickets for the same journey, but otherwise returns are normally double the price of singles. First-class fares cost about fifty percent on top of the regular fare. With any ticket, you're free to stop off anywhere en route and continue your journey later that day, but you're not allowed to backtrack. NS publishes a comprehensive and easy-to-use **timetable** (*spoorboekje*), which is available for €5.50 at all major stations, as well as mounds of information on its various services, passes and fares. Note, however, that you are not allowed to buy a ticket on the train and you cannot pay for a train ticket with a foreign debit card or, in most instances, a credit card.

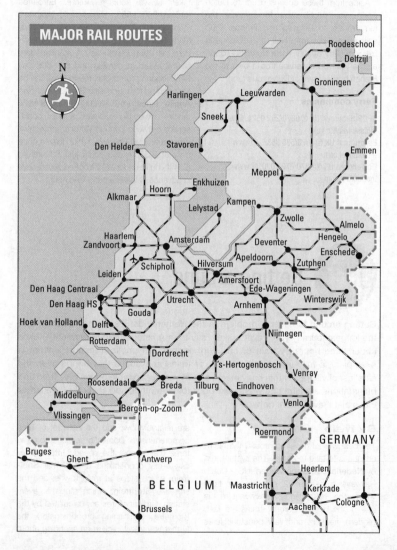

MAJOR RAIL ROUTES

N

Roodeschool
Delfzijl
Groningen
Harlingen
Leeuwarden
Sneek
Den Helder
Stavoren
Emmen
Meppel
Enkhuizen
Hoorn
Alkmaar
Kampen
Lelystad
Zwolle
Almelo
Haarlem
Hengelo
Zandvoort
Amsterdam
Deventer
Enschede
Schiphol
Hilversum
Apeldoorn
Zutphen
Leiden
Amersfoort
Den Haag Centraal
Ede-Wageningen
Winterswijk
Den Haag HS
Utrecht
Arnhem
Gouda
Hoek van Holland
Delft
Nijmegen
Rotterdam
Dordrecht
's-Hertogenbosch
Venray
Roosendaal
Breda
Tilburg
Eindhoven
Middelburg
Venlo
Bergen-op-Zoom
Vlissingen
Roermond
GERMANY
Bruges
Ghent
Antwerp
Heerlen
BELGIUM
Maastricht
Kerkrade
Cologne
Brussels
Aachen

Planning a journey

For pre-departure information on your train journey, the "**Planner Plus**" feature on the Dutch railways website (🖥 www.ns.nl) is hard to beat. Type in your departure and arrival points (train station, street address or even just the name of a museum or concert hall), and it will not only give you a street map to get to the nearest station, but will also tell you what platform your train leaves from, how many changes to make (and where, with platform numbers), and how much your ticket will cost. It even tells you how long your journey will take, factoring in how you get to and from the train station at either end – on foot, by bike, or on the bus.

Treintaxis

In NS's **treintaxi** scheme, rail passengers can be assured of a taxi to or from over 40 major stations. To get to the station at the start of your journey, call the local *treintaxi* number or ☎0900/873 4682 (premium line, only within the Netherlands), at least half an hour in advance; within the relevant city limits, the fare is a flat-rate €4.20. On arrival at the local station, you can either book a *treintaxi* at your destination station when you buy your ticket, or wait till you get there and pay the taxi driver. Most major stations have *treintaxi* buttons at the entrance, which you press to summon a *treintaxi* for your onward journey (within the city limits). Note that *treintaxis* are not the same as regular taxis – you may well, for instance, have to share with other people taking a similar route. The cabs are identifiable by a "*treintaxi*" sign on the roof and they have a separate rank outside train stations.

NS discount tickets and deals

NS offers a variety of **discount tickets and deals**, perhaps the most useful of which is the **Dagkaart** (Day Travel Card) for unlimited travel on any train in the system and costing just €40 in second-class; first-class is €65. The **Weekendretour** (Weekend Return) provides substantial discounts on weekend travel (up to forty percent); the family-orientated **Railrunner** charges just €2 per journey for up to three children aged 4–11 travelling with an adult; and the **Vordeelurenabonnement** (Off-peak Discount Pass) costs €55 and gives a discount of forty percent on all off-peak journeys (Mon–Fri after 9am and on the weekend) to the pass holder and three companions for that day. For further information, consult NS's website.

In addition to these, there's a host of pan-European rail passes. Some have to be bought before leaving home while others can be bought only in specific countries; for further details, see p.29.

By bus and tram

Supplementing the train network are buses – run by a patchwork of local companies but again amazingly efficient and reaching into every rural nook and cranny. Ticketing is straightforward, using **strippenkaarts** (see box, on p.34), though some long-distance buses don't accept them and you must pay the driver direct instead. Bear in mind also that in more rural areas some bus services only operate when passengers have made advance bookings. Local timetables indicate where this applies; regional bus timetable books, costing around €3, are sold at train station bookshops and many VVVs.

Within major towns, urban public transport systems are extensive, inexpensive and frequent, which makes getting around straightforward and hassle-free; most bus and tram services run from 6am until about midnight and *strippenkaarts* are valid except on special night buses (1–5am). Urban "Park and Ride" or **Transferium** schemes are commonplace.

By car

For the most part, driving around the Netherlands is pretty much what you would hope: smooth, easy and quick. The country has a uniformly good road network, with most of the major towns linked by some kind of motorway or dual carriageway, though snarl-ups and jams are far from rare. Rules of the road are straightforward: you drive on the right, and **speed limits** are 50kph in built-up

33

Travelling on a strippenkaart

Ticketing for all buses in the Netherlands, plus city metros and trams, is organized on a universal, nationwide system. You need to buy just one kind of ticket wherever you are – a **strippenkaart**, a piece of card made out of strips. The whole country is divided up into zones; you need to cancel one strip on your *strippenkaart* for yourself plus one for each of the zones you travel through. On city trams and metro systems you cancel the *strippenkaart* yourself by folding it over to the right place and inserting it into the date-stamping machines provided – but note that you only need to stamp the last of the strips you need. On buses, you usually hand the *strippenkaart* to the driver, who will do the stamping for you. In larger towns and cities, two or three strips is enough to take you anywhere in the centre. You can buy 2- and 3-strip *strippenkaarts* at a premium from bus drivers (€1.60/2.40), or pick up the better-value 15-strip (€6.70) or 45-strip (€19.80) *strippenkaarts* in advance from train stations, tobacconists and local public transport offices.

One *strippenkaart* can be used by any number of people, provided that the requisite number of strips is cancelled for each person's journey. Similarly, strips can be carried over from one *strippenkaart* to another: if you've used up, say, 14 of your 15 strips, you can stamp the 15th strip on one card and the first strip on another, new card in order to travel.

areas, 80kph outside, 120kph on motorways – though some motorways have a speed limit of 100kph, indicated by small yellow signs on the side of the road. Drivers and front-seat passengers are required by law to wear seatbelts, and penalties for drunk driving are severe. There are no toll roads, and although fuel is very expensive, at around €1.60 per litre (diesel €1.3), the short distances mean this isn't too much of a factor.

Most foreign **driving licences** are honoured in the Netherlands, including all EU, US and Canadian ones. If you're bringing your own car, you must have adequate insurance, preferably including coverage for legal costs, and it's advisable to have an appropriate breakdown policy from your home motoring organization too.

Renting a car

All the major international car **rental agencies** are represented in the Netherlands and a scattering of contact details are given in the "Listings" section at the end of the Guide accounts of major towns. To rent a car, you'll have to be 21 or over (and have been driving for at least a year), and you'll need a credit card – though some local agencies will accept a hefty cash deposit instead. Rental **charges** are fairly high, beginning around €300 per week for unlimited mileage in the

smallest vehicle, but include collision damage waiver and vehicle (but not personal) insurance. To cut costs, watch for special deals offered by the bigger companies. If you go to a smaller, local company (of which there are many), you should proceed with care: in particular, check the policy for the excess applied to claims and ensure that it includes a collision damage waiver (applicable if an accident is your fault) as well as adequate levels of financial cover.

If you break down in a rented car, you'll get roadside assistance from the particular repair company the rental firm has contracted. The same principle works with your own vehicle's breakdown policy providing you have coverage abroad.

Car rental agencies

Alamo US ☎1-800/462-5266, ⓦwww.alamo.com
Avis UK ☎0870/606 0100, Republic of Ireland ☎021/428 1111, US ☎1-800/230-4898, Canada ☎1-800/272-5871, Australia ☎136 333 or 02/9353 9000, New Zealand ☎09/526 2847 or 0800/655 111, ⓦwww.avis.com
Budget US ☎1-800/527-0700, Canada ☎1-800/268-8900, UK ☎0870/156 5656, Australia ☎1300/362 848, New Zealand ☎0800/283 438, ⓦwww.budget.com
Europcar UK ☎0870/607 5000, Republic of Ireland ☎01/614 2800, US & Canada ☎1-877/940 6900, Australia ☎393/306 160, ⓦwww.europcar.com

Hertz UK ☎020/7026 0077, Republic of Ireland ☎01/870 5777, US & Canada ☎1-800/654-3131, New Zealand ☎0800/654 321, ⓦwww.hertz.com
Holiday Autos (part of the lastminute.com group) UK ☎0870/400 4461, Republic of Ireland ☎01/872 9366, Australia ☎299/394 433, ⓦwww.holidayautos.co.uk
National UK ☎0870/400 4581, US ☎1-800/CAR-RENT, Australia ☎0870/600 6666, New Zealand ☎03/366 5574, ⓦwww.nationalcar.com **SIXT**, Republic of Ireland ☎1850/206 088, UK ☎0800/4747 4227, US ☎1-877/347-3227, ⓦwww.e-sixt.com
Suncars UK ☎0870/500 5566, Republic of Ireland ☎1850/201 416, ⓦwww.suncars.com

Cycling

One great way to see the Netherlands, whether you're a keen cyclist or an idle pedaller, is to travel by **bike** (*fiets*): cycle-touring can be a short cut into Dutch culture and you can reach parts of the country – its beaches, forests and moorland – that might otherwise be inaccessible.

To the Dutch, the bicycle is both a utility and recreational mode of transport. The mostly flat landscape makes travelling by bike an almost effortless pursuit, although you can find yourself battling against a headwind powering a wind farm, or swallowed up in a shoal of cyclists commuting to work. The short distances involved make it possible to see most of the country with relative ease, using the nationwide system of well-marked **cycle paths**. A circular blue sign with a white bicycle on it indicates an obligatory cycle lane, separate from car traffic. Red lettering on signposts gives distances for fairly direct routes; lettering in green denotes a more scenic (and lengthy) mosey. Long-distance (LF) routes weave through the cities and countryside, often linking up to local historic loops and scenic trails. The Dutch as a nation are celebrated touring cyclists, and bookshops are packed with cycling books; however, for all but the longest trips the maps and route advice provided by most VVVs (see p.53) are fine.

If you're looking for a **place to stay** after a day in the saddle, the best advice is to visit a member of the Vrienden op de Fiets (see p.37), who for a modest fee (❶) will put you up for the night in their home and feed you a princely breakfast the next morning. Many hosts are wonderfully warm and hospitable, as well as experts on cycling in their own country (and often many others).

Cycle rental

You can **rent a bike** from all main train stations for €6.50 a day or €32.50 per week, plus a €50 deposit (€100 in larger centres). Most bikes are single-speed, though there are some 3-speeds to be had, and even mountain bikes in the hillier south. You'll also need some form of **ID**. The snag is that cycles must be returned to the station from which they were rented, making onward hops by rented bike impossible. Most bike shops rent bicycles out for around the same amount, and they may be more flexible on deposits – some may accept a passport in lieu of cash. Wherever you're intending to rent your bike from, in summer it's a good idea to reserve one in advance. It is possible to take your bike on trains, and the bike carriages have a clear cycle symbol on the exterior. You'll need to buy a flat-rate ticket (*dagkaart fiets*) for your bike, which is valid for the whole day. Space can be limited, despite the variety of ingeniously folding bikes favoured by locals, and because of this you won't be allowed on at all during the morning and evening rush hours (6.30–9am and 5.30–6pm), except in July and August.

Note that in the larger cities in particular, but really anywhere around the country, you should never, ever, leave your bike unlocked, even for a few minutes – bike stealing is a big deal here. Almost all train stations have somewhere you can store your bike safely for less than a euro.

Accommodation

Inevitably accommodation is one of the major expenses of a trip to the Netherlands – indeed, if you're after a degree of comfort and style, it's going to be the costliest item by far. There are, however, budget alternatives, principally private rooms (broadly bed and breakfast arranged via the local tourist office), campsites and a scattering of HI-registered hostels. During the summer and over holiday periods vacant rooms can be scarce, so it's wise to book ahead. In Amsterdam, room shortages are commonplace throughout the year, so advance booking is always required; hotel prices are about thirty percent higher here than in the rest of the country.

Hotels

All **hotels** in the Netherlands are graded on a star system. One-star and no-star hotels are rare, and prices for two-star establishments start at around €60 for a double room without private bath or shower; count on paying at least €80 if you want en-suite facilities. Three-star hotels cost upwards of about €80; for four- and five-star places you'll pay €125-plus. Generally, the stated price includes breakfast, except in the most expensive and the very cheapest of hotels.

You can book ahead easily by calling the hotel direct; English is almost always spoken. You can also contact the Netherlands Reservations Centre, the NRC (☏0299/689 114, ⓔinfo@hotelres.nl), which coordinates the website ⓦwww.hotelres.nl, where you can view availability and prices and make hotel and apartment bookings online. In the Netherlands itself, you can make advance bookings in person through any VVV tourist office for a nominal fee. Two other useful booking websites are ⓦwww.weekendcompany.nl and ⓦwww.weekendjeweg.nl.

Private rooms

One way of cutting costs is to use **private accommodation** – rooms in private homes that are let out to visitors on a bed and breakfast basis, sometimes known as pensions. Prices are quoted per person and are normally around €20–25 with breakfast usually included. You mostly have to go

---

Accommodation price codes

All the hotels listed in this guide have been graded according to the following price codes, which indicate the price for the cheapest double room available during high season. In the case of hostels we've given the code if they have double rooms; otherwise, we've stated the price per dorm bed in euros. Single rooms generally cost between sixty and eighty percent of the double-room rate. These codes are above all a guide to price, and aren't intended to indicate the level of facilities available. You'll also find that many bottom-end hotels have a mixture of rooms, some with en-suite facilities, some without; thus, an establishment graded, for example, as a ❸ may also have plenty of more comfortable rooms at ❹. Most hotels only charge the full quoted rates at the very busiest times, which means that you'll often pay less than the price quoted in this book; it's always worth asking if there is any discount available either by phone or online, where many of the best deals are posted.

❶ up to €75	❹ €125–150	❼ €200–250
❷ €75–100	❺ €150–175	❽ €250–300
❸ €100–125	❻ €175–200	❾ Over €300

through local VVVs to find private rooms; they will either give you a list to follow up independently or will book the accommodation themselves and levy a minimal booking fee. Not all VVVs are able to offer private rooms; generally you'll find them only in the larger towns and tourist centres and characteristically a good way from the centre. In some of the more popular tourist destinations the details of B&Bs are listed in tourist brochures.

Vrienden op de Fiets

If you're cycling or walking around the Netherlands, you will find the organization **Vrienden op de Fiets** (Friends of the Bicycle; ☎030/267 9070, ⓦwww.vriendenopdefiets .nl) is an absolute bargain. For an annual joining fee of €9, you'll be sent a book of almost two thousand addresses in the Netherlands where you can stay the night in somebody's home for a maximum of €16 per person; all you have to do is phone 24 hours in advance. Accommodation can range from stylish town houses to suburban semis to centuries-old farmhouses – you don't know until you turn up – and staying in somebody's home can give a great insight into Dutch life. Hosts are usually very friendly, offer local information about the area and will provide a breakfast of often mammoth proportions to send you on your way.

Hostels

If you're travelling on a budget, a **hostel** is likely to be your accommodation of choice, whether you're youthful or not. They can often be extremely good value, and offer clean and comfortable dorm beds as well as a choice of rooms (doubles and sometimes singles) at rock-bottom prices. Both city and country locations can get very full between June and September, when you should book in advance. If you're planning on spending some nights in hostels, it makes sense to join your home HI organization (see below) before you leave in order to avoid paying surcharges.

Stayokay (ⓦwww.stayokay.com), the HI-affiliated Dutch youth hostel association, runs thirty hostels in the Netherlands. Dorm beds cost €20–25 per person per night including breakfast, depending on the season

and the hostel's facilities; there are no age restrictions. Accommodation is usually in small dormitories, though most hostels have single- and double-bedded rooms. Meals are often available – about €8 for a filling dinner – and in some hostels there are kitchens where you can cook your own food. Most Stayokay hostels accept online bookings. In addition to Stayokay HI hostels, the larger cities – particularly Amsterdam – have a number of private hostels offering dormitory accommodation (and invariably double- and triple-bedded rooms, too) at broadly similar prices, though standards vary enormously; we've given detailed reviews in the guide.

Youth hostel associations

Australia Youth Hostels Association ☎02/9565 1699, ⓦwww.yha.com.au
Hostelling International-American Youth Hostels ☎1-301/495-1240, ⓦwww.hiayh.org
Hostelling International Canada ☎1-800/663-5777, ⓦwww.hihostels.ca
Hostelling International Northern Ireland ☎028/9032 4733, ⓦwww.hini.org.uk
Irish Youth Hostel Association Republic of Ireland ☎01/830 4555, ⓦwww.irelandyha.org
Scottish Youth Hostel Association ☎01786/891 400, ⓦwww.syha.org.uk
Youth Hostel Association (YHA) England and Wales ☎0870/770 8868, ⓦwww.yha.org.uk
Youth Hostelling Association New Zealand ☎0800/278 299 or 03/379 9970, ⓦwww.yha.co.nz

Camping and trekkers' huts

If you are not too averse to rain, then **camping** is a viable proposition in the Netherlands: there are plenty of sites, most are very well equipped, and they are a cheap accommodation option. Prices vary greatly, mainly depending on the facilities available, but you can generally expect to pay around €3–5 per person, plus the same again for a tent, and another €3–5 or so if you have a car or motorbike. All VVVs have details of their nearest sites, and we've mentioned campsites in the Guide. A list of selected sites is available from the Dutch camping association, **Sticht-ing Vrije Recreatie**, Broakseweg 75–77, 4231 VD Meerkerk (☎0183/352 741, ⓦwww .svr.nl). If you don't mind having basic facilities, then look out for **minicampings**, which are generally signed off the main roads. These are often family-run – you may end up pitched next to a family's house – and are informal, cheap and friendly. Details of VVV-affiliated minicampings can be found in the accommodation sections of the provincial guides available in every VVV. Some campsites also offer **trekkers' huts** (*trekkershutten*) – frugally furnished wooden affairs that can house a maximum of four people for about €30 a night. You can get details of the national network, with good information in English, and a list of sites in each-province, from the **Stichting Trekkershutten Nederland** (ⓦwww.trekkershutten.nl).

Food and drink

The Netherlands may not be Europe's gastronomic heartland, but the food in the average Dutch restaurant has improved by leaps and bounds in recent years, and there are any number of places serving a good, inventive take on home-grown cuisine. All the larger cities also have a decent assortment of ethnic restaurants, especially Indonesian, Chinese and Thai, plus lots of cafés and bars that serve adventurous, reasonably priced food in a relaxed and unpretentious setting – often known as eetcafés. The Netherlands is also a great country to go drinking, with a wide selection of bars, ranging from the chic and urbane to the rough and ready. Considering the country's singular approach to the sale and consumption of cannabis, you might choose to enjoy a joint after your meal rather than a beer – for which you will have to go to a "coffeeshop" (see p.47).

Food

Dutch **food** tends to be higher in protein content than variety: steak, chicken and fish, along with filling soups and stews, are staples, usually served up in substantial quantities. It can, however, at its best, be excellent, with lots of restaurants – and even bars and eetcafés – offering increasingly adventurous crossovers with French cuisine at good-value prices.

Breakfast

In all but the cheapest and most expensive of hotels, **breakfast** (*ontbijt*) will be included in the price of the room. Though usually nothing fancy, it's always substantial: rolls, cheese, ham, hard-boiled eggs, jam and honey or peanut butter are the principal ingredients. Many bars and cafés serve rolls and sandwiches in similar mode, although few open much before 8 or 8.30am.

Dutch **coffee** is normally good and strong, served with a little tub of *koffiemelk* (evaporated milk); ordinary milk is rarely used. If you want coffee with warm milk, ask for a *koffie verkeerd*. Tea generally comes with lemon – if anything; if you want milk you have to ask for it. Chocolate (*chocomel*) is also popular, hot or cold; for a real treat, drink it hot with a layer of fresh whipped cream (*slagroom*) on top. Some cafés also sell aniseed-flavoured warm milk (*anijsmelk*).

Snacks and sandwiches

Dutch fast food has its own peculiarities. Chips/fries (*friet* or *patat*) are the most common standby; *vlaamse* or "Flemish" style sprinkled with salt and smothered with huge gobs of mayonnaise (*frietesaus*) are the best, or with curry, sateh, goulash or tomato sauce. If you just want salt, ask for *patat zonder*; fries with salt and mayonnaise are *patat met*. You'll also come across *kroketten*

– spiced minced meat (usually either veal or beef), covered with breadcrumbs and deep fried – and *fricandel*, a frankfurter-like sausage. All these are available over the counter at evil-smelling fast-food places, or, for a euro or so, from coin-op heated glass compartments on the street and in train stations.

Much tastier are the **fish specialities** sold by street vendors, which are good as a snack or a light lunch: salted raw herring, rollmops, smoked eel (*gerookte paling*), mackerel in a roll (*broodje makreel*), mussels and various kinds of deep-fried fish are all delicious. Look out, too, for "green" or *maatje* herring, eaten raw with onions in early summer: hold the fish by the tail, tip your head back and dangle it into your mouth, Dutch-style.

Another snack you'll see everywhere is *shoarma* or **shwarma** – another name for a doner kebab, shavings of lamb pressed into a flat pitta bread – sold in numerous Middle Eastern restaurants and takeaways for about €3. Other, less common, street foods include **pancakes** (*pannenkoeken*), sweet or spicy, also widely available at sit-down restaurants; waffles (*stroopwafels*), doused with syrup; and, in November and December, *oliebollen*, greasy doughnuts sometimes filled with fruit (often apple) or custard (as a *Berliner*) and traditionally eaten on New Year's Eve.

Bars often serve sandwiches and rolls (*boterham* and *broodjes*) – mostly open, and varying from a slice of tired cheese on old bread to something so embellished it's almost a complete meal – as well as more substantial dishes. A sandwich made with French bread is known as a *stokbrood*. In the winter, *erwtensoep* (or *snert*) – thick pea soup with smoked sausage, served with smoked bacon on pumpernickel – is available in many bars, and – for about €5 a bowl – makes a great buy for lunch. Alternatively, there's an *uitsmijter* (a "kicker-out", derived from the practice of serving it at dawn after an all-night party to prompt guests to depart): now widely available at all times of day, it comprises one, two or three fried eggs on buttered bread, topped with a choice of ham, cheese, or roast beef; at about €5, it's another good budget lunch.

Cakes and cookies

Dutch **cakes and cookies** are always good, best eaten in a *banketbakkerij* (patisserie) with a small serving area; or buy a bag and munch them on the hoof. Top of the list is the ubiquitous Dutch speciality *appelgebak* – chunky, memorably fragrant apple-and-cinnamon pie, served hot in huge wedges, often with whipped cream (*met slagroom*). Other nibbles include *speculaas*, a crunchy cinnamon cookie with gingerbread texture; *stroopwafels*, butter wafers sandwiched together with runny syrup; and *amandelkoek*, cakes with a crisp cookie outside and melt-in-the-mouth

Dutch cheese

Abroad, **Dutch cheeses** have an unjustified reputation for being bland – perhaps partly because the Dutch tend to export the lower-quality stuff and keep the best for themselves. On home turf, Dutch cheese can be delicious, although, to be fair, there certainly isn't the variety on show as there is, say, in France or Switzerland. Most Dutch cheeses vary little from the familiar pale yellow, semi-soft Gouda, within which differences in taste come with the varying stages of maturity: *jong* cheese has a mild flavour, *belegen* is much tastier, while *oud* can be pungent and strong, with a grainy, flaky texture. The best way to eat it is as the Dutch do, in thin slices (cut with a cheese slice, or *kaasschaaf*) rather than large hunks. Among other names to look out for, best known is Edam, also semi-soft in texture but slightly creamier than Gouda; it's usually shaped into balls and coated in red wax ready for export – it's not eaten much in the Netherlands. Leidse is simply a bland Gouda laced with cumin or caraway seeds; most of its flavour comes from the seeds. Maasdam is a Dutch version of Emmental or Jarlsberg, strong, creamy and full of holes, sold under brand names such as Leerdammer and Maasdammer. You'll also find Dutch-made Emmental and Gruyère.

almond paste inside. In and around Maastricht, don't miss *Limburgse Vlaai*, a pie with various fruit fillings.

Full meals

The majority of bars serve food, everything from sandwiches to a full menu – in which case they may be known as an **eetcafé**. This type of place is usually open all day, serving both lunch and an evening meal. Full-blown restaurants, on the other hand, tend to open in the evening only, usually from around 5.30pm or 6pm until around 10pm. Especially in the smaller towns, the Dutch eat early, usually around 7.30 or 8pm; after about 10pm you'll find many restaurant kitchens closed.

If you're on a budget, stick to the **dagschotel** (dish of the day) wherever possible, for which you pay around €10 for a meat or fish dish, heavily garnished with potatoes and other vegetables and salad; note, though, that it's often only served at lunchtime or between 6 and 8pm. Otherwise, you can pay up to €20 for a meat or seafood main course in an average restaurant.

Vegetarian dining isn't a problem. Many eetcafés and restaurants have at least one meat-free menu item, and you'll find a few veggie restaurants in most of the larger towns, offering full-course set meals for €7.50–10 – although bear in mind that they often close early (7/8pm).

As for foreign cuisines, the Dutch are particularly partial to **Indonesian** food and Indonesian restaurants are commonplace: *nasi goreng* and *bami goreng* (rice or noodles with meat) are good basic dishes, though there are normally more exciting items on the menu, some very spicy; chicken or beef in peanut sauce (*sateh*) is always available. Or you could try a **rijsttafel** – a sampler meal, comprising rice and/or noodles served with perhaps ten or twelve small, often spicy dishes and hot sambal sauce on the side. Usually ordered for two or more people, you can reckon on paying around €20–25 per person. **Surinamese** restaurants are much rarer, being largely confined to the big cities, but they offer a distinctive, essentially Creole cuisine – try *roti*, flat pancake-like bread served with a spicy curry, hardboiled egg and vegetables.

Italian food is ubiquitous with pizzas and pasta dishes starting at a fairly uniform €8 or so in most places. To eat **Spanish** costs a little more.

Drinking

Most **drinking** is done in the laidback surroundings of a brown bar (*bruin kroeg*) – so named because of the colour of the walls, often stained by years of tobacco smoke – or in more modern-looking places, everything from slick designer bars, minimally furnished and usually catering for a younger crowd, to cosy neighbourhood bars. Most bars **stay open** until around 1am during the week and 2am at weekends, though some don't bother to open until lunchtime, a few not until 4 or 5pm. Though they're no longer common, you may also come across *proeflokaalen* or tasting houses. Originally the sampling premises of small distillers, there are now small, old-fashioned bars that only serve spirits (and maybe a few beers) and sometimes close early (around 8pm).

Beer

The Netherlanders' favourite tipple is **beer**, mostly Pilsener-style lager usually served in a relatively small measure (just under a half-pint, with a foaming head on top) – ask for *een pils*. Prices are fairly standard: about €1.60–1.80 pretty much everywhere. Predictably, beer is much cheaper from a supermarket, most brands retailing at just under €1 for a half-litre bottle.

The most common Dutch brands are Heineken, Amstel and Grolsch, all of which you can find more or less nationwide. Expect them to be stronger and more distinctive than the watery approximations brewed abroad under licence. In the south of the country, you'll also find a number of good local brews – Bavaria from Noord-Brabant, De Ridder, Leeuw, Gulpen and Brand (the country's oldest brewer) from Limburg. For something a little less strong, look out for *donkenbier*, which is about half the strength of an ordinary Pilsener beer. There are also a number of seasonal beers: rich, fruity *bokbier* is fairly widespread in autumn, while year-round you'll see *witbier* (white beer) such as Hoegaarden, Dentergems or Raaf – refreshing and potent in equal measure, and often served with a slice of a lemon or lime.

Around the country, you'll also spot plenty of the better-known Belgian brands available on tap, like Stella Artois and the darker De Koninck, as well as bottled beers like Duvel, Chimay and various brands of the fruit-flavoured Kriek.

Wine and spirits

Wine is reasonably priced – expect to pay around €6 or so for an average bottle of French white or red in a supermarket; €15 in a restaurant. As for spirits, the indigenous drink is **jenever**, or Dutch gin – not unlike British gin, but a bit weaker and oilier, made from molasses and flavoured with juniper berries: it's served in a small glass (for around €2) and is traditionally drunk straight, often knocked back in one gulp with much hearty back-slapping. There are a number of varieties, principally *Oud* (old), which is smooth and mellow, and *Jong* (young), which

packs more of a punch – though neither is extremely alcoholic. The older *jenevers* (including *zeer oude*, very old) are a little more expensive but stronger and less oily. In a bar, ask for a *borreltje* (straight *jenever*) or a *bittertje* (with angostura); if you've a sweet tooth, try a *bessenjenever* (flavoured with blackcurrant). A glass of beer with a *jenever* chaser is a *kopstoot*. Imported spirits are considerably more expensive, and you can't buy spirits in supermarkets.

Other drinks include numerous Dutch **liqueurs**, notably *advocaat* or eggnog; sweet, blue *curaçao*; and luminous green *pisang ambon*. There is also an assortment of luridly coloured fruit brandies best left for experimentation at the end of an evening – or perhaps not at all – a Dutch-produced brandy, *Vieux*, which tastes as if it's made from prunes but is in fact grape-based, and various regional **firewaters**, such as *elske* from Maastricht – made from the leaves, berries and bark of alder bushes.

The media

English-speakers will find themselves quite at home in the Netherlands, as Dutch TV broadcasts a wide range of British programmes, and English-language newspapers from around the world are readily available.

Newspapers and magazines

British newspapers are on sale in every major city on the day of publication, for around €4. Newsagents located at train stations will almost always have copies if no one else does. Current issues of UK and US magazines are widely available too, as is the *International Herald Tribune*.

Of the **Dutch newspapers**, *NRC Handelsblad* is a right-of-centre paper that has perhaps the best news coverage and a liberal stance on the arts; *De Volkskrant* is a progressive, leftish daily; the popular right-wing *De Telegraaf* boasts the highest

circulation figures in the country and has a well-regarded financial section; *Algemeen Dagblad* is a right-wing broadsheet; while the middle-of-the-road *Het Parool* ("The Password") and the news magazine *Vrij Nederland* ("Free Netherlands") are the successors of underground Resistance newspapers printed during wartime occupation. The Protestant *Trouw* ("Trust"), another former underground paper, is centre-left in orientation with a focus on religion.

Bundled in with the weekend edition of the *International Herald Tribune* is *The Nether-lander*, a small but useful business-oriented review of Dutch affairs in English.

TV and radio

Dutch **TV** isn't the best, although the quantity of English-language programmes broadcast is high, and they're all shown in the original language. If you're staying somewhere with cable TV, it's also possible to find many foreign TV channels: Britain's BBC1 and BBC2 are available everywhere; popular cable offerings include the National Geographic channel, Eurosport and Discovery; and there's also a host of German, French, Spanish, Italian, Turkish and Arabic stations, some of which also show undubbed British and US movies. Other Dutch and Belgian TV channels, cable and non-cable, regularly run English-language movies with Dutch subtitles.

Dutch **radio** has loads of stations catering for every niche. Briefly, of the public service stations, Radio 1 is a news and sports channel, Radio 2 plays AOR music, Radio 3 plays chart music and Radio 4 classical, jazz and world music. Of commercial stations, some of the main nationwide players are Radio 538, Veronica, Sky Radio and Noordzee FM, and they all pretty much play current and past chart music.

There's next to no English-language programming, apart from the overseas-targeted Radio Netherlands (W www.rnw.nl), which broadcasts Dutch news in English, with articles on current affairs, lifestyle issues, science, health and so on.

The **BBC World Service** broadcasts pretty much all day in English on 648kHz (AM) around Amsterdam; it also occupies 198kHz (long wave) and 101.3 (FM).

Festivals and events

Across the Netherlands, most annual festivals are arts- or music-based affairs, confined to a particular town or city, though there is also a liberal sprinkling of folkloric events celebrating one local event or another – the Alkmaar cheese market (see p.150) being a case in point. Most festivals take place during the summer and the local VVV can be guaranteed to have all the latest details.

January

Elfstedentocht (Eleven Cities' Journey)
W www.elfstedentocht.nl. Annual ice-skating marathon along the frozen rivers of Friesland, starting and finishing in Leeuwarden. Held, weather permitting, sometime in January.

February

Holland Flowers Festival Bovenkarspel, near Enkhuizen; late Feb; W www.hollandflowersfestival .nl. The world's largest covered flower show held over ten days.
Lent carnivals late Feb to early March. At the beginning of Lent in Breda, 's Hertogenbosch, Maastricht and other southern towns.

March

Keukenhof Gardens Lisse; late March to late May; W www.keukenhof.nl. World-renowned floral displays in the bulbfields and hothouses of this 23-hectare park.

April

Alkmaar cheese market W www.vvvalkmaar .nl. Held every Friday (10am–12.30pm), from the first Friday in April to the first Friday in September. See p.150
Fortis Marathon Rotterdam W www .rotterdammarathon.nl, Held on a Sunday.
Queen's Day (Koninginnedag) April 30. Across the country, especially in Amsterdam – celebrated by street markets, processions, partying and fireworks.

May

Scheveningen Sand Sculpture Festival, May to early June; W www.sandsculptures.nl. Hard-working teams descend on the resort from all over

Europe to create amazing sand sculptures, which are left for three weeks for visitors to admire.

Herdenkingsdag (Remembrance Day) May 4. There's wreath-laying all over the country and a two-minute silence is widely observed in honour of the Dutch dead of World War II.

Bevrijdingsdag (Liberation Day) May 5. The country celebrates the 1945 liberation from German occupation with music, outdoor festivals and processions.

Breda Jazz Festival end May; Ⓦwww .bredajazzfestival.nl. With open-air concerts and street parades. See p.323.

Pinkpop festival Landgraaf, near Maastricht; end May; Ⓦwww.pinkpop.nl. A top-notch, three-day open-air rock festival. See p.336.

June

Holland Festival Amsterdam; Ⓦwww .hollandfestival.nl. This month-long performing arts festival covers all aspects of both national and international music, theatre, dance and the contemporary arts.

Oerol Festival Terschelling; mid- to late June; Ⓦwww.oerol.nl. A ten-day event featuring location theatre and stand-up comedy. See p.235.

July

North Sea Jazz Festival Rotterdam; mid-July; Ⓦwww.northseajazz.nl. Outstanding three-day jazz festival showcasing international names as well as local talent. Multiple stages and a thousand musicians. See p.199.

Woodstock69 Bloemendaal July–Aug; Ⓦwww .woodstock69.nl. Festival held on Bloemendaal beach and featuring live percussion, dance acts and plenty of revelry.

Internationale Vierdaagse Afstandmarsen Nijmegen; late July; Ⓦwww.4daagse.nl. One of the world's largest walking events, with over 30,000 participants walking 30–50km per day over four days. See p.300.

August

Sneek Week early Aug; Ⓦwww.sneekweek.nl. International sailing event in Sneek, with around 1000 boats competing in over thirty classes.

Amsterdam Pride 1st or 2nd weekend; Ⓦwww .amsterdamgaypride.nl.. The city's gay community celebrates, with street parties and performances, as well as a "Canal Pride" flotilla of boats parading along the Prinsengracht.

Grachtenfestival Amsterdam; 3rd week; Ⓦwww .grachtenfestival.nl. International musicians perform classical music at twenty historic locations in the city. Includes the Prinsengrachtconcert, one of the world's most prestigious open-air concerts, featuring a stage over the canal and a promenading audience.

September

Bloemencorso Aalsmeer; early Sept; Ⓦwww .bloemencorsoaalsmeer.nl. A flower parade that makes its way round the southwestern outskirts of Amsterdam in the vicinity of Schiphol airport.

Brabantse Fietsdag mid-Sept. For one day, one hundred cycle routes are laid out in Noord-Brabant, ranging in length from 15km to 50km.

October

Amsterdam city marathon early/mid-Oct; Ⓦwww.amsterdammarathon.nl.

November

Crossing Border The Hague; 2nd or 3rd week; Ⓦwww.crossingborder.nl. Four-day festival that aims to cross artistic boundaries with performances by over a hundred international acts presenting the spoken word in various forms, from rap to poetry.

December

Pakjesavond Dec 5. Presents are dropped down the chimney by Zwarte Piet (Black Pete) as Sinterklaas rides across the rooftops on his white horse. Traditionally, kids sing songs to make Sinterklaas happy in the weeks before Pakjesavond as there is always the chance of being caught by Zwarte Piet if you haven't been good and sent to Spain – where Sinterklaas lives – in a brown bag.

Shopping

The Netherlands has a flourishing retail sector and all of its large towns and cities are jammed with department stores and international chains. More distinctively, the big cities in general, but Amsterdam in particular, play host to scores of specialist shops selling everything from condoms to beads. There are certain obvious Dutch goods – tulips, clogs and porcelain windmills to name the big three – but it's the Dutch flair for design that is the most striking feature, whether it's reflected in furniture or clothes.

Normal opening hours are Monday to Friday 8.30/9am to 5.30/6pm and Saturday 8.30/9am to 4/5pm, with many shops opening late on Thursday or Friday evenings too. In the cities, Sunday opening is increasingly common in the larger stores (noon–5pm) and many supermarkets stay open till about 8pm every night. Equally, lots of smaller places don't bother with Monday mornings and, out in the sticks, Saturday afternoon can be a retail desert as well. In the cities, a handful of night shops – *avondwinkels*

Clothing and shoe sizes

Women's dresses and skirts

American	4	6	8	10	12	14	16	18
British	8	10	12	14	16	18	20	22
Continental	38	40	42	44	46	48	50	52

Women's blouses and sweaters

American	6	8	10	12	14	16	18
British	30	32	34	36	38	40	42
Continental	40	42	44	46	48	50	52

Women's shoes

American	5	6	7	8	9	10	11
British	3	4	5	6	7	8	9
Continental	36	37	38	39	41	42	43

Men's suits

American	34	36	38	40	42	44	46	48
British	34	36	38	40	42	44	46	48
Continental	44	46	48	50	52	54	56	58

Men's shirts

American	14	15	15.5	16	16.5	17	17.5	18
British	14	15	15.5	16	16.5	17	17.5	18
Continental	36	38	39	41	42	43	44	45

Men's shoes

American	7	7.5	8	8.5	9.5	10	10.5	11	11.5
British	6	7	7.5	8	9	9.5	10	11	12
Continental	39	41	41	42	43	44	44	45	46

Clogs

You'll see clogs – or *klompen* – on sale in all the main tourist centres, usually brightly painted and not really designed for wearing. It's estimated that about three million clogs are still made annually in the Netherlands. Interestingly, only about half are for the tourist market, the rest being worn mainly by industrial workers as foot protection – they pass all European safety standards.

– stay open into the small hours or round the clock.

Most towns have a **market day**, usually midweek (and sometimes Saturday morning), and this is often the liveliest day to visit, particularly when the stalls fill the central square, the *markt*.

Travel essentials

Addresses

These are written, for example, as Haarlem-merstraat 15 III, meaning the third-floor (US fourth-floor) apartment at no. 15 Haarlem-merstraat. The ground floor is indicated by hs (*huis*, "house") after the number; the basement is sous (*sousterrain*). The figures 1e, 2e, 3e and 4e before a street name are an abbreviation for Eerste, Tweede, Derde and Vierde, respectively – the first, second, third and fourth streets of the same name. Some sidestreets, rather than have their own name, take the name of the street that they run off, with the addition of the word dwars, meaning crossing – so Palmdwarsstraat is a sidestreet off Palmstraat. T/O (*tegenover*, "opposite") in an address shows that the address is a boat: hence "Prinsengracht T/O 26" would indicate a boat to be found opposite building no. 26 on Prinsengracht. Dutch postcodes – made up of four figures and two letters – can be found in the directory kept at post offices.

Children

In general terms at least, Dutch society is sympathetic to its **children** and the tourist industry follows suit. Extra beds in hotel rooms are usually easy to arrange; many

restaurants (but not the smartest) have children's menus; concessions for children are the rule, from public transport through to museums; and baby changing stations are commonplace. Pharmacists (*apotheek*) carry all the kiddy stuff you would expect – nappies, baby food and so forth.

Costs

Accommodation in the Netherlands is moderately expensive, and will probably prove to be your biggest expense, especially in Amsterdam where hotel prices are around thirty percent more than in the rest of the country. Public transport and food are reasonably priced. Eating out, most main courses cost €15–20. You can, of course, pay a lot more: a meal in a top restaurant can cost €60 head, and then some.

Travelling by bicycle, eating picnics bought from supermarkets and cooking your own food at campsites it's possible to keep costs down to €25 a day per person. If you don't want to lug camping equipment with you, cycling also entitles you to the creature comforts of the excellent Vrienden op de Fiets (see p.37), but you'll need to factor in another €15 to your daily budget. Moving up a notch, if you picnic at lunch, stick to less expensive bars and restaurants, and stay in cheap hotels or hostels, you could get by on around €50–60 a day. Staying in two-star hotels, eating out in medium-range restaurants and going to bars, you should reckon on about €120 a day, the main variable being the cost of your room – plus the higher prices in Amsterdam. On €150 a day and upwards, you'll be limited only by time, though if you're planning to stay in a five-star hotel anywhere in the country and have a big night out, this still won't be enough.

Crime and personal safety

By comparison with other parts of Europe, the Netherlands is relatively free of crime, so there's little reason why you should ever come into contact with the Dutch police force. However, there is more street crime than there used to be, especially in Amsterdam and the larger cities, and it's advisable to be on your guard against petty theft: secure your things in a locker when staying in hostel accommodation, and never leave any valuables in a tent or car. If you're on a bike, make sure it is well locked up: bike theft and resale is a major industry here. If you are robbed, you'll need to go to a police station to report it, not least because your insurance company will require a police report; remember to make a note of the report number – or, better still, ask for a copy of the statement itself. Don't expect a great deal of concern if your loss is relatively small – and don't be surprised if the process of completing forms and formalities takes ages.

As for personal safety, it's generally possible to walk around without fear of harassment or assault, but certain parts of all the big cities – especially Rotterdam and Amsterdam – are decidedly dodgy, and wherever you go at night it's always better to err on the side of caution. In particular, Amsterdam's Red Light District can have an unpleasant, threatening undertow (although the crowds of people act as a deterrent), while Rotterdam's docklands are similarly grim. Using public transport, even late at night, isn't usually a problem, but if in doubt take a taxi.

If you're detained by the police, you don't automatically have the right to a phone call, although in practice they'll probably phone your consulate for you – not that consular officials have a reputation for excessive helpfulness (particularly in drug cases). If your alleged offence is a minor matter, you can be held for up to six hours without questioning; if it is more serious, you can be detained for up to 24 hours.

Disabilities, travellers with

Despite its general social progressiveness, the Netherlands is only just getting to grips with the requirements of people with mobility problems. In Amsterdam and most of the other major cities the most obvious difficulty you'll face is in negotiating the cobbled streets and narrow, often broken pavements of the older districts, where the key sights are often located. Similarly, provision for people with disabilities on the country's urban **public transport** is only average, although improving – many new buses, for instance, are now wheelchair-accessible. And yet, while it can be difficult simply to get around, practically all **public buildings**, including museums, theatres, cinemas, concert halls and hotels, are obliged to provide access, and do. Places that have been certified wheelchair-accessible now bear an International Accessibility Symbol (IAS). Bear in mind, however, that a lot of the older, narrower **hotels** are not allowed to install lifts, so check first. If you're planning to use the Dutch train network during your stay and would appreciate assistance on the platform, phone the Bureau Assistentieverlening Gehandicapten (Disabled Assistance Office) on ☎030/235 7822 (🖷235 3033) at least three hours before your train departs, and there will be someone to meet and help you at the station (office open daily 7am–11pm). NS publishes information about train travel for people with disabilities online at ⊛www.ns.nl and in various leaflets, stocked at main stations.

Drugs

Thousands of visitors come to the Netherlands in general, and Amsterdam in particular, just to get stoned. This is the one

Coffeeshops

Dutch cities remain just about the only ones in the world where you can stand in a public place and announce in a loud, clear voice that you intend to buy and smoke a large, well-packed joint, and then do just that in front of the watching police. In theory, purchases of up to 5g of cannabis, and possession of up to 30g (the legal limit) are tolerated; in practice, many coffeeshops offer discounted bulk purchases of 50g with impunity (though bear in mind that if the police do search you, they're entitled to confiscate any amount they find). No one will ever call the police on you in the major cities for discreet, personal dope-smoking, but if in doubt about whether smoking is OK in a given situation, ask somebody – the worst you'll get will be a "no".

When you first walk into a coffeeshop, how you buy the stuff isn't immediately apparent – it's illegal to advertise cannabis in any way, which includes calling attention to the fact that it's available at all. What you have to do is ask to see the menu, which is normally kept behind the counter. This will list all the different hashes and grasses on offer, along with (if it's a reputable place) exactly how many grams you get for your money. The in-house dealer will be able to help you out with queries. Current prices per gram of hash and marijuana range from €10 for low-grade stuff up to €25 for top-quality hash and as high as €40 for really strong grass.

The hash you come across originates in various countries and is much like you'd find anywhere, apart from Pollem, which is compressed resin and stronger than normal. Marijuana is a different story, and the old days of imported Colombian, Thai and sensimelia are fading away; taking their place are limitless varieties of "Neder-wiet", Dutch-grown under UV lights and more potent than anything you're likely to have come across. Skunk, Haze and Northern Lights are all popular types of Dutch weed, and should be treated with caution – a smoker of low-grade British draw will be laid low (or high) for hours by a single spliff of skunk. You would be equally well advised to take care with spacecakes (cakes or biscuits baked with hash), which are widely available: you can never be sure exactly what's in them; they tend to have a delayed reaction (up to two hours before you notice anything strange – don't get impatient and gobble down another one!); and once they kick in, they can bring on an extremely intense, bewildering high – 10–12 hours is common. You may also come across cannabis seeds for growing your own: while locals are permitted to grow a small amount of marijuana for personal use, the import of cannabis seeds is illegal in any country, so don't even think about trying to take some home.

Finally a word of warning: since all kinds of cannabis are so widely available over-the-counter in coffeeshops, there's no need to buy any on the street. If you do, you're simply asking for trouble.

Western country where the purchase of cannabis is de-criminalized, and the influx of people drawn to the country by this fact creates problems: many Amsterdammers, for instance, get mightily hacked off with "drug tourism", as do folk in border towns, who have to deal with tides of people popping over the international frontier to the first coffeeshop they see.

The Dutch government's attitude to soft drugs is more complex than you might think: the use of **cannabis** is tolerated but not condoned, resulting in a rather complicated set of rules and regulations that can be safely ignored as long as you buy very small amounts for personal use only (see box, above). Buy in bulk, or sell to other people, and you become liable under Dutch criminal law. Needless to say, the one thing you shouldn't attempt to do is take any form of cannabis out of the country. A surprising number of people think (or claim to think) that if it's bought in the Netherlands it can be taken back home legally; this story won't wash with customs officials and drug enforcement officers, who will happily add your stash to the statistics of national drug seizures, and arrest you into the bargain.

Sniffer dogs invariably meet flights arriving from Dutch airports.

As far as other drugs go, the Dutch law surrounding **magic mushrooms** is that you can legally buy and possess any amount so long as they are fresh, but as soon as you tamper with them in any way (dry or process them, boil or cook them), they become as illegal as crack. Despite the existence of a lively and growing trade in **cocaine** and **heroin**, possession of either could mean a stay in one of the Netherlands' lively and growing jails. **Ecstasy**, **acid** and **speed** are as illegal in the Netherlands as they are anywhere else.

Electricity

220v AC. British equipment needs only a plug adaptor; American apparatus requires a transformer and an adaptor.

Embassies and consulates in the Netherlands

Australia Carnegielaan 4, 2517 KH Den Haag
℡070/310 8200, ⓦwww.netherlands.embassy.gov.au
Canada Sophialaan 7, 2514 JP Den Haag
℡070/311 1600, ⓦwww.canada.nl
Ireland Dr Kuijperstraat 9, 2514 BA Den Haag
℡070/363 0993, ⓦwww.irishembassy.nl
New Zealand Carnegielaan 10, 2517 KH Den Haag
℡070/346 9324, ⓦwww.nzembassy.com
UK Lange Voorhout 10, 2514 ED Den Haag
℡070/427 0427, ⓦwww.britain.nl; Consulate-General: Koningslaan 44, PO Box 75488, 1070 AL Amsterdam ℡020/676 4343
USA Lange Voorhout 102, 2514 EJ Den Haag
℡070/310 2209, ⓦwww.usemb.nl; Consulate General: Museumplein 19, 1071 DJ Amsterdam
℡020/575 5309

Entry requirements

Citizens of the UK, Ireland, Australia, New Zealand, Canada and the US do not need a visa to enter the Netherlands if staying for three months or less. However, you do need a passport valid for at least six months after your arrival, a return airline ticket and/or funds deemed to be sufficient for your stay.

If you intend to stay beyond three months, you must apply for a temporary residence permit (a "VTV") within three days of your arrival in the Netherlands. Go to your local Aliens Police office (*Vreemdelingenpolitie*) armed with your birth certificate and proof that you have the funds to finance your stay in the Netherlands, a fixed address, and health insurance. For further information, visit the Ministry of Foreign Affairs website ⓦwww.minbuza.nl.

If you intend to **work**, you will need a work permit, for which your employer must apply on your behalf. The exceptions to this rule are the work schemes set up for Australian, New Zealand and Canadian citizens aged 18–30, who can stay for up to 12 months in the Netherlands on a "Working Holiday Scheme", provided you can convince the authorities that your main priority is holidaying, not working. For further information, contact the Dutch embassies in Canberra, Wellington, Ottawa or London.

For those planning a long-term stay in the Netherlands, a good source of information is a non-profit organization called Access, Societeit de Witte, Plein 24, 2511 CS Den Haag (℡070/346 2525, ⓦwww.access-nl.org). They operate a very useful English-language information line on everything from domestic services to legal matters, as well as running courses on various aspects of Dutch administration and culture.

Dutch embassies abroad

Australia 120 Empire Circuit, Yarralumla, ACT 2600 ℡02/6220 9400, ⓦwww.netherlands.org.au
Canada 350 Albert St #2020, Ottawa, ON, K1R 1A4 ℡613/237 5030, ⓦwww.netherlandsembassy.ca
Ireland 160 Merrion Rd, Dublin 4 ℡01/269 3444, ⓦwww.netherlandsembassy.ie
New Zealand PO Box 480, Ballance/Featherston St, Wellington ℡04/471 6390 ⓦwww.netherlandsembassy.co.nz
South Africa 210 Queen Wilhelmina Ave, New Muckleneuk, Pretoria ℡012/425 4500, ⓦwww.dutchembassy.co.za
UK 38 Hyde Park Gate, London, SW7 5DP ℡020/7590 3200, ⓦwww.netherlands-embassy.org.uk
USA 4200 Linnean Ave NW, Washington, DC 20008 ℡202/244 5300, ⓦwww.netherlands-embassy.org

Flowers

It doesn't take long to notice the Dutch enthusiasm for flowers and plants of all kinds: windows are often festooned with blooms and greenery, and shops and markets sell sprays and bunches for next to nothing. Flowers are grown year-round, though spring is the best time to come if this is your interest, when the bulbfields (and glasshouses) of Noord- and Zuid-Holland are dense with colour – tulips, hyacinths and narcissi are the main blooms, most accessibly viewed at the Keukenhof Gardens (p.169). Later in the year there are rhododendrons and, in Friesland and Groningen, fields of yellow rapeseed; in summer roses appear, while the autumn sees late chrysanthemums.

Gay and lesbian travellers

The Netherlands ranks as one of the top gay-friendly countries in Europe. The superstar of the country's gay and lesbian scene is of course Amsterdam, where attitudes are tolerant, bars are excellent and plentiful, and support groups and facilities are unequalled.

In the other major cities of the Netherlands, while the scene isn't anywhere near as extensive, it's well organized: Rotterdam, The Hague, Nijmegen and Groningen each has a visible and enjoyable gay nightlife. The native lesbian scene is smaller and more subdued: many politically active lesbians move in close-knit communities, and it takes time for foreign visitors to find out what's happening.

The **COC** (Ⓦwww.coc.nl), the national organization for gay men and women, dates from the 1940s and is actively involved in gaining equal rights for gays and lesbians, as well as informing society's perceptions of homosexuality. The national HQ is at Rozenstraat 14 in Amsterdam (Mon–Fri 9am–5pm; ☏020/626 8300), and all cities of any size have a branch office which can offer help, information on events and promotions – and usually a sociable coffee bar. For more help and advice contact Amsterdam's Gay and Lesbian Switchboard on ☏020/623 6565. Gay legislation in the Netherlands is streets ahead of the rest of the world; same-sex marriage and adoption by same-sex partners were legalized in 2001, and within six months over two thousand couples had tied the knot. The age of consent is 16.

Consider timing your visit to coincide with Amsterdam's **Gay Pride** (Ⓦwww .amsterdampride.nl) on the first weekend

in August. Celebrations are unabashed, with music, theatre, street parties and floats parading through the canals. Other events of interest might include the Fetish Fantasy Weekend (end of March), Queen's Day (not that sort of queen, but with lots of gay parties anyway, on April 30) and Amsterdam's Leather Pride in late October. Contact the Tourism Board or COC for more details.

Health

As a member of the European Union, the Netherlands has free reciprocal health agreements with other member states. EU citizens are entitled to free treatment within the Netherlands' public health-care system on production of a **European Health Insurance Card** (EHIC), which you can obtain in the UK by picking up a form from a post office, by calling ☏0845 606 2030, or applying online at Ⓦwww.dh.gov.uk. Allow up to 21 days for delivery. The EHIC is free of charge and is valid for at least three years. Australians are able to receive treatment through a reciprocal arrangement with Medicare (check with your local office for details). Anyone planning to stay for three months or more is required by Dutch law to have private **health insurance**. Taking out private insurance means the cost of items not within the purview of the EU scheme, such as dental treatment and repatriation on medical grounds, will be covered. Non-EU residents, apart from Australians, will need to insure themselves against all eventualities, including medical costs. In the case of major expense, the more worthwhile policies promise to sort matters out before you pay rather than after, but if you do have to pay upfront, make very sure that you always keep full doctors' reports, signed prescription details and all receipts.

Minor ailments can be remedied at a **drugstore** (*drogist*). These sell non-prescription drugs as well as toiletries, tampons, condoms and the like. A **pharmacy** (*apotheek*) – generally open Mon–Fri 9.30am–6pm, but often closed Monday mornings – is where you go to get a prescription filled. There aren't many 24-hour pharmacies, but the local VVV (see p.53), as well as most of the better hotels, will supply addresses of ones that stay open till late.

In more serious cases, you can get the address of an English-speaking doctor from your local pharmacy, tourist office or hotel. The 24-hour medical helpline Centrale Doktorsdienst (☎0900/503 2042) can give general advice about medical symptoms and let you know the details of duty doctors. If you're entitled to free treatment under EU health agreements, double-check that the doctor is both working within, and regarding you as a patient of, the public health care system. Bear in mind though, that even within the EU agreement you may still have to pay a significant portion of the prescription charges (although senior citizens and children are exempt). Most private health insurance policies don't help cover prescription charges either, and although the "excesses" are usually greater than the cost of the medicines, it's worth keeping receipts just in case.

Minor accidents can be treated at the outpatients department of a **hospital** (*ziekenhuis*), but in **emergencies** phone ☎112. Again if you're reliant on free treatment within the EU health scheme, try to make this clear to the ambulance staff, and, if you're whisked off to hospital, to the medic you subsequently encounter. If possible, it's a good idea to hand over a photocopy of your EHIC on arrival in the hospital to ensure your status is clearly understood. In terms of describing symptoms, you can be pretty sure that someone will speak English. Without an EHIC you won't be turned away from a hospital, but you will have to pay for any treatment you receive and should therefore get an official receipt, a necessary preamble to the long-winded process of trying to get at least some of the money back.

Dental treatment is not within the scope of the EU health agreement: again, enquire at the local tourist office or your hotel reception for an English-speaking dentist.

Insurance

Even though EU health care privileges apply in the Netherlands, you'd do well to take out an insurance policy before travelling to cover against theft, loss and illness or injury. A typical policy usually provides cover for the loss of baggage, tickets and – up to a certain limit – cash or cheques, as well as cancellation or curtailment of your journey. Many policies can be chopped and changed to exclude coverage you don't need: sickness and accident benefits can often be excluded or included at will. If you need to make a claim, you should keep all receipts, and in the event you have anything stolen, you must obtain an official statement from the police.

Rough Guides has teamed up with Columbus Direct to offer you **travel insurance** that can be tailored to suit your needs. Products include a low-cost **backpacker option** for long stays; a **short break option** for city getaways; a typical **holiday package option**; and others. There are also annual **multi-trip policies** for those who travel regularly. Different sports and activities (trekking, skiing, etc) can be usually be covered if required. See our website (ⓦwww.roughguidesinsurance.com) for eligibility and purchasing options. Alternatively, UK residents should call ☎0870/033 9988; Australians should call ☎1300/669 999 and New Zealanders should call ☎0800/559 911. All other nationalities should call ☎+44 870/890 2843.

The Internet

The Netherlands, and particularly Amsterdam, is well geared up for Internet access. In most large cities you'll find Internet cafés, which charge around €0.20 for every twenty minutes spent online, but you'll often find that the local town library offers free access.

The useful website ⓦwww.kropla.com gives details of how to plug your laptop in when abroad, phone country codes around the world, and information about electrical systems in different countries.

Mail

The Netherlands has an efficient **postal system**. Post offices are plentiful and mostly open Monday to Friday 8.30am to 5pm, though some big-city branches also open on Saturday from 8.30am to noon. **Stamps** are sold at a wide range of outlets including many shops and hotels. Postboxes are everywhere, but be sure to use the correct slot – the one labelled *overige* is for post going outside the immediate locality.

Maps

Several **road maps** of the Netherlands are widely available abroad and in the country. The *Hallwag* offering is particularly good; it's also the most detailed, at 1:200,000, a feat it accomplishes by being double-sided, and it includes an index. Kümmerly & Frey's country map (1:300,000) uses the excellent ANWB (Royal Dutch Touring Club) cartography, giving good road coverage with detailed insets for The Hague, Amsterdam, Rotterdam and Utrecht. With Michelin, you can either go for the annually updated 1:400,000 red-covered Benelux, complete with index, or the two 1:200,000 yellow-covered indexed sheets covering the Netherlands only (Amsterdam–Groningen and Amsterdam–Maastricht). The ANWB publishes a broad variety of maps covering the country, ranging from three sectional maps (north, middle and south), to individual province maps and waterproof 1:100K sets specifically for cyclists. Of the city maps, Falk publish the best; others are the Cito series and Geocart. Finally, if you're after a **city map** of Amsterdam, look no further than our own Rough Guide city map, printed on indestructible paper and with recommendations listed in the chapter in this book keyed by location.

Money

The currency of the Netherlands – like much of the rest of the EU – is the euro (€), divided into 100 cents. At time of writing the exchange rates were €1.27 to $1 and €0.66 to £1. There are notes of €500, €200, €100, €50, €20, €10 and €5, and coins of €2, €1, 50c, 20c, 10c, 5c, 2c and 1c. Euro coins feature a common EU design on one face, but different country-specific designs on the other, but no matter what the design, all euro coins and notes are legal tender in all of the following countries as well as the Netherlands: Austria, Belgium, Finland, France, Germany, Greece, Ireland, Italy, Luxembourg, Portugal and Spain.

The Netherlands is a cash society; as a general rule, people prefer to pay for most things with notes and coins. However, debit cards are becoming increasingly popular, and most shops and restaurants accept these and credit cards.

You can use many Visa, Mastercard and UK debit cards (within the Cirrus, Plus or Maestro systems) to withdraw cash from ATMs – often the quickest and easiest way of obtaining money. There are dozens dotted across every major city and a reasonable number in smaller places too. They usually give instructions in a variety of languages. Otherwise Dutch banks and post offices usually offer the best deals on changing money. Banking hours are Monday to Friday 9am to 4pm, with a few big-city banks also open Thursday until 9pm or on Saturday morning; all are closed on public holidays (see p.52). Outside these times, changing money is rarely a problem: there's a nationwide network of GWK exchange offices, usually at train stations, which are open late every day – sometimes, as at Amsterdam Centraal Station and Schiphol Airport, even 24 hours. GWK offers competitive rates and charges reasonable commissions, but some other agencies do not, so be cautious. VVV tourist offices also change money, as do most hotels and campsites and some hostels, but their rates are generally poor.

Mosquitoes

These pesky blighters thrive in the Netherlands' watery environment and can be particularly bad at campsites. An antihistamine cream such as Phenergan is the best antidote, although this can be difficult to find – in which case preventative sticks like Autan or Citronella are the best idea.

Museumcards

If you're planning to visit even a handful of museums around the Netherlands, you'll save money with a **Museumjaarkaart** (Museum Yearcard), which gives free entry to over 400 attractions nationwide. It costs €30 for a year (€15 if you're 24 or under), plus a one-off fee of €4.95. Full details, including online ordering, are at ⓦwww.museumjaarkaart.nl, or you can purchase one at any participating museum – most major museums are in the scheme.

Opening hours and public holidays

The Dutch weekend fades painlessly into the working week with many smaller shops and businesses, even in Amsterdam, staying closed on Monday mornings until noon. Normal opening hours are, however, Monday to Friday 8.30/9am to 5.30/6pm and Saturday 8.30/9am to 4/5pm, and many places open late on Thursday or Friday evenings. Sunday opening is becoming increasingly common in larger stores, and in the bigger cities.

Most restaurants are open for dinner from about 6 or 7pm, and though many close as early as 9.30pm, a few stay open past 11pm. Bars, cafés and coffeeshops are either open all day from around 10am or don't open until about 5pm; all close at 1am during the week and at 2am at weekends. Nightclubs generally function from 11pm to 4am during the week, though a few open every night, and some stay open until 5am on the weekend.

Museums, especially those that are state-run (a *rijksmuseum*), tend to follow a pattern: closed on Monday, open Tuesday to Saturday from 10am to 5pm, and on Sundays from 1 to 5pm, although things are slowly changing in favour of seven-day opening. Though closed for Christmas and New Year, the state-run museums adopt Sunday hours on the remaining public holidays, when most shops and banks are closed. Galleries tend to be open from Tuesday to Sunday noon to 5pm. We've quoted precise opening hours throughout the guide.

Public holidays (*Nationale feestdagen*) provide the perfect excuse to take to the streets. The most celebrated of them all is Queen's Day – Koninginnedag – on April 30, which is celebrated everywhere but with particular vim and gusto in Amsterdam.

January 1 New Year's Day
Good Friday (although many shops open)
Easter Sunday
Easter Monday
April 30 Queen's Day
May 5 Liberation Day
Ascension Day
Whit Sunday and Monday
December 25 and 26 Christmas

Phones

The **International phone code** for the Netherlands is 31. Numbers prefixed ☎0800 are free; those prefixed ☎0900 are premium-rated – a (Dutch) message before you're connected tells you how much you will be paying for the call, and you can only call them from within the Netherlands.

Phone cards can be bought at many outlets, including post offices, tobacconists and VVV offices, and in several specified denominations, beginning at €5. However, phone boxes are provided by different companies and their respective phone cards are not mutually compatible. KPN phones (and cards) are the most common. The cheap-rate period for international calls is between 8pm and 8am during the week and all day at weekends. Although most hotel rooms have phones, there is almost always an exorbitant surcharge for their use.

Useful phone numbers

All emergencies (police, fire service, ambulance) ☎112
Or call ☎0900/8844 (premium line, within the Netherlands only) to be connected to your nearest police station.
Operator (domestic and international) ☎0800/0410
Directory enquiries domestic ☎0900/8008, international ☎0900/8418 The Dutch phone directory is also available (in Dutch) at ⓦwww .detelefoongids.nl

Calling home from abroad

Note that the initial zero is omitted from the area code when dialling the UK, Ireland, Australia and New Zealand from abroad.
Australia international access code + 61 + city code.
New Zealand international access code + 64 + city code.
Republic of Ireland international access code + 353 + city code.
South Africa international access code + 27 + city code.
UK international access code + 44 + city code.
US and Canada international access code + 1 + area code.

Sports and outdoor activities

Most visitors to the Netherlands confine their exercise to **cycling** (see p.35) and **walking**, both of which are ideally suited to the flatness of the terrain and, for that matter, the excellence of the public transport system. The Netherlands also offers all the sporting facilities you would expect of a prosperous, European country, from golf to gymnasia, swimming pools to horse riding. More individual offerings include **Korfbal** (ⓦwww.korfball.com), a home-grown sport, cobbled together from netball, basketball and volleyball, and played with mixed teams and a high basket; **canal ice skating**, though this is of course dependent on the weather being cold enough; and, cream of the idiosyncratic lot, **pole sitting**. The Netherlands also possesses some great sandy **beaches** on both its western and northern coasts, although it has to be admitted that the weather is notoriously unreliable – some say bracing – and the North Sea is really rather murky. There are a number of fully fledged seaside resorts – like Zandvoort and Scheveningen – but there are nicer, quieter stretches of coast, most notably amid the wild dunes and beaches that make up the **National Zuid-Kennemerland** (see p.132) near Haarlem and right across the islands of the Waddenzee from Texel to Schiermonnikoog, which are popular for **windsurfing** and **kitesurfing**. The lakes of Friesland and the IJsselmeer are good for **sailing**, particularly the yachting centre of Sneek, which hosts the annual Sneek Week sailing event.

The chief spectator sport is **football** and the teams that make up the country's two professional leagues attract a fiercely loyal following. Big-deal clubs include PSV Eindhoven (ⓦwww.psv.nl); Feyenoord from Rotterdam (ⓦwww.feyenoord.nl); and Amsterdam's Ajax (ⓦwww.ajax.nl). The football season runs from September to May, and matches are generally on Sunday at 2.30pm, with occasional games at 8pm on Wednesday. Tickets for key matches are notoriously hard to come by.

Time

The whole country is on Central European Time (CET) – one hour ahead of London, six hours ahead of New York, and eight hours behind Sydney.

Tourist information

The Netherlands' Board of Tourism's all-encompassing website ⓦwww.holland .com highlights upcoming events, and is particularly strong on practical information. It also publishes a wide range of brochures and guides.

Once in the Netherlands, almost every place you visit will have a tourist office, universally known as a **VVV** (pronounced *fay-fay-fay*), with a distinctive triangular logo. In towns, the VVV is usually either in the centre, often on the Grote Markt (the main square), or by the train station. Staff are nearly always enthusiastic and helpful, and speak excellent English. In addition to handing out basic maps (often for free) and English information on the main sights, many VVVs also keep lists of nearby accommodation, which they can book for you at a small fee (say €2.50). Quite often, these lists include lodgings in private houses (see p.36), which are accessible only through the VVV. Many VVV offices also keep information on neighbouring towns, which can be a great help for forward planning, particularly if the VVV in question has a counter of the Dutch motoring organization **ANWB**, where you'll find plenty of maps and touring information.

If you're roaming around a small area, the VVVs' chunky province guides can be useful, as they list every sort of accommodation from plush hotels to minicampings, albeit in Dutch. However, establishments must pay for inclusion, so there are many small hotels, pensions and campsites that are of perfectly good quality but which choose not to be represented in the official bumph.

War cemeteries

There was fierce fighting in parts of the Netherlands during World War II, notably at Arnhem (see p.292), where several thousand British and Polish servicemen are remembered at the Oosterbeek cemetery. There are other military cemeteries in the east and south of the country, not least at Margraten, where around eight thousand US soldiers lie buried.

Windmills

The best place to see windmills is at Kinderdijk near Dordrecht (see p.208) Some, too, have been moved and reassembled out of harm's way in the open-air museums at Zaanse Schans (see p.149) and the Open-Air Museum just outside Arnhem (see p.294).

Guide

Guide

Amsterdam

CHAPTER 1 # Highlights

✳ **Grachtengordel** Amsterdam's "girdle" of canals lattice the city centre – spend a snoozy afternoon viewing the grand facades from the water. See p.82

✳ **Anne Frank Huis** A poignant memorial to the Holocaust. See p.83

✳ **Jordaan** This picturesque quarter of tree-shaded canals makes an ideal setting for a stroll. See p.89

✳ **Rijksmuseum** World-class collection of Dutch paintings, including Rembrandt's *Night Watch*. See p.98

✳ **Van Gogh Museum** This fabulous collection of the master's paintings are well displayed in a modern, purpose built gallery. See p.98

✳ **Bars** Casual bar-hopping is one of the city's greatest pleasures. See p.106

✳ **Coffeeshops** Not all the city's cannabis "coffeeshops" feature shifty characters nodding along to Bob Marley; plenty offer a pleasant environment to sample high-quality dope. See p.108

△ Keizersgracht and Leliegracht canals, the Grachtengordel

Amsterdam

Amsterdam is a compact, instantly likeable city. It's appealing to look at and pleasant to walk around, an intriguing mix of the parochial and the international; it also has a welcoming attitude towards visitors and a uniquely youthful orientation, shaped by the liberal counter-culture that took hold in the 1960s. Also engaging are the buzz of open-air summer events and the intimacy of its clubs and bars, not to mention the Dutch facility with languages: just about everyone you meet in Amsterdam will be able to speak near-perfect English, on top of their own native Dutch, and often French and German too.

The city's layout is determined by a web of **canals**. The historical centre, which dates from the thirteenth century, is girdled by five concentric canals – the **Grachtengordel** – dug in the seventeenth century as part of a planned expansion to create a uniquely elegant urban environment. It is here that the city's merchant class built their grand mansions, typified by tall, gracefully decorated gables, whose fine proportions are reflected in the still, olive-green waters below. The city council exercised strict control over this expansion – proscribing, for example, the width and length of every building lot – resulting in the homogeneous architecture that survives today. With its antique houses, cobbled streets, humpback bridges and tree-lined canals, Amsterdam is – at its best – acutely beautiful. The conventional sights are for the most part low-key, the most promoted being the **Anne Frank Huis**. What sways the balance, however, is Amsterdam's world-class group of museums and galleries. For many, the **Van Gogh Museum** alone is reason enough to visit the city, but add to this the **Rijksmuseum**, with its collections of medieval and seventeenth-century Dutch paintings, and the contemporary and experimental art of the **Stedelijk Museum**, and the international quality of the art on display in the city is self-evident.

But it's Amsterdam's **population and politics** that constitute its most enduring characteristics. Notorious during the 1960s and 1970s as the zenith – or nadir – of radical permissiveness, the city mellowed only marginally during the Eighties, and, despite the gentrification of the last ten years or so, retains a uniquely laidback feel, with much to it that is both innovative and comfortably familiar. The city has certainly become a more urban, more homogenized place over the last decade or so, but Amsterdammers still make much of their city and its attractions being *gezellig*, a rather over-used Dutch word roughly corresponding to "cosy", "appealingly lived-in" and "warmly convivial" all at the same time. The city's unparalleled selection of *gezellig* drinking-places is a delight, whether you choose to visit a traditional, bare-floored **brown café** or one of the many designer bars and grand cafés. Furthermore, Amsterdam's unique approach to combating hard-drug abuse – embodied in the effective decriminalization of cannabis – has led to a proliferation of **coffeeshops** that sell high-quality marijuana and hashish. Entertainment has a similarly innovative edge, exemplified by **multimedia complexes**, whose offerings are at the forefront of contemporary European film, dance, drama and music. There is any amount of affordable **live music** from all genres – although the Dutch have a particular soft spot for jazz – and Amsterdam has one of the world's leading classical **orchestras**, with generously subsidized ticket prices. The **club** scene is by contrast relatively subdued, even modest by the standards of other capital cities, though **gay** men will find that Amsterdam has one of Europe's more active and convivial nightlife network, at least partly justifying its claim to be the "Gay Capital of Europe". Gay women, on the other hand, with far fewer options, may feel the tag to be unwarranted.

Arrival

Arriving in Amsterdam by train and plane could hardly be easier. Schiphol, Amsterdam's international airport, is a quick and convenient train ride away from Centraal Station, the city's international train station, which is itself just a ten-minute metro ride from Amstel Station, the terminus for long-distance and international buses. Centraal Station is also the hub of an excellent public transport network, whose trams, buses and metro combine to delve into every corner of the city and its suburbs.

By air

Amsterdam's international **airport**, Schiphol (℡0900/7244 7465, ⓦwww .schiphol.nl), is located about 15km southwest of the city centre. **Trains** run from there to Amsterdam Centraal Station every ten minutes during the day, every hour at night (midnight–6am); the journey takes 15–20 minutes and costs €3.60. There are plenty of **taxis**, and the fare from Schiphol to most parts of the city centre is €40–45, and also hotel shuttles like the *Connexxion* service (℡038/339 4741; ⓦwww.schipholhotelshuttle.nl), which departs from the designated bus stop outside the arrivals hall every half an hour (on the half-hour) from 6am to 9pm at a cost of €12 one-way, €19 return. The route varies with the needs of the passengers it picks up at the airport, but buses take about thirty minutes to get from the airport to the city centre. Tickets are available from the *Connexxion* desk in the arrivals hall.

By train and bus

Amsterdam's **Centraal Station** (CS) has regular connections with key cities in Germany, Belgium and France, as well as all the larger towns and cities of the Netherlands. Amsterdam also has several suburban train stations, but these are principally for the convenience of commuters. As you would expect, Centraal Station has a good spread of facilities, including ATMs, a bureau de change and coin-operated luggage lockers and a staffed left-luggage office (both daily 7am–11pm). Small coin-operated lockers cost €2.70, the larger ones €4.20 per 24 hours; left luggage costs €5.70 per item. In addition, there's a **VVV** tourist office (see opposite) on platform 2 and another directly across from the main station entrance on Stationsplein. Centraal Station is also the hub of the city's excellent public transport system: trams and buses depart from outside on Stationsplein, which is also the location of a metro station and a GVB public transport information office (see below). There's a taxi rank on Stationsplein too. For all rail enquiries contact NS (Netherlands Railways; international enquiries ℡0900/9296; domestic enquiries ℡0900/9292; ⓦwww.ns.nl). Eurolines (℡020/560 8788, ⓦwww.eurolines.nl) long-distance, international **buses** arrive at **Amstel Station**, about 3.5km to the southeast of Centraal Station. The metro journey to Centraal Station takes about ten minutes.

By car

Arriving **by car** on either the A4 (E19) from Den Haag (The Hague) or the A2 (E35) from Utrecht, you should experience few traffic problems, and the city centre is clearly signposted as soon as you approach Amsterdam's southern reaches. Both roads feed onto the A10 (E22) ring road; on its west side, leave the A10 at either the Osdorp or Geuzenveld exits for the city centre. However, be warned that driving in central Amsterdam – never mind parking – is extremely difficult; see box on p.63 for further details.

Information and tours

The VVV runs three **tourist offices** in the city centre: on platform 2 of Centraal Station (Mon–Sat 8am–8pm, Sun 9am–5pm); on Stationsplein, across from the entrance to Centraal Station (daily 9am–5pm); and on Leidsestraat, just off Leidseplein (daily 9am–5pm). These three offices share one premium-rate **information line** on ℡0900/400 4040 (calls cost €0.55 per minute) and a website at ⓦwww.visitamsterdam.nl. They take in-person bookings for canal cruises and other organized excursions and operate an extremely efficient accommodation reservation service for just €3 plus a refundable deposit that is subtracted from your final bill, but bear in mind that during peak periods the wait can be exhausting. They also sell tickets for most forthcoming performances, from rock and classical concerts through to theatre. For cultural events, go to the Amsterdam Uitburo, or **AUB**, operated by the city council, which has a walk-in booking centre tucked away in a corner of the Stadsschouwburg theatre on Leidseplein (Mon–Sat 10am–6pm, Thurs until 9pm, Sun noon–6pm; ℡0900/0191), at which you can get advice on anything remotely cultural, as well as tickets and copies of listings magazines (see p.110).

The VVV's much-touted **Amsterdam Card** provides free and unlimited use of the city's public transport network, a complimentary canal cruise and free admission to the bulk of the city's museums and attractions. It costs €33 for one day, €43 for two consecutive days and €53 for three. Altogether it's not a bad deal, but you have to work fairly hard to make it worthwhile. It's available from any branch of the VVV. Another option if you're staying for more than a couple of days is the **Museumkaart** (museum card), which gives free entry to most museums in the whole of the Netherlands for a year; it costs €29.95, slightly less for the under-25s and the over-60s.

Organized tours

No one could say the Amsterdam tourist industry doesn't make the most of its canals, with a veritable armada of glass-topped **cruise boats** shuttling along the city's waterways, offering everything from quick hour-long excursions to fully-fledged dinner cruises. There are several major operators and they occupy the prime pitches – the jetties near Centraal Station on Stationsplein, beside the

Damrak and on Prins Hendrikkade. Despite the competition, **prices** are fairly uniform with a one-hour tour costing around €10 per adult, €6 per child (4–12 years old), and around €25 (€15) for a two-hour cruise at night. The big companies also offer more specialized boat trips – dinner cruises from around €50, literary cruises, and most notably the weekly Architecture Cruise run by Lovers (☏020/530 1090, ⊛www.lovers.nl; €19.50/14.50). All these cruises – and especially the shorter and less expensive ones – are extremely popular and long queues are common throughout the summer. One way of avoiding much of the crush is to walk down the Damrak from Centraal Station to the jetty at the near end of the Rokin, where the first-rate Reederij P. Kooij (☏020/623 3810, ⊛www.rederijkooij.nl), which also has a jetty beside Centraal Station, offers all the basic cruises at slightly cheaper prices.

City transport

Almost all of Amsterdam's leading attractions are clustered in or near the city centre, within easy walking distance of each other. For longer jaunts, the city has a first-rate **public transport system**, comprising trams, buses, a pint-sized metro and four passenger ferries across the River IJ to the northern suburbs. Centraal Station is the hub of this transit system, which is run by the GVB. GVB's remit does not extend to the city's **canals**, which are mainly the haunt of cruise boats, but there are one or two interesting and reasonably economic options for getting round the city by boat. Amsterdam is also ideal for **cycling**, but **driving** – never mind parking – is a pain.

Trams, buses and the metro

Trams, **buses** and the **metro** operate daily between 6am and midnight, supplemented by a limited number of **nightbuses** (*nachtbussen*). All tram and bus stops display a detailed map of the network. For further details on all services, head for the main GVB information office (Mon–Fri 7am–9pm, Sat & Sun 8am–9pm; ☏0900/8011, ⊛www.gvb.nl) on Stationsplein. Their free, English-language *Tourist Guide to Public Transport* is very helpful, and they have free transport maps too.

The most common type of ticket, usable on all forms of GVB transport, is the **strippenkaart**, a card divided into strips: fold your *strippenkaart* over to expose the number of strips required for your journey and then insert it into the on-board franking machine. Amsterdam's public transport system is divided into zones, and one person making a journey within one zone costs two strips, two zones three strips. The "Centre" zone covers the city centre and its immediate surroundings (well beyond Singelgracht), and thus two strips will cover more or less every journey you're likely to make. If you travel into an additional zone, it costs three strips, and so on. More than one person can use a *strippenkaart*, as long as the requisite number of strips is stamped. After franking, you can use any GVB tram, bus and the metro for up to one hour. Currently, a two-strip *strippenkaart* costs €1.60, three-strip €2.40, and you can buy these on the bus or tram. However you're better off buying tickets in advance from tobacconists, the GVB, the VVV and metro stations – a fifteen-strip costs €6.70 and a 45-strip €19.80. You can opt instead for a **dagkaart** (day ticket), available from the same places, which gives unlimited access to the GVB system for up to a maximum of three days, and costs €6.30 for 24 hours, €10 for 48 hours and €13 for 72 hours.

Finally, note that the GVB tries hard to keep fare dodging down to a minimum and wherever you're travelling, and at whatever time of day, there's a reasonable chance you'll have your ticket checked. If you are caught without a valid ticket, you risk an on-the-spot fine.

Canal transport

One good way to get around Amsterdam's waterways is to take the **Canal Bus** (☎020/623 9886, ⓦwww.canal.nl). This operates on three circular routes, coloured green, red and blue, which meet at various places: at the jetty opposite Centraal Station beside Prins Hendrikkade; on the Singelgracht (opposite the Rijksmuseum), near the Leidseplein; and by the Stadhuis on Waterlooplein. There are fourteen stops in all and together they give easy access to all the major sights. Boats leave from opposite Centraal Station every half an hour or so during high season between 10am and 5.30pm, and a day ticket for all three routes, allowing you to hop on and off as many times as you like, costs €17 per adult, €11 for children (4–12 years old); it's valid until noon the following day and entitles the bearer to minor discounts at several museums. Two-day passes cost €28.50.

A similar boat service, the **Museumboot** (☎020/530 1090, ⓦwww.lovers .nl), calls at seven jetties located at or near many of the city's major attractions. It departs from opposite Centraal Station (every 30min; 10am–5pm) and a day ticket costs €15 children €13 (4–12 years old).

Finally **Canal Bikes** (daily 9am–6pm, July & August until 9.30pm; ☎020/626 5574, ⓦwww.canal.nl) are four-seater pedaloes which take a lifetime to get anywhere but are nevertheless good fun unless – of course – it's raining. You can rent them at four central locations: on the Singelgracht opposite the Rijksmuseum; the Prinsengracht outside the Anne Frank Huis; on Keizersgracht at Leidsestraat; and behind Leidseplein. Rental prices per person per hour are €7 (3–4 people) or €8 (1–2 people), plus a refundable deposit of €50; they can be picked up at one location and left at any of the others.

Bicycles

One of the most agreeable ways to explore Amsterdam is by **bicycle**. The city has an excellent network of designated bicycle lanes (*fietspaden*) and for once cycling isn't a fringe activity – there are cyclists everywhere. Indeed, much to the chagrin of the city's taxi drivers, the needs of the cyclist often take precedence over those of the motorist and by law if there's a collision it's always the driver's

Parking

On-street parking is very limited and quite expensive. Every city-centre street where parking is permitted is **metered** (Mon–Sat 9am–midnight, Sun noon–midnight), with a standard cost of €2.80 for one hour, €16.80 for a day (9am–5pm), €11.20 for the evening (7pm–midnight) or €25.20 for the full period. If you overrun your ticket, you can expect your vehicle to be clamped by eager-beaver traffic wardens; thereafter, if you don't follow the instructions posted on your windscreen promptly, your vehicle will be removed to the municipal pound. The good news is that signs on all the main approach roads to Amsterdam indicate which of the city's **car parks** have spaces. Car parks in the centre (see Listings on p.118) comparable rates to the metered street spaces, but those on the outskirts are a good deal less expensive and are invariably but a short journey from the centre by public transport. Note, too, that some of the better hotels either have their own parking spaces or offer special deals with nearby car parks.

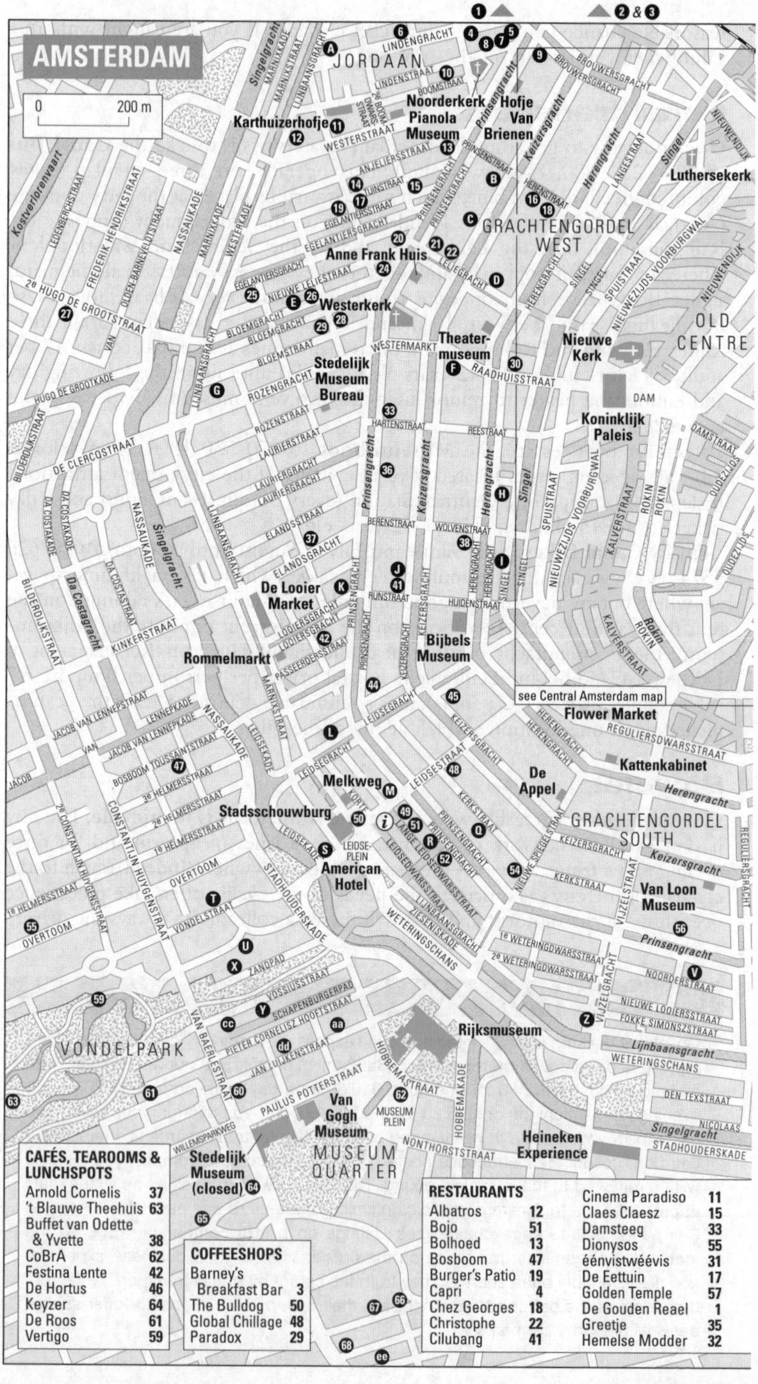
AMSTERDAM
0 200 m
JORDAAN
GRACHTENGORDEL WEST
OLD CENTRE
GRACHTENGORDEL SOUTH
VONDELPARK
MUSEUM QUARTER
Karthuizerhofje
Noorderkerk
Pianola Museum
Hofje Van Brienen
Luthersekerk
Anne Frank Huis
Westerkerk
Theatermuseum
Nieuwe Kerk
DAM
Koninklijk Paleis
Stedelijk Museum Bureau
De Looier Market
Rommelmarkt
Bijbels Museum
see Central Amsterdam map
Flower Market
Kattenkabinet
De Appel
Melkweg
Stadsschouwburg
LEIDSEPLEIN
American Hotel
Van Loon Museum
Rijksmuseum
Van Gogh Museum
MUSEUMPLEIN
Stedelijk Museum (closed)
Heineken Experience
CAFÉS, TEAROOMS & LUNCHSPOTS
Arnold Cornelis 37
't Blauwe Theehuis 63
Buffet van Odette & Yvette 38
CoBrA 62
Festina Lente 42
De Hortus 46
Keyzer 64
De Roos 61
Vertigo 59
COFFEESHOPS
Barney's Breakfast Bar 3
The Bulldog 50
Global Chillage 48
Paradox 29
RESTAURANTS
Albatros 12
Bojo 51
Bolhoed 13
Bosboom 47
Burger's Patio 19
Capri 4
Chez Georges 18
Christophe 22
Cilubang 41
Cinema Paradiso 11
Claes Claesz 15
Damsteeg 33
Dionysos 55
éénvistwéévis 31
De Eettuin 17
Golden Temple 57
De Gouden Reael 1
Greetje 35
Hemelse Modder 32

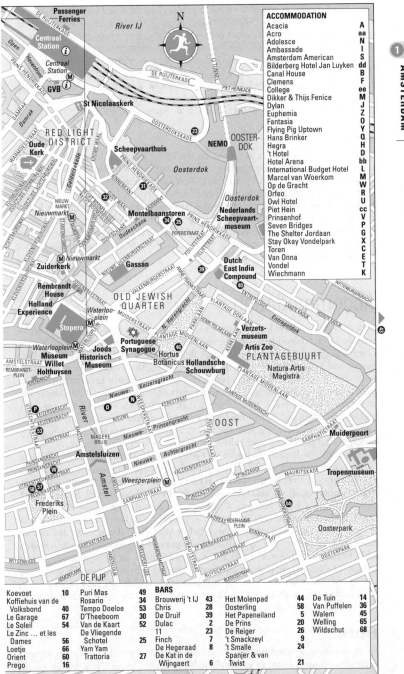

ACCOMMODATION

Acacia	A
Acro	aa
Adolesce	N
Ambassade	I
Amsterdam American	S
Bilderberg Hotel Jan Luyken	B
Canal House	F
Clemens	ee
College	M
Dikker & Thijs Fenice	J
Dylan	Z
Euphemia	O
Fantasia	Y
Flying Pig Uptown	Q
Hans Brinker	H
Hegra	D
't Hotel	bb
Hotel Arena	L
International Budget Hotel	M
Marcel van Woerkom	W
Op de Gracht	R
Orfeo	U
Owl Hotel	cc
Piet Hein	V
Prinsenhof	P
Seven Bridges	G
The Shelter Jordaan	X
Stay Okay Vondelpark	C
Toren	E
Van Onna	T
Vondel	K
Wiechmann	

Koevoet	10	Puri Mas	49	
Koffiehuis van de Volksbond	40	Rosario	34	
Le Garage	67	Tempo Doeloe	53	
Le Soleil	54	D'Theeboom	30	
Le Zinc … et les Dames	56	Van de Kaart	52	
Loetje	66	De Vliegende Schotel	25	
Orient	60	Yam Yam Trattoria	27	
Prego	16			

BARS

Brouwerij 't IJ	43	Het Molenpad	44	De Tuin	14
Chris	28	Oosterling	58	Van Puffelen	36
De Druif	39	Het Papeneiland	5	Walem	45
Dulac	2	De Prins	20	Welling	65
11	23	De Reiger	26	Wildschut	68
Finch	7	't Smackzeyl	9		
De Hegeraad	8	't Smalle	24		
De Kat in de Wijngaert	6	Spanjer & van Twist	21		

fault. **Bike rental** is straightforward. There are lots of rental companies (*fietsen-verhuur*) but MacBike (daily 9am–5.45pm; ☎020/620 0985, ⓦwww .macbike.nl) is perhaps the most convenient, with three rental outlets in central Amsterdam, one at the east end of Centraal Station, a second beside Water-looplein at Mr Visserplein 2, and a third near Leidseplein at Weteringschans 2. They charge €6 for three hours, €8.50 per day, €18 for three days and €30 for a week for a standard bicycle; 21-speed cycles cost about half as much again. All companies, including MacBike, ask for some type of security, usually in the form of a cash deposit (some will take credit card imprints) or passport.

Taxis

The centre of Amsterdam is geared up for trams and bicycles rather than cars, with motorists having to negotiate a convoluted one-way system, avoid getting boxed onto tram lines and steer round herds of cyclists. As such, **taxis** are not as much use as they are in many other cities. They are, however, plentiful: taxi ranks are liberally distributed across the city centre and they can also be hailed on the street. If all else fails, call ☎020/677 7777. **Fares** are metered and reasonably high, but distances are small: the trip from Centraal Station to the Leidseplein, for example, will cost around €12, €2 more to Museumplein – and about fifteen percent more late at night.

Accommodation

Despite a slew of new **hotels**, from chic designer places through to chain high-rises, hotel accommodation in Amsterdam can still be difficult to find, and is often a major expense, especially at peak times of the year – July and August, Easter and Christmas. Such is the popularity of Amsterdam as a short-break destination that you'd be well advised to make an advance **reservation** at any time of the year. In spite of this, most hotels only charge the full quoted rates at the very busiest times, which means that you'll often pay less than the peak season prices quoted in this book; it's certainly always worth asking if there is any discount available. At least the city's compactness means that you're pretty much bound to end up somewhere within easy reach of the centre.

The **VVV** will make advance bookings (☎(0031)20/551 2525, ⓦwww .amsterdamtourist.nl), and book rooms on the spot for a €3 fee, and you can also book through the **Netherlands Reservation Centre** (☎0299/689 144, ⓦwww.hotelres.nl), or via websites such as ⓦwww.bookings.nl. Something to bear in mind when choosing a hotel is the fact that many of Amsterdam's buildings have narrow, very steep staircases, and not all hotels have installed lifts. If this is a consideration for you, check before you book. If you arrive at Centraal Station, you'll probably be approached by **touts** offering rooms or beds in hostels and cheap hotels. Despite the fact that most of them are genuine enough, our advice is to steer clear. If the place they're offering is in our or the VVV's listings you can phone it directly yourself; if it isn't, it's been left out for a reason.

All accommodation listings are located on a map: the most central ones on p.72, the remainder on pp.64–65.

Hotels

In the main Amsterdam **hotels** are quite expensive – you'll need to pay around €100 for a double room in anywhere halfway decent, more if you want en-suite facilities. Usually some form of breakfast is included, except at the most expensive hotels. A number of hotels in Amsterdam also have large three- or four-bed family rooms available for around €150. The establishments listed below have something particular to recommend them over the rest – location, value for money or ambience. Don't be afraid to ask to see the room first, and to refuse it if you don't like it.

The Old Centre

Bellevue Martelaasrgracht 10 ☎020/707 4500, ⓦwww.bellevuehotel.nl. The rooms are newly renovated in a modern style and the location couldn't be more convenient, two minutes' from Centraal Station. Prices don't include breakfast. ❺

Le Coin Nieuwe Doelenstraat 5 ☎020/524 6800, ⓦwww.lecoin.nl. A good location opposite the swanky *Hotel de l'Europe*, but a quarter of the price. All rooms have kitchenettes and are kitted out in contemporary style. ❹

The Crown Oudezijds Voorburgwal 21 ☎020/626 9664, ⓦwww.hotelthecrown.com. Bang in the middle of the Red Light District, this is really a hotel for single people, and its pricing policy reflects that. The rooms at the back are dark and a bit austere; the ones at the front are nicer, but of course prone to noise from the busy canal outside. Still, if you're a single person wanting to meet other people you won't mind that. Very safe, and very friendly, despite the location. Late bar until 3am; five minutes from Centraal Station. ❷

Grand Hotel Krasnapolsky Dam 9 ☎020/554 9111, ⓦwww.nh-hotels.com. Located in a huge and striking mid-nineteenth-century building, this four-star hotel occupies virtually an entire side of Dam Square. Its rooms are nicely done, if unspectacular, though bargains are sometimes available. ❼

Hotel des Arts Rokin 154–56 ☎020/620 1558, ⓦwww.hoteldesarts.nl. The 22 rooms here are cosy and well furnished and the welcome is friendly. ❻

Hotel de l'Europe Nieuwe Doelenstraat 2–8 ☎020/531 1777, ⓦwww.leurope.nl. One of the city's top five hotels, and retaining a wonderful fin-de-siècle charm, with large, well-furnished rooms and an attractive riverside terrace. Great central location too – this is about as luxurious as the city gets. ❾

Misc Kloveniersburgwal 20 ☎020/330 6241, ⓦwww.hotel.misc.com. Very friendly hotel on the edge of the Red Light District with six good-sized rooms each with a different theme. Excellent value. ❹

Nes Kloveniersburgwal 137–39 ☎020/624 4773, ⓦwww.hotelnes.nl. This pleasant and quiet hotel, with helpful staff, is well positioned away from noise but close to shops and nightlife, and also has a lift. The size and quality of the rooms can vary quite a bit, so don't be afraid to ask to see another if you're disappointed. Prices vary as well and there are also triples and quads. ❹

NH City Centre Spuistraat 288 ☎020/420 4545, ⓦwww.nh-hotels.com. This appealing chain hotel occupies a sympathetically renovated 1920s Art Deco former textile factory, and is well situated for the cafés and bars of the Spui, and the Museum Quarter. Rooms vary in size, some have canal views, and all boast extremely comfy beds and good showers. The buffet breakfast is extra, but will set you up for the day. ❺

Rho Nes 5 ☎020/620 7371, ⓦwww.rhohotel.com. Built as a theatre in 1908, the lovely large high-ceilinged, fin-de-siècle lobby here gives a slightly misleading impression: the rooms are on the small side and have been unimaginatively modernized. Still, it's pleasant enough, and in a good central location just off Dam Square. Daily bike rental available. Breakfast included. ❸

Sint Nicolaas Spuistraat 1a ☎020/626 1384, ⓦwww.hotelnicolaas.nl. More characterful than many of the other budget hotels in the area, the *St Nicolaas*'s cosy downstairs bar-reception gives way to around 30 recently refurbished rooms all with baths. Very conveniently located too, just five minutes' walk from Centraal Station. ❸

Vijaya Oudezijds Voorburgwal 44 ☎020/626 9406, ⓦwww.hotelvijaya.nl. Right in the heart of the Red Light District, next door but one to the Amstelkring (see p.78), this is a warren of rooms spread over a couple of old canal houses. It's rather threadbare, but not bad for the price, and has a friendly charm that's only enhanced by the Indian restaurant downstairs. No lift. Ten minutes' walk from Amsterdam's Centraal Station. ❷

Winston Warmoesstraat 129 ☎020/623 1380, ⓦwww.winston.nl. This self-consciously young and cool hotel has funky rooms individually decorated with wacko art and a busy ground-floor bar that has occasional live music. It's a formula that works a treat; the *Winston* is popular and often full – though this is probably also due to its low prices. Lift and full disabled access. Ten minutes' walk from Amsterdam Centraal Station. ❷

The Grachtengordel

Agora Singel 462 ☏020/627 2200, @agora@
worldonline.nl. Nicely located, small and amiable
hotel right near the flower market. You'll pay more
for a canal view. ❸

Ambassade Herengracht 341 ☏020/555 0222,
Ⓦwww.ambassade-hotel.nl. Elegant canalside
hotel made up of ten seventeenth-century houses,
with smartly furnished lounges, a well-stocked
library and comfortable en-suite rooms. Friendly
staff and free 24-hour Internet access. Breakfast is
an extra €16, but well worth it. ❻

Amsterdam American Leidsekade 97 ☏020/556
3000, Ⓦwww.amsterdamamerican.com. Landmark
Art Deco hotel just off Leidseplein, which dates from
1902, though the large double-glazed bedrooms are
mostly kitted out in standard modern style. ❽

Canal House Keizersgracht 148 ☏020/622 5182,
Ⓦwww.canalhouse.nl. Intelligently restored seventeenth-century building, centrally located on one of
the principal canals. Comfortable rooms. ❹

Clemens Raadhuisstraat 39 ☏020/624 6089,
Ⓦwww.clemenshotel.nl. Friendly, well-run budget
hotel, with knowledgeable owner, close to the Anne
Frank Huis, this is one of the better options along
this busy main road. Prices stay the same
throughout the year. All rooms have free Internet
connection, and you can rent laptops for just a few
euros. ❷

Dikker & Thijs Fenice Prinsengracht 444
☏020/620 1212, Ⓦwww.dtfh.nl. Small and stylish
hotel not far from Leidseplein. Rooms vary in decor
but all include a minibar, telephone and TV – those
on the top floor have good views of the city. ❺

Dylan Keizersgracht 384 ☏020/530 2010,
Ⓦwww.dylanamsterdam.com. This stylish hotel is
housed in a seventeenth-century building that
centres on a beautiful courtyard and terrace. Its 41
sumptuous rooms range in style from opulent reds
or greens to minimal white and oatmeal shades,
and have flat-screen TVs and stereos. The restaurant combines French and African cuisine and the
bar is open to non-guests. The ambience is hip
without being pretentious, and that goes for the
staff too, making it popular, with many guests
returning. Breakfast €24 extra. ❾

Estherea Singel 303–9 ☏020/624 5146, Ⓦwww
.estherea.nl. This smart, standard-issue hotel
converted from a couple of canal houses is in a
great location, and although the rooms lack the
personal touch they are all perfectly adequate; the
best overlook the canal. ❽

Hegra Herengracht 269 ☏020/623 7877, Ⓦwww
.hegrahotel.com. Welcoming atmosphere and
relatively inexpensive for the location, on a
handsome stretch of canal near the Spui. Rooms

are small but comfortable, either en suite or with
shared facilities. ❷

Hoksbergen Singel 301 ☏020/626 6043,
Ⓦwww.hotelhoksbergen.nl. Agreeable hotel, with a
light and open breakfast room overlooking the
Singel canal. Basic en-suite rooms, all with
telephones and TVs; breakfast and tax included.
There are also self-catering apartments. ❷

't Hotel Leliegracht 18 ☏020/422 2741, Ⓦwww
.amsterdamby.com/thotel. Extremely appealing
hotel located in an old high-gabled house along a
quiet stretch of canal. The eight spacious rooms
are decorated in bright, modern style with large
beds and either bath or shower. No groups.
Minimum three-night stay at the weekend. ❹

Marcel van Woerkom Leidsestraat 87 ☏020/622
9834, Ⓦwww.marcelamsterdam.com. This well-
known, popular B&B is run by a graphic designer
and artist who attracts like-minded people to this
stylish restored house with four en-suite doubles
available for two, three or four people sharing.
Relaxing and peaceful amid the buzz of the city,
with regulars returning year after year, so you'll
need to book well in advance in high season.
Breakfast isn't included, but there are tea- and
coffee-making facilities. ❸

Op de Gracht Prinsengracht 826 ☏020/626 1937,
Ⓦwww.opdegracht.nl. This B&B run by the very
pleasant Jolanda Schipper is in a good-looking old
house on one of the main canals. The two rooms
are tastefully decorated, both with en-suite
bathrooms. Minimum stay two nights. ❷

Orfeo Leidsekruisstraat 14 ☏020/623 1347,
Ⓦwww.hotelorfeo.com. Very pleasant and
popular gay and lesbian hotel round the back of
Leidseplein, with decent breakfasts served until
midday. ❷

Prinsenhof Prinsengracht 810 ☏020/623 1772,
Ⓦwww.hotelprinsenhof.com. This tastefully
decorated hotel is one of the city's top budget
options. Booking essential. ❶

Seven Bridges Reguliersgracht 31 ☏020/623
1329, Ⓦwww.sevenbridgeshotel.nl. One of the
city's most charming hotels – and excellent value
for money too. It takes its name from its canalside
location, which affords a view of no fewer than
seven dinky little bridges. Beautifully decorated in
antique style, its spotless rooms are regularly
revamped. Small and popular, so advance reservations are pretty much essential. Breakfast is
included in the price and served in your room. ❸

🏃 **Toren** Keizersgracht 164 ☏020/622 6033,
Ⓦwww.hoteltoren.nl. The 40 bedrooms are
distributed between two sympathetically revamped
seventeenth-century canal houses just a few doors
away from each other. One of them – no.164 – was

once the home of a Dutch prime minister, and both are now popular with American visitors. The bedrooms themselves are large, modern and well appointed. Friendly and efficient staff. ❻

Wiechmann Prinsengracht 328–32 ☎020/626 3321, ⓦwww.hotelwiechmann.nl. Family-run for over fifty years, this medium-sized hotel occupies an attractively restored canal house, close to the Anne Frank Huis, with dark wooden beams and restrained style throughout. Large, bright rooms are in perfect condition with TVs and showers. Prices stay the same throughout the year. ❹

The Jordaan and the Western docklands

Acacia Lindengracht 251 ☎020/622 1460, ⓔacacia.nl@wxs.nl. Small hotel, situated in the heart of the Jordaan, right on a corner, so some of the rooms have wide views of the canal and its adjoining streets. Rooms, which sleep two to four people, are rather nondescript with small beds and a shower room. There are also self-catering studios. A fifteen-minute walk from Centraal Station. ❷

Van Onna Bloemgracht 102 ☎020/626 5801, ⓦwww.hotelvanonna.nl. A quiet, well-maintained place on a tranquil canal. The building dates back over three hundred years and still retains some of its original fixtures, though the rooms themselves are rather modest, with basic furniture and blankets on the beds. Simple setup – no TV, no smoking and cash payment only. Booking advised. Rooms sleeping up to four people for €45 per person, including breakfast.

The Old Jewish Quarter and the Oosterdok

Adolesce Nieuwe Keizersgracht 26 ☎020/626 3959, ⓦwww.adolesce.nl. Popular and welcoming hotel in an old canal house not far from Waterlooplein. There are ten neat and trim modern rooms and a large dining room. ❸

Fantasia Nieuwe Keizersgracht 16 ☎020/623 8259, ⓦwww.fantasia-hotel.com. Appealing, family-run hotel in an intelligently revamped old canal house on a broad, quiet canal just off the River Amstel; the eighteen en-suite rooms are all well maintained and the attic rooms are especially attractive. Doubles, triples and a four-bed family room are available. Closed Jan–March and most of Dec. ❸

Hotel Arena 's-Gravesandestraat 51 ☎020/850 2400, ⓦwww.hotelarena.nl. A little way east of the

centre, in a renovated old convent on the edge of the Oosterpark, this place has been thoroughly revamped, and is now a hip three-star hotel complete with split-level rooms and minimalist decor. Despite the odd pretentious flourish, it manages to retain a relaxed vibe attracting both businesspeople and travellers alike. Lively bar, intimate restaurant, and late-night club (Fri & Sat) located within the former chapel. ❸

The Museum Quarter and the Vondelpark

Acro Jan Luyckenstraat 44 ☎020/662 5538, ⓦwww.acro-hotel.nl. Small and fairly functional rooms, but a friendly welcome and a nice bar on the ground floor mean that this hotel gets booked up a long way in advance. ❸

Bilderberg Hotel Jan Luyken Jan Luykenstraat 58 ☎020/676 3841, ⓦwww.janluyken.nl. Good-sized rooms, nicely refurbished relatively recently, mark out this decent stab at a mini four-star, full-service hotel. A nice lounge and bar downstairs too. ❹

🎿 **College** Roelof Hartstraat 1 ☎020/571 1511, ⓦwww.thesteingroup.com/college. Converted from an old schoolhouse, *College* is one of the most elegant and original recent additions to Amsterdam's hotel scene. Original because it's largely run by students from the city's catering school; elegant because of the sheer class of the refurbishment. ❼

Owl Hotel Roemer Visscherstraat 1 ☎020/618 9484, ⓦwww.owl-hotel.nl. The reasonably priced doubles here are relatively blandly furnished, but its location is nice and quiet, with a downstairs lounge opening onto a lovely garden, and – run by the same family for nearly forty years – the staff are a welcoming bunch. ❹

Piet Hein Vossiusstraat 53 ☎020/662 7205, ⓦwww.hotelpiethein.nl. Five minutes' walk from Leidseplein, this sleek three-star hotel has large rooms with views over the entrance to the Vondelpark and slightly more expensive rooms in the modern annexe overlooking its peaceful back garden. Bar open till 1am. Lift access. ❹

🎿 **Vondel** Vondelstraat 18–30 ☎020/616 4075, ⓦwww.hotelvondel.com. This newly refurbished hotel tries hard to be cool and sleek, and mostly succeeds, with black paint and light natural wood characterizing lovely rooms with flatscreen TVs. There's a pleasant bar and breakfast room and modern art decorates the walls of the common areas. ❺

Hostels

The bottom line for most travellers is taking a dormitory bed in a **hostel**, and there are plenty to choose from: official HI places (dubbed "Stayokay"), unofficial private hostels, even Christian. Most hostels will provide either (relatively) clean bed linen or charge a few euros for it – so your own sleeping bag may be a better option. Many hostels also lock guests out for a short period each day to clean the place and some set a nightly curfew, though these are usually late enough not to cause too much of a problem. Prices start at just under €20 for a dormitory bed and rise to around €60-plus for a double room – which a number of hostels offer. Many hostels don't accept reservations from June to August.

Bob's Youth Hostel Nieuwezijds Voorburgwal 92 ☎020/623 0063, ⓦwww.bobshostel.nl. An old favourite with backpackers, Bob's is a lively place with small, basic dorm beds for €19 per person, including breakfast in the coffeeshop on the ground floor. They also let four apartments (€70 for two people, €80 for three). However, they kick everyone out at 10.30am to clean, which is not so good if you want a lie-in. Just 10 minutes' walk from Centraal Station.

Bulldog Low-Budget Hotel Oudezijds Voorburgwal 220 ☎020/620 3822, ⓦwww .bulldoghotel.com. Part of the *Bulldog* coffeeshop chain, and recently renovated, with a bar and DVD lounge downstairs complete with leather couches and soft lighting. Beds in dorms with TVs and showers start at €28, including breakfast, with linen €3 extra, and there are also double rooms for €90, as well as fully equipped apartments from €135 – all with bathrooms and TVs.

Euphemia Fokke Simonszstraat 1–9 ☎020/622 9045, ⓦwww.euphemiahotel.com. Situated a shortish walk from Leidseplein and the major museums, with a likeable laidback atmosphere and basic but large rooms. Doubles from €70, triples from €75. Breakfast €7. Booking advised.

Flying Pig Downtown Nieuwendijk 100 ☎020/420 6822, ⓦwww.flyingpig.nl. Clean, large and well run by ex-travellers familiar with the needs of backpackers. Free use of kitchen facilities, no curfew, there's a late-night coffeeshop next door and the hostel bar is open all night. Justifiably popular, and a very good deal, with mixed dorm beds from just €23 depending on the size of the dorm; queen-size bunks sleeping two also available; €10 deposit for sheets and keys. During the peak season you'll need to book well in advance. Just a five-minute walk from Centraal Station.

Flying Pig Uptown Vossiusstraat 46 ☎020/400 4187, ⓦwww.flyingpig.nl. The better of the two *Flying Pig* hostels, facing the Vondelpark and close to the city's most important museums. Immaculately clean and well maintained by a staff of travellers. Free use of kitchen facilities, no curfew and good tourist information. Fourteen-bed dorms start at €23.90 per person and there are a few two-person queen-size bunks, as well as double rooms. Great value.

Hans Brinker Kerkstraat 136 ☎020/622 0687, ⓦwww.hans-brinker.com. Well-established and raucously popular Amsterdam hostel, with around 600 beds. Dorms are basic and clean and beds go for around €21; singles, doubles and triples are also available. All rooms are en suite. The facilities are good: free Internet after 10pm, disco every night, and it's near to the buzz of Leidseplein too. A hostel to head for if you're out for a good time (and not too bothered about getting a solid night's sleep), though be prepared to change dorms during your stay. Walk-in policy only.

International Budget Hotel Leidsegracht 76 ☎020/624 2784, ⓦwww.internationalbudgethostel .com. An excellent budget option on a peaceful little canal in the heart of the city, with the same owners as the *Euphemia*, and young, friendly staff. Small, simple rooms sleeping up to four with shared facilities and costing €25–30 per person.

Shelter City Barndesteeg 21 ☎020/625 3230, ⓦwww.shelter.nl. A non-evangelical Christian youth hostel smack in the middle of the Red Light District. Beds in large dorms for €19, including bed linen, shower and sizeable breakfast, which makes this one of the city's best deals (€23 for a bed in a smaller dorm). Dorms are single-sex; lockers require a €5 deposit and there's a midnight curfew (1am at weekends). You might be handed a booklet on Jesus when you check in, but you'll get a quiet night's sleep and the sheets are clean. Metro Nieuwmarkt.

The Shelter Jordaan Bloemstraat 179 ☎020/624 4717, ⓦwww.shelter.nl. The second of Amsterdam's two Christian youth hostels. Great-value beds start from €19 per dorm bed (€16 in low season) including breakfast; bed linen is €2 extra. Fri & Sat €3 supplement. Dorms sleeping fourteen to twenty are single-sex and non-smoking; downstairs there's a decent café. Lockers require a €5 deposit. Sited in a particularly attractive and quiet part of the Jordaan, close to the Lijnbaansgracht canal.

Stay Okay Stadsdoelen Kloveniersburgwal 97 ☎020/624 6832, ⓦwww.stayokay.com /stadsdoelen. The closest to Centraal Station of the two official hostels, with clean, semi-private dorms at €20 for members, who get priority in high season; non-members pay €23.75. Price includes linen, breakfast and locker, plus use of communal kitchen. Guests get a range of discounts on activities in the city too, and you can also book Eurolines bus tickets here, with members receiving a ten-percent discount. The bar overlooks the canal and serves good-value if basic food, and there's a 2am curfew (though the door opens for three 15min intervals between 2am and 7am).

Stay Okay Vondelpark Zandpad 5 ⊕020/589 8996, ⊛www.stayokay.com/vondelpark. Well

located and, for facilities, the better of the city's two HI hostels, with a bar, restaurant, TV lounge, Internet access and bicycle shed, plus various discount facilities for tours and museums. Non-member rates are €23.75 per person in the dorms, including use of all facilities, shower, sheets and breakfast. Singles, doubles and rooms sleeping up to eight are also available, for prices ranging from €26 per person in an eight-person dorm to €75 or so for a double room. Secure lockers and no curfew. To be sure of a place in high season you'll need to book at least two months ahead.

Campsites

There are several **campsites** in and around Amsterdam, most of them easily accessible by car or public transport. The three listed below are recommended by the VVV; *Amstermse Bos* is suitable for families, or those touring with a caravan or camper, while the other two attract younger visitors. For information on city campsites throughout the Netherlands, take a look at ⊛www.stadscampings.nl.

Amsterdamse Bos Kleine Noorddijk 1, Aalsmeer ⊕020/641 6868, €camping@dab.amsterdam.nl. Facilities include a bar, shop and restaurant, but this campsite is a long way out, on the southern reaches of the lush and well-kept Amsterdamse Bos (forest). Rates are €5 per person per night (children under 3 are free), hot showers included, plus €3.50 for a car, €7 for a camper and €4.50 for a caravan. Huts sleeping up to four cost €45 a night, which includes a gas stove. Take yellow NZH bus #172 from Centraal Station to Amstelveen, then bus #171; from Schiphol you can take bus #199 direct. Exit 6 off the A9 towards Aalsmeer. April to mid-Oct.

Vliegenbos Meeuwenlaan 138 ⊕020/636 8855, ⊛www.vliegenbos.com. A relaxed and friendly site, just a 10-minute bus ride from the centre, in north Amsterdam. Facilities include a general shop, bar, restaurant and laundry. Rates are €8 per night per

person, hot showers included, plus €1–4 for a tent, €8 for a car. There are also huts with bunk beds and basic cooking facilities, for €68 per night for four people; phone ahead to check availability. Under-16s need to be accompanied by an adult; no pets. Bus #32 or #33 (nightbus #361) from Centraal Station, or ferries to Wilhelmina Dok leave you a fifteen-minute walk from the site. Exit S116 off the A10 motorway. April–Sept.

Zeeburg Zuider IJdijk 20 ⊕020/694 4430, ⊛www.campingzeeburg.nl. Slightly better equipped than *Vliegenbos*, rates here are €3–5 per person, plus €2.50–5 for a tent, €3 for a motorbike and €3–4 for a car. Hot showers are an extra €0.80. Cabins sleeping two to six are available for €25–120 per night, including bed linen. Tram #26 from Centraal Station, bus #37 from Amstel Station. Exit S114 off the A10. Open all year.

The City

Confined by the circuitous sweep of the Singelgracht canal, Amsterdam's compact centre contains most of the city's leading attractions but it takes only about forty minutes to stroll from one end to the other. **Centraal Station**, where you're most likely to arrive, lies on the centre's northern edge, its back to the River IJ, and from here the city fans south in a web of concentric canals, surrounded by expanding suburbs. The city centre readily divides into a network of distinct neighbourhoods, but it's small enough that just wandering around from one to another to get the flavour of the place is often the most enjoyable way to proceed.

At the heart of the city is Amsterdam's most vivacious district, the **Old Centre**, an oval-shaped area featuring a jumble of antique streets and beautiful, narrow little canals, some of which are the unlikely setting for the sleazy but

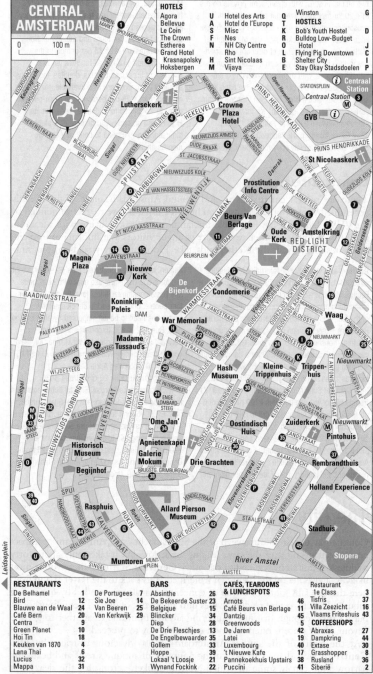

CENTRAL AMSTERDAM

0 — 100 m

HOTELS

Agora	U	Hotel des Arts	Q	Winston	G
Bellevue	A	Hotel de l'Europe	T	**HOSTELS**	
Le Coin	S	Misc	K	Bob's Youth Hostel	D
The Crown	F	Nes	R	Bulldog Low-Budget	
Estherea	N	NH City Centre	O	Hotel	J
Grand Hotel		Rho	L	Flying Pig Downtown	C
Krasnapolsky	H	Sint Nicolaas	B	Shelter City	I
Hoksbergen	M	Vijaya	E	Stay Okay Stadsdoelen	P

RESTAURANTS

De Belhamel	1	De Portugees	7
Bird	12	Sie Joe	14
Blauwe aan de Waal	24	Van Beeren	25
Café Bern	20	Van Kerkwijk	29
Centra	9		
Green Planet	10		
Hoi Tin	18		
Keuken van 1870	4		
Lana Thai	6		
Lucius	32		
Mappa	31		

BARS

Absinthe	26
De Bekeerde Suster	23
Belgique	15
Blincker	34
Diep	28
De Drie Fleschjes	13
De Engelbewaarder	35
Gollem	33
Hoppe	39
Lokaal 't Loosje	21
Wynand Fockink	22

CAFÉS, TEAROOMS & LUNCHSPOTS

Arnots	26
Café Beurs van Berlage	11
Dantzig	45
De Jaren	42
Latei	19
Luxembourg	40
't Nieuwe Kafe	17
Pannekoekhuis Upstairs	38
Puccini	41

Restaurant 1e Class	3
Tisfris	37
Villa Zeezicht	16
Vlaams Friteshuis	43
COFFEESHOPS	
Abraxas	27
Dampkring	44
Extase	30
Grasshopper	8
Rusland	36
Siberië	2

infamous Red Light District. Forming a ring around it is the first of the major canals, the Singel, followed closely by the Herengracht, Keizersgracht and Prinsengracht – collectively known as the **Grachtengordel**, or "Girdle of Canals". These were part of a major seventeenth-century urban extension and, with the interconnecting radial streets, form the city's distinctive web shape. This is the Amsterdam you see in the brochures: still, dreamy canals, crisp reflections of seventeenth-century town houses, cobbled streets, railings with chained bicycles – an image which, although perhaps a little too familiar, is still utterly authentic. Beyond the Grachtengordel, the **Jordaan** to the west grew up as a slum and immigrant quarter and remains the traditional heart of working-class Amsterdam, though in recent years it has experienced a measure of gentrification. Its mazy streets and narrow canals make it a pleasant area to wander. On the east side of the centre is the **Old Jewish Quarter**; since the Nazi occupation during World War II, this area has changed more than any other – its population gone and landscape altered – but there are several poignant reminders of earlier times, most notably the first-rate Jewish Historical Museum, and a rash of new development in the eastern docklands beyond. A couple of Amsterdam's leading museums can be found just beyond the southern boundary of the Grachtengordel, in what is sometimes known as the **Museum Quarter**, on the edge of Museumplein, which forms a cultural prelude to the sprawling greenery of the nearby **Vondelpark**, Amsterdam's loveliest park, and the residential neighbourhoods of the Old South beyond.

The Old Centre

The **Old Centre** was where Amsterdam began, starting out as a fishing village at the mouth of the River Amstel and then, when the river was dammed in 1270, flourishing as a trading centre and receiving its municipal charter from a new feudal overlord, the Count of Holland, in about 1300. Thereafter, the city developed in stages, each of which was marked by the digging of new canals and, after a particularly severe fire in 1452, by the abandonment of timber for stone and brick as the main building materials. Today, it's the handsome stone and brick buildings of subsequent centuries, especially the seventeenth, which provide the old centre with most of its architectural highlights.

Strolling across the bridge from Centraal Station brings you onto the **Damrak**, the spine of the Old Centre and the thoroughfare that once divided the **Oude Zijde** (Old Side) of the medieval city to the east from the smaller **Nieuwe Zijde** (New Side) to the west. The Damrak culminates in **Dam Square**, flanked by two of the city's most impressive buildings, the Koninklijk Paleis (Royal Palace) and the Nieuwe Kerk. To the east of Damrak is the **Red Light District**, which stretches up to Nieuwmarkt. It's here you'll find many of the city's finest buildings, though the seediness of the tentacular red-light zone dulls many charms. That said, be sure to spare time for the district's two delightful churches – the Amstelkring and the Oude Kerk. Just beyond the reach of the Red Light District is careworn **Nieuwmarkt**, an unappetizing start to the **Kloveniersburgwal**, which forms one of the most beguiling parts of the Old Centre, with a medley of handsome old houses lining the prettiest of canals. From here, it's a short walk west to the **Rokin**, a shopping boulevard running south from the Dam to **Muntplein**, a busy junction where you'll find the floating flower market.

Centraal Station and around

With its high gables and cheerful brickwork, the neo-Renaissance **Centraal Station** is an imposing prelude to the city. At the time of its construction in the

△ Clock face on Centraal Station

1880s, it aroused much controversy because it effectively separated the centre from the River IJ, source of the city's wealth, for the first time in Amsterdam's long history. Outside, **Stationsplein** is a messy open space, edged by ovals of water, packed with trams and dotted with barrel organs and chip stands – in the summer street performers complete the picture.

Across the water, to the southeast on Prins Hendrikkade, rise the whopping twin towers and dome of **St Nicolaaskerk** (Mon–Sat noon–3pm; free), the city's foremost Catholic church. Dating back to the 1880s, the cavernous interior holds some pretty dire religious murals, mawkish concoctions only partly relieved by swathes of coloured brickwork. Above the high altar is the crown of the Habsburg emperor Maximilian, very much a symbol of the city and one you'll see again and again. Amsterdam had close ties with Maximilian: in the late fifteenth century he came here as a pilgrim and stayed on to recover from an illness. The burghers funded many of his military expeditions and, in return, he let the city use his crown in its coat of arms – a practice that, rather surprisingly, survived the seventeenth-century revolt against Spain.

Damrak

From Stationsplein, **Damrak**, a wide but unenticing avenue lined with tacky restaurants, bars and bureaux de change, slices south into the heart of the city, first passing an inner harbour crammed with the bobbing canal boats of Amsterdam's considerable tourist industry. Just beyond the harbour is the imposing bulk of the **Beurs**, the old Stock Exchange – known as the "Beurs van Berlage" – a seminal work designed at the turn of the century by the leading light of the Dutch Modern movement, Hendrik Petrus Berlage (1856–1934). It's used for concerts and occasional exhibitions these days, so you often can't get in to see the graceful exposed ironwork and shallow-arched arcades of the main hall, but you can stop by the café that fronts onto Beursplein around the corner (see p.102) for a coffee and admire the tiled scenes of the past, present and the future by Jan Toorop.

Just along from the Beurs, the enormous and long-established De Bijenkorf – literally "beehive" – department store extends south along the Damrak. Amsterdam's most upmarket store, De Bijenkorf posed all sorts of problems for the Germans when they first occupied the city in World War II. It was a Jewish concern, so the Nazis didn't really want their troops shopping here, but it was just too popular to implement a total ban; the bizarre solution was to prohibit German soldiers from shopping on the ground floor, where the store's Jewish employees were concentrated, as they always had been, in the luxury goods section.

Dam Square

Situated at the heart of the city just beyond De Bijenkorf, **Dam Square** gave Amsterdam its name: in the thirteenth century the River Amstel was dammed here, and the fishing village that grew around it became known as "Amstelredam". Boats could sail into the square down the Damrak and unload right in the middle of the settlement, which soon prospered by trading herrings for Baltic grain. In the early fifteenth century, the building of Amsterdam's principal church, the Nieuwe Kerk, and thereafter the town hall (now the Royal Palace), formally marked the Dam as Amsterdam's centre, but since World War II it has lost much of its dignity. Today it's open and airy but somehow rather desultory, despite – or perhaps partly because of – the presence of the main municipal **war memorial**, a prominent stone tusk adorned by bleak, suffering figures and decorated with the coats of arms of each of the Netherlands' provinces (plus the ex-colony of Indonesia). The local branch of **Madame Tussaud's** waxworks is at no. 20 (daily 10am–6.30pm, July & Aug until 9pm; €19.95, children €14.95; ⓦ www.madame-tussauds.com).

Dominating the Dam is the **Koninklijk Paleis** or Royal Palace (July & Aug 11am–5pm, and occasionally at other times during the year; €4.50; ☎020/620 4060, ⓦ www.koninklijkhuis.nl). The title is deceptive, given that this vast sandstone structure started out as the city's Stadhuis (town hall) in the mid-seventeenth century, and only had its first royal occupant when Louis Bonaparte moved in during the French occupation (1795–1813). At the time of the building's construction, Amsterdam was at the height of its powers. The city was pre-eminent amongst Dutch towns, and had just resisted William of Orange's attempts to bring it to heel; predictably, the council craved a residence that was a declaration of the city's municipal power and opted for a startlingly progressive design by Jacob van Campen, who proposed a Dutch rendering of the Classical principles revived in Renaissance Italy. Initially, there was opposition to the plan from the council's Calvinist minority, who pointed out that the proposed Stadhuis would dwarf the neighbouring Nieuwe Kerk. However, when the Calvinists were promised a new church spire (it was never built) they promptly fell in line, and in 1648 work started on what was then the largest town hall in Europe, supported by no fewer than 13,659 wooden piles driven into the Dam's sandy soil – a number every Dutch schoolchild remembers by adding a "1" and a "9" to the number of days in the year. The poet Constantijn Huygens called the new building "The world's Eighth Wonder / With so much stone raised high and so much timber under".

The Stadhuis received its royal designation in 1808, when Napoleon's brother Louis, who had recently been installed as king, commandeered it as his residence. Lonely and isolated, Louis abdicated in 1810 and high-tailed it out of the country, leaving behind a large quantity of Empire furniture, most of which is exhibited in the rooms he converted. Possession of the palace subsequently reverted to the city, which sold it to the state in 1935, since when it has been used by royalty on very rare occasions.

The Nieuwe Kerk

Vying for importance with the Royal Palace is the adjacent **Nieuwe Kerk** (open for exhibitions; check hours and admission on ☏020/638 6909, ⓦwww .nieuwekerk.nl), which despite its name – "new church" – is an early fifteenth-century structure built in a late flourish of the Gothic style, with a forest of pinnacles and high, slender gables. Nowadays de-sanctified and used for temporary exhibitions, opening times vary according to what's on, and occasionally it's closed altogether. But it is worth going in if you can: its hangar-like interior holds a scattering of decorative highlights, such as the seventeenth-century tomb of Dutch naval hero Admiral Michiel de Ruyter, complete with trumpeting angels, conch-blowing Neptunes and cherubs all in a tizzy. Ruyter trounced in succession the Spaniards, the Swedes, the English and the French, and his rise from deck-hand to Admiral-in-Chief is the stuff of national legend. He was buried here with full military honours and the church is still used for state occasions: the coronations of queens Wilhelmina, Juliana and, in 1980, Beatrix, were all held here.

Across the street from the church, you can't miss the old neo-Gothic post office of 1899, now converted into the **Magna Plaza** shopping mall. The building is a grand affair, and makes an attractive setting for the numerous clothes chains that inhabit its redbrick interior.

The Red Light District

The area to the east of Damrak, between Warmoesstraat, Nieuwmarkt and Damstraat, is the **Red Light District**, known locally as "De Walletjes" (Small Walls) on account of the series of low brick walls that contains its canals. The district stretches across the two narrow canals that once marked the eastern part of medieval Amsterdam, **Oudezijds Voorburgwal** and **Oudezijds Achterburgwal**, with the far canal of Kloveniersburgwal forming its eastern boundary. The area is pretty seedy, although the legalized prostitution here has long been one of the city's most distinctive draws. It wasn't always so: the handsome facades of Oudezijds Voorburgwal in particular recall ritzier days, when this was one of the wealthiest parts of the city, richly earning its nickname the "Velvet Canal".

Oudezijds Voorburgwal and Oudezijds Achterburgwal, with their narrow connecting passages, are thronged with "window brothels", and at busy times the crass, on-street haggling over the price of sex is drowned out by a surprisingly festive atmosphere – entire families grinning more or less amiably at the women in the windows or discussing the specifications of the sex toys in the shops. There's a nasty undertow to the district, however, oddly enough sharper during the daytime, when the pimps hang out in shifty gangs and drug addicts wait anxiously, assessing the chances of scoring their next hit. Don't even think about taking a picture of one of the windows, unless you're prepared for some major grief from the camera-shy prostitutes and their minders.

Soliciting hasn't always been the principal activity on sleazy **Warmoesstraat**. It was once one of the city's most fashionable streets, home to Holland's foremost poet, **Joost van den Vondel** (1587–1679), who ran his hosiery business from no. 110 in-between writing and hobnobbing with the Amsterdam elite. Vondel is a kind of Dutch Shakespeare: his *Gijsbrecht van Amstel*, a celebration of Amsterdam during its Golden Age, is one of the classics of Dutch literature, and he wrote regular, if ponderous, official verses, including well over a thousand lines on the inauguration of the new town hall. He had more than his share of hard luck too. His son frittered away the modest family fortune and Vondel lived out his last few years as doorkeeper of the pawn shop on Oudezijds Voorburgwal, dying of hypothermia at what was then the remarkable age of 92.

Vondel's Warmoesstraat house was knocked down decades ago, and the street holds few attractions apart from the **Condomerie Het Gulden Vlies**, at no.141, which specializes in every imaginable design and make of condom, in sizes ranging from the small to the remarkable. Also, for the lowdown on the local sex industry, there's the **Prostitution Information Centre**, at Enge Kerksteeg 3, in-between Warmoesstraat and the Oude Kerk (Tues, Wed, Fri & Sat 11.30am–7.30pm), a charitable foundation set up to provide prostitutes, their clients and general visitors with information about prostitution, which sells books, pamphlets and souvenirs of the Red Light District.

The Oude Kerk

Just to the east of Warmoesstraat, the Gothic **Oude Kerk** is the city's most appealing church. There's been a church on this site since the middle of the thirteenth century, but most of the present building dates from a century later, funded by the pilgrims who came here in their hundreds following a widely publicized miracle. The story goes that in 1345 a dying man regurgitated the Host he had received here at Communion and when it was thrown on the fire afterwards, it did not burn. The unburnable Host was placed in a chest and eventually installed here, and although it disappeared during the Reformation, thousands of the faithful still come to take part in the annual commemorative **Stille Omgang** in mid-March, a silent nocturnal procession terminating at the Oude Kerk. Inside you can see the unadorned memorial tablet of Rembrandt's first wife, Saskia van Uylenburg, beneath the smaller of the organs, and three beautifully coloured stained-glass windows beside the ambulatory dating from the 1550s. They depict, from left to right, the Annunciation, the Adoration of the Shepherds and the Dormition of the Virgin. Outside, the Oude Kerk tower is open weekends between April and September (1–5pm; €5) and offers predictably great views – in a city with relatively few such opportunities.

The Amstelkring

The front of the Oude Kerk overlooks the northern reaches of **Oudezijds Voorburgwal**, where, at no. 40, is the clandestine **Amstelkring** (Mon–Sat 10am–5pm, Sun 1–5pm; €7; @ www.museumamstelkring.nl), which was once the city's principal Catholic place of worship and is now one of Amsterdam's most enjoyable museums. The Amstelkring – "Amstel Circle" – is named after the group of nineteenth-century historians who saved the building from demolition, but its proper name is Ons Lieve Heer Op Solder ("Our Dear Lord in the Attic"). The church dates from the early seventeenth century when, with the Protestants firmly in control, the city's Catholics were only allowed to practise their faith in private – such as here in this clandestine church, which occupies the loft of a wealthy merchant's house. The church's narrow nave has been skilfully shoehorned into the available space and, flanked by elegant balconies, there's just enough room for an ornately carved organ at one end and a mock-marble high altar, decorated with Jacob de Wit's mawkish *Baptism of Christ*, at the other. The rest of the house is similarly untouched, its original furnishings reminiscent of interiors by Vermeer or De Hooch.

Nieuwmarkt and Kloveniersburgwal

Nieuwmarkt was long one of the city's most important market squares and the place where gentiles and Jews from the nearby Jewish Quarter – just southeast along St Antoniebreestraat – traded. All that came to a traumatic end during World War II, when the Nazis cordoned off the Nieuwmarkt with barbed wire and turned it into a holding pen. After the war, the square's old exuberance never returned and these days its focus is the sprawling multi-turreted **Waag**, dating from the 1480s and with a chequered history. Built as one of Amsterdam's fortified gates, the city's expansion soon made it obsolete and the ground floor was turned into a municipal weighing-house (*waag*), with the rooms upstairs taken over by the surgeons' guild. It was here that the surgeons held lectures on anatomy and public dissections, the inspiration for Rembrandt's *Anatomy Lesson of Dr Tulp*, displayed in the Mauritshuis collection in Den Haag. Abandoned by the surgeons and the weigh-masters in the nineteenth century, the building eventually fell into disuse, until being renovated to house the café-bar and restaurant, *In de Waag*.

Nieuwmarkt sits at the head of the **Kloveniersburgwal**, a long, dead-straight waterway that was the outermost of the three eastern canals of the medieval city. The canal is framed by a string of old and dignified facades, one of which, the **Trippenhuis**, at no. 29, is a huge overblown mansion complete with Corinthian pilasters and a grand frieze built for the Trip family in 1662. One of the richest families in Amsterdam, the Trips were a powerful force among the Magnificat, a clique of families (Six, Trip, Hooft and Pauw) who shared power during the Golden Age. One part of the Trip family dealt with the Baltic trade, another with the manufacture of munitions (in which they had the municipal monopoly), but in addition to this they also had trade interests in Russia and the Middle East, much like the multinationals of today. Almost directly opposite, on the west bank of the canal, the **Kleine Trippenhuis**, at no. 26, is, by contrast, one of the narrowest houses in Amsterdam, albeit with a warmly carved facade. Legend asserts that Mr Trip's coachman was so taken aback by the size of the new family mansion that he exclaimed he would be happy with a home no wider than the Trips' front door – which is exactly what he got. His reaction to his new lodgings is not recorded.

Further along the canal, on the corner of Oude Hoogstraat, is the former headquarters of the Dutch East India Company, the **Oostindisch Huis**, a monumental redbrick structure built in 1605 shortly after the founding of the company. It was from here that the Company organized and regulated its immensely lucrative trading interests in the Far East, importing shiploads of spices, perfumes and exotic woods. This trade underpinned Amsterdam's Golden Age, but predictably the people of what is now Indonesia, the source of most of the raw materials, received little in return. These days the building is occupied by university classrooms and offices.

From the Oostindisch Huis, you can either proceed along Oude Hoogstraat to the Hash Museum or keep to Kloveniersburgwal, whose southern reaches are flanked by a comely collection of old canal houses interrupted by the occasional nineteenth-century extravagance. In particular, turn east across the canal along Staalstraat and stop at the second of the two little drawbridges for one of the finest views in the city down the slender **Groenburgwal**, with the Zuiderkerk looming beyond.

The **Zuiderkerk** (Mon 11am–4pm, Tues–Wed & Fri 9am–4pm, Thurs 9am–8pm; free), dating from 1611, was the first Amsterdam church built specifically for Protestants. It was designed by the prolific architect and sculptor, Hendrick de Keyser (1565–1621), whose distinctive – and very popular – style extrapolated elements of traditional Flemish design, with fanciful detail and frilly towers added wherever possible. The basic design of the Zuiderkerk is firmly Gothic, but the soaring tower is typical of his work, complete with balconies and balustrades, arches and columns. Now deconsecrated, the church has been turned into a municipal information centre, with displays on housing and the environment, plus temporary exhibitions revealing the city council's future plans. The **tower**, which has a separate entrance, can be climbed during the summer (June–Sept Wed–Sat 2–4pm; €3).

St Antoniesbreestraat and the Pintohuis

Stretching south from Nieuwmarkt, **St Antoniesbreestraat** once linked the city centre with the Jewish quarter, but its huddle of shops and houses was mostly demolished in the 1980s to make way for a main road. The plan was subsequently abandoned, but the modern buildings that now line most of the street hardly fire the soul, even if the modern symmetries – and cubist coloured panels – of the apartment blocks that spill along part of the street are at least visually arresting. One of the few survivors of this is the **Pintohuis** (Mon & Wed 2–8pm, Fri 2–5pm, Sat 11am–4pm; free), at no. 69, now a public library. Easily spotted by its off-white Italianate facade, the mansion is named after Isaac De Pinto, a Jew who fled Portugal to escape the Inquisition and subsequently became a founder of the East India Company. Pinto bought this property in 1651 and promptly had it remodelled in grand style, the facade interrupted by six lofty pilasters, which lead the eye up to the blind balustrade. The mansion was the talk of the town, even more so when Pinto had the interior painted in a similar style to the front – pop in to look at the birds and cherubs of the original painted ceiling.

The Hash Marihuana Hemp Museum and around

From the Oostindisch Huis (see above), it's a couple of minutes' walk west to the **Hash Marihuana Hemp Museum**, Oudezijds Achterburgwal 148 (daily 11am–10pm; €5.70), which features displays on different kinds of dope and the huge number of ways to imbibe and otherwise use it. Amsterdam's reliance on imported dope ended in the late 1980s when it was discovered that a reddish weed bred in America – "skunk" – was able to flourish under artificial lights; nowadays over half the dope sold in the coffeeshops is grown in the Netherlands. There's also an indoor marijuana garden here, samples of textiles and paper made with hemp, and pamphlets explaining the medicinal properties of cannabis, and the museum's shop sells pipes, books, videos and plenty of souvenirs.

Doubling back to Kloveniersburgwal, turn right for the **Oudemanhuis-poort**, a covered passageway leading off the street that is lined with secondhand bookstalls (Mon–Sat 10am–4pm); it was formerly part of an almshouse complex for elderly men – hence the unusual name. The buildings on either side are part of the **University of Amsterdam**, which dominates this part of town, and you can either wander through its peaceful precincts, taking in the red-shuttered, mullion-windowed seventeenth-century **Huis op de Drie Grachten**, or "House on the Three Canals", sitting prettily on the corner of Oudezijds Achterburgwal and Oudezijds Voorburgwal, or, just beyond, cross the south end of Kloveniersburgwal, to one of the prettiest corners of the city – a small pocket of placid waterways and old canal houses that extends east to Zwanenburgwal.

Rokin, Muntplein and the flower market

Rokin picks up where the Damrak leaves off, cutting south from Dam Square in a wide sweep that follows the former course of the River Amstel. This was the business centre of the nineteenth-century city, and although it has lost much of its prestige it is still flanked by an attractive medley of architectural styles incorporating everything from grandiose nineteenth-century mansions to more utilitarian modern stuff. Running parallel, pedestrianized **Kalverstraat** is a busy shopping street that has been a commercial centre since medieval times, when it was used as a calf market; nowadays it's home to many of the city's chain stores and clothes shops – you could be anywhere in Holland really.

The **Allard Pierson Museum**, off Rokin at Oude Turfmarkt 127 (Tues–Fri 10am–5pm, Sat & Sun 1–5pm; €4.30; ⓦ www.uba.uva.nl/apm), is a good, old-fashioned archeological museum in a solid Neoclassical building. The collection is spread over two floors and has a wide-ranging, if fairly small, assortment of finds. The particular highlight is the museum's Greek pottery, with fine examples of both the black- and red-figured wares produced in the sixth and fifth centuries BC. Look out also for the Roman sarcophagi, especially a marble whopper decorated with Dionysian scenes and a very unusual wooden coffin from around 150 AD, which is partly carved in the shape of the man held within.

Past the museum, it's a brief stroll to **Muntplein**, a dishevelled square where the **Munttoren** of 1480 was originally part of the old city wall. Later, it was adopted as the municipal mint – hence its name – a plain brick structure to which Hendrik de Keyser, in one of his last commissions, added a flashy spire in 1620. A few metres away, the floating **Bloemenmarkt** (Flower Market; daily 9am–5pm, though some stalls close on Sun), extends along the southern bank of the Singel west as far as Koningsplein. Popular with locals and tourists alike, the market is one of the main suppliers of flowers to central Amsterdam; its blooms and bulbs now share stall space with souvenir clogs, garden gnomes and Delftware.

Spui and the Begijnhof

The west end of the **Spui** (rhymes with "cow") opens out into a wide, tram-clanking square flanked by bookshops and popular café-bars. In the middle is a cloying statue of a young boy, known as **'t Lieverdje** ("Little Darling" or "Loveable Scamp"), a gift to the city from a cigarette company in 1960. It was here in the mid-1960s, with the statue seen as a symbol of the addicted consumer, that the playful Sixties pressure group, the **Provos**, organized some of their most successful *ludiek* ("pranks").

A fancy little gateway on the north side of the Spui leads into the **Begijnhof** (daily 10am–5pm; free), where a huddle of immaculately maintained old houses looks onto a central green, their backs to the outside world; if this door is locked, try the main entrance, just a couple of hundred metres north of Spui on Gedempte Begijnensloot. The Begijnhof was founded in the fourteenth-century as a home for the *beguines* – members of a Catholic sisterhood living as nuns, but without vows and with the right of return to the secular world. The original medieval complex comprised a series of humble brick cottages, but these were mostly replaced by the larger, grander houses of today shortly after the Reformation, though the secretive, enclosed design survived. A couple of pre-Reformation buildings remain, including the **Houten Huys**, at no. 34, whose wooden facade dates from 1477, the oldest in Amsterdam, and erected before the city forbade the construction of timber houses as an essential precaution against fire. Of the two churches here, the **Engelse Kerk** (English Reformed Church) is of medieval construction too, but it was taken from the *beguines* and given to Amsterdam's English community during the Reformation. Plain and unadorned, the church is of interest for its carefully worked pulpit panels, several of which were designed by a youthful Piet Mondrian (1872–1944), the leading De Stijl artist. After they had lost their church, the *beguines* were allowed to celebrate Mass inconspicuously in the clandestine Catholic **chapel** (Mon 1–6pm, Tues–Sun 9am–6pm; free), which they established in the house opposite their old church. It's still used today, a cosy little place with some terribly sentimental religious paintings, one of which – to the left of the high altar – depicts the miracle of the unburnable Host (see The Oude Kerk, p.77).

Amsterdams Historisch Museum

Emerging from the east side of the Begijnhof, turn left onto narrow Gedempte Begijnensloot and nearby is the **Schuttersgalerij** – the Civic Guard Gallery.

△ The Begijnhof

Here, an assortment of huge group portraits of the Amsterdam militia, ranging from serious-minded paintings of the 1540s through to lighter affairs from the seventeenth century, is displayed for free in a glassed-in passageway. The Schuttersgalerij is part of the **Amsterdams Historisch Museum** (Mon–Fri 10am–5pm, Sat & Sun 11am–5pm; €6; ⓦwww.ahm.nl), which occupies the smartly restored but rambling seventeenth-century buildings of the municipal orphanage. This museum surveys the city's development with a scattering of artefacts and lots of paintings from the thirteenth century onwards. It's a slightly difficult collection to navigate, and you need to pay close attention to the colour-coded signs that attempt to guide you through chronologically – and the labelling, which is in English and Dutch. High points include a number of paintings from the city's Golden Age – Rembrandt's wonderful *Anatomy Lesson of Dr Jan Deijman* stands out – and the section entitled "Social Care & Stern Discipline", where the harsh paternalism of the city's merchant oligarchy is examined with paintings depicting the regents of several orphanages, self-contented bourgeois in the company of the grateful poor.

The Grachtengordel

Medieval Amsterdam was enclosed by the Singel, part of the city's protective moat, but this is now just the first of five canals that reach right around the city centre, extending anticlockwise from Brouwersgracht to the River Amstel in a "girdle of canals" or **Grachtengordel**. This is without doubt the most charming part of the city, its lattice of olive-green waterways and dinky humpback bridges overlooked by street upon street of handsome seventeenth-century canal houses, almost invariably undisturbed by later development. It's a subtle cityscape – full of surprises, with a bizarre carving here, an unusual facade there – but architectural peccadilloes aside, it is the district's overall atmosphere that appeals rather than any specific sight – with the notable exception of the **Anne Frank Huis**. There's no obvious walking route around the Grachtengordel, and indeed you may prefer to wander around as the mood takes you, but the description we've given below goes from north to south, taking in all the highlights on the way. On all three of the main canals – **Herengracht**, **Keizersgracht** and **Prinsengracht** – street numbers begin in the north and increase as you go south.

Brouwersgracht to Leliegracht

Running east to west along the northern edge of the three main canals is leafy **Brouwersgracht**, one of the most picturesque waterways in the city. In the seventeenth century, Brouwersgracht lay at the edge of Amsterdam's great harbour. This was where many of the ships returning from the East unloaded their silks and spices, and as one of the major arteries linking the open sea with the city centre it was lined with storage depots and warehouses. Breweries flourished here too, capitalizing on their ready access to shipments of fresh water. Today, the harbour bustle has moved elsewhere, and the warehouses, with their distinctive spout-neck gables and shuttered windows, formerly used for the delivery and dispatch of goods by pulley from the canal below, have been converted into apartments, some of the most expensive in Amsterdam. There are handsome merchants' houses here as well, plus moored houseboats and a string of quaint little swing bridges.

Strolling south along **Prinsengracht** from Brouwersgracht, past smart canal houses and tumbledown houseboats, it only takes a minute or two to reach the **Hofje Van Brienen**, at Prinsengracht 85–133, which you can walk around for

The canals

The **canals of the Grachtengordel** were dug in the seventeenth century as part of a comprehensive plan to extend the boundaries of a city no longer able to accommodate its burgeoning population. Increasing the area of the city from two to seven square kilometres was a monumental task, and the conditions imposed by the council were strict. The three main waterways – Herengracht, Keizersgracht and Prinsengracht – were set aside for the residences and businesses of the richer and more influential Amsterdam merchants, while the radial cross-streets were reserved for more modest artisans' homes; meanwhile, immigrants, newly arrived to cash in on Amsterdam's booming economy, were assigned, albeit informally, the Jodenhoek (see p.91) and the Jordaan (see p.89).

Of the three main canals, **Herengracht**, the "Gentlemen's Canal", was the first to be dug, followed by the **Keizersgracht**, the "Emperor's Canal", named after the Holy Roman Emperor and fifteenth-century patron of the city, Maximilian. Further out still, the **Prinsengracht**, the "Princes' Canal", was named in honour of the princes of the House of Orange. The merchants who dominated Amsterdam soon lined the three with their mansions; the grandest concentrated on Herengracht, where the stretch of water between Leidsegracht and the Amstel was soon nicknamed the "**Golden Bend**" (De Gouden Bocht).

In the Grachtengordel, everyone, even the wealthiest merchant, had to comply with a set of strict and detailed planning regulations. In particular, the council prescribed the size of each building plot – the frontage was set at thirty feet, the depth two hundred – and although there was a degree of tinkering, the end result was the loose conformity you can see today: tall, narrow residences, whose individualism is mainly restricted to the stylistic permutations among the gables.

The earliest extant **gables**, dating from the early seventeenth century, are crow-stepped gables, but these were largely superseded from the 1650s onwards by neck gables and bell gables. Some are embellished, others aren't, many have decorative cornices, some don't, and the fanciest, which almost invariably date from the eighteenth century, sport full-scale balustrades. The plainest gables are those of former **warehouses**, where the deep-arched and shuttered windows line up on either side of loft doors, which were once used for loading and unloading goods, winched by pulley from the street down below. Indeed, outside **pulleys** remain a common feature of houses and warehouses alike, and are often still in use as the easiest way of moving furniture into the city's myriad apartments.

free. This is one of the prettiest of the city's *hofjes*, or courtyard almshouses, built in 1804. Continue walking for a few metres more and you'll come to the first cross-street connecting the main canals, **Prinsenstraat**, which quickly runs into **Herenstraat**, an appealing little street of flower shops and cafés, greengroceries and secondhand clothes shops. At the east end of Herenstraat, turn right onto **Herengracht** and it's a short walk to the **Leliegracht**, one of the tiny radial canals that cut across the Grachtengordel, and home to a number of bookshops and canal-side bars. Though there are precious few extant examples of Art Nouveau and Art Deco architecture in Amsterdam, one of the finest is the tall and striking building at the Leliegracht–Keizersgracht junction. The building was designed by Gerrit van Arkel in 1905.

Anne Frank Huis

In 1957, the Anne Frank Foundation set up the **Anne Frank Huis** in the house at Prinsengracht 267 (daily: mid-March to mid-Sept 9am–9pm; mid-Sept to mid-March 9am–7pm; closed Yom Kippur; €7.50, 10- to 17-year-olds

€3.50, under-9s free; ☎020/556 7100, ⑩www.annefrank.nl), where the young diarist and her family were in hiding for two years (see box below). Since the posthumous publication of her diaries, Anne Frank has become extraordinarily famous, in the first instance for recording the iniquities of the Holocaust, and latterly as a symbol of the fight against oppression and, in particular, racism. The house is now one of the most popular attractions in town, so try to go early (or late) to avoid the crowds.

Anne Frank's **diary** was among the few things left behind in the annexe. It was retrieved by one of the people who had helped the Franks and handed to Anne's father on his return from Auschwitz; he later decided to publish it. Since its appearance in 1947, the diary has been constantly in print, translated into over sixty languages, and has sold millions of copies worldwide. The rooms the Franks lived in for two years are left much the same as they were during the war, even down to the movie star pin-ups in Anne's bedroom and the marks on the wall recording the children's heights. Remarkably, despite the number of visitors, there is a real sense of intimacy here and only the coldest of hearts could fail to be moved. Apposite video clips on the family in particular and the Holocaust in general give the background. Anne Frank was only one of about 100,000 Dutch Jews who died during World War II, but this, her final home, provides one of the most enduring testaments to its horrors. Her diary has been a source of inspiration to many, including Nelson Mandela.

The story of Anne Frank

The story of Anne, her family and friends is well known. Anne's father, **Otto Frank**, was a well-to-do Jewish businessman who ran a successful spice-trading business and lived in the southern part of Amsterdam. After the Nazi occupation of the Netherlands, he felt – along with many other Jews – that he could avoid trouble by keeping his head down. However, by 1942 it was clear that this was not going to be possible: Amsterdam's Jews were isolated and conspicuous, being confined to certain parts of the city and forced to wear a yellow star. Roundups, too, were becoming increasingly commonplace. In desperation, Otto Frank decided – on the advice of two Dutch friends, Mr Koophuis and Mr Kraler – to move the family into the unused back room of his company's warehouse on the Prinsengracht. The Franks went into hiding in July 1942, along with a Jewish business partner and his family, the Van Daans. They were separated from the eyes of the outside world by a bookcase that doubled as a door. As far as everyone else was concerned, they had fled to Switzerland. So began the two-year occupation of the *achterhuis*, or back annexe. The two families were joined in November 1942 by a Mr Dussel, a dentist friend. Koophuis and Kraler, who continued working in the front office, regularly brought supplies and news of the outside world. In her diary Anne Frank describes the day-to-day lives of the inhabitants of the annexe: the quarrels, frequent in such a claustrophobic environment; celebrations of birthdays, or of a piece of good news from the Allied Front; and her own, slightly unreal, growing-up (much of Anne's description of which was edited out by her father, but restored to later editions). Two years later, the atmosphere was optimistic: the Allies were clearly winning the war and liberation seemed within reach. It wasn't to be. One day in the summer of 1944 the Franks were betrayed by a Dutch collaborator and the Gestapo arrived and forced Mr Kraler to open up the bookcase. Thereafter, the occupants of the annexe were all arrested and quickly sent to Westerbork (see p.259) – the transit camp in the north of the country where all Dutch Jews were processed before being moved to Belsen or Auschwitz. Of the eight from the annexe, only Otto Frank survived; Anne and her sister died of typhus within a short time of each other in Belsen, just one week before the German surrender.

The Westerkerk, Westermarkt and around

Immediately to the south of the Anne Frank Huis, the **Westerkerk** (April–Sept Mon–Fri 11am–3pm; free) dominates the district, its 85-metre tower (May–Sept Mon–Sat 10am–5pm; €5) – without question Amsterdam's finest – soaring imperiously above the gables of Westermarkt. On its top perches the crown of the Habsburg Emperor Maximilian, a constantly recurring symbol of Amsterdam and the finishing touch to what was only the city's second place of worship built expressly for Protestants. The church was designed by Hendrik de Keyser and completed in 1631 as part of the general enlargement of the city, but whereas the exterior is all studied elegance, the interior – as required by the Calvinist congregation – is bare and plain. The church is also the reputed resting place of **Rembrandt**, though the location of his pauper's tomb is not known. Instead, the painter is commemorated by a small memorial in the north aisle, close to which his son Titus is buried. Rembrandt adored his son – as evinced by numerous portraits – and the boy's death dealt a final crushing blow to the ageing and embittered artist, who died just over a year later.

Westermarkt, an open square in the shadow of the Westerkerk, possesses two evocative statues. At the back of the church, beside Keizersgracht, are the three pink granite triangles (one each for the past, present and future) of the **Homo-Monument**. The world's first memorial to persecuted gays and lesbians, commemorating all those who died at the hands of the Nazis, it was designed by Karin Daan and recalls the pink triangles that homosexuals were forced to sew into and display on their clothes during the occupation. The monument's inscription, by the Dutch writer Jacob Israel de Haan, translates as "Such an infinite desire for friendship". Nearby, on the south side of the church by Prinsengracht, is a small but beautifully crafted **statue of Anne Frank** by the gifted Dutch sculptor Mari Andriessen (1897–1979), who is also the creator of the dockworker statue outside Amsterdam's Portuguese Synagogue (see p.94).

A few metres away at Herengracht 168, is the **Theatermuseum** (Mon–Fri 11am–5pm, Sat & Sun 1–5pm; €4.50; ☎020/551 3300, ⓦwww.tin.nl), which holds an enjoyable collection of theatrical bygones, from props through to stage sets, with a particularly good section devoted to puppets and puppetry. The museum, which spreads over into the adjoining building, also offers a lively programme of temporary exhibitions, but it's the house itself that is perhaps of most interest. Dating from 1638, Herengracht 168 has a fetching sandstone facade to a design by Philip Vingboons, the most talented architect involved in the creation of the Grachtengordel. The house was built for Michael de Pauw, a leading light in the East India Company, and the interior sports a riot of flamboyant stuccowork, romantic Italianate wall paintings and a splendid spiral staircase.

Raadhuisstraat to Leidsegracht

Westermarkt flows into **Raadhuisstraat**, the principal thoroughfare into the Old Centre, running east to Dam Square. South of here the main canals are less appealing than the narrow cross-streets, many of which are named after animals whose pelts were used in the local tanning industry – Reestraat ("Deer Street"), Hartenstraat ("Hart Street") and Berenstraat ("Bear Street"), to name but three. The tanners are thankfully long gone, but they've been replaced by some of the most pleasant shopping streets in the city, known collectively as the "Nine Streets", selling everything from carpets and handmade chocolates to designer toothbrushes and beeswax candles. The area's southern boundary is marked by **Leidsegracht**, a mostly residential canal, lined with chic town houses and a medley of handsome gables.

The **Woonbootmuseum**, Prinsengracht 296 (March–Oct Tues–Sun 11am–5pm; Nov–Feb Fri–Sun 11am–5pm; €3; Ⓦ www.houseboatmuseum.nl), is a 1914 Dutch houseboat that doubles as a tourist attraction with a handful of explanatory plaques about life on the water. Nearby, the **Bijbels Museum** at Herengracht 366, just north of Leidsegracht (Mon–Sat 10am–5pm, Sun 11am–5pm; €6; Ⓦ www.bijbelsmuseum.nl), occupies two of four matching stone mansions, frilled with tendrils, carved fruit and scrollwork and graced by dinky little bull's-eye windows and elegant gables. They were built in the 1660s for one of Amsterdam's wealthy merchant families, the Cromhouts, and contain an extravagant painted ceiling portraying Classical gods and goddesses – the work of Jacob de Wit. On display in the museum is a splendid selection of old bibles, including the first Dutch-language Bible ever printed, dating from 1477, and a series of idiosyncratic models of Solomon's Temple and the Jewish Tabernacle plus a scattering of archeological finds from Palestine and Egypt brought to the Netherlands in the nineteenth century.

Leidseplein and around

Lying on the edge of the Grachtengordel, **Leidseplein** is the bustling hub of Amsterdam's nightlife, a rather cluttered and disorderly open space that has never had much character. The square once marked the end of the road in from Leiden and, as horse-drawn traffic was banned from the centre long ago, it was here that the Dutch left their horses and carts – a sort of equine car park. Today, it's quite the opposite: continual traffic made up of trams, bikes, cars and pedestrians gives the place a frenetic feel, and the surrounding side streets are jammed with bars, restaurants and clubs in a bright jumble of jutting signs and neon lights. On a good night, however, Leidseplein can be Amsterdam at its carefree, exuberant best.

The square has a couple of buildings of architectural note. The grandiose **Stadsschouwburg**, a neo-Renaissance edifice dating from 1894, was so widely criticized for its clumsy vulgarity that the city council of the day temporarily withheld the money for decorating the exterior. Home to the National Ballet and Opera until the Muziektheater (see p.92) was completed on Waterlooplein in 1986, it is now used for theatre, dance and music performances, as well as hosting visiting English-language theatre companies. However, its most popular function is as the place where the Ajax football team gather on the balcony to wave to the crowds whenever they win anything – as they often do. Almost next door, the **American Hotel** is one of the city's oddest buildings, a monumental and slightly disconcerting rendering of Art Nouveau, with angular turrets, chunky dormer windows and fancy brickwork. Completed in 1902, the present structure takes its name from its demolished predecessor, which was decorated with statues and murals of North American scenes. Inside the present hotel is the *Café Americain*, once the fashionable haunt of Amsterdam's literati, but now a mainstream location for coffee and lunch. The Art Nouveau decor is well worth a peek – an artful combination of stained glass, shallow arches and geometric patterned brickwork.

Heading northeast from Leidseplein, **Leidsestraat** is a crowded shopping street, a long, slender gauntlet of fashion and shoe shops of little distinction that leads across the three main canals up towards the Singel and the Flower Market (see p.80). En route, at the corner of Keizersgracht, is **Metz & Co** department store, which was, when it was built, the tallest commercial building in the city – one reason why the owners were able to entice Gerrit Rietveld, the leading architectural light of the De Stijl movement, to add a rooftop glass and metal showroom in 1933. The showroom has survived and is now a café offering one of the best views over the centre in this predominantly low-rise city. One block east of Metz & Co, along Keizersgracht, is Nieuwe Spiegelstraat, an appealing mixture of bookshops and corner cafés that extends south into Spiegelgracht to form the **Spiegelkwartier** – home to the pricey end of Amsterdam's antiques trade. It's a lovely district to browse around, and while you're here be sure to pop into **De Appel**, a lively centre for contemporary art at Nieuwe Spiegelstraat 10 (Tues–Sun 11am–6pm; €4; ⓦwww.deappel.nl).

The Golden Bend

Strolling southeast from Leidsegracht, the elegant sweep of the main **Herengracht** canal reaches the so-called "**Golden Bend**" (De Gouden Bocht), where the canal is overlooked by a long sequence of double-fronted mansions, some of the most opulent dwellings in the city. Most of the houses here date from the eighteenth century, with double stairways leading to the entrance, underneath which the small door was for the servants. Classical references are common, both in form – pediments, columns and pilasters – and decoration, from scrolls and vases through to geometric patterns inspired by ancient Greece. One of the first buildings to look out for on the north side of the canal is **no. 475**, an extravagant edifice surmounted by a slender French-style balustrade and decorated with twin caryatids. It was completed in 1672, whereas the comparable residence at **no. 493**, complete with its good-looking balcony, was finished in the 1730s. In a rather more modest mansion a couple of doors down, at no. 497, is the peculiar **Kattenkabinet** (Tues–Fri 10am–2pm, Sat & Sun 1–5pm; €5; ⓦwww.kattenkabinet.nl), an enormous collection of art and artefacts relating to cats installed by a Dutch financier, whose own cherished moggy, John Pierpont Morgan, died in 1984; feline fanatics will be delighted. Metres away, at the corner of Vijzelstraat, **no. 507** is an imposing building too, all Neoclassical pilasters and slender windows; it was once the home of Jacob Boreel, the one-time major whose attempt to impose a burial tax prompted a riot during which the mob ransacked his house. Opposite, across the canal, is the mammoth lumpiness of the former ABN–AMRO bank, a broadly Expressionist structure dating to 1923.

Rembrandtplein and around

Pushing on along the north side of Herengracht, it takes a couple of minutes to reach pedestrianized **Thorbeckeplein**, a scrawny adjunct to **Rembrandtplein**, itself a dishevelled bit of greenery that was formerly Amsterdam's butter market, renamed after the artist in 1876. Rembrandtplein is one of the city's nightlife centres, though the crowded restaurants are firmly tourist-targeted. The great man's statue stands in the middle, his back wisely turned against the square's worst excesses, which include live (but deadly) outdoor music. Of the prodigious number of cafés and bars here, only the bar of the **Schiller Hotel** at no. 26 stands out, with an original Art Deco interior reminiscent of an ocean liner.

Tacky **Reguliersbreestraat**, leading off the northwest corner of Rembrandtplein, is notable only for the city's most extraordinary cinema, the **Tuschinski**, at nos. 26–28, which boasts a marvellously well-preserved Art Deco interior. Opened in 1921 by a Polish Jew, Abram Tuschinski, the cinema boasts Expressionist paintings, coloured marbles and a wonderful carpet, handwoven in Marrakesh to an original design. Tuschinski died in Auschwitz in 1942, and there's a plaque in the cinema's foyer in his memory. Back on the Herengracht, near the River Amstel, the **Museum Willet-Holthuysen** at no. 605 (Mon–Fri 10am–5pm, Sat & Sun 11am–5pm; €4; ⓦwww.museumwilletholthuysen.nl) is billed as "a peep behind the curtains into an historic Amsterdam canal house", which just about sums it up. The coal-trading Holthuysen family occupied this elegant, late-seventeenth-century mansion until the last of the line, Sandra Willet-Holthuysen, gifted her home and its contents to the city in 1895. Modified and renovated on several occasions, the interior has largely been returned to its original eighteenth-century Rococo appearance – a flashy and ornate style that the Dutch merchants held to be the epitome of refinement and good taste. The house also displays a small collection of glass, silver, majolica and ceramics assembled by Sandra's husband, Abraham Willet. At the back of the house are the formal gardens, a neat pattern of miniature hedges graced by the occasional stone statue.

The Museum Van Loon

Southwest of Rembrandtplein, on Keizersgracht, is the **Museum Van Loon** at no. 672 (Mon & Fri–Sun 11am–5pm; also March–May, July & Aug Wed & Thurs 11am–5pm; €6; ⓦ www.museumvanloon.nl), which has perhaps the finest accessible canal house interior in Amsterdam. Built in 1672, the first tenant of the property was the artist Ferdinand Bol, who seems to have been one of the few occupants to have avoided some sort of scandal. The Van Loons occupied the house from 1884 to 1945, and the last member of the family to live here was Willem van Loon, a banker whose wife, Thora van Loon-Egidius, was *dame du paleis* to Queen Wilhelmina. Of German extraction, Thora was proud of her roots and allegedly entertained high-ranking Nazi officials here during the occupation – a charge of collaboration that led to the Van Loons being shunned by polite society. Recently renovated, the interior of the house has been returned to something akin to its eighteenth-century appearance, with acres of wood panelling and fancy stuccowork. Look out also for the ornate copper balustrade on the staircase, into which is worked the name "Van Hagen-Trip" (after a one-time owner of the house); the Van Loons later filled the spaces between the letters with iron curlicues to prevent their children falling through. The top-floor landing has several pleasant paintings sporting Roman figures, and one of the bedrooms – the "painted room" – is decorated with a Romantic painting of Italy – a favourite motif in Amsterdam from around 1750 to 1820. The oddest items are the fake bedroom doors: the eighteenth-century owners were so keen to avoid any lack of symmetry that they camouflaged the real bedroom doors and created imitation, decorative doors in the "correct" position instead.

The River Amstel

The main canals come to an abrupt halt beside the wide and windy **River Amstel**, which was long the main route into the interior, with goods arriving by barge and boat to be traded for the imported materials held in Amsterdam's many warehouses. Turning left from Herengracht takes you to the **Blauwbrug** ("Blue Bridge") and the Old Jewish Quarter (see p.91), while further down the **Magere Brug** ("Skinny Bridge") is arguably the cutest of the city's many swing bridges. From here, it's a few metres further to the **Amstelsluizen**, the Amstel Locks. Every night, the municipal water department closes these locks to begin the process of sluicing out the canals. A huge pumping station on an island out to the east of the city then starts to pump fresh water into the canal system from the IJsselmeer (see p.134); similar locks on the west side of the city are left open for the surplus to flow into the IJ and, from there, out to sea via the North Sea Canal. The watery contents of the canals is thus regularly refreshed – though, what with three centuries of algae, prams, shopping trolleys and a few hundred rusty bikes, the water is appealing just as long as you're not in it.

The Jordaan and the Western Docklands

Lying to the west of the city centre and the Grachtengordel, its boundaries clearly defined by the Prinsengracht and the Lijnbaansgracht, the **Jordaan** is a likeable and easily explored area of slender canals and narrow streets flanked by an agreeable mix of architectural styles, from modern terraces to handsome seventeenth-century canal houses. In all probability the district takes its name from the French word *jardin* ("garden"), since the area's earliest settlers were Protestant Huguenots, who fled here to escape persecution in the sixteenth and seventeenth centuries. Another possibility is that it's a corruption of the Dutch word for Jews, *joden*. Whatever the truth, the Jordaan developed from open country – hence the number of streets and canals named after flowers and plants – into a refugee enclave, a teeming, cosmopolitan quarter beyond the pale of bourgeois respectability. Indeed, when the city fathers planned the expansion of the city in 1610, they made sure the Jordaan was kept outside the city boundaries. Consequently, the Jordaan was not subject to the rigorous planning restrictions of the Grachtengordel, and its lattice of narrow streets followed the lines of the original polder drainage ditches rather than any municipal outline. This gives the district its distinctive, mazy layout, and much of its present appeal.

Traditionally the home of Amsterdam's working class, the Jordaan has in recent years been transformed by a middle class influx, with the district now one of the city's most sought-after residential neighbourhoods. Before then, and until the late 1970s, the Jordaan's inhabitants were primarily stevedores and factory workers, earning a crust among the docks, warehouses, factories and boatyards that extended north beyond Brouwersgracht, the Jordaan's northern boundary and nowadays one of Amsterdam's prettiest canals. Specific sights are few and far between but it's still a pleasant area to wander.

Rozengracht to Westerstraat

The streets and canals extending north from **Rozengracht** to **Westerstraat** form the heart of the Jordaan and hold the district's prettiest moments. Beyond Rozengracht, the first canal is the **Bloemgracht** (Flower Canal), a leafy waterway dotted with houseboats and arched by little bridges, its network of cross streets sprinkled with cafés, bars and idiosyncratic shops. There's a warm, relaxed community atmosphere here which is really rather beguiling, not to mention a clutch of old and handsome canal houses. Pride of architectural place goes to nos. 89–91, a sterling Renaissance building of 1642 complete with mullion windows, crowstep gable, brightly painted shutters and distinctive facade stones, representing a *steeman* (city-dweller), *landman* (farmer) and a *seeman* (sailor). Next door, nos. 85–87 were built a few decades later, two immaculately maintained canal houses adorned by the bottleneck gables typical of the period.

From Bloemgracht, it's a few metres north to **Egelantiersgracht** (Rose-Hip Canal), where, at no. 12, *Café 't Smalle* is one of Amsterdam's oldest cafés, opened in 1786 as a *proeflokaal* - a tasting house for the (long-gone) gin distillery next door. In the eighteenth century, when quality control was intermittent, each batch of *jenever* (Dutch gin) could turn out very differently, so customers insisted on a taster before they splashed out. As a result, each distillery ran a *proeflokaal* offering free samples and this is a rare survivor. The café's waterside terrace remains an especially pleasant spot to take a tipple (see p.107).

A narrow cross-street – Tweede Egelantiersdwarsstraat and its continuation Tweede Tuindwarsstraat and Tweede Anjeliersdwarsstraat – runs north from Bloemgracht flanked by many of the Jordaan's more fashionable stores and clothing shops as well as some of its liveliest bars and cafés. At the end is workaday **Westerstraat**, a busy thoroughfare, which is home to the small but fascinating **Pianola Museum** at no. 106 (Sun 2–5pm; €5; Ⓦ www.pianola.nl), whose collection of pianolas and automatic music-machines dates from the beginning of the twentieth century. Fifteen have been restored to working order. These machines, which work on rolls of perforated paper, were the jukeboxes of their day, and the museum has a vast collection of 14,000 rolls of music, some of which were "recorded" by famous pianists and composers – Gershwin, Debussy, Scott Joplin, Art Tatum and others. Nearby, and also of some interest, is the largest of the Jordaan's *hofjes*, the **Karthuizerhofje**, Karthuiz-ersstraat 89–171, a substantial courtyard complex established as a widows' hospice in the middle of the seventeenth century, though the present buildings are much later.

The Noorderkerk and around

At the east end of Westerstraat, overlooking the Prinsengracht, is Hendrik de Keyser's **Noorderkerk** (Mon, Thurs & Sat 11am–1pm, Wed 11am–3pm, Sun 1.30–4pm), the architect's last creation and probably his least successful, finished two years after his death in 1623. A bulky, overbearing brick building, it represented a radical departure from the conventional church designs of the time, having a symmetrical Greek-cross floor plan, with four equally proportioned arms radiating out from a steepled centre. Uncompromisingly dour, it proclaimed the serious intent of the Calvinists who worshipped here in so far as the pulpit – and therefore the preacher proclaiming the Word of God – was at the centre and not at the front of the church, a symbolic break with the Catholic past. Nevertheless, it's still hard to understand quite how Keyser, who designed such elegant structures as the Westerkerk (see p.85), could have ended up designing this.

The **Noordermarkt**, the somewhat inconclusive square outside the church, holds a statue of three figures bound to each other, a poignant tribute to the bloody Jordaanoproer riot of 1934, part of a successful campaign to stop the government cutting unemployment benefit during the Depression. The inscription reads: "The strongest chains are those of unity". The square also hosts two of Amsterdam's best open-air **markets**: an antiques and general household goods market on Monday mornings (9am–1pm) and a popular Saturday farmers' market, the Boerenmarkt (9am–3pm), a lively affair selling organic fruit and vegetables, freshly baked breads and a plethora of oils and spices. Cross an unmarked border though and you'll find yourself in the middle of a Saturday bird market, which operates on an adjacent patch at much the same time, and is not everyone's cup of tea.

Just to the north of the Noorderkerk, the **Lindengracht** ("Canal of Limes") lost its waterway decades ago, but has had a prominent role in local folklore since the day in 1886 when a policeman made an ill-advised attempt to stop an eel-pulling contest. Horrible as it sounds, eel-pulling was a popular pastime hereabouts with tug-o'-war teams holding tight to either end of the poor creature, which was smeared with soap to make the entertainment last a little longer. The crowd unceremoniously bundled the policeman away, but when reinforcements arrived, the whole thing got out of hand and there was a full-scale **riot** – the Paling-Oproer – which lasted for three days and cost 26 lives.

The Scheepvaartsbuurt and the Western Docklands

Brouwersgracht marks both the northern edge of the Jordaan and the southern boundary of the **Scheepvaartsbuurt** – the Shipping Quarter – an unassuming neighbourhood that focuses on Haarlemmerstraat and Haarlemmerdijk, a long, rather ordinary thoroughfare lined with bars, cafés and food shops, the architectural high point being the Art Deco interior of *The Movies* cinema (see p.113) at Haarlemmerdijk 161. In the eighteenth and nineteenth centuries, this district boomed from its location between the Brouwersgracht and the **Westerdok**, a narrow parcel of land dredged out of the River IJ immediately to the north and equipped with docks, warehouses and shipyards. The construction of the artificial islands took the pressure off Amsterdam's congested maritime facilities and was necessary to sustain the city's economic success. The Westerdok hung on to some of the marine trade until the 1960s, but today – bar the odd small boatyard – industry has to all intents and purposes disappeared and the area is busy reinventing itself. There is still an air of faded grittiness here, but the old forgotten warehouses – within walking distance of the centre – are rapidly being turned into bijou studios, and dozens of plant-filled houseboats are moored along the Westerdok itself and the adjoining Realengracht. Nearby, **Westerpark** provides a touch of green for locals, running alongside a slither of a canal.

On the north side of the Westerpark, a pedestrian tunnel leads you to **Het Schip**, the seminal Amsterdam School municipal housing block by Michael de Klerk at Spaarndammerplantsoen 140 (Wed–Sun 1–5pm; €5; ⓦwww.hetschip .nl) that takes its name from its ship-like shape and is graced by all manner of decorative details such as wavy brick facades and misshaped windows – reachable direct by bus #22 from Centraal Station. Housed inside the complex's former post office, the Museum Het Schip explores the history of the architectural movement and provides information on the site's main distinguishing features. Regular half-hour guided tours (€2.50) take you inside one of the restored residences – the block is still used as social housing today – and up to the main turret.

The Old Jewish Quarter and the Eastern Docklands

Originally one of the marshiest parts of Amsterdam, prone to regular flooding, the narrow slice of land sandwiched between the curve of the Amstel, Kloveniersburgwal and the Nieuwe Herengracht was the home of Amsterdam's Jews from the sixteenth century up until World War II. By the 1920s, this **Old Jewish Quarter**, or the Jodenhoek ("Jews' Corner"), was crowded with tenement buildings and smoking factories, but in 1945 it lay derelict – and postwar redevelopment has not treated it kindly either. Its focal point, **Waterlooplein**, has been overwhelmed by a whopping town hall and concert hall complex, which caused much controversy at the time of its construction, and the once-bustling Jodenbreestraat is now bleak and very ordinary, with Mr Visserplein, at its east end, one of the city's busiest traffic junctions. Picking your way round these obstacles is not much fun, but you should persevere – among all the cars and concrete are several moving reminders of the Jewish community that perished in the war.

Immediately to the east of the Old Jewish Quarter lies the **Plantagebuurt**, a trim district centred around the **Plantage Middenlaan**, a wide boulevard that was constructed in the mid-nineteenth century as the first part of the creation of this leafy suburb – one of Amsterdam's earliest. The avenue borders the city's largest botanical gardens, the **Hortus Botanicus**, and runs close to both the **Artis Zoo** and the first-rate **Verzetsmuseum** (Dutch Resistance Museum). Just slightly to the north of here are the artificial islands that comprise the **Oosterdok** (East Dock) quarter, dredged out of the River IJ to accommodate warehouses and docks in the seventeenth century. These islands once formed part of a vast maritime complex that spread right along the River IJ. Industrial decline set in during the 1880s, but the area is currently being redefined as a residential district, while its nautical heyday is recalled by the **Nederlands Scheepvaartmuseum** (Netherlands Maritime Museum).

Jodenbreestraat and Rembrandthuis

St Antoniesbreestraat runs into **Jodenbreestraat**, the "Broad Street of the Jews", and once the main centre of Jewish activity. Badly served by postwar development, this ancient thoroughfare is now short on charm, but in these unlikely surroundings, at no. 6, stands **Het Rembrandthuis** (daily 10am–5pm, but times may vary with exhibitions; €7.50; ☎020/520 0400, ⓦwww .rembrandthuis.nl), whose intricate facade is decorated by pretty wooden shutters and a small pediment. Rembrandt bought this house at the height of his fame and popularity, living here for over twenty years and spending a fortune on furnishings – an expense that ultimately contributed to his bankruptcy. An inventory made at the time details the huge collection of paintings, sculptures and art treasures he'd amassed, almost all of which was confiscated after he was declared insolvent and forced to move to a more modest house on Rozengracht in the Jordaan in 1658. The city council bought the Jodenbreestraat house in 1907 and has subsequently revamped the premises on several occasions, most recently in 1999. A string of period rooms now gives a clear impression of Rembrandt's life and times, while the adjoining modern wing displays an extensive collection of Rembrandt's etchings as well as several of the original copper plates on which he worked. The biblical illustrations attract the most attention, though the studies of tramps and vagabonds are equally appealing. An accompanying exhibit explains Rembrandt's engraving techniques and there are also regular temporary exhibitions on Rembrandt and his contemporaries; to see his major paintings, however, you'll have to go to the Rijksmuseum (see p.98).

Next door, the multimedia **Holland Experience** (daily 10am–6pm; €8.50; ⓦwww.holland-experience.nl.) is a kind of sensory-bombardment movie about Amsterdam and the Netherlands, with synchronized smells and a moving floor – not to mention special 3D effects. The experience lasts thirty minutes and is especially popular with kids.

The Stadhuis and Muziektheater

Jodenbreestraat runs parallel to the **Stadhuis en Muziektheater**, a sprawling and distinctly underwhelming modern complex dating to the 1980s and incorporating the city hall and a large auditorium. The Muziektheater offers a varied programme of theatre, dance and ballet as well as opera from the country's first-rate Netherlands Opera (ⓦwww.dno.nl), but tickets go very quickly. One of the city's abiding ironies is that the title of the protest campaign aiming to prevent the development in the 1980s – "Stopera" – has passed into common usage to describe the finished item. Inside, there are a couple of minor attractions, beginning with the glass columns in the public passageway towards the rear of the complex. These give a salutary lesson on the fragility of the Netherlands: two contain water indicating the sea levels in the Dutch towns of Vlissingen and IJmuiden (below knee level), while another records the levels experienced

△ Rembrandthuis

during the 1953 flood disaster (way above head height). Downstairs a concrete pile shows what is known as "Normal Amsterdam Level" (NAP), originally calculated in 1684 as the average water level in the river IJ and still the basis for measuring altitude above sea level across Europe.

Waterlooplein

The Stadhuis complex dominates **Waterlooplein**, a rectangular parcel of land that was originally swampy marsh. This was the site of the first Jewish Quarter, but by the late nineteenth century it had become an insanitary slum, home to the poorest of the Ashkenazi Jews. The slums were cleared in the 1880s and thereafter the open spaces of the Waterlooplein hosted the largest and liveliest marketplace in the city, the place where Jews and Gentiles met to trade. In World War II, the Nazis used the square to round up their victims, but despite these ugly connotations the Waterlooplein was revived in the 1950s as the site of the city's main **flea market** and remains so to this day (Mon–Sat 9am–5pm). The market is nowhere as large as it once was thanks to the town hall and concert hall development, but nonetheless it's still the final resting place of many a pair of yellow corduroy flares and has some wonderful antique and junk stalls to root through – and secondhand vinyl too.

Mr Visserplein, the Esnoga and JD Meijerplein

Just behind the Muziektheater, **Mr Visserplein** is a busy junction for traffic speeding towards the IJ tunnel. It takes its name from Mr Visser, president of the Supreme Court of the Netherlands in 1939. He was dismissed the following year when the Germans occupied the country, and became an active member of the Jewish resistance, working for the illegal underground newspaper *Het Parool* ("The Password") and refusing to wear the yellow Star of David. He died in 1942, a few days after publicly – and famously – denouncing all forms of collaboration.

Unmissable on the corner of Mr Visserplein is the brown and bulky brickwork of the **Esnoga** or **Portuguese synagogue** (Mon–Thurs & Sun 10am–4pm, Fri 10am–3pm; closed Yom Kippur; €6.50; Ⓦwww.esnoga.com), completed in 1675 for the city's Sephardic Jews. One of Amsterdam's most imposing buildings, the central structure, with its grand pilasters and blind balustrade, was built in the broadly Neoclassical style that was then fashionable in Holland. It is surrounded by a courtyard complex of small outhouses, where the city's Sephardim have fraternized for centuries. Barely altered since its construction, the synagogue's lofty interior follows the Sephardic tradition in having the *hechal* (the Ark of the Covenant) and *tebah* (from where services are led) at opposite ends. Also traditional is the seating, with two sets of wooden benches (for the men) facing each other across the central aisle – the women have separate galleries up above. A set of superb brass chandeliers holds the candles, which remain the only source of artificial light. When it was completed, the synagogue was one of the largest in the world, its congregation almost certainly the richest; today, the Sephardic community has dwindled to just 250 families, most of whom live outside the city centre. In one of the outhouses, a video sheds light on the history of the synagogue and Amsterdam's Sephardim; the mystery is why the Nazis left it alone. No one knows for sure, but it seems likely that they intended to turn it into a museum once all the Jews had been polished off.

Next to the synagogue is **Jonas Daniel Meijerplein**, a scrawny triangle of gravel named after the eponymous lawyer, who in 1796, at the age of just 16, was the first Jew to be admitted to the Amsterdam Bar. It was here in February 1941 that around 400 Jewish men were forcibly loaded up on trucks and taken to their deaths at Mauthausen concentration camp, in reprisal for the killing of a Dutch Nazi during a street fight. The arrests sparked off the February Strike (*Februaristaking*), a general strike in protest against the Germans' treatment of the Jews. It was organized by the outlawed Communist Party and spearheaded by Amsterdam's transport workers and dockers – a rare demonstration of solidarity with the Jews whose fate was usually accepted without visible protest in all of occupied Europe. The strike was quickly suppressed, but is still commemorated by an annual wreath-laying ceremony on February 25, as well as by Mari Andriessen's statue of the **Dokwerker** (Dockworker) here on the square.

The Joods Historisch Museum

Across J.D. Meijerplein, on the far side of the main road at Nieuwe Amstelstraat 1, the **Joods Historisch Museum** (daily 11am–5pm, closed Yom Kippur; €6.50; Ⓦ www.jhm.nl) is cleverly shoehorned into four Ashkenazi synagogues dating from the late seventeenth century. For years after World War II these buildings lay abandoned, but they were finally refurbished – and connected by walkways – in the 1980s to accommodate a Jewish resource centre and exhibition area. A second renovation is currently under way and at present the highlight of a visit is the display on Jewish life exhibited in the main body of the handsome **Grote Synagoge**. This includes a fine collection of religious silverware as well as a handful of paintings plus all manner of antique artefacts illustrating religious customs and practices.

Hortus Botanicus and the Hollandsche Schouwburg

From Mr Visserplein, it's a short walk east along Muiderstraat to the lush **Hortus Botanicus** at the corner of Plantage Middenlaan and Plantage Parklaan (Mon–Fri 9am–5pm, Sat & Sun 10am–5pm; July & Aug until 9pm; Dec & Jan closes 4pm; €6; Ⓦ www.hortus-botanicus.nl), the city's botanical gardens, founded in 1682 as medicinal gardens for the use of the city's physicians and apothecaries. Thereafter, many of the city's merchants made a point of bringing back exotic species from the East, the result being the 6000-odd plant species exhibited today. The gardens are divided into several distinct sections, each clearly labelled and its location pinpointed by a map available at the entrance kiosk. There's also a three-climates glasshouse, where the plants are arranged according to their geographical origins, a capacious palm house, an orchid nursery and a butterfly house. It's all very low-key – and none the worse for that – and the gardens make a relaxing break on any tour of central Amsterdam, especially as the café, in the old orangery, serves up tasty sandwiches, coffee and cakes (see p.102).

Continue down the right-hand side of Plantage Middenlaan to reach another sad relic of the war, **De Hollandsche Schouwburg**, at no. 24 (daily 11am–4pm; closed Yom Kippur; free). Formerly a Jewish theatre, the building became the main assembly point for Amsterdam Jews prior to their deportation. Inside, there was no daylight and families were interned in conditions that foreshadowed those of the camps they would soon be taken to. The building has been refurbished to house a small exhibition on the plight of the city's Jews, but the old auditorium out at the back has been left as an empty, roofless shell. A memorial column of basalt on a Star of David base stands where the stage once was, an intensely mournful monument to suffering of unfathomable proportions.

Artis Zoo

A brief walk northeast along Plantage Kerklaan is the **Artis Zoo** (daily: April to mid-Oct 9am–6pm; mid-Oct to March 9am–5pm; €16, 3- to 9-year-olds €12.50; Ⓦ www.artis.nl). Opened in 1838, the zoo has long been one of the city's top tourist attractions and its layout and lack of bars and cages mean that it never feels overcrowded. Highlights include an African savanna environment, a seventy-metre-long aviary, aquaria and a South American zone with llamas and the world's largest rodent, the capybara. Feeding times – always popular – include: 11am birds of prey; 11.30am and 3.45pm seals and sea lions; 2pm pelicans; 2.30pm crocodiles (Sun only); 3pm lions and tigers (not Fri); and 3.30pm penguins. In addition, the on-site **Planetarium** has five or six shows daily, all in Dutch, though you can pick up a leaflet with an English translation from the desk.

The Verzetsmuseum

Near the zoo, at Plantage Kerklaan 61, is the excellent **Verzetsmuseum** (Mon, Sat & Sun noon–5pm; Tues–Fri 10am–5pm; €5.50; Ⓦwww.verzetsmuseum .org), which outlines the development of the Dutch Resistance from the Nazi invasion of the Netherlands in May 1940 to the country's liberation in 1945. Thoughtfully presented, the main gangway examines the experience of the majority of the population, dealing honestly with the fine balance between co-operation and collaboration. Side rooms are devoted to different aspects of the resistance, from the brave determination of the Communist Party, who went underground as soon as the Germans arrived, to more ad hoc responses like the so-called Milk Strike of 1943, when hundreds of milk producers refused to deliver. Interestingly, the Dutch Resistance proved especially adept at forgery, forcing the Nazis to make the identity cards they issued more and more complicated – but without much success. Fascinating old photographs illustrate the (English and Dutch) text along with a host of original artefacts, from examples of illegal newsletters to signed German death warrants. Apart from their treatment of the Jews, which is detailed here, perhaps the most chilling feature of the occupation was the use of indiscriminate reprisals to terrify the population. For the most part it worked, though there were always a minority courageous enough to resist. The museum has dozens of little metal sheets providing biographical sketches of the members of the Resistance – and it's this mixture of the general and the personal that is its real strength.

Entrepotdok

At the northern end of Plantage Kerklaan, just beyond the Dutch Resistance Museum, a footbridge leads over to **Entrepotdok**, on the nearest, and most interesting, of the Oosterdok islands. On the far side of the bridge, old brick warehouses stretch right along the quayside, distinguished by their spout gables, multiple doorways and overhead pulleys. Built by the Dutch East India Company in the eighteenth century, they were once part of the largest warehouse complex in continental Europe, a gigantic customs-free zone established for goods in transit. On the ground floor, above the main entrance, each warehouse sports the name of a town or island; goods for onward transportation were stored in the appropriate warehouse until there was enough to fill a boat or barge. The warehouses have been tastefully converted into offices and apartments, a fate that must surely befall the central East India Company compound, whose chunky Neoclassical entrance is at the west end of Entrepotdok on Kadijksplein, from where it's a couple of minutes' walk to the Maritime Museum.

Nederlands Scheepvaartmuseum

The **Nederlands Scheepvaartmuseum** (Dutch Maritime Museum; Tues–Sun 10am–5pm; mid-June to mid-Sept also Mon 10am–5pm; €9; Ⓦwww .scheepvaartmuseum.nl) occupies the old arsenal of the Dutch navy, a vast sandstone structure built in the Oosterdok on Kattenburgerplein. It's underpinned by no fewer than 18,000 wooden piles driven deep into the riverbed at enormous expense in the 1650s. The building's four symmetrical facades are dour and imposing despite the odd stylistic flourish, principally some small dormer windows and Neoclassical pediments, and they surround a central, cobbled courtyard. It's the perfect location for a maritime museum – or at least it would be if the museum's collection, spread over three floors, was larger; in the event the collection seems a little forlorn, rattling around a building that's just too big.

The ground floor displays a flashy gilded barge built for King William I in 1818 and is used to host temporary exhibitions. The next floor up, devoted to shipping in the seventeenth and eighteenth centuries, is the most diverting. It includes garish ships' figureheads, examples of early atlases and navigational equipment, and finely detailed models of the clippers of the East India Company, then the fastest ships in the world.

Contemporary shipbuilders tried hard to make the officers' quarters as domestic as possible – literally a home-from-home – and the fancifully carved, seventeenth-century stern which dominates one of the rooms comes complete with a set of dainty mullion windows. There are oodles of nautical paintings too, some devoted to the achievements of Dutch trading ships, others showing heavy seas and shipwrecks and yet more celebrating the successes of the Dutch Navy. Willem van de Velde II (1633–1707) was the most successful of the Dutch marine painters of the period and there's a small sample of his work here – canvases that emphasize the strength and power of the Dutch warship, often depicted in battle or amid turbulent seas. Outside, moored at the museum jetty, is a full-scale replica of an East Indiaman, the *Amsterdam*.

NEMO

Strolling west along the waterfront Prins Hendrikkade, the foreground is dominated by a massive elevated hood that rears up above the entrance to the IJ tunnel. A good part of this hood is occupied by the large and lavish **NEMO** centre, Prins Hendrikkade (Tues–Sun 10am–5pm; during school holidays and July & Aug also Mon 10am–5pm; €11.50; ☎0900/919 1100 premium line, ⓦ www.e-nemo.nl) – just follow the signs for the ground-floor entrance. Recently rebranded, this is a young kids' attraction par excellence, with all sorts of interactive science and technological exhibits spread over six floors.

Stedelijk Museum

Just over the footbridge from NEMO, the collection of Amsterdam's modern art museum – the **Stedelijk** – is currently housed in the former postal building on Oosterdokskade near Centraal Station (daily 10am–6pm; €9; ⓦ www .stedelijk.nl). It's a good choice – the building is a classic 1960s tower block of industrial proportions and the move has proved so popular that there is a chance the collection may never return to its old premises in the Museum Quarter. Since the move, the museum has focused on cutting-edge temporary exhibitions of modern art – from photography and video through to sculpture and collage – to such an extent that the permanent collection rarely gets much of an outing; this includes drawings by Picasso, Matisse and their contemporaries, as well as paintings by Manet, Monet, Bonnard, Ensor, Cézanne, and of course Mondrian, from his early, muddy-coloured abstractions to the cool, boldly coloured rectangular blocks for which he's most famous. The museum also owns a good sample of the work of Kasimir Malevich, his dense attempts at Cubism leading to the dynamism and bold, primary tones of his "Suprematist" paintings, several Marc Chagall paintings, and a number of pictures by American Abstract

Expressionists Mark Rothko, Ellsworth Kelly and Barnett Newman, plus works by other American artists such as Lichtenstein, Warhol and Jean Dubuffet.

The Museum Quarter and the Vondelpark

Just south of Leidseplein, the wide lawns of **Museumplein** extend south from the Rijksmuseum to Van Baerlestraat, and are used for a variety of outdoor activities, from visiting circuses to political demonstrations. The largest of the museums that give it its name is the **Rijksmuseum**, which occupies a huge late nineteenth-century edifice built in an inventive historic style by Petrus Josephus Hubertus Cuypers, also the creator of Centraal Station, in the early 1880s. The museum possesses one of the most comprehensive collections of seventeenth-century Dutch paintings in the world, with twenty or so of Rembrandt's works, plus a healthy sample of canvases by Steen, Hals, Vermeer and their leading contemporaries. There are also representative displays of every other pre-twentieth-century period of Dutch and Flemish painting. On the right, looking south, the **Van Gogh Museum** boasts the finest assortment of Van Gogh paintings in the world, while the **Stedelijk Museum**, just beyond, focuses on modern and contemporary art, although it's semi-permanently closed and its collection currently relocated (see p.97). From Museumplein, it's a brief walk northwest along Van Baerlestraat to the sprawling greenery of the **Vondelpark**, Amsterdam's loveliest park.

The Rijksmuseum

The **Rijksmuseum** (entrance on Jan Luijkenstraat; daily 9am–6pm, Fri until 10pm; €10, combined ticket with Van Gogh Museum, including current exhibition, €25; Ⓦwww.rijksmuseum.nl) is without question the country's foremost museum, with an extravagant collection of Dutch art, as well as a vast hoard of applied art and sculpture. The bad news is that there's a major renovation going on at the moment and most of the museum is closed, probably until 2009. The exception is the Rijksmuseum's Philips Wing, whose smallish but eclectic "Masterpieces" exhibition, scheduled to last until the rest of the museum is reopened, is devoted to the paintings of Amsterdam's Golden Age. Bear in mind, though, that queues can be long, especially in summer and at weekends, so try to book online first.

It's worth the wait, as the selection on display is superb. There are paintings by Rembrandt's pupils – Ferdinand Bol, Gerard Dou and Gabriel Metsu; several wonderful canvases by Frans Hals, such as his scatological *Merry Drinker*; the cool interiors of Vermeer, Gerard ter Borch and Pieter de Hooch; soft, tonal river scenes by the Haarlem artist Salomon van Ruysdael and by Albert Cuyp; the cool church interiors of Pieter Saenredam; and the popular carousing peasants of Jan Steen. However, it's the Rembrandts that steal the show, especially *The Night Watch* of 1642 – perhaps the most famous and probably the most valuable of all the artist's pictures – plus other key works, like a late *Self-Portrait*, a touching depiction of his cowled son, Titus, the arresting *Staalmeesters* and *The Jewish Bride*, one of his very last pictures, finished in 1667.

The Van Gogh Museum

The **Van Gogh Museum**, comprising a fabulous collection of the artist's (1853–90) work, is one of Amsterdam's top attractions (daily 10am–6pm, Fri until 10pm; €10, children 13–17 years €2.50, combined ticket with Rijksmuseum, including current exhibition, €25; Ⓦwww.vangoghmuseum.nl). It occupies two modern buildings, with the kernel of the collection housed in an angular building designed by a leading light of the De Stijl movement, Gerritt Rietveld, and opened to the public in 1973. Well conceived and beautifully presented, this part of the museum provides an introduction to the man and his art based on paintings that were mostly inherited from Vincent's art-dealer brother Theo.

The **ground floor** of the main museum displays works by some of Van Gogh's well-known friends and contemporaries, many of whom influenced his work – Gauguin, Millet, Anton Mauve, Charles Daubigny and others – while the **first floor** has paintings by the artist himself, displayed chronologically, starting with the dark, sombre works of the early years like *The Potato Eaters* and finishing up with the asylum years at St Rémy and the final, tortured paintings done at Auvers, where Van Gogh lodged for the last three months of his life. It was at Auvers that he painted the frantic *Ears of Wheat* and *Wheatfield with a Reaper*, in which the fields swirl and writhe under weird, light-green, moving skies. A few weeks after completing these last paintings that Van Gogh shot and fatally wounded himself.

The two floors above provide back-up to the main collection. The **second floor** has a library and study area with access to a detailed computerized account of Van Gogh's life and times, plus a number of sketches and a handful of less familiar paintings. The **third floor** features more drawings and sketches from the permanent collection as well as notebooks and letters. This floor also affords space to relevant temporary exhibitions illustrating Van Gogh's artistic influences, or his own influence on other artists.

To the rear of Rietveld's building, and connected by a ground-floor-level escalator, is the ultra-modern curved annexe, an aesthetically controversial structure completed in 1998. Financed by a Japanese insurance company – the same conglomerate who paid $35 million for one of Van Gogh's *Sunflowers* canvases in 1987 – this provides temporary exhibition space. Most of these exhibitions focus on one aspect or another of Van Gogh's art and draw heavily on the permanent collection, which means that the paintings displayed in the older building are regularly rotated.

The Concertgebouw

Across Van Baerlestraat is the **Concertgebouw** (Concert Hall), home of the famed – and much recorded – Royal Concertgebouw Orchestra (tours Sun 9.30am, €4, though you have to buy a ticket for the Sun 11am concert too, €13; ℡020/671 8345, ⓦwww.concertgebouw.nl). When the German composer Brahms visited Amsterdam in the 1870s he was scathing about the locals' lack of culture and in particular their lack of an even halfway suitable venue for his music. In the face of such ridicule, a consortium of Amsterdam businessmen got together to fund the construction of a brand-new concert hall and the result was the Concertgebouw, completed in 1888. Since then it has become renowned among musicians and concertgoers for its marvellous acoustics, and after a facelift and the replacement of its crumbling foundations in the early 1990s it is looking and sounding better than ever. The acoustics of the Grote Zaal (Large Hall) are unparalleled, and the smaller Kleine Zaal regularly hosts chamber concerts, often by the resident Borodin Quartet. Prices are very reasonable at €30–50; there are free Wednesday lunchtime concerts from September to May, and in July and August they put on a heavily subsidized series of summer concerts. **Tours** last a little over an hour and take in the Grote Zaal, the Kleine Zaal, and the various backroom activities behind all this – control rooms, piano stores, dressing rooms and the like.

The Vondelpark

Amsterdam's city centre is short of green spaces, which makes the leafy expanses of the **Vondelpark**, just beyond Museumplein, doubly welcome. This is easily the largest and most popular of the city's parks, its network of footpaths used by a healthy slice of the city's population. The park dates back to 1864, when a group of leading Amsterdammers clubbed together to transform the soggy marshland that lay beyond the Leidsepoort into a landscaped park. The group, who were impressed by the contemporary English fashion for natural (as distinct from formal) landscaping, gave the task of developing the new style of park to the Zocher family, big-time gardeners who set about their task with gusto, completing their work in 1865. Named after the seventeenth-century poet Joost van den Vondel, the park proved an immediate success and was expanded to its present size (45 hectares) in 1877. It now possesses over 100 species of tree, a wide variety of local and imported plants, and – among many incidental features – a **bandstand** and excellent **rose garden**. Neither did the Zochers forget their Dutch roots: the park is latticed with ponds and narrow waterways, home to many sorts of wildfowl. There are other animals too: cows, sheep, hundreds of squirrels plus a large colony of bright-green parakeets. The Vondelpark has several different children's **play areas** and during the summer regularly hosts free concerts and theatrical performances, mostly in its own specially designed **open-air theatre**.

De Pijp

Across Boerenwetering, the canal to the east of the Rijksmuseum and Museumplein, lies the busy heart of the **Oud Zuid** (Old South), and specifically the district known as **De Pijp** ("The Pipe"), Amsterdam's first real suburb. New development beyond the Singelgracht began around 1870, but

△ Vondelpark

after laying down the street plans, the city council left the actual house-building to private developers. They made the most of the arrangement and constructed long rows of cheaply built and largely featureless five- and six-storey buildings, and it is these that still dominate the area today. The district's name comes from the characteristically narrow terraced streets running between long, sombre canyons of brick tenements: the apartments here were said to resemble pipe-drawers, since each had a tiny street frontage but extended deep into the building. De Pijp remains one of the city's more closely knit communities, and is home to a large proportion of new immigrants – Surinamese, Moroccan, Turkish and Asian.

Albert Cypstraat market

Ferdinand Bolstraat, running north–south, is De Pijp's main street, but the long, slim east–west thoroughfare of **Albert Cuypstraat** is its heart. The general market (daily except Fri 10am–5pm) held here – which stretches for over a kilometre between Ferdinand Bolstraat and Van Woustraat – is the largest in the city, with a huge array of stalls selling everything from cut-price carrots and raw-herring sandwiches to saucepans and Day-Glo thongs. Check out, too, the ethnic shops that flank the market on each side, and the Indian and Surinamese restaurants down the side streets – they're often cheaper than their equivalents in the city centre.

The Heineken Experience

On the northern edge of De Pijp, the former Heineken brewery, a whopping modern building beside the Singelgracht canal at Stadhouderskade 78, now holds the **Heineken Experience** (tram #16, #24 or #25 from CS; Tues–Sun 10am–6pm; €10; ⓦ www.heinekenexperience.com). The brewery was Heineken's headquarters from 1864 to 1988, when the company was restructured and brewing was moved to a more efficient location out of town. Since then, Heineken has developed the site for tourists with lots of gimmicky but fun attractions such as virtual reality tours and displays on the history of Heineken from advertising campaigns to beer-making. The old brewing facilities with its vast copper vats are included on the tour, but for many the main draw is the free beer you get to quaff at the end in the bar – three drinks, and a souvenir glass, which isn't bad value.

Eating

Amsterdam has never been one of Europe's culinary hotspots, but there has been a resurgence of interest in Dutch cooking in recent years and the city has accumulated a string of excellent homegrown **restaurants**. It's also a city of tremendous diversity, and as well as having some of the best Indonesian food outside Indonesia, at hard-to-beat prices, there are lots of ethnic choices, from French, Iberian and Italian, to Thai, Middle Eastern and Indian. Amsterdam also excels in the quantity and variety of its **eetcafés and bars**, which serve increasingly adventurous and inexpensive food in a wide range of attractive settings. The city's **cafés and tearooms** – calling themselves this to steer clear of druggy "**coffeeshop**" connotations – correspond to the normal idea of a café: they are generally open all day, might serve alcohol but definitely aren't bars, don't allow dope-smoking, and serve up good coffee, sandwiches, light snacks and cakes.

All the following listings are on the maps on pp.64–65 and p.72.

Cafés, tearooms and lunchspots

The Old Centre

Arnots Singel 441. A basement café serving some of the best coffee in town along with wholemeal sandwiches and freshly squeezed apple juice. A great summertime spot with people spilling out onto the pavement. Mon–Fri 11.30am–4.30pm.

Café Beurs van Berlage Beurssplein 1. The best chance to glimpse the interior of the Beurs (see p.75), and an elegantly furnished place to drink coffee or eat lunch. Tables outside too. Tues–Sun 10am–6pm.

De Jaren Nieuwe Doelenstraat 20. One of the grandest of the grand cafés, overlooking the Amstel next to the university, with three floors, two terraces and a cool, light feel. A great place to nurse the Sunday papers – unusually you'll find English ones here. It serves reasonably priced food too, and there's a great salad bar.

Latei Zeedijk 174. Homely shop and café that sells bric-a-brac as well as serving good coffee and decent lunches. Quite a find if you fancy something different from the Chinese restaurants that dominate this end of Zeedijk. Mon–Wed 8am–6pm, Thurs & Fri 8am–10pm, Sat 9am–10pm, Sun 11am–6pm.

Luxembourg Spui 22. Crowded, trendy grand café with a long and deep bar, a good selection of snacks, and possibly the best hamburgers in town. Daily 9am–1am, Fr & Sat until 2am.

't Nieuwe Kafe Eggerstraat 8. Beside the Nieuwe Kerk, this bistro-style café is popular with shoppers and tourists, serving good, reasonably priced breakfasts, lunches, light meals and great pancakes too. Daily 9am–6pm.

Pannekoekhuis Upstairs Grimburgwal 2. Minuscule place in a tumbledown house, in the old centre opposite the university buildings, with sweet and savoury pancakes at low prices. Student discount. Wed–Fri noon–7pm, Sat & Sun noon–6pm.

Puccini Staalstraat 21. Lovely café that serves great salads, sandwiches and cakes and pastries, a few doors down from its sister chocolate shop (see p.117).

Restaurant 1e Class Platform 2b, Centraal Station. More of a fully-fledged restaurant than a café, and with a huge menu to prove it. But its location in Centraal Station means that you're more likely to choose to enjoy its sumptuous turn-of-the-century interior and solid menu of omelettes, sandwiches or more substantial meat and fish offerings at lunchtime, and it's certainly the best option in the station's immediate vicinity. Daily 8.30am–11pm.

Villa Zeezicht Torensteeg 4. Excellent sandwiches and light lunches, and some of the best apple cake in the city. Mon–Fri 8am–6.30pm, Sat & Sun 9am–6.30pm.

Vlaams Friteshuis Voetboogstraat 33. This hole-in-the-wall take-away has a long-established and pretty much undisputed reputation for serving the best *frites* in town. Mon–Sat 11am–6pm, Sun noon–5.30pm.

The Grachtengordel

Buffet van Odette & Yvette Herengracht 309. Just walking past will get your taste buds going: lots of tasty sandwiches, cakes and other good things – a perfect lunch-stop. Mon–Fri 8.30am–5pm, Sat 10am–5pm & Sun noon–5pm.

Greenwood's Singel 103. Small, English-style teashop in the basement of a canal house. Pies and sandwiches, pots of tea – and a decent breakfast. Daily 9.30am–7pm.

The Jordaan and the Western Docklands

Arnold Cornelis Elandsgracht 78. Long-established confectioner and patisserie with a mouth-watering display of pastries and cakes. Take-away or eat in the snug tearoom out the back. Mon–Fri 8.30am–6pm, Sat 8.30am–5pm.

Festina Lente Looiersgracht 40b. Relaxed, mezzanine neighbourhood café-bar with mismatched furniture and armchairs to laze about on. The outside tables overlooking the canal are a suntrap in the summer when the locals come out to relax with friends for the afternoon; inside is equally cosy in the winter, and there's a good selection of board games. Service can be slow at the weekends though. Mon 2pm–1am, Tues–Fri 10.30am–1/3am, Sat 11am–3am, Sun noon–1am.

The Old Jewish Quarter and the Eastern Docklands

Dantzig Zwanenburgwal 15. Easy-going grand café, right on and across the water from Waterlooplein. Comfortable chairs, friendly service and a low-key, chic atmosphere. Daily 11am–10pm – kitchen open all day, except 5–6pm.

De Hortus Plantage Middenlaan 2a. The amenable café in the orangery of the Hortus Botanicus (see p.95) serves a good range of tasty sandwiches and rolls plus the best cheesecake in the western world. Unfortunately, you have to pay to get into the gardens to get to the café. Mon–Fri 9am–4.30pm,

Sat & Sun 10am–4.30pm; Dec & Jan closes 3.30pm; July & Aug until 8.30pm.

Tisfris St Antoniesbreestraat 142. Colourful, New Age-ish split-level café-cum-bar near the Rembrandthuis. Youthful and popular. Daily 9am–7pm.

The Museum Quarter and Vondelpark

't Blauwe Theehuis Vondelpark 5. These days this is a slightly shabby tearoom/café/bar in the middle of the Vondelpark, but its building dates from the De Stijl period. Downstairs it's a regular self-service park café; upstairs it's a nice circular bar that hosts DJs on Friday and Saturday nights. Daily 11am–10pm.

CoBrA Hobbemastraat 18. This standalone asymmetric structure behind the Rijksmuseum mainly caters for tourists wanting a convenient place for a drink or quick bite between exhibitions. It's also a popular late-night hangout, open from 10am until 3am at weekends, otherwise until 9pm.

Keyzer Van Baerlestraat 96. In operation since 1905, and right next to the Concertgebouw, this café-restaurant exudes a fin-de-siècle charm, with ferns, gliding bow-tied waiters and a dark carved-wood interior. It's open all day, and you can come here for dinner, but these days it's best as a venue for lunch or coffee. Mon–Sat 10am–11pm, Sun 11am–11pm.

De Roos PC Hooftstraat 183. The downstairs café at this New Age centre on the edge of the Vondelpark is one of the most peaceful spots in the city, selling a range of drinks and organic snacks and meals. There's also an upstairs bookshop, and any number of courses in yoga and meditation. Mon–Fri 8.30am–9.30pm, Sat & Sun 8.30am–5.30pm.

Vertigo Vondelpark 3. Attached to the Film museum, this is a pleasant place to while away a summer afternoon at the tables outside, overlooking the park, or take refuge in winter in the cosy basement interior. Good food, too, at all times of day. Daily 10am–1am.

Restaurants

The Old Centre

Bird Zeedijk 77 ☎020/420 6289. This Thai canteen is always packed, and rightly so, drawing people from far and wide for its cheap and authentic Thai fare. Its big brother across the road serves much the same food in slightly more upscale surroundings, if that's what you're after. Daily noon–10pm.

Blauwe aan de Waal Oudezijds Achterburgwal 99 ☎020/330 2257. Quite a haven, situated down an alley in the heart of the Red Light District, with tremendous French–Dutch food and a wonderfully soothing environment after the mayhem of the streets outside. Not cheap, but worth every cent. Mon–Sat 6–11pm.

Café Bern Nieuwmarkt 9 ☎020/622 0034 Casual and inexpensive brown café patronized by a predominantly arty clientele. Run by a native of Switzerland, its speciality is, not surprisingly, excellent and alcoholic cheese fondue. Daily 6–11pm.

Centra Lange Niezel 29 ☎020/622 3050. This authentic Spanish cantina is a long-standing Red Light District favourite, with a wonderful selection of Spanish food, masterfully cooked and genially served. Daily 1–11pm.

Green Planet Spuistraat 122 ☎020/625 8280. Cute mezzanine café with lots of tofu dishes and a varied international menu. Cash only. Daily 5.30pm–midnight.

Hemelse Modder Oude Waal 9 ☎020/624 3203. Tasty meat, fish and vegetarian food in French–Italian style at reasonable prices in an informal atmosphere. Very popular. Tues–Sun 6–11pm.

Hoi Tin Zeedijk 122 ☎020/625 6451. You can always trust a restaurant where you have to walk through the kitchen to get to your table, and this one is no exception: a constantly busy Chinatown favourite with an enormous menu (in English too). Dim sum at lunchtime. Daily noon–midnight.

Keuken van 1870 Spuistraat 2 ☎020/620 4018 This big light restaurant has been serving hearty Dutch food to cheapskates for years and continues – justifiably – to thrive. Its three-course €7.50 menu is one of the city's best bargains. Mon–Sat 4–10.30pm.

Lana Thai Warmoesstraat 10 ☎020/624 2179. Among the best Thai restaurants in town, with seating overlooking the water of Damrak. Quality food and chic surroundings but high prices. Mon & Wed–Sun 5–11pm.

Lucius Spuistraat 247 ☎020/624 1831. This long-established restaurant has been uneven over the years but when it gets it right – as it usually does – it's one of the best fish restaurants in town. Daily 5pm–midnight.

Mappa Nes 59 ☎020/528 9170. Classic Italian food with some inventive twists, incorporating good home-made pasta dishes and excellent service in an unpretentious and modern environment. Daily noon–10.30pm.

De Portugees Zeedijk 39 ⓣ020/427 2005. Truly a little piece of Portugal on the Zeedijk, with chaotic service and authentically hearty and filling (rather than gourmet) food – tasty fish stews, garlicky sausages, salt cod and eggs. Daily 6–10.30pm.

Sie Joe Gravenstraat 24 ⓣ020/624 1830. Small Indonesian café-restaurant whose great value-for-money menu is far from extensive but comprises well-prepared, simple dishes such as *gado gado*, *sateh* and *rendang*. Mon–Sat 11am–7pm, Thurs until 8pm.

Van Beeren Koningstraat 54 ⓣ020/622 2329. This eetcafé serves a satisfying mixture of Dutch staples and modern European fare in relaxed surroundings. Daily 5.30–10.15pm.

Van Kerkwijk Nes 41 ⓣ020/620 3316. It looks like a bar but is more of a restaurant these days, serving steaks, fish and so on from an ever-changing menu that isn't written down but is heroically memorized by the attentive waiting staff. Good food, and cheap too – mains from €10. Daily noon–10pm.

The Grachtengordel

De Belhamel Brouwersgracht 60 ⓣ020/622 1095. Smashing restaurant where the Art Nouveau decor makes a delightful setting and the menu is short but extremely well chosen, mixing Dutch with French dishes. Main courses at around €20–25. Daily 6–10pm.

Bojo Lange Leidsedwarsstraat 51 ⓣ020/622 7434. Possibly the best-value – though certainly not the best – Indonesian place in town. The food is very much a hit-and-miss affair, and you'll have to wait a long time both for a table and service. Mon–Wed 4pm–2am, Thurs & Sun noon–2am, Fri & Sat noon–4am.

Bolhoed Prinsengracht 60 ⓣ020/626 1803. Something of an Amsterdam institution, the daily changing menu here features familiar vegan and vegetarian options, with organic beer to wash it down. Mains at around €14. Daily noon–10pm.

Chez Georges Herenstraat 3 ⓣ020/626 3332. This much-lauded Belgian restaurant offers immaculately presented dishes from a well-chosen menu. The premises are decorated in brisk modern style and main courses cost €20 and up. Daily from 6pm except Wed & Sun.

Christophe Leliegracht 46 ⓣ020/625 0807. Classic Michelin-starred restaurant, whose gastronomic subtleties draw inspiration from the olive-oil-and-basil flavours of southern France and the chef's early years in North Africa. The aubergine terrine with cumin has been dubbed the best vegetarian dish in the world. Attractive canalside premises too. Advance reservations

essential; main courses €25 and up. Tues–Sat 6.30–10.30pm.

Cilubang Runstraat 10 ⓣ020/626 9755. Tiny but much liked Indonesian restaurant, with a friendly atmosphere, serving well-presented, spicy dishes at reasonable prices, with mains hovering around €14. Tues–Sun 6–11pm.

Damsteeg Reestraat 28 ⓣ020/627 8794. First-rate, French-inspired cuisine with more than the occasional Dutch gastronomic flourish, served up in a charmingly renovated old canal house. Mains are around €20. Mon–Sat 2pm–11pm.

Golden Temple Utrechtsestraat 126 ⓣ020/626 8560. Laidback place with a little more soul than the average Amsterdam veggie joint. Well-prepared food and pleasant, attentive service. No alcohol and non-smoking throughout. Daily 5–9pm.

Le Soleil Nieuwe Spiegelstraat 56 ⓣ020/622 7147. Dinky little inexpensive pancake house (once visited by the Queen) that does what it does outstandingly well – even in this the land of the pancake. Daily 10am–6pm.

Le Zinc … et les Dames Prinsengracht 999 ⓣ020/622 9044. Wonderfully atmospheric little place serving good-quality, simple fare with main courses averaging €20–25; there's a particularly good wine list too. Mon–Sat 5.30–11pm.

Prego Herenstraat 25 ⓣ020/638 0148. Informal French restaurant with sharp modern decor offering an exceptionally inventive menu including such delights as stuffed guinea fowl and chicory cooked every which way. Mains €20 and up. Daily from 6pm.

Puri Mas Lange Leidsedwarsstraat 37 ⓣ020/627 7627. Exceptionally good value for money Indonesian, on a street better known for rip-offs. Friendly and informed service preludes spectacular *rijsttafels*, both meat and vegetarian. Daily from 5pm.

Tempo Doeloe Utrechtsestraat 75 ⓣ020/625 6718. Reliable, reasonably priced quality place close to Rembrandtplein. As with all Indonesian restaurants, be guided by the waiter when choosing – some of the dishes are very hot indeed. Daily from 6pm.

D'Theeboom Singel 210 ⓣ020/623 8420. Traditional French restaurant in an old and attractive canal house a short walk from Dam Square. Relaxed atmosphere; attentive service. Mains from around €20. Daily 6–10pm.

Van de Kaart Prinsengracht 512 ⓣ020/625 9232. Slick and chic restaurant, with an excellent and enterprising French-inspired menu including such delights as lobster carpaccio, home-cured bacon and pumpkin-stuffed ravioli. The selection of wines complements with vim and gusto. Mon–Sat 6.30–11pm.

The Jordaan and the Western Docklands

Albatros Westerstraat 264 ☏ 020/627 9932. This nautically adorned fish restaurant serves exceptionally good food, making it a great place to splash out and linger over a meal. Mains from €20; three-course menu of the day €30. Mon & Thurs–Sun 6pm–11pm.

Burger's Patio 2e Tuindwarsstraat 12 ☏ 020/623 6854. Despite the name (the site used to be occupied by a butchers), there isn't a burger in sight in this long-established convivial restaurant, which has managed to maintain its informal atmosphere without compromising on taste. Italian-inspired dishes are wonderfully presented with a good choice of daily specials. Mains from €15. Daily 6pm–late.

Capri Lindengracht 61 ☏ 020/624 4940. Large café-restaurant serving pizza and pasta at reasonable prices (from €7). Saturdays are usually busy with much of the joyful atmosphere of the neighbouring market, while evenings are popular with local families. Daily 5–9pm, Sat from 9am.

Cinema Paradiso Westerstraat 186 ☏ 020/623 7344. Slick, fast-moving restaurant covering all the Italian classics with vim and gusto. It's in a former moviehouse and very popular, so you may have to shout to be heard. Dress to kill/thrill. Main courses kick off at around €15. Tues–Sun 6pm–11pm.

Claes Claesz Egelantiersstraat 24 ☏ 020/625 5306. This exceptionally friendly Jordaan restaurant attracts a mixed crowd and serves excellent Dutch food. Fridays and Saturdays feature various Dutch theatrical and musical acts between the courses. Choose between two- and four-courses €25–30. Wed–Sun 6–11pm.

De Eettuin 2e Tuindwarsstraat 10 ☏ 020/623 7706. Hefty and eminently affordable portions of Dutch food, with salad from a serve-yourself bar. Non-meat eaters can content themselves with a choice of tasty vegetarian options, and all mains (from €13) come with a choice of rice or potato. Daily 5.30–11.30pm.

De Gouden Reael Zandhoek 14 ☏ 020/623 3883. Fine French food in a unique setting up in the Westerdok. Its relaxed mezzanined interior is a good place for a coffee any time of day. The bar, as described in the novel of the same name by Jan Mens, has a long association with the dockworkers. Main courses hover around €15–20. Daily 11am–12pm.

Koevoet Lindenstraat 17 ☏ 020/624 0846. The "Cow's-Foot" – or, alternatively, the "Crowbar" – is a traditional Jordaan eetcafé with a creative French menu and very tasty, moderately priced food. Wed–Sat 6–11pm.

De Vliegende Schotel Nieuwe Leliestraat 162 ☏ 020/625 2041. Perhaps the pick of the city's cheap and wholesome vegetarian restaurants, the "Flying Saucer" serves delicious food in large portions. Lots of space, a peaceful ambience – and a good notice board. Mains around €10. Daily from 4pm.

Yam Yam Trattoria Frederik Hendrikstraat 90 ☏ 020/681 5097. Top pizzeria and trattoria in a simple, traditional dining room, with wipe-clean table covers and an open kitchen. It attracts couples and all the hip young parents from the neighbourhood with its excellent pizza toppings, including fresh rocket and truffle sauce. Booking advised. Pizzas €10–12. Tues–Sun 6–10pm.

The Old Jewish Quarter and the Eastern Docklands

éénvistwéévis Schippersgracht 6 ☏ 020/623 2894. An uncomplicated fish restaurant serving an interesting selection of seafood, such as oyster and mussel soup for starters and sea bass with rosemary and thyme for main courses. Mains at around €20. Tues–Sun 6–10pm.

Greetje Peperstraat 23 ☏ 020/779 7450. New kid on the gastronomic block, *Greetje* is a cosy, busy restaurant and bar that serves up Dutch staples with a modern twist. A changing menu reflects the seasons and the favourite dishes of the owners' mother – a native of the southern Netherlands. Great, home cooking in a great atmosphere. Wed–Sun 5–10pm; bar Wed–Fri & Sun 5pm–1am, Sat 5pm–3am.

Koffiehuis van de Volksbond Kadijksplein 4 ☏ 020/622 1209. Formerly a Communist Party café and apparently the place where the local dockworkers used to receive their wages, this is now an Oosterdok neighbourhood café-restaurant – and a good place to try sauerkraut and pork. Daily 6–10pm.

Rosario Peperstraat 10 ☏ 020/627 0280. This very attractive trattoria occupies smart canalside premises and serves up excellent Italian food – especially the ravioli. Mains around €20. Mon–Sat 6–11pm.

The Museum Quarter and Vondelpark

Bosboom Bosboom Toussaintstraat 29 ☏ 020/683 6854 Owned by the same people who own the *Toussaint Café* across the road, this bright, welcoming restaurant serves food, especially fish, with a Mediterranean slant. Three-course menus are €25. Wed–Sun 5.30–10.30pm.

Dionysos Overtoom 176 ☏ 020/689 4441. Inexpensive Greek restaurant just west of the Vondelpark, with the distinct added advantage of serving until 1am. Daily 5pm–1am.

Le Garage Ruysdaelstraat 54 ☏ 020/679 7176. This elegant restaurant, with an eclectic French and Italian menu, is popular with a media crowd, since it's run by a well-known Dutch TV cook. Call to reserve a week ahead and dress to impress. Prices are moderate to high, with two-course menus for around €40, three courses for €50. Daily 6–11pm, Mon–Fri also noon–2pm.

Loetje J. Vermeerstraat 52 ☏ 020/662 8173. Excellent steaks, fries and salads are the thing at this eetcafé. The service can be touch-and-go, but the food is great, and fairly inexpensive. Mon–Fri 11am–10pm, Sat 6–10pm.

Orient Van Baerlestraat 21 ☏ 020/673 4958. Moderately priced Indonesian restaurant. Excellently prepared dishes, with a wide range to choose from; vegetarians are very well taken care of, and the service is generally good. Expect to pay around €22 for a *rijsttafel*. Daily 5–10pm.

Drinking

Amsterdam's selection of **bars** and **café–bars** is one of the real pleasures of the city. There are traditional, so-called brown cafés, so called because of the dingy colour of their walls, stained by years of tobacco smoke, and slick, self-consciously modern **designer bars**, which tend to be as un-brown as possible and geared towards a young crowd. We've included details of the more established ones, although these places come and go – something like seventy percent are said to close down within a year of opening. Most **café–bars** (often called **eetcafés**) and some bars sell food – anything from snacks to an extensive menu. Another type of drinking spot, though increasingly rare, is the **tasting-house** (*proeflokaal*), originally the sampling rooms of small private *jenever* distillers, now tiny, stand-up places that often only sell spirits and close around 8pm. For listings of gay bars, see p.114.

All the following listings are on the maps on pp.64–65 and p.72.

The Old Centre

Absinthe Nieuwezijds Voorburgwal 171 ☏ 020/777 4870. Small, late-night basement lounge bar that specializes in – you guessed it – absinthe, or at least the turn-of-the-century decadence that's associated with it. DJs at the weekend.

De Bekeerde Suster Kloveniersburgwal 6. Don't waste your time in the unappealing drinkeries of the Red Light District proper; this place is a few steps away and offers home-brewed beer, a good bar menu and a very convivial atmosphere, just off the top end of Nieuwemarkt.

Belgique Gravenstraat 2. Tiny bar behind the Nieuwe Kerk that serves up Belgian brews with cubes of cheese.

Blincker St Barberenstraat 7. Hi-tech theatre bar just south of the Red Light District that also serves decent food.

Diep Nieuwezijds Voorburgwal 256. Not much more than an ordinary brown café during the day, but a hip hangout with DJs at night.

De Drie Fleschjes Gravenstraat 18. Tasting house for spirits and liqueurs, which once would have been made on the premises. Clients tend to be well heeled or well soused (often both). Mon–Sat noon–8.30pm, Sun 3–8pm.

De Engelbewaarder Kloveniersburgwal 59. Once the meeting place of Amsterdam's bookish types, this is still known as a literary café. It's relaxed and informal, with live jazz on Sunday afternoons.

Gollem Raamsteeg 4. Small and intimate bar with a superb selection of Belgian beers – and with the correct glasses to drink them from. The genial barman will help you choose.

Hoppe Spui 18. One of Amsterdam's longest-established and best-known bars, frequented by the city's businessfolk on their wayward way home. Summer is especially good, when the throngs spill out onto the street.

Lokaal 't Loosje Nieuwmarkt 32. Quiet old-style brown café that's been here for two hundred years and looks it. Wonderful for late breakfasts and pensive afternoons.

Wynand Fockink Pijlsteeg 31. Small and cosy bar hidden just behind the *Krasnapolsky* hotel off Dam Square. One of the older *proeflokalen*, it offers a vast range of its own flavoured *jenevers* that used to be distilled down the street.

The Grachtengordel

De Hegeraad Noordermarkt 34. Lovingly maintained, old-fashioned brown café with a loyal clientele. The back room with red plush furnishings and paintings is the perfect place to relax with a hot chocolate.

🚶 **Het Molenpad** Prinsengracht 653. This is one of the most appealing brown cafés in the city – a long, dark bar that fills up fast with a young, professional crowd after 6pm.

Oosterling Utrechtsestraat 140. Stone-floored, neighbourhood bar-cum-off-licence that's been owned by the same family for donkeys' years. Kitted out in attractive traditional style, it specializes in *jenever* with dozens of brands and varieties. No mobile phones.

Het Papeneiland Prinsengracht 2. With its wood panelling, antique Delft tiles and ancient stove, this is one of the cosiest bars in the Grachtengordel, though it does get packed late at night with a garrulous crew.

De Prins Prinsengracht 124. With its well-worn decor and chatty atmosphere, this popular and lively brown bar offers a wide range of drinks and a well-priced bar menu with food served from 10am to 9pm.

't Smackzeyl Brouwersgracht 101. Uninhibited drinking hole on the fringes of the Jordaan – on the corner of Prinsengracht. One of the few brown cafés to have Guinness on tap; also an inexpensive menu of light dishes.

Spanjer & van Twist Leliegracht 60. Hip café-bar with an arty air and brisk modern fittings. Tasty snacks and light meals plus an outside mini-terrace right on the canal. Lunch served daily 10am–4pm, evening meals from 6pm.

Van Puffelen Prinsengracht 377. This long-established and popular spot is divided into two with a brown café-bar on one side and a (very average) restaurant on the other. The café-bar (daily 3pm to 1 or 2am) is an appealing place to drink, with a good choice of international brews.

Walem Keizersgracht 449. A chic café-bar – cool, light, and vehemently un-brown. The clientele is stylish, and the food is a kind of hybrid French–Dutch; there's also a wide selection of newspapers and magazines, including some in English. Breakfast in the garden during the summer is a highlight. Usually packed. Kitchen daily 10am–10pm.

The Jordaan and the Western Docklands

Chris Bloemstraat 42. Very proud of itself for being the Jordaan's (and Amsterdam's) oldest bar, dating from 1624. Comfortable, homely atmosphere.

Dulac Haarlemmerstraat 118. A very appealing Art Deco grand café, with lots of nooks to sit in, housed in what was an old city bank – the metal cage doors remain but now the only money changing hands is at the bar, especially on weekends when it stays open till 3am. DJs from Thursday to Saturday play a mixture of jazz, funk and Seventies and Eighties tunes.

Finch Noordermarkt 5. This smart and cosy café-lounge bar situated near the Noorderkerk attracts a stylish, relaxed crowd, drawn by the design-school ambience, good tunes and superb location overlooking the Prisengracht. Lunch from noon, dinner from 6pm.

De Kat in de Wijngaert Lindengracht 160. With the enticing name "Cat in the Vineyard", this small bar is the epitome of the Jordaan local, and quiet enough for conversation.

🚶 **De Reiger** Nieuwe Leliestraat 34. Situated in the thick of the Jordaan, this is one of the area's many meeting places, an old-style café filled with modish Amsterdammers and with faded portraits on the walls. Dinner around €18.

't Smalle Egelantiersgracht 12. Candle-lit and comfortable, with a pontoon on the canal out front for relaxed summer afternoons. One of Amsterdam's oldest cafés, it opened in 1786 as a *proeflokaal* – a tasting house for the (long gone) gin distillery next door.

De Tuin 2e Tuindwarsstraat 13. The Jordaan has some marvellously unpretentious bars, and this is one of the best: agreeably unkempt and always filled with locals.

The Old Jewish Quarter and the Eastern Docklands

Brouwerij 't IJ De Gooyer Windmill, Funenkade 7. About ten minutes' walk east of the Maritime Museum along Hoogte Kadijk. Cosy old-fashioned bar and mini-brewery adjacent to the De Gooyer windmill. Serves up an excellent range of brews, including the thunderously strong Columbus (at nine per cent). Wed–Sun 3–8pm.

🚶 **De Druif** Rapenburgerplein 83. Possibly the city's oldest bar, and certainly one of its more beguiling, this neighbourhood joint pulls in an easy-going crowd.

🚶 **11** Oosterdokskade 3 ☎020/625 5999. One of the hippest joints in town, this sprawling bar-club-restaurant has bare minimalist-industrial decor inherited from its previous incarnation as the top floor of the old postal building – above the Stedelijk Museum (see p.97). The views out over the city centre are second to none and the journey up in one of the enormous old postal lifts is good fun, but the food doesn't match the setting and really the place is best used as a bar and club. Mon–Wed & Sun 11am–10pm, Thurs–Sat club nights 11am–4am (kitchen till 10pm).

De Sluyswacht Jodenbreestraat 1 This pleasant little bar occupies an old and now solitary gabled house that stands sentry by the lock gates opposite the Rembrandthuis. A smashing spot to nurse a beer on a warm summer's night, gazing down the canal towards the Montelbaanstoren.

The Museum Quarter and Vondelpark

Welling J.W. Brouwersstraat 32. Situated right behind the Concertgebouw, this traditional haunt of gloomy Amsterdam intellectuals is usually packed solid with performers and visitors alike before and after evening performances.

Wildschut Roelof Hartplein 1. Not far from the Concertgebouw this bar is famous for its Art Deco trimmings, and its congenial large interior and outside seating in summer. Much the nicest place to drink in the area, and with a decent menu too.

Coffeeshops

In Amsterdam a "**coffeeshop**" is advertising just one thing: **cannabis**. You might also be able to get coffee and a slice of cake, but the main activity in a coffeeshop is smoking. There are almost as many different kinds of coffeeshops as there are bars: some are neon-lit, with loud music and Day-Glo decor, but there are plenty of others that are quiet, comfortable places to have a relaxed smoke and take it easy. See p.47 for more advice on what to expect, including a rundown on the legal situation and how to go about making your purchase. The establishments listed here are better than the average, and most of them open around 10am or 11am and close around midnight.

All the following listings are on the maps on pp.64–65 and p.72.

Abraxas Jonge Roelensteeg 12. Quirky, mezzanine coffeeshop with spiral staircases that are challenging after a spliff. The hot chocolate with hash is not for the susceptible. Daily 10am–1am.

Barney's Breakfast Bar Haarlemmerstraat 102. Something of an Amsterdam institution, this extremely popular café-cum-coffeeshop is simply the most civilized place in town to enjoy a big hit with a fine breakfast – at any time of the day. A few doors down, at no. 98, *Barney's Brasserie* affords a nice sunny spot in the morning and serves alcohol. Daily 7am–10pm.

The Bulldog Leidseplein 15. The biggest and most famous of the coffeeshop chains, and a long way from its pokey Red Light District-dive origins. This, the main Leidseplein branch (the *Palace*), housed in a former police station, has a large cocktail bar, coffeeshop, juice bar and souvenir shop, all with separate entrances. It's big and brash, not at all the place for a quiet smoke, though the dope they sell (packaged up in neat little brand-labelled bags) is reliably good. Daily 9am–1am.

Dampkring Handboogstraat 29. Colourful coffeeshop with a laidback atmosphere that is known for its good-quality hash. Sun–Thurs 10am–1am, Fri & Sat 10am–2am.

Extase Oude Hoogstraat 2. Part of a chain run by the initiator of the Hash Museum (see p.79).

Considerably less chi-chi than a lot of coffeeshops but a handy Red Light District standby. Daily 9am–1am.

Global Chillage Kerkstraat 51. A celebrated slice of Amsterdam dope culture, always comfortably filled with tie-dyed stone-heads propped up against the walls, so chilled they're horizontal. Daily 1pm–1am.

Grasshopper Oudebrugsteeg 16. Multi-levelled coffeeshop, with bar, sports screen and restaurant. One of the city's more welcoming places, although its proximity to Centraal Station means that at times it can be overwhelmed by tourists. Another location at Nieuwezijds Voorburgwal 57. Mon–Thurs & Sun 8am–1am, Fri & Sat 7am–3am.

Paradox 1e Bloemdwarsstraat 2. If you're fed up with the usual coffeeshop food offerings, Paradox satisfies the munchies with outstanding natural food, including spectacular fresh fruit concoctions and veggie burgers. Daily 10am–8pm.

Rusland Rusland 16. One of the first Amsterdam coffeeshops, a cramped but vibrant place that's a favourite with both dope fans and tea addicts (it has 43 different kinds). A cut above the rest. Daily 10am–1am.

Siberië Brouwersgracht 11. Very relaxed, very friendly, and worth a visit whether you want to smoke or not. Mon–Thurs & Sun 11am–11pm, Fri & Sat 11am–midnight.

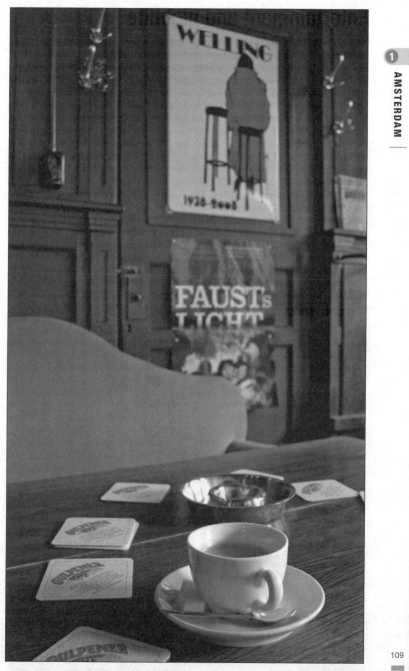

△ Welling

Entertainment and nightlife

Although Amsterdam is not generally considered one of the world's major cultural centres, the quality and quantity of **music**, **dance** and **film** on offer are high – largely thanks to the government's long-term subsidy to the arts. For information about what's on, try the Amsterdam Uitburo, or **AUB**, the cultural office of the city council, which is housed in a corner of the Stadsschouwburg theatre on Leidseplein (Mon–Sat 10am–7.30pm, Sun noon–7.30pm). You can get advice here on anything remotely cultural, as well as tickets and copies of listings magazines. Tickets for most performances can be bought at the Uitburo (for a €2 fee) and VVV offices, or reserved by phone through the AUB Uitlijn (☎0900/0191 at €0.40 per minute) for a one-percent booking fee, but the cheapest way to obtain tickets is to turn up at the venue itself.

For information about what's on, the monthly *Uitkrant* is comprehensive and free, but in Dutch, or there's the VVV's English-language *What's On In Amsterdam*, though this is rather bland. Take a look, too, at the AUB's *Uitlijst* notice boards, which include music gigs, or grab a copy of the cigarette-sponsored *Camel Uitlijst* from any café for the latest live music events. The Dutch newspaper *Het Parool* has a Wednesday entertainment supplement, *Uit en Thuis*. In addition, cinemas stock the fold-out "Week Agenda", which gives details of all films showing in the city that week (Thurs to Wed).

Rock, jazz and folk

Amsterdam is a regular tour stop for many major artists, and something of a testing ground for current rock bands. **Dutch rock** was formerly dire, but local groups can nowadays lay claim to both quality and originality. Bear in mind, too, that Amsterdam is often on the tour circuit of up-and-coming British bands – keep a sharp eye on the listings. With the construction of the 50,000-seat ArenA out in the southeastern suburbs, Amsterdam has finally gained the stadium **rock venue** it has craved for years. However, it's taking some time to catch on, and, aside from the Tina Turner brand of superstar, most major touring acts still choose to play at Rotterdam's Ahoy sports hall. The three dedicated music venues in Amsterdam city centre – the **Paradiso**, the **Melkweg** and the **Arena** (not to be confused with the ArenA) – are all much smaller, and supply a constantly changing seven-days-a-week programme of music to suit all tastes and budgets. Alongside the main venues, the city's clubs, bars and multimedia centres sporadically host performances by live bands. As far as **prices** go, for big names you'll pay anything between €25 and €50 a ticket; ordinary gigs cost €6–15, although some places charge a membership (*lidmaatschap*) fee on top. If no price is listed, entrance is usually free.

Arena 's-Gravensandestraat 51, tram #7 from Centraal Station. ☎020/850 2400, ☻www .hotelarena.nl. Hip club set within in a restored chapel adjoining a hotel that used to be an orphanage and asylum. Open Fridays and Saturdays, with occasional salsa nights and special parties hosted on a Sunday. International DJs sometimes drop by – and that's when you can expect the entrance fee to jump from around €11 to €20. Fri & Sat 10pm–4am.

Bimhuis Piet Heinkade 3, east of Centraal Station ☎020/788 2188, ☻www.bimhuis.nl. In 2004 the city's premier jazz and improvised music venue moved to its spanking new building next to the Muziekgebouw (see p.112), featuring events from Dutch and international artists throughout the week, as well as jam sessions and workshops; there are free improv workshops on Tuesdays. There's also a modern bar and restaurant for concert-goers with fantastic views over the water.

Café Alto Korte Leidsedwarsstraat 115 ☎ 020/626 3249, 🌐 www.jazz-cafe-alto.nl. It's worth hunting down this legendary little jazz bar just off Leidseplein for its quality modern jazz, performed every night from around 10pm until 3am (even later at the weekend). It's big on atmosphere, though slightly cramped, but entry is free. Daily from 9pm.

Maloe Melo Lijnbaansgracht 163 ☎ 020/420 4592, 🌐 www.maloemelo.nl. Dark, low-ceilinged bar, with a small back room featuring lively local blues acts every day of the week. Jam sessions Monday to Thursday.

Melkweg Lijnbaansgracht 234a ☎ 020/531 8181, 🌐 www.melkweg.nl. Probably Amsterdam's most famous entertainment venue, plus one of the city's prime multimedia arts centres, with a young, hip clientele. A former dairy (hence the name) just round the corner from Leidseplein, with two separate halls for live music, putting on a broad range of bands covering everything from reggae to rock, all of which lean towards the "alternative". Excellent DJ sessions go on late at the weekend, with Que Pasa providing a Latino flavour to Friday

nights and anything from dancehall to indie pop thrown down on Saturdays. There's also a monthly film programme, a theatre, gallery and café-restaurant (Marnixstraat entrance; Wed–Sun noon–9pm).

Paradiso Weteringschans 6–8 ☎ 020/626 4521, 🌐 www.paradiso.nl. A converted church near the Leidseplein, revered by many for its atmosphere and excellent programme, featuring local and international bands ranging from the newly signed to the more established. Popular club nights such as Friday's Paradisoul still draw in the crowds, and look out too for DJ sets featuring live performances on Saturdays. It has been known to host classical concerts, as well as debates and multimedia events (often in conjunction with the nearby Balie centre, see p.112).

Winston Warmoesstraat 123 ☎ 020/623 1380, 🌐 www.winston.nl. Adventurous small venue, next to a hotel, featuring everything from live Ghanean percussion and symphonic rock to R&B, punk/ noise and club nights. Poetry night once a month on Monday.

Classical music and opera

There's no shortage of **classical music** concerts in Amsterdam, with two major orchestras based in the city, plus regular visits by other Dutch orchestras. Amsterdam's Royal Concertgebouw Orchestra (🌐 www.concertgebouworkest .nl) remains one of the most dynamic in the world, and occupies one of the finest concert halls to boot. The other resident orchestra is the Dutch Philharmonic (🌐 www.orkest.nl), based at the Beurs van Berlage concert hall, which has a wide symphonic repertoire and also performs with the Dutch Opera (🌐 www.dno.nl) at the Muziektheater. As far as smaller classical ensembles go, Dutch musicians pioneered the use of period instruments in the 1970s, and Ton Koopman's Amsterdam Baroque Orchestra (🌐 www.tonkoopman.nl) and Frans Brüggen's Orchestra of the Eighteenth Century (🌐 www.orchestra18c .com) are two internationally renowned exponents. Koopman's Amsterdam Baroque Choir and the Amsterdam Bach Soloists are also pre-eminent. As well as the main concert halls, a number of Amsterdam's churches (and former churches) host regular performances of classical and chamber music; both types of venue are listed below. The most prestigious venue for **opera** is the Muziektheater (otherwise known as the Stopera) on Waterlooplein, which is home to the Dutch Opera company as well as the National Ballet. Visiting companies sometimes perform here, but more often at the Stadsschouwburg and the Carré Theatre.

The best multi-venue event is June's annual **Holland Festival** (🌐 www .hollandfestival.nl), which attracts the best domestic mainstream and fringe performers in all areas of the arts, as well as an exciting international line-up. One of the more interesting music-oriented events is the **piano recital** held towards the end of August on a floating stage outside the *Pulitzer Hotel* on the Prinsengracht. The whole area is floodlit and filled with small boats, and every available spot on the banks and bridges taken up – altogether a thoroughly atmospheric evening.

Beurs van Berlage Damrak 213 ☎020/521 7575 or 530 4141, ⊛www.beursvanberlage.nl. The splendid interior of the former stock exchange (see also p.75) has been put to use as a venue for theatre and music, among other things, and there are regular concerts in its various impressive halls.

Carré Theatre Amstel 115–25 ☎0900/252 5255, ⊛www.theatercarre.nl. A splendid hundred-year-old structure (originally built for a circus) which represents the ultimate venue for Dutch folk artists, and hosts all kinds of top international acts, anything from Swedish gospel to Carmen, with reputable touring orchestras and opera companies squeezed in between.

Concertgebouw Concertgebouwplein 2–6 ☎020/671 8345, ⊛www.concertgebouw.nl. After a recent facelift, the Concertgebouw is now looking – and sounding – better than ever. There are two halls here and both boast a star-studded international programme. Prices are very reasonable, rarely over €35, and around €15 for Sunday-morning events. Free lunchtime concerts are held from September to May every Wednesday at 12.30pm. For more, see p.99.

Muziekgebouw Pietheinkade 1 ☎020/788 2000, ⊛www.muziekgebouw.nl. This massive new development of two new medium-sized concert halls has given new impetus to the redevelopment going on alongside the IJ, as its top-quality programmes of opera and orchestral music draw a highbrow crowd to this part of town. Worth a visit for the building alone. The same development also includes the relocated Bimhuis.

Muziektheater Amstel 3 ☎020/625 5455 or 551 8100, ⊛www.muziektheater.nl. Part of the €150 million complex that includes the city hall. The theatre's resident companies, Netherlands Opera and National Ballet, offer the fullest, and most reasonably priced, programme of opera and dance in Amsterdam. Tickets go very quickly. See also p.92.

Oude Kerk Oudekerksplein 23 ☎020/625 8284, ⊛www.oudekerk.nl. Hosts organ and carillon recitals, as well as occasional choral events. In summer, in conjunction with the Amstelkring Museum (see p.78), the church organizes a series of "walking" concert evenings, consisting of three separate concerts at different venues, with time for coffee and a stroll between each.

Stadsschouwburg Leidseplein 26 ☎020/624 2311, ⊛www.stadsschouwburgamsterdam.nl. These days somewhat overshadowed by the Muziektheater, but still staging significant opera and dance (it's the home theatre of the Hague's innovative company, the Dutch Dance Theatre), as well as visiting English-language theatre companies.

Waalse Kerk Oudezijds Achterburgwal 159 ☎020/623 2074. Tickets €10–15. Weekend afternoon and evening concerts of early and chamber music.

Theatre, cabaret and film

Surprisingly for a city that functions so much in English, there is next to no English-language **theatre** – though English-speaking touring companies do regularly visit. The Stalhouderij is the only company working in English, performing in a broom-cupboard of a theatre in the Jordaan. English-language **comedy** and **cabaret**, on the other hand, has become a big thing in Amsterdam, spearheaded by the resident and extremely successful Boom Chicago comedy company. During the summer in particular, a number of small venues host mini-seasons of English-language stand-up comedy and cabaret featuring touring British performers. As for cinema, most of Amsterdam's commercial cinemas are huge, multiplex picture palaces showing a selection of general releases, but there is also a scattering of film houses (*filmhuizen*) showing revival and art films and occasional retrospectives. All foreign movies playing in Amsterdam (almost no Dutch movies turn up anyway) are shown in their original language and subtitled in Dutch. Amsterdam's only regular film event is the fascinating International Documentary Film Festival in November/December (info ☎020/627 3329, ⊛www.idfa.nl), during which two hundred documentaries from all over the world are shown in ten days.

De Balie Kleine Gartmanplantsoen 10 ☎020/553 5100, ⊛www.balie.nl. A multimedia centre for culture and the arts, located off the Leidseplein, which often plays host to drama, debates, international symposia and the like, sometimes in conjunction with the *Paradiso* (see p.111) next door.

Boom Chicago Leidseplein 12 ☎020/423 0101, ⊛www.boomchicago.nl. Something of a phenomenon in Amsterdam, this rapid-fire improv comedy troupe hailing from the US performs at the Leidseplein Theater nightly to crowds of tourists and locals alike. With inexpensive food, cocktails and beer served in pitchers, the comedy need not be funny – but it is.

Cinecenter Lijnbaansgracht 236 ⊕ 020/623 6615, ⓦ www.cinecenter.nl. Opposite the *Melkweg*, this shows independent and quality commercial films, the majority originating from non-English-speaking countries. Shown with an interval.

Filmmuseum Vondelpark 3 ⊕ 020/589 1400, ⓦ www.filmmuseum.nl. The Filmmuseum holds literally tens of thousands of prints, and although Dutch films show regularly, there are also regular screenings of all kinds of movies from all corners of the world. Silent movies often have live piano accompaniment, and on summer weekend evenings there are free open-air screenings on the terrace. Tickets €7–8.

Kriterion Roeterstraat 170 ⊕ 020/623 1708, ⓦ www.kriterion.nl. Stylish duplex cinema close to Weesperplein metro that shows arthouse and quality commercial films, with late-night cult favourites. Friendly bar attached. Trams #6, #7 or #10.

Melkweg Lijnbaansgracht 234a ⊕ 020/531 8181, ⓦ www.melkweg.nl. As well as music, art and dance (see p.111), the Melkweg manages to maintain a consistently good monthly film and video programme, ranging from mainstream fodder through to obscure imports.

The Movies Haarlemmerdijk 161 ⊕ 020/624 5790, ⓦ www.themovies.nl. A beautiful Art Deco cinema, and a charming setting for independent films. Worth visiting for the bar and restaurant alone. "Filmdiinner" nights Mon–Thurs include a three-course meal plus film for €29. Late shows at the weekend.

Nachttheater Sugar Factory Lijnbaansgracht 238 ⊕ 020/627 0008, ⓦ www.sugarfactory.nl. Busy Leidseplein's latest addition is the recently opened "theatrical nightclub", which hosts a stimulating programme of cabaret, live music, poetry and theatre, plus a late-night club that kicks off after the show. Pulls in a young and artistic crowd, and features up to two events per evening. Closed Tues.

Clubs

Clubbing in Amsterdam used to be a relatively low-key affair, but in recent years the city has established itself as more of a clubbers' city, with a good array of decent venues that are just as style-conscious as those in other European capitals, as well as plenty of bars hosting regular DJs – most playing variations on house, trance, garage and techno. Although all the places listed open at either 10pm or 11pm, there's not much point turning up anywhere before midnight; unless stated otherwise, everywhere stays open until 5am on Friday and Saturday nights, 4am on other nights.

Bitterzoet Spuistraat 2 ⊕ 020/521 3001, ⓦ www.bitterzoet.com. Bar-cum-club with DJs every night and sometimes live music too – reggae, hip-hop, dance. No entrance fee if you arrive before 11pm. Daily 8pm–3am, 4am at weekends.

Dansen bij Jansen Handboogstraat 11–13 ⊕ 020/620 1779, ⓦ www.dansenbijjansen.nl. Club with upstairs bar that was founded by – and for – students. It's very popular, playing a mixture of pop, chart and R&B. though officially you need student ID to get in. Daily 10pm–4am, Sat & Sun until 5am. €2 Mon–Wed & Sun, €4 Thurs–Sat.

Escape Rembrandtplein 11 ⊕ 020/622 1111, ⓦ www.escape.nl. This vast club has space enough to house 2000 people, but its glory days – when it was home to Amsterdam's cutting edge Chemistry nights – are long gone and it now focuses on weekly club nights that pull in crowds of mainstream punters. Thurs–Sun 11pm–4/5am.

Exit Reguliersdwarsstraat 42 ⊕ 020/625 8788. A classic gay club ideally situated for the fall-out from the surrounding nightlife, with four bars playing different music from R&B to house. Attracts an upbeat, cruisey crowd. Predominantly male, though women are admitted. Thurs 11pm–4am, Fri & Sat midnight–5am.

Jimmy Woo Korte Leidsedwarsstraat 18 ⊕ 0202/626 3150. Intimate and stylish club spread over two floors. Upstairs, the black lacquered walls, Japanese lamps and cosy booths with leather couches ooze sexy chic, while downstairs a packed dance floor throbs under hundreds of oscillating lightbulbs studded into the ceiling. Popular with young, well-dressed locals so look smart if you want to join in. Wed–Sat 11am–3/4am, Sun 8pm–1am.

Melkweg Lijnbaansgracht 234a, near Leidseplein ⊕ 020/624 1777, ⓦ www.melkweg.nl. After the bands have finished, this multimedia centre plays host to some of the most enjoyable theme nights around, everything from African dance parties to experimental jazz-trance.

Ministry Reguliersdwarsstraat 12 ☎020/623 3981, ⓦwww.ministry.nl. A flourishing club near Rembrandtplein that tries to catch a wide brand of party people and featuring quality DJs playing speed garage, house and R&B. Monday night jam session with the local jazz talent. Open late.

Odeon Singel 460 ☎020/521 8555, ⓦwww .odeontheater.nl. Originally a brewery, this beautifully restored old canal house has since been a theatre, cinema and concert hall until it was gutted in a fire in 1990. Rescued, it's now a stylish nightclub and restaurant, with a splendidly decorated bar overlooking the canal. Club Thurs–Sat 11pm–4/5am, bar Wed–Sun 6pm till late; restaurant Thurs–Sat from 6.30pm.

Panama Oostelijke Handelskade 4 ☎020/311 8686, ⓦwww.panama.nl. Host to a wide variety of funky gigs and themed club nights, also with a theatre and restaurant. Well out from the centre in the Oosterdok.

Paradiso Weteringschans 6–8 ☎020/623 7348, ⓦwww.paradiso.nl. One of the principal venues in the city, which on Fridays hosts an unmissable club night, from midnight onwards. Also hosts one-off events – check listings. Near Leidseplein.

Vrankrijk Spuistraat 216 ⓦwww.squat.net /vrankrijk. Regular club nights at this squat club and café – as you might expect the emphasis is on punk, speed garage, and the like.

Gay and lesbian Amsterdam

Amsterdam boasts one of the largest gay populations in Europe, and one of the most dynamic gay scenes, with a dense sprinkling of advice centres, bars and clubs. The COC (pronounced "say-oh-say"), the national gay and lesbian pressure group (see below), is one of the longest-lived, and largest, groups of its kind in the world. The city has four recognized gay areas: Reguliersdwarsstraat with its trendy bars and clubs tends to attract a young, lively crowd, while quieter Kerkstraat is populated as much by locals as visitors. The streets just north of Rembrandtplein and along Amstel are a camp focus, as well as being home to a number of rent-boy bars, while Warmoesstraat, in the heart of the Red Light District, is cruisey and mainly leather- and denim-oriented. Many bars and clubs have darkrooms, which are legally obliged to provide safe-sex information and condoms. The **bars and clubs** listed below cater either predominantly or exclusively to a gay clientele. Some venues have both gay only and mixed gay/straight nights; there are, however, very few **lesbian**-only nights or clubs and bars.

Gay information and bookshops

COC Rozenstraat 14 ☎020/626 3087, ⓦwww .cocamsterdam.nl. Amsterdam branch of the national gay and lesbian organization, offering advice and contacts. Mon–Fri 10am–4pm.

Gay and Lesbian Switchboard ☎020/623 6565, ⓦwww.switchboard.nl. Mon–Fri noon–10pm, Sat & Sun 4–8pm. An English-speaking service, which provides help and advice.

Intermale Spuistraat 251 ☎020/625 0009, ⓦwww .intermale.nl. Well-stocked gay bookshop, with a wide selection of English, French, German and Dutch

literature, as well as cards, newspapers and magazines. They have a worldwide mail order service.

MVS Radio ⓦwww.mvs.nl. Amsterdam's gay and lesbian radio station, broadcasts daily 7–8pm on 106.8FM (or 88.1 via cable) – try and catch the English-language talk show *Aliens* (Sun 6–8pm).

Vrolijk Paleisstraat 135 ☎020/623 5142, ⓦwww .vrolijk.nu. "The largest gay and lesbian bookstore on the continent", with a vast stock of new and secondhand books and magazines, as well as music and videos.

Gay bars and clubs

April Reguliersdwarsstraat 37. On the itinerary of almost every gay visitor to Amsterdam, it's lively and cosmopolitan, with a good selection of foreign newspapers, cakes and coffee, and a

small dance floor at the back. Happy hour Mon–Sat 6–7pm & 11pm–midnight and special two-for-one deals on Sun 6–8pm. Opens 2pm.

Argos Warmoesstraat 95. Europe's oldest gay leather bar, with two bars and a raunchy cellar. Not for the faint-hearted. Mon–Thurs & Sun 10pm–3am, Fri & Sat 10pm–4am.

Cockring Warmoesstraat 96. Amsterdam's most popular – and very cruisey – gay men's disco, open nightly, with a light show and bars on two levels. Get there early at the weekend to avoid queuing. Free.

Cuckoo's Nest Nieuwezijds Kolk 6. A cruisey gay leather bar with a long reputation, this is described as "the best place in town for chance encounters". Vast and infamous darkroom.

Exit Reguliersdwarsstraat 42. ☎ 020/625 8788. A classic gay club ideally situated for the fall-out of the area's surrounding bars and cafés, with four bars each playing different music from R&B to house to an upbeat, cruisey crowd. Predominantly male, though women are admitted. Thurs 11pm–4am, Fri & Sat midnight–5am.

Saarein Elandsstraat 119 ☎ 020/623 4901. Known for years for its stringent women-only policy, *Saarein* finally opened its doors to men. Though some of the former glory of this café is gone, it's still a warm, relaxing place to take it easy, with a cheerful atmosphere. Also a useful starting point for gay contacts and information. Opens 5pm; closed Mon.

Vive la Vie Amstelstraat 7. Small, campy bar, patronized mostly, but not exclusively, by women. Quiet during the week, it steams on the weekend.

The Web St Jacobsstraat 6. Leather and denim bar that attracts an older crowd. Darkrooms and a pool table. From 2pm.

Why Not Nieuwezijds Voorburgwal 28 ⊛ www .whynot.nl. Long-standing, intimate bar which puts on live shows, with a porno cinema and "boys' club" above. Terrace open in summer. Shows Fri & Sat from 9pm. Mon–Thurs & Sun noon–1am, Fri & Sat noon–2am

You II Amstel 178. Amsterdam's first and long-awaited official lesbian and members-only dance club. Men are in fact welcome, as long as they're under female supervision. Fri & Sat 10pm–5am; entry Sat €5.

Shopping

Amsterdam has some excellent, unusual **speciality shops** and a handful of great **street markets**. Where the city scores most though is in its convenience – the centre concentrates most of what's interesting within its tight borders, and the majority of shops are still individual businesses rather than chains, which makes a refreshing change from many big cities.

Broadly, the **Nieuwendijk/Kalverstraat** strip is where you'll find mostly dull, high-street fashion and mainstream department stores. Here, just off Dam Square, is **Magna Plaza**, a massive shopping mall spread over five floors, complete with espresso bars and teenagers joy-riding on the escalators. Elsewhere, **Koningsplein** and **Leidsestraat** used to be home to the most exclusive shops, but many of them have fled south, though there is still a surprisingly good selection of affordable designer shoe- and clothes-stores here. The **Jordaan**, by comparison, is where many local artists have set up shop and you can find much original stuff of genuine interest here, from arts and crafts to adventurous clothes shops and affordable antiques. Less affordable antiques – the cream of Amsterdam's renowned trade – can be found in the **Spiegelkwartier**, centred on Nieuwe Spiegelstraat, while to the south, **P.C. Hooftstraat** and **Van Baerlestraat** play host to designer clothiers, upmarket ceramics stores and confectioners.

Books and magazines

American Book Center Kalverstraat 185. Vast stock, all in English, with lots of imported US magazines and books. Especially good gay section. Students get a ten-percent discount.

Athenaeum Spui 14. Excellent all-round bookshop with an adventurous stock, though mostly in Dutch. Also the best source of international newspapers and magazines.

The English Bookshop Lauriergracht 71 ☎ 020/626 4230. Stocks a well-chosen collection of titles on a wide range of subjects, in particular literature, many of which you won't find elsewhere.

Amsterdam markets

Visiting an Amsterdam market is a must. There's a fine central flea market on Waterlooplein, a number of vibrant street markets selling fresh veggies as well as clothes plus smaller, specialist markets devoted to everything from stamps to flowers.

Albert Cuypmarkt Albert Cuypstraat, between Ferdinand Bolstraat and Van Woustraat. The city's principal general goods and food market, with some great bargains to be had. Mon–Sat 9am–5pm. South of the city centre; trams #4, 16, 20, 24 or 25 from Centraal Station.

Amstelveld Prinsengracht. Flowers and plants in a pleasant canalside location near Utrechtsestraat, but much less of a scrum than the Bloemenmarkt. Friendly advice on what to buy too. Mon 10am–3pm.

Bloemenmarkt Singel. Stretching between Koningsplein and Muntplein, this very popular market specializes in flowers and plants, ostensibly for tourists, but is frequented by locals too. Bulbs for export (with health certificate). Mon–Sat 9am–5pm, but some stalls open on Sunday as well.

Boekenmarkt Spui. Wonderful rambling collection of secondhand books, with many an interesting find lurking in the unsorted boxes. Fri 10am–3pm.

Boerenmarkt Noordermarkt. Next to the Noorderkerk, this organic farmers' market offers all kinds of organically grown produce, fresh bread, exotic fungi and fresh herbs. Sat 9am–4pm.

Kunstmarkt Spui & Thorbeckeplein. Low-key but high-quality art market in two locations, with much lower prices than you'll find in the galleries; prints and occasional books as well. Neither operates during the winter. Both Sun 10am–3pm.

Noordermarkt Noordermarkt. Next to the Noorderkerk, this is a junk-lover's goldmine, with a general market on Mondays full of all kinds of bargains, tucked away beneath piles of useless rubbish. Get there early. There's also a farmers' produce market (Sat 9am–4pm; see Boerenmarkt above) and a bird market (Sat 8am–1pm).

Waterlooplein Behind the Stadhuis. A real Amsterdam institution, sprawling and chaotic, this is the final resting-place of vintage clothes, antique junk and secondhand records. Mon–Sat 9am–5pm.

Jacob van Wijngaarden Overtoom 97, west across the Singelgracht from Leidseplein. The city's best travel bookshop, with knowledgeable staff and a huge selection of books and maps.

Scheltema Koningsplein 20, just south of Spui. Amsterdam's biggest and best bookshop. Six floors of absolutely everything, including reasonable English book sections. Open late and on Sundays.

Waterstones Kalverstraat 152. Dutch branch of the UK high-street chain, with four floors of books and magazines. A predictable selection perhaps, but prices are sometimes cheaper here than elsewhere.

Department stores

De Bijenkorf Dam 1. Dominating the northern corner of Dam Square, this is the city's biggest and most diverse department store, a huge bustling place that has an indisputably wide range and little snobbishness. Departments to head for include household goods, cosmetics and kids' wear; there's also a good range of newspapers and magazines.
HEMA Nieuwendijk 174. A kind of Dutch Woolworth's, but of a better quality: good for stocking up on toiletries and other essentials, and occasional designer delights – it's owned by De Bijenkorf, and you can sometimes find the same items at knockdown prices. Surprises include wine and cheese in the back of the shop.
Metz & Co Keizersgracht 455. Classic store, with the accent on Liberty prints, stylish ceramics and designer furniture of the kind that's exhibited in modern art museums: just the place to pick up a

Rietveld chair. If your funds won't stretch quite that far, settle for a cup of coffee in the top-floor restaurant, which gives great views over the city.

Vroom & Dreesmann Kalverstraat 203, entrance also from Rokin. The main Amsterdam branch of a middle-of-the-road nationwide chain, just near Muntplein. It's pretty unadventurous, but check out the listening stands in the CD section on the top floor – the best place for a free Mozart recital with a canal view.

Food and drink

Albert Heijn Koningsplein 4, just west of Muntplein, ⓦwww.ah.nl. Amsterdam's main branch of a nationwide supermarket chain, but still small and crowded. There are other central branches at Nieuwmarkt 18 and Waterlooplein 131, but prices are marginally lower in those further out of the centre – Vijzelstraat 117 and Westerstraat 79 for instance. Variable opening hours; currently the Koningsplein branch operates Mon–Sat 10am–10pm, Sun noon–6pm.

J.G. Beune Haarlemmerdijk 156. Age-old chocolatier with exquisite confectionery and enticing window displays.

De Bierkoning Paleisstraat 125. The "Beer King" is aptly named: 950 different beers, with the appropriate glasses to drink them from.

Gimsel Huidenstraat 19. Very central, with a good selection of fruit and vegetables and excellent bread. A short walk west of Spui.

Jacob Hooij Kloveniersburgwal 1. In business at this address since 1778, this is a traditional homeopathic chemist with any amount of herbs and natural cosmetics, as well as a huge stock of *drop* (Dutch liquorice).

De Kaaskamer Runstraat 7. Friendly cheese shop, with tapas and olives too.

Kwekkeboom Reguliersbreestraat 36 & Ferdinand Bolstraat 119. One of the city's most famous pastry shops, showered with awards. Serves coffee too.

De Natuurwinkel Weteringschans 133. Main branch of a chain selling only organic food – and thus a little more expensive than the mainstream.

Paul Année Runstraat 25. The best wholegrain and sourdough breads in town, bar none – all made from organic grains. Try their home-made muesli.

Puccini Staalstraat 17. Perhaps the best chocolate shop in town – all handmade, with an array of fantastic and imaginative fillings.

Miscellaneous shops

Boudisque Haringpakkersteeg 10–18. One of the city's best record stores, with a good selection of metal, reggae, world music and dance.

Broekmans & Van Poppel Van Baerlestraat 92. Classical music specialist, with historical recordings, smaller labels, opera and sheet music.

Concerto Utrechtsestraat 54. New and used records and CDs in all categories; equally good on baroque as on grunge. The best all-round selection in the city, with the option to listen before you buy.

Condomerie Het Gulden Vlies Warmoesstraat 141. Condoms of every shape, size and flavour imaginable, in the heart of the Red Light District. All in the best possible taste.

Frozen Fountain Prinsengracht 465. Great houseware and furniture store selling wonderful examples of modern Dutch and Scandinavian design.

Geels & Co Warmoesstraat 67. Oddly situated among Warmoesstraat's loud bars and porn shops, this is one of the city's oldest and best-equipped coffee and tea specialists, and has a small museum of coffee upstairs.

Gerda's Runstraat 16. Amsterdam is full of flower shops, but this one is the most imaginative and sensual.

1001 Kralen Rozengracht 54. "Kralen" means beads, and 1001 would seem a conservative estimate in this place in the Jordaan, which sells nothing but.

P.G.C. Hajenius Rokin 92. Long-established tobacconist selling its own and other brands of cigars, tobacco, smoking accessories, and every make of cigarette you can think of.

Posthumus Sint Luciensteeg 23. Posh stationery, cards and, best of all, a choice of hundreds of rubber stamps.

't Winkeltje Prinsengracht 228. Jumble of cheap glassware and crockery, candlesticks, antique tin toys, kitsch souvenirs, old apothecaries' jars and flasks. Perfect for browsing.

Witte Tandenwinkel Runstraat 5. The "White Teeth Shop" sells wacky toothbrushes and just about every dental hygiene accoutrement you could ever need.

Listings

Banks and exchange Bureaux de change are scattered around town – GWK has 24-hour branches at Centraal Station and Schiphol Airport and offers competitive rates compared with the others. The VVV tourist office also changes money.

Bike rental Bike City, Bloemgracht 70 ☎020/626 3721; Damstraat Rent-a-Bike, Damstraat 20 ☎020/625 5029; Holland Rent-a-Bike, Damrak 247 ☎020/622 3207; Koenders Take-a-Bike, Stationsplein 12 ☎020/624 8391; MacBike, Mr Visserplein 2 ☎020/620 0985; Macbike Too, Marnixstraat 220 ☎020/626 6964 (see also p.63).

Car parks The following are all 24hr city-centre car parks: De Bijenkorf, Beursplein, off Damrak; Byzantium, Tesselschadestraat 1, near Leidseplein; De Kolk, Nieuwezijds Kolk 20; Muziektheater, Waterlooplein (under City Hall); Parking Plus Amsterdam Centraal, Prins Hendrikkade 20a, east of Centraal Station.

Car rental Avis, Nassaukade 380 ☎020/683 6061; Budget, Overtoom 121 ☎020/612 6066; Europcar, Overtoom 51 ☎020/683 2123; Hertz, Overtoom 333 ☎020/612 2441.

Consulates and embassies UK, Koningslaan 44, Amsterdam ☎020/676 4343; USA, Museumplein 19, Amsterdam ☎020/575 5309. For embassies in the Hague see Basics p.48.

Doctors/dentists Your hotel or the VVV should be able to provide the address of an English-speaking doctor or dentist if you need one. Otherwise call Central Doctors Service ☎020/592 3434 or ☎0900/503 204

Hospitals Ones with A&E units include: Academisch Medisch Centrum, Meibergdreef 9 ☎020/566 9191; Onze Lieve Vrouwe Gasthuis, 1e Oosterparkstraat 279 ☎020/599 9111; Sint Lucas Ziekenhuis Jan Tooropstraat 164 ☎020/510 8911.

Internet Amsterdam has a healthy supply of Internet cafés; most hotels provide Internet access for their guests for free or for a small charge and many are beginning to install WiFi networks. A couple of central Internet cafés are: EasyInternetcafé, Damrak 33 ⓦwww.easyeverything.com (daily 9am–10pm); and Internetcafe, Martelaarsgracht 11 ☎020/627 1052, ⓦwww.internetcafe.nl (daily 9am–1am, Fri & Sat until 3am), just 200m from Centraal Station and serving alcoholic drinks as well as the usual juice and coffee; reasonable rates – €1 per hour, including a drink.

Left luggage Centraal Station has both coin-operated luggage lockers (daily 7am–11pm) and a staffed left-luggage office (daily 7am–11pm). Small coin-operated lockers cost €3.70, the larger ones €5.90 per 24 hours.

Lost property For items lost on the trams, buses or metro, contact GVB Head Office, Prins Hendrikkade 108–114 (Mon–Fri 9am–4pm; ☎020/460 5858). For property lost on a train, go to the Gevonden Voorwerpen office at the nearest station; Amsterdam's is at Centraal Station, near the left-luggage lockers (☎020/557 8544).

Pharmacies You'll need an *apotheek* (usually Mon–Fri 9am–6pm, but may be closed Mon mornings) for minor ailments or to get a prescription filled. A complete list – with many opening hours – can be found in the city's yellow pages under "*Apotheken*". Most of the better hotels will be able to assist too.

Police There are city centre police stations at Elandsgracht 115, Beurrstraat 33, NZ Voorburgwal 104, Lijnbaansgracht 219 and Marnixstraat 148. Or call ☎0900/8844 if it's not an emergency.

Post Post offices are open Mon–Fri 9am–5pm, with larger ones also open Sat 9am–noon. The main post office (Mon–Fri 9am–6pm, Thurs till 8pm, Sat 10am–1.30pm; ☎020/556 3311) is at Singel 250, on the corner with Raadhuisstraat. Stamps are sold at a wide range of outlets including many shops and hotels. Post boxes are everywhere, but be sure to use the correct slot – the one labelled *overige* is for post going outside the immediate locality.

Travel details

Trains

Amsterdam CS (Centraal Station) to: Alkmaar (every 15min; 30–40min); Amersfoort (every 10min; 30–40min); Apeldoorn (every 30min; 1hr); Arnhem (every 20min; 1hr 10min); Den Helder (every 30min; 1hr 10min); Dordrecht (every 20min; 1hr 20min); Eindhoven (every 30min; 1hr 30min); Enkhuizen (every 30min; 1hr); Groningen (every 30min; 2hr 20min); Haarlem (every 10min; 15min); The Hague/Den Haag (every 15min; 50min); Hoorn (every 30min; 40min); Leeuwarden (every 30min; 2hr 20min); Leiden (every 15min; 40min); Maastricht (every 30min; 2hr 30–2hr 45min); Nijmegen (every 15min; 1hr 40min); Rotterdam (every 15min; 1hr); Schiphol Airport (every 15min; 20min); Utrecht (every 15min; 30min); Vlissingen (every 20min; 2hr 45min); Zwolle (every 30min; 1hr 10min).

Buses

Amsterdam CS (Centraal Station) to: Edam (#110; hourly; 40min); Marken (#111; every 30min; 30min); Monnickendam (#111; every 30min; 20min); Volendam (#110; hourly; 30min).
Amsterdam Amstel Station to: Muiden (#136; every 30min; 40min); Naarden (#136; every 30min; 55min).

Noord-Holland

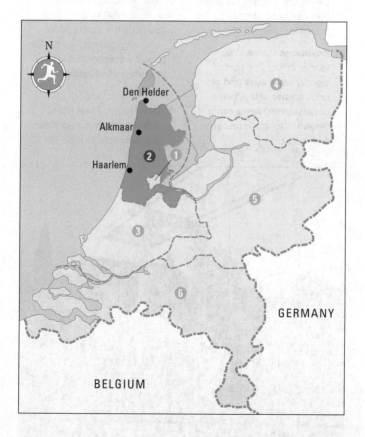

CHAPTER 2 # Highlights

* **Haarlem** This good-looking old town is home to the outstanding Frans Hals Museum. See p.125

* **Edam** Archetypal Dutch country town of narrow canals and antique cottages that was once famous for its mermaids. See p.135

* **Enkhuizen** Handsome, former Zuider Zee port of slender waterways and old brick houses with a brace of outstanding restaurants thrown in for good measure. See p.142

* **Alkmaar cheese market** Much hyped cheesy spectacle that is still good fun despite the crowds. See p.150

* **De Brede Duinen route** Among North Holland's myriad cycle routes, this is perhaps the pick, a 42km-long loop through the pristine coastal scenery that lies to the west of Alkmaar. See p.154

* **Den Hoorn, Texel** Island hideaway near a magnificent sandy beach. See p.156

△ Edam

Noord-Holland

Stretching north from Amsterdam to the island of Texel, the province of **Noord-Holland** (ⓦwww.noord-holland-tourist.nl) remains largely rural, its polder landscapes of green, pancake-flat fields intercepted by hundreds of drainage canals and ditches, its wide horizons only interrupted by the odd farmhouse or windmill. The province's **west coast** is defended from the ocean by a long belt of sand dunes, which is itself shielded by long and broad **sandy beaches** and it's these that attract holidaying Netherlanders in their hundreds. Very different is the **east coast**, much of which has been reclaimed from what was once the saltwater Zuider Zee and is now, after the construction of two complementary **dykes**, the freshwater Markermeer and IJsselmeer. Here, along this deeply indented coast, lies a string of old seaports – primarily Hoorn and Enkhuizen – which flourished from the fourteenth to the eighteenth century on the back of the sea trade with the Baltic.

Noord-Holland's urban highlight is undoubtedly **Haarlem**, an amenable old town just fifteen minutes by train from Amsterdam. Haarlem has more than its fair share of Golden Age buildings, possesses the province's best art gallery in the **Frans Hals Museum**, and gives ready access to some wild stretches of dune and beach in the **Nationaal Park Zuid-Kennemerland** as well as one of the country's largest coastal resorts, **Zandvoort**.

For investigating the rest of the province, there are two obvious **routes** out of Amsterdam – one along the east coast, the other inland from Zaandam through to Texel, with possible detours to the coast along the way. The east-coast route starts with the villages nearest Amsterdam – **Marken** and **Volendam** – kitsch places full of tourists in search of clogs and windmills during summer, but – in the case of Marken – with considerable charm if you can visit off-season. Neighbouring **Edam** is, however, even better – indeed, it's one of the region's most appealing country towns and one that has somehow managed to elude the tourist hordes. Further north, **Hoorn** and **Enkhuizen** were once major Zuider Zee ports, whose historic wealth is reflected in a liberal scattering of handsome old buildings. Modern development has hacked Hoorn around, but Enkhuizen remains a fascinating town and the possessor of one of the country's best open-air museums, the **Zuiderzeemuseum**.

The inland route starts a short train ride from Amsterdam in the **Zaanstad** conurbation, whose chief attraction is the antique windmills and canals of the over-visited, over-hyped **Zaanse Schans**. Further up the line, **Alkmaar** has a much touted summer cheese market, but is worth a longer visit if you're keen to experience small-town life. Alkmaar also makes a good base for investigating the west coast, especially the network of footpaths and cycle trails that crisscross two protected coastal zones, the **Noordhollands Duinreservaat** (North

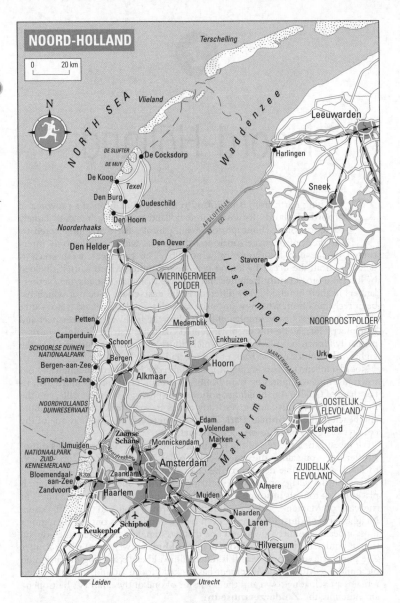

Holland Dune Reserve) and the **Schoorlse Duinen Nationaalpark**. Beyond, in the far north of the province, lies the island of **Texel**, the most accessible of the Waddenzee islands. It's very crowded during summer, but don't be put off: with a bit of walking – or cycling – you can soon find some solitude, and the hamlet of **Den Hoorn** is a simply delightful place to stay.

Most of Noord-Holland is located, logically enough, north of Amsterdam, but the borders of the province also dip round the city, taking in an assortment of leafy suburbs. Those to the southeast of Amsterdam are collectively known as **Het Gooi**, where the highlight is the old fortified town of **Naarden**.

Getting around Noord-Holland by **public transport** is easy enough, with **trains** linking all the major settlements and **buses** filling in the gaps. Distances are small, so the majority of Noord-Holland is easily visited on day-trips from Amsterdam, but to make the most of the province you're much better off **staying over** at least a couple of nights – Haarlem, Edam, Enkhuizen and Den Hoorn on Texel are the four most appealing bases. If you want to continue north or east, the two dykes that enclose the Markermeer and the IJsselmeer carry handy road links. The former, the **Markerwaarddijk**, connects Enkhuizen with Lelystad on the reclaimed Flevoland polders (see p.269), and the latter, the **Afsluitdijk**, makes the thirty-kilometre trip from Den Oever to the province of Friesland (see Chapter 4).

Haarlem and around

Though only fifteen minutes from Amsterdam by train, **HAARLEM** has a very different pace and feel from its big-city neighbour, being an easy-going, medium-sized town of around 150,000 souls, and with an old and good-looking centre that is easily absorbed in a few hours or on an overnight stay. Founded on the banks of the River Spaarne in the tenth century, the town first prospered when the counts of Holland decided to levy shipping tolls here, but later it developed as a cloth-making centre. In 1572, the townsfolk sided with the Protestant rebels against the Habsburgs, a decision they must have regretted when a large Spanish army besieged them in December of the same year. The siege was a desperate affair that lasted for eight months, but finally the town surrendered after receiving various assurances of good treatment – assurances which the Spanish commander, Frederick of Toledo, promptly broke, massa-cring over two thousand of the Protestant garrison and all their Calvinist ministers to boot. Recaptured by the Protestants five years later, Haarlem went on to enjoy its greatest prosperity in the seventeenth century, becoming a centre for the arts and home to a flourishing school of **painters**, whose canvases are displayed at the outstanding **Frans Hals Museum**, located in the almshouse where Hals spent his last, and for some his most brilliant, years.

Haarlem is also within easy striking distance of the **coast**: every half-hour trains make the ten-minute trip to the clumsy modern resort of **Zandvoort-aan-Zee**, and there are frequent buses to the huddle of fast-food joints that make up **Bloemendaal-aan-Zee** just to the north. Neither is particularly endearing in itself, but both are redeemed by the long sandy beach that stretches for miles along this part of the coast. Equally enticing – perhaps more so – is the **Nationaal Park de Zuid Kennemerland**, a strip of pristine dune and lagoon, crisscrossed by footpaths and cycling trails, that backs onto Bloemendaal-aan-Zee.

Arrival, information and accommodation

With fast and frequent services from Amsterdam, Haarlem's handsome **train station**, in a Dutch version of the Arts and Crafts style, is located on the north side of the city centre, about ten minutes' walk from the main square, the Grote Markt. The **bus station** is in front of the train station on Stationsplein and the **VVV** is next door (April–Sept Mon 1–5.30pm, Tues–Fri 9am–5.30pm, Sat 10am–4pm; Oct–March Mon–Fri 9.30am–5pm, Sat 10am–2pm; ℡0900/616

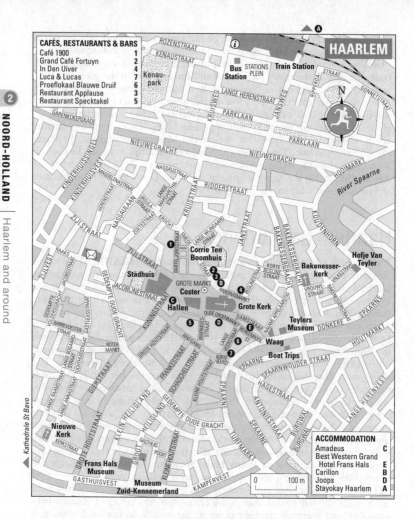

CAFÉS, RESTAURANTS & BARS

Café 1900	1
Grand Café Fortuyn	2
In Den Uiver	4
Luca & Lucas	7
Proeflokaal Blauwe Druif	6
Restaurant Applause	3
Restaurant Specktakel	5

HAARLEM

ROZENSTRAAT
KENAUSTRAAT
Kenau-park
STATIONS PLEIN
Bus Station
STATIONS Train Station
STRAAT
RIPPERDA
GONNETSTRAAT
N

GAARENKOKERSKADE
LANGE HERENSTRAAT
KRUISWEG
JANSWEG
PARKLAAN
NIEUWEGRACHT
NIEUWEGRACHT
HOOIMARKT
River Spaarne

KINDERHUISSINGEL
KINDERHUISVEST
MAGDALENASTRAAT
HERENSTRAAT
NASSAULAAN
NASSAUSTRAAT
LANGE MARGARETHA STRAAT
URSULA STRAAT
KROCHT
SMEE
LANGE WIJNGAARD STRAAT
KRUISSTRAAT
RIDDERSTRAAT
JANSSTRAAT
BAKENESSERGRACHT
KOUDENHORN

ZIJLSTRAAT
RAAKS
ZOETESTRAAT
ZIJLSTRAAT
BARTELJORISSTRAAT

Corrie Ten Boomhuis

ZUIVELVEST
JACOBSTRAAT
KORTE VEERSTRAAT
GEDEMPTE OUDE GRACHT
JACOBIJNESTRAAT
KONINGSTRAAT

Stadhuis
Coster
GROTE MARKT
Hallen

KORTE BEGIJNE STRAAT
BEGIJNESTRAAT
Bakenesser-kerk
Hofje Van Teyler
VROUWE STRAAT
BAKENESSERGRACHT
RIVIERVISMARKT
Grote Kerk
DAMSTRAAT
SPAARNE

GEDEMPTE
VOLDERSGRACHT
BARREVOESTER STRAAT
GASTHUISSTRAAT
BOTER MARKT
GIERSTRAAT
FRANKESTRAAT
SCHAGCHELSTRAAT
OUDE GROENMARKT
WARMOES STRAAT
ANEGANG
LANGE
KORTE
Teylers Museum
DONKERE
HOUTMARKT
Waag
Boat Trips
SPAARNWOUDER STRAAT

KLEINE HOUTSTRAAT
GEDEMPTE OUDE GRACHT
SPAARNE
HAGESTRAAT
ANTONIESTRAAT
BURGWAL
BURGWAL
LANGE HERENVEST

LANGE RAAMSTRAAT
LANGE ANNASTRAAT
TUCHTHUISSTRAAT
KLEIN HEILIGLAND
KLEIN HEILIGLAND
GASTHUIS POORT
GROOT HEILIGLAND
SPAARNE
TURFMARKT

Kathedrale St Bavo

Nieuwe Kerk
KERKSTRAAT
Frans Hals Museum
GASTHUISVEST
Museum Zuid-Kennemerland
KAMPERVEST

0 ___ 100 m

ACCOMMODATION

Amadeus	C
Best Western Grand Hotel Frans Hals	E
Carillon	B
Joops	D
Stayokay Haarlem	A

1600 premium line, Ⓦwww.vvvzk.nl). Woltheus Cruises, by the river at Spaarne 11 (☎023/535 7723, Ⓦwww.woltheuscruises.nl), operates **boat trips** in and around Haarlem, including a ninety-minute afternoon cruise with "English High Tea" (1 weekly; €23); advance reservations are recommended. The VVV issues free city maps and brochures, has details of some **rooms** (❶) in private houses, mostly on the outskirts of town, and can provide hotel information. **Bike rental** is available at the train station.

Hotels

Amadeus Grote Markt 10 ☎023/532 4530, Ⓦwww.amadeus-hotel.com. Homely, medium-sized hotel with plain but perfectly comfortable en-suite rooms. The front bedrooms have enjoyable views over the main square. ❶

Best Western Grand Hotel Frans Hals Damstraat 10 ☎023/518 1818, Ⓦwww .bestwestern.com. Brand new chain hotel, right in the centre of town, and offering 79 smart and well-appointed modern rooms. Rack rates are expensive but discounts commonplace. ❼

Carillon Grote Markt 27 ☎023/531 0591, ⓦwww
.hotelcarillon.com. Inexpensive place opposite the
Grote Kerk, with spartan modern rooms but friendly
atmosphere. ❷
Joops Oude Groenmarkt 20 ☎023/532 2008,
ⓦwww.joopshotel.com. Large if somewhat austere
modern en-suite rooms in a recently renovated
building immediately behind the Grote Kerk, though
to be fair the public rooms are bright and cheerful.
Internet facilities. ❷

Hostel

Stayokay Haarlem Jan Gijzenpad 3 ☎023/537
3793, ⓦwww.stayokay.com. Spick and span
modern HI hostel near the sports stadium about
3km north of the town centre. To get there, take
bus #2 from the station – a ten-minute journey.
Dorm beds €27.

The Town

At the heart of Haarlem is the **Grote Markt**, a wide and attractive open space
flanked by an appealing ensemble of Gothic and Renaissance architecture,
including an intriguing if exceptionally garbled **Stadhuis**, whose turrets and
towers, balconies and galleries were put together in piecemeal fashion between
the fourteenth and the seventeenth centuries. At the other end of the Grote
Markt stands a **statue** of a certain Laurens Coster (1370–1440), who, Haarlem-
mers insist, is the true inventor of printing. Legend tells of Coster cutting a
letter "A" from the bark of a tree, dropping it into the sand by accident, and,
hey presto, he realized how to create the printed word. The statue shows him
earnestly holding up the wooden letter concerned, but most historians agree
that it was actually the German Johannes Gutenberg who invented printing, in
the early 1440s.

The Grote Kerk

The Coster statue stands in the shadow of the **Grote Kerk** or **Sint Bavokerk**
(Mon–Sat 10am–4pm; €2), a soaring Gothic structure supported by mighty
buttresses that dwarfs the surrounding clutter of ecclesiastical outhouses. If
you've been to the Rijksmuseum in Amsterdam (see p.98), the church may
seem familiar, at least from the outside, since it turns up in several paintings of
Haarlem by the seventeenth-century artist Gerrit Berckheyde – only the black-
coated burghers are missing. Finished in 1538, and 150 years in the making, the
church is surmounted by a good-looking lantern tower, which perches above
the transept crossing; the tower is made of wood clad in lead, a replacement for
a much grander stone tower that had to be dismantled in 1514 when its
supports began to buckle.

    Entry to the church is round the back, on Oude Groenmarkt, with a humble
passageway leading to the southeast end of the **nave**, whose towering beauty is
enhanced by the creaminess of the stone and the bright simplicity of the white-
washed walls. The Protestants cleared the church of most of its decoration
during the Reformation, but the splendid wrought-iron **choir screen** has
survived as have the choir's wooden **stalls** with their folksy misericords. In front
of the screen is the conspicuous Neoclassical **tomb** of Haarlem's own Chris-
tiaan Brunings (1736–1805), a much-lauded hydraulic engineer and director of
Holland's water board, who devised a detailed strategy for controlling the waters
of the lower Rhine.

    Close by, next to the south transept, is the **Brewers' Chapel**, where the
central pillar bears two black markers – one showing the height of a local giant,
the 2.64m-tall Daniel Cajanus, who died in 1749, the other the 0.84m-high
dwarf Simon Paap from Zandvoort. Further west still, on the north side of the
nave, is the pocket-sized **Dog Whippers' Chapel**, built for the men employed

127

△ Statue of Laurens Coster and the Grote Kerk, Haarlem

to keep dogs out of the church, and now separated from the nave by an iron grille. At the west end of the church, the mighty Christian Müller **organ** was manufactured in Amsterdam in the 1730s. It is said to have been played by Handel and Mozart (the latter on his tour of the country in 1766, at the age of 10) and is one of the biggest in the world, with over five thousand pipes and loads of snazzy Baroque embellishment. Hear it at work at one of the free organ recitals held in the summer (mid-May to mid-Oct Tues 8.15pm, July & Aug also Thurs 3pm). Beneath the organ, Jan Baptist Xavery's lovely group of draped marble figures represent Poetry and Music offering thanks to the town, which is depicted as a patroness of the arts – in return for its generous support in the purchase of the organ.

Around the Grote Markt

Back outside, just beyond the western end of the church, the rambling **Hallen** divides into two: first up is the old meat market, the **Vleeshal**, which boasts a flashy Dutch Renaissance facade and a basement given over to a modest **Archeologisch Museum** (Wed–Sun 1–5pm; free). A couple of doors along is the **Kunstcentrum De Hallen** (Tues–Sat 11am–5pm, Sun noon–5pm; €5), an art gallery where the emphasis is on temporary exhibitions of modern and contemporary art and photography.

After these modest attractions, you'll probably want to push on south to Haarlem's star turn, the Frans Hals Museum, but you might consider a brief detour north from the Grote Markt to the **Corrie Ten Boomhuis**, Barteljorisstraat 19 (April–Oct Tues–Sat 10am–3.30pm; Nov–March Tues–Sat 11am–2.30pm; 1hr guided tours only; free; ⑳www.corrieteboom.com), where a Dutch family – the Booms – hid fugitives, Resistance fighters and Jews alike, above their watchmaking shop during World War II. There is not too much to actually look at, but the guided tour is instructive and moving if a little drawn out. The family, whose bravery sprang from their Christian faith, was betrayed to the Gestapo in 1944 and only one, Corrie Boom, survived.

The Frans Hals Museum

Haarlem's biggest draw, the **Frans Hals Museum** (Tues–Sat 11am–5pm, Sun noon–5pm; €7; ⑳www.franshalsmuseum.nl), is a five-minute stroll south of the Grote Markt at Groot Heiligland 62: to get there, take pedestrianized Warmoesstraat and keep going. The museum occupies an old almshouse complex, a much modified red-brick *hofje* with a central courtyard, where the aged Hals lived out his last destitute years on public funds. The collection comprises a handful of prime works by Hals along with a small but eclectic sample of Dutch paintings from the fifteenth century onwards, all immaculately presented and labelled in English and Dutch. There's also a small separate section consisting of a life-size replica of a seventeenth-century Haarlem street.

Little is known about **Frans Hals** (c.1580–1666). Born in Antwerp, the son of Flemish refugees who settled in Haarlem in the late 1580s, his extant oeuvre is relatively small – some two hundred paintings, and nothing like the number of sketches and studies left behind by his contemporary, Rembrandt. His outstanding gift was as a portraitist, showing a sympathy with his subjects and an ability to capture fleeting expression that some say even Rembrandt lacked. Seemingly quick and careless flashes of colour characterize his work, but they are always blended into a coherent and marvellously animated whole.

The museum begins with the work of other artists: first comes a small group of early sixteenth-century paintings, the most prominent of which, displayed in Room 2, is a triptych from the **School of Hans Memling**. In the same room is a curious painting by Haarlem-born **Jan Mostaert** (1475–1555), his *West Indian Scene* depicting a band of naked, poorly armed natives trying to defend themselves against the cannon and sword of their Spanish invaders; the comparison with the Dutch Protestants was obvious. Next door, Room 3 displays two works by **Jan van Scorel** (1495–1562): a polished *Adam and Eve* and *Pilgrims to Jerusalem*, one of the country's earliest group portraits.

The adjacent Room 4 features *the Wedding of Peleus and Thetis* by **Cornelis Cornelisz van Haarlem**'s (1562–1638) , an appealing rendition of what was then a popular subject, though Cornelisz gives as much attention to the arrangement of his elegant nudes as to the subject. This marriage precipitated civil war among the gods and was used by the Dutch as a warning against discord, a call for unity during the long war with Spain. Similarly, and also in Room 4, the same artist's *Massacre of the Innocents* connects the biblical story with the Spanish siege of Haarlem in 1572. Moving on, Rooms 6 and 7 hold several paintings by the **Haarlem Mannerists**, including two tiny and precise works by **Karel van Mander** (1548–1606), leading light of the Haarlem School and mentor of many of the city's most celebrated painters, including Hals. There's more Cornelis Cornelisz van Haarlem in Room 7 too, most notably an early militia group portrait and a Mannerist Biblical work entitled *Worshipping the Golden Calf*.

The **Hals paintings** begin in earnest in **Room 14** with a set of five "Civic Guard" portraits – group portraits of the militia companies initially formed to defend the country from the Spanish, but which later became social clubs for the gentry. Getting a commission to paint one of these portraits was a well-paid privilege – Hals got his first in 1616 – but their composition was a tricky affair and often the end result was dull and flat. With great flair and originality, Hals made the group portrait a unified whole instead of a static collection of individual portraits, his figures carefully arranged, but so cleverly as not to appear contrived. For a time, Hals himself was a member of the Company of St George, and in the *Officers of the Militia Company of St George* he appears in the top left-hand corner – one of his few self-portraits. Hals' later paintings are darker, more contemplative works, closer to Rembrandt in their lighting and increasingly sombre in their outlook. In **Room 18**, among several portraits of different groups of regents, is Hals' *Regents of St Elizabeth Gasthuis*, a serious but benign work of 1641 with a palpable sense of optimism, whereas his twin *Regents* and *Regentesses of the Oudemannenhuis*, currently displayed in **Room 19**, is deep with despair. The latter were commissioned when Hals was in his 80s, a poor man despite a successful painting career, hounded for money by the town's tradesmen and by the mothers of his illegitimate children. As a result he was dependent on the charity of people like those depicted here: their cold, self-satisfied faces staring out of the gloom, the women reproachful, the men only marginally more affable. Incidentally, although the character just right of centre in the *Regents* painting looks drunk, it is inconceivable that Hals would have depicted him in this condition; it's more likely that he was suffering from some kind of facial paralysis, and his jauntily cocked hat was simply a popular fashion of the time. There are those who claim Hals had lost his touch by the time he painted these pictures, yet their sinister, almost ghostly, power suggests quite the opposite. Van Gogh's remark that "Frans Hals had no fewer than 27 blacks" suddenly makes perfect sense.

Finally, just before you exit, look out for the berserk *Dutch Proverbs* by **Pieter Brueghel the Younger** (1564–1638), illustrating a whole raft of contemporary proverbs – a detailed key next to the painting gives the low-down.

Along the River Spaarne

Across the road from the Frans Hals Museum, at Groot Heiligland 47, stands the **Historisch Museum Zuid-Kennemerland** (Tues–Sat noon–5pm, Sun 1–5pm; €2), which tracks through a really rather pedestrian history of Haarlem, in premises that were once used as a women's almshouse. From here, stroll south down Groot Heiligland and turn left at the end along the canal and you soon

reach the **River Spaarne**, whose wandering curves mark the eastern per.
of the town centre. Turn left here, along riverside Turfmarkt and its continu
Spaarne, to reach the surly stonework of the **Waag** (Weigh House) and then t.
country's oldest museum, the **Teylers Museum**, located in a grand Neoclassica.
building at Spaarne 16 (Tues–Sat 10am–5pm, Sun noon–5pm; €5.50; ⓦwww
.teylersmuseum.nl). Founded in 1774 by a wealthy local philanthropist, Pieter
Teyler van der Hulst, the museum is delightfully old-fashioned, its wooden
cabinets crammed with fossils, bones, crystals and rocks, medals and coins, all
displayed alongside dozens of antique scientific instruments of lugubrious
appearance and uncertain purpose. The finest room is the rotunda – **De Ovale
Zaal** – a handsome, galleried affair with splendid wood-panelling, and there is
also a room of nineteenth-century and early twentieth-century Dutch paintings,
featuring the likes of Breitner, Israëls, Weissenbruch and, not least, Wijbrand
Hendriks (1774–1831), who was once the keeper of the art collection here.

Teyler also bestowed his charity on the riverside **Hofje van Teyler**, a little way
east around the bend of the Spaarne at Koudenhorn 64. Unlike most other *hofjes*,
which are decidedly cosy, this is a grandiose building, a Neoclassical edifice dating
from 1787 and featuring solid columns and cupolas. Nearby, the elegant fifteenth-
century tower of the **Bakenesserkerk** (no public access), on Vrouwestraat, is a
flamboyant, onion-domed affair poking high above the Haarlem skyline.

Eating and drinking

The pick of the town's **restaurants** and **bars** are conveniently clustered on or
within easy walking distance of the Grote Markt and Oude Groenmarkt, round
the back of the Grote Kerk.

Café 1900 Barteljorisstraat 10. With a smashing
1930s interior, right up to the swishing ceiling fans,
this has long been a popular café-bar, serving
drinks and reasonably tasty light meals. Mon & Sun
11am–midnight, Tues–Sat 9am–midnight.
Grand Café Fortuyn Grote Markt 21. A popular
café-bar with charming 1930s decor, including a
tiled entrance and dinky little glass cabinets
preserved from the building's days as a shop.
In Den Uiver Riviervismarkt 13. Just off the Grote
Markt, this lively and extremely appealing bar is
decked out in traditional Dutch brown style; it also
showcases occasional live music.
Luca & Lucas Lange Veerstraat 51 ☎023/534
1855. Upmarket Italian restaurant with a menu that

covers all the favourites and then some. Main
courses from €15, pizzas from €12. Daily noon–
10pm.
Proeflokaal Blauwe Druif Lange Veerstraat 7.
Intimate and amenable bar – typically Dutch.
Restaurant Applause Grote Markt 23a
☎023/531 1425. A chic little bistro serving up
Italian food with excellent main courses hovering
around €15. Closed Mon & Tues.
Restaurant Specktakel Spekstraat 4 ☎023/532
3841. Inventive little place that tries its hand at an
international menu – everything from kangaroo to
antelope. Mostly the main courses are very
successful, and cost around €17. Daily from 5pm,
plus Sat noon–4pm.

Around Haarlem: Zandvoort and the Nationaal Park Zuid-Kennemerland

The suburbs of Haarlem ramble out almost as far as **ZANDVOORT-AAN-
ZEE**, a major seaside resort just 5km away to the west. As Dutch resorts go,
Zandvoort is pretty standard – packed in summer, dead and gusty in winter –
and its agglomeration of modern apartment blocks hardly cheers the heart, but
its **beach** is wide and sandy, it musters up a casino and a car-racing circuit and
it is one of the few places in the Netherlands where the rail network reaches
the coast: there's a half-hourly service from Haarlem, and Zandvoort train
station is merely a five-minute walk (if that) from the beach.

If, however, you're after more than just a few hours sunbathing, the better
option when it comes to exploring the coast is to delve into the pristine woods,
dunes and lagoons of the **Nationaal Park Zuid-Kennemerland**, which stretches
north from Zandvoort all the way up to the eminently missable industrial town of
IJMUIDEN, at the mouth of the Nordzeekanaal; maps of the park are available at
Haarlem VVV (see p.125). Hourly **bus #81** from Haarlem bus station travels west to
cut across the national park along the **N200** before reaching the coast at the
minuscule beachside settlement of **Bloemendaal-aan-Zee**; it then proceeds
the 4km south to Zandvoort bus station, on Louis Davidsstraat, a short,
signposted walk from the train station. En route, between Haarlem and
Bloemendaal-aan-Zee, several bus stops give access to the clearly marked
hiking trails that pattern the national park, but the best option is to get off at
the **Koevlak** entrance – ask the driver to let you off. Three colour-coded
hiking routes are posted at Koevlak and the most appealing is the 9km (3hr)
jaunt west through pine wood and dune to the seashore at the *Parnassia* **café**
(April–Nov), where you can wet your whistle gazing out across the North Sea.
From the café, it's 2km by minor road to Bloemendaal-aan-Zee, where you can
catch bus #81 back to Haarlem.

The east coast

The turbulent waters of the **Zuider Zee** were once busy with Dutch trading
ships plying to and from the Baltic. This trade was the linchpin of Holland's
prosperity in the Golden Age, revolving around the import of huge quantities
of grain, the supply of which was municipally controlled to safeguard against
famine. The business was immensely profitable and its proceeds built a string of
prosperous seaports – most notably Volendam, Hoorn and Enkhuizen – and
nourished market towns like Edam, while the Zuider Zee itself supported a
batch of fishing villages such as Marken and Urk. In the eighteenth century the
Baltic trade declined and the harbours silted up, leaving the ports economically
stranded, and, with the rapid increase in the Dutch population during the
nineteenth century, plans were made to reclaim the Zuider Zee and turn it into
farmland. In the event, the Zuider Zee was only partly reclaimed (see box on
p.134), creating a pair of freshwater lakes – the **Markermeer** and **IJsselmeer**.
These placid, steel-grey lakes are popular with day-tripping Amsterdammers,
who come here in their droves to sail boats, observe the waterfowl, and visit a
string of dinky little towns and villages. These begin on the coast just a few

kilometres north of Amsterdam with the picturesque old fishing village of **Marken** and the former seaport of **Volendam** just up along the coast. From Volendam, it's a couple of kilometres more to **Edam**, the pick of the local bunch, a small and infinitely pretty little town of narrow canals and handsome old houses.

A little way north of Edam, the Markermeer shore curves east to form a jutting claw of land at the base of which is **Hoorn**, an old and once important Zuider Zee port whose compact centre, with its slender harbour and narrow streets, boasts a diverting assortment of Golden Age buildings. Though worth an hour or two of anyone's time, Hoorn is best viewed as a stop on the way to **Enkhuizen**, perhaps the prettiest town hereabouts, boasting an especially engaging ensemble of narrow cobbled streets and slender waterways plus the open-air **Zuiderzeemuseum** celebrating the region's heritage. Enkhuizen is also within easy striking distance of another old seaport, **Medemblik**, as well as the Afsluitdijk over to Friesland (see Chapter 4).

There are fast and frequent **buses** from Amsterdam's Centraal Station to Marken and an equally efficient service to Volendam and Edam. More poetically, a seasonal **passenger ferry**, the Marken Express (April–Oct daily 11am–5pm, every 30–45min; 30min; €6.50 return, €4 single, bikes €1 one-way; T029/936 3331, Wwww.markenexpress.nl), skittles along the coast between Marken and Volendam, giving a taste of the pond-like Markermeer. Finally, there are hourly **trains** from Amsterdam's Centraal Station to Hoorn and Enkhuizen.

Marken

Once an island in the Zuider Zee, **Marken** was, until its road connection to the mainland in 1957, pretty much a closed community, supported by a small fishing industry. Despite its proximity to Amsterdam, its biggest problem was the genetic defects caused by close and constant intermarrying, but now it's how to contain the tourists, whose numbers can reach alarming proportions on summer weekends. That said, there's no denying the picturesque charms of the island's one and only village – also called **MARKEN** – where the immaculately maintained houses, mostly painted in deep green with white trimmings, cluster on top of artificial mounds raised to protect them from the sea. There are two main parts to the village, **Havenbuurt**, behind the harbour, and **Kerkbuurt** around the **church** (mid-May to Oct Mon–Sat 10am–5pm; free), an ugly 1904 replacement for its nineteenth-century, sea-battered predecessor. Of the two, Kerkbuurt is the less touristy, its narrow lanes lined by ancient dwellings and a row of old eel-smoking houses, now the **Marker Museum**, Kerkbuurt 44 (April–Sept Mon–Sat 10am–5pm, Sun noon–4pm; Oct Mon–Sat 11am–4pm; €2.50), devoted to the history of the former island and its fishing industry. Over in the Havenbuurt, one or two of the houses are open to visitors, proclaiming themselves to be "typical" of Marken, and the waterfront is lined by snack bars and souvenir shops, often staffed by locals in traditional costume. It's all a tad prosaic, but now and again you get a hint of how hard life used to be – many of the houses on the waterfront are raised on stilts and although these are now panelled in, they were once open, allowing the sea to roll under the floors in bad weather, enough to terrify most people half to death.

Practicalities

Marken is accessible direct from Amsterdam on **bus #111**, departing from outside Centraal Station (every 30min); the journey takes forty minutes. The bus drops

The closing of the Zuider Zee

The towns and villages that string along the east coast of **Noord-Holland** flourished during Amsterdam's Golden Age, their economies buoyed up by shipbuilding, the Baltic Sea trade and the demand for herring. They had access to the open sea via the waters of the **Zuider Zee** (Southern Sea) and, to the north, the connecting **Waddenzee** (Mud Sea). Both seas were comparatively new, created when the North Sea broke through from the coast in the thirteenth century: the original coastline is marked by Texel and the Frisian Islands. However, the Zuider Zee was shallow and tidal, part salt and part freshwater, and accumulations of silt began to strangle its ports – notably Hoorn and Enkhuizen – from the end of the seventeenth century, and shortly afterwards the Baltic trade slipped into decline. Indeed, by the 1750s the Zuider Zee ports were effectively marooned and the only maritime activity was fishing – just enough to keep a cluster of tiny hamlets ticking over, from Volendam and Marken on the sea's western coast, to Stavoren and Urk on the eastern side.

The Zuider Zee may have provided a livelihood for local fishermen, but most of the country was more concerned by the danger of flooding it posed, as time and again storms and high tides combined to breach the east coast's defences. The first plan to seal off and reclaim the Zuider Zee was proposed in 1667, but the rotating-turret windmills that then provided the most efficient way of drying the land were insufficient for the task and matters were delayed until suitable technology arrived – in the form of the steam-driven pump. In 1891, **Cornelis Lely** (1854–1929), after whom Lelystad was named, proposed a retaining dyke and his plans were finally put into effect after devastating floods hit the area in 1916. Work began on this dyke, the **Afsluitdijk**, in 1920 despite some uncertainty among the engineers, who worried about a possible rise in sea level around the islands of the Waddenzee. In reality, their concerns proved groundless and, on May 28, 1932, the last gap in the dyke was closed and the Zuider Zee simply ceased to exist, replaced by the freshwater **IJsselmeer**.

The original plan was to reclaim all the land protected by the Afsluitdijk, turning it into farmland for settlers from the country's overcrowded cities, starting with three large-scale land-reclamation schemes that were completed over the next forty years: **Noordoostpolder** in 1942 (48,000 hectares), **Oostelijk Flevoland** in 1957 (54,000 hectares) and **Zuidelijk Flevoland** in 1968 (44,000 hectares). In addition, a second, complementary dyke linking Enkhuizen with Lelystad was finished in 1976, thereby creating lake **Markermeer** – a necessary prelude to the draining of another vast stretch of the IJsselmeer. The engineers licked their contractual lips, but they were out of sync with the majority of the population, who were now opposed to any further draining of the lake. Partly as a result, the grand plan was abandoned and, after much governmental huffing and puffing, the Markermeer was left alone and thus most of the old Zuider Zee remained water.

There were many economic benefits to be had in the closing of the Zuider Zee. The threat of flooding was removed, the country gained great chunks of new and fertile farmland and the roads that were built along the top of the two main retaining dykes brought Noord-Holland within twenty minutes' drive of Friesland. The price was the demise of the old Zuider Zee **fishing fleet**. Without access to the open sea, it was inevitable that most of the fleet would go down the pan, though some skippers wisely transferred to the north coast before the Afsluitdijk was completed. Others learnt to fish the freshwater species that soon colonized the Markermeer and IJsselmeer, but in 1970 falling stocks prompted the government to ban trawling. This was a bitter blow for many fishermen and there were several violent demonstrations before they bowed to the inevitable. Today, villages such as Marken and Urk (see p.269) are shadows of their former selves, forced to rely on tourist kitsch to survive.

passengers beside the car park on the edge of Marken village, from where it's a five-minute walk to the lakeshore. Marken does not have a **VVV**. In season a **passenger ferry** links Marken with Volendam (see below), but otherwise it's a fiddly bus trip involving a change of buses – and bus stops – at **MONNICKENDAM**, itself a former Zuider Zee port, but now a busy sailing centre: the Amsterdam–Marken bus #111 stops on the southern edge of Monnickendam at the **Swaensborch stop**, from where it's a ten-minute walk across Monnickendam to the **Bernhardbrug stop** for bus #110 or #118 north to Volendam and Edam.

Volendam

The former fishing village of **VOLENDAM**, just up along the coast from Monnickendam, has had, by comparison with its neighbours, some rip-roaring cosmopolitan times. In the early years of the twentieth century it became something of an artists' retreat, with both Picasso and Renoir spending time here, along with their assorted acolytes. The artists are, however, long gone and nowadays Volendam is crammed with day-tripping tourists bobbing in and out of the souvenir stalls that run the length of the cobbled main street, whose perky gables line up behind the harbour. It's a pleasant enough scene, if you don't mind crowds, and the antique public rooms of the *Best Western Hotel Spaander*, on the waterfront at Haven 15 (☏029/936 3595, ⓦwww.hotelspaander.com; ❷), with their creaking wooden floors, low ceilings, paintings and sketches, are pleasant reminders of more artistic times. The hotel was opened in 1881 and its first owner, Leendert Spaander, was lucky to have seven daughters, quite enough to keep a whole bevy of artists in lust for a decade or two. Some of the artists paid for their lodgings by giving Spaander paintings – hence today's collection.

In Volendam, **bus #110** and **118** from Amsterdam and Monnickendam drops passengers on Zeestraat, just across the street from the **VVV**, at Zeestraat 37 (Mon–Sat: mid-March to Oct 10am–5pm; Nov to mid-March 10am–3pm; ☏029/936 3747, ⓦwww.vvvvolendam.nl). From the VVV, it's a five-minute walk to the waterfront, from where, in the summertime, there is a regular **passenger ferry** to Marken (see above).

Edam

Just 3km from Volendam, you might expect **EDAM** to be jammed with tourists considering the international fame of the rubbery red balls of cheese that carry its name. In fact, Edam usually lacks the crowds and remains a delightful, good-looking and prosperous little town of neat brick houses, high gables, swing bridges and slender canals. Founded by farmers in the twelfth century, it experienced a temporary boom in the seventeenth as a shipbuilding centre with river access to the Zuider Zee. Thereafter, it was back to the farm – and the excellent pasture land surrounding the town is still grazed by large herds of cows, though nowadays most Edam cheese is produced elsewhere, even in Germany ("Edam" is the name of a type of cheese and not its place of origin). This does, of course, rather undermine the authenticity of Edam's open-air **cheese market**, held every Wednesday morning in July and August on the Kaasmarkt, but it's still a popular attraction and the only time the town heaves with tourists.

The Town

At the heart of Edam is the **Damplein**, a pint-sized main square where an elongated humpbacked bridge has long vaulted the Voorhaven **canal**, which now connects the town with the Markermeer and formerly linked it to the Zuider Zee. At a stroke, the bridge stopped the canal flooding the town, as it

The Edam mermaid

A number of **mermaid legends** have grown up around the coastal towns of northern Holland, but Edam's is the best. In 1403, two milkmaids were rowing across the lake to the north of Edam to get to their cows, when they spied a mermaid, who they agreed must have been washed up over the sea dyke during a storm. Later, they returned to fish the mermaid out of the lake and, in the way of such things, blushes were saved all round by the layer of seaweed and moss hiding the creature's remarkable curves and contours. Back in town, the mermaid willingly enough slipped into a dress, and soon picked up all the necessary domestic and devotional skills, learning how to spin, cook and kiss the crucifix. Some versions, however, feature a less obliging mermaid who didn't take kindly to her chores and was forever trying to escape. The mermaid is supposed to have lived on in Edam for fifteen years, and one of the now-demolished town gates was decorated with a mermaid statue. More important was the municipal subtext: the legend portrayed the women of Edam as so kind and the town so pleasant that even a slippery siren was prepared to hole up here.

had done with depressing regularity, but local ship builders hated the thing as it restricted navigation, and on several occasions they launched night-time raids to break it down, though eventually they bowed to the will of the local council. Facing the bridge is the **Edams Museum** (mid-April to Oct Tues–Sat 10am–4.30pm, Sun 1–4.30pm; €3), which occupies an attractive old house whose crow-stepped gables date back to 1530. Inside, a series of cramped and narrow rooms holds a modest display on the history of the town as well as an assortment of local bygones, including a couple of splendid box beds. The museum's pride and joy is, however, its floating cellar, supposedly built by a retired sea captain who could not bear the thought of sleeping on dry land, but actually constructed to stop the house from flooding. Across the square – over the bridge – stands Edam's eighteenth-century **Stadhuis**, a severe Louis XIV-style structure whose plain symmetries culminate in a squat little tower. The ground floor of the Stadhuis is home to the VVV and upstairs is the second part of the Edams Museum (same times & ticket), comprising a handful of old Dutch paintings; the most curious is the portrait of Trijntje Kever (1616–33), a local girl who ended up being over two and a half metres (9 feet) tall; displayed in front of the portrait is a pair of her specially made shoes.

From Damplein, it's a short walk along Grote Kerkstraat to the rambling **Grote Kerk** (April–Oct daily 2–4.30pm; free), on the edge of the fields to the north of town. This is the largest three-ridged church in Europe, a handsome, largely Gothic structure whose strong lines are disturbed by the almost comically stubby spire, which was shortened to its present height after a lightning strike started a fire in 1602. The church interior is distinguished by its magnificent **stained-glass windows**, which date from the early seventeenth century and sport both heraldic designs and historical scenes, and by its whopping organ.

Stroll back from the church along Matthijs Tinxgracht, just to the west of Grote Kerkstraat, and you soon reach the **Kaasmarkt**, site of the summer **cheese market** (July to mid-Aug Wed 10.30am–12.30pm). It's a good deal more humble than Alkmaar's (see p.150), but follows the same format, with the cheeses laid out in rows before the buyers sample them. Once a cheese has been purchased, the cheese porters, dressed in traditional white costumes and straw boaters, spring into action, carrying them off on their gondola-like trays. Overlooking the market is the **Kaaswaag** (Cheese Weighing House), whose decorative panels feature the town's coat of arms, a bull on a red field with three stars.

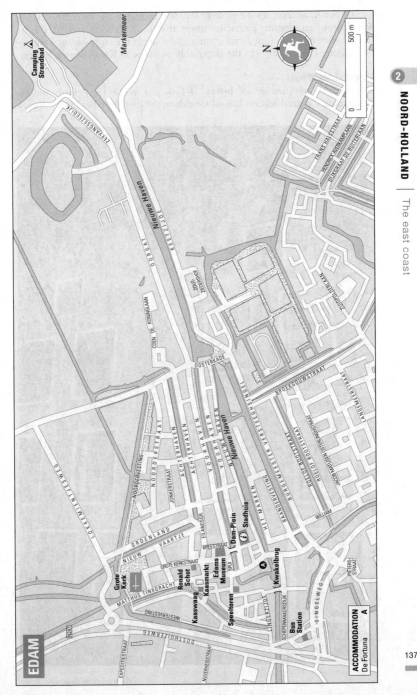

EDAM

Markermeer

Camping
Strandbad

N

500 m

0

ZEEVANGSZEEDIJK

OORGAT

Nieuwe Haven

KEETZIJDE

TRANS HASTRAAT

HENDRICK ANDRIANPLAAN

DIJKGRAAF DE RUITERLAAN

ZUIDPOLDERLAAN

COEN DE KONINGLAAN

ZOUT-
ZIEDERSHOF

OOSTERKADE

BROEKGOUWSTRAAT

LANGEMEERSTRAAT

NOORDERVESTING

NOORDERSTRAAT

JONKERSTRAAT

ACHTERHAVEN

ACHTERHAVEN

VOORHAVEN

VOORHAVEN

Nieuwe Haven

BURGEMEESTER VERSTEEGHSINGEL

BLANDERVESTING

ROLOF BOOLSTRAAT

ROELOF BOOLSTRAAT

JACOB MATHIJSEN OOSTRHUISSTRAAT

WILLIAM

HET MARKEN

LOKHORSTENEWEG

GROENLAND

VAARTJE

EILANDSGR

SPUI

Dam-Plein

Stadhuis

NIEUW

GROTE KERKSTRAAT

BREESTRAAT

MATTHIJS TINXGRACHT

Grote
Kerk

Ronald
Schot

Kaasmarkt

Edams
Museum

Kaaswaag

Speeltoren

Kwakelbrug

LINGERTZIJDE

SCHEPENMAKERSDIJK

Bus
Station

SINGELWEG

PIETERS-
STRAAT

WESTERVESTING

OOSTHUIZERWEG

N247

EXPEDITIESTRAAT

NUHERNERSTRAAT

ACCOMMODATION
De Fortuna   A

From the Kaasmarkt, it's a couple of hundred metres to the fifteenth-century **Speeltoren**, an elegant, pinnacled tower that is all that remains of Edam's second most important medieval church, and roughly the same distance again – south along Lingerzijde – to the impossibly picturesque **Kwakelbrug** bridge.

Practicalities

Every thirty minutes or so, **buses #110** and **#118** leave from outside Amsterdam Centraal Station bound for Edam; the journey takes forty minutes.

△ Buildings in the Kaasmarkt, Edam

Edam's **bus station** is on the southwest edge of town, on Singelweg, a five- to ten-minute walk from Damplein, where the **VVV**, in the Stadhuis (mid-March to Nov Mon–Sat 10am–5pm, July & Aug also Sun 1–4.30pm; Nov to mid–March Mon–Sat 10am–3pm; ☎0299/315 125, ⓦwww.vvv-edam.nl), issues town maps and brochures. The VVV also has details of – and takes bookings for – local **boat trips**, both along the town's canals and out into the Markermeer. **Bike rental** is available at Ronald Schot, in the town centre at Grote Kerkstraat 7 (Tues–Fri 8.30am–6pm, Sat 8.30am–5pm; €6.50 per day; ☎0299/372 155, ⓦwww.ronaldschot.nl).

The VVV has a small supply of **rooms** in private houses (❶), which they will book on your behalf for no extra charge. The best **hotel** in Edam is the charming ⚜ *De Fortuna*, which abuts a narrow canal just round the corner from the Damplein at Spuistraat 3 (☎0299/371 671, ⓦwww.fortuna-edam.nl; ❷). This three-star establishment is the epitome of cosiness, its 23 guest rooms distributed among two immaculately restored old houses and three cottage-like buildings round the back. The nearest **campsite**, *Strandbad*, is east of town on the way to the lakeshore at Zeevangszeedijk 7A (☎0299/371 994, ⓦwww.campingstrandbad.nl; April–Sept) – a twenty-minute walk east along the canal from Damplein.

For **food**, *De Fortuna* has a first-rate restaurant, a lively and eminently agreeable spot decorated in traditional style and with an imaginative, modern menu featuring local ingredients; main courses average around €20; reservations, especially on the weekend, are well-nigh essential.

Hoorn

The old Zuider Zee port of **HOORN**, some 15km north of Edam, "rises from the sea like an enchanted city of the east, with its spires and its harbour tower beautifully unreal" – or at least it did when the English travel writer E.V. Lucas passed through here in 1905. The trouble is that Hoorn has spent much of the last fifty years accruing humdrum suburbs and the town has now lost most of its looks. Nevertheless, there's no gainsaying its splendid past nor the fine ensemble of old merchants' houses whose tall and slender gables flank the convoluted streets down near the harbour. During the seventeenth century this was one of the richest of the Dutch ports, referred to by the poet Vondel as the "trumpet" of the Zuider Zee, handling the important Baltic trade and that of the Dutch colonies. The Dutch East India Company had one of its centres of operation here; *The Tasman* left Hoorn to "discover" Tasmania and New Zealand; and in 1616 William Schouten sailed out of Hoorn to navigate a passage around South America, calling its tip "Cape Hoorn" after his native town. The good times ended in the early eighteenth century when the harbour silted up, strangling the trade on which the town was reliant and turning Hoorn into one of the so-called "dead cities" of the Zuider Zee – a process completed with the creation of the IJsselmeer in 1932 (see box on p.134).

The Town: Rode Steen and the Westfries Museum

At the centre of Hoorn is **Rode Steen**, literally "red stone", an unassuming square that used to hold the town scaffold and now zeroes in on a swashbuckling **statue** of Jan Pieterszoon Coen (1587–1629), founder of the Dutch East Indies Empire and one of the town's big shots in its seventeenth-century heyday. Coen was a headstrong and determined leader of the Dutch imperial effort and under him the country's Far East colonies were consolidated, and rivals, like the English, kept at bay. His settling of places like the Moluccas and

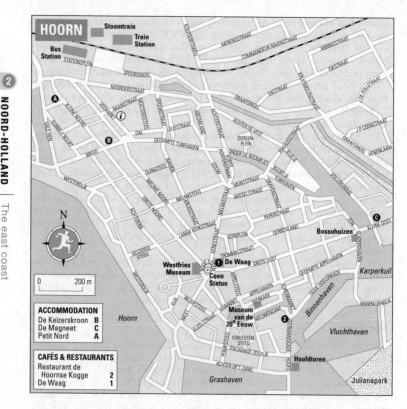

Batavia was something of a personal crusade, and his austere, almost puritanical way of life was in sharp contrast to the wild and unprincipled behaviour of many of his fellow colonialists. On one side of Rode Steen stands the early seventeenth-century **Waag**, whose handsome stone symmetries were designed by Hendrik de Keyser (1565–1621), one of the leading architects of his day. The Waag now accommodates a café-bar, which is enjoyable for its setting, amid the ponderous wood and iron appliances that once weighed the cheese, and its food (see p.142).

On the other side of Rode Steen, the **Westfries Museum** (Mon–Fri 11am–5pm, Sat & Sun 2–5pm; €3.50; ⓦwww.wfm.nl) is housed in the former West Friesland government building of 1632, an imposing stone structure whose facade is decorated with the coats of arms of the house of Orange-Nassau and the region's towns. Now a district within the province of Noord-Holland, West Friesland incorporates the chunk of land between Alkmaar, Hoorn and Enkhuizen, but its origins were much grander. The **Frisians**, who speak a distinctive German dialect, once controlled a narrow sliver of seaboard stretching west from Bremerhaven in Germany to Belgium. Charlemagne conquered them in the 780s and incorporated their territory into his empire, chopping it down in size and dividing the remainder into seven regions, two of which – West Friesland and Friesland – are now in the Netherlands. **Inside the museum**, where the labelling is only in Dutch, the ground floor holds a string of period rooms that re-create the flavour of the seventeenth- and eighteenth-century seaport and along the way are numerous paintings, most memorably the militia portraits of **Jan Rotius** (1624–66) in the old Council Chamber (Room 7). Walk past the figure in the far right of the central painting opposite the fireplace and you'll see his foot change position from left to right – a nifty little trick that was much admired by Rotius's contemporaries. Upstairs, the second floor weighs in with more period rooms as well as discrete collections of all sorts of things from church and guild silverware through to antique furniture and paintings. In the particular, Room 14, the **Chirurgijnskamer** (literally Surgeon's Room, but also, in medieval times, the barber's, the alchemist's and the pharmacist's), holds a mock-up of a medieval "medical" workshop, complete with skeletons, skulls and, curiously enough, a stuffed dodo, while Room 16 has a splendid wooden fireplace carved with tiny scenes of a whaling expedition – Hoorn was once a whaling port of some importance.

Down to the harbour

Strolling east from Rode Steen, **Grote Oost** is shadowed by fine old mansions, one or two of which sport neat rococo balustrades. The most appealing among them is the **Bossuhuizen**, right at the end on the corner with Slapershaven, its facade decorated with a long and slender frieze depicting a sea battle of 1573 – which Admiral Bossu actually lost. Continuing down **Slapershaven**, past some of the most comfortable houseboats imaginable – some even have garages – you soon reach the inner harbour, the **Binnenhaven**, with its clutter of sailing boats and antique barges. Overlooking the harbour, on **Oude Doelenkade**, are two immaculately restored old warehouses, with their prim shutters and crow-stepped gables, whilst, just over the swing bridge and also beside the Binnen-haven, **Veermanskade** is fringed by elegant merchants' houses mostly dating from the seventeenth century. In particular, look out for the birthplace of **Willem Ysbrantzoon Bontekoe** (1587–1657), at Veermanskade 15 – the facade stone shows a particularly ugly spotted cow, as in *bonte* ("spotted") and *koe* ("cow"). A sea captain with the East India Company, Bontekoe published his journals in 1646, a hair-raising account of his adventures that proved immensely popular. Portraying himself as astute and brave in equal measure, Bontekoe's most eventful voyage included the snapping of the mainmast, an epidemic of scurvy and an explosion that forced the crew to abandon ship, all en route from Hoorn to Jakarta. At the end of Veermanskade rises the solid brickwork of the **Hoofd-toren**, a defensive watchtower from 1532, and at its base you'll find a friendly bronze sculpture of 1968 entitled *Three Ships' Boys*, by Jan van Druten.

The Stoomtram

Hoorn is the starting point for the **Stoomtram**, an antiquated steam tram/train that chugs north out of Hoorn, travelling across open countryside before ending up at Medemblik, another old seaport about 14km away (see p.146). It's a popular family excursion and there are between one and three departures per day in July and August and the same from mid-April to June and in September except on Mondays. Advance booking is recommended on ☎0229/214 862, ⓦwww.museumstoomtram .nl. The journey takes one hour and a return ticket costs €15 (children 4–12 years, €12), one-way €9.30 (€7); the starting point is beside Hoorn railway station.

You can make a whole day of it by continuing on from Medemblik by passenger ferry to Enkhuizen (April–Oct 2–3 daily; 1hr 30min; €8 one-way, €12 return), from where there is an hourly train service back to Hoorn (and Amsterdam).

Doubling back along Veermanskade, turn left at the swing bridge along **Nieuwendam** and it's a couple of minutes' walk round the canal to Appelhaven and the **Museum van de Twintigste Eeuw** (Museum of the Twentieth Century; Tues–Fri 10am–5pm, Sat & Sun noon–5pm; €83.50; ⑩ www .museumhoorn.nl), housed in two former cheese warehouses of 1903 at Bierkade 4. Its permanent displays of daily life, though not exactly gripping, are supplemented by changing exhibits with titles such as "Travel Posters – A Nostalgic Journey" and "100 Years of Blokker" (Blokker is the Dutch equivalent of Woolworth's). A scale model of Hoorn in 1650 and an audiovisual display describing the role of the town in the Dutch Golden Age are perhaps a little more diverting. From the museum, it's a couple of minutes' walk back to Rode Steen.

Practicalities

The easiest way to reach Hoorn from Amsterdam is by train (every 30min; 40min); from Edam, take bus #114 from the bus station (every 30min, hourly on Sun; 30min). Hoorn's combined **bus and train station** is on the northern edge of town about ten minutes' walk from the centre. To get to Rode Steen from here, veer right across the square in front of the station, turn left along Veemarkt, right at Breed and left again along Grote Noord, the main shopping street. The **VVV** is near the train station at Veemarkt 4 (May–Aug Mon 1–6pm, Tues–Fri 9.30am–6pm, Sat 9.30am–5pm; Sept–April Mon 1–5pm, Tues–Sat 9.30am–5pm; ☎ 072/511 4284, ⑩ www.vvvhoorn.nl).

With Enkhuizen and Edam so near, there's no strong reason to overnight in Hoorn, but the VVV does have a small supply of **rooms** (❶) in private houses and there are three decent **hotels** in the town centre. First up is the three-star *De Keizerskroon*, in a well-kept, two-storey brick building near the station at Breed 31 (☎ 0229/212 717; ❷). Alternatively, there's the *Petit Nord*, a smart four-star hotel in a humdrum location on the main shopping street at Kleine Noord 53 (☎ 0229/212 750, ⑩ www.hotelpetitnord.nl; ❷), and the well-maintained, three-star *De Magneet*, in modest, modern premises beside a busy road down near the harbour at Kleine Oost 5 (☎ 0229/215 021, ⑩ www.hoteldemagneet.nl; ❷).

For **food**, *De Waag*, right in the centre of town on Rode Steen, offers a tasty line in snacks and lunches amidst all the antiquated paraphernalia of the old municipal weigh house (Mon noon–6pm, Tues 11am–6pm, Wed–Sun 11am–11pm). Moving up-market, *Restaurant De Hoornse Kogge*, Nieuwendam 2 (daily except Tues from 5pm; ☎ 0229/219 309), in a sympathetically revamped old building down by the harbour, offers first-rate French cuisine with main courses hovering around €20; it is strong on seafood and has a good range of vegetarian dishes too.

Enkhuizen

The lovely little town of **ENKHUIZEN**, just 19km east of Hoorn and 25 minutes by train, was once one of the country's most important seaports. From the fourteenth to the early eighteenth century, when its harbour silted up, it prospered from both the Baltic sea trade and the North Sea herring fishery – and indeed its maritime credentials were second to none: Enkhuizen was home to Holland's largest fishing fleet and its citizens were renowned for their seamanship, with the Dutch East India Company always keen to recruit here. Enkhuizen was also the first town in Noord-Holland to rise against Spain, in 1572, but, unlike many of its Protestant allies, it was never besieged – its northerly location kept it safely out of reach of the Habsburg army. Subsequently, Enkhuizen slipped into a long-lasting economic reverie, becoming a remote and solitary backwater until,

During the summer, there are **passenger ferries** east across the IJsselmeer from Enkhuizen to either **Stavoren** (late April Tues–Sun 1 daily; May & Sept Tues–Sun 3 daily; June–Aug 3 daily; early Oct 3 weekly; 1hr 30min; €8.50 one-way, €11.50 day-return; ☎0228/326 667, ⊛www.veerboot.info) or **Urk** (late June to Aug Mon–Sat 3 daily; 1hr 30min; €8 one-way, €12 day-return; ⊛www.urk-enkhuizen.nl). Ferries leave from behind the train station, and you can buy tickets from the VVV, which also has timetables.

in recent years, tourism has revived its fortunes. About twenty minutes' walk from end to end, the town centre, with its ancient streets and slender canals, has preserved its medieval shape, a rough circle with a ring of bastions and moat on one side, and the old sea dyke on the other. The town also possesses no fewer than three pretty harbours and a major attraction in the extensive **Zuiderzeemuseum**, which details the history and cultural significance of the sea to the region. The museum divides into two parts: the indoor **Binnenmuseum** and the rather more interesting **Buitenmuseum**, a well-conceived re-creation of life in the old Zuider Zee ports between 1880 and 1932. The town is also a good place to visit for its summer passenger **ferry** connections across the IJsselmeer to Stavoren (see p.243) and Urk (see p.269).

Arrival and information

Trains to Enkhuizen, which is at the end of the line, stop right opposite the head of the main harbour – the Buitenhaven, at the southern end of town. **Buses** stop beside the train station, and the **VVV** (April–Oct daily 9am–5pm; Nov–March Mon 1–5pm, Tues–Fri 10am–12.30pm & 1–5pm, Sat 10am–12.30pm & 1.30–3pm; ☎0228/313 164, ⊛www.vvvenkhuizen.nl) is about 100m to the east, on the harbourfront at Tussen Twee Havens 1. The VVV sells maps and town brochures and has details of local boat trips.

Accommodation

The VVV has details of some **rooms** in private houses (❶). They also have a list of all the holiday cottages and hotels in the area; there are three good **hotels** in the town centre. In addition, there are two summer-only **campsites** handily located on the edge of the centre. The nearest is the *Enkhuizer Zand* on the far side of the Zuiderzeemuseum at Kooizandweg 4 (☎0228/317 289, ⊛www.campingenkhuizerzand.nl; April–Sept). The other is the plainer *De Vest*, Noorderweg 31 (☎0228/321 221; April–Sept), which fits snugly onto one of the old bastions. To get there, follow Vijzelstraat north off Westerstraat, continue along Noorderweg, and turn left by the old town ramparts; from the train station to the campground is about 1.5km.

Appartement Hotel Driebanen Driebanen 59 ☎0228/316 381, ⊛www.hoteldriebanen.com. Modest, three-star hotel with spick and span modern rooms, as well as apartments for longer stays, in the centre near the Westerkerk. Rooms with private facilities ❷, without ❶
Recuer Dos Westerstraat 217 ☎0228/562 469, ⊛www.recuerdos.nl. The best hotel in town by a long chalk, offering just three double rooms in an immaculate Victorian residence on the west side of

the centre. Cosy, well-appointed rooms, an outside terrace and garden. Reflecting the owner's interests, there are regular Spanish guitar concerts in the hotel's purpose-built guitar salon. ❷
Het Wapen van Enkhuizen Breedstraat 59 ☎0228/313 434, ⊛www.wapenvanenkhuizen.nl. Unassuming, three-star hotel in a modern, two-storey building right in the centre of town by the Stadhuis. The bedrooms are kitted out in proficient modern style. ❶

The Town

A good place to start an exploration of Enkhuizen's compact centre is **Wester-straat**, the town's spine, a busy pedestrianized street that is home to most of its shops and stores. About halfway along stands the **Westerkerk**, an early fifteenth-century, redbrick Gothic church whose free-standing wooden tower is painted in violently incongruous colours – orangey-beige and green. The bare interior of the church, with its three naves of equal height, is distinguished by its **rood-screen**, a mid-sixteenth century extravagance whose six intricately carved panels show biblical scenes in dramatic detail – Moses with the Tablets, St John on Patmos and so forth. From the Westerkerk, it's a couple of minutes' walk south to the **Oude Haven** (old harbour) and its jangle of sailing boats and low-slung barges. The harbour stretches east in a gentle curve that leads round to the conspicuous **Drommedaris**, a heavy-duty brick watchtower built in 1540 to guard the harbour entrance. Immediately to the east is the oldest part of town, an extraordinarily pretty lattice of alleys, quays, canals and antique houses among which nestles the pocket-sized **Flessenscheepjesmuseum**, at Zuiderspui 1 (daily 1–5pm; €3), which is devoted to that ubiquitous maritime curiosity, the ship-in-a-bottle. Well presented and labelled, the exhibits are fascinating, with vessels ranging from East Indiamen to steamboats, and containers from a tiny scent bottle to a thirty-litre wine flagon.

Walk north from the museum along Zuider Havendijk and turn left at the end of the canal to get to the **Zuiderkerk**, a hulking Gothic pile with a massive brick tower that was erected in 1518 – the octagon and then the cupola on top were added later. Close by, just to the east, is the solid, classically styled mid-seventeenth-century **Stadhuis**, an elegant and imposing Neoclassical edifice that still houses the city council.

The Zuiderzeemuseum

From the Stadhuis, it's a short walk east to the indoor section of the **Zuiderzeemuseum**, the **Binnenmuseum**, at Wierdijk 18 (June–Aug daily

△ Enkhuizen harbour

10am–5pm; Sept–May Tues–Sun 10am–5pm; €7, joint ticket with Buiten-museum €11.50; Ⓦwww.zuiderzeemuseum.nl). This has nine separate sections on different aspects of Zuider Zee life, including trade and transport, boats and shipbuilding, fishing and whaling, land reclamation and the East India Company. One of the more curious exhibits is an ice-cutting boat from Urk, once charged with the responsibility of keeping the shipping lanes open between the island and the mainland. There are also several sections devoted to applied art, most notably some extravagant regional costumes, complete with fancy Dutch caps, and several beautiful examples of the painted furniture traditionally carved in Hindeloopen (see p.241).

However, most people give the indoor museum a miss and instead make straight for the picture-postcard **Buitenmuseum** (late April to May, Sept & Oct Tues–Sun 10am–5pm, June–Aug daily 10am–5pm; joint ticket with Binnenmuseum €11.50), whose main entrance is about 100m to the north along Wierdijk. The Buitenmuseum stretches north along the seaward side of the old dyke that once protected Enkhuizen from the turbulent waters of the Zuider Zee. It contains over 130 dwellings, stores, workshops and even streets that have been transported here from every part of the region and together they provide the flavour – albeit rather antiseptically – of life hereabouts from 1880 to 1932. Highlights include a reconstruction of Marken harbour as of 1900, a redbrick chapel and assorted cottages from Den Oever, old fishermen's houses from Urk, a herring smokehouse, a post office and a schoolhouse. There are also regular demonstrations of traditional crafts, and goats and sheep roam the surrounding meadows.

Eating and drinking

For a small town, Enkhuizen has a first-rate supply of **restaurants**. Handy, town-centre options include the excellent ⚶ *De Smederij*, Breedstraat 158 (daily except Wed & Thurs Nov–Mar 5–10pm; ℡0228/314 604), which occupies smart premises kitted out in traditional Dutch style – wooden beams and so forth – and offers inventive, modern Dutch cuisine. Lamb and fish both feature on the menu and the mustard soup, when it's on, is simply stunning; main courses average around €20. A second great choice is the harbourside ⚶ *Die Drie Haringhe*, Dijk 28 (daily except Tues noon–2pm & 5–10pm; ℡0228/318 610), whose imaginative menu is strong on seafood with main courses in the region of €20–25. Housed in an immaculately renovated, seventeenth-century building, complete with antique furnishings and modern paintings, this is the best place to try the local delicacy IJsselmeer pike (*snoek*), when it's on the menu. A third – and far more economic – option is *Vishandel Theo Schilder*, Dijk 48 (Mon–Sat 9am–6pm, Sun noon–7pm), a fish shop with a pint-sized café that offers filling seafood snacks for €10. Finally, a good spot for a **drink** is the *'t Ankertje* pub at Dijk 4, an atmospheric, old-fashioned kind of place with nautical knick-knacks hanging on the walls.

Medemblik

Nautical **MEDEMBLIK**, just over 20km north along the coast from Enkhuizen, is one of the oldest towns in the Netherlands, a seat of Frisian kings until the seventh century and later a Zuider Zee port of some importance. Unfortunately, there's not a great deal to entice you here nowadays unless you're into yachts: the town's several waterways, harbour and marina are jam-packed with leisure craft. The only significant reminder of Medemblik's past is the **Kasteel Radboud**, a dinky little, moated fortress set beside the entrance to the harbour on Oudevaartsgat (May to mid-Sept Mon & Wed–Sat 11am–5pm, Sun 2–5pm; €4). The castle is named after the last Frisian king to hold sway here, though the structure that survives is not his at all, but a much-modified thirteenth-century fortress built by a Count of Holland, **Floris V** (1254–96), one of the most celebrated of the country's medieval rulers. Nicknamed "God of the Peasants" (Der Keerlen God) for his attempts to improve the lot of his humbler subjects, Floris spent most of his time fighting his enemies, both the nobles within his territories and his archenemy the Duke of Flanders. In the end, it was his own nobles who did for him, capturing Floris when he was out hunting and then murdering him during a skirmish when the peasantry came to the rescue. As for the castle itself, it owes much of its present appearance to Petrus J.H. Cuypers (1827–1921), who repaired and rebuilt what had by then become a dilapidated ruin; Cuypers was a leading architect of his day, who was also responsible – among many other commissions – for Amsterdam's Centraal Station and the Rijksmuseum. Inside the castle, exhibits outline the fort's turbulent history and there's a ragbag of archeological finds from local sites.

Castle apart, Medemblik is short on sights, though the main drag, **Nieuwstraat**, is wide and well appointed and the town is home to a large lakeside building that was once the main pumping station hereabouts and is now the **Nederlands Stoommachinemuseum**, on the town's southeasterly outskirts at Oosterdijk 4 (Dutch Steam Engine Museum; mid-Feb to Sept Tues–Sun 10am–5pm; €5; ⓦwww.stoommachinemuseum.nl), the proud possessor of a batch of antique steam engines.

Practicalities

Buses to Medemblik, as well as the **Stoomtram** from Hoorn (see p.141), pull in on the Dam, at the north end of the town centre – and at the top of Nieuwstraat. The **VVV** is five minutes' walk away, at the foot of Nieuwstraat at Kaasmarkt 1 (April–June, Sept & Oct Mon–Sat 10am–4pm; July & Aug Mon–Sat 9.30am–5pm; ☎072/511 4284, ⓦwww.medemblik.nl) – and midway between the Dam and the castle. The VVV sells town maps and has a small supply of **rooms** in private houses (❶). The *Medemblik*, Oosterhaven 1 (☎0227/543 844, ⓦwww.hetwapenvanmedemblik.nl; ❷), is a medium-sized **hotel** in neat and trim premises across the street from the VVV.

North of Medemblik

North of Medemblik, the **Wieringermeer Polder** was reclaimed in the 1920s, filling in the gap between the former Zuider Zee island of Wieringen and the mainland. Towards the end of World War II, just three weeks before their surrender, the Germans flooded the polder, boasting they could return the Netherlands to the sea if they so wished. After the war, it was drained again, leaving a barren, treeless terrain that had to be totally replanted. Almost sixty years later, it's indistinguishable from its surroundings, a familiar landscape of flat, geometric fields, highlighted by neat and trim farmhouses. The polder leads north to the **Afsluitdijk** highway over to Friesland (see Chapter 4). The sluices on this side of the Afsluitdijk are known as the **Stevinsluizen**, after **Hendrick Stevin**, the seventeenth-century engineer who first had the idea of reclaiming the Zuider Zee. At the time, his grand plan was impracticable – the technology wasn't up to it – but his vision lived on, to be realized by **Cornelis Lely** (see box on p.134), though he too died before the dyke was completed. There's a **statue** of Lely by the modern Dutch sculptor Mari Andriessen at the west end of the dyke. Further out along the dyke, at the point where the barrier was finally closed, there's an observation point on which an inscription reads "A nation that lives is building for its future" – a linking of progress with construction that read well in the 1930s, but seems rather more dubious today.

North from Zaandam to Texel

The inland route through the province of Noord Holland begins with the pile-up of settlements collectively known as Zaanstad, which trails northwest of Amsterdam on the far side of the River IJ. Amid all the concrete, there's not much to wet the appetite, though **Zaandam**, the urban core of Zaanstad, does possess the unusual **Czaar Peterhuisje**, where the eponymous tsar hunkered down when he was working in the shipyards here, and is near the over-hyped and over-visited windmills that trail along the polder canals at neighbouring **Zaanse Schans**. Stay on the train and it's another thirty minutes or so to **Alkmaar**, a pleasant old town with a clutch of handsome Golden Age buildings and a traditional open-air cheese market that is much admired by tourists. Nearby is the leafy, well-heeled village of **Bergen**, home to the enjoyable Museum Kranenburgh of fine art and pleasantly located on the edge of the woods, coastal dunes and long sandy beach of the **Noordhollands Duinn-reservaat**. From Alkmaar, it's another short haul to **Den Helder**, a humdrum port that is useful for the ferry over to the green fields and sandy dunes and beaches of **Texel**, a popular Dutch holiday spot.

A fast and frequent **train** service runs north from Amsterdam linking Zaandam, Koog-Zaandijk (for Zaanse Schans), Alkmaar and Den Helder. From each train station, **buses** run to the smaller communities roundabout, usually every hour or half-hour.

Zaandam

As observed from the train heading north out of Amsterdam, the largely modern town of **ZAANDAM** is not especially alluring, but it does deserve a brief stop. The town was a popular tourist hangout in the nineteenth century, when it was known as "La Chine d'Hollande" for the faintly oriental appearance of its windmills, canals and row upon row of brightly painted houses. Monet spent some time here in the 1870s, and, despite being under constant police surveillance as a suspected spy, went on to immortalize the place in a series of paintings. Monet's Zaandam is long gone, but the town is home to one real curiosity in **Czaar Peterhuisje**, at Krimp 23 (Tues–Sun 1–5pm; €2), where the Russian Tsar Peter the Great stayed incognito in 1697. Earlier that year, Peter had attached himself to a Russian trade mission to Holland as an ordinary sailor, Peter Mikhailov. The Russians came to Zaandam, which was then an important shipbuilding centre, and the Tsar bumped into a former employee, one Gerrit Kist. Swearing Kist to the utmost secrecy, the Tsar moved into Kist's simple home and, perhaps more to the point, worked at a local shipyard where he learnt as much as he could about shipbuilding. Now renamed Czaar Peterhuisje, Gist's old home is a tottering wooden structure enclosed within a brick shelter. It comprises little more than two small rooms, decorated with a handful of portraits of a benign-looking emperor and the graffiti of tourists going back to the mid-nineteenth century. Among the few things to see is the cupboard bed in which Peter is supposed to have slept, together with the calling cards and pennants of various visiting Russian delegations; around the outside of the house is a display on the shipbuilding industry in Zaandam and the history of the house. Napoleon is said to have remarked on visiting, "Nothing is too small for great men."

Czaar Peterhuisje is only about 600m east of Zaandam train station, but it's poorly signed and can be difficult to find: from the station, cross the main road and walk south until you reach Hogendijk, where you turn left. Proceed along this street and take the fourth turning on the left – Lage Horn – and Krimp is a few metres away on the left again.

Zaanse Schans

From Zaandam, it's about 4km north to **ZAANSE SCHANS** (ⓦwww .zaanseschans.nl), a sort of re-created Dutch village whose antique houses, shops, warehouses and windmills, mostly dating from the eighteenth century, were brought here from all over the region about forty years ago and re-erected amid a network of narrow canals beside the River Zaan. The problem is its popularity: Zaanse Schans literally swarms with day-trippers and at the height of the season it's really rather unpleasant. A visit starts at the **information centre** (daily 9am–5pm), on the east side of the "village" beside the car park, where you can pick up free maps. From here, it's a short stroll to a string of minor attractions such as the Klompenmakerij (clog-making workshop), the Bakkerij (bakery) and Kaasboerderij (cheese-making plant); opening times vary – the information centre has the details – but these three and almost every other building are open from April to October daily (10am–5pm), with limited winter hours, often weekends only. The particular highlight is the eight **windmills** that string along the River Zaan, giant, insect-like affairs still used – among other things – to cut wood, grind mustard seeds and produce oil. This is the closest place to Amsterdam to see windmills working. Finally, there are also pleasant, 45-minute-long **boat trips** on the River Zaan from the jetty near the De Huisman mustard windmill (April–June & Sept Tues–Sun 11am–4pm, July & Aug daily 11am–4pm; €5).

The nearest **train station** is Koog-Zaandijk, two stops up the line from Zaandam. From the station, it's a fifteen-minute walk east across the River Zaan to Zaanse Schans – just follow the signs.

Alkmaar and around

Forty minutes north from Amsterdam by train, the amenable little town of **ALKMAAR** has preserved much of its medieval street plan, its compact centre surrounded by what was once the town moat and laced with spindly canals. The town is also dotted with fine old buildings, but is best known for its much-touted **cheese market**, an ancient affair that these days ranks as one of the most extravagant tourist spectacles in Noord Holland. Alkmaar was founded in the tenth century in the middle of a marsh – hence its name, which is taken from the auk, a diving bird which once hung around here in numbers, as in *alkeen meer*, or auk lake. Just like Haarlem, the town was besieged by Frederick of Toledo, but heavy rain flooded its surroundings and forced the Spaniards to withdraw in 1573, an early Dutch success in their long war of independence. At the time, Alkmaar was small and comparatively unimportant, but the town prospered when the surrounding marshland was drained in the 1700s and it received a boost more recently when the northern part of the old moat was incorporated into the Noordhollandskanaal, itself part of a longer network of waterways running north from Amsterdam to the open sea.

Alkmaar is also within easy striking distance of **Bergen**, a pretty little village halfway between Alkmaar and the North Sea coast, whose immediate hinterland,

Alkmaar's cheese market

Cheese has been sold on Alkmaar's main square since the 1300s, and although it's no longer a serious commercial concern, the **kaasmarkt** (cheese market; Fri 10am–12.30pm, from the first Friday in April to the first Friday in Sept) continues to pull the crowds – so get there early if you want a good view. The ceremony starts with the buyers sniffing, crumbling, and finally tasting each cheese, followed by intensive bartering. Once a deal has been concluded, the cheeses – golden discs of Gouda mainly, laid out in rows and piles on the square – are borne away on ornamental carriers by groups of four **porters** (*kaasdragers*) for weighing. The porters wear white trousers and shirt plus a black hat whose **coloured bands** – green, blue, red or yellow – represent the four companies that comprise the cheese porters' guild. Payment for the cheeses, tradition has it, takes place in the cafés around the square.

with its woods and dunes, is protected in the **Noordhollands Duinreservaat** (North Holland Dune Reserve) and, just to the north, the **Schoorlse Duinen Nationaalpark** (Schoorl Dunes National Park). Both the reserve and the park are latticed by hiking and cycling routes, and bike rental is available at Alkmaar and Bergen.

Arrival, information and accommodation

From Alkmaar's **train** and **bus station**, it's a ten-minute walk to the centre of town: outside the station head straight along Spoorstraat, hang a left at the end onto Geestersingel and then turn right over the bridge onto Kanaalkade; keep going along Kanaalkade until you reach Houttil Pieterstraat, which leads straight to the main square, Waagplein, where you'll find the **VVV** (Mon–Fri 10am–5.30pm, Sat 9.30am–5pm; ☎072/511 4284, Ⓦwww.vvvalkmaar.nl). They sell a useful town brochure, have details of the area's walking and cycling routes, and can tell you where to rent a bike. Among several places, **cycle rental** is available at the train station and at de Kraak, Nieuwstraat 39 (☎072/512 5840).

Alkmaar only takes an hour or two to explore, but if you decide to stay the VVV has plenty of **rooms** in private houses (❶), including breakfast, though most places are on the outskirts of town. The *Best Western Amrath Hotel Alkmaar*, in a strikingly modern building just across the canal from the west end of the centre at Geestersingel 15 (☎072/518 6186, Ⓦwww.bestwestern.com; ❷) has sixty rooms decorated in crisp, modern chain-hotel style. A pleasant alternative is *Hotel Te Laat*, whose seven spacious and modern, en-suite rooms are located in an older building right in the centre at Laat 117 (☎072/512 5506, Ⓦwww .telaat.com; ❶).

The Town

Even if you've only come for the cheese market (see box above), it's well worth seeing something of the rest of the town before you leave. On the main square, the **Waag** (Weighing House) was originally a chapel dedicated to the Holy Ghost – hence the imposing tower – but was converted and given its delightful east gable shortly after the town's famous victory against the Spanish. The gable is an ostentatious Dutch Renaissance affair bedecked with allegorical figures and decorated with the town's militant coat of arms. The Waag holds the VVV and the **Hollands Kaasmuseum** (Cheese Museum; April–Oct Mon–Thurs & Sat 10am–4pm, Fri 9am–4pm; €2.50), with predictable displays on the history of cheese, cheese-making equipment and such like.

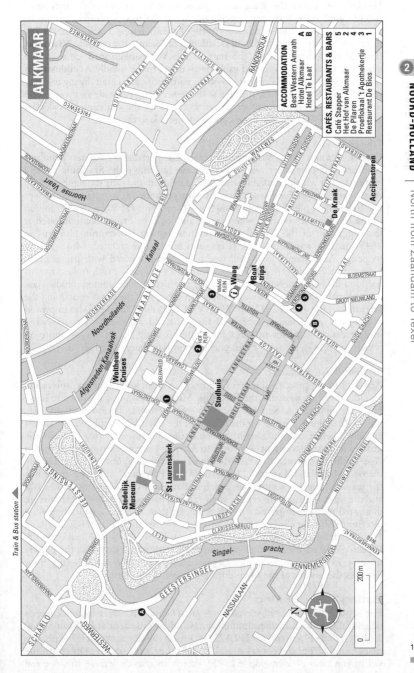

ALKMAAR

ACCOMMODATION
Best Western Amrath — A
Hotel Alkmaar —
Hotel Te Laat — B

CAFÉS, RESTAURANTS & BARS
Café Stapper — 5
Het Hof van Alkmaar — 2
De Pilaren — 4
Proeflokaal 't Apothekertje — 3
Restaurant De Bios — 1

Train & Bus station

N

0   200 m

Heading south from the Waag along Mient, it's a few metres to the jetty from where **canal trips** leave for a quick zip round the town's central canals – an enjoyable way to spend 40 minutes (April–Oct daily, hourly 11am–5pm; €4.70); tickets are on sale at the VVV. At the south end of Mient is the open-air **Vismarkt** (Fish Market), which marks the start of the **Verdronkenoord** canal, whose attractive medley of facades and gables leads down to the spindly **Accijnstoren** (Excise Tower), part harbour master's office, part fortification built during the long struggle with Spain in 1622. Turn left at the tower along Bierkade and you'll soon reach **Luttik Oudorp**, another attractive corner of the old centre, its slender canal jammed with antique barges and leading back to the Waag.

The Stadhuis and St Laurenskerk

One block south of the Waag, pedestrianized **Langestraat** is Alkmaar's main and mundane shopping street, whose only notable building is the **Stadhuis**, a florid edifice, half of which (the Langestraat side) dates from the early sixteenth century. At the west end of Langestraat lurks **St Laurenskerk** (early April to early Sept Fri 10am–5pm, plus June–Aug Tues–Sun 10am–5pm; €2.50), a Gothic church of the late fifteenth century whose pride and joy is its **organ**, commissioned at the suggestion of the diplomat and political bigwig Constantijn Huygens in 1645. The case was designed by Jacob van Campen, the architect who was later to design Amsterdam's town hall (see p.92), and decorated with paintings by Caesar van Everdingen (1617–78). The artist's seamless brushstrokes, not to mention his willingness to kowtow to the tastes of the burgeoning middle class, were to make Everdingen a wealthy man. In the apse is the tomb containing the intestines of the energetic Count Floris V of Holland (1254–96), who improved the region's sea defences, succoured the poor and did much to establish the independence of the towns hereabouts until his untimely demise (for more on which, see p.147); the rest of him ended up in Rijnsburg, near Leiden.

The Stedelijk Museum

Across from the church, Alkmaar's Cultureel Centrum holds a theatre, offices and a mildly diverting museum, the **Stedelijk Museum** (Municipal Museum; Tues–Fri 10am–5pm, Sat & Sun 1–5pm; €4.50; Ⓦwww.stedelijkmuseumalkmaar.nl), whose three floors hone in on the history of the town. Well displayed, but almost entirely labelled only in Dutch, the collection begins with two floors – the ground floor and basement – devoted to Alkmaar's seventeenth-century Golden Age. In the basement, a large assortment of archeological finds is divided up by theme – "Light and Warmth", "Blue and White Porcelain" and so forth – while the ground floor has sections on different aspects of the town, from trade, war and the militias through to replica scenes and scenarios. Many of the exhibits are illustrated by **paintings** and highlights among them include a typically precise interior of Alkmaar's St Laurenskerk by Pieter Saenredam (1597–1665), a striking *Holy Family* by the Mannerist Gerard van Honthorst (1590–1656), who usually kept to glossy portraits of high officials, and a huge canvas depicting the bloody siege of 1573 by the medievalist Jacobus Hilverdink (1809–64). The top floor explores the history of the town during the twentieth century.

Eating and drinking

For **food**, Alkmaar is well served by ⚘ *Het Hof van Alkmaar*, which occupies a delightfully restored medieval nunnery just off Nieuwesloot at Hof van Sonoy 1 (daily noon–10pm; ☎072/512 1222). During the day they offer inexpensive snacks, sandwiches and pancakes, and at night they serve up tasty Dutch cuisine with main courses averaging €15–20; there's an outside terrace too. A good second choice is *Restaurant De Bios*, in modern premises just along the street at Gedempte Nieuwesloot 54 (Tues–Sat noon–10pm; ☎072/512 4422), where the menu has a Mediterranean slant.

Alkmaar has two main groups of **bars**, one on Waagplein, the other just a couple of minutes' walk away around the Vismarkt. Among the former, the pick is *Proeflokaal 't Apothekertje*, an old-style bar, open until 2am, with an antique-cluttered interior and a laidback atmosphere. On the Vismarkt, *De Pilaren* is a livelier, more youthful spot catering to a cooler crowd, some of whom take refuge in the *Café Stapper* next door if the music gets too much.

Around Alkmaar: Bergen and Bergen-aan-Zee

Out towards the coast, just 5km northwest of Alkmaar, lies the village of **BERGEN**, a cheerful, leafy sort of place whose main square, the **Plein**, is an amiable affair crowded by cafés and restaurants. Bergen has been something of a retreat for artists since the late nineteenth century and the **Museum Kranenburgh** (Tues–Sun 1–5pm; €5; ⓦwww.museumkranenburgh.nl), in a Neoclassical villa about 700m southwest of the Plein, features the work of the Expressionist Bergen School, which was founded here in 1915. Greatly influenced by the Post-Impressionists, especially Cézanne, none of the group is original enough to stand out, but taken as a whole it's a delightful collection and one that is supported by an imaginative programme of temporary exhibitions. These often focus on the two contemporaneous Dutch schools that were to have much more artistic impact – De Ploeg and De Stijl (see p.382). Warming to this artistic heritage, the local council organizes all sorts of cultural events in Bergen, including open-air sculpture displays and concerts, and the village also boasts a scattering of chi-chi commercial galleries. Bergen has one other museum of some note, the **Gemeentemuseum Het Sterkenhuis**, in a seventeenth-century manor house about 100m from the west end of Plein at Oude Prinsweg 21 (early May to Oct Tues–Sat 1–5pm; July & Aug also Sun 1–5pm; €2). The museum holds regular exhibitions of work by contemporary Dutch artists, has a string of period rooms and features a local history section, including a display on a largely forgotten episode in the Napoleonic Wars, when a combined army of 30,000 English and Russian soldiers were defeated by a Franco-Dutch force here in 1799.

Bus #160 leaves Alkmaar train station every thirty minutes or so – hourly on Sunday – for the ten-minute ride to Bergen, dropping passengers in the centre on Plein, a few metres from **Bergen VVV**, Plein 1 (Mon–Sat 10am–5pm; July & Aug also Sun 11am–3pm; ☎072/581 3100, ⓦwww.vvvnoordzeekust.nl). They sell maps of the hiking and cycling routes that crisscross the coastal woods and dunes just to the west of the village – both in the Noordhollands Duinreservaat and the Schoorlse Duinen Nationaalpark. **Bike rental** is available in Bergen, at, among several places, Fietsenverhuur Bergen, just north of Plein at Breelaan 46 (☎072/589 8248).

Bergen-aan-Zee and the coast

From Bergen, it's just 5km to **BERGEN-AAN-ZEE**, a sprawling, modern resort that dips and bucks over the dunes. There's nothing special about the place, apart from the sheer volume of holiday cottages, and the first-rate **beach**, a strip of golden sand extending as far as the eye can see to north and south. The resort also marks the northerly limit of the **Noordhollands Duinreservaat** (North Holland Dune Reserve), whose bumpy sand dunes stretch north from the suburbs of IJmuiden, and the southern boundary of the **Schoorlse Duinen Nationaalpark** (Schoorl Dunes National Park), where a band of sweeping, wooded dunes, up to 5km wide, extends north as far as Camperduin – one of the widest undeveloped portions of the whole Dutch coastline. The dune reserve and the national park are both crisscrossed by footpaths and cycling trails, but the most lauded route is the well-signposted, 42km-long **De Brede Duinen route** that takes cyclists on a loop between Alkmaar, Bergen, Bergen-aan-Zee, Schoorl and Camperduin, passing the highest of the national park's sand dunes (54m) on the way. Both Bergen and Alkmaar VVV sell detailed **maps** of local hiking and cycling routes.

Local **buses** make the trip from the Plein in Bergen to Bergen-aan-Zee every hour or so.

Den Helder

The gritty port, oil supply centre and naval base of **DEN HELDER**, some forty minutes north from Alkmaar by train, was little more than a fishing village until 1811, when Napoleon, capitalizing on its strategic position at the very tip of Noord-Holland, built a fortified dockyard here. It's still the principal home of the Dutch navy, and **national fleet days**, or *Vlootdagen*, are held in the harbour on one weekend during the summer – usually in July – when, should you so desire, you can check out the bulk of the Dutch navy; for further details, contact the VVV. Otherwise, the town holds little of interest with the possible exception of the **Marinemuseum**, on the seafront – in-between the train station and the ferry terminal – at Hoofdgracht 3 (Tues–Fri 10am–5pm, Sat & Sun noon–5pm; May–Oct also Mon 10am–5pm; €4.50; ⓦwww.marinemuseum.nl), which makes a gallant attempt to conjure interest in what is, for most people, hardly a riveting subject. Nevertheless, the sections tracking through the history of the Dutch navy are well presented and entertaining and in particular you might look out for the stuff on the naval heroes of yesteryear, especially Admiral Michiel de Ruyter (1607–76), who trounced in succession the Spaniards, the Swedes, the English and the French. His most daring exploit was a raid up the River Thames to Medway in 1667 and the seizure of the Royal Navy's flagship, *The Royal Charles*, a raid that drove Charles II almost to distraction. There's lots of technical information too – on shipbuilding techniques and the like – and several decommissioned vessels, including a 1960s submarine, the *Tonijn*, and the veteran World War II minesweeper, the *Abraham Crijnssen*.

It's a five-minute walk north from Den Helder **train and bus station** to the **VVV**, Bernhardplein 18 (Mon 10.30am–5.30pm, Tues–Sat 9.30am–5pm; ⓣ0223/625 544, ⓦwww.vvvkopvannoordholland.nl), and just under 2km to the Texel ferry terminal (for ferry details, see opposite); alternatively, you can miss the town altogether by taking a bus direct from the train station to the ferry dock.

The island of Texel

Stuck out in the Waddenzee, **Texel** (pronounced "tessel") is the westernmost of the string of islands that band the northern coast of the Netherlands. Some 25km long and up to 9km wide, Texel is mostly reclaimed polder, a flattened landscape of green pasture land dotted with chunks of woodland, speckled with small villages and protected in the east by long sea defences. The west coast boasts a magnificent sandy **beach** that stretches from one end of the island to the other, its numbered markers (*paal*) – from 6 in the south to 33 in the north – distinguishing one bit from another. Behind the beach, a belt of sand dunes widens as it approaches both ends of the island. In the north it spreads out into two nature reserves – **De Muy** and **De Slufter** – and the latter incorporates Texel's finest scenery in **De Slufter**, a tidal inlet where a deep cove of salt marsh, lagoon and dune has been left beyond the sea defences exposed to the willfulness of the ocean. The beach, combined with the island's laidback rural charms, attracts holidaying Netherlanders here in their hundreds and the island has scores of holiday bungalows and cottages, plus a scattering of hotels and campsites. As for the island's **villages**, they are disappointingly humdrum with the notable exception of **Den Hoorn**, easily the prettiest place on the island with **De Cocksdorp** a distant runner up.

Arrival, information and island transport

Car ferries (Mon–Sat 6.30am–9pm, Sun 7.30am or 8.30am–9pm; ☎0222/369 600, ⓦwww.teso.nl) leave Den Helder for Texel hourly, sometimes every half-hour in season, and the journey takes about twenty minutes. **Return tickets** cost just €3 for foot passengers and €2.50 for cycles, whereas cars are charged

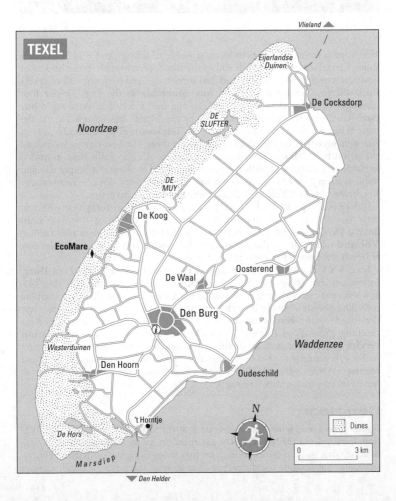

△ Horses on Texel island

€35 at peak times, which includes most weekend sailings, and €24.50 at other times. Ferries dock at the south end of the island, pretty much in the middle of nowhere, but there is a good **island bus** service to – and between – all of Texel's main villages.   Pick up an island **bus timetable** at the Den Helder foot passenger ticket window, where you can also buy a one-day, island-wide **bus pass** for €4.50, though passes are sold by the island's bus drivers too. At the same ticket window, you can arrange for a **Telekomtaxi** (☎0222/322 211) to take you anywhere on the island once you get there. The best way to get around the island is by **bike** – Texel has about 130km of cycle path. **Bike rental** is available at a number of locations across the island at about €4.50 per day and there is a very convenient outlet beside the Texel ferry dock – Fietsverhuur Veerhaven Texel (☎0222/319 588); reservations aren't necessary.

De Vriendschap (☎0222/316 451) is a seasonal passenger **ferry** (early May to early July & Sept 2 daily on 4 days weekly; mid-July to Aug 4 daily; 30min) linking De Cocksdorp, at the northern tip of Texel, with the next island along, **Vlieland** (see p.236). A day return costs €20, single fare is €13, and bikes cost €7 each way; note that Vlieland is car free.

Texel **VVV** is on the southern edge of the island's largest village, **Den Burg**, Emmalaan 66 (Mon–Fri 9am–5.30pm, Sat 9am–5pm; ☎0222/314 741, Ⓦwww.vvv.texel.net). Staff here issue or sell a wide range of island information, including booklets detailing **cycling routes**, as well as the best places to view the island's many **bird colonies** – the island is one of the most important breeding grounds in Europe. The VVV also operates an **accommodation service**, which is especially useful in the height of the summer when spare rooms can get mighty thin on the ground. The VVV has a substantial supply of **rooms** in private houses (❶–❷) which supplement the island's dozen or so hotels and myriad summer cottages.

Den Hoorn

Ferries from Den Helder (see p.154) dock at the south end of Texel, about 4km from the hamlet of **DEN HOORN**, a leafy little place whose rustic cottages, some of which date back to the eighteenth century, string along the main street, Herenstraat, and out towards the dunes, just 2km away to the west; the beach another

2km further on (at *paal* 10). There are two very appealing **hotels** in the village, beginning with *Loodman's Welvaren*, Herenstraat 12 (☎0222/319 228, ⓦwww .welvaarttexel.nl; ❷), which has nine spick and span, modern doubles in a sympathetically modernized old building. Similarly enticing is 🍴 *Bij Jef*, in another old building just along the street at Herenstraat 34 (☎0222/319 623, ⓦwww.bijjef.nl; ❷), though here the rooms are a little more stylish. There's also a large **campsite**, *Loodsmansduin*, Rommelpot 19 (☎0222/317 208, ⓦwww.rsttexel.nl; April–Oct), with plenty of space for tents and caravans on the edge of the dunes just to the southwest of Den Hoorn. As for **food**, the restaurant of the *Bij Jef Hotel* (Mon–Sat noon–2pm & 6–10pm, Sun noon–9pm; ☎0222/319 623) has an island-wide reputation for its excellent Franco-Dutch cuisine; main courses are from €19 to €30 and reservations are strongly recommended. A more economic option is *Klif 23*, on the west side of the village at Klif 23 – Klif being the road running west towards the dunes – where they offer over 150 different sorts of pancake.

Bike rental is available in Den Hoorn at *Vermeulen Bikes*, Herenstraat 69 (☎0222/319 213); there are hourly **bus** connections between Den Hoorn and the ferry port Monday through Saturday, 5 daily on Sundays.

North from Den Hoorn to De Cocksdorp

From Den Hoorn, it's about 5km northeast to **DEN BURG**, the island's main village and home to the VVV (see opposite), and another 4km or so north to **DE KOOG**, Texel's busiest resort, equipped with lots of restaurants and hotels, plus a small army of campsites. Pressing on, the coastal road north from De Koog leads, after about 4km, past the first of two turnings that cut down to the sea wall behind **De Slufter** nature reserve, a beautiful tidal inlet, whose assorted lagoons, marshes and dunes are exposed to the ocean's tides. Steps enable visitors to clamber up and over the sea wall to the footpaths beyond: it is perhaps the prettiest spot on the island.

Beyond, near the northern tip of Texel, is **DE COCKSDORP**, a middling sort of village, whose wedge of mostly modern houses trail along a slender inlet, all protected by a sea wall. The village has a handful of **hotels**, the pick of which is *'t Anker*, a cosy, unassuming little place in a pair of oldish cottages on the main street at Kikkertstraat 24 (☎0222/316 274, ⓦwww.t-anker.texel.com; ❷). There's also a **campsite**, *De Robbenjager*, to the north of the village at Vuurtorenweg 148 (☎0222/316 258; April–Oct).

De Cocksdorp heaves with **cafés** and restaurants, and one good choice is the *Pangkoekehuus*, Kikkertstraat 9, where they serve up a great line in pancakes from €6 – and then deliver your bill to the table inside a tiny clog.

Ferries to Vlieland (see p.236) leave from the jetty about 1.5km north of De Cocksdorp and there's an hourly **bus** service between De Cocksdorp, De Koog and the ferry dock.

Het Gooi

Known collectively as **Het Gooi**, the sprawling suburbs that spread southeast from Amsterdam towards Amersfoort (see p.214) and Utrecht (see p.209) are interrupted by open heaths, lakes, canals and woods, reminders of the time when this was a sparsely inhabited district largely devoted to sheep farming. The turning point was the construction of the Amsterdam–Amersfoort railway in 1874, which allowed hundreds of bourgeois Amsterdammers to build their country homes here, nowhere more so than in well-heeled **Hilversum**, long the area's main settlement and nowadays pretty much a dormitory town despite the best efforts of the Dutch media, much of which is encamped here. Hilversum is a possible target for a day trip on account of its modern architecture, most notably the work of Willem Dudok, as are Het Gooi's two other prime attractions, the immaculate star-shaped fortifications of **Naarden** and the handsome medieval castle at **Muiden**.

The most useful **train line** across Het Gooi passes through Weesp, where there are connecting buses onto Muiden, and then proceeds onto Naarden-Bussum (for Naarden) and Hilversum.

Muiden

MUIDEN, just to the north of the A1 motorway about 10km to the southeast of Amsterdam, straddles the River Vecht as it approaches the Markermeer, its several waterways crowded with pleasure boats and yachts. At the far end of the town is the **Muiderslot** (April to mid-Oct Mon–Fri 10am–5pm, Sat & Sun noon–6pm; Nov–March Sat & Sun noon–6pm; €7; ⓦ www.muiderslot.nl), one of the country's most visited castles, a handsome red-brick structure whose imposing walls are punctuated by mighty circular towers, all set behind a reedy moat. The Muiderslot was built by Count Floris V of Holland (1254–96) – for more on whom, see p.147 – but it has been rebuilt or remodelled on several occasions, most recently after World War II when the interior was returned to its seventeenth-century appearance in honour of the poet Pieter Hooft, one of its most celebrated occupants. Hooft was chatelain here from 1609 to 1647, a sinecure that allowed him to entertain a group of artistic and literary friends who became known as the Muiden Circle, and included Grotius, Vondel, Huygens and other Amsterdam luminaries. The obligatory guided tour focuses on this clique and the restoration is both believable and likeable.

To get to Muiden by **public transport**, take the train from Amsterdam Centraal Station to Weesp (every 15min; 15min) and then catch the hourly local bus #110 on from there, a thirty-minute journey. In Muiden, the bus drops you on the edge of town, a short, signposted walk from the Muiderslot.

Naarden

Look at a postcard of **NAARDEN**, about 8km east along the A1 from Muiden, and it seems as if the old town was created by a giant pastry-cutter, its gridiron of streets encased within a double ring of ramparts and moats that were engineered with geometrical precision between 1675 and 1685 to defend the eastern approaches to Amsterdam. These formidable defences were used right up until the 1920s, and one of the fortified spurs, on Westwalstraat, is now the wonderfully explorable **Nederlands Vestingmuseum** (Dutch Fortress Museum; March–Oct Tues–Fri 10.30am–5pm, Sat & Sun noon–5pm; Nov–Feb Sun noon–5pm; €5; ⓦ www.vestingmuseum.nl), whose claustrophobic underground passages demonstrate how the garrison defended the town for nigh-on 300 years.

Within the ramparts, Naarden's attractive and architecturally harmonious centre mostly dates from the late sixteenth century, its small, low houses erected after the Spanish sacked the town in 1572. Fortunately, the Spaniards spared the late Gothic **Grote Kerk** (June to mid-Sept Wed–Sun noon–5pm; free) and its superb vault paintings. Based on drawings by Dürer, these 22 rectangular wooden panels were painted between 1510 and 1518 and show Old Testament scenes on the south side, New Testament on the north; there are also five triangular panels at the east end of the church. To study the paintings without cricking your neck, borrow a mirror at the entrance. The church is also noted for its wonderful acoustics: every year there are several acclaimed performances of Bach's *St Matthew Passion* in the Grote Kerk in the days leading up to Easter – details from the VVV. A haul up the 235 steps of the Grote Kerk's massive square **tower** gives the best view of the fortress. The elaborately step-gabled building opposite the church is the **Stadhuis** (April–Sept Mon–Sat 1.30–4.30pm; free), built in 1601 and still in use by the town council today.

Naarden also possesses the mildly absorbing **Comenius Museum**, in the centre at Kloosterstraat 33 (late May to mid-Sept Wed–Sun noon–5pm; €2.50; @www .comeniusmuseum.nl). Jan Amos Komenski (1592–1670), his name latinized as Comenius, was a philosopher, cartographer and educational reformer who was born in Moravia, then part of the Holy Roman Empire and today part of the Czech Republic. A Protestant, he was expelled from the empire for his religious beliefs in 1621 and spent the next 36 years wandering round Europe preaching and teaching before finally settling in Amsterdam. The museum outlines Comenius' life and times and takes a stab at explaining his work, notably his plan to improve the Swedish educational system and his 1658 *Orbis Pictus* ("The World in Pictures"), the first-ever picture-book for children. Further sections relate his work to that of other philosophers of the day, principally the Frenchman René Descartes, who also lived in Amsterdam (from 1629 to 1649). After his death, Comenius was, for some unexplained reason, buried here in Naarden, his **mausoleum** placed in what had once been the chapel of a Franciscan convent; the museum followed. In the 1930s the Dutch authorities refused the Czechoslovak government's request for the repatriation of the philosopher's remains, and instead sold them the building (and the land it stood on) for the symbolic price of one guilder: the mausoleum remains a tiny slice of Czech territory to this day.

Practicalities

There are three **trains** hourly from Amsterdam Centraal Station to Naarden-Bussum train station, about 4km from the old town – Naarden has spread well beyond its original fortifications. Local buses link the train station with the old town, but it's far easier to buy a **train and taxi ticket**, which costs an extra €5, but includes the onward taxi ride (for more on train and taxi tickets, see Basics p.31). Naarden's old town is readily explored on foot – it's only 1km long and about 800m wide – and maps are available at the **VVV**, on the south side of the old town at Adriaan Dortsmanplein 1B (May Tues–Fri 11am–3pm & Sat 10am–2pm; June to early Sept Mon–Fri 11am–3pm & Sat 10am–2pm; early Sept to April Sat 10am–2pm; ☎035/694 2836, @www.vvvnaarden.nl). The VVV has a small supply of **rooms** in private houses (❶), though most of these are out of the old town, and there is one central **hotel**, *Poorters*, in a trim, two-storey older house at Marktstraat 66 (☎035/694 4868, @www.poorters.nl; ❶); the hotel has just five double rooms decorated in modest modern style and advance reservations are advised.

For **food**, there's a concentration of places along the main shopping street, Marktstraat. **Café** options here include the *Salon de Thé Sans Doute* at no. 33, great for sandwiches and coffee, and the *Café De Doelen*, next to the Grote Kerk on the south side at no. 7, perfect for an inexpensive meal. The best **restaurant** in town is *Het Arsenaal*, in the old arsenal on the west side of the centre at Kooltjesbuurt 1 (Mon–Fri noon–4pm & daily from 6pm; ☎035/694 9148), where the excellent Franco–Dutch main courses start at around €20.

Hilversum

Sprawling, leafy **HILVERSUM**, some 10km south of Naarden, is the main town of Het Gooi and a prosperous, commuter suburb with a population of around 90,000. Many locals love the place, but for the casual visitor Hilversum is mainly of interest for its modern architecture – or to be precise the work of **Willem Marinus Dudok** (1884–1974), the director of public works and town architect for over thirty years. Hilversum possesses several dozen buildings by Dudok, who was much influenced by the American Frank Lloyd Wright, but pride of place among them goes to the **Raadhuis** (town hall), about 700m northwest of the train station at Dudopark 1. Dating from 1931, the structure's design is based on a deceptively simple progression of straw-coloured blocks rising to a clock tower, with long, slender bricks giving it a strong horizontal emphasis. The interior is well worth seeing too: essentially a series of lines and boxes, its marble walls are margined with black, like a monochrome Mondrian painting, all coolly and immaculately proportioned. Dudok also designed the interior decorations, and though some have been altered, his style prevails, right down to the ashtrays and lights. If the Raadhuis whets your appetite, the **Dudok Centrum**, in the basement of the Raadhuis (Wed, Fri & Sun noon–4.30pm; free), presents an overview of Dudok's life and work and issues a free leaflet outlining the **Dudok Route**, which meanders around Hilversum taking in a goodly number of his buildings – a pleasant enough way to spend a couple of hours; the leaflet is also available at the VVV.

Trains leave Amsterdam's Centraal Station twice an hour for Hilversum, and take about thirty minutes to get there. From Hilversum's combined **train and bus station**, it's a short walk west to the **VVV**, not far from the Raadhuis at Kerkbrink 6 (Mon–Sat 10am–5pm; ℡035/629 2810, ⓦwww.vvvhilversum .nl). They have a small supply of **rooms** in private houses (①) and there are a couple of central chain **hotels** too – including the *Best Western Grand Hotel Gooiland*, in a Dudok-inspired 1930s building about 600m south of the station at Emmastraat 2 (℡035/621 2331, ⓦwww.bestwestern.nl; ②) – but with Amsterdam so close, and connections to more interesting towns so easy, there's little reason to stay. You can rent bikes, as usual, from the train station.

Travel details

Trains

Alkmaar to: Haarlem (every 30min; 30min); Hoorn (every 30min; 25min).
Amsterdam CS to: Alkmaar (every 30min; 30min); Den Helder (every 30min; 1hr); Enkhuizen (every 30min; 1hr); Haarlem (every 15min; 15min); Hilversum (every 30min; 30min); Hoorn (every 30min; 40min); Koog-Zaandijk (every 15min; 15min); Naarden-Bussum (every 20min; 20min); Weesp (every 15min; 15min); Zaandam (every 15min; 10min).
Haarlem to: Alkmaar (every 30min; 30min); Hoorn (every 30min; 25min); Zandvoort (every 30min; 10min).
Hilversum to: Amersfoort (every 30min; 15min); Utrecht (every 20min; 20min).

Buses

Alkmaar to: Bergen (every 30min, hourly on Sun; 10min).

Amsterdam to: Edam (every 30min; 40min); Marken (every 30min; 30min); Volendam (every 30min; 30min).
Edam to: Hoorn (every 30min; 25min).
Haarlem to: Bloemendaal-aan-Zee (every 30min to 1hr; 15min).
Hoorn to: Medemblik (every 30min to 1hr; 30–40min).
Marken to: Monnickendam (every 30min; 15min).
Monnickendam to: Volendam (every 30min; 15min).

Ferries

Den Helder to: Texel (hourly; 20min).
Enkhuizen to: Medemblik (April–Oct 2–3 daily; 1hr 30min); Stavoren (late April 1 daily; May & Sept 3 daily except Mon; June–Aug 3 daily; early Oct 3 weekly; 1hr 30min); Urk (late June to Aug Mon–Sat 3 daily; 1hr 30min).
Marken to: Volendam (April–Oct daily 11am–5pm, every 30–45min; 30min).

Zuid-Holland and Utrecht

CHAPTER 3 # Highlights

✳ **Leiden** Patterned by canals, this old university town has, among its several attractions, some delightful botanical gardens in the Hortus Botanicus. See p.165

✳ **Den Haag** Fascinating city that boasts the Mauritshuis, arguably the country's most impressive art gallery. See p.171

✳ **Delft** A lovely little town, and one-time home of Vermeer, with one of the prettiest market squares in the whole of the Netherlands. See p.184

✳ **Rotterdam** This gritty and boisterous port city has resurrected itself in flash modern style after extensive war damage, complete with its own Museumpark. See p.191

✳ **Gouda** Archetypal Dutch country town, home of the famous round cheese and a splendid set of stained-glass windows in St Janskerk. See p.200

✳ **Utrecht** Admire Gerrit Rietveld's De Stijl furniture design and architecture in his home town. See p.209

△ Windmills of the Kinderdijk

Zuid-Holland and Utrecht

Z uid-Holland, or South Holland, is the most densely populated province of the Netherlands, incorporating a string of towns and cities that make up most of what is commonly called the **Randstad** (literally "Rim-Town"). By and large, careful urban planning has succeeded in stopping this from becoming an amorphous conurbation, however, and each town has preserved a pronounced identity. A short hop from Amsterdam is **Leiden**, a university town par excellence, with an antique centre latticed by canals and dotted with fine old buildings. **Den Haag** (The Hague) was once a humdrum government town but has jazzed itself up and is now a very likeable city with a string of good museums and an appealing bar and restaurant scene. **Delft**, a smaller place with just 100,000 inhabitants, possesses an extremely pretty centre, replete with handsome seventeenth-century buildings, in stark contrast to the rough and tumble of big-city **Rotterdam**, the world's biggest port, where an adventurous city council has stacked up a string of first-rate attractions, from fine art through to harbour tours. It's a short journey inland from here to **Gouda**, a good-looking country town historically famed for its cheese market, and to the somnambulant charms of rural **Oudewater**. Back on the coast, **Dordrecht** marks the southern edge of the Randstad and is of interest as an ancient port and for its location, within easy striking distance of the windmills of the **Kinderdijk** and the creeks and marshes of the **Biesbosch**. Finally, the province of **Utrecht** holds two places of some interest: Utrecht itself, a sprawling city with a dramatic history and a bustling, youthful centre, and **Amersfoort**, half the size of its neighbour and home town of Piet Mondrian.

Historically, Zuid-Holland is part of what was once simply **Holland**, the richest and most influential province in the country. Throughout the Golden Age, Holland dominated the political, social and cultural life of the Republic, overshadowing its neighbours whose economies were dwarfed by Holland's success. There are constant reminders of this pre-eminence in the province's buildings: elaborate town halls proclaim civic importance and even the usually sombre Calvinist **churches** allow themselves decorative excesses – the later windows of Gouda's Janskerk being a case in point. Many of the great Dutch **painters** either came from or worked here, too – Rembrandt, Vermeer, Jan Steen – a tradition that continued into the nineteenth century with the

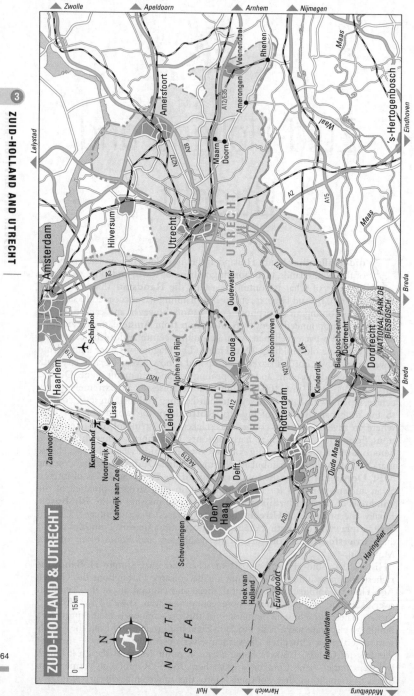

ZUID-HOLLAND & UTRECHT

0 — 15 km

N

NORTH
SEA

paintings of the Hague School. All the towns offer good **museums** and galleries, most notably The Hague's Mauritshuis and Rotterdam's Boijmans Van Beuningen. In addition, the coastal cities – especially Leiden and Den Haag – are only a short bus or tram ride from the wide sandy **beaches** of the North Sea coast, while the pancake-flat Randstad landscape is at least brightened by rainbow flashes of **bulbfields** in spring with the **Keukenhof gardens**, near Leiden, having the finest display.

A fast and efficient rail network makes travelling around Zuid-Holland extremely easy, and where the trains fizzle out, buses take over.

Leiden and around

LEIDEN, just 30km to the south of Amsterdam – and forty minutes by train – is a lively and energetic city of around 120,000 souls, which makes for an enjoyable day trip or overnight stay. At its heart, the city's antique, sometimes careworn centre is a maze of narrow lanes that wriggle and worm their way around a complicated network of canals, one of which marks the line of the medieval walls. It's all very appealing – and appealingly unfussy – with Leiden's multitude of bars and cafés kept afloat by the thirsty students of the city's one great institution, its university, one of Europe's most prestigious seats of learning. As for specific sights, top billing goes to the magnificent ancient Egyptian collection at the **Rijksmuseum van Oudheden** (National Museum of Antiquities) and the seventeenth-century Dutch paintings of the **Stedelijk Museum de Lakenhal**, though, perhaps surprisingly, given that this was his home town, the museum is very short of Rembrandts. Leiden is also within easy striking distance of the Dutch bulbfields and the showpiece **Keukenhof gardens** as well as the amenable North Sea resort of **Katwijk-aan-Zee** and its long sandy beach

It may well have been the **Romans** who founded Leiden as a forward base on an important trade route running behind the dunes, but, whatever the truth, it was certainly fortified in the ninth century when a local lord built a castle here on an artificial mound. Flemish weavers migrated to Leiden in the fourteenth century and thereafter the town prospered as a minor cloth-making centre, but things didn't really take off until the foundation of its university in 1575. It was **William the Silent** who chose Leiden as the home of the university as a reward for the city's bravery during the rebellion against Spain: Leiden had declared for William in 1572, but a Habsburg army besieged the city in October 1573. The siege, which lasted a whole year, was a desperate affair during which hundreds of city folk starved to death, but William the Silent finally sailed to the rescue on October 3, 1574, cutting through the dykes around the town and vanquishing the Spaniards in one fell swoop. The event is still commemorated with an annual fair, fireworks and the consumption of two traditional dishes: herring and white bread, which the fleet brought with them, and *hutspot*, a vegetable and potato stew, a cauldron of which was found simmering in the abandoned Spanish camp outside the walls.

Arrival, information and accommodation

Leiden's ultra-modern **train station** is next to the **bus station** on the northwest edge of town, a five-minute walk from the Beestenmarkt at the west end of the centre. Halfway between is the **VVV**, at Stationsweg 2 (Mon 11am–5.30pm,

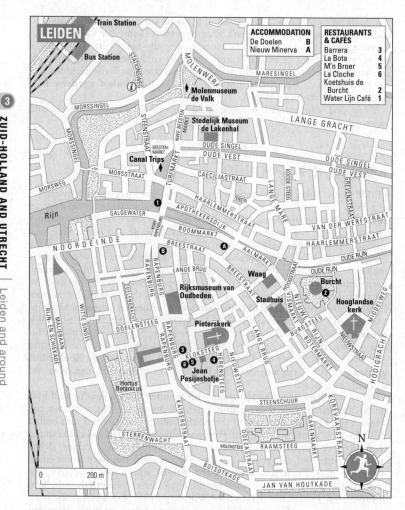

LEIDEN

Train Station

Bus Station

ACCOMMODATION	
De Doelen	**B**
Nieuw Minerva	**A**

RESTAURANTS & CAFÉS	
Barrera	**3**
La Bota	**4**
M'n Broer	**5**
La Cloche	**6**
Koetshuis de Burcht	**2**
Water Lijn Café	**1**

Molenmuseum de Valk

Stedelijk Museum de Lakenhal

Canal Trips

Rijn

Molenmuseum van Oudheden

Waag

Burcht

Hooglandse kerk

Pieterskerk

Stadhuis

Jean Pesijnshofje

Hortus Botanicus

0   200 m

N

JAN VAN HOUTKADE

Tues–Fri 9.30am–5.30pm, Sat 10am–4.30pm; also April–Aug Sun 11am–3pm; ☏071/516 1211, ⓦwww.leiden.nl), which has all manner of local information, including city maps and brochures, as well as an excellent range of walking and touring maps covering most of the country.

Of the town's **hotels**, easily the most appealing is the excellent ⚜ *Nieuw Minerva*, a cosy, very Dutch hotel that occupies a sequence of old canalside houses in the centre at Boommarkt 23 (☏071/512 6358, ⓦwww.nieuwminerva.nl; ❸). All their rooms are comfortable, in an undemanding sort of way, but the "honeymoon room" (❺) is up a notch, boasting a four-poster bed and fancy drapes. A reasonable second choice is the three-star *De Doelen*, which occupies a grand if somewhat faded old house by another of the town's central canals at Rapenburg 2 (☏071/512 0527, ⓦwww.dedoelen.com; ❸); there are sixteen guest rooms, all kitted out in plain modern style.

The Town

The obvious place to start an exploration of the centre is the **Beestenmarkt**, a large and really rather ugly open space that's long been a major meeting point. The square is also the starting point for **canal trips** around the centre – a pleasant enough way to spend forty minutes (April–Sept 3–5 daily; €6). From here, it's a hop and a jump to **Rapenburg**, a gentle, curving canal lined by some of Leiden's grandest mansions. In one of the largest, at no. 28, is the town's most important museum, the **Rijksmuseum van Oudheden** (National Museum of Antiquities; Tues–Fri 10am–5pm, Sat & Sun noon–5pm; €7.50; Ⓦ www.rmo .nl), a leading archeological museum, whose three floors hold extensive Egyptian and classical collections. On the ground floor, the museum kicks off in style with the squat and sturdy **Taffeh Temple**, a gift from the Egyptian government in gratitude for Dutch help with the 1960s UNESCO excavations that saved scores of ancient monuments from the rising waters of the Nile following the construction of the Aswan dam. Dating back to the first century AD, the Taffeh Temple was originally part of a fortress that guarded the southern border of the Roman province of Egypt. Initially, it was dedicated to Isis, the goddess of love and magic, but in the fourth century it was turned into a Christian church.

The next floor up exhibits oodles of classical Greek and Roman sculptures, including stolid busts, statues and friezes from Imperial Rome, but it is the **Egyptian artefacts** that really catch the eye. This wide-ranging collection features wall reliefs, statues, stele and sarcophagi from a variety of tombs and temples, plus a set of mummies as complete as you're likely to see outside Egypt. Particular highlights include the wonderfully ornate mummy cover of the priest Panehsy; magnificent stele from the temple at Abydos; and the exceptionally well-preserved double sculpture of *Maya and Merit*, Maya being the minister of finance under Tutankhamen, Merit his wife. Moving on, the top floor holds a Netherlands archeological section, which tracks through the history of the country from prehistoric to medieval times, but inevitably this suffers by comparison with what has gone before.

Hortus Botanicus

Further along Rapenburg, at no. 73, a three-sided courtyard complex includes – on the left – the building that became the university's first home, after previously being part of a medieval monastery. Through the courtyard is the **Hortus Botanicus** (April–Oct daily 10am–6pm; Nov–March Mon–Fri & Sun 10am–4pm; €5; Ⓦ www.hortusleiden.nl), lushly planted and subtly landscaped botanical gardens that stretch along the Witte Singel canal. Planted in 1587, this is one of the oldest botanical gardens in Europe, a mixture of carefully tended beds of shrubs and hothouses full of tropical foliage.

Pieterskerk

On the east side of Rapenburg, across from the botanical gardens, lies the network of narrow streets that once constituted the medieval town and now converges on the Gothic **Pieterskerk** (daily 1.30–4pm; free), Leiden's principal church. Deconsecrated now, it has an empty warehouse-like feel, but among the fixtures that remain are a simple and beautiful Renaissance rood screen and a host of memorials to the sundry notables buried here – including one to John Robinson (1575–1625), leader of the Pilgrim Fathers. Robinson lived in a house on the site of what is now the **Jean Pesijnshofje** at Kloksteeg 21, right beside the church. A curate in England at the turn of the seventeenth century, he was suspended from preaching in 1604, later fleeing with his congregation to pursue his Puritanism in the more amenable atmosphere of Calvinist Holland. Settling in Leiden, Robinson acted as pastor to growing numbers, but even here he found himself at odds with the religious establishment. In 1620, one hundred of his followers – the "**Pilgrim Fathers**" – sailed via Plymouth for the untrammelled wilderness of America, though Robinson died before he could join them; he's buried in the church.

The Stadhuis and the Waag

From the church, it's a short stroll east to **Breestraat**, marking the southern edge of Leiden's present commercial centre but undistinguished except for the **Stadhuis**, an imposing edifice whose Renaissance facade is a copy of the late sixteenth-century original destroyed by fire in 1929. Behind the Stadhuis, the canals that cut Leiden's centre into pocket-sized segments converge at the busiest point in town, tiny **Hoogstraat**, the focus of a vigorous general **market** on Wednesdays and Saturdays. Around Hoogstraat, a tangle of narrow bridges is flanked by a number of fetching buildings, ranging from overblown Art Nouveau department stores to modest terrace houses. Here also, on Vismarkt, is the **Waag**, built to a design by Pieter Post (1608–69) and fronted with a naturalistic frieze showing a merchant watching straining labourers. Post was a successful architect, but his artist brother Frans was even better known for his major contribution to the *Historia Naturalis Brasiliae*, an influential ethnographic study of eastern Brazil, a Dutch colony from 1630 to 1654.

The Hooglandsekerk and the Burcht

Stretching southeast from Vismarkt, the **Nieuwe Rijn** is one of the town's prettiest canals, the first of its several bridges topped off by a matching pair of Neoclassical porticoes dating from 1825. Turn left along Burgsteeg, and then right at the end for the **Hooglandsekerk** on Nieuwstraat (mid-May to mid-Sept Mon 1–5pm, Tues–Fri 11am–3.30pm, Sat 11am–4pm; free), a light and lofty Gothic structure built in stages over a couple of hundred years. The church holds a monument to Pieter van der Werff, the heroic burgomaster of Leiden at the time of the 1573–74 siege. When the situation became so desperate that the people were all for giving up, the burgomaster, no doubt remembering the massacre at Haarlem (see p.125), offered up his own body to be eaten. The invitation was declined, but it inspired new determination in the town's flagging citizens.

Doubling back to the end of Burgsteeg, go through the gateway and you'll soon pass the steps up to the top of the artificial mound where Leiden's first castle stood, though the stone remains that occupy the site today, known as the **Burcht** (daily 10am–10pm; free), are disappointingly paltry. At the far end of the alley is the **Oude Rijn** canal, on the other side of which lies the blandly pedestrian **Haarlemmerstraat**, the town's main shopping street.

The Stedelijk Museum de Lakenhal

From Haarlemmerstraat, it's a short walk north to Leiden's **Stedelijk Museum de Lakenhal** (Tues–Sun 10am–5pm, Sat & Sun noon–5pm; €4; Ⓦwww .lakenhal.nl), housed in the old Cloth Hall and its modern extension at Oude Singel 32. The museum's ground floor displays a healthy sample of local sixteenth- and seventeenth-century paintings, including examples of the work of Jacob van Swanenburgh (first teacher of the young Rembrandt), Jan Lievens (with whom Rembrandt shared a studio), and Gerrit Dou (1613–75), whose exquisite *Astrologer* is in Room 8. Rembrandt's first pupil, Dou, began by imitating his master but soon developed his own style, pioneering the Leiden

The Battle with the Sea

As your plane comes in to land at Schiphol it's worth remembering that two hundred years ago the runway would have been situated under a lake. Large parts of the country have been reclaimed from the sea and two-thirds of the country would be flooded without its dykes. Everywhere the Netherlands' land- and cityscapes are defined by this fact: its chequered farmland, divided by drainage ditches; the windmills that still speckle the skyline; and of course the canals that skewer the centres of most Dutch towns. It's testament to the ingenuity of the Dutch that they have turned these measures to their advantage: at the same time as ensuring the safety of their people they have created vital new land in what is one of the most congested countries in the world.

Water, water, everywhere

The first inhabitants of the land must have been a wretched but resourceful lot, gathering together in communities on higher ground, known as terpen, and catching fish in the flooded areas all around. Eventually, to protect themselves from flooding, the Dutch began to build dykes, and in order to cultivate the land efficiently they drained it by whatever means they could. They were still vulnerable, however, facing regular threats from breaks in the dykes, with some floods more disastrous than others. After the first St Elizabeth Day Flood of 1404, which mainly affected Zeeland, many dykes were reinforced, only to be breached again when North Sea storms flooded much of the drained land of South Holland and Zeeland with the second St Elizabeth Day Flood in 1421. This caused 10,000 casualties, and created the wetlands around Dordrecht, the Biesbosch, a strange, other-worldly area that you can still visit today. In 1916 the areas around the Zuider Zee were inundated, causing a number of fatalities, but the worst floods in recent memory took place in 1953, when on February 1 a combination of unusually high tides and heavy storms broke through the North Sea dykes twice, causing nearly 2000 deaths in Zeeland, North Brabant and South Holland, and displacing around 70,000 people. It's these two events, more than any others, that have determined Dutch water planning in the modern age.

Draining away

The first big drainage and land reclamation projects were undertaken in the early 1600s, and were the work of one Jan Adriaanszoon, an engineer who devised the method of draining land using windmills. He patented this in 1605, taking the name Leeghwater – literally "empty

water". Drained land became known as **"polders"**, and the first polder, the Beemster, north of Amsterdam, was completed in 1612. Leeghwater was also an advocate of draining of the large Haarlemermeer, to the south and west of Amsterdam, although this didn't happen until the 1850s. It's here, among the dormitory towns and suburbs of ever-expanding Amsterdam that they decided to site Schiphol in

▲ The IJsselmeer

1916 – now one of the largest airports in the world, and the most tangible testament to the Dutch success in taming their watery landscape.

The Zuider Zee

These days the **IJsselmeer** is a shallow lake that lies at the centre of the Netherlands, but it was formerly the **Zuider Zee**, or "southern sea" – an inlet of the North Sea that reached deep into Dutch territory and left its low-lying areas especially vulnerable to flooding. In 1932 the creation of the Afsluitdijk bridged the gap at the northern end and formally cut its connection to the sea, reclaiming land and creating the polderlands that unite western and eastern Netherlands. A massive project, the largest ever undertaken, the polders it created included the **Wieringermeer**, north of Enkhuizen, the **North East Polder**, drained in 1942, encompassing the two former islands of Schokland and Urk, and two large polders to the south, creating the new province of **Flevoland**, with its capital Lelystad. The final part of the plan for a new dyke joining Lelystad to Enkhuizen was begun in 1976. However, there was huge opposition to this from the towns north of Amsterdam who wanted to keep their coastal position, plus the money began to run out, and it was finally abandoned at the end of the last century, leaving just the new and separate lake and reservoir of the **Markermeer**.

The Delta Project

Planned after the inundation of Zeeland in 1953, the **Delta Project** is essentially a complicated series of new dams, designed to shorten the Dutch coastline in Zeeland and to

provide protection from high tides and storm surges. It was over thirty years in the making, partly because of the sheer size of the undertaking and partly because it ran into opposition from environmental groups concerned about local bird habitats and fishermen whose livelihoods were threatened. However, with the completion of the **Stormvloedkering** or "Storm Surge barrier", an ingenious gate designed to only shut when water levels are especially high, in 1986 it was finally finished, and has kept this part of the country safe ever since.

▲ The Delta Project

To drain or not to drain?

The Netherlands' success in overcoming the sea is an inspiring one. But it's also a story of delay and procrastination. The plan to dam and reclaim the Zuider Zee was hatched as long ago as 1667, but it wasn't until the early 1900s, and several floods later, that the Dutch parliament finally approved the scheme. Similarly with the Delta Project: it was known long before the devastating floods of 1953 that the safety of the people living in the low-lying areas of Zeeland and South Holland could not be guaranteed in the event of a major storm, but it took the disaster to force the Dutch government to take action.

And it's not over yet. Climate change means that in coming years the Netherlands may have to rise to meet new challenges. It's reckoned that the sea level around the country will rise by up to 90 centimetres in the next century; plus the ground is sinking, because of the Dutch success in draining it. And the threat isn't only from the sea. Higher rainfall – the summer of 2004 was the wettest since 1951 – could easily cause widespread flooding in an already waterlogged landscape.

On the water

In a country so defined by its relationship with water, it's no surprise that there are many opportunities for watersports. The lakes of Friesland are prime sailing territory, centring on the yachting centre of Sneek, and the IJsselmeer also provides a beautiful and sheltered area for sailing, with lots of safe harbours – and plenty of places that rent boats. The lakes south of Amsterdam and around Utrecht are good for windsurfing and gentle water-based activities, particularly around Loosdrecht, while the Frisian islands are popular with windsurfers – and more recently kitesurfers. Finally, of course, there are the canals countrywide, which provide waterborne holidays for nautical novices; lots of operators rent boats and, again, the best places are either up in Friesland, or in south Holland around Utrecht and Leiden.

tradition of small, minutely detailed pictures of enamel-like smoothness. There's also Lucas van Leyden's (1494–1533) alarming and spectacularly unsuccessful *Last Judgement* triptych in Room 6, several paintings devoted to the siege of 1574 and the heroics of burgomaster Werff, plus mixed rooms of furniture, silver, tiles, glass and ceramics. **Rembrandt** (1606–69) himself, though a native of Leiden, is poorly represented; he left his home town at the tender age of 14, and, although he returned in 1625, he was off again six years later, this time to settle permanently in Amsterdam. Only a handful of his Leiden paintings survive, but there's one here, *Agamemnon before Palamedes*, a stilted and rather unsuccessful rendition of the classical tale, painted in 1626.

The other floors of the museum are of cursory interest only: the first floor is devoted to Leiden textiles, the second is used for temporary exhibitions (which often increase the price of admission), and the top floor has a series of modest displays on the town's history.

The Windmill

West along Oude Singel from the Stedelijk Museum, and then right at the end it's a couple of hundred metres to the **Molenmuseum de Valk** (Valk Windmill Museum; Tues–Sat 10am–5pm, Sun 1–5pm; €3), a restored grain mill that is the last survivor of the twenty-odd windmills built on the town's outer fortifications in the eighteenth century. On the ground floor are the millers' living quarters, furnished in simple period style, while upstairs are several different displays, one of which is a slide show and exhibition recounting the history of Dutch windmills.

Eating and drinking

Leiden's crowded centre heaves with inexpensive **cafés** and **café-bars**, and there's a cluster of top-flight **restaurants** too. Many of the more interesting places are concentrated in the immediate vicinity of Pieterskerk, among the ancient brick houses that make up this especially pretty quarter of the city.

Barrera Rapenburg 56. A fashionable café-bar and student favourite with a good beer menu and a pavement terrace. Opposite the entrance to the Hortus Botanicus.

Koetshuis de Burcht Burgsteeg 13. Just below the Burcht, this busy bistro-style restaurant has a wide-ranging menu featuring all the Dutch (as well as some French) favourites. Daily noon–9.30pm.

La Bota Herensteeg 9 ☎071/514 6340. Popular, very informal restaurant serving up some of the best-value Dutch food in town as well as an excellent range of beers. Mains from €11. Daily 5–10pm.

La Cloche Kloksteeg 3 ☎071/512 3053. Small and smart French restaurant with a well-chosen

menu featuring local ingredients – try the Texel lamb (€24). Tues–Sat 5–10pm.

M'n Broer Kloksteeg 7 ☎071/512 5024. Agreeable, low-key café-restaurant kitted out in traditional style and offering a tasty range of light snacks and full meals, with Italian dishes high up on the agenda. Main courses €12–18, veggie options €11. Mon–Fri 6–10pm, Sat & Sun 5–10pm.

Water Lijn Café Turfmarkt. Modern, floating café, where the food is routine, if perfectly OK, but the views of the boats and barges on the busy Galgewater more than compensate.

North of Leiden: The Keukenhof gardens

If you're after bulbs, then make a beeline for the bulb growers' showcase, the **Keukenhof gardens** (late March to late May daily 8am–7.30pm; €12.50, ⓦ www.keukenhof.com), located on the edge of the little town of **LISSE**, beside the N208 about 15km north of Leiden. The largest flower gardens in the world, dating back to 1949, the Keukenhof was designed by a group of prominent bulb growers to convert people to the joys of growing flowers from bulbs in their own gardens. Literally the "kitchen garden", its site is the former estate of a fifteenth-century countess, who used to grow herbs and vegetables for her dining table. Several million flowers are on show for their full flowering period, complemented, in case of especially harsh winters, by thousands of square metres of glasshouse holding indoor displays. You could easily spend a whole day here, swooning with the sheer abundance of it all, but to get the best of it you need to come early, before the tour buses pack the place. There are several restaurants in the grounds, and a network of well-marked footpaths explores every horticultural nook and cranny.

To get to the Keukenhof by **public transport** from Leiden, catch **bus #54** (every 30min; 30min) from the main bus station. To get there from Haarlem, the easiest way is to take the train to Leiden (every 20min; 20min) and then the bus.

Northwest of Leiden: Katwijk-aan-Zee

Leiden is just a few kilometres from the North Sea coast, where the prime target is **KATWIJK-AAN-ZEE**, an amenable little resort whose low-slung houses string along behind a wide sandy beach with a pristine expanse of beach and dune beckoning beyond – and stretching south towards Scheveningen (see p.184). Here and there, a row of cottages recalls the time when Katwijk was a busy fishing village, but there are no real sights as such with the possible exception of a chunky, old **lighthouse**, by the beach on the southern edge of the resort, and the Katwijk sluices, on the north side of Katwijk. Completed in 1807, this chain of sluice gates regulates the flow of the Oude Rijn as it

---

The Dutch bulbfields

The pancake-flat fields stretching north from Leiden towards Haarlem (see p.125) are the heart of the Dutch **bulbfields**, whose bulbs and blooms support a billion-euro industry and some ten thousand growers, as well as attracting tourists in their droves. Bulbs have flourished here since the late sixteenth century, when one **Carolus Clusius**, a Dutch botanist and one-time gardener to the Habsburg emperor, brought the first **tulip bulb** over from Vienna, where it had – in its turn – been brought from Asia Minor by an Austrian aristocrat. The tulip flourished in Holland's sandy soil and was so highly prized that it fuelled a massive **speculative bubble**. At the height of the boom – in the mid-1630s – bulbs were commanding extraordinary prices: the artist Jan van Goyen paid 1900 guilders and two paintings for ten rare bulbs, while a bag of one hundred bulbs was swapped for a coach and horses. When the government finally intervened in 1636, the industry returned to reality with a bang, leaving hundreds of investors ruined – much to the satisfaction of the country's Calvinist ministers who had long railed against the excesses.

Other types of bulbs apart from the tulip have also been introduced, and nowadays the spring flowering season begins in mid-March with **crocuses**, followed by **daffodils** and yellow **narcissi** in late March, **hyacinths** and **tulips** from mid-April through to May, and **gladioli** in August. The views of the bulbfields from any of the trains heading southwest from Schiphol airport can often be sufficient in themselves, the fields divided into stark geometric blocks of pure colour, but, with your own transport – either cycle or car – you can take in their particular beauty by way of special routes marked by hexagonal signposts; local VVVs sell pamphlets describing the routes in detail. You could also drop by the bulb growers' showpiece, the **Keukenhof** gardens (see p.169). Bear in mind also that there are any number of local flower festivals and parades in mid- to late April; every local VVV has the details of these too.

approaches the sea. Around high tide, the gates are closed, and when they are reopened the pressure of the accumulated water brushes aside the sand deposited at the mouth of the river. This simple system has effectively fixed the course of the Oude Rijn, which for centuries had been continually diverted by the sand deposits, flooding the surrounding area with depressing regularity.

Katwijk is a thirty-minute **bus** ride from Leiden bus station (every 15min, half-hourly on Sunday). The resort's **VVV** is on the main street, a short walk from the beach at Voorstraat 41 (Mon–Fri 10am–5.30pm, Sat 9.30am–5pm; ☎071/407 5444, ⓦwww.hollandrijnland.nl). They have a supply of **rooms** in private houses (❶), as well as a list of hotels and pensions, but even they may struggle to find a vacancy in July and August.

Den Haag

DEN HAAG (The Hague) is markedly different from any other Dutch city. In a country built on civic independence and munificence, it's been the focus of national institutions since the sixteenth century, but it is not – curiously enough – the capital, which is Amsterdam. Frequently disregarded until the development of central government in the nineteenth century, Den Haag's older buildings are a comparatively subdued and modest collection, with little of Amsterdam's flamboyance. Indeed, the majority of the canal houses are demurely classical and exude that sense of sedate prosperity which prompted Matthew Arnold's harsh estimation of 1859: "I never saw a city where the well-to-do classes seemed to have given the whole place so much of their own air of wealth, finished cleanliness, and comfort; but I never saw one, either, in which my heart would so have sunk at the thought of living."

Nevertheless, much has changed since Arnold's days. His "well-to-do classes" – now mostly diplomats and top-flight executives – are still in evidence, inflating city-centre prices, but parts of the centre are now festooned with slick government high-rises and, more promisingly, Den Haag now holds a slew of lively and reasonably priced bars and restaurants. A creative city council has done much to jazz the city up, too, organizing a lively programme of concerts and events, and it boasts a veritable battery of outstanding museums, principally the wonderful Dutch paintings of the **Mauritshuis**, and more modern works of art at the **Gemeentemuseum**. Den Haag is also a brief tram ride from **Scheveningen**, a sprawling kiss-me-quick resort with a long, sandy beach.

Arrival, information and city transport

The city has two **train stations**: Den Haag HS (Hollands Spoor) and Den Haag CS (Centraal Station). Of the two, Den Haag CS is the more convenient, sited five minutes' walk east of the town centre; Den Haag HS is 1km to the south. There are frequent rail services between the two as well as trams from Den Haag HS to the centre – several services make the five-minute journey, so check the destination sign before hopping on.

Den Haag's main **VVV** is right in the centre of the city, a five- to ten-minute walk west from Den Haag CS at Hofweg 1 (Mon–Fri 10am–6pm, Sat 10am–5pm, Sun noon–5pm; ☎0900/340 3505 premium line, ⓦwww.denhaag.com). They provide a wide range of information on the city and its surroundings, will help with accommodation and stock several free listings magazines.

Most of the city's principal sights are in or within easy walking distance of the centre, but this is the country's third-largest city and you may need to catch a

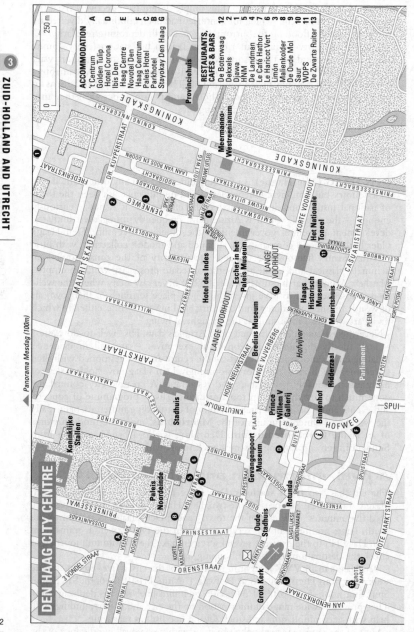

DEN HAAG CITY CENTRE

▲ Panorama Mesdag (100m)

ACCOMMODATION

't Centrum	A
Golden Tulip	D
Hotel Corona	D
Ibis Den	E
Haag Centre	E
Novotel Den	F
Haag Centrum	C
Paleis Hotel	B
Parkhotel	B
Stayokay Den Haag	G

RESTAURANTS, CAFÉS & BARS

De Boterwaag	12
Deksels	2
Djawa	1
HNM	5
De Landman	4
Le Café Hathor	7
Le Haricot Vert	6
Limón	3
Malienkolder	8
De Oude Mol	9
Saur	10
WDPS	11
De Zwarte Ruiter	13

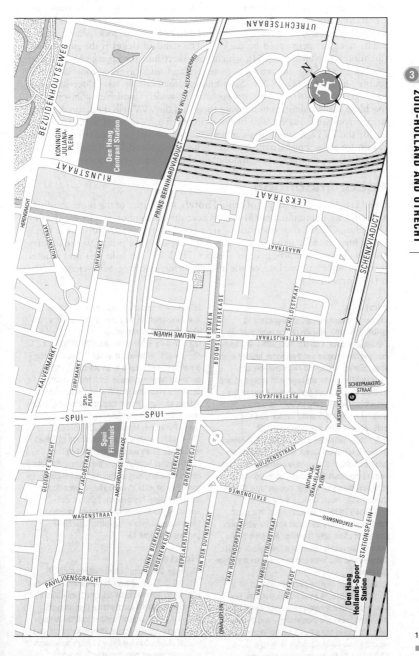

3

tram or bus if you're after visiting the more outlying attractions. The twin hubs of the tram system, which covers most of where you're likely to want to go, are Centraal Station and the Spui, in the centre of town just south of the VVV. The city and its immediate environs are divided into twelve or so zones, shown on the public transport map issued by the VVV. The standard **ticket** is the *strippenkaart* (for more on which, see p.34), which you insert into the appropriate franking machine, cancelling one strip per passenger and one for every zone crossed: a journey from Den Haag CS to Scheveningen, for example, takes three strips per passenger per journey. The *strippenkaart* is widely available: coin-operated machines at the train stations dispense them and the VVV sells them too. A three-strip *strippenkaart* costs €1.60, a fifteen-strip one €6.70. To avoid all this stamping, go for the VVV's *dagkaart* (day-card; €5.90), which grants unlimited use of the system for a day. Finally, tram #1 links Scheveningen and Den Haag with Delft (see p.184), an alternative to – and slightly cheaper than – the train.

Accommodation

Den Haag has a good supply of central **hotels**, with many of the more comfortable (and sometimes luxurious) dotted near the Binnenhof, just to the west of Den Haag CS. Advance reservations are a good idea especially during the week when business folk arrive in numbers, pushing up hotel prices: weekend rates are usually around thirty percent cheaper. The VVV can help you find a hotel room in either Den Haag or the neighbouring resort of Scheveningen (see p.184) for a small fee.

Hotels

Carlton Ambassador Hotel Sophialaan 2 ☎070/363 0363, ⊛www.carlton.nl/ambassador. Deluxe, executive, four-star hotel with every mod-con you can imagine and then some, located in an immaculately maintained nineteenth-century mansion. The rooms are large, well appointed, and all decorated in plush, period style. Banquet-like breakfasts included and an open-air terrace. Sophialaan is a smart residential avenue about 1km north of the centre (see map p.180). ❻

't Centrum Veenkade 5 ☎070/346 3657, ⊛www .hotelhetcentrum.nl. Small, unassuming but cosy two-star hotel in a three-storey terrace house just west of the Paleis Noordeinde. All the rooms are en suite and decorated in neat modern style. ❷

Golden Tulip Hotel Corona Buitenhof 39 ☎070/363 7930, ⊛www.corona.nl. In a great location just across the street from the Binnenhof, this smart chain hotel has large and extremely comfortable double rooms at a rack rate of €170, but weekend discounts and special deals are often available. ❹

Ibis Den Haag Centre Jan Hendrikstraat 10 ☎070/318 4318, ⊛www.accorhotels.com. Few would say that Ibis hotels have much character, but they are reliable and inexpensive – and this one with 200 rooms has a handy central location too. ❶

Novotel Den Haag Centrum Hofweg 5 ☎070/364 8846, ⊛www.accorhotels.com.

Efficient, four-star chain hotel with very comfortable rooms right in the centre of things, across the street from the Binnenhof. ❹

Paleis Hotel Molenstraat 26 ☎070/362 4621, ⊛www.paleishotel.nl. This charming, privately owned hotel is in an old, mostly eighteenth-century town house. Each of the twenty bedrooms is decorated with style and panache – antique furniture, French fabrics and so forth. Great central location as well. ❻

Parkhotel Molenstraat 53 ☎070/362 4371, ⊛www.parkhoteldenhaag.nl. Smart and immaculately maintained chain hotel in a handy central location. From the outside, the hotel doesn't look anything special, but the interior is graced by all sorts of wonderful Art Deco flourishes. The hotel has over one hundred well-appointed rooms decorated in brisk modern style. Some rooms overlook the Paleis Noordeinde gardens next door. ❺

Hostel

Stayokay Den Haag Scheepmakersstraat 27 ☎070/315 78 88, ⊛www.stayokay.com. This large and comfortable HI hostel is located just 400m east of – and across the canal from – Den Haag HS station. A good range of facilities includes luggage and bicycle storage, a café, Internet terminals, and a small library. Doubles ❶; €21 (€25 mid-March to Oct) for a dorm bed; breakfast is included.

The city centre

The prettiest spot in the centre of Den Haag – and the logical place to start a visit – is the north side of the **Hofvijver** (Court Pond), a placid lakelet that mirrors the attractive, vaguely Ruritanian symmetries of the extensive **Binnenhof** (Inner Court) beyond. Long home to the country's bicameral parliament, the Binnenhof occupies the site of the medieval castle where Den Haag began. The first fortress was raised by William II, Count of Holland – hence the city's official name, *'s Gravenhage*, literally "Count's Hedge", but more precisely "Count's Domain". William's descendants became the region's most powerful family, simultaneously acting as Stadholders (effectively provincial governors) of most of the seven United Provinces, which rebelled against the Habsburgs in the sixteenth century. In due course, one of the family, Prince Maurice of Orange-Nassau (1567–1625), established his main residence in Den Haag, which had effectively become the country's political capital. As the embodiment of central rather than municipal power, the Binnenhof was at times feted, at others virtually ignored, until the nineteenth century when Den Haag officially shared political capital status with Brussels during the uneasy times of the United Kingdom of the Netherlands (1815–30). Thereafter it became the seat of government and home to a functioning legislature.

The lack of prestige in the low-slung brick buildings of the Binnenhof long irked Dutch parliamentarians and finally, in 1992, they moved into a flashy new extension next door. Without the politicians, the original Binnenhof became somewhat redundant, but it's still an eye-pleasing architectural ensemble, comprising a broadly rectangular complex built around two connecting court-yards. The main sight as such is the **Ridderzaal** (Knights' Hall), an imposing twin-turreted structure that looks distinctly church-like, but was built as a banqueting hall for Count William's son, Floris V, in the thirteenth century. Now used for state occasions, it's been a courtroom, market and stable, and so often renovated that little of the original remains, but there are regular guided tours

△ The Binnenhof, Den Haag

leaving from the information office round the side at Binnenhof 8 (Mon–Sat 10am–4pm, last tour 3.45pm; 30min; €5; ⓦwww.binnenhofbezoek.nl).

The Mauritshuis

To the immediate east of the Binnenhof, the **Mauritshuis**, Korte Vijverberg 8 (Tues–Sat 10am–5pm, Sun 11am–5pm; April–Sept also Mon 10am–5pm; €9.50; ☎070/302 3435, ⓦwww.mauritshuis.nl), is located in an elegant seventeenth-century mansion. The gallery is famous for its eclectic collection of Flemish and Dutch paintings from the fifteenth to the eighteenth century, based on the hoard accumulated by Prince William V of Orange (1748–1806). The collection has examples of the work of all the major Dutch artists, but the Mauritshuis runs an ambitious programme of temporary exhibitions, so quite what paintings are on display – and in which room – varies enormously. Neither are the rooms numbered, except on the free map issued at reception, which can be confusing, though the museum is not large – just two medium-sized floors – and multilingual cards in many of the rooms give the artistic lowdown. The **museum entrance** is on the east side of the building in the basement; from here, you head up the stairs to reach the **ground floor**, where the medieval paintings are usually displayed; the later paintings either share the same floor or are exhibited on the **upper floor**. The description below focuses on those key paintings from the permanent collection you can expect to see. Finally, the museum shop sells an excellent guidebook detailing the permanent collection for €12.50 and you can book your own one-hour **guided tour** with the Mauritshuis for €50.

The ground floor

On the ground floor, the room to the left (east) of the old front doors usually holds a small but exquisite sample of late medieval Flemish art. Highlights include *Portrait of a Man* by **Hans Memling** (1440–94), a typically observant work, right down to the scar on the nose, and *The Lamentation of Christ* by **Rogier van der Weyden** (1400–64), a harrowing picture of death and sorrow. Weyden has Christ's head hanging down toward the earth, surrounded by the faces of the mourners, each with a particular expression of anguish and pain. Here also should be *Descent from the Cross* by **Quentin Matsys** (1465–1530), in which Christ's suffering body, bent under the weight of the Cross, is contrasted with the grinning, taunting onlookers behind. An influential figure, Matsys was the first major artist to work in Antwerp, where he was made a Master of the Guild in 1519.

Proceeding in a counterclockwise direction, through a series of rooms on either side of the Italianate dining room, you should soon spy a giant allegorical canvas by Jan Sanders van Hemessen (1500–66) and **Lucas Cranach the Younger**'s (1515–86) piercing *Man with a Red Beard*. There are also the busy, stick-like figures of *Winter Scene* by **Hendrick Avercamp** (1585–1634), an artist from Kampen, and two fine canvases by **Hans Holbein the Younger** (1497–1543): a striking *Portrait of Robert Cheeseman*, where all the materials – the fur collar, the falcon's feathers and the cape – seem to take on the appropriate texture; and a *Portrait of Jane Seymour*, one of several pictures commissioned by Henry VIII, who sent Holbein abroad to paint matrimonial candidates. Holbein's vibrant technique was later to land him in hot water: an over-flattering portrait of Anne of Cleves swayed Henry into an unhappy marriage with his "Flanders mare" that was to last only six months.

The gallery holds three paintings by **Adriaen Brouwer** (1605–38), two of which – *Fighting Peasants* and *Inn with Drunken Peasants* – are typical of his style, with thick, rough brushstrokes recording contemporary Flemish lowlife. Brouwer could approach this subject with some authority, as he spent most of his brief life in either a tavern or prison. **Peter Paul Rubens** (1577–1640), the acclaimed painter and diplomat, was a contemporary of Brouwer, though the two could hardly be more dissimilar. Rubens moved in much more elevated circles and his *Portrait of Michael Ophovius*, a leading churchman, is a rather formal, somewhat statuesque work, not nearly as intriguing as the dappled, evocative shade and light of his *Old Woman and a Boy with Candles*.

Rubens' chief assistant was **Anthony van Dyck** (1599–1641), a portrait specialist who found fame at the court of the English king Charles I. His *Peeter Stevens of Antwerp* and *Anna Wake* are good examples of his tendency to flatter and ennoble – which doubtless helped his career prospects no end. Also demonstrating the influence of Rubens are two canvases by **Jacob Jordaens** (1593–1678), the more robust of which is the *Adoration of the Shepherds*.

The upper floor

The Mauritshuis owns no fewer than twelve paintings by **Rembrandt** (1606–69) and these are almost always exhibited on the upper floor. Pride of place among them goes to the *Anatomy Lesson of Dr Tulp*, the artist's first commission in Amsterdam, dating from 1632. The peering pose of the students who lean over the corpse solved the problem of emphasis falling on the body rather than the subjects of the portrait, who were members of the surgeons' guild. Hopefully Tulp's skills as an anatomist were better than his medical advice, which included the recommendation that his patients drink fifty cups of tea a day. Very different is the artist's hauntingly gloomy *Saul and David*, completed when Rembrandt was in his 40s.

Look out also for *Young Bull* by **Paulus Potter** (1625–54), a massive canvas that includes the smallest details, from the exact hang of the testicles to the dung at the rear end, while **Frans Hals** (1582–1666) chimes in with the broad brush-strokes of *Laughing Boy* – a far cry from the restrained style he was forced to adopt in his famous paintings of the Haarlem gentry. By contrast, **Gerard Ter Borch** (1617–81) concentrated on domestic scenes with a sentimental undertow, as in the *Lice Hunt* and the *Woman Writing a Letter*, whereas Delft's **Gerard Houckgeest** specialized in church interiors, like *The Tomb of William of Orange*, a minutely observed study of architectural lines lightened by expanses of white marble.

Carel Fabritius (1622–54), a pupil of Rembrandt and (possibly) a teacher of Vermeer, was killed in a gunpowder explosion at Delft when he was only 22. Few canvases of his survive but an exquisite exception is *The Goldfinch*, a curious, almost impressionistic work, with the bird reduced to a blur of colour. The Fabritius is usually displayed in the same room as two of the museum's most trumpeted paintings, **Johannes Vermeer's** (1632–75) *Girl with a Pearl Earring* and the same artist's *View of Delft*. The former is not – as is often thought – a portrait, but a "tronie", that is an illustration of a mood or emotion based on a real-life model. In this particular case, the girl looks back over her shoulder expectantly, wide-eyed and with her lips parted, the turban on her head and the sheer size of her earring suggesting her exoticism – as distinct from the rest of her attire, which is ordinary and workaday: Dutch women of the time just did not wear turbans or large pearl earrings. The second Vermeer, the superb and somehow thrilling *View of Delft*, is similarly deceptive: the fine lines of the city are pictured beneath a cloudy sky, a patchwork of varying light and shade, but once again all is not quite what it seems. The painting may look like the epitome of realism, but in fact Vermeer doctored what he saw to fit in with the needs of his canvas, straightening here, lengthening there, to emphasize the horizontal. Interestingly, the detached vision implicit in the painting has prompted some experts – like Wilenski – to suggest that Vermeer viewed his subject through a fixed reducing lens or maybe even a mirror.

Finally, dotted throughout the museum are no fewer than fourteen paintings by **Jan Steen** (1625–79), including a wonderfully riotous picture carrying the legend "The way you hear it, is the way you sing it" – a parable on the young learning bad habits from the old – and a typically salacious *Girl Eating Oysters*.

The Haags Historisch Museum

Strolling north from the Mauritshuis, it's a few metres to the **Haags Historisch Museum**, Korte Vijverberg 7 (City Historical Museum; Tues–Fri 10am–5pm, Sat & Sun noon–5pm; €4; ⓦwww.haagshistorischmuseum.nl), which occupies a handsome Neoclassical mansion that was originally home to the city's leading militia company, the so-called Archers of St Sebastian. The museum's various displays trace the convoluted history of the city in particular and the country in general, but it's the paintings that catch the eye, most notably those by Jan Steen and his father-in-law, Jan van Goyen (1596–1656). A pioneer of realistic landscape painting, Goyen is especially well represented by the tonal palette and earthy hues of his *River View with Sentry Post*.

Lange Voorhout

Across the street from the Historical Museum are the trees and cobblestones of **Lange Voorhout**, a wide L-shaped street-cum-square overlooked by a string of ritzy Neoclassical mansions, many of which have become embassies and consulates. Most conspicuous is the *Hotel des Indes*, an opulent hotel where the ballerina Anna Pavlova died in 1931 and where today you stand a fair chance of being flattened by a chauffeur-driven limousine. Just up along the square, at no. 74, the **Escher in het Paleis Museum** (Tues–Sun 11am–5pm; €7.50; ⓦwww.escherinhetpaleis.nl) occupies another of these grand mansions and was a favourite royal residence from 1901 to 1934. Nowadays, it's devoted to the vibrantly kaleidoscopic work of the Dutch graphic artist, M.C. Escher (1898–1972).

Museum Bredius

Doubling back to the north side of Lange Vijverberg, it's only a couple of minutes' walk to the delightful **Museum Bredius**, Lange Vijverberg 14 (Tues–Sun noon–5pm; €4.50; ⓦwww.museumbredius.nl), which displays the collection of paintings bequeathed to the city by art connoisseur and one-time director of the Mauritshuis, Abraham Bredius, in 1946. Squeezed together in this fine old house, with its stuccowork and splendid staircase, are some exquisite paintings, notably two canvases by **Rembrandt**, a *Christ's Head* and a *Raising of the Cross*, whose glutinous paintwork forms one of the artist's darkest, most melancholic works. Among the genre paintings is a characteristic *Boar Hunt* by **Roelandt Savery** (1576–1639), all green foliage and fighting beasts, and the careful draughtsmanship of **Aert van de Neer** (1603–77) in his *Winter Landscape*. There are also two noteworthy paintings by **Jan Steen**, the fruity *Couple in a Bedchamber* and the curious *Satyr and the Peasant*, a representation of a well-known Aesop fable in which the satyr, sitting at the table with his hosts, is bemused by human behaviour. The creature's confusion is symbolically represented by the surrounding figures – the man blowing on his soup to cool it down, the woman with the basket of fruit on her head.

Museum Gevangenpoort

A short walk from the Bredius Museum, on the west side of the Hofvijver, the **Museum Gevangenpoort**, Buitenhof 33 (Prison Gate Museum; guided tours only: Tues–Fri 10am–5pm, Sat & Sun noon–5pm; hourly tours on the hour, last tour 4pm; €4; Ⓦ www.gevangenpoort.nl), occupies the old town prison, which is itself squeezed into one of Den Haag's medieval, fortified gates. The big pull here is the museum's collection of instruments of torture, interrogation and punishment, which – for some unaccountable reason – goes down a storm with visiting school parties. Several of the prison's old cells have survived too, including the *ridderkamer* for the more privileged captives. Here Cornelis de Witt, Burgomaster of Dordrecht, was imprisoned before he and his brother Johan, another staunch Republican and leader of the States of Holland, were dragged out and murdered by an Orangist mob in 1672. The brothers were shot, beheaded and cut into pieces that were then auctioned to the crowd; Johan's tongue can be seen in the Haags Historisch Museum, along with the toe of poor old Cornelis.

Galerij Prince Willem V

Just along the street at Buitenhof 35, the **Galerij Prins Willem V** (closed for refurbishment at the time of writing) was created in 1773 as the private picture gallery of the eponymous prince and Stadholder of the United Provinces. On display is a diverting collection of seventeenth-century paintings including examples of the work of the prolific Jan Steen as well as Jacob Jordaens and Paulus Potter. There's also the folksy *Girl with a Lamp* by Gerard Dou (1613–75), a pupil and companion of the young Rembrandt, and one of Willem van de Velde's (1633–1707) most successful maritime paintings, the *Warship at Sunset*. However, the gallery is perhaps more interesting as an example of an eighteenth-century "cabinet" picture gallery: the fashion then was to sandwich paintings together in a cramped patchwork from floor to ceiling, and this is precisely how it is arranged, though this does make viewing a trifle difficult for eyes more used to spacious modern galleries.

The Oude Stadhuis and Grote Kerk

The cobweb of narrow, mostly humdrum streets and squares stretching west of the Buitenhof zeros in on the flamboyant Dutch Renaissance facade of the sixteenth-century **Oude Stadhuis** (Old City Hall), a good-looking affair complete with mullioned windows, shutters and decorative carvings. To the rear are the plodding symmetries of a later extension, and next door rises St Jacobskerk, or the **Grote Kerk** (July & Aug Mon–Fri 11am–4pm; free; Ⓦ www .grotekerkdenhaag.nl). Dating from the middle of the fifteenth century and easily the best of Den Haag's old churches, the building's cavernous interior, with its three naves of equal height, has an exhilarating sense of breadth and handsome timber vaulting. Like most Dutch churches, it's short on decoration, but there are one or two highlights, notably the **stained-glass windows** in the choir ambulatory. Two are particularly exquisite and may well be the work of Dirk Crabeth, one of the craftsmen responsible for the windows in Gouda's St Janskerk (see p.200). Of the two, one depicts the Annunciation, the other shows the Virgin descending from heaven to show the infant Jesus to a kneeling Emperor Charles V, who footed the bill for the windows. Nearby, in the choir, stands a memorial to Admiral Jacob van Opdam, who was blown up with his ship during the little-remembered naval battle of Lowestoft in 1665. Also look out for the Renaissance pulpit: similar to the one in Delft's Oude Kerk (see p.188), it has carved panels framing the apostles in false perspective. The church is also open when it hosts art exhibitions and is used for classical music concerts throughout the year.

From the Grote Kerk, it's a short walk north to the sixteenth- and seventeenth-century **Paleis Noordeinde** (no public access), the grandest of several royal buildings that lure tourists onto the expensive "Royal Tours" of Den Haag and its surroundings. Outside the palace's main entrance, on Noordeinde, is a jaunty equestrian statue of Holland's main hero, William the Silent.

North of the city centre

Ten minutes' walk north of the Paleis Noordeinde, and accessible by tram #10 from Centraal Station and tram #1 and #10 from the Buitenhof, the **Panorama Mesdag**, Zeestraat 65 (Mon–Sat 10am–5pm, Sun noon–5pm; €5; Ⓦ www .panorama-mesdag.com), was designed in the late nineteenth century by Hendrik Mesdag (1831–1915), banker-turned-painter and local citizen-become-Hague School luminary. For the most part, Mesdag painted unremarkable seascapes tinged with a bourgeois sentimentality, but there's no denying the achievement of his panorama, a depiction of Scheveningen as it appeared in

1881. Completed in four months with help from his wife and the young George Hendrik Breitner (1857–1923), the painting is so naturalistic that it takes a few moments for the skills of lighting and perspective to become apparent, though the wearing canvas is in need of some tender care.

Museum Mesdag and the Peace Palace

From the panorama, it's another ten-minute walk north to the house Mesdag bought as a home and gallery at Laan van Meerdervoort 7f, now the **Museum Mesdag** (Tues–Sun noon–5pm; €5; ⓦ www.museummesdag.nl). At the time, Mesdag had a view over the dunes, the inspiration for many of his canvases, but the house and its environs were gobbled up by the city long ago and today it is visited for its easily assimilated collection of nineteenth- and early twentieth-century paintings, especially those of the Hague School, whose artists – like Mesdag – took local land and seascapes as their favourite subject. The Dutch canvases are supplemented by a modest collection of French paintings from the likes of Corot, Rousseau, Delacroix and Millet, though none of them represents the artists at their peak.

Round the corner from the Mesdag Museum, framing the Carnegieplein, the **Vredespaleis**, or Peace Palace (guided tours usually Mon–Fri 10am, 11am, 2pm, 3pm & 4pm; €5; advance reservations required on ☏070/302 4137, ⓦ www.vredespaleis.nl) is home to the International Court of Justice, the principal judicial organ of the United Nations, and, for all the wrong reasons, a monument to the futility of war. Toward the end of the nineteenth century, Tsar Nicholas II called an international conference for the peaceful reconciliation of national problems. The result was the First Hague Peace Conference of 1899, whose purpose was to "help find a lasting peace and, above all, a way of limiting the progressive development of existing arms". This in turn led to the formation of a Permanent Court of Arbitration housed obscurely in Den Haag until the American industrialist Andrew Carnegie gave $1.5 million for a large new building – the Peace Palace. These honourable aims came to nothing with the onset of World War I: just as the donations of tapestries, urns, marble and stained glass were arriving from all over the world, so Europe's military commanders were preparing their offensives. Backed by a massive law library, fifteen judges still sit today, conducting trade matters in English and diplomatic affairs in French. Widely respected and generally considered neutral, their judgments are nevertheless not binding.

To reach the Peace Palace and the Museum Mesdag by **public transport**, take tram #10 from Centraal Station or tram #1 and #10 from the Buitenhof.

Gemeentemuseum Den Haag

About 1.5km northwest of the Peace Palace, the **Gemeentemuseum Den Haag**, Stadhouderslaan 41 (Tues–Sun 11am–5pm; €8; ⓦ www.gemeentemuseum .nl), reached by tram #17 from Centraal Station and the Buitenhof, is easily the largest and most diverse of Den Haag's many museums. Designed by Hendrik Petrus Berlage (1856–1934) and completed in 1935, the building itself is often regarded as his masterpiece, an austere but particularly appealing structure with brick facings superimposed on a concrete shell. Inside, the museum displays a regularly rotated selection from its vast permanent collection and also offers an ambitious, headline-making programme of temporary exhibitions. Among much else, there is a large and diverting section on fashion, another devoted to old musical instruments, and a third concentrating on the decorative arts, including an especially fine Delft pottery collection. The modern art section outlines the development of painting since the early nineteenth century and although the bulk of the paintings are Dutch, there's a liberal sprinkling of international artists too. The museum is especially strong on the land and seascape painters of the **Hague School**, which flourished here in the city from 1860 to 1900, and the **De Stijl** movement, that loose but influential group of Dutch painters, sculptors, designers and architects who developed their version – and vision – of modern art and society between the two world wars. The museum has the world's largest collection of paintings from the most famous member of the group, **Piet Mondrian** (1872–1944), and although much of it consists of unfamiliar early works, painted before he evolved the abstraction of form into geometry and pure colour for which he's best known, it does possess *Victory Boogie Woogie*, his last and – some say – finest work.

On the same campus as the Gemeentemuseum, at Stadhouderslaan 43, is **GEM, Museum voor Actuele Kunst** (Tues–Sun noon–6pm; €5; ⓦwww .gem-online.nl), a gallery of contemporary art featuring an enterprising programme of temporary exhibitions. In the same complex – and costing no extra – is the **Fotomuseum** (Photography Museum; same hours; ⓦwww .fotomuseumdenhaag.com), which puts on a minimum of four exhibitions a year and in between times displays photographs from the Gemeentemuseum's permanent collection.

Also on the Gemeentemuseum campus, at Stadhouderslaan 37, is the **Museon** (Tues–Sun 11am–5pm; €7.50, children under 12 years €4; ⓦwww.museon.nl), a sequence of non-specialist exhibitions dealing with human activities and the history of the earth – everything from rock formations to the use of tools. Self-consciously internationalist, it's aimed at school parties, as is the neighbouring **Omniversum**, at President Kennedylaan 5 (Mon noon–5pm, Tues–Wed 10am–5pm, Thurs–Sun 10am–10pm; €9, children under 12 years €7.50; programme on ⓣ0900/666 4837 premium line, ⓦwww.omniversum.nl), an IMAX cinema in all but name.

The Madurodam miniature town

Halfway between Den Haag and Scheveningen, the **Madurodam miniature town** (daily: April–June 9am–8pm; July & Aug 9am–11pm; Sept–March 9am–6pm; €12.50, children under 12 years €9; ⓦwww.madurodam.nl), reachable on tram #9 from Centraal Station, is heavily plugged hereabouts, though its origins are more interesting than the rather trite and expensive present, a stylized version of a Dutch town constructed on a 1:25 scale. The money was put up by one J.M.L. Maduro, who wished to establish a memorial to his son, George, who had distinguished himself during the Nazi invasion of 1940 and died in Dachau concentration camp five years later. There's a memorial to him just by the entrance, and profits from the Miniature Town are still used for general Dutch social and cultural activities. The replica town itself is extremely popular – so be prepared to queue.

Eating and drinking

Den Haag has an excellent range of **restaurants**, and although some are aimed squarely at the expense account, many more are very affordable, with main courses hovering between €15 and €20. There is a cluster of first-rate places just beyond Lange Voorhout along and around Denneweg and Frederikstraat, and another on Molenstraat, near the Paleis Noordeinde: frankly, you need look no further. These two areas are good for **cafés** and **café-bars** too, though the liveliest **bars** are concentrated on and around the Grote Markt, south of the Grote Kerk, and the Plein, near the Mauritshuis.

Restaurants

Dekxels Denneweg 130 ☎070/365 9788. This highly recommended, coolly decorated, chic restaurant serves a superb range of international and Dutch dishes. Main courses average €22. Daily 5.30–10/11pm.

Djawa Mallemolen 12a ☎070/363 5763. A favourite with many locals, this long-established Indonesian restaurant offers a tasty range of traditional dishes in smart, modern premises. Full meals for around €30. Mon–Sat 5.30–11pm.

HNM Molenstraat 21 ☎070/365 6553. Imaginatively decorated café serving a tasty range of Dutch, Indonesian, French and Italian snacks and meals. The daily specials are especially good value, beginning at just €10. No mobiles. Daily noon–3.30pm & 5.30–9.30pm.

Le Haricot Vert Molenstraat 9 ☎070/365 2278. Cosy French restaurant decorated in traditional bistro style. All the classics and then some. Main courses in the region of €20–25. Daily 6–11pm.

Limón Denneweg 39a ☎070/356 1465. Pastel-painted Spanish tapas restaurant catering to a fashionable, youngish crowd. Good food – though admittedly not all the tapas turn out as well as each other; a very popular spot. Tapas from as little as €3. Daily 5–11pm, midnight at weekends.

Malienkolder Maliestraat 9 ☎070/364 5542. Inexpensive, informal bistro-style restaurant with a tasty range of French and Dutch dishes. A few metres from the end of Denneweg. Mains from €15. Tues–Sun 5–10.30pm.

Saur Lange Voorhout 47 ☎070/346 2565. This smart and formal, old-fashioned restaurant, with its Art Deco flourishes and French menu, serves some of the best steaks in town. The attached brasserie is a new, ultra-modern and informal addition – and the steaks are just as good. Main courses average €25. Mon–Fri noon–2.30pm & 6–10.30pm, Sat 6–10.30pm.

WDPS Schouwburgstraat 4 ☎070/356 1122. Fashionable (in an alternative sort of way) café-restaurant in deep, dark premises not far from the Mauritshuis. Serves up a wide range of reasonably priced Dutch favourites plus veggie and pasta dishes. WPDS stands for "Wat De Pot Schaft" – "Whatever is left in the pot". Main courses €12–16. Mon–Sat 5.30–10.30/11.30pm.

Café-bars and bars

De Boterwaag Grote Markt 8a. Immensely appealing café-bar housed in an old and cavernous brick-vaulted weigh house. It's very popular with a youthful crowd and offers a wide range of beers as well as inexpensive bar food, though this hardly inspires the palate. Large terrace, which fills up quick when the sun pops out.

De Landman Denneweg 48. Mellow brown(ish) bar near the southern end of Denneweg with dark panelling and a lively crew. Gay friendly.

Le Café Hathor Maliestraat 22. Just 100m or so from the south end of Denneweg, this agreeable, laidback café-bar with a convivial atmosphere occupies charming old premises and has a pleasant canalside terrace to boot.

De Oude Mol Oude Molstraat 61. Good old traditional bar and neighbourhood joint down a narrow sidestreet. Oodles of atmosphere and an enjoyable range of beers. Upstairs is a tiny tapas bar, and they also serve tapas downstairs.

De Zwarte Ruiter Grote Markt 27. This fashionable bar boasts a good selection of beers and ales, and positively heaves on the weekend. Large terrace as well.

Listings

Bike rental From either of Den Haag's train stations at standard rates.

Car rental Europcar, Binckhorstlaan 297 ☎070/381 1811; Hertz, Binckhorstlaan 318 ☎070/381 8989. For others – and there are lots of them – look up Autoverhuur in the yellow pages.

Embassies and consulates Australia, Carnegielaan 4 ☎070/310 8200; Canada, Sophialaan 7 ☎070/311 1600; Ireland, Dr Kuyperstraat 9 ☎070/363 0993; New Zealand, Carnegielaan 10 ☎070/346 9324; UK, Lange Voorhout 10 ☎070/427 0427; US, Lange Voorhout 102 ☎070/310 9209.

Markets Food market just south of the VVV on Markthof, Gedempte Gracht/Spui (Mon 11am–6pm, Tues–Fri 9am–6pm, Thurs until 9pm & Sat 9am–5pm). Antiques, books and curios markets are on Lange Voorhout (mid-May to late Sept Thurs 10am–6pm & Sun 10am–6pm) and on Plein (Oct–May Thurs 10am–6pm).

Pharmacy Hofstad Apotheek, right in the centre at Korte Poten 7a (Mon–Fri 8.30am–6pm, Sat 10am–2pm). For information on night services, call ☎070/345 1000.

Post office Main post office on Kerkplein (Mon–Fri 9am–6pm, Thurs until 8pm, Sat 9am–4pm).

Taxi HTMC ☎070/390 7722.

Scheveningen

Wedged against the seashore about 4km north of the centre of Den Haag, the old fishing port of **SCHEVENINGEN** is now the Netherlands' biggest coastal resort, a sometimes tacky, often breezy place that attracts more than nine million visitors a year. It also has one curious claim to fame: during World War II, resistance groups tested suspected Nazi infiltrators by getting them to say "Scheveningen" – an impossible feat for Germans, apparently, and not much easier for English-speakers either (try a throaty *s-khay-ve-ning-uh*). A thick strip of forested dune once separated Den Haag from Scheveningen, but nowadays it's hard to know where one ends and the other begins. There is, however, no mistaking Scheveningen's principal attraction, its **beach**, a long expanse of golden sand that is hard to resist on a warm day, especially as it only takes about ten minutes to get there on **tram #1** from the Spui and from outside the VVV.

Scheveningen's handiest tram stop is a couple of hundred metres from its most impressive building, the **Kurhaus**, a grand hotel of 1885, built when this was one of the most fashionable resorts in Europe. Pop inside for a peek at its central hall, a richly decorated affair with pendulous chandeliers and rich frescoes bearing mermaids and semi-clad maidens cavorting high above the diners and coffee-drinkers. Most of Scheveningen's other attractions are within easy walking distance of the Kurhaus: the **casino** is across the street; it's east along the seashore to the **pier** and its amusement arcades; and west to **Sea Life**, Strandweg 13 (daily: Jan & Feb 10am–6pm; March–June & Sept–Dec 10am–7pm; July & Aug 10am–8pm; €11.50, children €8; ⓦwww.sealifeeurope.com), a glorified aquarium complete with a sea-bed walkway and coral reef. Much more original, and about 200m west of Sea Life, is the **Museum Beelden-aan-Zee**, at Harteveltstraat 1 (Tues–Sun 11am–5pm; €6; ⓦwww.beeldenaanzee.nl). This features an intriguing assortment of modern sculptures arranged around a pavilion built by King William I for his ailing wife, Wilhelmina, in 1826. There are examples of the work of many leading sculptors, including Karel Appel and Wim Quist, Man Ray and Fritz Koenig, and although there is supposed to be a unifying theme – the human experience – it's the variety of forms and materials that impresses.

Practicalities

Scheveningen is best visited on a day-trip from Den Haag, but if you do decide to stay, the **VVV**, by the seafront just east of the Kurhaus at Gevers Deynootweg 1134 (Mon–Fri 9.30am–5.30pm, Sat 10am–5pm, Sun 11am–4pm; ☎0900/340 3505 premium line, ⓦwww.denhaag com), issues a free brochure listing all the resort's **hotels** and **pensions**. Out of season, there are oodles of vacant rooms, but in the summer it's best to use the VVV's accommodation booking service.

Scheveningen also hosts a lively programme of special events, most memorably an international **sand sculpture** competition held in early May.

Delft

Pint-sized **DELFT**, in between Den Haag and Rotterdam, has a beguiling centre, a pastel-shaded medley of red-tiled houses set beside tree-lined canals interrupted by the cutest of bridges. With justification, it's one of the most visited spots in the Netherlands, but most tourists come here for the day, and

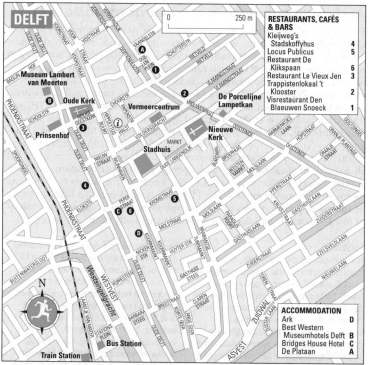

RESTAURANTS, CAFÉS & BARS

Kleijweg's Stadskoffyhus	4
Locus Publicus	5
Restaurant De Klikspaan	6
Restaurant Le Vieux Jen	3
Trappistenlokaal 't Klooster	2
Visrestaurant Den Blaeuwen Snoeck	1

ACCOMMODATION

Ark	D
Best Western Museumhotels Delft	B
Bridges House Hotel	C
De Plataan	A

Koninklijke Porceleyne Fles ▼

in the evening, even in the summer, the town can be surprisingly – and mercifully – quiet. Delft boasts a clutch of fascinating old buildings and one of them – the **Prinsenhof** – holds an enjoyable collection of Golden Age paintings, but nevertheless it's still the general flavour of the place that appeals rather than any specific sight. That said, the two big pulls, as far as the day-trippers are concerned, are the **Delftware factories**, stuffed with the blue and white ceramics for which the town is famous, and the **Johannes Vermeer** (1632–75) connection. Precious little is known about Vermeer, but he was certainly born in the town and died here too, leaving a wife, eleven children and a huge debt to the local baker. He had given the baker two pictures as security, and his wife subsequently bankrupted herself trying to retrieve them. Vermeer's most celebrated painting is his 1661 *View of Delft*, now displayed in the Mauritshuis in Den Haag (see p.176), but if you're after a townscape that even vaguely resembles the picture, you'll be disappointed – it doesn't exist and in a sense it never did, no matter how many "Vermeer walks" Delft lays on. Vermeer made no claim to be a realist and his *View* accorded with the landscape traditions of his day, presenting an idealized Delft framed by a broad expanse of water and dappled by a cloudy sky. There is a cool detachment here that Vermeer also applied to those scenes of contemporary domestic life which are more typical of his oeuvre – though only 36 Vermeers survive – as exemplified by *The Love Letter*, in Amsterdam's Rijksmuseum (see p.98).

Arrival, information and accommodation

From either of Den Haag's train stations, it only takes a few minutes to reach Delft **train station**, from where it's a ten-minute walk north to the main square, the Markt; Delft **bus station** is in front of the train station. You can also make the trip on **tram #1**, which runs south from Scheveningen to the centre of Den Haag (Spui and Buitenhof) before proceeding on to Delft, where it rattles along Phoenixstraat/Westvest between the train station and the centre.

Delft VVV has turned itself into a **Toeristen Informatie Punt (TIP)** and it's located just north of the Markt at Hippolytusbuurt 4 (April–Sept Mon & Sun 10am–4pm, Tues–Fri 9am–6pm, Sat 10am–5pm; Oct–March Mon 11am–4pm, Tues–Sat 10am–4pm, Sun 10am–3pm; ☎0900/515 1555 premium line, ☎(0)15/215 4051 from abroad; ⓦwww.delft.nl). They issue free city maps, sell all manner of local brochures and operate an **accommodation booking service**, which can be very useful in the height of the summer when spare rooms are thin on the ground. The TIP also has the details of a light scattering of **rooms** in private houses (❶–❷), though most of these are on the outskirts of town, whereas Delft's dozen or so **hotels** are mostly in the old centre.

Hotels

Ark Koornmarkt 65 ☎015/215 7999, ⓦwww .deark.nl. Attractive four-star hotel occupying three tastefully restored seventeenth-century canal houses. The bedrooms are perhaps more spartan than you might expect from the public areas, but they are comfortable and well appointed. ❹

Best Western Museumhotels Delft Phoenix-straat 50 ☎015/215 3070, ⓦwww.museumhotel .nl. There are two separate sections to this smart, four-star hotel – one in an eighteenth-century building, the other in its grander, seventeenth-century neighbour. Great location, backing onto the Oude Delft canal just along from the Prinsenhof, though the guest bedrooms are themselves uninspiringly modern. ❻

Bridges House Hotel Oude Delft 74 ☎015/212 4036, ⓦwww.bridges-house.com.

This medium-sized, privately owned hotel occupies an old town house that was once the home of the artist Jan Steen. There's no chain-hotel standardization here and neither is the place excessively spick and span, but the best guest rooms are large, well equipped and have good views of the Oude Delft canal. It has an ideal location, too, the briefest of walks from the Markt. ❸, suites ❹

De Plataan Doelenplein 10 ☎015/212 6046, ⓦwww.hoteldeplataan.nl. A little off the beaten track, but still within easy walking distance of the Markt, this three-star hotel has really pushed the decorative boat out, from the cheerful colours of the regular rooms through to the four theme rooms, including a "Garden of Eden" and a "Desert Island" – great fun. ❸, theme rooms ❼

The Town

The obvious place to start an exploration of Delft is the **Markt**, a handsome square and central point of reference with the Stadhuis at one end and the Nieuwe Kerk at the other, with cafés and restaurants and a **statue** of Delft's own Hugo Grotius lined up in between. A well-known scholar and statesman, Grotius (1583–1645) was sentenced to life imprisonment by Maurice of Orange-Nassau during the political turmoil of the 1610s, but was subsequently rescued by his wife who smuggled him out of jail in a chest. Unfortunately, it didn't save Grotius from a sticky end – he died of exposure after being shipwrecked near Danzig.

The **Nieuwe Kerk** (Mon–Sat: April–Oct 9am–6pm; Nov–March 11am–4pm; €3, including Oude Kerk) is new only in comparison with the Oude Kerk, as there's been a church on this site since 1381. Most of the original structure was destroyed in the great fire that swept through Delft in 1536, and the remainder in an explosion a century later – a disaster, incidentally, which claimed the life of the artist Carel Fabritius, Rembrandt's greatest pupil and (debatably) the

Delftware

The clunky ceramics known as **delftware** traces its origins to the Balearic island of Mallorca, where craftsmen had earlier developed **majolica**, a type of porous pottery that was glazed with bright metallic oxides. During the Renaissance, these techniques were exported to Italy from where they spread north, first to Antwerp and then to the United Provinces. Initially, delft pottery designs featured Dutch and Italian landscapes, portraits and biblical scenes, but the East India Company's profitable import of Chinese ceramics transformed the industry. Delft factories freely copied Chinese designs and by the middle of the seventeenth century they were churning out blue-and-white tiles, plates, panels, jars and vases by the boat load – even exporting to China, where they undercut Chinese producers.

From the 1760s, however, the delft factories were themselves undercut by British and German workshops, and by the time Napoleon arrived they had all but closed down. There was a modest revival of the industry in the 1870s and there are several local producers today, but it's mostly cheap mass-produced stuff of little originality. Delft's souvenir shops are jam-packed with delftware, but if that isn't enough, head for the factory of **Koninklijke Porceleyne Fles** (Mon–Sat 9am–5pm; April–Oct also Sun 9am–5pm; frequent guided tours €4; ⊛www.royaldelft.com), the leading local manufacturer, where they still produce hand-painted pieces. The factory is located a good twenty minutes' walk south of the centre at Rotterdamseweg 196; alternatively, take bus #63 or #129 from Delft train station and get off at Jaffalaan, from where it's a five-minute walk. More conveniently, **De Porcelijne Lampetkan**, just behind the Nieuwe Kerk at Vrouwenregt 5 (☏015/212 1086, ⊛www.antiquesdelft.com), is an appealing little shop selling a good range of antique delftware at (comparatively) reasonable rates.

teacher of Vermeer. The most striking part of the restoration is the most recent, the church's 100-metre **spire** (same hours; €2.50 extra), replaced in 1872 and from whose summit there's a great view over the town. Otherwise, apart from the sheer height of the nave, the interior is mainly distinguished by the **mausoleum of William the Silent**, a prodigiously elaborate marble structure built on the orders of the States General between 1614 and 1623. The mausoleum holds two effigies of William, one in his pomp, seated and dressed in his armour, the other showing him recumbent on his deathbed. This second carving is exquisite, down to the finest details of his face, and at his feet is his faithful dog, who – so legend has it – refused to eat or drink after William's death, thereby rejoining his master in quick time. The two effigies are surrounded by bronze allegorical figures, representing the likes of Liberty and Justice, but the statue of **Fame**, standing on tiptoe behind the recumbent William, caused all sorts of problems: it fell over and the cost of the repairs pushed the whole project way over budget. Look out also for the attractive Art Deco **stained-glass windows** in the north transept and chancel. Inserted between 1927 and 1936, they are a mixed bunch, some illustrating Biblical themes, but most singing the praises of the House of Orange, many of whom are interred in the **burial vault** beneath the nave (no public access).

Directly opposite the Nieuwe Kerk is the **Stadhuis**, whose delightful facade of 1618 is equipped with pert dormer windows, shutters, fluted pilasters and shell decoration. Most of its medieval predecessor was incinerated in the fire of 1536, but the stern stone tower of the earlier building survived and was incorporated – none too successfully – into the later design.

From the Markt, it's a few metres to Voldersgracht 21, where the brand new **Vermeercentrum** (⊛www.vermeerdelft.nl) is – or at least will be – an

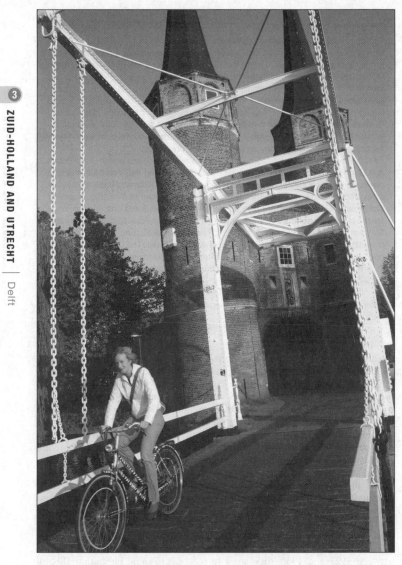

△ Bridge in Delft

all-singing, all-dancing visitor and interpretation centre that makes the most of the town's links with Vermeer. The centre is currently under construction; it's scheduled to be open in late 2007.

The Oude Kerk

From behind the Stadhuis, it's a short but pretty walk north to the **Oude Kerk** (Mon–Sat: April–Oct 9am–6pm; Nov–March 11am–4pm; €3, including

Nieuwe Kerk), a rambling Gothic pile whose discordant lines are redeemed by the most magnificent of church towers, with soaring columns rising high above the town. Despite its dense buttressing, the tower has long been subject to subsidence and the angle of its lean has been measured by generations of worried town architects. Indeed, there have been periodic panics about its safety, not least in the 1840s when the council almost decided to pull it down; the last repairs were undertaken in the 1990s. Inside, the church boasts a splendid vaulted timber ceiling and a fine set of modern **stained-glass windows**, which mostly depict Biblical scenes, the key exception being the intense "Liberation Window", installed in the north transept in 1956 to celebrate the expulsion of the German army at the end of World War II. Also of interest is the **pulpit**, whose five intricately carved panels depict John the Baptist and the four evangelists in false perspective; dating from 1548, the pulpit did well to survive the attentions of the Protestants when they ransacked the church in the Icono-clastic Fury of 1565 (see p.360). Among the assorted **tombs** there is a plain floor plaque in honour of Vermeer just to the west of the pulpit and a flashy marble memorial to **Admiral Maarten Tromp** (1598–1653) close by, next to the north transept. One of the country's most successful admirals, Tromp was captured twice at sea – once by the English and once by Tunisian Arabs – but survived to lead the Dutch fleet at the start of the First Anglo-Dutch War (1652–54). Tromp famously hoisted a broom at his masthead to "sweep the seas clear of the English", but the Royal Navy had its revenge, shooting him down during a sea battle off Scheveningen in 1653. It's this last battle that is depicted on Tromp's tomb alongside an effigy of the man himself, dressed up in his armour beneath a flock of bawling, trumpeting cherubs. Perhaps surprisingly, the marble carving depicting the battle, which shows the British fleet burning away, was much admired by no less than Samuel Pepys, who wrote "the smoke [was] the best expressed that ever I saw".

The Prinsenhof

Down a passageway opposite the Oude Kerk, in what was originally a convent, is **Het Prinsenhof** (Tues–Sat 10am–5pm, Sun 1–5pm; €5, €6 with Museum Lambert van Meerten; Ⓦwww.prinsenhof-delft.nl), which served as the main residence of William the Silent of Orange-Nassau from 1572 to 1584. A sprawling, somewhat confusing building spread over two floors, it was here that William coordinated the Dutch resistance to the Habsburgs and it was here too that he was assassinated. Today, the building holds the **municipal art collec-tion**, an appealing jumble of works mostly dating from the sixteenth and seven-teenth centuries and arranged by theme rather than chronology.

The first few rooms (Rooms 2–8) concentrate on the life and turbulent times of William with portraits of some of the protagonists and, in Room 6, the curious *Wretched State of the Netherlands*. This inflammatory canvas by an unknown seventeenth-century Protestant depicts the Habsburg commander, the Duke of Alva, in cahoots with the devil and the pope, enslaving the Low Countries with each province represented by one of the seventeen chained women before him. Meanwhile, in the background, Margaret of Parma, the region's Habsburg governor, can be seen fishing in a pool of blood. Close by, in Room 8, the bottom of the old wooden staircase marks the spot where **William the Silent was assassinated** on July 10, 1584. A former army commander of both Charles V and Philip II, William turned against the Habsburgs during Alva's persecution of the Protestants in 1567. He went on to lead the Protestant revolt against Philip, mustering a series of armies and organ-izing the *Watergeuzen*, a guerrilla unit that played a key role in driving back the imperial army. In return, Philip put a bounty of 25,000 gold crowns on William's head, but in the event the man who shot him was not a professional assassin but a fanatical Catholic, Balthazar Gerard, who did the deed for his religion. Gerard's two bullets passed right through William and the **bullet holes** are now protected by a glass sheet, put there to stop curious fingers enlarging them. Protestant legend asserts that the dying William asked for his assassin to be treated mercifully, but no such luck: Gerard was tortured in the Markt for four whole days.

Upstairs, Room 13 holds a selection of militia paintings, the pick of which is *Banquet of the Delft Militia* by Michiel van Miereveld (1567–1641). During the long war with Spain, every Dutch city had its own militia, but as the Habsburg threat diminished the militias devolved into social clubs, each of them keen to immortalize their particular company in a group portrait like these on display here. Nearby, Rooms 16 and 17 also exhibit paintings from Delft's seventeenth-century heyday, including a splendidly realistic, almost pointilist canvas entitled *The Disbanding of the Mercenaries in Utrecht, 1618* by Paulwels van Hillegaert. In what now seems a very strange state of affairs, the mercenaries had been hired by Utrecht city council to keep the peace between those Protestants who asserted the primacy of predestination over free will and those who believed it was the other way round. Before matters got even worse, William the Silent's son, Maurits, rode to the rescue. He restored order, disarmed the mercenaries – and gave Hillegaert the chance to produce another of his sycophantic paintings in praise of the House of Orange. Finally, Room 21 has a small but eclectic collection of anatomy paintings, with *The Anatomy Lesson* by Cornelis de Man (1621–1706) being especially striking.

Museum Lambert van Meerten

A few metres north of the Prinsenhof, the canalside **Museum Lambert van Meerten**, at Oude Delft 199 (Tues–Sat 10am–5pm, Sun 1–5pm; €3.50, €6 with Prinsenhof; ⓦ www.lambertvanmeerten-delft.nl), exhibits the town's best collection of delftware. There are jars and vases, plates and panels, but the museum's speciality is its tiles – a fabulous hoard collected by the eponymous nineteenth-century industrialist who once lived in this grand mansion and gifted the house and its contents to the town when he died. In particular, look out for the vibrant tile picture of the Battle of La Hogue – in which an Anglo-Dutch fleet worsted the French in 1692 – displayed on the staircase.

Eating and drinking

Many of Delft's **cafés** and **restaurants** are geared up for the day-trippers and serve up some pretty routine stuff, but there are also several excellent places dotted within easy strolling distance of the Markt. The same applies to the town's **bars**.

Kleijweg's Stadskoffyhus Oude Delft 133. Popular café both inside, in a cosily kitted out old terrace house near the Markt, and outside, on a patio-barge. The best pancakes in town, for €4–9. Mon–Fri 9am–8pm & Sat 9am–6pm.

Locus Publicus Brabantse Turfmarkt 67. You don't come to Delft for the nightlife, but this is one of the town's busiest and most youthful bars and it offers a wide range of beers.

Restaurant De Klikspaan Koornmarkt 85 ☏ 015/214 1562. Smart and polished restaurant in an old canalside town house just south of the Markt. The food is broadly French, though Dutch dishes do pop up now and then, and you can eat outside on their patio-barge during the summer. Mains €23–27. Wed–Sun 1–11pm.

Restaurant Le Vieux Jen Heilige Geestkerkhof 3 ☏ 015/213 0433. Immaculate French restaurant serving *nouvelle cuisine* with care and precision. Main courses €23–27; excellent cellar too. Tues–Fri noon–2.30pm & 6–10.30pm, Sat 6–10.30pm.

Trappistenlokaal 't Klooster Vlamingstraat 2. Smashing little neighbourhood bar with traditional decor and an excellent range of Belgian beers, both on tap and bottled.

Visrestaurant Den Blaeuwen Snoeck Verwersdijk 14 ⓣ015/213 8850. This sedate restaurant, with its neat, vaguely nautical decor and classical music as the backdrop, is the only specialist seafood place in town. Prices are very reasonable, with mains averaging around €20, though the range of fish on offer is not extensive.

Rotterdam

ROTTERDAM lies at the heart of a maze of rivers and artificial waterways that together form the outlet of the rivers Rijn (Rhine) and Maas (Meuse). After devastating damage during World War II, Rotterdam has grown into a vibrant, forceful city dotted with first-division cultural attractions. Neither has redevelopment obliterated the city's earthy character: its tough grittiness is part of its appeal, as are its boisterous bars and clubs.

An important **port** as early as the fourteenth century, Rotterdam was one of the major cities of the United Provinces and shared its periods of fortune and decline until the nineteenth century when it was caught unawares. The city was ill prepared for the industrial expansion of the Ruhr, the development of larger ships and the silting up of the Maas, but prosperity did finally return in a big way with the digging of an entirely new ship canal (the "Nieuwe Waterweg") between the city and the North Sea in the 1860s. Rotterdam has been a major seaport ever since, though it has had difficult times, especially during World War II, when the Nazis bombed the city centre in 1940 and, in retreat, destroyed much of the harbour four years later, with Allied bombing doing much damage in between.

The postwar period saw the rapid reconstruction of the **docks** and, when huge container ships and oil tankers made the existing port facilities obsolete, Rotterdammers promptly built an entirely new deep-sea port, the **Europoort**, jutting out into the North Sea, some 25km to the west of the old town. Completed in 1968, the Europoort can accommodate the largest of ships and now Rotterdam is the largest port in the world, handling some 350 million tonnes of goods a year, with more than half of all goods heading into Europe passing through it. The same spirit of enterprise was reflected in the council's plans to rebuild the devastated **city centre**. There was to be no return to the crowded terrace houses of yesteryear, but instead the centre was to be a modern extravaganza of concrete and glass, high-rise and pedestrianized areas. Decades in the making, parts of the plan work very well indeed – like the *kubuswoningen* ("cube houses") of the Blaak district – but others, such as the Lijnbaan shopping precinct, look tired and sad.

All this modernity may sound unalluring, but Rotterdam's attractions are enticing, most notably the **Kunsthal**, exhibiting contemporary art, and the **Museum Boijmans Van Beuningen**, which has an outstanding art collection holding representative works from almost all the most important Dutch painters; both are in the city's designated culture zone, the **Museumpark**. Other city highlights include **Oude Haven**, the city's oldest harbour, ravaged during World War II but sympathetically redeveloped, and **Delfshaven**, an antique harbour that managed to survive the bombs pretty much intact.

Arrival, information and city transport

Rotterdam has several train stations, but the one you want for the centre is **Centraal Station**, which adjoins Stationsplein, the hub of the RET public

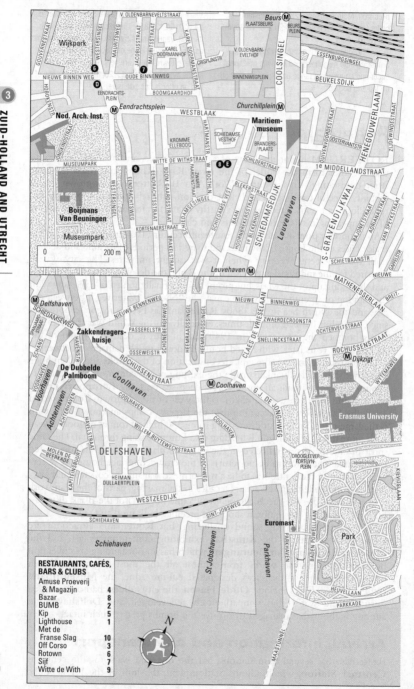

Wijkpark

GOUDERNESTRAAT

WESTERSINGEL

MAURITSWEG

JACOBUSSTRAAT

MAURITSSTRAAT

V. OLDENBARNEVELTSTRAAT

KAREL DOORMANSTRAAT

KAREL DOORMANHOF

CRISPIJNSTR

PLAATSBEURS

Beurs Ⓜ

BEURS PLEIN

ESSENBURGSINGEL

6

7

OUDE BINNENWEG

NIEUWE BINNEN WEG

Ⓓ

EENDRACHTS-PLEIN

BOOMGAARDHOF

V. OLDENBARN-EVELTHOF

BINNENWEGPLEIN

COOLSINGEL

BEUKELSDIJK

Ⓜ *Eendrachtsplein*

Ned. Arch. Inst.

WESTBLAAK

Churchillplein Ⓜ

Maritiem-museum

HENEGOUWERLAAN

JONCKBLOETSTRAAT

KROMME ELLEBOOG

HARTMANSTR

SCHIEDAMSE VESTHOF

BRANDERS-PLAATS

DUYVENVOORDESTRAAT

OOSTERVANTSTR

ZIJDEWINDESTRAAT

MUSEUMPARK

WESTERSINGEL

EENDRACHTSWEG

WITTE DE WITHSTRAAT

BOOM GAARDSTRAAT

ZWARTE PAARDENSTRAAT

W. BOOTHLN

SCHILDERSTRAAT

8 Ⓔ

10

1e MIDDELLANDSTRAAT

9

EENDRACHTSSTRAAT

SCHIEDAMSESINGEL

SCHIEDAMSE VEST

BLEKERSTRAAT

HOORNBREKERSTRAAT

1e BLEKERHOF

SCHIEDAMSEDIJK

LEUVEHAVEN

'S-GRAVENDIJKWAL

BAJONETSTRAAT

ADRIANASTRAAT

VAN SPEYKSTRAAT

Boijmans Van Beuningen

BRAKELSTRAAT

KORTENAERSTRAAT

LAAN

SCHIETBAANSTR

GAFFELSTR

Museumpark

0 ——— 200 m

Leuvehaven Ⓜ

NIEUWE

MATHENESSERLAAN

BREIT.

Ⓜ *Delfshaven*

SCHIEDAMSEWEG

SPANJAARD STRAAT

SCHANS

NIEUWE BENNENWEG

PASSERELSTR

SCHONEBERGERWEG

HEEMRAADSSINGEL

HEEMRAADSSINGEL

NIEUWE

BINNENWEG

ZWAERDECROONSTR

CLAES DE VRIESELAAN

SNELLINCKSTRAAT

OCHTERVELTSTRAAT

ROCHUSSENSTRAAT

Ⓜ *Dijkzigt*

WITTEWEG

Zakkendragers-huisje

HAVENSTR

VOORHAVEN

OSSEWEISTR

ROCHUSSENSTRAAT

De Dubbelde Palmboom

Coolhaven

ACHTERHAVEN

COOLHAVEN

Ⓜ *Coolhaven*

G.J. DE JONGHWEG

Erasmus University

ACHTERHAVEN

HAVELSTRAAT

WILLEM BUYTEWECHSTRAAT

COOLHAVEN

PIETER DE HOOCHWEG

KIEVITSLAAN

MOLEN DE BEERKADE

KAPITEINBUURT

DELFSHAVEN

HEIMAN DULLAERTPLEIN

DROOGLEEVER FORTUYN-PLEIN

WESTZEEDIJK

SCHIEHAVEN

SINT-JOBSWEG

Euromast

PARKHAVEN

BADEN POWELLLAAN

Park

HEUVELLAAN

Schiehaven

St. Jobshaven

Parkhaven

PARKKADE

RESTAURANTS, CAFÉS, BARS & CLUBS

Amuse Proeverij & Magazijn	4
Bazar	8
BUMB	2
Kip	5
Lighthouse	1
Met de Franse Slag	10
Off Corso	3
Rotown	6
Sijf	7
Witte de With	9

N

MAASTUNNEL

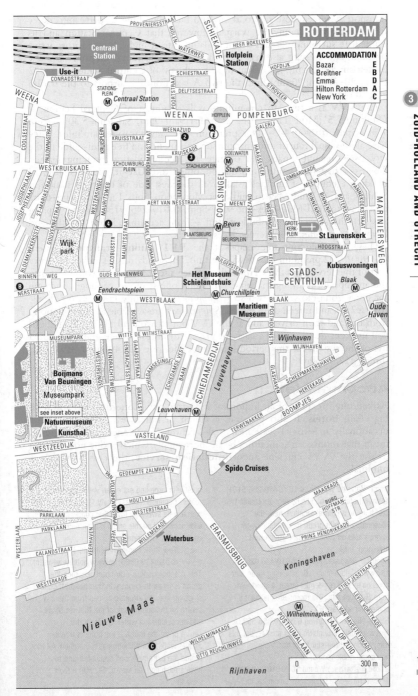

ROTTERDAM

Centraal
Station

Use-it

Hofplein
Station

CONRADSTRAAT

STATIONS-
PLEIN

Ⓜ Centraal Station

WEENA

PROVENIERSSTRAAT

WATERWEG

SCHIEKADE

HEER BOKELWEG

HOFDIJK

STROYER

WEENA

HOFPLEIN

POMPENBURG

GALERIJ

KRUISSTRAAT

WEENAZUID

DOELWATER

Ⓜ Stadhuis

COOLSINGEL

Stadhuis

SCHOUWBURG
PLEIN

KRUISKADE

STADHUISPLEIN

LIJNBAAN

AERT VAN NESSTRAAT

MEENT

LOMBARDKADE

MEENT

GROTE-
KERK-
PLEIN

St Laurenskerk

Ⓜ Beurs

PLAATSBEURS

BEURSPLEIN

HOOGSTRAAT

Kubuswoningen

Wijk-
park

BULGERSTEYN

KEIZERSTRAAT

STADS-
CENTRUM

Blaak Ⓜ

Het Museum
Schielandshuis

Ⓜ Churchillplein

OUDE BINNENWEG

Eendrachtsplein Ⓜ

WESTBLAAK

Maritiem
Museum

BLAAK

Oude
Haven

WITTE DE WITHSTRAAT

Wijnhaven

WIJNHAVEN

Boijmans
Van Beuningen

Museumpark

see inset above

Leuvehaven Ⓜ

BOOMPJES

Spido Cruises

Natuurmuseum
Kunsthal

WESTZEEDIJK

VASTELAND

Waterbus

ERASMUSBRUG

Koningshaven

Nieuwe Maas

Ⓜ Wilhelminaplein

WILHELMINAKADE

OTTO REUCHLINWEG

Rijnhaven

0   300 m

transport system, whose metro, trams and buses combine to delve into every urban nook and cranny. Be warned, however, that Centraal Station and its immediate surroundings can be intimidating late at night. Most visitors arrive by train, but the city also has its own (rapidly expanding) **airport** (Ⓦwww .rotterdam-airport.nl), just 10km or so northwest of Centraal Station; bus #33 (every 10–20min; 20min) links the two. A taxi from the airport to the station costs about €25.

The **VVV** is a five- to ten-minute walk southeast of Centraal Station, at Coolsingel 5 (Mon–Thurs 9am–6pm, Fri 9am–9pm, Sat 9am–5.30pm, Sun 10am–5pm; Ⓣ0900/403 4065 premium line, Ⓦwww.rotterdam.info). They have all the usual tourist information, supply a useful and free mini-guide to the city, issue free city maps and operate an accommodation booking service. There's a first-rate youth information office too, **Use-it**, in a red-painted building a couple of minutes' walk from the west side of the train station at Schaatsbaan 41 (mid-May to mid-Sept Mon noon–5pm, Tues–Sun 9am–6pm; mid-Sept to mid-May Tues–Sat 9am–5pm; Ⓣ010/240 9158, Ⓦwww.jip.org /use-it); they specialize in budget stuff – from accommodation to cafés and beyond – and offer free internet access too.

They also dole out free maps of the **RET public transport** system (Ⓣ0900/9292 premium line, Ⓦwww.ret.nl). The standard RET ticket, on every part of the network, is the **strippenkaart** (see also p.34), which you insert into the appropriate franking machine, cancelling one strip per passenger and one for every zone crossed. A two-strip *strippenkaart* currently costs €1.60, three-strip €2.40, and fifteen-strip €6.70. *Strippenkaart* are available at metro stations, from bus and tram drivers and at the VVV, but to avoid all this fiddling about you may decide to opt for a *dagkaart* (day-card) instead. These grant unlimited use of the system for the period specified, either one (€6.40), two (€9.60) or three (€12.80) days.

Accommodation

As you might expect of an important industrial city, Rotterdam has a slew of big chain **hotels**. It also possesses a clutch of much less expensive places, occasionally in – or at least near – the centre. Conferences and congresses mean that rooms can sometimes be in short supply, which is one good reason to use the VVV's efficient **accommodation service**, the cost of which is minimal.

Bazar Witte de Withstraat 16 Ⓣ010/206 5151, Ⓦwww.hotelbazar.nl. Lively, very agreeable two-star hotel in a central location, near the Museumpark, with great, modernistic decor. There's also an excellent café-restaurant adjoining it. ❷

Breitner Breitnerstraat 23 Ⓣ010/436 0262, Ⓦwww.hotelbreitner.nl. Unassuming three-star hotel on a quiet residential street, a short walk from Museumpark. The rooms are pleasant if somewhat spartan. ❸

Emma Nieuwe Binnenweg 6 Ⓣ010/436 5533, Ⓦwww.hotelemma.nl. No great shakes, but this trim, modern three-star hotel has a central location and comfortable rooms. ❸

Hilton Rotterdam Weena 10 Ⓣ010/710 8000, Ⓦwww.rotterdam.hilton.com. Luxurious four-star hotel with large and extremely well-appointed rooms. Occupies a classic early 1970s tower block with a wide sweeping foyer that comes complete with oceans of marble and a broken mirror motif on the walls. First-rate. ❺

New York Koninginnenhoofd 1 Ⓣ010/439 0500, Ⓦwww.hotelnewyork.nl. This prestigious four-star hotel occupies the grand nineteenth-century former head office of a shipping line. It's situated across from the city centre on the south bank of the Nieuwe Maas, and accessible via water taxi from the centre or on the metro – the hotel is a five-minute walk from Wilhelminaplein station. All the rooms are extremely well appointed and most have smashing river views. ❷, with a river view ❺

Leaving from beside Rotterdam's Erasmusbrug, the **Waterbus passenger ferry** (T 0900/266 6399 premium line, W www.waterbus.nl) takes an hour to zip down the rivers Nieuwe Maas and Noord bound for Dordrecht (see p.204). It's a great way to see this part of the country and fares are very reasonable – a single to Dordrecht costs just €3.80, €6.60 return; boats leave every half-hour from 7am to 7pm on weekdays, 9.30am to 7pm on Saturdays and 11.30am to 6pm on Sundays. Furthermore, connecting ferries make side journeys to – among several places – the Kinderdijk (see p.208) and the Dordrecht Biesbosch (see p.207).

The City

From **Stationsplein**, outside Centraal Station, Kruisplein and then Westersingel/Mauritsweg cut south, dividing this part of the city into two: to the west is a largely working-class residential area, while to the east, hemmed in by Weena, Coolsingel and Westblaak, lies a jangle of modern high-rises and shopping streets. The layout is a tad baffling, but the focus of this second area – if indeed there is one – is the **Lijnbaan**, Europe's first pedestrianized shopping precinct, completed in 1953. The Lijnbaan is interesting as a prototype, but the dimensions are disconcerting: the street is too wide and the buildings are too low to create any sense of intimacy. Developers learnt lessons here.

To the east of Coolsingel, just north of Hoogstraat, is the fifteenth-century **St Laurenskerk** or Grote Kerk (Tues–Sat 10am–4pm; free), a mighty brick pile rebuilt after bomb damage in 1940. The church, which now hosts cultural events, has splendid bronze doors, the work of Giacomo Manzu in the 1960s, and you can climb the tower on the third Saturday of the month (April–Sept only, noon–2pm; free).

From the back of St Laurenskerk, it's a short walk south along the wide and windy Binnenrotte to **Blaak**, a compact, one-time working-class district that was comprehensively levelled in World War II, but has since been rebuilt in a full flush of modern design. The architectural high point is a remarkable series of cube-shaped houses, the *kubuswoningen*, completed in 1984 to a design by the architect Piet Blom. One of them, the **Kijk-Kubus** (Show Cube; March–Dec daily 11am–5pm; Jan & Feb Fri–Sun 11am–5pm; €2; W www.kubuswoning.nl), at Overblaak 70, near Blaak train and metro station, is open to visitors, offering a somewhat disorientating tour of what amounts to an upside-down house.

Behind the cube houses is the **Oude Haven**, the city's first harbour, built in 1325, and now flanked by cafés and crowded with antique barges and boats.

The Maritiem Museum and the Museum Het Schielandshuis

Heading west from the Kijk-Kubus, it's about 600m along Blaak boulevard to Churchillplein and the **Maritiem Museum** (Tues–Sat 10am–5pm, Sun 11am–5pm, July & Aug also Mon 10am–5pm; €5; W www.maritiemmuseum.nl), situated beside the waters of the city's first harbour, the **Leuvehaven**. The museum has an interesting display on the history of Rotterdam as a seaport and shipbuilding centre plus an entertaining section on the life of sea men in the seventeenth and eighteenth centuries. The outside area has been spruced up for the museum's prime exhibit, the *Buffel*, an immaculately restored mid-nineteenth-century ironclad ship, complete with communal sinks shaped to match the angle of the bows and a string of luxurious officers' cabins.

△ Cube houses, Rotterdam

There's more on the history of Rotterdam at the **Museum Het Schielandshuis** (Tues–Fri 10am–5pm, Sat & Sun 11am–5pm; €3; ⓦwww .historischmuseumrotterdam.nl), housed in a seventeenth-century mansion at Korte Hoogstraat 31 – a brief stroll north of the Maritiem Museum on the far

Spido cruises

The shape and feel of the Leuvehaven, Rotterdam's first artificial harbour, has been transformed by the Boompjes freeway, which scoots along the top of the old enclosing sea dyke. Beside the Boompjes, at the south end of the Leuvehaven, is the departure point for Spido cruises (℡010/275 9988, ⓦwww.spido.nl). They have several different tours of the surrounding waterways and port facilities, heading off past the wharves, landings, docks and silos of this, the largest port in the world, but the standard harbour tour costs just €9 (April–Oct 5–10 daily; Nov–March Thurs–Sun 3–4 daily; 1hr 15min). In July and August, there are also longer trips to several destinations, most notably the series of colossal dams that make up the Delta Project, along the seaboard southwest of Rotterdam (July & Aug 1 weekly; 6hr 30min; €42). For more on the Delta Project and Delta Expo, see p.318.

side of Blaak boulevard. The main historical display features original footage of the bombing of the city in World War II and the museum is also home to the *Atlas van Stolk* collection of drawings and prints, which includes fascinating sketches of pre-colonial Indonesia.

Museumpark

Tram #8 (direction Spangen) links Centraal Station and Coolsingel/Schiedam-sedijk with the southern edge of **Museumpark**, a designated cultural zone where a string of museums fringe a wide, open area. In the south, bordering Westzeedijk, are the **Natuurmuseum** (Tues–Sat 10am–5pm, Sun 11am–5pm; €4; ⓦwww.nmr.nl), where all sorts of stuffed animals are displayed, and the excellent **Kunsthal** (Tues–Sat 10am–5pm, Sun 11am–5pm; €8.50; ⓦwww .kunsthal.nl), which showcases first-rate exhibitions of contemporary art, photography and design.

Museum Boijmans Van Beuningen

A few minutes' walk from the Kunsthal, on the northern edge of Museumpark within shouting distance of Eendrachtsplein metro stop, is Rotterdam's top attraction, the **Museum Boijmans Van Beuningen** (Tues–Sun 11am–5pm; €8; ⓦwww.boijmans.nl). Recently revamped, the museum spreads over two floors with the ground floor used for temporary exhibitions, the first floor for the vast permanent collection. The older paintings are in one wing of the first floor, and those from the late nineteenth century onwards in the other. The information desk provides an updated and simplified diagrammatic outline of the museum, necessary because the exhibits are frequently rotated.

Among the museum's earlier paintings is an excellent **Flemish and Nether-landish** section, where one highlight is the sumptuous *Christ in the House of Martha and Mary* by Pieter Aertsen (1508–75). There are also four exquisite works by Hieronymus Bosch (1450–1516). Usually considered a macabre fantasist, Bosch was actually working to the limits of oral and religious tradition, where biblical themes were depicted as iconographical representations, laden with explicit symbols. In his *St Christopher*, the dragon, the hanged bear and the broken pitcher lurk in the background, representations of danger and uncertainty, whereas the Prodigal Son's attitude to the brothel behind him in *The Peddler* is deliberately ambivalent. Bosch's technique never absorbed the influences of Renaissance Italy, and his figures in the *Marriage Feast at Cana* are static and unbelievable, uncomfortably arranged around a distorted table. Other works in this section include paintings by Jan van Scorel (1495–1562), who was more willing to absorb Italianate styles as in his *Young Scholar in a Red Cap*; the Bruges artist Hans Memling (1433–94), whose capacity for detail can be seen in his *Two Horses in a Landscape*; (1525–69) the mysterious, hazy *Tower of Babel* by Pieter Brueghel the Elder; and Geertgen tot Sint Jans (1460–90) beautiful, delicate *Glorification of the Virgin*.

Moving on, a fascinating selection of **Dutch genre** paintings reflects the tastes of the emergent seventeenth-century middle class. The idea was to depict real-life situations overlaid with a symbolic moral content as typified by Jan Steen's (1625–79) *Extracting the Stone* and his *Sick Woman*. There's also *The Quack* by Gerrit Dou (1613–75), ostensibly just a passing scene, but littered with small cameos of deception – a boy catching a bird, the trapped hare – that refer back to the quack's sham cures. In this section also are a number of **Rembrandts**, including two contrasting canvases: an analytic *Portrait of Alotta Adriaensdr*, her ageing illuminated but softened by her white ruff, and a gloomy, powerfully indistinct *Blind Tobias and his Wife* painted twenty years later. His intimate *Titus at his Desk* is also in marked contrast to the more formal portrait commissions common to his era. Most of the work of Rembrandt's pupil Carel Fabritius (1622–54) was destroyed when he was killed in a Delft gunpowder explosion in 1654; an exception is his *Self-Portrait*, reversing his master's usual technique by lighting the background and placing the subject in shadow.

The museum's collection of **modern paintings** is perhaps best known for its Surrealists. *De rigueur* for students' bedrooms in the 1970s, it's difficult to appreciate Salvador Dalí's *Spain* as anything more than the painting of the poster, but other works by the likes of René Magritte, Max Ernst and Giorgio de Chirico still have the power to surprise. Surrealism was never adopted by Dutch artists, though the Magic Realism of Carel Willink (1900–83) has its similarities in the precise, hallucinatory technique he uses to distance the viewer in *Self Portrait with a Pen*. *Three Generations* by Charley Toorop's (1891–1955) is also Realism with an aim to disconcert: the huge bust of her father, Jan, looms in the background and dominates the painting. In this section, look out also for paintings from many of Europe's most famous artists, including Monet, Van Gogh, Picasso, Gauguin, Cézanne and Munch, as well as a representative sample of the Barbizon and Hague schools, notably *Strandgezicht* by J.H. Weissenbruch (1822–80), a beautiful gradation of radiant tones.

Delfshaven

If little in Rotterdam city centre can exactly be called picturesque, **DELFSHAVEN**, a couple of kilometres southwest of Centraal Station, goes part of the way to make up for it: to get there from the station, catch tram #8 (direction Spangen) and get off at Spanjaardstraat tram stop, or take the metro to Delfshaven. Once the harbour that served Delft, it was from here that the **Pilgrim Fathers** set sail in 1620, changing to the more reliable *Mayflower* in Plymouth before continuing onward to the New World. Nevertheless, despite this substantial claim to fame, Delfshaven was long a neglected corner until finally, in the 1970s, the city recognized its tourist potential and set about conserving and restoring. Most of the buildings lining the two narrow canals that comprise Delfshaven are eighteenth- and nineteenth-century warehouses, with the more fetching facades on the more westerly Voorhaven. It's here, at no. 12, you'll find the **Museum de Dubbelde Palmboom** (Tues–Fri 10am–5pm, Sat & Sun 11am–5pm; €3; ⓦwww.dedubbeldepalmboom.nl), once a *jenever* distillery and now a historical museum, with a wide-ranging, if unexceptional collection of objects representing work and leisure in the Maas delta. A few metres to the north, at Voorstraat 13, is the **Zakkendragershuisje** (Tues–Fri 10am–5pm, Sat 11am–5pm; free), originally the guild room of the Grain Sack Carriers, who decided the allocation of duties by dice. Today, it's a privately owned, fully operational tin foundry, selling a variety of items made in the old moulds.

Eating, drinking and nightlife

Handy for many of the sights, the Oude and Nieuwe Binneweg are two of the Rotterdam's grooviest streets, lined with recommendable **cafés**, **café-bars** and **restaurants**. Similarly enticing is Witte de Withstraat, where you'll also find one of the city's more amenable **cannabis coffeeshops**, the *Witte de With*, at no. 92.

Amuse Proeverij & Magazijn Van Oldenbarneveltstrat 139 ☏ 010/280 7206. Attractive, bistro-style café very much in the French manner with a simple, tasty and inexpensive menu – set meals start at just €15. Wed 11am–9pm, Thurs–Sat 11am–11pm, Sun noon–6pm.

Bazar Witte de Withstraat 16. Big and bustling North African restaurant with a good sideline in vegetarian dishes. Laidback (some would say cool) atmosphere. Daily 9am–11pm.

Kip Van Vollenhovenstraat 25 ☏ 010/436 9923. This smooth and chic restaurant in classy premises, kitted out in a modern version of Golden Age style, has won all sorts of gastronomic awards. Finessed food at its finest and at a price – mains from €25 to €50. Tues–Sun 6–10pm.

Lighthouse Restaurant *Hotel Westin Rotterdam*, Weena 686 ☏ 010/430 2000. This tower-block hotel has a well-regarded if somewhat staid first-floor restaurant with enjoyable views back over to the station. The menu is international and main courses average around €20–25. Mon–Sat noon–3pm & 5–11pm.

Met de Franse Slag Schilderstraat 20a ☏ 010/413 0143. Delicious French cuisine at this popular café-restaurant, where you sit surrounded by modern paintings and sculptures. Main courses are a very reasonable €15 or so.

Rotown Nieuwe Binnenweg 17. Lively café-bar attracting an alternative crew and serving up a wide variety of snacks and light meals from as little as €3. Regular live music too.

Sijf Oude Binnenweg 115, corner of Jacobstraat. Downbeat café-bar with entertaining decor, it serves filling Dutch snacks and light meals. Kitchen open daily noon–2pm & 5–11pm.

Clubs

Rotterdam has a great **club scene**. Two current hotspots are *Off Corso*, near Centraal Station at Kruiskade 22 (Fri & Sat 11pm–4/5am; Ⓦ www.off-corso.nl), with top DJs and even art exhibitions, and *BUMB* (Thurs–Sat midnight–4/5am; Ⓦ www.bumb.nl), underground in a disused underpass at the north end of the Lijnbaan. **Tickets** for gigs and concerts are on sale at the VVV (see p.194), which is an authorized outlet for Ticket Service, a Ticketmaster company (Ⓦ www.ticketmaster.nl).

Listings

Airport enquiries Rotterdam Airport ☏010/446
3444, Ⓦwww.rotterdam-airport.nl.
Car rental Hertz, Schiekade 986 ☏010/404 6088
& at the airport ☏010/415 8239; Europcar, Walen-
burghof 17 ☏010/465 6400.
Football The main local team is Feyenoord
(☏010/292 3888, Ⓦwww.feyenoord.nl), one of
Europe's most prestigious clubs. To get to the
club's stadium, which is well to the west of the
centre, take tram #23 from Rotterdam Centraal

Station. Most games are on Sundays; the VVV has
details.
Internet Free email and Internet access at Use-it,
the youth information office (see p.194).
Post office Coolsingel 42 (Mon–Fri 9am–6pm, Sat
9am–1pm).
Taxis Rotterdamse Taxi Centrale NV ☏010/462
6060; Rotterdamse Taxi Centrale RTC ☏010/262
1173.

Gouda and around

GOUDA, a pretty little place some 25km northeast of Rotterdam, is everything you'd expect of a Dutch country town, with its ring of quiet canals encircling ancient buildings set amid a tangle of narrow lanes and alleys. More surprisingly, its **Markt** is the largest in the Netherlands, a wide and airy piazza that remains an attractive reminder of the town's prominence as a centre of the medieval cloth trade, and later of its success in the manufacture of cheeses and that old Dutch favourite, the clay pipe.

Gouda's main claim to fame is its **cheese market**, held on the Markt every Thursday morning (10am–12.30pm) from the middle of June to late August. Traditionally, some one thousand local farmers brought their home-produced cheeses here to be weighed, tested and graded for moisture, smell and taste. These details were marked on the cheeses, and formed the basis for negotiation between buyer and seller, the exact price confirmed by an elaborate code of hand-claps. Today, however, the cheese market is a shadow of its former self, comprising a few locals in traditional dress standing outside the Waag with their cheeses, all surrounded by modern, open-air stands. It's mercilessly milked by tour operators, who herd their crowds into this scene every week – but don't let this put you off a visit to the town, since Gouda's charms lie elsewhere, especially in the splendid stained-glass windows of **St Janskerk**. Gouda is also a short bus ride from the hamlet of **Oudewater**, home to the curious **Heksen-waag** (witches' weigh house), where many medieval women were saved from certain death when it was "proved" they were not witches.

The Town

Slap-bang in the middle of the Markt, the **Stadhuis** is an elegant Gothic structure whose soaring stonework, with its spiky towers and cheerful dormer windows, dates from 1450. Statues of counts and countesses of Burgundy decorate the building's facades and on its east side is the dinkiest of carillons, where the tiny figures play up and around every half-hour. Nearby, on the north side of the square, is the **Waag**, a tidy seventeenth-century building adorned by a detailed relief of cheese-weighing and now holding a moderately interesting **Kaaswaag** (Cheese Weigh House museum; April–Oct Tues, Wed & Fri–Sun 1–5pm, Thurs 10am–5pm; €2.50).

St Janskerk

To the south, just off the Markt, the lumpy **St Janskerk** (Mon–Sat: March–Oct 9am–5pm; Nov–Feb 10am–4pm; €2.50) was founded in the thirteenth century,

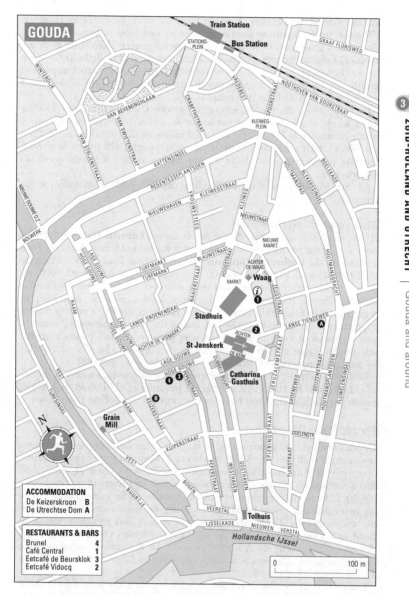

GOUDA

Train Station
Bus Station

STATIONS-
PLEIN

GRAAF FLORISWEG

VREEBEEST

NOOTHOVEN VAN GOORSTRAAT

SPOORSTRAAT

CRABETHSTRAAT

WINTERDIJK

VAN BEVEMINGHLAAN

KLEIWEG-
PLEIN

VAN SWIETENSTRAAT

VAN STRIJENSTRAAT

KATTENSINGEL

HOUTMANSPAD

BLEKERSSINGEL

BOELEKADE

NIEUWE GOUWE O.Z.

REGENTESSEPLANTSOEN

KLEIWEGSTRAAT

KLEIWEG

NIEUWEHAVEN

VROUWESTEEG

NIEUWSTRAAT

NIEUWE
MARKT

BOLWERK

LAGE GOUWE

HOGE GOUWE

TURFMARKT

BLAUWSTRAAT

HOOGSTRAAT

ACHTER
DE WAAG

Waag

HOUTMANSGRACHT

MARKT
ⓘ
Ⓐ LANGE TIENDEWEG

RAAM

LANGE GROENENDAAL

MAAIERSTRAAT

ACHTER DE VISMARKT

Stadhuis

②

ACHTER
DE KERK

JERUZALEMSTRAAT

HOUTMANSPLANTSOEN

GEUZENSTRAAT

VEST

TURFSINGEL

LAGE GOUWE

HOGE GOUWE

St Janskerk

PEPERSTRAAT

④③

DUBBELE BUURT

Catharina
Gasthuis

GROENEWEG

FLUWEELENSINGEL

N

KEIZERSTRAAT

Ⓑ

DOELENSTR

Grain
Mill

SPIERINGSTRAAT

DOELENSTR

KUIPERSTRAAT

VEST

PEPERSTRAAT

WESTHAVEN

OOSTHAVEN

TUINSTRAAT

BOGEN

BUURTJE

VEERSTAL

NIEUWEN

VERSTAL

ACCOMMODATION
De Keizerskroon   B
De Utrechtse Dom   A

Tolhuis

IJSSELKADE

Hollandsche IJssel

RESTAURANTS & BARS
Brunel   4
Café Central   1
Eetcafé de Beursklok 3
Eetcafé Vidocq   2

0   100 m

but the present structure mostly dates from the second half of the sixteenth century, when it was rebuilt following a dreadful fire. The church is famous for its magnificent and stunningly beautiful **stained-glass windows**, which coincidentally witness the move from Catholicism to Calvinism. The biblical themes executed by Dirk and Wouter Crabeth between 1555 and 1571, when Holland was still Catholic, are traditional in content, but they have an amazing clarity of detail and richness of colour. Their last work, *Judith Slaying Holofernes* (Window no. 6), is perhaps the finest, the story unfolding in intricate perspective – and a gruesome tale it was too: the Assyrian general Holofernes made the mistake of sharing his tent with Judith, a Jewish woman from Bethulia, the town he was besieging; he made things worse by drinking himself into a stupor and Judith, not one to look a gift horse in the mouth, lopped off his head and carried it back to Bethulia in triumph.

By comparison, the post-Reformation windows, which date from 1572 to 1603, adopt an allegorical and heraldic style typical of a more secular art. A prime illustration is *The Relief of Leiden* (Window no. 25), which shows William the Silent retaking the town from the Spanish, though Delft and its burgomasters take prominence – no doubt because they paid the bill for the window's manufacture.

All the windows are numbered and a detailed guide is available at the entrance.

The rest of the centre

By the south side of the church, the fancily carved **Lazarus Gate** of 1609 was once part of the town's leper hospital, until it was moved here to form the back entrance to the **Catharina Gasthuis** (Tues–Sat 11am–5pm; €2.50), a hospice till 1910 and now a fine art museum. The collection, which spreads over two floors is really rather confusing and short of major paintings, but the Gasthuiskapel (Chapel, Rooms 12 and 13) does hold a pleasant assortment of sixteenth- and seventeenth-century Dutch paintings, notably a sterling biblical triptych by Dirck Barendsz (1534–92), and, in the corridor between Rooms 10 and 11, is a set of four striking Civic Guard group portraits. Upstairs, a modest selection of Hague and Barbizon School canvases is given a bit of artistic sparkle by four, small paintings of rural idylls by Anton Mauve (1838–88).

With time to spare, you might stroll south along Westhaven, a winsome jumble of old canalside buildings that rambles off towards the old Tolhuis (toll house) beside the Hollandsche IJssel river, on the southern edge of the town centre.

Practicalities

Gouda's **train** and **bus stations** are to the immediate north of the town centre, ten minutes' walk from the **VVV**, at Markt 27 (Mon–Fri 9am–5pm, Sat 10am–4pm; July & Aug also Sun noon–3pm; ☎0900/4683 2888 premium line, Ⓦ www.vvvgouda.nl). They have a limited supply of **rooms** in private houses (❶–❷), and will make hotel reservations on your behalf for a small charge. There are two reasonably priced **hotels** in the centre, the more enjoyable of which is the excellent-value *De Utrechtsche Dom*, in an airy and pleasantly renovated building five minutes' walk from the Markt at Geuzenstraat 6 (☎0182/528 833, Ⓦ www.hotelgouda.nl; ❷). A second choice is *De Keizerskroon*, an unassuming family-run hotel in a terrace house to the west of Westhaven at Keizerstraat 11–13 (☎0182/528 096; ❶).

You don't come to Gouda for the nightlife, but there are several good **cafés**, beginning with *Café Central*, Markt 23 (daily 9am–midnight), where they rustle up a tasty and filling range of Dutch standbys in resolutely old-fashioned premises – there's been no tacky modernization here, witness the wood panelling. There's more good-quality Dutch cuisine at the popular *Eetcafé De Beursklok*, in an attractively converted old shop at Hoge Gouwe 19 (daily 5–10.30pm), and at *Eetcafé Vidocq*, Koster Gijzensteeg 8 (daily 5–10.30pm) – both eetcafés are also pleasant places for a drink. The best **restaurant** in town is

Brunel, a smart French split-level joint at Hoge Gouwe 23 (☎0182/518 979; daily 5–10pm), where main courses average about €20.

Around Gouda: Oudewater

Pocket-sized **OUDEWATER**, deep in the countryside about 11km east of Gouda, is a compact and delightful little town that holds a unique place in the history of Dutch witchcraft (see box below). The town's sixteenth-century Waag has survived, converted into the **Heksenwaag** (Witches' Weigh House; April–Oct Tues–Sat 11am–5pm, Sun 11am–5pm; €2.50; ⓦwww.heksenwaag.nl), a family-run affair, where you can be weighed on the original rope and wood balance, as were women accused of witchcraft. The owners dress up in national costume and issue a certificate in olde-worlde English that states nothing much in particular, but does so very prettily. There's not much else to see in Oudewater, but it is a pleasant little place, whose traditional stepped gables spread out along the River Hollandsche IJssel as it twists its way through town.

Oudewater is readily reached on **bus** #180 linking Gouda with Utrecht (every 30min, hourly on Sun; 30min from Gouda). The **VVV** is a brief stroll south of the Heksenwaag at Kapellestraat 2 (April–Sept Tues–Sat 10am–4pm, Sun 1–3pm; Oct–March Tues–Sat 10am–1pm; ☎0348/564 636, ⓦwww.vvvoudewater.nl).

Oudewater and Dutch witch-hunts

It's estimated that over a million European women were burned or otherwise murdered in the widespread **witch-hunts** of the sixteenth century – and not just from quasi-religious fear and superstition: anonymous accusation to the authorities was an easy way of removing a wife, at a time when there was no divorce. Underlying it all was a virulent misogyny and an accompanying desire to terrorize women into submission. There were three main methods for investigating accusations of witchcraft: in the first, **trial by fire**, the suspect had to walk barefoot over hot cinders or have a hot iron pressed into the back or hands. If the burns blistered, the accused was innocent, since witches were supposed to burn less easily than others; naturally, the (variable) temperature of the iron was crucial. **Trial by water** was still more hazardous: dropped into water, if you floated you were a witch, if you sank you were innocent – though very probably dead by drowning. The third method, **trial by weight**, presupposed that a witch would have to be unduly light to fly on a broomstick, so many Dutch towns – including Oudewater – used the Waag (town weigh-house) to weigh the accused. If the weight didn't accord with a notional figure derived from a person's height, the woman was burned. The last Dutch woman to be burned as a witch was a certain Marrigje Ariens, a herbalist from Schoonhoven in Zuid-Holland, whose medical efforts, not atypically, inspired mistrust and subsequent persecution. She died in 1597.

The Emperor Charles V (1516–52) made Oudewater famous after seeing a woman accused of witchcraft in a nearby village. The weigh-master there, who'd been bribed, stated that the woman weighed only a few pounds, but Charles was dubious and ordered the woman to be weighed again in Oudewater, where the officials proved unbribable, pronouncing a normal weight and acquitting her. The probity of Oudewater's weigh-master impressed Charles, and he granted the town the privilege of issuing certificates, valid throughout the empire, stating: "The accused's weight is in accordance with the natural proportions of the body." Once in possession of the certificate, a woman could never be brought to trial for witchcraft again. Not surprisingly, thousands of women came from all over Europe for this life-saving piece of paper, and, much to Oudewater's credit, no one was ever condemned here.

They have lots of local information including bus timetables. For **food**, try *Joia*, a smart, modern brasserie serving Dutch dishes a brief walk west of the VVV at Havenstraat 1–2 (☎0348/567 150; Tues–Sun noon–5pm & 6–9pm); main courses here cost €16–21.

Dordrecht and around

Some 20km southeast of Rotterdam, the ancient port of **DORDRECHT**, or "Dordt" as it's often called, sits beside one of the busiest waterway junctions in the world, where tankers and containers from the north pass the waterborne traffic of the Maas and Rijn. Eclipsed by the expansion of Rotterdam – and barely touched by World War II – Dordrecht's old centre has survived in excellent nick, its medley of eighteenth- and nineteenth-century warehouses, town houses and workers' terraces strung along its innermost canals and harbours. It takes about three hours to cover all of the town's main sights, which makes a day-trip the most obvious choice, especially as good hotels are thin on the ground. If, however, you're after exploring the sprawling marshes and tidal flats of the wilderness **Nationaal Park de Biesbosch** just south of town, then Dordrecht is the obvious base, though a long day-trip from, say, Rotterdam, Delft or Den Haag is quite feasible. The other main pull hereabouts is the windmills of the **Kinderdijk**.

Granted a town charter in 1220, Dordrecht was the most important and powerful town in Holland until well into the sixteenth century. One of the first cities to declare against the Habsburgs in 1572, it was the obvious site for the first meeting of the Free Assembly of the United Provinces, and for a series of doctrinal conferences that tried to solve a whole range of theological differences among the various Protestant sects. The Protestants may have hated the Catholics, but they inherited the medieval church's enthusiasm for theological debate; in 1618, at the Synod of Dordt, the Remonstrants argued with the Calvinists over the definition of predestination – pretty weighty stuff compared with the Synod of 1574, when one of the main rulings demanded the dismantling of church organs. From the seventeenth century, Dordrecht lost ground to its great rivals to the north, slipping into comparative insignificance, though it did manage to hold on to enough trade and shipbuilding to keep its economy afloat.

Arrival and information

Well connected by train to all of the Randstad's major cities, Dordrecht's adjoining **train** and **bus** stations are a ten-minute walk from the town centre: to get there, head straight down Stationsweg/Johan de Wittstraat and left at the end along Bagijnhof/Visstraat. On the way, just a couple of minutes from the station, you'll pass the **VVV**, at Stationsweg 1 (Mon noon–5.30pm, Tues–Fri 9am–5.30pm, Sat 10am–4pm; ☎0900/463 6888 premium line ⓦwww.vvvzhz .nl), which carries a good range of information about the town and its surroundings – including the Biesbosch – and operates an accommodation service. There's also a **Waterbus** passenger ferry service from Rotterdam (see p.195) that drops passengers within easy walking distance of the old centre, a couple of hundred metres from the **Groothoofdspoort**.

Accommodation

The VVV has a small supply of **rooms** in private houses (①), which it will reserve on your behalf for a nominal fee. Alternatively, there is one good central

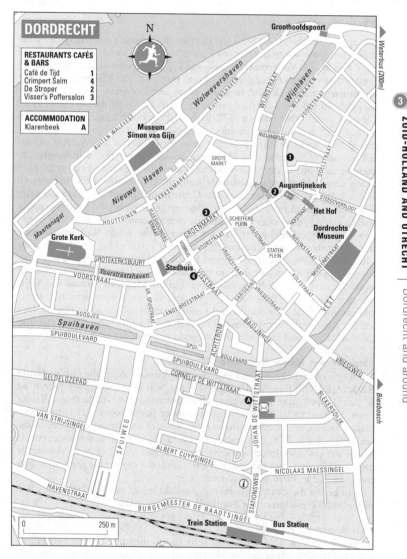

hotel, the *Klarenbeek*, a medium-sized place with modest, modern rooms metres from the VVV at Johan de Wittstraat 35 (☏078/614 4133, ⓦwww .hotelklarenbeek.nl; ❷). Dordrecht also has an HI **hostel**, but it's way out in the boon docks, on the edge of the Biesbosch about 6km east of town on Baanhoekweg (☏078/621 2167, ⓦwww.stayokay.com; double room (❶), dorm bed €22–27). To get there by public transport, take bus #5 from the station and tell the driver you want to change to the "Biesbus", which takes you on to the hostel. There's a small **campsite** at the hostel, one of several dotted around the peripheries of the Biesbosch.

The Town

Jutting out into the River Maas, the old part of Dordrecht is interrupted by the three concentric waterways that once protected it from assault. The middle canal runs beside the **Voorstraat**, today's main shopping street, and here, at the junction of Voorstraat and Visstraat, sitting pretty on the **Visbrug**, is a clunky **monument** to the de Witt brothers, Johan and Cornelius, prominent Dutch Republicans who paid for their principles when they were torn to pieces by an Orangist mob in Den Haag in 1672. To the right of the Visbrug, Voorstraat wends its way northeast, a chaotic mixture of the old, the new and the restored, intersected by a series of tiny alleys that once served as the town's docks. About halfway along Voorstraat the Wijnbrug bridge crosses the **Wijnhaven**, the harbour used by the city's merchants to control the import and export of wine when they held the state monopoly from the fourteenth to the seventeenth century. At the end of Voorstraat, the **Groothoofdspoort** was once the main city gate, its grand brick facade of 1618, complete with bronze-green cupola, staring down at the barges and boats that shuttle across the adjacent waterways.

From the Groothoofdspoort, it's a few metres to the slender **Wolwevershaven**, the first of the two small harbours that together make up the town's innermost canal. The Wolwevershaven is home to an eye-catching mixture of old boats and barges, some of which date back to the 1880s, and is framed by several fine old mansions, one of which has been turned into the **Museum Simon van Gijn**, Nieuwe Haven 29 (Tues–Sun 11–5pm; €6; ⓦ www.simonvangijn.nl), whose collection of local memorabilia and period rooms is of moderate interest. Best are the eighteenth-century Brussels tapestries and a fine Renaissance chimney piece of 1550, transferred from the old guild house of the arquebusiers.

The Grote Kerk and the Stadhuis

Lording it over the Nieuwe Haven, the next harbour along, the Gothic **Grote Kerk** (April–Oct Tues–Sat 10.30am–4.30pm, Sun noon–4pm; Nov–March Sat & Sun 1–4pm; free; ⓦ www.grotekerk-dordrecht.nl) is visible from all over town, its truncated, fourteenth-century **tower** (same hours; €1) topped with incongruous seventeenth-century clocks. One of the largest churches in the country, it was built to emphasize Dordrecht's wealth and importance, but it's heavy and dull, despite its attractive environs, and there's only an elaborately carved choir inside to hold your interest. Climb the tower for a great view over the town and its surrounding waterways.

From beside the church, the harmonious old gables of Grotekerksbuurt lead to the stolid classicism of the **Stadhuis**, on the Voorstraat.

Dordrechts Museum

From the Stadhuis, it's a ten-minute walk east to the town's premier art gallery, the **Dordrechts Museum**, at Museumstraat 40 (Tues–Sun 11am–5pm; €6; ⓦ www.dordrechtsmuseum.nl). Well presented and clearly labelled (in Dutch), the museum has a lively programme of temporary exhibitions and a strong permanent collection focused on local artists from the seventeenth century onwards. The paintings from the permanent collection are regularly rotated, but you can expect to see certain high points, beginning with a couple of finely drawn portraits by Jacob Cuyp (1594–1651), specifically pictures of a very young *Michiel Pompe* and of the eminently bourgeois *Anthonis Repelaer*. Jacob's son, Aelbert Cuyp (1620–91) is well represented too – by four romanticized land- and seascapes, whose soft, yellowish tones were much influenced by those of his contemporaries who had visited Italy.

Jan van Goyen (1596–1656), on the other hand, remained firmly within the Dutch landscape tradition, as illustrated by the detailed realism of his exquisite *View of Dordrecht*, the city flat and narrow beneath a wide, cloudy sky. In its turn, Goyen's vision of Dordrecht bears interesting comparison with Adam Willaertz's (1577–1664) massive *Gezicht op Dordt* (View of Dordt), in which the painter abandons proper scale to emphasize the ships in front of the city.

A student of Rembrandt, Nicolaes Maes (1634–93) first specialized in informal domestic scenes, as in *The Eavesdropper*, before turning his skills to portrait painting after his visit to Antwerp in 1670. More curiously, *De Dordtse Vierling* ("The Dordt Quadruplets") is an odd, unattributed seventeenth-century painting of a dead child and her three swaddled siblings, a simple, moving tribute to a lost daughter.

On the second floor, there's a selection of work by the later and lesser Ary Scheffer (1795–1858), who was born in Dordrecht, but lived in Paris from 1811. His much-reproduced *Mignon Pining for her Native Land* struck a chord in the sentimental hearts of the nineteenth-century bourgeoisie. Jozef Israels' (1824–1911) *Midday Meal at the Inn*, a scream against poverty, and G.H. Breitner's (1857–1923) *Amsterdam's Lauriergracht* are among a small collection of Amsterdam and Hague School paintings.

Eating and drinking

Dordrecht is not overly endowed with good **cafés** and **restaurants**, but there are certainly enough to be going on with, kicking off with *Visser's Poffersalon*, an old-fashioned café on the Groenmarkt (Tues & Wed 9am–6pm, Thurs 9am–9pm, Fri & Sat 9am–11pm), which does an especially fine line in pancakes. A second good choice is *De Stroper*, a smart seafood restaurant in modern, well-turned-out premises at Wijnbrug 1 (☎078/613 0094; Mon–Fri 11am–2pm & 5–10pm, Sat & Sun 5–10pm); main courses cost €20–25. There's also the *Crimpert Salm*, a French-style café and restaurant near Visbrug at Visstraat 5 (☎078/614 5557; Tues–Sat 10am–1am), where they serve snacks and light meals during the day and dinner in the evening; the *Crimpert* occupies a handsome old building that once housed the fish merchants' guild.

For **drinking**, the best place in town is *Café de Tijd*, a laidback, brown bar at Voorstraat 170 (daily except Tues from 3pm or 4pm till late) and with a first-class range of brews, both bottled and on tap.

East of Dordrecht: the Nationaal Park de Biesbosch

On November 18, 1421, Zuid-Holland's sea defences gave way and the St Elizabeth Day flood formed what is now the Hollands Diep sea channel and the **Biesbosch** (Reed Forest), an expanse of river, creek, marsh and reed covering around fifteen square kilometres to the south and east of Dordrecht. It was a disaster of major proportions, with seventy towns and villages destroyed, and a death toll of around 100,000. The effect on the region's economy was catastrophic, too, with the fracturing of links between Zuid-Holland and Flanders accelerating the shift in commercial power to the north. Those villages that did survive took generations to recover, subjected, as they were, to raids by the wretched refugees of the flood.

Inundated twice daily by the tide, the Biesbosch produced a particular **reed culture**, its inhabitants using the plant for every item of daily life, from houses to baskets and boats, and selling excess cuttings at the local markets. It was a harsh existence that lasted well into the nineteenth century, when machine-manufactured goods largely rendered the reeds redundant. Today, the Biesbosch is protected as a national park, but its delicate ecosystem is threatened by the very scheme that aims to protect the province from further flooding. The dams of the Delta Project (see p.318) have controlled the rivers' flow and restricted the tides' strength, forcing the reeds to give ground to other forms of vegetation incompatible with the area's bird and plant life. Large areas of reed have disappeared, and no one seems to know how to reconcile the nature reserve's needs with those of the seaboard cities, but vigorous attempts are being made.

The national park divides into two main sections, north and south of the Nieuwe Merwede waterway. The undeveloped heart of the park is the **Brabantse Biesbosch**, the chunk of land to the south, whereas almost all tourist facilities have been carefully confined to the north, on a strip just east of Dordrecht, along the park's perimeter.

Practicalities

The **Biesboschcentrum Dordrecht**, 7km or so east of town at Baanhoekweg 53 (Visitor Centre; Jan–April & Sept–Dec Tues–Sun 9am–5pm; May & June Mon 10am–5pm & Tues–Sun 9am–5pm; July & Aug daily 9am–6pm; Ⓦwww .biesbosch.org; free), has displays on the flora and fauna of the region and a beaver observatory. Frankly, this is pretty dull stuff, but it's here, from the jetty beside the visitor centre, that you can take a **boat trip** into the untouched reaches of the park, where deep and dense tracts of forest are crisscrossed by narrow waterways inhabited by all manner of wildfowl. Prices vary according to the itinerary, starting at €15 for the day ("Dagtochten") or €6 for an hour-long excursion ("Rondvaarten"), and you should check what's on offer – and make an advance booking – at Dordrecht VVV (see p.204) before you set out. If you fancy doing it under your own steam, note that there is boat and kayak here too.

The other way of visiting the park is by **bike**, for rent at standard rates from Dordrecht train station. The VVV sells detailed maps of the national park and brochures on suggested cycle routes. The ride from town to the Kop van 't Land dock, where ferries shuttle over to the Brabantse Biesbosch, takes about half an hour.

North of Dordrecht: the Kinderdijk

Some 12km north of Dordrecht, the **Kinderdijk** (Child's Dyke; Ⓦwww .kinderdijk.nl) sits at the end of a long drainage channel that feeds into the River Lek, whose turbulent waters it keeps in check. Sixteenth-century legend suggests it takes its name from the time when a cradle, complete with cat and kicking baby, was found at the precise spot where the dyke had held during a particularly bad storm. A mixture of symbols – rebirth, innocence and survival – the story encapsulates the determination with which the Dutch fought the floods for hundreds of years. Today, the Kinderdijk is famous for its picturesque, quintessentially Dutch **windmills**, all nineteen lining the main channel and its tributary beside the Molenkade for some three kilometres. Built around 1740 to drive water from the Alblasserwaard polders, the windmills are put into operation every Saturday afternoon in July and August and, in addition, one of the windmills is open to visitors from April through October (Mon–Sat 9.30am–5.30pm; €3).

Easily the best way to get to – and get around – the Kinderdijk is by **bike** (follow signs from Dordrecht). It is also possible to travel here on the **Waterbus** passenger ferry (see p.195) and by **Arriva bus**, though the bus service from Utrecht (bus #154: hourly, 1hr 30min) and Rotterdam's Zuidplein (bus #154: hourly, 50min) is much better than that from Dordrecht (bus #251; 3 daily, 40min): indeed, the bus timetable from Dordrecht means that it is often impossible to visit on a day-trip. There are also boat trips to the Kinderdijk from Rotterdam (see p.195).

Utrecht

"I groaned with the idea of living all winter in so shocking a place," moaned Boswell when he arrived in **UTRECHT** in 1763, a harsh judgement perhaps, but even today the mammoth shopping centre that encloses the city's train station is not an encouraging start. But persevere: much of Utrecht's old centre has survived intact, its network of canals, cobbled lanes and old gabled houses at their prettiest around the **Domkerk**, the city's cathedral. Domkerk apart, it's the general appearance and university atmosphere of the old town that is its appeal rather than any specific sight – and indeed Utrecht's two key museums, the **Centraal** and the **Catharijne Convent**, both of which have an enjoyable collection of old Dutch paintings, are out of the immediate centre to the south. Utrecht was also the long-time home of the De Stijl luminary **Gerrit Rietveld**, whose assorted furniture decorates the Centraal Museum, which pays further tribute to the man by organizing bus trips to the house that Rietveld built – the **Rietveld Schröderhuis**.

Founded by the **Romans** in the first century AD, Utrecht only came to prominence in the eighth century after the consecration of its first **bishop**. Thereafter, a long line of powerful bishops made Utrecht an independent city-state under the auspices of the German emperors and extended their control over the surrounding region. In 1527, the bishop, seeing which way the historical wind was blowing, sold off his secular rights to the Habsburg Emperor Charles V, and shortly afterwards the town council enthusiastically joined the revolt against Spain. Indeed, the **Union of Utrecht**, the agreement that formalized the opposition to the Habsburgs, was signed here in 1579. The seventeenth century witnessed the foundation of **Utrecht University** and the eighteenth saw Utrecht pop up again as the place where the **Treaty of Utrecht** was signed in 1713, thereby concluding decades of dynastic feuding between Europe's rulers. Today, with a population of around quarter of a million, Utrecht is one of the country's most important cities, its economy buoyed up by light industry and IT.

Arrival and information

Utrecht's **train and bus stations** both lead into the sprawling **Hoog Catharijne** shopping centre, on the western edge of the city centre; the main **VVV** office is a five- to ten-minute walk away at Vinkenburgstraat 19 (Mon noon–6pm, Tues–Fri 10am–6pm, Sat 9.30am–5pm; ☏0900/128 8732 premium line, Ⓦwww.utrechtstad.com). They have a range of information on the city and its surroundings, provide city maps and operate an accommodation booking

---

Canal trips

Throughout the summer, Schuttevaer (Ⓦwww.schuttevaer.com, ☏030/272 0111) operates enjoyable, hour-long **canal trips** (daily 11am–5pm; €7) around the centre of the city. Departures are from Oude Gracht, just south of the Lange Viestraat/ Potterstraat junction.

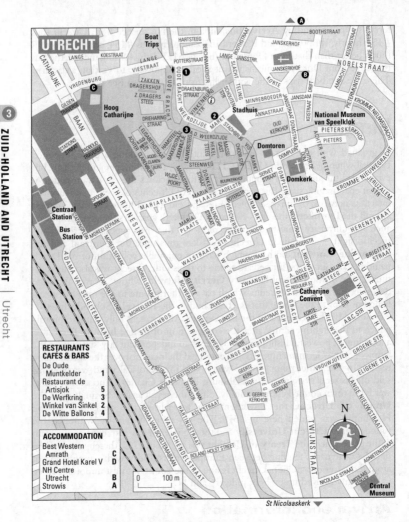

RESTAURANTS CAFÉS & BARS

De Oude Muntkelder	1
Restaurant de Artisjok	5
De Werfkring	3
Winkel van Sinkel	2
De Witte Ballons	4

ACCOMMODATION

Best Western Amrath	C
Grand Hotel Karel V	D
NH Centre Utrecht	B
Strowis	A

St Nicolaaskerk ▼

service. The best way to explore the city centre is on foot, but **bikes** can be rented from the train station at standard rates.

Accommodation

As you might expect of a big city, Utrecht has a battery of chain **hotels**. Some occupy big modern blocks, but one or two are rather more distinctive, and the city also has a great-value **hostel**.

Hotels

Best Western Amrath Hotel Vredenburg 14
℡030/233 1232, ⓦwww.amrathutrecht.nl.
Popular with visiting business folk, this smart and modern chain hotel has a handy central location. ❺

Grand Hotel Karel V Geertebolwerk 1
℡030/233 7555, ⓦwww.karelv.nl. Opened in 1999, the *Karel V* is the plushest hotel in town, a five-star extravagance on the site of what was once the headquarters of the Knights of the Teutonic Order and partly occupying the infirmary of a

nineteenth-century military hospital. The interior is, as you might expect, immaculate, all wooden floors and white walls with the odd suit of armour propped up here and there for good measure. The more expensive rooms are in the former infirmary, the less expensive in the modern annexe. A seven-minute walk south of the train station. ❻
NH Centre Utrecht Hotel Janskerkhof 10 ☎030/231 3169, ⓦwww.nh-hotels.com. Well-equipped chain hotel in a sympathetically converted old building from the 1870s. The 45 guest rooms are kitted out in brisk, modern style. A fifteen-minute walk east of the train station. ❹

Hostel

Strowis Boothstraat 8 ☎030/238 0280, ⓦwww.strowis.nl. This pleasant hostel in a seventeenth-century town house has a good range of facilities, including a small library, bike rental, a self-catering kitchen and free Internet access. The bedrooms, which range from single rooms to 14-bed dorms, are well kept and painted in cheerful colours. The *Strowis* is situated in the old centre near St Janskerk, 1km east of the station. Dorm beds €14–17, doubles ❶

The Town

The obvious place to start a visit to the city is the **Domtoren**, at over 112m the highest church bell tower in the country. It's one of the most beautiful, too, its soaring columns and arches rising to a delicate, octagonal lantern, which was added in 1380 some sixty years after the rest of the tower was completed. Hour-long guided tours (April–Sept Mon & Sun noon–5pm, Tues–Sat 11am–5pm; Oct–March Mon–Fri & Sun noon–5pm, Sat 10am–5pm; tours hourly, every 30min in July & Aug; €7.50; ⓦwww.domtoren.nl) take you unnervingly near to the top, from where on a clear day you can see Rotterdam and Amsterdam. Below, only the eastern part of the great cathedral – the **Domkerk** – remains, the nave having collapsed during a storm in 1674. It's worth peeking inside (May–Sept Mon–Sat 10am–5pm, Sun 2–4pm; Oct–April Mon–Sat 11am–4pm, Sun 2–4pm; free) to get a sense of the hangar-like space the building once had. The adjacent cloisters, the fourteenth-century **Kloostergang**, link the cathedral to the chapterhouse and their gardens, the **Kloostertuin**, are generally reckoned to be the best place to listen to the carillon concerts of the Domtoren.

Just to the east of the Domtoren, **Kromme Nieuwegracht** is one of the city's most delightful streets, its string of fine old buildings overlooking a slender, tree-lined canal. Follow the canal round and eventually you reach Jansstraat, from where it's a hop, skip and a jump to the grandiose nineteenth-century **Stadhuis**, on a bend in the Oude Gracht. The Stadhuis is also close to the unusual **Nationaal Museum van Speelklok tot Pierement**, Steenweg 6 (Tues–Sat 10am–5pm, Sun noon–5pm; €7), a collection of fairground organs and ingenious musical boxes worth an hour of (almost) anyone's time. The museum is housed in the **Buurkerk**, once the home of one sister Bertken, who was so ashamed of being the illegitimate daughter of a cathedral priest that she hid away in a small cell here for 57 years, until her death in 1514.

The Museum Catharijne Convent

The national collection of ecclesiastical art, the **Museum Catharijne Convent** (Tues–Fri 10am–5pm, Sat & Sun 11am–5pm; €8.50; ⓦwww.catharijneconvent.nl), 500m south of the Domtoren at Lange Nieuwstraat 38, has a mass of paintings, manuscripts and church ornaments from the ninth century on, brilliantly exhibited in a complex built around the old convent. This excellent collection of paintings includes work by Geertgen tot Sint Jans, Rembrandt, Hals and, perhaps best of all, a luminously beautiful *Virgin and Child* by Joos Van Cleve (1485–1540). The convent incorporates the late Gothic **St Catharijnekerk**, whose radiant white interior is enhanced by floral decoration.

Centraal Museum – and the Rietveld Schröderhuis

From the Catharijne Convent, it's about 400m south along Lange Nieuwstraat to the **Centraal Museum** at Nicolaaskerkhof 10 (Tues–Sun noon–5pm, Fri till 9pm; €8; Ⓦwww.centraalmuseum.nl). The museum's claim to hold "25,000 curiosities" may be exaggerated, but it does have a good collection of paintings by Utrecht artists of the sixteenth and seventeenth centuries. One of the most interesting of them is Jan van Scorel (1495–1562), who lived in Utrecht before and after he visited Rome, from where he brought the influence of the Renaissance back home to his fellow painters. A prime example of this mix of native Dutch observation and Renaissance style is Scorel's vivid *Portraits of Twelve Members of Utrecht's Jerusalem Brotherhood*, in which, incidentally, the fifth figure from the right is the artist himself. Scorel is also thought to have made a trip to Jerusalem sometime in the 1520s and this may well account for his unusually accurate drawing of the city in the *Lokhorst Triptych: Christ's Entry into Jerusalem*.

A later generation of city painters fell under the influence of Italian art in general and Caravaggio (1572–1610) in particular. Known as the **Utrecht School**, one of the group's leading practitioners was Gerrit van Honthorst (1590–1656), whose *Procuress* adapted Caravaggio's chiaroscuro technique to a genre subject and also developed an erotic content that would itself influence later genre painters like Jan Steen and Gerrit Dou. Even more skilled and realistic is Hendrick Terbrugghen's (1588–1629) *The Calling of St Matthew*, a beautiful balance of gestures dramatizing Christ summoning the tax collector to become one of the twelve disciples.

Gerrit Rietveld (1888–1964), the celebrated De Stijl architect and designer, lived and worked in Utrecht and the museum has a fine collection of his furniture, especially the brightly coloured geometrical chairs for which he is perhaps best known. The chairs are quite simply beautiful, but although part of the De Stijl philosophy (see Contexts, p.382) was the need for universality, they are undoubtedly better to look at than to actually sit on. Rietveld fans will also be keen to catch the museum **shuttle bus** (Tues–Sun 4 daily) over to the **Rietveld Schröderhuis** (€8 extra, including bus; reservations recommended, during museum opening hours on ☏030/236 2310; Ⓦwww .rietveldschroderhuis.nl), a couple of kilometres to the east at Prins Hendrik-laan 50. Rietveld designed and built the house in 1924 for one Truus Schröder and her family. It's hailed as one of the most influential pieces of modern architecture in Europe, demonstrating the organic union of lines and rectangles that was the hallmark of the De Stijl movement. The ground floor is the most conventional part of the building, since its design had to meet the rigours of the building licence; however, Rietveld was able to let his imagination run riot with the top floor living space, creating a flexible environment where only the outer walls are solid – indeed the entire top floor can be subdivided in any way, simply by sliding the modular walls. The excursion also includes a quick gambol round the modernist terrace Rietveld designed on neighbouring Erasmuslaan.

Back at the Centraal Museum, it's a few metres over to the **Dick Bruna Huis**, Agnietenstraat 2 (Tues–Sun 10am–5pm; €8; Ⓦwww.dickbrunahuis.com), which celebrates the life and work of Dick Bruna (b.1927), who has established an international reputation for his children's picture books in general and for his star creation, *Miffy* the rabbit, in particular.

From the Dick Bruna Huis, it takes about fifteen minutes to return to the Domtoren, a pleasant stroll along either the Oude Gracht or the Nieuwe Gracht canals.

△ Utrecht centre

Eating and drinking

There are lots of inexpensive places to **eat and drink** along Oude Gracht, both on the street and below at canal level – on the Werf – where the brick cellars, which were once used as warehouses, have been converted into a string of cafés, bars and restaurants. Options here include the inexpensive pancake house *De Oude Muntkelder*, Oude Gracht – Werf 112 (daily noon–9pm), and the vegetarian *De Werfkring*, Oude Gracht – Werf 123 (Mon–Sat noon–2pm & 5–8pm). For something a little more upmarket, you might try the *Restaurant de Artisjok*,

Nieuwegracht 33 (daily 5–10pm; ☎030/231 7494), a smart but cosy little place with an imaginative, international menu; main courses hover around €20.

Among Oude Gracht's many **bars and café-bars**, there's *Winkel van Sinkel*, Oude Gracht 158, a large and often crowded bar with regular weekend dance nights, plus a chill-out room downstairs in the cellars. A second good choice is *De Witte Ballons*, a friendly, low-key bar at Lijnmarkt 10–12. Most of Utrecht's thirty-odd **cannabis coffeeshops** are on the outskirts of town, but one city-centre option is *Andersom*, at Vismarkt 23 (Mon–Sat 10am–11pm, Sun 11am–11pm).

East of Utrecht: Amersfoort, Doorn and Rhenen

Stretching east from Utrecht's trailing suburbs, the **Utrechtse Heuvelrug** (Utrecht Ridge) is a pleasant wooded district that is popular with walkers and cyclists alike. **Amersfoort**, twenty minutes by train from Utrecht, is the main town hereabouts – an amenable, easygoing place with a clutch of medieval buildings as well as the Mondriaanhuis, where the artist Piet Mondrian was born and raised. Otherwise, the area's high points are to the south of Amersfoort in the medieval castle turned chateau at **Doorn**, where Kaiser Bill spent his exile after World War I, and the little town of **Rhenen**, which pulls in tourists aplenty to view the fifteenth-century church of St Cunera. There is a direct train from Utrecht to Rhenen, which takes thirty minutes and passes through Maarn, just 4km from Doorn.

Amersfoort

The middling town **of AMERSFOORT**, some 15km to the east of Utrecht, was first fortified in the eleventh century, but its salad days came later, from the sixteenth century onwards, when it prospered from the brewing of beer, the making of cloth and the processing of tobacco. The town centre is still ringed by what was once its medieval moat and holds a string of old buildings, but the prime attraction is the **Modriaanhuis**, where the eponymous artist was born and raised.

The Town

At the centre of Amersfoort is the **Hof**, a pleasant square edged by the giant hulk of **St Joriskerk** (mid-June to mid-Sept Mon–Sat 2–4.30pm; free), a predominantly Gothic edifice finished in 1534. Unusually, the nave and aisles are of equal height, and only the south porch stops the exterior from resembling an aircraft hangar. Like most churches of the period, it was an enlargement of an earlier building, but here the original Romanesque tower was left inside the later fifteenth-century construction. From the church, it's a few minutes' walk northeast along Langestraat to the **Kamperbinnenpoort**, a turreted thirteenth-century gate, extensively renovated in the 1930s. To the north and south of the gate runs **Muurhuizen** – literally "wall houses", after the habit of attaching dwellings to what was once the city's medieval rampart. Head north along Muurhuizen and it takes about ten minutes to reach the town's principal museum, the **Museum Flehite**, at Westsingel 50 (Tues–Fri 11am–5pm, Sat & Sun noon–5pm; €5; ⓦ www.museumflehite.nl). The museum occupies a good-looking, fancifully gabled building beside one of the town's canals, but the collection within focuses on the history of Amersfoort, something of a specialist subject. Rather more engaging, and about 300m north of the museum, is the **Koppelpoort**, an elaborate, fifteenth-century town gate whose assorted defences straddle what was once the main waterway into the city.

Doubling back to the Museum Flehite, it's another 400m or so south along Westsingel to the fifteenth-century **toren** (tower; July & Aug Tues–Sat 10am–5pm; €4), which is all that remains of Amersfoort's other main church, the **Onze Lieve Vrouwekerk** – the rest was accidentally blown up in 1797. The original church was paid for by pilgrims visiting the Amersfoort Madonna, a small and much-revered medieval wooden figure. Legend has it that, in 1444, a young girl threw the statuette into the town canal when she was on her way to enter one of the city's convents. It wasn't that she minded becoming a nun, but rather that she was ashamed of the simplicity of her Madonna. In the manner of such things, a dream commanded her to retrieve the statue, which subsequently demonstrated miraculous powers. Part-morality play, part-miracle, the story fulfilled all the necessary criteria to turn the figure into a revered object, and the town into a major centre of medieval pilgrimage.

Piet Mondrian (1872–1944), the leading light of De Stijl, was a native of Amersfoort and the house where he was born, along with the adjacent school where his father was the headteacher, have been turned into the **Mondriaanhuis**, located by the canal a five- to ten-minute walk southeast of the Onze Lieve Vrouwekerk at Kortegracht 11 (Tues–Fri 10am–5pm, Sat & Sun 1–5pm; €3.75; ⓦwww.mondriaanhuis.nl). The museum holds an enjoyable retrospective of the artist's life and work, and although the exhibits are regularly rotated, you can expect to see prime examples of the geometric paintings for which Mondrian was internationally famous.

Practicalities

Amersfoort **train station** and **VVV**, Stationsplein 9 (May–Sept Mon–Fri 9am–5.30pm, Sat 10am–4pm; Oct–April Mon–Fri 9am–5.30pm, Sat 9am–2pm; ⓣ0900/112 2364, ⓦwww.vvvamersfoort.nl), are located to the west of the town centre, about 1km from the Hof. The town has several reasonably priced **hotels**, the best being the *Logement de Gaaper* (ⓣ033/453 1795, ⓦwww.degaaper.nl; ❷), in an attractively renovated older building plumb in the centre at Hof 39.

As regards **food** and **drink**, the best place to head for is *Het Filmhuis*, a combined café, restaurant (Tues-Sat 6–10pm; ⓣ033/465 5550, ⓦwww.hetfilmhuis.nl), cinema and art gallery in tastefully modernized premises just east off the Hof at Groenmarkt 8. Finally, *Trenchtown*, just north of the Hof at Krommestraat 41, is an agreeable and handy **cannabis coffeeshop**.

Doorn

Some 15km east of Utrecht, the workaday town of **DOORN** is home to the **Kasteel Huis Doorn** (mid-March to Oct Tues–Sat 10am–5pm, Sun 1–5pm; Nov to mid-March Tues–Sun 1–5pm, last entry 1hr before closing, guided tours only; €5.50; ⓣ0343/421 020, ⓦwww.huisdoorn.nl), a medieval castle that was converted into a staid and really rather pedestrian manor house in two stages – one at the end of the eighteenth century, the other in the middle of the nineteenth. That might well have been it, except that **Kaiser Wilhelm II** bought the property after the German surrender at the end of World War I and lived here in exile from 1920 until his death in 1941. The Dutch had remained neutral in World War I and they stuck to the same policy in peace time, consistently refusing to extradite Wilhelm for trial as a war criminal, though in truth the French and British were not overly disappointed; quite what they would have done with a guilty ex-Kaiser is hard to conceive. Later, in the 1930s, Wilhelm entertained hopes that Hitler would revive the monarchy, and although this proved to be a pipe dream, Wilhelm did die with German guards at his gates, courtesy of the occupying forces of World War II.

The **guided tour** takes in the usual trappings of a stately home – elegantly decorated rooms, furnished here in the style of the 1920s – and among Wilhelm's personal souvenirs is a fine collection of snuffboxes from the era of Frederick the Great. There's a bust of the Kaiser in the gardens and House of Hohenzollern tea cosies in the souvenir shop.

Rhenen

Tiny **RHENEN**, strategically positioned on the north bank of the Rhine 19km east of Doorn, has ancient origins – as evidenced by the prehistoric pottery and burial urns displayed at the enjoyable **Gemeentemuseum Het Rondeel**, Kerkstraat 1 (Tues–Fri noon–5pm, Sat 1–5pm; July & Aug also Sun 1–5pm; €1.50). The museum also holds Merovingian weapons and jewellery plus a collection of gargoyles and assorted statuary brought here from the town's **Sint Cunerakerk** (July to mid-Sept Mon–Sat 2–3.30pm; free), a late Gothic church with an imposing 84-metre tower. According to legend, St Cunera was a fifth-century English princess, who was kidnapped when she was on a pilgrimage to Rome. Radboud, king of Rhenen, promptly rode to the rescue and afterwards Cunera decided to hang around, becoming hugely popular on account of her work with the poor and the sick – though Radboud's wife was distinctly unimpressed. Green with envy, the queen had Cunera murdered, but that was just the beginning of her problems. Cunera's ghost appeared again and again, churning out the odd medical miracle and attracting so many pilgrims that Rhenen was able to build the Cunerakerk in honour of the saint.

Travel details

Trains

Amersfoort to: Amsterdam CS (every 20min; 40min); Den Haag CS (every 30min; 1hr); Utrecht (every 15min; 15min); Zwolle (every 30min; 35min).
Amsterdam CS to: Amersfoort (every 20min; 40min); Den Haag CS (every 30min; 50min); Leiden (every 30min; 40min); Utrecht (every 15min; 30min).
Delft to: Den Haag CS (every 15min; 12min); Dordrecht (every 15min; 25min); Rotterdam (every 15min; 10min).
Den Haag CS to: Amersfoort (every 30min; 1hr); Amsterdam CS (every 30min; 50min); Delft (every 15min; 12min); Dordrecht (every 30min; 35min); Gouda (every 20min; 20min); Leiden (every 30min; 20min); Rotterdam (every 15min; 25min); Utrecht (every 20min; 40min).
Dordrecht to: Delft (every 15min; 25min); Den Haag CS (every 30min; 35min); Rotterdam (every 15min; 15min).

Leiden to: Amsterdam CS (every 30min; 40min); Den Haag CS (every 30min; 20min).
Rotterdam to: Delft (every 15min; 10min); Den Haag CS (every 15min; 25min); Dordrecht (every 15min; 15min); Gouda (every 20min; 25min); Utrecht (every 20min; 45min).
Utrecht to: Amersfoort (every 15min; 15min); Amsterdam CS (every 15min; 30min); Arnhem (every 30min; 40min); Den Haag (every 20min; 40min); Leeuwarden (hourly; 2hr); Maarn (for Doorn; every 30min; 15min); Rhenen (every 30min; 30min); Rotterdam (every 20min; 45min); Zwolle (every 30min; 1hr).

Buses

Dordrecht to: Kinderdijk (3 daily; 40min).
Gouda to: Oudewater (every 30min, hourly on Sun; 30min).
Rotterdam to: Kinderdijk (hourly; 50min).
Utrecht to: Kinderdijk (hourly; 1hr 30min).

The north and the Frisian Islands

CHAPTER 4

Highlights

* **Fries Museum, Leeuwarden** A fine insight into the culture of Friesland, in the heart of this easygoing market town. See p.226

* **Harlingen** Far-flung harbour, with a long history of traditional barge-building. See p.230

* **Terschelling** The most alluring of the Frisian islands, wild and wind-blown. See p.232

* **Vlieland** Tranquil, low-key island of woods and dunes. See p.236

* **Sneek** This prosperous shipbuilding town of old is now famous as the location for the Sneek Week sailing regatta every August. See p.237

* **Groningen** Dynamic university town in the far north, with a cosmopolitan outlook and the memorable Groniger Museum of art and culture. See p.247

* **Schiermonnikoog** Atmospheric, little-visited island off the far northern coast. See p.256

* **Wadlopen** The best way to experience the northern landscapes is to copy the Dutch and take a guide for *wadlopen* – mudflat walking. See p.256

△ Schiermonnikoog island

The north and the Frisian Islands

U ntil the early twentieth century, the north of the Netherlands was a relatively remote area, a distinct region of small provincial towns far removed from the mainstream life of the Randstad. The year 1932 saw the opening of the **Afsluitdijk**, a 30-kilometre-long sea wall bridging the mouth of the Zuider Zee, once the corridor for the great trading ships of the Golden Age. Since the completion of the dyke, the cultural gap between the north and west of the Netherlands has narrowed, and now fashion and custom seem all but identical. The main exception is linguistic: Friesland has its own language, more akin to Low German than Dutch, and its citizens are keen to use it.

One of the three northern provinces, **Friesland**, is a deservedly popular tourist stopover. Attracting an increasing number of visitors, it offers the cluster of duneswept **Frisian Islands** and a chain of eleven immaculate, history-steeped "cities", such as **Hindeloopen**, **Stavoren** and **Sloten**, each with a distinct charm and trade. Church towers, cobbled streets, narrow canals, wooden barges and bright window-boxes are typical details that add colour to these smartly kept settlements. Like much of the Netherlands, the scenery is predominantly green, bisected by a network of canals and dotted with black and white cattle – Friesians, of course – and pitch-black Frisian horses. Breaking the dead flat monotony of the landscape, sleek wind turbines, or American windmills as they're called, make the most of the strong westerlies, a modern counterpart to the last working windmills in the area.

East of Friesland, the province of **Groningen** has comparatively few attractions. But while its villages are less charismatic and more suburban, the university town of Groningen more than makes up for them with its vibrant ambience, contemporary fashions, an array of affordable bars and restaurants, a growing international performance-art festival and the best nightlife in the region. It's also home to the Groninger Museum, a striking and controversial vision of urban architecture and art, and a definite highlight of the region.

South of Groningen lies **Drenthe**, little more than a barren moor for much of its history. During the nineteenth century, the face of much of the province was changed by the founding of innumerable peat colonies, whose labourers drained the land and dug the peat to expose the subsoil below. As a result of

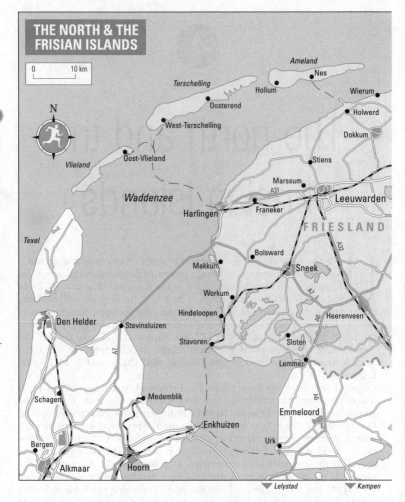

THE NORTH & THE
FRISIAN ISLANDS

0   10 km

N

Ameland
Nes

Terschelling
Hollum
Wierum

Oosterend
Holwerd

West-Terschelling
Dokkum

Vlieland
Oost-Vlieland
Stiens

Texel
Marssum
A31
Leeuwarden

Waddenzee
Franeker

Harlingen
FRIESLAND

Bolsward

Makkum
Sneek

Workum
A7

Hindeloopen
A6
Heerenveen

Den Helder
Stevinsluizen

Stavoren
Sloten

Lemmer
A6

Schagen
Medemblik

Emmeloord

Enkhuizen

Bergen
Urk

Alkmaar   Hoorn

▼ *Lelystad*   ▼ *Kampen*

their work, parts of Drenthe are given over to prosperous farmland, with agriculture the dominant local industry. Sparsely populated and the least visited of the Dutch provinces, today Drenthe is popular with homegrown tourists, who are drawn by its quiet natural beauty, swathes of woods, wide cycling paths and abundant walking trails. The two main towns have only a couple of attractions that might bring you this far off the beaten track: the capital **Assen** has the Drents Museum, with a superb collection of prehistoric finds, while **Emmen** is the best place to see Drenthe's most original feature – its *hunebeds*, or megalithic tombs.

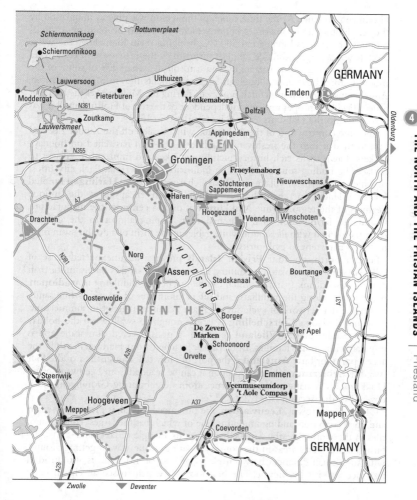

Friesland

A region that prospered during the sixteenth-century heyday of the Zuider Zee trade, **Friesland** is focused around eleven historic cities and seven lakes, the latter symbolized by the seven red hearts on the region's flag, which proudly flutters in many a back garden.

Friesland once occupied the whole of the north. In the eighth century, Charlemagne recognized three parts: West Frisia, equivalent to today's West Friesland, across the IJsselmeer; Central Frisia, today's Friesland; and East Frisia, now

Groningen province. At the time, much of the region was prey to inundation by the sea. Houses and sometimes entire settlements would be built on artificial mounds or *terpen*, as long ago as 500 BC, bringing them high above the water level. It was a tough existence, and not surprisingly the Frisians soon built dykes to keep the water out permanently. You can still see what's left of some of the mounds around the area, though in large settlements they're mostly obscured. Always a maverick among Dutch provinces, during the Middle Ages the area that is now Friesland proper remained independent of the rest of Holland, until it was absorbed into the Habsburg empire by Charles V in 1523.

Since the construction of the Afsluitdijk, which sealed off the Zuider Zee and transformed it into the freshwater IJsselmeer, Friesland has relied on holiday-makers drawn to its rich history, picturesque lakes and immaculate villages to replace the trading routes and fishing industries of yesteryear. Each city (most of which are town- or village-sized) has a charm of its own: **Harlingen** is noted for its splendid merchant houses; **Hindeloopen** encapsulates the antique neatness of the region; while **Makkum** was once a centre of tile manufacture. Grand old farmhouses, their thatched roofs sloping almost to the ground, remain crowned with *úleboerden*, white gables in the form of a double swan once used as a deterrent to evil spirits.

Further north, the four **Frisian Islands** preserve an unexpected sense of wilderness in so populated a country. Each strand of land is barely more than elongated sandbank (parts of which can be reached by indulging in **wadlopen**, hearty walks along the mudflats) and offers kilometres of hourglass-fine sandy beaches and a network of cycleways to roam. A tourist magnet in summertime, busy and developed **Terschelling** is large enough to swallow up the holiday crowds, while car-free **Vlieland** resembles a grass-covered dunescape and is popular with young families. Both can be reached from Harlingen, while the access point for busy **Ameland** is the port of Holwerd. The smallest of the four islands is **Schiermonnikoog**; although it can be reached from Leeuwarden and Dokkum, it's actually a shorter journey from neighbouring Groningen, and is covered in that section (see p.256).

Of the larger towns, **Leeuwarden**, the provincial capital, is pleasant if sedate, and boasts two outstanding museums, one of which has the largest collection of tiles in the world. Nearby **Sneek** has access to a tangle of lakes and canals, the busiest watersports areas in the country. Boating is one way of getting around; with such small distances between places of interest, Friesland is also an ideal province to visit by bicycle. The best loop by which to see all eleven cities

Frisian sports and traditions

The Frisians have several unusual sports and traditions that can raise eyebrows in the rest of the country. Using a large pole to jump over wet obstacles was once a necessity in the Frisian countryside, but the Frisians turned it into a sport: **Fierljep-pen**. Today Frisian and Dutch pole jumpers compete for the honour during the annual Frisian championships held in Winsum, always on the second Saturday of August.

Skûtjesilen, a fourteen-day sailing race held throughout Friesland in July or August, is another regional rarity. *Skûtjes* are large cargo vessels, but they went out of use after World War II and are now only used for contests and recreational purposes. The VVV in Sneek (see p.238) can give more information on where to see the contest. Last but not least **kaatsen**, a Frisian version of tennis, with over 2000 contests held every year. Instead of a racket a *kaatser* uses a handmade glove to hit the handmade ball with; a team of *kaatsers* always has three players.

follows the 220-kilometre-long route of the **Elfstedentocht**, a marathon ice-skating race held during winters cold enough for the canals to freeze over. Most VVVs stock maps and guides for cycling, in-line skating, driving or sailing the route all year round.

Leeuwarden

An old market town at the heart of an agricultural district, **LEEUWARDEN** was formed from the amalgamation of three *terpen* that originally stood on an expanse of water known as the Middelzee. Later it was the residence of the powerful Frisian Stadholders, who vied with those of Holland for control of the United Provinces; tracks from this period can still be found in Leeuwarden. These days it's Friesland's capital, a university town with a provincial air, its centre a discordant blend of modern glass architecture and traditional design. While it lacks the concentrated historic charm of many other Dutch towns, it does have a number of grand buildings and two outstanding museums. Most appealing is a compact town centre, almost entirely surrounded and dissected by water, along which big barges nudge their way through.

Arrival, information and accommodation

Leeuwarden's **train** and **bus stations** virtually adjoin each other, five minutes' walk south of the town centre. There's no cheap **car parking** near the station, but you can park for free in the residential area around it. The **VVV** is on the ground floor of the Achmea Tower, the grey skyscraper 200m north of the train station at Sophialaan 4 (Mon noon–5.30pm, Tues–Fri 9.30am–5.30pm, Sat 10am–3pm; June–Aug Sat until 4pm; ☎0900/202 4060). They publish a map detailing walking tours of the centre (€1.15, ask for accompanying English leaflet) and have a short list of private **rooms** that covers the whole of Friesland, as well as information on guided boat trips to the Frisian lakes or canal trips through Leeuwarden.

There are a few reasonably priced **hotels** in town: the *Eurohotel,* Europaplein 30 (☎058/213 1113, ⓦwww.eurohotel.nl; ❷), located outside the city centre, is a good option when travelling by car (free parking); the *Hotel 't Anker*, Eewal 69–75 (☎058/212 5216, ⓦwww.hotelhetanker.nl; ❶), is popular and more central, though it does need some refurbishing. The *Bastion* is a reliable fallback, though it's a good walk south of town at Legedijk 6 (☎058/289 0112, ⓦwww .bastionhotels.nl; ❶). A plusher option is *Eden Oranje*, Stationsweg 4 (☎058/212 6241, ⓦwww.edenhotelgroup.com; ❷), near the train station, with a large restaurant. By far the most luxurious option is the four-star *Stadhouderlijk Hof*, Hofplein 29 (☎058/216 2180, ⓦwww.stadhouderlijkhof.nl; ❸), which offers rooms with Jacuzzi for a decadent stay. There's **camping** at *De Kleine Wielen*, De Groene Ster 14 (☎0511/431 660, ⓦwww.dekleinewielen.nl; April–Sept), about 6km out towards Dokkum, nicely sited by a lake; take bus #10, #13, #51 or #62 from the station.

The Town

If you've just arrived from Friesland's immaculate coast and countryside towns, Leeuwarden is initially a bit of a disappointment, with the southern part of the town centre near the station an indeterminate, careless mixture of the old and new. Heading north, high-rise blocks and shopping centres line Wirdumerdijk

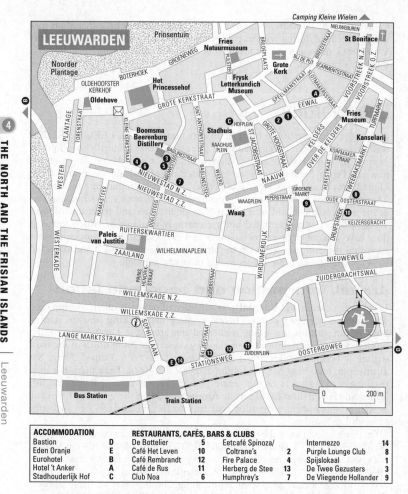

LEEUWARDEN

Camping Kleine Wielen ▲

Prinsentuin
Fries Natuurmuseum
Noorder Plantage
St Boniface
NIEUWEBUREN
BREEDPLAATS
BIJ DE PUT
SCARMENTSSTRAAT
Grote Kerk
BOTERHOEK
GROENEWEG
PIJSTEEG
SPEELMANSTRAAT
ROTMAKERSTRAAT
BREESTEEG N.Z.
VOORSTREEK N.Z.
VOORSTREEK O.Z.
OLDEHOOFSTER KERKHOF
Het Princessehof
Frysk Letterkundich Museum
EEWAL
Oldehove
GROTE KERKSTRAAT
SINT ANTHONYSTRAAT
HOFPLEIN
Fries Museum
TURFMARKT
Boomsma Beerenburg Distillery
Stadhuis
ST JACOBSSTRAAT
GROTE HOOGSTRAAT
KELDERS
OVER DE KELDERS
Kanselarij
RAADHUIS PLEIN
BAGIJNESTRAAT
BAGIJNESTEEG
KORFMAKER-STRAAT
TWEEBAKSMARKT
WEERD
NAAUW
HERESTRAAT
OUDE OOSTERSTRAAT
NIEUWESTAD N.Z.
NIEUWESTAD Z.Z.
WAAGPLEIN
PEPERSTRAAT
GROENTE MARKT
DRUIFSTREEK
KEIZERSGRACHT
Waag
WEAZE
HAMASTEEG
DOELESTEEG
RUITERSKWARTIER
Paleis van Justitie
ZAAILAND
WILHELMINAPLEIN
WIRDUMERDIJK
NIEUWEWEG
ZUIDERGRACHTSWAL
WESTERKADE
WESTER
PLANTAGE
TORENSTRAAT
KLEINE KERKSTRAAT
PRINS HENDRIK-STRAAT
ZUIDERSTRAAT
WILLEMSKADE N.Z.
WILLEMSKADE Z.Z.
LANGE MARKTSTRAAT
SOPHIALAAN
STATIONSWEG
BALLESTRAAT
ZUIDERPLEIN
OOSTERGOWEG
N
Bus Station
Train Station
0   200 m

ACCOMMODATION
Bastion   D
Eden Oranje   E
Eurohotel   B
Hotel 't Anker   A
Stadhouderlijk Hof   C

RESTAURANTS, CAFÉS, BARS & CLUBS
De Bottelier   5
Café Het Leven   10
Café Rembrandt   12
Café de Rus   11
Club Noa   6
Eetcafé Spinoza/
  Coltrane's   2
Fire Palace   4
Herberg de Stee   13
Humphrey's   7
Intermezzo   14
Purple Lounge Club   8
Spijslokaal   1
De Twee Gezusters   3
De Vliegende Hollander   9

into the centre of town at **Waagplein**, a long, narrowing open space cut by a canal and flanked by cafés and large department stores. The **Waag** itself, now converted into a restaurant, dates from 1598. Walking west, **Nieuwestad** is Leeuwarden's main shopping street, from where Kleine Kerkstraat, a turn on the right, leads to the **Oldehoofster Kerkhof**, a large square-cum-car park near the old city walls, at the end of which stands the precariously leaning **Oldehove**. Something of a symbol for the city, this is part of a cathedral started in 1529 but never finished because of subsidence, a lugubrious mass of disproportion that defies all laws of gravity and geometry. To the right stands a statue of the Frisian politician and trade unionist P.J. Troelstra, who looks on impassively, no doubt admonishing the city fathers for their choice of architects. For a better view, climb the 40m-high tower (May–Sept Tues–Sat 2–5pm; €1.20).

A little further east is the **Prinsentium**, a small park that was once the pleasure garden of the ruling Nassaus. It is still a quiet place to wander by the river and admire, on the other side, the rather thoughtful bronze Friesian cow, called *Ús Mem* (Our Mother), donated to the city by the Frisian Cattle Syndicate. *Ús Heit* (Our Father) is also present in Leeuwarden – a statue of Regent Willem Lodewijk, a Frisian hero, which stands on the Gouveneursplein, in front of the majestic Stadhouderlijk Hof hotel.

Het Princessehof

Grote Kerkstraat leads east from the Oldehoofster Kerkhof, following the line of the track that connected two of Leeuwarden's original *terpen*, Oldehove and Nijehove. Near the square, at Grote Kerkstraat 11, is **Het Princessehof** (Tues–Sun 11am–5pm; €6; ⓦ www.princessehof.nl), a house from 1650 that was once the residence of the Stadholder William Friso and also the birthplace of graphic artist M.C. Escher. It's now a completely renovated ceramics museum, with the largest collection of tiles in the world.

Of the many displays, two are outstanding. The first is the collection of **Chinese, Japanese** and **Vietnamese ceramics**, which outlines the rise and fall of Far Eastern china production. In the sixteenth century Portuguese traders began to bring back Chinese porcelain for sale in Europe, which proved tremendously popular, and by the seventeenth century the Dutch, among others, had muscled in. European factories began to reproduce their goods, and the Dutch soon modified the original, highly stylized designs to more naturalistic patterns with a lighter, plainer effect, with the result that Chinese producers had to change their designs to fit Western tastes.

Some of the earliest pieces on display in this section date from the sixteenth century, notably several large blue and white plates of naive delicacy, decorated with swirling borders and surrealistic dragons. Some of the most exquisite examples of Chinaware date from as late as the middle of the eighteenth century – not least those from the Dutch merchantman *Geldermalsen*, which sank in the waters of the South China Sea in 1752 and was salvaged in 1983. Some 150,000 items of cargo were retrieved, and there's a small sample here, including a magnificent dish of bright-blue entwined fish bordered by a design of flowers and stems.

The second are the rooms devoted to the development of **Chinese porcelain** from prehistory onward, with representative examples illustrating major trends. The finest work dates from the Ming Dynasty (1368–1644), with powerful open-mouthed dragons, billowing clouds, and sharply drawn plant tendrils.

Another section you shouldn't miss, is the magnificent array of **Dutch tiles**, with good examples of all the classic designs – soldiers, flowers, ships and so forth – framed by uncomplicated borders. Well documented and clearly laid out, the earliest tiles date from the late fifteenth century, the work of Italians based in Antwerp who used a colourful and expensive tin-glazing process. By the seventeenth century thousands of identical tiles were churned out by dozens of Dutch factories: there were seven in Friesland alone. The emphasis was on very simple designs, characteristically blue-on-white, the top end of the market distinguished by extra colours or the size of the design: the more tiles it took to make the "picture", the more expensive the tile.

The collection of **European ceramics and porcelain** slots awkwardly around the other exhibits; best are the Art Deco and Art Nouveau pieces. More interesting, is the small collection of **Middle Eastern tiles**, including thirteenth-century pieces from Persia and a few flamboyant sixteenth-century Iznik tiles.

Along Grote Kerkstraat

East of the museum along Grote Kerkstraat, the **Frysk Letterkundich Museum** (Frisian Literary Museum; Mon–Fri 9am–12.30pm & 1.30–5pm;

€0.90) is housed at no. 212 in the building where Mata Hari, something of a local heroine, spent her early years. Her old home has become a repository for a whole range of Frisian documents and a handful of pamphlets in English on the Frisian language. A permanent display details P.J. Troelstra, the Frisian socialist politician and poet, who set up the Dutch Social Democratic party in 1890 and headed the Dutch labour movement until 1924.

At the far end of Grote Kerkstraat, the **Grote** or **Jacobijner Kerk** (June Sat 11am–4pm; July–Aug Tues–Thurs & Sat 11am-4pm, Fri 1–4pm), though restored in recent years, remains an unremarkable Gothic construction. Another victim of subsidence, the whole place tilts slightly toward the newer south aisle, where you can see some fragmentary remnants of sixteenth-century frescoes. In front of the church a modernistic monument remembers Leeuwarden's wartime Jewish community, based on the classroom registers of 1942; it's an imaginative and harsh reminder of suffering and persecution. A few minutes' walk west of the church, the **Fries Natuurmuseum**, Schoenmakersperk 2 (Tues–Sat 10am–5pm & Sun 1–5pm; €5; ⓦwww.natuurmuseumfryslan.nl), has exhibitions on local flora and fauna. A short walk towards the Nieuwestad will lead you to the **Boomsma Beerenburg Distillery**, Bagijnestraat 42a (Tues–Sat 10am–5pm; €1; ⓦwww.boomsma.net), where you can get a tour of the small museum and taste the herb-flavoured gin that is a regional speciality.

The Fries Museum

East of here, on Turfmarkt 11, the **Fries Museum** (Tues–Sun 11am–5pm; €6; ⓦwww.friesmuseum.nl) is one of the Netherlands' best regional museums. Founded by a society that was established in the nineteenth century to develop interest in the language and history of Friesland, the museum traces the development of Frisian culture from prehistoric times up until the present day. It also incorporates the Frisian Resistance Museum, with its story of the local resistance to Nazi occupation, and an exhibition on the infamous Mata Hari.

The main entrance is next to the **Kanselarij**, a superb gabled Renaissance structure of 1571, which has a slightly off-centred gable and corresponding double stairway – not in the original plan, which had them in the centre, but the money ran out before the work was finished – which houses some of the museum.

The museum's extensive collection of **silver** is concentrated in the basement of the Kanselarij. Silversmithing was a flourishing Frisian industry throughout the seventeenth and eighteenth centuries, most of the work commissioned by the local gentry, who were influenced by the fashions of the Frisian Stadholder and his court.

The top floor of the Kanselarij has a chronological exhibition tracing the early days of the **Nazi invasion**, through collaboration and resistance on to the Allied liberation. A variety of photographs, Nazi militaria, Allied propaganda and tragic personal stories illustrate the text, but the emphasis is very much on the local struggle rather than the general war effort.

Back by the ticket desk downstairs, a passage leads through to the museum's second building, the **Eysingahuis**, where you'll find the exhibition on **Mata Hari**. A native of Leeuwarden, Mata Hari's name has become synonymous with the image of the *femme fatale*. A renowned dancer, she was arrested in 1917 by the French on charges of espionage and subsequently shot, though what she actually did remains a matter of some debate. In retrospect it seems likely that she acted as a double agent, gathering information for the Allies while giving snippets to the Germans. Photographs, letters and other mementoes illustrate the rather pathetic story.

△ Painted Hindeloopen tray from the Fries Museum, Leeuwarden

Upstairs, on the first floor, the most interesting rooms are those devoted to the painted **furniture** of Hindeloopen: rich, gaudy and intense, patterned with tendrils and flowers on a red, green or white background. Most peculiar of all are examples of the bizarre headgear of eighteenth-century Hindeloopen women: large cartwheel-shaped hats known as *Duitse muts* and the less specifically Frisian *oorijzers*, gold or silver helmets that were an elaborate development of the hat-clip or brooch.

Around the Fries Museum

Just south of the Fries Museum, at Turfmarkt 48, the wonderful 1930s **Utrecht Building** today contains a restoration workshop. A little way north of Turfmarkt is the Catholic church of **St Boniface**, a belated apology to an English missionary killed at nearby Dokkum, along with 52 other Christians, by the pagan Frisians in 754. It's a neo-Gothic building of 1894 designed by P.J.H. Cuypers, its ornamented spire imposing itself on what is otherwise a rather flat skyline. The spire was almost totally destroyed in a storm of 1976 and many people wanted to take the opportunity to pull the place down altogether – even to replace it with a supermarket. Fortunately the steeple was replaced at great expense and with such enormous ingenuity that its future seems secure, making it one of the few Cuypers churches left in the Netherlands.

Eating, drinking and nightlife

Although Leeuwarden does not have a university, it is a real student town, attracting over 16,000 pupils each year. And where there are students, there are cheap place to eat. Expect to find a good range of **cafés** serving a quick bite at **Nieuwstad**, while along **Eewal** you are in the right place for a more intimate dinner. There are also a few places for a good meal and some night time excitement near the station at **Stationweg**.

Café Het Leven Druifstreek 57–59. This rather smart café is the right place for steaks, stews and the occasional curry.

Eetcafé Spinoza Eewal 50–52. One of the most popular places to eat in Leeuwarden, this is a youthful, reasonably priced restaurant with daily specialities for around €7 and a range of vegetarian dishes. The hidden inner courtyard is a well-kept treasure.

Humphrey's Nieuwstad 91. Although part of a chain, *Humphrey's* offers great value for money in a cosy atmosphere, with a three-course meal for the fixed price of €19.95.

Intermezzo, Stationsweg 6. Another stylish establishment near the station, *Intermezzo* is popular with business people during lunch and a

slightly younger crowd at night, with its flashy pink and black interior. Mains like shrimps with coriander or steak with red port sauce cost around €17.

Purple Lounge Club Tweebaksmarkt 49. Expect Asian-style food in a trendy setting; at weekends a DJ takes over later on in the evening.

🏃 **Spijslokaal** Eewal 54. The intimate *Spijslokaal* serves great Mediterranean food with accompanying wines, with mains for €15 and a three-course meal for €24.50. The owner's personal touch gives this restaurant a homey feel.

De Vliegende Hollander Berlikumermarkt 15. Serves daily specialities starting from €7.50 and a wide variety of soups, stews and *schnitzels*.

Nightlife

There are several attractive places for a good night out on the town. For **drinking**, there is a series of lively bars on Doelesteeg, most with loud music; quieter drinking spots across the bridge on Nieuwesteeg include *De Bottelier* and *De Twee Gezusters*. Near the station *Café Rembrandt*, with occasional live music, *Café De Rus* and *Herberg De Stee,* a typical brown café, are all lively options, all located on the Stationsweg. *Coltrane's*, in the basement of restaurant *Spinoza,* started as a jazz club but now serves all tastes. *Club Noa* hosts Holland's better-known DJs on weekends, while the *Fire Palace* (a former prison), Nieuwstad N.Z. 49, is a big bar that doubles as disco at weekends.

Listings

Bike rental From the *Fietspoint* next to the train station (€6.50/day).

Books Van der Velde, Nieuwstad 90, has a good stock of English-language titles.

Car rental AutoRent, Valeriusstraat 2 ☎058/299 8882, ⊛www.autorent-europaservice.nl.

Internet access At the VVV and the Bibliotheek, Wirdumerdijk 34 ☎058/234 7777.

Market General market on Fridays and Saturdays at Wilhelminaplein.

Pharmacy Details of nearest (emergency) pharmacy on ☎058/213 5295.

Police Holstmeerweg 1 ☎058/213 2423.

Post office Oldehoofster Kerkhof 4 (Mon–Fri 7.30am–6pm, Thurs until 8pm, Sat 7.30am–1.30pm).

Taxi Taxi Leeuwarden ☎058/216 1716.

Popta Slot

On the western outskirts of Leeuwarden, the tiny village of **MARSSUM** incorporates **Popta Slot** (guided tours only: April & Oct Mon–Fri by appointment; May, June & Sept Mon–Fri 2.30pm; July & Aug Mon–Sat hourly 11am–4pm; €4; ⊛www.poptaslot.nl), a trim, onion-domed eighteenth-century manor house that sits prettily behind its ancient moat; inside, the period rooms are furnished in the style of the local gentry. Dr Popta was an affluent lawyer who spent some of his excess wealth on the neighbouring **Popta Gasthuis**, neat almshouses cloistered behind an elaborate portal of 1712. Bus #71 heads to Marssum from Leeuwarden bus station, departing each hour.

West of Leeuwarden

West of Leeuwarden, the train line heads straight for **Harlingen**, though the small town of **Franeker**, with its fascinating eighteenth-century planetarium, makes a worthwhile detour. Seventeenth-century Harlingen was very much a naval centre and it remains an important port today, primarily to ferry tourists from the mainland to the Frisian islands of **Terschelling** and **Vlieland**. With a resurgence in the last few decades in its tradition of ceramic manufacture, and a strong maritime heritage, Harlingen makes a pleasant stopover for the night en route to the islands.

Franeker

About 17km west of Leeuwarden, **FRANEKER** was the cultural hub of the northern Netherlands until Napoleon closed the university in 1810. Nowadays it's a quiet country town with a spruce old centre, the highlight of which is its intriguing Planetarium. The **train station** is five minutes' walk southeast of the centre; follow Stationsweg round to the left and over the bridge, first left over the second bridge onto Zuiderkade and second right along Dijkstraat. Buses from Leeuwarden drop off passengers on Kleijenburg, at the northwest corner of the old town centre.

All the key sights are beside or near the main street, **Voorstraat**, a continuation of Dijkstraat, which runs east–west to end in a park, **Sternse Slotland** – the site of the medieval castle. Near the park is the **Waag** of 1657 and heading east along Voorstraat you will find **Museum Martena** (Tues–Fri 10am–5pm, Sat & Sun 1–5pm; €2; ⓦ www.coopmanshus.nl) in the old **Martenahuis** of 1498, with bits and pieces relating to the former university and its obscure alumni. Past the Martenahuis, the Raadhuisplein branches off to the left; opposite, above the Friesland Bank, is the **Kaatsmuseum** (May–Sept Tues–Sat 1–5pm; €2), devoted to the Frisian sport of *Kaatsen* ("Frisian tennis"; see box on p.222). The nearby **Stadhuis** (Mon–Fri 1.30–5.30pm; free), with its twin gables and octagonal tower, is rather more interesting. It's a magnificent mixture of Gothic and Renaissance styles built in 1591 and worth a peek upstairs for the leather-clad walls – all the rage until French notions of wallpaper took hold in the eighteenth century.

Opposite the Stadhuis, at Eise Eisingastraat 3, there's the fascinating eighteenth-century **Planetarium** (Tues–Sat 10am–5pm, Sun 1–5pm; April–Oct also Mon 1–5pm; €3.50; ⓦ www.planetarium-friesland.nl) built by a local woolcomber, Eise Eisinga, and now the oldest working planetarium in the world. Born in 1744, Eisinga was something of a prodigy: he taught himself mathematics and astronomy, and published a weighty arithmetic book when aged only 17. In 1774, the unusual conjunction of Mercury, Venus, Mars and Jupiter under the sign of Aries prompted a local paper to predict the end of the world. There was panic in the countryside, and an appalled Eisinga embarked on the construction of his planetarium, in order to dispel superstition by demystifying the workings of the cosmos. It took him seven years, almost as long as he had to enjoy it before his disdain for the autocratic Frisian Stadholder caused his imprisonment and exile. His return signalled a change of fortunes. In 1816 he was presented with the order of the Lion of the Netherlands, and, two years later, a royal visit persuaded King Willem I to buy the planetarium for the state, granting Eisinga a free tenancy and a generous annual stipend until his death in 1828.

The planetarium isn't of the familiar domed variety but was built as a false ceiling in the family's living room, a series of rotating dials and clocks indicating the movement of the planets and associated phenomena, from tides to star signs. The whole apparatus is regulated by a clock, driven by a series of weights hung in a tiny alcove beside a half-size cupboard-bed. Above the face of the main dials, the mechanisms – hundreds of handmade nails driven into moving slats – are open for inspection. A detailed guidebook explains every aspect and every dial and there's an explanatory video in English, shown on request.

Practicalities

Franeker's **VVV** is at Dijkstraat 26 in Blaauw bookshop (Mon 1–6pm, Tues–Thurs 9am–6pm, Fri 9am–9pm, Sat 9am–5pm; ☎0517/394 394 & ☎0900/540 0001, ⓦwww.friesekust.nl). Of the town's **hotels**, your first choice should be the friendly *De Stadsherberg*, on the continuation of Stationsweg at Oude Kaatsveld 8, situated next to the canal (☎0517/392 686, ⓦwww.stadsherbergfraneker.nl; ❷); failing that, try *Pension De Klokgevel*, opposite the modern church at Godsacker 20 (☎06/1465 9800; ❶). The town **campsite**, *Bloemketerp* (☎0517/395 099, ⓦwww.bloemketerp.nl), is ten minutes' walk north of the station at Burg. J. Dijkstraweg 3: head up Stationsweg, Oud Kaatsveld and Leeuwarderweg, then turn left.

For **snacks**, try the croissanterie *La Terraz*, Zilverstraat 7, or coffee and cakes at *De Tuinkamer*, beside the Planetarium at Eise Eisingastraat 2 – the building dates back to 1745, and has fine wooden counters, a mosaic floor and original coffee cabinets from 1910, as well as a beautiful back garden. Of the **restaurants**, the upmarket, canalside *De Grillerije*, Groenmarkt 14, offers mains like stew, catch of the day and mixed grill for around €17, or you could try *De Doelen*, a hotel and grand café on the same square, which has main courses for around €15. *De Bogt Fen Gune*, Vijverstraat 1, is the oldest student **bar** in the country, and worth dropping in for a drink.

Harlingen

Just north of the Afsluitdijk, 30km west of Leeuwarden, **HARLINGEN** is a more compelling stop than Franeker. An ancient and historic port that serves as the ferry terminus for the islands of Terschelling and Vlieland, Harlingen is something of a centre for traditional Dutch **sailing barges**, a number of which are usually moored in the harbour. A naval base from the seventeenth century, the town straddles the Vliestroom channel, once the easiest way for shipping to pass from the North Sea through the shallows that surround the Frisian islands and on into the Zuider Zee. Before trade moved west, this was the country's lifeline, where cereals, fish and other foodstuffs were brought in from the Baltic to feed the expanding Dutch cities.

Harlingen has two **train stations**: one on the southern edge of town for trains from Leeuwarden; the other, Harlingen Haven, right next to the docks, handling trains connecting with boats to the islands. From Harlingen Haven the old town spreads east, sandwiched between the pretty Noorderhaven and more functional Zuiderhaven canals, a mass of sixteenth- to eighteenth-century houses that reflect the prosperity and importance of earlier times. However, Harlingen is too busy to be just another cosy tourist town: there's a fishing fleet, a small container depot, a shipbuilding yard and a resurgent ceramics industry. The heart of town is the **Voorstraat**, a long, tree-lined avenue that's home to an elegant eighteenth-century **Stadhuis** and the **Hannemahuis Museum** at no. 56 (April–June & mid-Sept to mid-Nov Tues–Sat 1.30–5pm; July to mid-Sept Tues–Sat 10am–5pm & Sun 1.30–5pm; €1.55). Sited in an eighteenth-century merchant's house, the museum concentrates on the history of the town

△ Harlingen harbour

and includes some interesting displays on shipping and some lovely locally produced tiles.

Harlingen's tile-making industry flourished until it was undermined by the rise of cheap wallpaper. The last of the old factories closed in 1933, but the demand for traditional crafts later led to something of a recovery, and the opening of new workshops during the 1970s. If you like the look of Dutch tiles, this is a good place to buy. The **Harlinger Aardewerk en Tegelfabriek**, Voorstraat 84, sells an outstanding range of contemporary and traditional styles – if you've got the money (Dutch handicrafts don't come cheap). On Thursdays in summer Voorstraat fills with market stalls selling cheap clothing and general bric-a-brac, with food stalls at the fringes (July & Aug 1.30–9pm).

Practicalities

Harlingen has a wide range of accommodation, most of it situated near the water. The **VVV**, Noorderhaven 50 (May–Oct Mon 1–5pm, Tues–Fri 10am–noon & 1–5pm, Sat 10am–4pm; Nov–April Tues–Fri 1–4pm, Sat 10am–2pm; ☎0900/540 0001, Ⓦwww.friesekust.nl), has a list of **rooms** and **pensions**, many of which you'll spot by walking down Noorderhaven. Of the **hotels**, the *Heerenlogement* is on the eastern continuation of Voorstraat, at Franekereind 23 (☎0517/415 846, Ⓦwww.heerenlogement.nl; ❷), with 24 smartly decorated rooms, while the slightly more expensive *Anna Casparii* (☎0517/412 065, Ⓦwww.annacasparii.nl; ❷), located in three historical buildings on the north bank of the canal at Noorderhaven 67–71, has well-equipped rooms. A more picturesque option is the *Stadslogement Harlingen*, Kruisstraat 8–14, situated in a seventeenth-century warehouse (☎0517/417 706, Ⓦwww.stadslogementharlingen.nl; ❶). Central and close to the ferry is the *Zeezicht*, by the harbour at Zuiderhaven 1 (☎0517/412 536, Ⓕ419 001, Ⓦwww.hotelzeezicht.nl; ❷).

If you are looking for a really special experience, try sleeping in a lighthouse or a harbour crane. Both options are possible in Harlingen although a room with a view does not come cheap and you do need to book in advance (☎0515 540 550, Ⓦwww.vuurtoren-harlingen.nl; ❼–❽). The lighthouse went out of service after 25 years in 1998, and its future was uncertain until someone decided to make a hotel out of it. Now the three storeys offer luxury and a spectacular view over the surrounding area. The view from the harbour crane is less stunning, but the fact that you can rotate the crane by hand makes it every little boy's dream.

The nearest **campsite**, *De Zeehoeve* (☎0517/413 465, ⓦwww.zeehoeve.nl; April–Sept), is a twenty-minute walk along the sea dyke to the south of town at Westerzeedijk 45 – follow the signs from Voorstraat. If you've got your own transport, you're better off heading about 4km south to Kimswerd, to the delightful mini-camping *Popta Zathe* (☎0517/641 205; also a cheap B&B; ❶), something of a metropolis close to the sea wall. There's a small plot of grass, a beautiful garden and bike rental; the sunsets are great and it's a lovely bike ride along the top of the dyke into town.

As you'd expect, Harlingen's speciality is fresh **fish**, and there are fish stands, fish restaurants and snack bars dotted around the centre of town. A good but pricy choice with mains around €25 is *De Gastronoom,* at the Voorstraat 38, although you do get treated with oysters, bouillabaisse and scallops in a classy environment. An alternative is *De Tjotter* on the edge of the Noorderhaven at St Jacobstraat 1, a combined snack bar and restaurant with a wide range of North Sea delicacies. *Café 't Noorderke* at Noorderhaven 17–19 has good-value daily specials (fresh herring in season) and a view of the boats passing by from the terrace.

Nightlife is quiet but there are several decent **bars**, including *'t Skutsje* on the corner of Frankereind and Heiligeweg, and music café *De Wachter,* Voorstraat 64, with a terrace boat in the canal. More trendy options can be found at the Grote Bredeplaats, at the other end of the Voorstraat: *Nooitgedagt* and *Eigentijds* are hip venues, attracting Harlingen's younger crowd.

The islands of Terschelling and Vlieland

A highlight of any visit to Friesland is a trip to **Terschelling** or **Vlieland**, two of the five inhabited islands strung out along the Netherlands' north coast that include neighbouring Texel in Noord-Holland (see p.154). With kilometres of empty beach and grass-covered dunes, these low-lying sandbanks are popular with Dutch tourists in the holiday season, and havens too for scores of plants and animals that thrive in their unique ecological habitat. Known for their unpredictable weather, the islands are frequently swept by storms throughout the year, though the summer months can boast high temperatures and clear blue skies.

Ferries to Terschelling and Vlieland

From Harlingen, **ferries** cross to Terschelling and Vlieland at least three times daily in summer and twice daily in winter (1hr 45min). A return fare is €19.75 for either island (not including nominal taxes), plus €10.85 per bike. Boats dock at West-Terschelling and Oost-Vlieland, the islands' main settlements. There's also a fast **hydrofoil** service from Harlingen (May–Sept 3 daily to Terschelling, 2 daily to Vlieland; Oct–April 2 daily to Terschelling only). It costs an extra €7.90 return, but saves you an hour each way in travelling time, so is worth it if you're planning a day trip.

From May to the end of September there's also a ferry running between Terschelling and Vlieland, once or twice a day (€5.85 one-way, €6.50 for a bike).

Less than a two-hour ferry ride from Harlingen, both islands preserve a sense of isolated wilderness. Of the two, Terschelling is by far the more developed, and busier for it. Visitors' cars are not allowed on smaller and quieter Vlieland, but in any case the best way of exploring all the Frisian islands is by **bike**. There are rental companies near the ferry terminals on both islands, charging roughly €5 per day for a basic bike – although given the sometimes steep, stony hills, it's worth shelling out a bit more for a machine with decent gears.

Terschelling

Of all the Frisian Islands, **TERSCHELLING** is both the largest – some 30km long and 3.5km wide –and the easiest to reach. Despite its reputation as a teenage hangout in summer months, it does offer wilderness, peace and tranquillity: you just have to head away from main centres to find them. Quite simply, the further east you go the more attractive the island becomes; eighty percent of the island is a nature reserve area, dominated by beach, dunes, forest and polder. Although summer temperatures can soar, out of season Terschelling's wild weather seems to mirror its wild landscape, storms lending it a brooding air.

The ferry docks next to the colourful fishing harbour at **WEST-TERSCHELLING**, a tourist resort in its own right that's packed throughout the summer with tourists sampling the restaurants and bars that line the main streets, Torenstraat in particular. West-Terschelling today is a rather unappealing sprawl of chalets, bungalows and holiday complexes that spread out from what remains of the old village, belying its past importance as a port and safe anchorage on the edge of the Vliestroom channel, the main shipping lane from the Zuider Zee. This strategically positioned town boomed throughout the seventeenth century as a centre for the supply and repair of ships and with its own fishing and whaling fleets; it paid the price for its prominence when the British razed it in 1666. The islanders were renowned sailors, much sought after by ships' captains who also needed them to guide vessels through the treacherous shallows and shifting sandbanks that lay off the Vliestroom. Shipwrecks were common all along the island's northern and western shores; the most famous victim was the *Lutine*, which sank while carrying gold and silver to British troops stationed here during the Napoleonic wars. The wreck lies still at the bottom of the sea, and only the ship's bell was recovered – now in Lloyd's of London, it's still rung whenever a big ship goes down.

The best place to investigate Terschelling's past is the excellent **Museum 't Behouden Huys**, near the ferry terminus at Commandeurstraat 30 (April–Oct Mon–Fri 10am–5pm & Sat 1–5pm; mid-June to Sept also Sun 1–5pm; €3; ⊛www.behouden-huys.nl). Prime exhibits here include maps of the old coastline illustrating Terschelling's crucial position, various items from the whaling fleet, lots of sepia photos of bearded islanders and a shipwreck diving room. There's also a rather half-hearted tribute to the local explorer Willem Barents, who hit disaster when pack ice trapped his ship in the Arctic in 1595. Undaunted, he and his crew managed to survive the whole winter on the ice, sailing back in the spring. Barents mounted other, more successful expeditions into the Arctic regions, discovering Spitzbergen and naming the Barents Sea, all in the fruitless search for the northwest passage to China. He died in the Arctic in 1597. If you're extra-keen on things aquatic, aim for the tiny **Museum "Aike van Stien"**, a fishing museum at the back of a shop on Raadhuisstraat (May–Oct Mon–Sat 10am–12.30pm & 2–5.30pm; Nov–April Thurs & Sat 2–5pm; €2; ⊛www.visserijmuseumaikevanstien.nl), as well as,

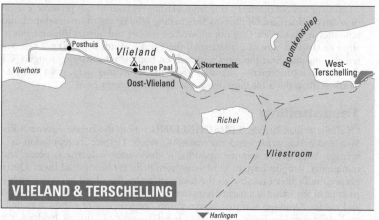

Posthuis

Vlieland

Vlierhors

△Lange Paal △ **Stortemelk**

Oost-Vlieland

Boomkensdiep

West-
Terschelling

Richel

Vliestroom

VLIELAND & TERSCHELLING

▼ *Harlingen*

just east of town, the **Centrum voor Natuur en Landschap**, Burgemeester
Reedekerstraat 11 (Nature and Landscape; April–Oct Mon–Fri 9am–5pm, Sat
& Sun 2–5pm; check hours at local VVV out of season; €4.50; @www
.natuurmuseumterschelling.nl), which contains a decent aquarium.

West-Terschelling practicalities

The **VVV** (summer Mon–Sat 9.30am–5.30pm; winter Mon–Fri 9.30am–5pm,
Sat 10am–3pm; ☏0562/443 000, @www.vvv-terschelling.org), near the ferry
port, provides a full list of **pensions** and **rooms** and operates a booking service.
They also take bookings for the rest of the island, offer a variety of walking
tours, sell a good **map** of the island (€2.75) that includes towns, beaches and
cycleways, and can give information on cycling routes and seal-watching
excursions.

You can **rent bikes** from Haantjes, located 50m to the right of the ferry
terminal, beyond the VVV – either single-speed (€5/day, €20/week) or geared
bikes (€6.50/day, €27.50/week); they have various drop-off points around the
island, and a handy cycling map. There are other bike-rental shops down by the
harbour and at the ferry terminal. The island's **bus** service leaves from right next
to the ferry terminus (every 1hr 10min), taking 30 minutes to travel along the
south coast to Oosterend.

Accommodation in West-Terschelling is hard to come by in July and August
when all the cheaper places tend to be booked up months in advance. At other
times you have a wide choice – try the *Hotel Buren*, Burgemeester Mentzstraat
20 (☏0562/442 226, @www.hotel.buren.op-terschelling.nl; ❷), or the similarly
priced *Pension Altijd Wad*, Trompstraat 6 (☏0562/442 050, @www.altijdwad.nl;
❷), both not far from the ferry terminus. There's a HI **hostel** overlooking the
harbour at Burgemeester van Heusdenweg 39 (☏0562/442 338, @www
.stayokay.com), with dorm beds (€25) and en-suite doubles (1x): it's a 1.5km
walk eastwards along the coast, or you can take any bus to the Dellewal stop.
There are also a number of shoreside **campsites** east of town that are popular
with the hordes of partying teenagers who descend on the island in summer.

For a quick bite to **eat**, the fish-and-chips takeaway at Boomstraat 12 offers
the usual fishy suspects fresh from the North Sea, including fried *lekkerbek*, a
typical Dutch fried fish speciality, for €2.75. At *Strandpaviljoen De Walvis*, at

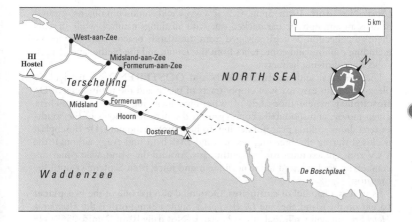

Groene Strand on the western edge of West-Terschelling, you can buy snacks and drinks while taking in the sea view, and *Brasserie De Brandaris*, Boomstraat 3 has a suitably nautical atmosphere, mains for around €17 and a typical Terschelling cheese platter for dessert.

Around the island

From West-Terschelling, plenty of visitors cycle off for the day to the beach 5km away at **WEST-AAN-ZEE** where there's a café, *Zilver Meeuw*, and as much empty beach as you're prepared to look for. There are two cycle routes to get there, the more northerly passing through a cemetery in a wood, with a small Commonwealth forces graveyard; as ever, the inscriptions make sad reading, with few of the downed bombardiers aged more than 25. Further round is the *Palm Café* at the Kaap Hoorn beach pavilion, reachable only by bicycle along a narrow forested trail from Hoorn, the variety of bikes locked around trees proof of its popularity.

Terschelling's other villages stretch out along the southern part of the island, sheltered from winter storms by the sand dunes and occasional patches of forest that lie to the immediate north. Cycle routes are almost always traffic-free. For peace and quiet, aim to stay in one of the pensions between the villages of Formerum and Oosterend, far enough east to escape most of the crowds; the VVV in West-Terschelling has details. Definitely worth a visit in **FORMERUM** is the delightful **Wrakkenmuseum "De Boerderij"**, Formerum Zuid 13

Terschelling Oerol Festival

Every year around June, Terschelling celebrates the beginning of the milder season with the Oerol Festival (ⓦ www.oerol.nl). Oerol, "everywhere" in Terschelling dialect, is the name of an ancient tradition, when the arrival of spring's better weather meant cattle could be released from their winter stables. The Oerol Festival reflects the joyful sight of cattle grazing, announcing the longed for summer season after the cold of winter. Over 50,000 people transform Terschelling into a big festival area, with the island serving as both inspiration and stage for theatre producers, musicians and graphic artists. Finding accommodation is almost impossible during the ten-day festival, so book ahead.

(April–Nov daily 10am–5pm; €2; ⓦwww.wrakkenmuseum.nl); its ground floor is an atmospheric bar decked out with all things nautical, while upstairs there's a collection of items salvaged from the island's beaches and shipwrecks, including cannons and coins, relics from the *Lutine*, and the Netherlands' largest collection of diving helmets.

The two final settlements, **HOORN** and **OOSTEREND**, are particularly pleasant, within easy reach of empty tracts of beach and the nature reserve **De Boschplaat**, where thousands of waterfowl, including gulls, oystercatchers, green plovers and spoonbills, congregate in the marshy shallows of the south-eastern shore, seeking peaceful nesting. To help protect the birds, De Boschplaat is closed during the breeding season (mid-March to mid-Aug), although the VVV runs guided tours for bird enthusiasts. Around the island, wild American cranberries are harvested for wine, liqueur and juice, from September until the first frost.

As well as a handful of **campsites**, Oosterend also has one of the best **places to eat** on the island, the café *De Boschplaat*. Signed 2km north is the *Heartbreak Hotel*, Strandpaviljoen Tordelenweg 2 (March–Nov daily 10am–2am; ☎0562/448 634), an American-style **diner**, decorated with wall-to-wall 1950s memorabilia, and sited in a superb location overlooking kilometres of white sand and sea; meals are around €12–18, and there is a live Fifties band every night during July and August. It's a great spot to relax in the dunes with a bottle of wine and watch the sun slipping into the sea. Live music can also be found in Hoorn at *Café De Groene Weide*, Dorpsstraat 79–81, where owner Hessel (a famous local artist) sings his songs live for the crowd.

Vlieland

Compared with its lively neighbour, **VLIELAND** is laid-back and low key. All but car free, it has just one settlement, **OOST-VLIELAND** – little more than a tree-lined street with a string of pavement cafés, bike-rental agencies and a few hotels and B&Bs. Historically isolated by a complex pattern of sandbanks, the island was of minor importance during the Zuider Zee trade; its only other village was swept away by the sea in the eighteenth century and never rebuilt. These days, there's not much to do but enjoy the country walks and relax along the 12km of sandy beach – a sedate lifestyle that is popular with Dutch families, who load up their bikes with panniers, tents, children and animals, and head for one of the island's two campsites.

Oost-Vlieland offers all the necessities, including a choice of eateries, bars and supermarkets. There's also a maritime centre geared towards children, the **Centrum "De Noordwester"**, Dorpsstraat 150 (July & Aug Mon–Fri 10am–5pm, Sat 2–5pm & Sun 1–4pm; hours vary out of season; €2.50; ⓦwww.denoordwester.nl), displaying an assortment of shells, an explanation of dune formation, a couple of aquariums with crabs and rays, and an unexpected elf forest (information is in Dutch only). The village's **Tromps Huys** museum, Dorpsstraat 99 (May–Sept Tues–Sat 11am–5pm, Sun 2–5pm; Oct–April Tues–Sat 2–5pm; €2.50), has a collection of antiques and Vlieland bygones.

Accommodation is limited, and virtually impossible to find throughout the summer unless you're camping. The **VVV**, Havenweg 10 (Mon–Fri 9am–12.30pm & 1.30–5.30pm, also open for brief periods daily to coincide with ferry arrivals; ☎0562/451 111, ⓦwww.vlieland.net), does its best with the few private rooms, and will help groups rent apartments and "dune houses"; it also has information on birdwatching expeditions. Vlieland has several cheap **hotels** and pensions. One of them is the *Duin en Dal*, Dorpsstraat 163 (☎0562/451 684; ❶);

along the road is the more comfortable *Badhotel Bruin*, Dorpsstraat 88 (☎0562/451 301, ⓦwww.badhotelbruin.nl; ❶), and the smart *De Wadden*, Dorpsstraat 61 (☎0562/452 626, ⓦwww.westcordhotels.nl; ❷). The **campsite** *De Stortemelk*, Kampweg 1 (☎0562/451 225, ⓦwww.stortemelk.nl), is on the dunes behind the beach, about half an hour's walk or a ten-minute bike ride northeast of the village. More peaceful is the Staatsbosbeheer site a few kilometres west at *Lange Paal* (☎0562/451 639, ⓦwww.langepaal.com); it's set in the forest clearing of a nature reserve, with carved log furniture and vine-like ropes for children to swing on. Facilities are simple but clean and there's a relaxed, friendly atmosphere. Bring some insect repellent though: the mosquitoes here are ruthless.

To explore the island's woods and dunes, follow one of the many **bike** routes that run the length of the island, crisscrossing a succession of wide sandy beaches on the northern shore. The VVV can provide you with details in English of two routes, and there are also plenty of marked **walking** trails. You can rent bikes, tandems and trailers – for kids as well as canines – all over town. A limited **bus** service travels along the southern shore from near the ferry terminus. Private operators organize day-trips to the northern tip of the neighbouring island of **Texel** by means of a tractor-like lorry, which crosses the great expanse of sand (the "Vliehors") on Vlieland's western extremity to connect with a boat (May–Sept; €20 for a round trip to Texel; ⓦwww.waddenveer.nl).

Southwest Friesland

Trains from Leeuwarden to **Stavoren** pass through a series of small Frisian towns with a speed that gainsays the earlier isolation of these places. Until well into the nineteenth century, the lakes, canals and peat diggings south and east of Sneek made land communications difficult, and the only significant settlements were built close to the sea or on major waterways. Dependent on water-borne commerce, these communities declined with the collapse of the Zuider Zee trade, but, because of their insularity, some maintained particular artistic and cultural traditions – from the painted furniture and distinctive dialect of **Hindeloopen** to the style and design of many of **Makkum**'s tiles. Passing through by train, the tiny old towns resemble what in fact they once were: islands in the shallow marshes. Nowadays all are popular holiday destinations; **Sneek**, the centre of a booming pleasure-boat industry, is by far the busiest.

Sneek

Twenty minutes by train from Leeuwarden, **SNEEK** (pronounced *snake*) was an important shipbuilding centre as early as the fifteenth century, a prosperous maritime town protected by an extensive system of walls and moats. Postwar development has robbed the place of some of its charm but there are still some buildings of interest. At the beginning of August, crowds flock in for **Sneek Week**, an annual regatta, when the flat green expanses around town are thick with the white of slowly moving sails.

Sneek's train and bus stations are five minutes' walk from the old centre. Stationsstraat leads to the main square, **Martiniplein**, whose ponderous sixteenth-century **Martinikerk** (mid-June to mid-Sept Tues–Sat 2.30–5pm; mid-July to mid-Aug also Tues–Thurs 7–9pm; free) is edged by an old wooden belfry. Around the corner at the end of Grote Kerkstraat, the **Stadhuis**, Marktstraat 15 (mid-July to mid-Aug Mon–Thurs 2–4pm; free), is all extravagance, from the Rococo facade to the fanciful outside staircase; inside there's an indifferent display of ancient weapons in the former guardroom. Heading east along Marktstraat, veer right after the VVV and follow the signs to the nearby **Scheepvaart Museum en Oudheidkamer**, Kleinzand 14 (Mon–Sat 10am–5pm, Sun noon–5pm; €3; ⓦwww .friesscheepvaartmuseum.nl), a well-displayed collection of maritime models, paintings and related miscellany. There's also a room devoted to the Visser family, who made a fortune during the eighteenth century by transporting eels to London. A little further along, at Kleinzand 32, the Weduwe Joustra shop has an original nineteenth-century interior, worth a glance for its old barrels and till, even if you decide not to indulge in a bottle of *Beerenburg*, a herb flavoured gin that is a regional speciality. Turn right at the end of Koemarkt and you reach the grandiose **Waterpoort**, all that remains of the seventeenth-century town walls.

To see more of the lakes outside town, **boat trips** (July & Aug) leave from the Oosterkade, over the bridge by the east end of Kleinzand. Itineraries and prices vary and there's no fixed schedule of sailings: you can request anything from a quick tour of the town's canals to venturing out into the open sea. Contact the VVV or the boat owners at the dock for up-to-date details. At the local VVV you can also obtain a free map with an overview of the best ways to explore southwest Friesland, either by foot, inline skate, horse or canoe (ⓦwww.routezuidwestfriesland.nl).

Practicalities

Sneek can get exceptionally busy, and accommodation is impossible to find during Sneek Week in early August. At other times, the central **VVV**, near the Stadhuis at Marktstraat 18 (Mon–Fri 9.30am–6pm, Sat 9.30am–5pm; summer Thurs till 9pm; ⓣ0515/414 096, ⓦwww.vvvsneek.nl), can arrange private **rooms** for a small fee. For **hotels**, *Daaldersplaats*, by the station at Stationsstraat 66 (ⓣ0515/413 175, ⓦwww.daaldersplaats.nl; ❷), is comfortable, and also has a restaurant which serves a very cheap four-course meal, while *De Wijnberg*, Marktstraat 23 (ⓣ0515/412 421, ⓦwww.hoteldewijnberg.nl; ❶–❷), is good value and central with a big restaurant and pub. A bit further from the centre, the four-star *Amicitia* hotel, Graaf Adolfstraat 67 (ⓣ0515/436 800, ⓦwww .amicitiahotel.nl; ❷), has themed rooms ranging from James Dean to original Hindeloopen. The HI **hostel** *Wigledam*, Oude Oppenhuizerweg 20 (ⓣ0515/412 132, ⓦwww.stayokay.com; April–Oct; €24.25), is some 2km southeast of the centre; head east to the end of Kleinzand, turn right down Oppenhuizerweg, and it's the first major road on the left (bus #99 from the station). The nearest **campsite** is *De Domp*, Domp 4 (ⓣ0515/412 559, ⓦwww.dedomp.nl; April– Oct), 2km northeast of the centre on Sytsingawiersterleane, a right turn off the main road to Leeuwarden; no buses run near.

Sneek has a large number of **restaurants**, few of which have much character. The most appealing is *De Wijsneus*, at Grote Kerkstraat 16, with a French-style garden and a four-course menu for around €30. *Hinderlooper Kamer*, Oosterdijk 10, is a smart, cheerful bistro with reasonably priced Dutch food; *Klein Java*, Wijde Noorderhorne 18, offers Indonesian meals. Nightlife is nothing special but if you do wish to explore Sneek **by night** you can do so around Kleine Kerkstraat and Kruizebroederstraat. *Ludiek*, Kruizebroederstraat 77, is a bar with dancing after dark while the *Alcatraz*, a former jail at Kleine Kerkstraat 4/B, does not open until late.

Bolsward

Some 10km west of Sneek, and served by regular bus #99 from Sneek train station, **BOLSWARD** (pronounced *bozwut* in the local dialect) is less touristy and has a wider ethnic diversity than the surrounding villages and towns. Founded in the seventh century, this was a bustling and important textile centre in the Middle Ages, though its subsequent decline has left a population of around ten thousand and only a handful of worthwhile sights. Your first stop should be the **Stadhuis**, Jongemastraat 2 – a magnificent red-brick, stone-trimmed Renaissance edifice of 1613. The facade is topped by a lion holding a coat of arms over the head of a terrified Turk, and below a mass of twisting, curling carved stone frames a series of finely cut cameos, all balanced by an extravagant external staircase. Inside there's a small **museum** (April–June, Sept & Oct Mon 2–4pm, Tues–Fri 9am–noon & 2–4pm; July & Aug Mon–Sat 10am–5pm; €1) of local historical bits and pieces. Ten minutes' walk away the fifteenth-century **Martinikerk** at Groot Kerkhof (Mon–Fri 10am–noon & 2–4pm; €1.20) was originally built on an earthen mound for protection from flooding. Some of the wood carving inside is quite superb: the choir with its rare misericords from 1470 and, particularly, the seventeenth-century pulpit, carved by two local men from a single oak tree. Its panels depict the four seasons: the Frisian baptism dress above the young eagle symbolizes spring, while the carved ice skates (winter) on the other side are thought to be unique. The stone font dates from around 1000, while the stained-glass windows at the back depict occupation by the Nazis and subsequent liberation by the Canadians.

Bolsward is also home to the **Friese Bierbrouwerij**, Snekerstraat 43 (Frisian Brewery; Mon, Tues, Thurs & Fri 3–6pm, guided tour at 4pm; Sat 10am–6pm, guided tours hourly; €5, drink included; Ⓦwww.bierbrouwerij-usheit.nl). The smallest brewery in the country produces eight different kinds of *Us Heit* beer and several whiskys. You can learn all about the production process before sampling the product. The brewery also has a small museum inside.

The **VVV**, Marktplein 1 (mid-June to mid-Sept Mon 1.30–5.30pm, Tues–Fri 10am–noon & 1.30–5.30pm, Sat 10am–1pm, hours vary out of season; ☎0515/577 701), has details of a handful of private **rooms**. There are two convenient **hotels**, the *Stadsherberg Heeremastate*, Heeremastraat 8 (☎0515/573 063, Ⓦwww.publiciteit.nl/heeremastate; ❸), which although central is very quiet and has a cosy terrace and billiards table, and *De Wijnberg*, Marktplein 5 (☎0515/572 220, Ⓦwww.wijnbergbolsward.nl; ❶–❷), more centrally located with a terrace right on the marked square.

Makkum

Immaculate houses, church towers, cobbled streets, flower pots and wooden boats sum up the agreeable town of **MAKKUM**. It's saved from postcard prettiness by a working harbour, although, as the centre of traditional Dutch **ceramics** manufacture, the town can be overwhelmed by tourists in summer. The local product rivals the more famous delftware in quality, varying from the bright and colourful to more delicate pieces. Ceramic enthusiasts can visit the Tichelaar family **workshops**, Turfmarkt 65 (Mon–Fri 9am–5pm, Sat 10am–5pm; ☎0515/231 341, Ⓦwww.tichelaar.nl), take a guided tour (Mon–Thurs 11am, 1.30pm & 3pm, Fri 11am & 1.30pm; €3.50), or just browse through their shop.

Makkum is served by the irregular **minibus** #102 from Workum train station, and by the much better bus #98 from Bolsward. Makkum **VVV**,

Pruikmakershoek 2 (April–June Mon–Fri 10am–5pm, Sat 10am–4pm; July & Aug Mon–Sat 10am–5pm; Sept & Oct Mon–Sat 10am–4pm; closed for lunch on weekdays; ☎0515/231 190, ⓦwww.friesekust.nl), is sited in the old Waag and can arrange **private rooms** for a €2.50 fee. The **campsite** *De Weeren* (☎0515/321 374), 2km out of town on the road to Wons (bus #98 or #99 towards Bolsward), is basic but clean and quiet. Otherwise, try the central but not very charming **hotel** *De Waag*, Markt 13 (☎0515/231 447, ⓦwww .hoteldewaagmakkum.nl; ❶), with a low-priced **restaurant**. *It Posthus*, in the old post office building at Plein 15, has scallops, salads and even curries in a bright and pleasant setting with mains averaging around €17.

Museumroute Aldfaerserf

If you take the scenic route from Makkum to Workum, you will pass the **Museumroute Aldfaerserf** (April–Oct daily 10am–5pm; Exmorra, Ferwoude and Piaam closed in April and Oct; €8.50; ⓦwww.aldfaerserf.nl). The villages of Exmorra, Allingawier, Ferwoude and Piaam now serve as open-air museums showing Frisian life in the eighteenth and nineteenth centuries. Historical buildings have been restored and refurbished, regaining their historical functions as bakeries, carpenters' shops and smithies. The 25-kilometre route can be done by car or bicycle (which can be rented at Allingawier). In Makkum you can rent a bike at Venema, Voorstraat 7 (☎0515/231 484; €4).

Workum

Ten minutes southwest of Sneek by train, **WORKUM**, a long, straggly town with an attractive main street, has the appearance of a comfortable city suburb, protected by several kilometres of sea defences. In fact, until the early eighteenth century it was a seaport, though nowadays indications of a more adventurous past are confined to the central square, 2km from the train station, with its seventeenth-century **Waag** at Merk 4, which contains a standard nautical-historical collection (April–Oct Tues–Sun 1pm–5pm; €2). Immediately behind, the **St Gertrudskerk** (Mon–Sat 11am–5pm; hours vary out of season; €1), the largest medieval church in Friesland, contains a small collection of mostly eighteenth-century odds and ends. If you're into religious art, explore the **Museum Kerkelijke Kunst** in the neo-Gothic St Werenfridus Kerk, Noard 175 (June to mid-Sept Mon–Sat 11am–5pm; €2). Just down the road at Noard 6, the likeable **Jopie Huisman Museum** (April–Oct Mon–Sat 10am–5pm, Sun 1–5pm; March & Nov daily 1–5pm; €4; ⓦwww.jopiehuismanmuseum.nl) is devoted to paintings by Huisman, a contemporary local artist, most of which have an appealingly unpretentious focus on Frisian life.

The **VVV** (April & May Tues–Fri 9.30am–5pm, Sat 9.30am–4pm; June–Sept Mon–Fri 9.30am–5.30pm, Sat 9.30am–4pm; Oct Mon 1.30–5pm, Tues–Fri 9.30am–5pm, Sat 9.30am–4pm; Nov–March Tues–Fri 9.30am–4pm, Sat 9.30am–2pm; closed for lunch on weekdays; ☎0515/540 550, ⓦwww .friesekust.nl), across from the Merk at Noard 5, has a limited number of **private rooms**. Alternatively, head for the *Gulden Leeuw*, Merk 2 (☎0515/542 341, ⓦwww.deguldenleeuw.nl; ❶), where facilities include a decent **restaurant** with mainly fish specialities, or the *Herberg van Oom Lammert en Tante Klaasje*, next door at Merk 3 (☎ & ☏0515/541 370, ⓦwww.oomlammert.nl; ❶), where you can sleep in a *bedstee* (something like an elevated closet Frisian style). The **campsite** *It Soal* (☎0515/541 443, ⓦwww.itsoal.nl; April–Oct) is located on the IJsselmeer, 3km south of the centre.

The Elfstedentocht

The **Elfstedentocht** ("Eleven Towns Race") is Friesland's biggest spectacle, a gruelling **ice-skating** marathon around Friesland that dates back to 1890, when one Pim Muller, a local sports journalist, skated his way around the eleven official towns of the province, simply to see whether it was possible. It was, and twenty years later the first official Elfstedentocht was born, contested by 22 skaters. Weather – and ice – permitting, it has taken place just fifteen times in the last hundred years, most recently in 1997, and attracts skaters from all over the world.

The race is organized by the Eleven Towns Association, of which you must be a member to take part; the high level of interest in the race means that membership is very difficult to obtain. The route, which measures about 200km in total, takes in all the main centres of Friesland, starting in Leeuwarden in the town's Expo Centre, from where the racers sprint – skates in hand – 1500m to the point where they get onto the ice. The first stop after this is Sneek, after which the race takes in Hindeloopen and the other old Zuider Zee towns before finishing in Dokkum in the north of the province. The event is broadcast live on national TV, the route lined with spectators. Of the 17,000 or so people who take part, usually no more than three hundred are professional skaters. Casualties are inevitably numerous; the worst year was 1963, when 10,000 skaters took part and only seventy finished, the rest beaten by the fierce winds, extreme cold and snowdrifts along the way. Generally, however, something like three-quarters of the starters make it to the finishing line.

If you're not around for the race itself, the route makes a popular bike ride and is signposted by the ANWB as one of their national cycling routes; four or five days will allow enough time to sightsee as well as cycle.

From Workum, it's just 6km to Hindeloopen, a pleasant bike-ride across fields, past a windmill and along a dyke. It's a popular route with families, well signposted and it steers clear of busy roads.

Hindeloopen

Next stop down the rail line, the village of **HINDELOOPEN** juts into the IJsselmeer, twenty minutes' walk west of its train station. A highlight of the tour bus trail during the summer months, it's an appealing little town that blossoms with elderly visitors on sunny weekends. A tidy jigsaw of old streets, canals and wooden bridges make an attractive stroll, but unless you visit out of high season it's too quaint and touristy to linger for long.

Until the seventeenth century, Hindeloopen prospered as a Zuider Zee port, concentrating on trade with the Baltic and Amsterdam. The combination of rural isolation and trade created a specific culture within this tightly knit community, with a distinctive dialect (Hylper – Frisian with Scandinavian influences) and sumptuous local **dress**. Adopting materials imported into Amsterdam by the East India Company, the women of Hindeloopen dressed in a florid combination of colours where dress was a means of personal identification: caps, casques and trinkets indicated marital status and age, and the quality of the print indicated social standing. Other Dutch villages adopted similar practices, but nowhere were the details of social position so precisely drawn. However, the development of dress turned out to be a corollary of prosperity, for the decline of Hindeloopen quite simply finished it off. Similarly, the local **painted furniture** showed an ornate mixture of Scandinavian and Oriental styles superimposed on traditional Dutch carpentry. Each item was covered from head to toe with painted tendrils and flowers on a red, green or white background, though again the town's decline resulted in the lapsing of the craft. Tourism has revived local furniture-making, and countless shops now line the main street selling modern versions, though even the smallest items aren't cheap, and the florid style is something of an acquired taste.

Hindeloopen's characterful **church** – a seventeenth-century structure with a wonky medieval tower – has some graves of British airmen who perished in the Zuider Zee, while the small **Schaats Museum**, Kleine Wiede 1 (Mon–Sat 10am–6pm & Sun 1–5pm; €1.50; Ⓦwww.schaatsmuseum.nl), displays some skating mementoes relating to the great Frisian ice-skating race "De Friese Elfst-edentocht" (see box on p.241), as well as plenty of painted Hindeloopen-ware in its shop. You can see original examples of this in the small village museum, the **Hidde Nijland Stichting Museum**, beside the church (April–Oct Mon–Fri 11am–5pm, Sat & Sun 1.30–5pm; €3; Ⓦwww.museumhindeloopen.nl), although there's a wider display at the Fries Museum in Leeuwarden.

Hindeloopen's popularity makes finding **accommodation** a problem during the summer and the town's lodgings tend to fill up early. By far the most characteristic option is to sleep in the old ⚓ *Likhus* at Tuinen 5–7 (Ⓣ0514 523 208, Ⓦwww.thuismetkunst.nl; ❻). This tiny house used to serve as a residence for the wives and children of ships' captains when they were at sea; the entire place is decorated in old Hindeloopen style. Alternatively, *De Stadsboerderij*, Nieuwe Weide 9 (Ⓣ0514/521 278, Ⓦwww.destadsboerderij.nl; ❶), and *Pension De Twee Hondjes*, Paardepad 2 (Ⓣ0514/522 873, Ⓦwww .detweehondjes.nl; ❶), both offer the option to sleep in an original *bedstee* (an elevated Frisian-style closet). If you're really caught short, try the prefab *Skips Appartementen & Dormettes*, in the yachting marina at Oosterstrand 22 (Ⓣ0514/524 500, Ⓦwww.skipsmaritiem.nl; ❶). The **VVV**, Nieuwstad 26 (April & May Mon, Wed & Sat 11am–4pm; June Mon–Sat 10am–12.30pm & 1–5pm; July & Aug Mon–Sat 10am–12.30pm & 1–5pm; Sept & Oct Mon, Wed & Sat 10.30am–4pm; Ⓣ0514/522 550, Ⓦwww.friesekust.nl), can organize the odd private **room**. The only alternative is the **campsite** *Hindeloopen* (Ⓣ0514/521 452, Ⓕ523 221; April–Oct), 1km or so south near the coast at Westerdijk 9.

For **eating**, the smart *De Gasterie*, just off the harbour at Kalverstraat 13, is a lovely place to dine on the terrace in the evening, although it's not cheap, with a three-course meal starting from €31; *De Brabander*, Nieuwe Wiede 7, has main dishes for under €20 and a wide array of excellent pancakes for under €5. Failing that, the stands on the harbour serve fresh fishy snacks during the day for around €5, with grassy verges to picnic on and plenty of passing boat trade for people-watching.

Sloten

With its thicket of boat masts poking out above the rooftops, it's easy to spot **SLOTEN** from afar. It's something of a museum piece, though the village's 700 inhabitants are proud to call Sloten one of Friesland's eleven "cities", and a medieval one at that. The town comprises little more than a few pavement cafés fronting a central canal, strips of manicured lawn, a windmill, old locks and colourful flower boxes, although it's encircled by water and is a popular spot with Dutch and German tourists. The adjoining milk-powder factory may seem a blip in this picture-perfect setting, but if anything it lends the place a welcome sense of realism.

Reaching Sloten by public transport can be a little awkward; the easiest way is to take bus #42 from Sneek train station to the bus change-over point on the motorway at Spannenburg (takes 35min), where connecting service #41 continues west to Sloten, and #44 runs on to Sloten and Bolsward. Alternatively, it's a nineteen-kilometre bike ride from Sneek.

There's a small **museum** (April–Oct Tues–Fri 11am–5pm, Sat & Sun 1–5pm; out of season by appointment; €3) in the town hall on Heerenwal, but otherwise it's just a case of wandering the cobbled alleyways and admiring the gabled facades. The **VVV**, located in the town hall (April–Oct Tues–Fri 11am–5pm, Sat & Sun 1–5pm; ℡0514/531 583 or 0900/540 0001, @www.friesekust .nl), can suggest a few **places to stay**, including the *Pension 't Brechje*, Voorstreek 110 (℡0514/531 298; ●). A couple of **restaurants** by the bridge on the canal do good light lunches and more expensive evening meals, and have nice outdoor seating.

The closest **campsite** is *Lemsterpoort*, Jachthaven 3 (℡0514/531 668), but if you have your own transport, it's worth striking out 2km to neighbouring Wijckel: turn left opposite the church, bear right at the first fork, follow the road round, and just past the cow postbox lies the friendly mini-camping *De Tjasker*, Iwert 17 (℡0514/605 869), with its own thatched barn and spotless lawn.

Stavoren

Named after the Frisian god Stavo, **STAVOREN** is the oldest town in Friesland and was once a prosperous port; it's now the point from where **ferries** make the crossing to Enkhuizen (see p.143 for frequencies and prices, and connecting trains to Amsterdam). Strung out along the coast, Stavoren is an eclectic mix of old and new: the harbour is flanked by modern "Legoland" housing while the shipyards are linked by cobbled backstreets. Popular with yachty types, it's a great place to admire the painstakingly restored seventeenth- to nineteenth-century vessels that once plied the Zuider Zee, now moored up and awaiting hire. On a sunny day, watching the old wooden ships go by and listening to the clink of halyards is as an enjoyable pastime as any. At the southern end of town, squat turbines encased in glass, once the largest in the world, can be seen pumping water out of Friesland and into the IJsselmeer.

The glass-shelled **VVV** is on the harbour, two minutes' walk from the station (opening hours correspond with ferry departures and arrivals; ℡0900/540 0001, @www.friesekust.nl), and has details of pensions and private rooms (around €20). Next door Zeilvloot Lemmer-Stavoren (℡0514/681 818, @www.zeilvloot.nl) can provide details on renting **sailboats**, though ideally you'll need to be in a group: keeping up tradition doesn't come cheap.

The best place to **stay** is the hotel *De Vrouwe van Stavoren*, Havenweg 1 (℡0514/681 202, @www.hotel-vrouwevanstavoren.nl; ●), attractively sited by the harbour and surprisingly good value. Try sleeping in one of their wine barrels, as long as you're not claustrophobic. Nearby Smidstraat has a pizzeria, café, ice-cream shop and supermarket; Vishandel Doede Bleeker, at no. 21 (daily 11am–6.30pm), offers a platter of tasty fish and chips for €5.

Situated at the end of the train line, Stavoren is a good base for **cycling**. Options include following the coastal cycleway north 10km to Hindeloopen, or south 5km to Laaksum, past dark green and marine blue lagoons with banks of reeds rustling in the wind. For a longer ride, continue through Laaksum and pick up the signposts to Oudemirdum, with its swathes of forest crisscrossed by cycleways and wooden bridges spanning pea-soupy canals. This 40-kilometre loop makes a pleasant day-trip, but bear in mind the winds can be forceful along the coast, and generally blow from the southwest.

North Friesland

Edged by the Lauwersmeer to the east and protected by interlocking sea-dykes to the north, the strip of Friesland **north of Leeuwarden** is dotted with tiny agricultural villages that were once separated from each other by swamp and marsh. The area was sparsely inhabited, and the first settlers were forced to confine themselves to whatever higher ground was available, the *terpen* which kept the treacherous waters at bay. It's home to one of Friesland's oldest towns, **Dokkum**; of interest too are the coastal hamlets of **Moddergat** and **Wierum**. Further west, the unprepossessing port of **Holswerd** provides access to the island of **Ameland**, reached directly from Leeuwarden by a bus service that connects with the ferry. Note too that while the island of Schiermonnikoog can also be reached from Dokkum and Leeuwarden, the quickest and most direct route is from Groningen (for full information on Schiermonnikoog, see p.256).

Dokkum

From Leeuwarden, the scenic national **bike** route LF3b heads northeast, following the contours of a meandering canal; flat, narrow and predominantly carless, its only challenges are the minute (but near-vertical) wooden humpback bridges, hiccups in the surrounding calm. Before you reach Holwerd, follow signs branching off to **DOKKUM**, half an hour from Leeuwarden by buses #50 and #51. This is the only significant settlement in the area, and one of Friesland's oldest towns: the English missionary St Boniface and 52 of his companions were murdered here in 754 while trying to convert the pagan Frisians to Christianity. In part walled and moated, Dokkum has kept its shape as a fortified town, best appreciated by the side of the Het Grootdiep canal, which cuts the town into two distinct sections. This was the commercial centre of the old town and is marked by a series of ancient gables, including that of the **Admiraliteitshuis** which serves as the town's **museum** (Tues–Sat 1–5pm; €2.50; Ⓦwww .museumdokkum.nl). There's not much else: a couple of windmills, quiet walks along the old ramparts and all sorts of things named after St Boniface.

The **VVV**, Op de Fetze 13 (Mon 1–5.30pm, Tues–Fri 9am–5.30pm, Fri also 7–9pm, Sat 9am–5pm; Ⓣ0519/293 800, Ⓦwww.vvvdokkum.nl), has a map of the city that covers the outlying towns of Holwerd and Wierum too, as well as a supply of private rooms. The best-value **hotel** is the *Van der Meer*, Woudweg 1 (Ⓣ0519/292 380, Ⓦwww.hotelvandermeer.nl; ❶). The closest campsite, *Harddraverspark* (Ⓣ0519/294 445, Ⓦwww.campingdokkum.nl), is just five minutes' walk east of the centre at Harddraversdijk 1a. At **lunchtime** *De Waegh*, Grote Breedstraat 1, serves medieval-style food – big servings of mostly meat, bread and potatoes – and large cups of coffee; *'t Keerpunt*, a lunch and snack bar a few doors further – along at no. 13, offers a selection of pancakes and soups, while in the evening your best bet is *'t Raedhus* on Koningstraat 1 (also a hotel), or *Pizzeria Romana* (closed Mon), just off the main canal at Koornmarkt 8.

Moddergat and Wierum

Of all the tiny hamlets in north Friesland, two of the most interesting lie on the Waddenzee. **MODDERGAT**, the more easterly of the two, spreads out along the road behind the sea wall 10km north of Dokkum, merging with the village of Paesens. At its western edge, a memorial commemorates the 1883 tragedy when seventeen ships sank during a storm, with the loss of 83 lives. Opposite, **'t Fiskerhuske Museum**, Fiskerpad 4–8 (March–Oct Mon–Sat 10am–5pm;

€2.50; ⓦwww.museummoddergat.nl), comprises three restored fishermen's cottages with displays on the history and culture of the village and details of the disaster: as such small museums go, it's pretty good. Huddled behind the sea dyke 5km to the west, **WIERUM** has one main claim to fame: its twelfth-century church with a saddle-roof tower and (as in Moddergat) a golden ship on the weather vane. The dyke offers views across to the islands and holds a monument of twisted anchors to the fishermen who died in the 1883 storm and the dozen or so claimed in the century since. The **Wadloopcentrum Fryslân** here (ⓣ0519/562 516, ⓦwww.wadlopen.net) organizes guided walks across the mud flats: times vary with conditions and tides.

Moddergat and Wierum are on the same **bus #52** route from Dokkum (you must book on ⓣ0900/1969 at least an hour in advance of the scheduled time to ensure that the bus will arrive at the stop). If you've rented a bicycle from Leeuwarden and ridden to Dokkum, follow the signposted cycleway; it's around 8km to Moddergat and a few kilometres more to Wierum. There are a couple of **places to stay**: the farmhouse pension *Recreatiebedrijf Meinsma*, Meinsmaweg 5 in Moddergat (ⓣ0519/589 396; ❶), which also offers a small campsite, and self-contained bungalows, or the pension *'t Sloepke*, Pastoriestraat 1 in Wierum (ⓣ0519/589 727, ⓦwww.sloepke.nl; ❶), also with some camping.

The island of Ameland

Easy to reach from the tiny port of Holwerd, a few kilometres from Wierum, the island of **AMELAND** is one of the major tourist resorts of the north Dutch coast, with a population that swells from 3000 to a staggering 35,000 during summer weekends. Not that the sun is always shining: at times, clouds bustle for position and the colour of the sky can mirror that of the water. It's during the storms that the island is at its moodiest, the flatness of the land accentuating the action in the sky above.

Boats dock near the main village, **NES**, a tiny place that nestles among the fields behind the dyke. Once a centre of the Dutch whaling industry, Nes has its share of cafés, hotels and tourist shops, though quite a bit of the old village survives. High-rise development has been forbidden, and there's a focus instead on the seventeenth- and eighteenth-century captains' houses, known as *Commandeurshuizen*, which line several of the streets. Perhaps surprisingly, the crowds rarely seem to overwhelm the village, but rather to breathe life into it – which is just as well as there's not a lot to do other than wander the streets and

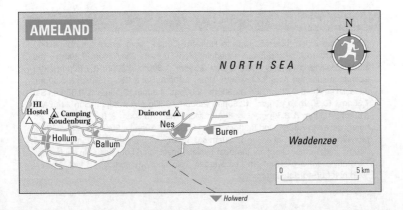

linger in cafés. Even if you do hit peak season, it's fairly easy to escape the crowds on all but the busiest of days, and you can **rent bikes** at a number of shops in the village. If it's raining, you might consider the **Natuurcentrum**, Strandweg 38 (mid-April to June, Sept & Oct Mon–Fri 10am–5pm, Sat & Sun 1–5pm; July & Aug Mon–Fri 10am–7pm, Sat & Sun 10am–5pm; Nov to mid-April Wed–Sat 1–5pm; €3.75; ⓦwww.amelandermusea.nl), an aquarium and natural history museum – look out for the life-size whale – with no information in English.

Nes practicalities

Nes has a wide range of **accommodation**, but prices do rise dramatically in summer, when many places are full. You should call ahead if you're visiting in July or August. For a small charge, the **VVV**, Bureweg 2 (Mon–Fri 9am–12.30pm & 1.30–6pm, Sat 10am–3.30pm; ⓣ0519/546 546, ⓦwww.vvvameland.nl) will fix you up with a pension or private **room** anywhere on the island. Failing that, you could try the central and family run hotel *De Jong*, Reeweg 29 (ⓣ0519/542 016, ⓦwww.hoteldejong.nl; ❷), or the luxurious *Golden Tulip Resort Noordsee*, Strandweg 42 (ⓣ0519/546 600, ⓦwww.westcordhotels.nl; ❹). The best-appointed **campsite** is the sprawling *Duinoord* at Jan van Eijckweg 4 (ⓣ0519/542 070, ⓦwww.duinoord.net; April–Oct); go 1km north out of Nes, then follow Strandweg all the way to the sea, bearing left to enter the camping complex.

A summer **bus** service, connecting with ferry arrivals, runs to the principal villages. There's a variety of **boat** excursions from Nes, including trips to the islands of Terschelling (see p.232) and Schiermonnikoog (see p.256), and to the sandbanks to watch seals. Details can be had from the VVV or tour operators in Nes.

Around the island

Ameland is just 2km wide but 25km long, and its entire northern shore is made up of a fine expanse of sand and dune laced by foot and cycle paths. The east end of the island is the most deserted, and you can cycle by the side of the marshy shallows that once made up the whole southern shore before the sea dyke was built.

Of the smaller villages that dot the island, the prettiest place to stay is **HOLLUM**, a sedate settlement of old houses and farm buildings west of Nes. Its **VVV**, Fabrieksweg 6 (April–Aug Mon–Fri 9am–noon & 1.30–5.30pm, Sat 10am–noon; Sept–March Mon–Fri 9am–noon, Sat 10am–noon; ⓣ0519/546 546), can offer the

---

Ferries to Ameland

From Leeuwarden, bus #66 runs to Holwerd (30min), from where the connecting ferry departs to Ameland (basic schedule: Mon–Fri every 2hr 7.30am–7.30pm – the 3.30pm sailing is Fri only – Sat & Sun 9.30am, 1.30pm, 5.30pm & 7.30pm; extra sailings in summer: April & May Mon–Thurs 3.30pm, Sat & Sun 11.30am & 3.30pm; June Mon–Thurs 3.30pm, Fri 12.30pm, 2.30pm, 4.30pm, 6.30pm & 8.30pm, Sat 7.30am, 10.30am, 11.30am, 12.30pm, 2.30pm, 3.30pm & 4.30pm, Sun 11.30am, 3.30pm, 4.30pm & 6.30pm; July & Aug Mon–Thurs 10.30am & 3.30pm, Fri & Sat hourly between 7.30am and 8.30pm, Sun 11.30am, 3.30pm, 4.30pm & 6.30pm; Sept Mon–Thurs 3.30pm, Sat & Sun 11.30am & 3.30pm; Oct Sat 11.30am; 45min; €11.25 return). In the other direction, the boat leaves Ameland an hour earlier in each case. Timetables are available from Leeuwarden train and bus stations. Check ⓦwww.wpd.nl for up-to-date information.

same services as the Nes VVV and is generally less crowded. If you're an aquatic addict there are a couple of small museums here: the **Sorgdragermuseum**, Herenweg 1 (July to late Aug Mon–Fri 10am–5pm, Sat & Sun 1.30–5pm; check hours with the VVV out of season; €2.50; W www.amelandermusea.nl), an old *Commandeurshuis*, the **Reddingsmuseum Abraham Fock**, Oranjeweg 18 (same hours; €2.50; W www.amelandermusea.nl), devoted to the local lifeboat teams and the horses that used to drag the boats to the sea and the **lighthouse** which was built in 1880 and gives a good view of the island (July to late Aug Tues–Sat 10am–5pm & 7–10pm, Sun from 1pm, April–June, Sept & Oct closes 9pm, check hours with the VVV out of season; €3.50; W www.amelandermusea.nl).

Hollum's best-value place to stay is the homely *Pension Ambla*, Westerlaan 33a (T 0519/554 537, W www.ambla.nl; ❶–❷). Alternatives include the **campsite** *Koudenburg Oosterhiemweg* (T 0519/554 367, W www.koudenburg.nl), by the heath to the north at Oosterhemweg 2. Further west, situated dramatically at the tip of the island past the lighthouse and between pine forest and dunes, is the *Waddencentrum Ameland* – a good HI **hostel** (T 0519/555 353, W www.stayokay.com; dorm bed €25), with bike-rental. To get there take bus #130 to the last stop.

Groningen

Once known as East Frisia, **Groningen** has relatively little to offer compared with other Dutch provinces: its landscape isn't abundant, and it is traditionally the province with the highest unemployment rate. There are, however, a few highlights that make a visit to the province worthwhile, especially the vibrant **city** that shares its name. The name Groningen dates back to 1040, when "Villa Cruoninga" was first mentioned in a letter by the German emperor. In the thirteenth century Groningen grew into a powerful trading centre that had its own laws and jurisdiction and a city wall for protection. Nowadays Groningen is a lively student centre, with over 180,000 inhabitants.

Northwest of the city, located on the Groningen–Frisian border, the **Lauwersmeer National Park** is home to an extensive range of wildlife and is a popular place for fishing, windsurfing and cycling. Further north lies **Schiermonnikoog**, the smallest Friesland island, less visited than the others but still popular and attractive. Also up north is the **seal sanctuary** of Pieterburen, where sick or underfed seals are nursed until they can be released back into the Waddenzee, and where you can watch the young seal pups being fed.

To the southeast of the province's capital, the village of **Bourtange** has been restored into its old glory and includes centuries-old defences and bastions, offering an insight into eighteenth-century life in a fortified town, and attracting mainly German tourists. South of Bourtange is the **monastery of Ter Apel**, now serving as a museum, which, extremely unusually for the region, survived the Reformation intact. Of the approximately 200 old **estate houses**, which served as hideouts for the rich during the Middle Ages, only sixteen have survived. They are scattered around Groningen, and one of the most famous is the **Menkemaborg** in Uithuizen.

Groningen

The most exciting city in the north Netherlands, **GRONINGEN** comes as something of a surprise in the midst of the province's quiet, rural surroundings. Hip, streetwise fashions, a cosmopolitan feel and thriving student life imbue the city with vigour. Competitively priced restaurants dish up exotic curries and fresh falafel alongside the standard Dutch staples, and the arts scene is vibrant, particularly during the academic year. Virtually destroyed during the Allied liberation in 1945, Groningen is now a jumble of arts and architectures: from traditional canal-side townhouses to colourful Art Deco tile work parading along the upper facades of the shopping streets. This eclecticism culminates in the innovative Groninger Museum, resplendent in acid-greens and golds on its

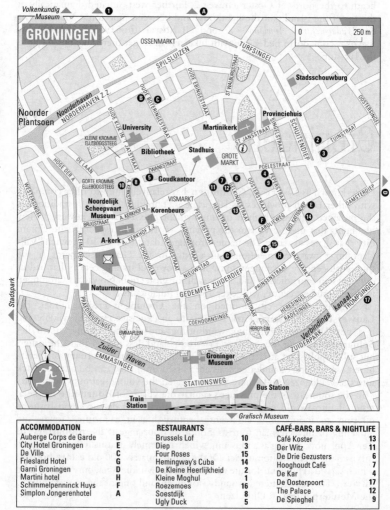

ACCOMMODATION		RESTAURANTS		CAFÉ-BARS, BARS & NIGHTLIFE	
Auberge Corps de Garde	B	Brussels Lof	10	Café Koster	13
City Hotel Groningen	E	Diep	3	Der Witz	11
De Ville	C	Four Roses	15	De Drie Gezusters	6
Friesland Hotel	G	Hemingway's Cuba	14	Hooghoudt Café	7
Garni Groningen	D	De Kleine Heerlijkheid	2	De Kar	4
Martini hotel	H	Kleine Moghul	1	De Oosterpoort	17
Schimmelpenninck Huys	F	Roezemoes	16	The Palace	12
Simplon Jongerenhotel	A	Soestdijk	8	De Spieghel	9
		Ugly Duck	5		

own little island; its controversial design encases a superb collection of contemporary art, set off by numerous and varied exhibitions.

Groningen was once an important centre of trade, nominally a fiefdom of the bishops of Utrecht from 1040 until 1536, but in reality an autonomous merchant state ruled by a tightly defined oligarchy, whose power was exercised through the city council, or *Raad*. In 1536 Charles V forced the town to submit to his authority, but Groningen was nevertheless still hesitant in its support of the Dutch rebellion against his successors. The dilemma for the city fathers was that, although they stood to gain economically from independence, the majority of the town's citizens were Catholic, deeply suspicious of their Protestant neighbours. In the end, the economic argument won the day, and the town became the capital of its own province in 1594.

Although Groningen does not have a rich culinary tradition, the **Hooghoudt brewery** (call ☎050/542 0000 for excursions every Tues, Wed & Fri; €5.50 with drink included; ⓦwww.hooghoudt.nl) is known throughout the country and dates back to 1888. The brewery is most famous for its *Graanjevener*, but they also produce *Beerenburg* and other liquors like the *Wilhelmus Orange Liquor*, which is traditionally served at Queen's Day.

Arrival, information and tours

Groningen's **bus** and **train** stations are side by side on the south side of town. The VVV is ten minutes' walk away in the centre at Grote Markt 25 (Mon–Fri 9am–6pm, Sat 10am–5pm; July & Aug also Sun 11am–3pm; ☎0900/202 3050, ⓦwww.groningen.nl/tourism). It offers a range of services, from tourist information on the town and province to online reservations of hotel rooms and tickets for visiting bands, theatre groups and orchestras. Also available is a brochure of city walks for €1.50 and information on exploring Groningen by boat (ⓦwww.rondvaartbedrijfkool.nl) or canoe. As well as information on the larger hotels, the VVV has a short list of **private rooms** in both Groningen and the surrounding area, though hardly any are near the centre.

Accommodation

Groningen has plenty of good, reasonably priced **accommodation**, though it's a good idea to call ahead to reserve a room. Many hotels offer free bicycles on loan for their guests.

If you're **camping**, *Stadspark*, Campinglaan 6 (☎050/525 1624, ⓦwww.campingstadspark.nl; mid-March to mid-Oct), is the best option, within walking distance of the city centre.

Auberge Corps de Garde Oude Boteringestraat 72–74 ☎050/314 5437, ⓦwww.corpsdegarde.nl. A central option located in a seventeenth-century building, close to the Grote Markt. ❷

City Hotel Groningen Gedempte Kattendiep 25 ☎050/588 6565, ⓦwww.edenhotelgroup.com. Modern and well equipped with a stunning view over the city from the roof terrace. ❷–❸

De Ville Oude Boteringestraat 43 ☎050/318 1222, ⓦwww.deville.nl. Even though now part of a chain, this hotel has maintained its intimate feel with friendly staff and fine Baroque interior. The cosy courtyard is also a great location for a romantic dinner. ❹

Friesland Hotel Kleine Pelsterstraat 4 ☎ & ⒻF050/312 1307, ⓦwww.hotelfriesland.nl. A budget choice, right next to the main shopping street. The rooms don't have private showers or bathrooms. ❶

Garni Groningen Damsterdiep 94 ☎050/313 5435. Ten minutes' walk east of Gedempte Zuiderdiep, a street of cheap eating places that get scruffier the further east you go, the *Groningen* is friendly if a little spartan, and a good alternative if the more central hotels are full. ❶

Martini hotel Gedempte Zuiderdiep 8 ☎050/312 9919, ⓦwww.martinihotel.nl. Large and central with Martini memorabilia on the walls and a huge

grand café with fireplace and piano for an intimate atmosphere. **①–②**
Schimmelpenninck Huys Oosterstraat 53 ☎050/318 9502, ⓦwww.schimmelpenninckhuys .nl. Listed as a state monument, the origins of this hotel date back to 1100, and there is a fourteenth-century wine cellar and an Art Deco lounge. By far the prettiest inner courtyard in town. **④**

Simplon Jongerenhotel Boterdiep 73 ☎050/313 5221, ⓦwww.simplon-jongerenhotel.nl. The lowest prices in town can be found at the edge of the city, with clean doubles as well as well-kept dorms (€13); from the Grote Markt follow Oude Ebbingestraat north over the canal, turn first right and then first left. **①**

The City

Groningen's canal forms a moat encircling the compact city centre, making all the main sights in easy walking distance from each other. To the south of the centre is Groningen's **train station**, which was built in 1896 at enormous cost; it was one of the grandest of its day, decorated with the strong colours and symbolic designs of Art Nouveau tiles from the Rozenburg factory in The Hague. The grandeur of much of the building has disappeared under a welter of concrete, glass and plastic suspended ceilings, but the old first- and second-class waiting rooms have survived pretty much intact, and have been refurbished as restaurants. The epitome of high Gothic style, the oak-panelled walls are edged by extravagantly tiled chimneypieces, while a central pillar in each room supports a papier-mâché fluted ceiling.

The Groninger Museum

The town's main draw is the excellent **Groninger Museum** (Tues–Sun 10am–5pm; July & Aug also Mon 1–5pm; €6; ⓦwww.groningermuseum.nl), set on its own island on the southern edge of the centre, directly across from the train station. It consists of six pavilions, each designed in a highly individual style. The museum entrance is under the shimmering golden tower of the central pavilion: think Gaudí on holiday in Miami, and you'll have some inkling of the interior decor. In-between the stylish café and museum shop, a striking mosaic stairwell flummoxes most visitors by sweeping downwards, depositing you among two bulbous lemon-yellow pillars on a baby-blue floor. From here moat-level corridors head off to pavilions either side: east to Mendini, Mendini 1 and Coop Himmelb(l)au, west to Starck and De Ploeg.

Highlights of the museum include Rubens' energetic *Adoration of the Magi* among a small selection of seventeenth-century works, Isaac Israels' inviting *Hoedenwinkel* from a modest sample of Hague School paintings, and a number of later works by the Expressionists of the Groningen *De Ploeg* association, principally Jan Wiegers, whose *Portrait of Ludwig Kirchner* is typically earnest.

Pedal power in Groningen

One of the best things about Groningen is the lack of motor traffic: much of the centre is **car-free**, the result of municipal decisions dating back to the mid-1970s, when the city suffered some of the worst road congestion in Europe. In typically bold but sensible Dutch fashion, local authorities dismantled a huge motorway intersection in the city centre, closed most of its roads to cars and invested heavily in a network of cycle paths and bus lanes. Today the park-and-ride scheme goes from strength to strength and two-thirds of residents travel regularly by **bike**, the highest percentage in the country. Groningen is now one of the most popular and appealing cities in the Netherlands in which to live, and the council is planning even more restrictions on cars.

An adventurous acquisition policy has led the museum to dabble in some of the more unusual trends in modern art, like Carel Visser's 1983 collage *Voor Dali* and the bizarre *Can the Bumpsteers While I Park the Chariot* by Henk Tas. The paintings are regularly revolved, so don't pin your hopes on catching any particular item.

To the west, the **Philippe Starck pavilion** is a giant disc clad in vertical aluminium plating. A simple vase motif on the exterior hints at the collection of **Chinese and Japanese porcelain** within, beautifully displayed in circular glass cases, softened by gauzy drapes.

Starck's disc pavilion sits atop the **De Ploeg pavilion**, created by Michele De Lucchi in the form of a trapezium constructed from red bricks, a traditional local building material. The De Ploeg art movement began in Groningen in 1918, and is characterized by intense colour contrasts, exaggerated shapes and depiction of landscapes. As founding member Jan Altink put it: "There wasn't much going on in the way of art in Groningen, so I thought of cultivation and thus also of ploughing. Hence the name *De Ploeg*." The group often depicted the landscape north of Groningen in their works; the museum information desk can provide cycle routes which take in scenes depicted in the art collection.

To the east of the mosaic stairway, three pavilions house the museum's collection of **contemporary art**. On the lower and ground levels, the **Mendini pavilion** is dedicated to temporary exhibitions.

The **Mendini 1 pavilion**, on the first floor, displays a selection of the museum's collection of contemporary visual art, with particular emphasis on art, architecture, design, graffiti and photography. The galleries are individually colour-schemed: cool blues and purples, or toastier cherry and peach.

A large concrete stairway links Mendini 1 to the final, and most controversial, pavilion. Designed by Wolfgang Prix and Helmut Swiczinsky, who together call themselves **Coop Himmelb(l)au**, this is a Deconstructivist experiment: double-plated steel and reinforced glass jut out at awkward angles, and skinny aerial walkways crisscross the exhibition space. It all feels – probably deliberately – half-built. Look out for the glass walkholes, where the concrete floor stops and suddenly between your feet the canal gapes, two storeys below. This pavilion is given over to temporary exhibitions which exist in a harsh industrial soundscape, created by the movement of visitors through metal doors and on the unworked concrete and resonating steel gantries.

Grote Markt and around

The effective centre of town is **Grote Markt**, a wide open space that was badly damaged by wartime bombing and has been rather unimaginatively reconstructed. At its northeast corner is the tiered tower of the **Martinikerk** (June to mid-Sept Tues–Sat noon–5pm; at other times, check hours with VVV; €1; ⓦ www.martinikerk.nl). Though the oldest parts of the church go back to 1180, most of it dates from the mid-fifteenth century, the nave being a Gothicized rebuilding undertaken to match the added choir. The vault paintings in the nave are beautifully restored, and in the old choir there are two series of frescoes on the walled-up niches of the clerestory. On the right, a series of eight depicts the story of Christmas, beginning with an Annunciation and ending with a portrayal of the young Christ in the temple.

Adjoining the church is the essentially seventeenth-century **Martinitoren** (April–Nov Mon–Sat 11am–5pm; July & Aug also Sun 11am–5pm; rest of year Mon–Sat noon–4pm; €3), which offers a view that is breathtaking in every sense of the word. Behind the church is the lawn of the Kerkhof, an ancient piece of common land that's partly enclosed by the Provinciehuis, a rather grand neo-Renaissance building of 1915, seat of the provincial government. On the opposite side of the Grote Markt, the classical **Stadhuis** dates from 1810, tucked in front of the mid-seventeenth-century **Goudkantoor** (Gold Office); look out for the shell motif above the windows, a characteristic Groningen decoration.

Around the A-kerk

From the southwest corner of the Grote Markt, the far side of Vismarkt is framed by the **Korenbeurs** (Corn Exchange) of 1865. The statues on the facade represent, from left to right, Neptune, Mercurius (god of commerce) and Ceres (goddess of agriculture). Just behind, the **A-kerk** is a fifteenth-century church with a Baroque steeple, attractively restored in tones of yellow, orange and red. The church's full name is Onze Lieve Vrouwekerk der A ("Our Dear Lady's Church of the A"), the A being a small river which forms the moat encircling the town centre.

Just west of the church along A-Kerkhof N.Z., the **Noordelijk Scheepvaart Museum**, Brugstraat 24–26 (Tues–Sat 10am–5pm, Sun 1–5pm; €3; ⓦ www .noordelijkscheepvaartmuseum.nl), is one of the best-equipped and most comprehensive maritime museums in the country, tracing the history of north Holland's shipping from the sixth to the twentieth centuries. Housed in a warren of steep stairs and timber-beamed rooms, each of the museum's twenty displays deals with a different aspect of shipping, including trade with the Indies, the development of peat canals and a series of reconstructed nautical workshops. The museum's particular appeal is its imaginative combination of models and original artefacts, which are themselves a mixture of the personal (seamen's chests, quadrants) and the public (figureheads, tile designs of ships). In the same building is the much smaller **Niemeyer Tabaksmuseum** (same hours and ticket), devoted to tobacco smoking. Exhibits include a multitude of pipes and a great collection of snuff paraphernalia in all sorts of materials, from crystal and ivory to porcelain and silver. The Niemeyer family built their fortune on the tobacco trade, and here you can see the origins of those familiar blue tobacco packets.

Smaller museums

Of the city's smaller museums, there's contemporary art at the **Centrum Beeldende Kunst** (Visual Arts Centre) in the Oosterpoort, Trompsingel 27 (Wed–Sun 1–5pm; free; ⓦwww.cbkgroningen.nl), while the **Grafisch Museum**, Rabenhauptstraat 65 (Graphic Museum; Tues–Sun 1–5pm; €3.50; ⓦwww.grafischmuseum.nl), southeast of the train station, has everything from a nineteenth-century steam-driven printing press to word-processors.

Northwest of Grote Markt, down a passage off Zwanestraat, the **Universiteitsmuseum** (Tues–Sun 1–5pm; €2.50; ⓦwww.rug.nl/museum) gives a taste of the university's history, with exhibits ranging from scientific equipment to photos of derby-hatted students clowning around at the turn of last century. Last but not least, the **Nederlands Stripmuseum** (Dutch Comics Museum), Westerhaven 71 (Tues–Sun 10am–5pm; €7; ⓦwww.nederlandsstripmuseum.nl), is a good option when travelling with children although the museum is mainly aimed at Dutch visitors.

Eating, drinking and nightlife

As Groningen is a student town without official closing hours, there are many budget options for a decent meal, and nightlife is vibrant round the clock. The nicest places to **eat and drink** can be found around the **Poelestraat**, just east of Grote Markt, where an array of open-air cafés pulls in a mainly young crowd. The south side of the **Grote Markt** serves all tastes with large terraces and loud music at night, while in the **Kleine or Grote Kromme Elleboog** area you are in the heart of the university district. The **Schuitendiep** was run-down a few years ago, but renovations have made this a pleasant area with a wide range of restaurants and bars, all overlooking the water.

The free *Uitgaanskrant* has listings of all events. There are several **music venues** in the city, and the main **theatre**, the Stadsschouwburg, is located in a historical building overlooking the water, at Turfsingel 86 (☎050/312 5645). Most plays are in Dutch, but they also have contemporary dance and music performances.

Restaurants

Brussels Lof A-Kerkstraat 24 ☎050/312 7603. Serves a wide range of vegetarian dishes and good fondues, but also known for fresh fish; pure and simple cuisine with mains like tuna, artichoke pie or scallops for around €17.

 Diep Schuitendiep 44 ☎050/589 0009. Once a residence for monks, now a stylish restaurant with lime-green accents and a hidden inner courtyard. The friendly staff serve mains like salmon filet, steak Japanese-style and goat's cheese salad for around €16.

Four Roses Oosterstraat 71 ☎050/314 3887. Tex-Mex food like nacho's, burritos and rib-eyes at the junction of Oosterstraat and Gedempte Zuiderdiep. Also great cocktails.

Hemingway's Cuba Gedempte Kattendiep 23/1
☏050/589 3409. This restaurant is part of the Via
Vecchia, consisting of three restaurants located
around a tiny Mediterranean-style alley. It serves
tapas Cuban style and steaks with Caribbean
vegetables for around €18.

De Kleine Heerlijkheid Schuitendiep 42
☏050/313 1370. Located in one of the oldest
buildings just outside the city walls, the smallest
restaurant in Groningen serves mains for around
€15 in an agreeable atmosphere.

Kleine Moghul Nieuwe Boteringestraat 62
☏050/318 8905. A ten-minute walk north from the
Grote Markt is this excellent-value and busy Indian
takeaway and restaurant that's well worth the trek
for its kitsch decor.

Roezemoes Gedempte Zuiderdiep 15 ☏050/314
8854. For an original *stamppot* (mashed potatoes
with veggies and meat) you're in the right place –
they even serve this typical Dutch winter dish in
summer. There are also non-mashed mains on the
menu for around €10.

Soestdijk Grote Kromme Elleboog 6 ☏050/314
5050. A bit pricier and posher than average with
paintings on the walls, and *sateh* chicken skewers,
steaks and lamb racks on the menu.

Ugly Duck Zwanestraat 28 ☏050/312 3192. If you
don't mind the plastic ducks serving as decoration
staring at you this is a good place for a basic but
decent meal with daily specials around €11, and a
wide range of salads, fish and Dutch food.

Café-bars, bars and nightlife

Café Koster Hoogstraat 7. Hidden down an alley,
this music café focuses on live blues, funk and
rock music.

Der Witz Grote Markt 47. This German-style brown
café has eight different beers on draft and some
strong chilled *korns* (the German version of the
Dutch *jenever*).

De Drie Gezusters Grote Markt 39. A civilized bar
with a great old interior that interlinks with neighbouring bars – handy on cold winter nights. Also
has a non-smoking area.

Hooghoudt Café Grote Markt 42. Located in the
old Lloyds Insurance building with a huge terrace
and attractively priced daily specials.

De Kar Peperstraat 15. A popular bar among
students, it's also open late during weekdays and
has dancing. Closed Sun.

De Oosterpoort Trompsingel 27 ☏050/313 1044.
A well-known and modern music centre, just east
of the train station, hosting many of the bigger
visiting bands.

The Palace Gelkingestraat 1. A good club that
occasionally hosts live bands and attracts a
younger crowd.

De Spieghel Peperstraat 11. This jazz café has
live performances most nights, including some
reasonably big names, and a nice terrace in
summer.

Listings

Bike rental At the train station (€6.50/day, €21/
week; ☏050/312 4174).

Boat trips Along the old town moat (€7.50 for 1hr
15min). Bookings and schedules at the VVV.

Books There's a good range of English-language
titles at Scholtens-Wristers on Guldenstraat.

Cinema Images, Poelestraat 30 (☏050/312 0433,
ⓦwww.images.nu) is an arthouse cinema with a
pleasant open-air café. Mainstream films are
shown at the Pathé Megabioscoop, Gedempte
Zuiderdiep 78 (☏050/584 4050).

Internet access Bibliotheek, Oude Boteringestraat
14 ☏050/368 3683.

Laundry Self or service wash at Handy Wash,
Schuitendiep 56 ☏050/318 7587.

Markets Vegetables, fruit, flowers, fish and fabrics
at A-Kerkhof (Tues, Fri & Sat 9am–5pm). Organic
food market at Vismarkt (Wed 9am–5pm). Non-food
general market at the Grote Markt (Thurs 1–9pm).

Pharmacy Apotheek Hanzeplein, Hanzeplein 122
(open 24hr; ☏050/311 5020).

Police Rademarkt 12 ☏0900/8844.

Post office By the A-kerk on Munnekeholm (Mon
10am–6pm, Tues–Fri 9am–6pm, Sat 10am–
1.30pm).

Taxi TaxiCentrale ☏050/366 6663.

Around Groningen

A patchwork of industrial complexes and nondescript villages, Groningen
province has few major attractions; unless you fancy a night in the country near
the old monastery at Ter Apel or prefer the tranquillity of Schiermonnikoog,
there's nowhere that really warrants a stay.

The easiest trip is to the **botanical gardens** at **HAREN** (daily 9.30am–5pm; €4.50; ⓦ www.hortusharen.nl) a few kilometres south by train or bus #50, #51, #54 or #58. From the train station it's a signed, 25-minute walk. There's a small Chinese garden, an English garden and some extensive rose gardens. At the time of writing, the tropical greenhouse complex, with a range of cacti and some wonderful old cycads, as well as the more familiar palms, bananas and ferns was closed and being renovated.

Uithuizen

For day-tripping from Groningen city, the most agreeable journey is to the village of **UITHUIZEN**, 25km north, where the moated manor house of **Menkemaborg** (March & April Tues–Sun 10am–noon & 1–4pm; May–Sept daily 10am–5pm; Oct–Jan Tues–Sun 10am–noon & 1–4pm; €4.50; ⓦ www .menkemaborg.nl) is a signed ten-minute walk from the station. Dating from the fifteenth century and surrounded by formal gardens in the English style, the house has a sturdy, compact elegance and is one of the very few mansions, or borgs, of the old landowning families to have survived. The interior consists of a sequence of period rooms furnished in the style of the seventeenth century, displaying some of the Groninger Museum's applied art and history collection.

The trip to Uithuizen can be combined with *wadlopen* (see box on p.256) – a guided walk across the coastal mud flats to the uninhabited sand-spit island of **Rottumeroog**. Excursion buses head out to the coast from Menkemaborg three or four times monthly (June–Sept); the trip costs from €22.50 per person, and booking is essential – contact Stichting Uithuizer Wad (ⓦ www.wadlopen.nl). Without a guide, it's too dangerous to venture onto the mud flats, but it is easy enough to **walk** along the enclosing dyke that runs behind the shoreline for the whole length of the province. There's precious little to see, but when the weather's clear, the browns, blues and greens of the surrounding land and sea are unusually beautiful. From Uithuizen, it's a good hour's stroll north to the nearest point on the dyke, and you'll need a large-scale map (available from Groningen VVV) for directions.

Pieterburen

The first thing that comes in mind to a Dutch person when you mention Pieterburen, 27km north from Groningen, is the **seal sanctuary** (Zeehonden-creche Pieterburen; daily 9am–6pm; €2; ⓦ www.zeehondencreche.nl). Founded 35 years ago by Lenie 't Hart, a local animal welfare heroine, the sanctuary rescues abandoned or weak seals with the purpose of releasing them back to the wild. The best time to see seal pups is during the summer, when many will be nursed and fed until they are strong enough to make it on their own.

Pieterburen is also the start and end point for the longest unbroken walking tour in the Netherlands, the 464-kilometre long **Pieterpad** to Maastricht. More information and a walking route can be obtained at the VVV, Hoofdstraat 83 (☎ 0595/528 522).

Just 5km from Pieterburen you will find the smallest hotel in the world, mentioned in the Guinness Book of Records. *De Kromme Raake* (☎ 0595/491 600, ⓦ www.hoteldekrommeraake.nl; ⑤) in **Eenrum** is an old grocery shop transformed into a hotel with nothing more than a reception and one room.

The Lauwersmeer National Park

Some 35km northwest of Groningen, the **Lauwersmeer National Park** is a broken and irregular lake that spreads across the provincial boundary into neighbouring Friesland. Once an arm of the sea, it was turned into a freshwater lake by the construction of the Lauwersoog dam, a controversial 1960s project that was vigorously opposed by local fishermen, who ended up having to move all their tackle to ports on the coast. Spared intensive industrial and agricultural development because of the efforts of conservationists, it's a quiet and peaceful region with a wonderful variety of sea birds, and increasingly popular with anglers, windsurfers, sailors and cyclists.

The local villages are uniformly dull, however; the most convenient base is **ZOUTKAMP**, near the southeast corner of the lake on the River Reitdiep, accessible by bus #65 from Groningen. The **VVV**, Reitdiepskade 11 (May–Oct Mon–Fri 9am–5pm, Sat 10am–4pm; Nov–April Mon–Fri 10am–noon &1–3pm; ☎0595/401 957; ⑩www.vvvlauwersland.nl), has a limited supply of private rooms, which can be reserved here or at Groningen VVV.

At the mouth of the lake, some 10km north of Zoutkamp, the desultory port of **LAUWERSOOG** is where **ferries** leave for the fifty-minute trip to the island of Schiermonnikoog.

The island of Schiermonnikoog

Until the Reformation, the island of **SCHIERMONNIKOOG** belonged to the monastery of Klaarkamp on the mainland; its name means literally "island of the grey monks". Nothing remains of the monks, however, and these days Schiermonnikoog's only settlement is a prim and busy village bordering on long stretches of muddy beach and sand dune to the north and farmland and mud flats to the south. At low tide, these motionless pools of water reflect the colours in the sky, particularly atmospheric at dawn and dusk. Schiermonnikoog is the smallest of the Frisian islands at 16km long and 4km wide, and, once you're clear of the weekend homes that fringe the village, it's a wild,

---

Wadlopen

Wadlopen, or mud-flat walking, is a popular and strenuous Dutch pastime, and the stretch of coast on the northern edge of the provinces of Friesland and Groningen is one of the best places to do it: twice daily, the receding tide uncovers vast expanses of mud flat beneath the Waddenzee. It is, however, a sport to be taken seriously, and far too dangerous to do without an experienced guide: the depth of the mud is variable and the tides inconsistent. In any case, channels of deep water are left even when the tide has receded, and the currents can be perilous. The timing of treks depends on weather and tidal conditions, but most start between 6am and 10am. It's important to be properly equipped; recommended gear includes shorts or a bathing suit, a sweater, wind jacket, knee-high socks, high-top trainers and a complete change of clothes stashed in a watertight pack. In recent years, wadlopen has become extremely popular, and as excursions are infrequent, between May and August it's advisable to book a place at least a month in advance.

Prices are €15–25 a head, and include the cost of a return ferry crossing; the VVVs in Leeuwarden, Dokkum and Groningen can provide details, or you could contact one of the wadlopen organizations direct: Dijkstras Wadlopencentrum, Hoofdstraat 118, Pieterburen (☎0595/528 345, ⑩www.wadloop-dijkstra.nl), has the most multilingual guides; there's also Stichting Wadloopcentrum Pieterburen, Hoofdstraat 105, Pieterburen (☎0595/528 300, ⑩www.wadlopen.com). The Wadloopcentrum Fryslân (☎0519/562 516, ⑩www.wadlopen.net) is based in Wierum (see p.245).

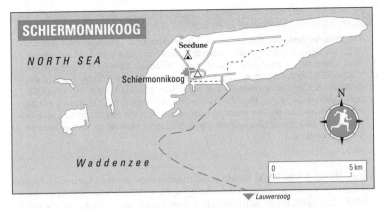

uncultivated place, crisscrossed by cycle paths – a popular spot for day-trippers.

Ferries from Lauwersoog (see box on p.258) dock at the island jetty, some 3km from the village; a connecting bus drops you off outside the VVV in the centre. It's even possible to walk to the island across the mud flats from Kloosterburen, a distance of about 8km, but you must do this accompanied by a guide; see the box opposite for details.

Finding **accommodation** is difficult in season, when prices rise sharply; it's essential to ring ahead. The **VVV** (Mon–Fri 9am–12.30pm & 1.30–6pm, Sat 9.30am–12.30pm & 1.30–4.30pm; Oct Mon–Fri closes 30min earlier; ☎0519/531 900, ⓦwww.vvvschiermonnikoog.nl) will help by booking private **rooms** and pensions. The large *Van der Werff*, Reeweg 2 (☎0519/531 203, ⓦwww.hotelvanderwerff.nl; ❶) is the cheapest **hotel** in town; the *Strandhotel Noderstraun* (☎0519/531 111, ⓦwww.strandhotel.nl; ❹–❺), about twenty minutes' walk from the VVV and overlooking the beach at Badweg 32, is a more luxurious alternative; the recently renovated *De Tjattel* (☎0519/531 133, ⓦwww.detjattel.nl; ❷), in the heart of the village at Langestreek 94, is a third possibility, with a large restaurant and bar. On the east side of the village at Knuppeldam 2, fifteen minutes' walk from the VVV, is the *Herberg Rijsbergen* (☎0519/531 257, ⓦwww.rijsbergen.biz; ❶), located in a historical building with a huge grass lawn around it. Schiermonnikoog's **campsite**, *Seedune* (☎0519/531 398, ⓦwww.seedune.nl), is to the north, in the woods just east of Badweg at Seeduneweg 1.

The *Strandhotel* has windsurfing equipment for rent; bikes are available from several small shops in the village, and the VVV sells good maps. Places to eat and drink are scattered along Langestreek and Badweg to the north of the VVV.

Bourtange

Some 60km southeast of Groningen close to the German frontier, **BOURTANGE** (ⓦwww.bourtange.nl) is a superbly restored fortified village. Founded by William of Orange in 1580 to help protect the eastern approaches to Groningen, Bourtange fell into disrepair during the nineteenth century, only to be entirely refurbished as a tourist attraction in 1964. The design of the village is similar to that of Naarden, outside Amsterdam, and is best appreciated as you walk round the old bastions of the star-shaped fortress. You enter the village through the **VVV** building and information centre (April–Oct Mon–Fri 9am–5.30pm, Sat & Sun 11am–5.30pm; Nov–March Mon–Fri 9am–noon; ☎0599/354 600). Entry to the village is free, but there is a charge of €4 if you want to see the slide-show, which gives a history of Bourtange and to visit the various exhibitions depicting traditional life in the village. There's a **campsite**, *'t Plathuis*, Vlagtwedderstraat 88 (☎0599/354 383, Ⓦwww.campingplathuis.nl; Apr–Oct), and one **hotel**, *De Staakenborgh*, up the road at no. 33 (☎0599/354 216, Ⓦwww.staakenborgh.nl; ❶).

Ter Apel

South from Bourtange in the small town of **TER APEL** near the German border, the **Museum Klooster** (Tues–Sat 10am–5pm, Sun 1–5pm; €4.50; Ⓦwww.museumklooster-terapel.com) is a definite highlight of this part of the country. This was the monastery of the Crutched Friars, built in 1465, and probably unique among rural monasteries in surviving the Reformation intact, after the enlightened local authorities allowed the monks to remain here during their lifetimes. The chapel, superbly restored, preserves a number of unusual features, including the tripartite sedilia, where the priest and his assistants sat during Mass, and a splendid rood screen that divides the chancel from the nave. Elsewhere, the east wing is a curious hybrid of Gothic and Rococo styles, the cloister has a small herb garden and the other rooms are normally given over to temporary exhibitions of religious art. The monastery is surrounded by extensive beech woods and magnificent old horse-chestnut trees; follow one of the marked walks or simply ramble at your leisure. Opposite, the **hotel** and **restaurant** *Boschhuis* (☎0599/581 208, Ⓦwww .hotelboschhuis.nl; ❶) is ideal for a good meal, or for spending a quiet night in the country.

Drenthe

Until the early nineteenth century, the sparsely populated province of **Drenthe** was little more than a flat expanse of empty peat bog, marsh and moor. Today it's the country's least populated province, popular with visitors for its woods and countryside. Its only conspicuous geographical feature is a ridge of low hills that runs northwest for some 50km from Emmen toward Groningen. This ridge, the **Hondsrug**, was high enough to attract prehistoric settlers whose *hunebeds* (megalithic tombs) have become Drenthe's main tourist attraction. **Assen**, the provincial capital, is a dull place with a good museum, and **Emmen**, the other major town, can only be recommended as a convenient base for visiting some of the *hunebeds* and three neighbouring open-air folk culture museums.

Governed by the bishops of Utrecht from the eleventh century, Drenthe was incorporated into the Habsburg Empire in 1538. The region sided with the Protestants in the rebellion against Spain, but it had little economic or military muscle and its claim to provincial status was ignored until the days of the Batavian Republic. In the nineteenth century, work began in earnest to convert the province's peat bogs and moors into farmland. *Veenkolonies* (peat colonies) were established over much of the south and east of Drenthe, where the initial purpose of the labourers was to dig drainage canals and cut the peat for sale as fuel to the cities. Once cleared of the peat, the land could be used to grow crops, and today the region's farms are some of the most profitable in the country.

Assen

ASSEN, about 16km south of Groningen, is a possible first stop, though not somewhere you're likely to want to stay. Its train and bus station are about five minutes' walk from the centre of town, moving straight ahead across the main road down Stationsstraat. On the eastern side of the central square, Brink square, is home to both parts of the **Drents Museum** (Tues–Sun 11am–5pm; €6; ⓦwww.drentsmuseum.nl), which, spread over a pleasant group of old houses, is the only thing that makes a stop in town worthwhile. The museum's most valuable asset is the assortment of prehistoric bodies of the early settlers who built the *hunebeds*. There is also the much vaunted Pesse Canoe, the oldest water vessel ever found dating from about 6800 BC and looking its age.

Assen's **VVV**, Marktstraat 8–10 (Mon 1–6pm, Tues–Fri 9am–6pm, Sat 9am–5pm; ⓣ0900/202 2393, ⓦwww.vvvassen.nl), is located in the main shopping street. The only **hotel** in the centre of town is *Hotel de Jonge*, Brinkstraat 85 (ⓣ0592/312 023, ⓦwww.hoteldejonge.nl; ❶–❷), which has a reasonable **restaurant** and terrace.

If you have your own transport, you might want to detour to the **Herinneringscentrum Kamp Westerbork** (Mon–Fri 10am–5pm, Sat & Sun 1–5pm; July & Aug Sat & Sun also 11am–1pm; €4.50; ⓦwww.kampwesterbork.nl), a little south of town on the road between the villages Amen and Hooghalen. It was here during World War II that the Nazis assembled Dutch

---

Motor racing in Assen

The only time Assen is the centre of attention in Dutch and international media is during the **TT Assen** (ⓦwww.tt-assen.com), the only Grand Prix motor racing in the Netherlands. More than 100,000 people visit the circuit on the last Saturday in June, making the TT the largest one-day sports event in the Netherlands. The nights before the TT, Assen's centre is packed with people enjoying live music and lots of beer. If you are visiting while it's on, make sure to book accommodation ahead.

Jews before transporting them to the death camps in the east. Although little remains of the camp itself, the documents and artefacts on display are deeply affecting.

Emmen and around

To all intents and purposes **EMMEN** is a new town, a twentieth-century amalgamation of strip villages that were originally peat colonies. The centre is a modernistic affair, mixing the remnants of the old with lumpy boulders, trees and shrubs and a job lot of concrete and glass.

Emmen is known for two things: its *hunebeds* and its zoo. The **zoo** (daily 10am–6pm; March–May & Oct closes 5pm, Sept closes 5.30pm, Nov–Feb closes 4.30pm; €17; ⓦwww.noorderdierenpark.nl), right in the middle of town at Hoofdstraat 18, boasts an imitation African savanna, where the animals roam "free", a massive sea-lion pool and a giant hippo house. In the newer part of the park you can find Humboldt penguins.

The best of Emmen's *hunebeds* is **Emmerdennen Hunebed**, in the woods 1km or so east of the station along Boslaan. This is a so-called passage-grave, with a relatively sophisticated entrance surrounded by a ring of standing stones. The other interesting *hunebed* within easy walking distance is the **Schimmer-Es**, a large enclosure containing two burial chambers and a standing stone about 2km north of the centre; to get there follow Hoofdstraat north from the VVV, take a left down Noorderstraat, right along Noordeinde, left along Broekpad, and first right at Langgrafweg. The VVV sells detailed maps of a circular car route along the minor roads to the north of town that covers all the principal remains.

Emmen's **train** and **bus** stations adjoin each other, five minutes' walk north of the town centre: head straight down Stationsstraat into Boslaan and turn left down Hoofdstraat, the main drag. The **VVV**, Hoofdstraat 22 (Mon 1–5.30pm, Tues–Fri 9.30am–5.30pm, Sat 10am–4pm; ☏0900/202 2393, ⓦwww .vvvemmen.nl), can arrange **accommodation** at pensions, private rooms and hotels. A cheap hotel-pension is *De Wanne*, Stortweg 1 (☏0591/611 250, ⓦwww.hoteldewanne.nl; ❶), 1.5km southwest of the zoo. Up a notch in price is hotel *Boerland*, Hoofdstraat 57 (☏0591/613 746, ⓦwww.stads-hotelboerland .nl; ❶–❷), which is across the street from the zoo. For a decent meal try the café of the *Boerland*.

Around Emmen

BORGER, some 20km northwest of Emmen, has the largest *hunebed* in the country on the northeast edge of the village, at 22.5m long; its origins are explained at the adjoining information centre (Mon–Fri 10am–5pm, Sat & Sun 11am–5pm; €4.50, ⓦwww.hunebedcentrum.nl). You'll need to use your imagination: these bulges in the ground, sprouting tufts of grass and small trees, aren't up to much. Back in town, the *hunebed* theme is everywhere, from street names and pancakes to special menus. Should you decide to stay, the **VVV**, Grote Brink 2a (Mon–Wed & Fri 9.30am–4pm, Sat 9.30am–3pm; Sept–March Sat 9.30am–12.30pm; ☏0599/234 855, ⓦwww.vvvborger-odoorn.nl), has a list of private rooms, or you could try the hotel-pension *Nathalia*, Hoofdstraat 87 (☏0599/234 791; ⓦwww.hotelpensionnathalia.nl; ❶). For **camping**, *Minicamping de Zwerfkei*, Strengenweg 6 (☏0599/234 925), is friendly and not that far out of town: from the centre, head west under the N34 road, and at the junction to Rolde cross straight over onto Stregenweg, and the campsite is 1.5km down the road on the right. As well as producing potatoes, sweet beet and maize, the farmers of Borger also make a mean football pitch – the immaculate, billiard-green fields around you are where the turf used for pitches around the country originates. Bus #59 runs to Borger on its way between Emmen and Groningen; from Assen, take bus #24.

About 11km east of Emmen, toward the German border, the **Veenpark** (daily Easter–Oct 10am–5pm; July & Aug until 6pm; €10.75; Ⓦwww.veenpark.nl), served by bus #45 hourly from Emmen station (25min) followed by a forty minute walk, is a massive open-air museum-village that traces the history and development of the peat colonies of the moors of southern Groningen and eastern Drenthe. The colonies were established in the nineteenth century, when labour was imported to cut the thick layers of peat that lay all over the moors. Isolated in small communities, and under the thumb of the traders who sold their product and provided their foodstuffs, the colonists were harshly exploited and lived in abject poverty until well into the 1930s. Built around some old interlocking canals, the museum consists of a series of reconstructed villages that span the history of the colonies. It's inevitably a bit folksy, but very popular, with its own narrow-gauge railway, a canal barge, and working period bakeries, bars and shops. A thorough exploration takes a full day.

Some 13km northwest of Emmen, on the northern edge of the village of **SCHOONOORD** and served by bus #21 from Emmen, **Ellert en Brammert** (April–Oct daily 9am–6pm; €4.50; Ⓦwww.ellertenbrammert.nl) is another open-air museum concerned with life in Drenthe. Exhibits here concentrate on the late nineteenth century and cover a wide range of traditional community activities – from sheep farming to education and carpentry. About 7km west, tiny **ORVELTE** (May–Oct Tues–Sun 11am–5pm; July & Aug also Mon 11am–5pm; €8; Ⓦwww.orvelte.net) is another village-museum, fully operational and actually inhabited, though certain buildings may be closed at any time. Owned by a trust, which exercises strict control over construction and repair, Orvelte's buildings date from the seventeenth to the nineteenth centuries and include examples of a tollhouse, a dairy, a farmhouse and a number of craft workshops. Most are open to the public, but you really need a car to get here: otherwise take bus #27 from Emmen to Zweeloo (20min) and then bus #22 to Orvelte (10min), but you should call ☎0900/9292 for up-to-date information before setting off to improve your chances of making successful connections.

Travel details

Trains

Emmen to: Zwolle (every 30min; 50–60min).
Groningen to: Amsterdam (every 30min; 2hr 20min); Assen (every 20min; 20min); Leeuwarden (every 30min; 50min); Uithuizen (hourly; 35min); Zwolle (every 20min; 1hr 10min).
Leeuwarden to: Amsterdam (every 30min; 2hr 20min); Franeker (every 30min; 15min); Groningen (every 30min; 50min); Harlingen (every 30min; 25min); Hindeloopen (hourly; 40min); Sneek (every 30min; 20min); Stavoren (hourly; 50min); Zwolle (every 30min; 50min–1hr 5min).

Buses

Bolsward to: Makkum (Mon–Sat hourly; Sun 7 daily; 20min).
Bourtange to: Ter Apel (Mon–Fri hourly, Sat every 2hr; Sun 3 daily; 30min).
Dokkum to: Wierum & Moddergat (Mon–Sat hourly, Sun 5 daily; 25min & 35min).
Groningen to: Bourtange (Mon–Fri hourly; 1hr); Emmen (hourly; 1hr 10min); Zoutkamp (hourly; 1hr).
Leeuwarden to: Dokkum (Mon–Fri 3 per hour, Sat & Sun hourly; 30–50min); Franeker (hourly; 40min);

Marssum (Mon–Sat every 30min, Sun hourly; 10min).

Sneek to: Bolsward (Mon–Sat every 30min, Sun hourly; 15min).

Workum to: Makkum (Mon–Fri every 2–3hr; 30min).

Buses to connecting ferries

Groningen to: Lauwersoog (bus #163: 7 daily; 1hr) for boats to Schiermonnikoog.

Leeuwarden to: Holwerd (bus #66: hourly; 50min) for boats to Ameland; and to Lauwersoog (bus #51: 6 daily; 1hr 30min) for boats to Schiermonnikoog.

Ferries and hydrofoils

Harlingen to: Terschelling (2–3 ferries daily; 1hr 45min; 3–4 hydrofoils daily; 50min direct, 1hr 20min via Vlieland); Vlieland (2–3 ferries daily; 1hr 45min; 2–3 hydrofoils daily; 45min direct, 1hr 30min via Terschelling).

Holwerd to: Ameland (4–14 ferries daily; 45min).

Lauwersoog to: Schiermonnikoog (3–6 ferries daily; 45min).

Stavoren to: Enkhuizen (May–Sept 3 ferries daily; 1hr 20min).

Terschelling to: Vlieland (1–2 hydrofoils daily; 30min).

Vlieland to: Terschelling (1–2 hydrofoils daily; 30min).

The eastern
Netherlands

CHAPTER 5

Highlights

✳ **Giethoorn** A postcard-pretty hamlet set amid lakes and wetlands, Giethoorn is an ideal place for pottering around on the water. See p.277

✳ **Blokzijl** Lovely little town and former Zuider Zee port perched on the edge of moors and wetlands. See p.279

✳ **Zutphen** Quintessential Dutch country town tucked up against the River IJssel. See p.281

✳ **Paleis Het Loo, Apeldoorn** Grand seventeenth-century palace that was formerly home to the Dutch royal family. See p.285

✳ **Arnhem** This garden city with a tragic wartime history makes a good base for exploring this attractive region. See p.287

✳ **Hoge Veluwe National Park** Spacious area of heath and forest, crossed by footpaths and cycle routes galore. See p.295

✳ **Kröller-Müller Museum** Outstanding museum of modern European art, with a large sculpture garden and impressive collection of works by Van Gogh. See p.296

✳ **Nijmegen** The Netherlands' oldest town, with a ruined castle at its core. See p.297

△ The sculpture garden at the Kröller-Müller Museum

The eastern Netherlands

n the **eastern Netherlands** the flat polder landscapes of the west gradually give way as the countryside ripples up towards the border with Germany. Arriving from Amsterdam, the first province you reach is **Flevoland**, whose three pancake-flat, reclaimed polders – the twin Flevoland polders and the Noordoostpolder – are decidedly tedious. Neither is the main town, modern **Lelystad**, of much appeal, though at least the fishing village of **Urk**, an island until the damming of the Zuider Zee (see p.134), is of some interest.

The boundary separating Flevoland from the province of **Overijssel** runs along the old Zuider Zee shoreline and it's here that the region comes up trumps with a string of former seaports, most strikingly the pretty little towns of **Elburg** (in Gelderland) and **Kampen**, **Vollenhove** and **Blokzijl**. These four, along with nearby **Zwolle**, the provincial capital, enjoyed a period of immense prosperity during the heyday of the Zuider Zee trade, from the fourteenth to the sixteenth centuries, but the bubble burst in the seventeenth when the great merchant cities of Zuid- and Noord-Holland simply out-played and undercut them. Later, these five towns – along with neighbouring **Deventer** and **Zutphen** – were bypassed by the Industrial Revolution, one happy consequence being that all of them boast a medley of handsome late medieval and early modern houses and churches. Vollenhove and Blokzijl also share their part of the province – **northwest Overijssel** – with the lakes and waterways that pattern the hamlet of picture-perfect **Giethoorn**, the region's most popular tourist target. By contrast, the district of **Twente**, which makes up southeast Overijssel, is an industrial region of one-time textile towns that remains one of the least visited parts of the country and with good reason: only **Enschede**, the main town, provides a reason to visit, with an excellent museum and an enjoyable set of distinctive 1930s public buildings.

The third province covered in this chapter, **Gelderland**, spreads east from Utrecht to the German frontier, taking its name from the German town of Geldern, its capital until the late fourteenth century. As a province it's a bit of a mixture, varying from the uninspiring agricultural land of the **Betuwe** (Good Land), south of Utrecht, to the more distinctive – and appealing – **Veluwe** (Bad Land), an expanse of heath, woodland and dune that sprawls down from the old Zuider Zee coastline to **Arnhem**. Infertile and sparsely populated in medieval times, today the Veluwe constitutes one of the most popular holiday destinations

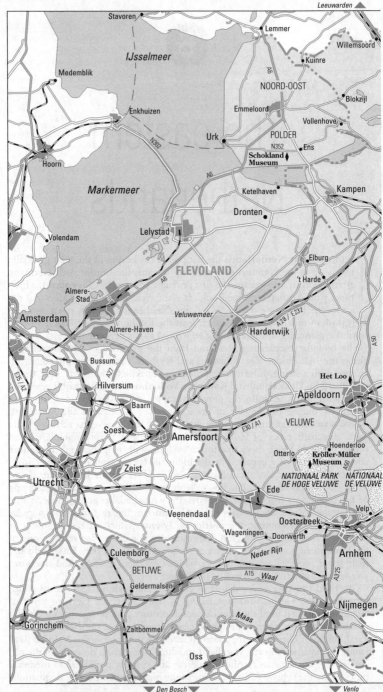

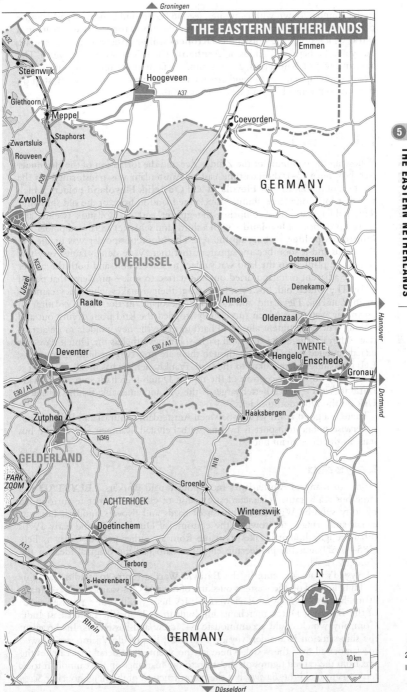

in the country, strewn with campsites, second homes and bungalow parks. Some people use **Apeldoorn** as a base to visit the fine **Hoge Veluwe National Park**, which holds the outstanding **Kröller-Müller Museum** of modern art, but you'd be better off choosing **Arnhem**, which is considerably livelier. The ancient town of **Nijmegen**, 21km south, is a fashionable university city, with a lively contemporary music and arts scene, and makes a good, if brief, stop on the way south into Limburg (see Chapter 000).

⑤ Flevoland

Following the damming of the Zuider Zee and the formation of the IJsselmeer (see box on p.134), the coastline east of Amsterdam was transformed by the creation of the **Zuidelijk Flevoland** and **Oostelijk Flevoland** polders, which together form one large chunk of reclaimed land in front of the old shoreline. This polder-island also comprises the greater part of Holland's twelfth and newest province – **Flevoland** – with a third (and separate) reclaimed polder, the **Noordoostpolder**, making up the rest. The Noordoostpolder was drained in the 1930s and it soon became apparent that there were design faults: very few trees were planted, so the land was subject to soil erosion, and both the polder and the adjacent mainland dried out and started to sink – problems that persist today. The Dutch did, however, learn from their mistakes when they came to drain Zuidelijk Flevoland and Oostelijk Flevoland in the 1950s, creating an encircling waterway, which successfully stopped the land from drying out and sinking. The government also tried hard to make the new polders more attractive – they're fringed by trees and parks – but nevertheless the Dutch have not exactly queued up to live here, though there are now two medium-sized towns, **Lelystad** and Almere, 20km to the west. Frankly, neither has much going for it – with the possible exception of the replica Dutch merchant ship at Lelystad's **Batavia Werf** – and a better target is the old and amenable fishing village of **Urk** on the Noordoostpolder.

There is a good **train** service between Amsterdam Centraal and Lelystad, but otherwise public transport is by **bus** with Lelystad, Kampen and Zwolle bus stations the three main hubs.

Lelystad

Home to many of Amsterdam's most poorly paid workers, **LELYSTAD** is a large but really rather characterless expanse of glass and concrete surrounded by leafy suburbs. With its mishmash of roads and flyovers, modern housing, canals and bridges, the town is the epitome of Dutch 1960s and early 1970s urban design, though it takes its name from an earlier period: Cornelis Lely (1854–1929) was the pioneering engineer who had the original idea for the Zuider Zee scheme.

Lelystad's main attraction is the **Batavia Werf**, a centre for traditional shipbuilding located on the western outskirts of town at Oostvaardersdijk 1–9 (daily 10am–5pm; €9; ⓦwww.bataviawerf.nl). It's here you'll find a precise replica of the *Batavia*, a Dutch merchant ship built in 1628 for the Dutch East India Company, which could accommodate 341 crew and passengers. In the event the ship sank on its maiden voyage with great loss of life. Visitors are allowed to clamber all over the vessel, where it's the attention to detail that catches the eye, from the carved figures on the stern to the markings on the cannon. It took ten years to build the *Batavia*, but the reconstruction of the neighbouring *Seven*

Wind turbines

Strung along the shores of the IJsselmeer, and popping up on many rural horizons, **wind turbines** dot the Dutch landscape from Friesland to Zeeland. In the countryside, solitary turbines provide electricity for farmers, while on the coast and out to sea, banks of turbines harness the incoming weather systems, providing electricity for thousands of households. Erected in the 1930s, the first wind turbines provided electricity for remote communities in the USA and the Australian outback. However, their full potential wasn't realized until research into cleaner forms of energy, carried out in Denmark and Germany during the 1970s, produced mechanisms that were both more efficient and more powerful. Ideally suited to the flat, windswept polders of the Netherlands, the first Dutch turbines generated 40 kilowatts of electricity; output is now a beefier 600 kilowatts – enough for a single wind farm of 50 turbines to provide power to 6500 households.

Provinces, the seventeenth-century flagship of Admiral Michiel Ruyter, will take even longer – 2015 is the latest target date for completion.

There are fast and frequent **trains** to Lelystad train station from Amsterdam Centraal (40min). From Lelystad station, **bus #F** runs to Batavia Werf, 5km away, in fifteen minutes. Lelystad **VVV** is about 400m east of the train station, right in the heart of town at Stadhuisplein 2 (Mon–Fri 9am–5pm, Sat 10am–4pm; ☎0320/278 222, ⓦwww.vvvflevoland.nl).

The Noordoostpolder

Drained in the early 1930s, the **Noordoostpolder** was the first major chunk of land to be reclaimed after the damming of the Zuider Zee (see p.134). The original aims of the scheme were predominantly agricultural with the Noordoostpolder providing 119,000 acres of new farmland, which the government then handed out to prospective smallholders. Little consideration was given to the needs of the new settlers, however, and even now most of the Noordoostpolder remains dull in the extreme. If you're looking for a crumb of scenic comfort, then at least the wide skies – and wide-skied sunsets and sunrises – can be breathtaking, and **Urk** makes for a pleasant detour.

Schokland Museum

The southern reaches of the Noordoostpolder incorporate the former Zuider Zee islets of Urk and **Schokland**, though the latter was abandoned in the nineteenth century because of the threat of flooding. Given the turbulent waters of the Zuider Zee, it's a wonder that the islanders hung on for as long as they did and the main reminder of those perilous days is the church of 1834, which has been turned into the **Schokland Museum** (April–Oct Tues–Sun 11am–5pm; July & Aug also Mon 11am–5pm; Nov–March Fri–Sun 11am–5pm; €3.50; ⓦwww.schokland.nl), with displays of all sorts of bits and pieces found during the draining of the polders. From beside the museum, a circular foot- and cycle-path follows the old Schokland shoreline, a distance of about 10km.

It's an awkward journey without a car: the museum is located some 3km west of Ens – and about 400m south of the minor road between Ens and Nagele/Urk. **Buses** from Lelystad go to Kampen (see p.270), where you change for Ens bus station, but then you have to walk the remaining 3km.

Urk

The only place really worth a visit on the Noordoostpolder is **URK**, a trim harbour and fishing port, where a series of narrow lanes – and tiny terraced houses – indicate the extent of the old village. Before it was pressed into the mainland, centuries of hardship and isolation had bred a tight-knit island community here, one that had a distinctive dialect and its own version of the national costume. Most of Urk's individuality may have gone, but its earlier independence does still resonate, rooted in a fishing industry that marks it out from the surrounding agricultural communities. As if to prove the point, quite a few of the islanders still wear traditional costume, further examples of which are on display in the **Museum Het Oude Raadhuis**, Wijk 2, no. 2 (April–Sept Mon–Fri 10am–5pm; €3).

There are regular **buses** to Urk from Kampen and Zwolle, but be sure to ask the driver to drop you off near the harbourside (Wijk 1) as the bus cuts a circuitous route through the village. During the summer, there are also **passenger ferries** east across the IJsselmeer from Enkhuizen to Urk (late June to Aug Mon–Sat 3 daily; 1hr 30min; €8 one-way, €12 day-return; Ⓦwww.urk-enkhuizen.nl) – check with the VVV for times and prices.

Urk's **VVV**, just up from the harbour by the museum at Wijk 2 no.2 (April–Oct Mon–Fri 10am–5pm; Nov–March Mon–Fri 10am–1pm; ☎0527/684 040), will help arrange **accommodation**, an especially useful service in the summer when spare rooms are thin on the ground. Among several inexpensive pensions within easy walking distance of the harbour, the pick is *De Kaap*, Wijk 1, no.5 (☎0527/681 509, Ⓦwww.restaurantdekaap.nl; ❶), which has a few straightforward, modern rooms.

Urk is a great place to eat **fresh fish**: *De Kaap* does good lunch specials and all-you-can-eat deals in the evening and has fine views over the IJsselmeer from its window tables; there is also the more expensive *De Zeebodem*, by the harbour at Wijk 1, no.67; main courses here start at €14. **Rollmop** enthusiasts may also want to know that Urk's fish processing plants make it the rollmop capital of the Netherlands.

Elburg

Once a Zuider Zee port of some importance, tiny **ELBURG**, about 30km east of Lelystad and 10km south of Kampen, abuts the Veluwemeer, the narrow waterway separating the mainland from the Oostelijk Flevoland polder. In recent years, the town has become a popular day-trip destination, awash with visitors who come here to wander Elburg's old streets, tour the homeopathic gardens on its outskirts, and taste the local delicacy, **smoked eel**.

Elburg was a successful port with its own fishing fleet from as early as the thirteenth century, but the boom times really began in the 1390s when the governor, a certain Arent thoe Boecop, redesigned the whole place in line with the latest developments in town planning with a central grid of streets encircled by a protective wall and moat. Not all of Elburg's citizens were overly impressed – indeed the street by the museum is still called Ledige Stede, literally "Empty Way" – but the basic design, with the notable addition of sixteenth-century ramparts and gun emplacements, survived the decline that set in when the harbour silted up, and can still be observed today. Elburg's two main streets are **Beekstraat**, which forms the north–south axis, and **Jufferenstraat/Vischpoortstraat**, which runs east–west; they intersect at right angles to form the main square, the Vischmarkt.

Urk irked

The damming of the Zuider Zee (see box on p.134) posed special problems for the deep-sea fishermen of Urk and it's hardly surprising that they opposed the IJsselmeer scheme from the beginning. Some villagers feared that when the Noordoostpolder was drained they would simply be overwhelmed by new settlers, but the fishermen were really irritated by the loss of direct access to the North Sea. After futile negotiations at national level, the fishermen of Urk decided to take matters into their own hands: the larger ships of the fleet were sent north to fish from ports above the line of the Afsluitdijk, particularly Delfzijl, and transport was organized to transfer the catch straight back for sale at the Urk fish auctions. In the meantime, other fishermen decided to continue to fish locally and adapt to the freshwater species of the IJsselmeer. These were not comfortable changes for the islanders and the whole situation deteriorated after the Dutch government passed new legislation banning trawling in the IJsselmeer in 1970. When the inspectors arrived in Urk to enforce the ban, years of resentment exploded in ugly scenes of dockside violence and the government moved fast to sweeten the pill by offering substantial subsidies to compensate those fishermen affected. This arrangement continues today and the focus of conflict has moved to the attempt to impose EU quotas on the catch of the deep-sea fleet.

The Town

Entering Elburg from the south, it's a few metres from the moat to the mildly enjoyable **Gemeentemuseum**, Jufferenstraat 6–8 (Tues–Fri 10am–5pm; joint ticket including Vischpoort & Kazematten €3), which is housed in an old convent and offers period rooms and objects of local interest. Heading north across Jufferenstraat from here, you soon reach **St Nicolaaskerk** (June–Aug Mon–Fri 2–4.30pm, Tues also 10am–noon), a lumpy fourteenth-century structure that dominates the landscape, even without its spire, which was destroyed by lightning in 1693. West of the church, down Van Kinsbergenstraat, is the old **Stadhuis**, which once served as Boecop's home. At the end of Van Kinsbergenstraat, turn left into Beekstraat for the town's main square, the **Vischmarkt**, from where Vischpoortstraat leads straight to the best preserved of the medieval town gates, the **Vischpoort**, a much restored brick rampart tower dating from 1594 (Tues–Fri 10am–5pm; joint ticket as above).

Beyond the gate, the pattern of the sixteenth-century defensive works is clear to see – from interior town wall, to dry ditch, to earthen mound and moat. One of the subterranean artillery casements – **Kazematten** – is open in summer (mid-June to Aug Mon 2–5pm, Tues–Fri 10am–5pm; joint ticket as above); cramped and poorly ventilated, it's easy to see why the Dutch called such emplacements Moortkuijl, literally "Pits of Murder". From the Kazematten, a stroll right around the ramparts takes about an hour.

Alfred Vogel Tuinen

Ten minutes' walk northwest from the Vischpoort – turn right along Havenkade and take the second left – lie the **Alfred Vogel Tuinen** (Homeopathic Gardens; April–Oct Mon–Fri 10am–5pm; June–Aug also Sat 10am–5pm; €3), six hectares of land that hold a comprehensive collection of homeopathic plants. The Bezoekerscentrum (visitors' centre), at Industriestraat 5, has a variety of illustrative displays and a mock-up of an old chemist's, but it's all in Dutch and the surrounding gardens are of far more interest. They form part of a successful business and are Elburg's main tourist attraction; in

ject to demand, there are free two-hour guided tours, starting
' centre. It's easy to tag onto any of the groups visiting the
you may want to call ahead (☎0525/687 200) to enquire
urs in English.

...ies

...e train network, but **bus** #100 (hourly, less on Sun) links it
with Zwolle train station to the east (35min) and Nunspeet train station to the
west (20min). Buses drop passengers just outside the southern entrance to the
old town, a couple of minutes' walk from Elburg **VVV**, which is around the
corner from the Gemeentemuseum at Ledige Stede 31 (May–Aug Mon–Fri
9am–5pm & Sat 10am–4pm; Sept–April Mon noon–5pm, Tues–Fri 9am–5pm,
Sat noon–4pm; ☎0525/681 520, ⓦwww.vvvelburg.nl). They have a long list
of private rooms (❶) and will phone around to make a booking; try to get a
room in the old centre and come early in the day in high season, when accommodation gets tight. Elburg has one **hotel**, the three-star *Elburg*, Smedestraat 5
(☎0525/683 877, ⓦwww.hotelburg.nl; ❷), in a pleasantly maintained, eighteenth-century building in the old town just off Beekstraat. The VVV also has
the details of **boat trips** along the Veluwemeer, or you can go it alone by hiring
a sailing boat from any one of several companies – again the VVV has the latest
information.

Of Elburg's many **restaurants** it's difficult to find any of real note, though *'t
Olde Regthuys*, in the old town at Beekstraat 33, does serve a reasonable range
of fish dishes with mains around €17–20. The town's favourite nibble, smoked
eel in jelly, is available at any number of pavement stalls and is sold by weight
– a *pond* is 500g.

Zwolle

A major railway junction, **ZWOLLE** is the compact capital of Overijssel. An
ancient town, it achieved passing international fame when Thomas à Kempis
settled here in 1399 and it went on to prosper throughout the fifteenth century
as one of the principal towns of the Hanseatic League, its burghers commission-
ing an extensive programme of public works designed to protect its citizens and
impress their rivals. Within the city walls, German textiles were traded for Baltic
fish and grain, or more exotic products from Amsterdam, like coffee, tea and
tobacco. The boom lasted for some two hundred years, but by the middle of the
seventeenth century the success of Amsterdam and the general movement of
trade to the west had undermined its economy – a decline reflected in Zwolle's
present-day status as a small market town of middling significance.

Strategically important, medieval Zwolle was protected by a strong **city wall**, a
small section of which has survived on the north side of town, but the star shape
of today's town centre, comprising nine roughly triangular earthen bastions that
encircle the old town and its harbour, mostly dates from the seventeenth century.
The approach from the train station is particularly pleasant, as fountains play in
the moat and the city's fortifications are clearly visible among the trees.

The Town

Right in the middle of Zwolle is the **Grote Markt**, a large and somewhat
discordant square that surrounds the sandstone mass of the **Grote Kerk**, one

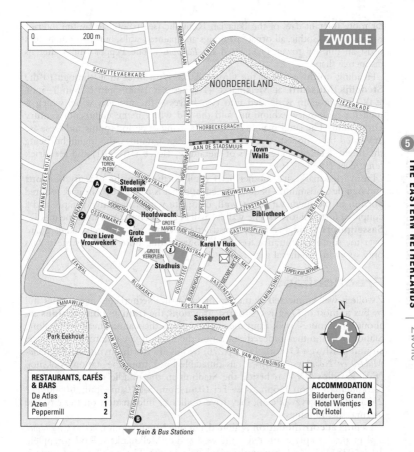

ZWOLLE

0   200 m

SCHUTTEVAERKADE

NOORDEREILAND

DIEZERKADE

DIJKSTRAAT

THORBECKEGRACHT

AAN DE STADSMUUR — **Town Walls**

RODE TOREN PLEIN

NIEUWSTRAAT

Stedelijk Museum

MELKMARKT

NIEUWSTRAAT

VOORSTRAAT

DIEZERSTRAAT

Hoofdwacht

Bibliotheek

OSSENMARKT

GROTE MARKT OUDE VISMARKT

GASTHUISPLEIN

Onze Lieve Vrouwekerk

Grote Kerk

Karel V Huis

GROTE KERKPLEIN

SASSENSTRAAT

NIEUWE MKT

Stadhuis

GOUDSTEEG

BLOEMENDALSTR

BLIJMARKT

KOESTRAAT

TERPELKWIJKPARK

WILHELMINASINGEL

EMMAWIJK

BURG. VAN ROIJENSINGEL

Sassenpoort

N

Park Eekhout

BURG. VAN ROIJENSINGEL

STATIONSWEG

PANNE KOEKENDIJK

IJSSEL

EEKWAL

SPIEGELSTRAAT

KERKSTRAAT

ZAMENHOF

REMBRANDTLAAN

DIEZERKADE

RESTAURANTS, CAFÉS & BARS

De Atlas	3
Azen	1
Peppermill	2

ACCOMMODATION

| Bilderberg Grand Hotel Wientjes | B |
| City Hotel | A |

▼ Train & Bus Stations

of the unluckiest churches in Overijssel: the townsfolk were once inordinately proud of the church's soaring bell tower, but after it had been hit by lightning no fewer than three times (in 1548, 1606 and 1669), they gave up and sold the bells instead. Inside, you'll find the familiar austerity of Dutch Protestantism, with the cavernous nave bare of decoration and the seats arranged on a central pulpit plan. The pulpit itself is an intricate piece of Renaissance carving, but it's the Baroque organ of 1721 that really catches the eye, a real musical whopper with four thousand pipes. Attached to the outside of the church is the **Hoofd-wacht**, an ornately gabled building of 1614, which once served as the munici-pal guardhouse. Public executions took place in front of the Hoofdwacht and the building bears the inscription *Vigilate et Orate* ("Watch and Pray"), a stern warning to the crowds who gathered to witness the assorted mutilations.

A little way to the west, down an alley off the Grote Markt, the prim and proper **Onze Lieve Vrouwekerk** (Mon 1–4.30pm, Tues–Sat 11am–4.30pm; free; tower €2) has had some hard times too: in the sixteenth century, the congregation stuck to their Catholic faith, so the Protestants closed the place down and the last priest had to hot-foot it out of town after he delivered a final sermon in 1580. Thereafter, the church was used for all sorts of purposes – including a cart shed and a musket range – until it was returned to the Catholics in 1809 during the

273

far more tolerant days of the Batavian Republic (see p.366). Today, the interior is firmly neo-Gothic, all ornate paintings and painted walls, but the church does boast an unusual tower, nicknamed *De Peperbus* ("The Pepper Mill") after its distinctive shape.

Heading northwest from the Grote Markt, it's a brief stroll through to the **Stedelijk Museum**, at Melkmarkt 41 (Tues–Sat 10am–5pm & Sun 1–5pm; €4). The museum is divided into two halves – the modern wing, which is used for temporary exhibitions, and the old wing in the eighteenth-century Drostenhuis. The latter mainly consists of a string of period rooms and these are enlivened by a modest selection of Golden Age paintings, the highlights being the finely detailed genre scenes of Gerard ter Borch (1617–81) and Hendrick ten Oever (1639–1716).

From Melkmarkt, it's another brief stroll northeast to the old city **harbour** and Aan de Stadsmuur, a pedestrianized lane that is flanked by a heavily restored portion of the medieval **town wall**, complete with a defensive parapet and a couple of fortified towers. The wall is small beer in comparison with the massive **Sassenpoort**, a mighty brick construction whose spiky turrets stands guard over the southern entrance to the old town; dating from 1409, it's the town's only surviving medieval gate.

Practicalities

Zwolle is well connected by train to many of the Netherlands' major cities and by bus to most of Overijssel's tourist attractions; the **train** and **bus stations** are about ten minutes' walk from the centre – from the stations head north along Stationsweg and then proceed east round the moat. If you're intending to travel around northwest Overijssel (see p.276) by bus, it's worth buying the *Flevoland-Midden en Noordwest Overijssel* bus timetable book from the station bookshop (€3). Zwolle's **VVV** is beside the Stadhuis in the middle of town at Grote Kerkplein 15 (Mon 1–5pm, Tues–Fri 10am–5pm, Sat 10am–4pm; ℡0900/112 2375, ⊛www.vvvzwolle.nl); they have oodles of information on the city and its rural surroundings.

Central **accommodation** is limited, but one bargain option is the *City Hotel*, a plain, modern place situated at the west end of Melkmarkt at Rodetorenplein 10 (℡038/421 8182, ⊛www.hotelzwolle.com; ❶). The best hotel in town is the four-star *Bilderberg Grand Hotel Wientjes*, which occupies a big old villa near the station at Stationsweg 7 (℡038/425 4254, ⊛www.bilderberg.nl; ❸); the *Bilderberg* has recently been revamped and has 57 bright and modern guest rooms.

Arguably the pick of Zwolle's **restaurants** is the *Azen*, Melkmarkt 47 (daily 5.30–10pm; ℡038/429 0634), a slick, modern place in a handsome old mansion that offers an international menu with mains from about €17. A good second bet is the cosy *Peppermill*, Jufferenwal 21 (daily 5–10pm; ℡038/423 8285), a self-styled "American restaurant" with an idiosyncratic menu featuring the likes of a "Country Stew from the Great Plains"; main courses here start at around €17. Zwolle has something of a **bar** scene with *De Atlas*, a large and youthful café-bar at Ossenmarkt 9, leading the alcoholic rush.

Kampen

Sleepy **KAMPEN**, just ten minutes by train from Zwolle, strings along the River IJssel, its bold succession of towers and spires recalling headier days when the

town was a bustling seaport with its own fleet. Th
end in the sixteenth century, however, as rival ar
the IJssel silted up, and then Amsterdam mopped u₁
its trade prices. Things have never been the same si
experience a minor boom on the back of its **ciga**
century, the place is fairly subdued today, the main
scores of late medieval and early modern buildings

Beside the Bovenk
fourteenth-centur
spoort and th
lie on the w
via Scho

P

EASTERN NETHERLANDS | Kampen

The Town

Not much more than six roughly parallel streets ed₁
takes a couple of hours to explore and the logica.
bridge that hits the town about halfway along –
Stadhuis, which is divided into two: the redbrick C᎐ᴗᴗ Raaanuis, dating from
1543 and topped by a distinctive onion-shaped dome, and the Neoclassical
Nieuwe Raadhuis, which was built in the eighteenth century. Of the two, the
Oude Raadhuis (limited opening hours; details from the VVV) has more to
offer, namely the **Schepenzaal** ("Magistrates' Hall"), a claustrophobic medieval
affair with dark-stained walls capped by a superbly preserved barrel-vault roof.
The magnificent stone chimneypiece – a grandiloquent, self-assured work – was
carved by Colijn de Nole in tribute to the Habsburg Charles V in 1545, though
the chimney's typically Renaissance representations of Justice, Prudence and
Strength speak more of municipal pride than imperial glory. To the right, the
magistrate's bench is the work of an obscure local carpenter, a Master Frederik,
who didn't get on with de Nole at all: angry at not getting the more important
job of the chimneypiece; his legacy can be seen on the left-hand pillar, where a
minute, malevolent satyr laughs maniacally at the chimney.

Just across the street from the Oude Raadhuis is a second tower, the seventeenth-century **Nieuwe Toren**, which becomes Kampen's main attraction for
one morning each year, usually in mid-July (contact the VVV for the exact date
and time), when the "Kampen cow" is pulled up to its top. The story goes that
when grass began growing at the top of the tower, a local farmer asked if he
could graze his cattle up there. To commemorate this daft request, an animal
has been hoisted up the tower every year ever since, though thankfully it's now
a plastic model rather than a real cow.

From the Nieuwe Toren, it's the briefest of strolls west to the **Kamper
Tabaksmuseum**, which occupies an old cigar factory at Botermarkt 3 (April–
Oct Thurs–Sat 11am–12.30pm & 1.30–5pm; €1.20). The museum makes a
gallant attempt to make its assorted tools and smoking paraphernalia interesting,
but frankly it's an uphill struggle.

The Bovenkerk

The Raadhuis and the Nieuwe Toren straddle Kampen's innocuous main street,
pedestrianized **Oudestraat**, which runs south to St Nicolaaskerk, or **Bovenkerk**
(Easter to early Sept Mon & Tues 1–4.30pm, Wed–Fri 10am–4.30pm; free), a
finely proportioned Gothic church with a light and spacious interior. Generally
regarded as one of the most important of the country's medieval churches, its
choir – with thirteen radiating chapels – was the work of Rotger of Cologne,
a member of the Parler family of masons who worked on Cologne Cathedral
among other commissions. In the south transept an urn contains the heart of
Admiral de Winter, a native of Kampen who loathed the House of Orange. A
staunch Republican, he took part in the successful French invasion of 1795 that
created the Batavian Republic; the rest of him lies in the Pantheon in Paris.

...rk is the earliest of Kampen's three surviving gates, the ... **Koornmarktspoort**. The others – the **Cellebroeder-** ... **Broederpoort** – are of a later, more ornamental design and ... st side of town along Ebbingestraat, reached from the Bovenkerk ... straat.

acticalities

Trains leave Zwolle for end-of-the-line Kampen every half-hour, hourly on Sundays, and the journey takes ten minutes. From Kampen **train station**, it's a five-minute walk over the bridge to the town centre, where the **VVV**, on the main street just along from the Stadhuis at Oudestraat 151 (mid-April to Sept Mon–Fri 9.30am–5.30pm & Sat 10am–4pm; Oct to mid-April Mon & Wed–Fri 10am–5pm, Tues 10am–1pm & Sat 10am–4pm; ☎0900/112 2375, Ⓦwww.vvvkampen.nl), has a short list of private rooms (❶). There's only one **hotel** in the centre, the riverside *Van Dijk*, an amenable, modern, three-star place near the bridge at IJsselkade 30 (☎038/331 4925, Ⓦwww.hotelvandijk .nl; ❷); advance reservations are advised.

For **food**, there are tasty pancakes and snacks at *'t Trappetje*, a pleasant little café at Oudestraat 25, and quality fish dishes for around €22 at *D'Olde Vismark*, near the bridge at IJsselkade 45 (daily noon–2.30pm & 5–10pm; ☎038/331 3490).

Northwest Overijssel

The closing of the Zuider Zee and the draining of the Noordoostpolder (see p.269) transformed **northwest Overijssel**, that parcel of land lying beyond Kampen and Zwolle: not only were the area's old seaports cut off from the ocean, but – as if to add injury to insult – they were placed firmly inland with only a narrow channel – the Vollenhover Kanaal – separating them from the new polder. In the event, however, it all turned out rather well: **Vollenhove** and **Blokzijl**, the two main seaports concerned, speedily reinvented themselves as holiday destinations and today hundreds of Dutch city folk come here to sail and cycle.

Traditionally, both Vollenhove and Blokzijl looked firmly out across the ocean, doing their best to ignore the moor and marshland villages that lay just **inland**. They were not alone: for many years this was one of the most neglected corners of the country and things only began to pick up in the nineteenth century, when the "Society of Charity" established a series of agricultural colonies here. The Dutch bourgeoisie were, however, as apprehensive of the unemployed pauper as their Victorian counterparts in Britain and the 1900 Baedeker, when surveying the colonies, noted approvingly that "the houses are visited almost daily by the superintending officials and the strictest discipline is everywhere observed". The villagers were reliant on **peat** for fuel and their haphazard diggings helped create the canals, lakes and ponds that now lattice the area, attracting tourists by the boat load. The big pull is picture-postcard **Giethoorn**, whose mazy canals are flanked by splendid thatched cottages, but try to avoid visiting in the height of the season when the crowds can get oppressive.

Buses crisscross Northwest Overijssel (see box opposite), but you really won't get the full flavour of the area unless you take at least one **boat** ride – or, even better, paddle away under your own steam: boat rental hereabouts is well-nigh ubiquitous.

From Steenwijk train station bus #70 (Mon–Fri hourly) goes to Giethoorn (10min), Zwartsluis (30min) and Zwolle (1hr 10min). Bus #75 (Mon–Fri hourly) goes to Blokzijl (20min) and Marknesse (30min).

From Zwolle train station bus #70 (Mon–Fri hourly) goes to Zwartsluis (40min), Giethoorn (1hr) and Steenwijk (1hr 10min). Bus #71 (Mon–Sat every 30min, Sun hourly) goes to Zwartsluis (30min), Vollenhove (50min), Marknesse (55min) and Emmeloord on the Noordoostpolder (1hr 15min).

Giethoorn

GIETHOORN's origins are really rather odd. No one gave much thought to this marshy, infertile chunk of land until the thirteenth century, when the local landowner gifted it to an obscure religious sect. Perhaps to his surprise, the colonists made a go of things, eking out a living from local peat deposits and discovering, during their digs, the horns of hundreds of goats, which are presumed to have been the victims of prehistoric flooding; duly impressed, the residents named the place Geytenhoren ("goats' horns"). Later, the colonists dug canals to transport the peat and the diggings flooded, thus creating the watery network that now attracts herds of day-trippers, the scenic supplement being the village's thatched cottages and dinky, humpbacked footbridges.

Running parallel to – and just east of – the **N334**, which links Zwartsluis (see p.278) and Steenwijk, Giethoorn is about 3km from north to south and up to 800m wide. **Bus #70** travels the length of the N334, pulling in at Ds. Hylkemaweg, Kerkweg and the hotel *De Harmonie* (see below). **Ds. Hylkemaweg**, the nearest stop to the old part of the village, is about 800m long and runs east from the N334 to lake Bovenwijde, on the east side of Giethoorn. The Kerkweg stop is near the **VVV** at Eendrachtsplein 1 (April to mid-May, Sept & Oct Mon–Fri 9am–5pm, Sat 10am–4pm; mid-May to June Mon–Sat 9am–5pm, Sun 10am–4pm; July & Aug Mon–Sat 9am–6pm, Sun 10am–4pm; Nov–March Mon–Fri 9am–5pm; ☏0900/567 4637, ⊛www.kopvanoverijssel.nl).

The VVV has a long list of **private rooms** (❶), though only a few of them are in the old part of Giethoorn, which is where you want to be; accommodation is very tight between June and August. Giethoorn's smartest **hotel** is the four-star ⚓ *De Harmonie*, a modern place by the canal at the north end of the village at Beulakerweg 55 (☏0521/361 372, ⊛www.harmonie-giethoorn.nl; ❷). An excellent alternative is the nearby ⚓ *Hotel De Jonge* (☏0521/361 360, ⊛www.dejonge-giethoorn.nl; ❷), which occupies several intelligently converted old buildings at Beulakerweg 30. Lake Bovenwijde has no fewer than six **campsites** on its western shore, including the well-kept *Botel Giethoorn*, at Binnenpad 49 (☏0521/361 332, ⊛www.botel-giethoorn.nl; April to mid-October).

Water taxis leave from pretty much everywhere and cost about €6 per hour for a trip round the village. Most of the campsites and hotels **rent boats**, in a variety of shapes and sizes, from canoes to motorboats and dinghies (and the VVV can provide details of more than a dozen other operators). Prices vary, but reckon on €10–15 per hour for a whisper boat (a quiet, environmentally friendly, electric-powered motorboat) down to €6–8 per hour for a canoe.

Both *De Harmonie* and the *Hotel De Jonge* have very competent **restaurants**, serving a good range of Dutch dishes from €17, but the best-known **café** hereabouts is the *Eetcafé Fanfare*, Binnenpad 68, which offers inexpensive food and an interior decorated with old photos of the village.

△ Giethoorn lake

Zwartsluis and Vollenhove

Heading south from Giethoorn, the N334 travels the length of the dyke that borders lakes Beulakerwijde and Belterwijde before clipping down into **ZWARTSLUIS**, once the site of an important fortress at the junction of waterways from Zwolle and Meppel. There's nothing much to the place today, but a couple of minutes' walk east of the bus station, at the bottom of Dawarsstraat, off Handelskade, is a small Jewish **cemetery** with a touching memorial to those locals who died in the concentration camps.

The pretty little town of **VOLLENHOVE**, some 10km west of Zwarts-luis, was once a Zuider Zee port of some significance, but the remains of its bastions and ramparts now nudge up against the Vollenhover Kanaal, separating the mainland from the Noordoostpolder. The old **harbour** has survived, too, a cramped, circular affair encased in steep grass banks, and just to the south, flank-ing Kerkplein, is a clutch of handsome old buildings, most notably the elegant, arcaded **Raadhuis**, the Gothic **St Nicolaaskerk** and the seventeenth-century **Latin School**, now a bank, which boasts charming crow-stepped gables.

Buses stop on Clarenberglaan, a five-minute walk from Kerkplein, straight up Doelenstraat and then Kerkstraat. The **VVV** is beside the harbour, just north of Kerkplein at aan Zee 4 (May–June Mon–Fri 10am–12.30pm & 2–4pm & Sat 10.30am–12.30pm; July & Aug Mon–Sat 10am–12.30pm & 1.30–4.30pm; ℡0900/567 4637, ⓦwww.kopvanoverijssel.nl). There's just one **hotel** in Vollenhove, the modest and unassuming *De Herberg*, at Kerkstraat 1 (℡0527/243 466, ⓦwww.de-herberg.nl; ❶). Of the two local **campsites**, the nearest is *'t Akkertien op de Voorst*, ten minutes' walk southwest of Kerkplein at Noordwal 3 (℡0527/241 378, ⓦwww.akkertien.nl).

The **restaurant** *De Vollenhof*, Kerkplein 12, serves good fish dishes from €14. More appealing – and more expensive – is the *Seidel* restaurant in the old Raad-huis at Kerkplein 3, which is worth popping into, even for just a coffee – the decor is delightfully antique.

Blokzijl

BLOKZIJL, some 5km north of Vollenhove, is just as comely as its near neighbour, its cobweb of narrow alleys and slim canals surrounding a trim little harbour. Formerly a seaport, it now finds itself pushed up against the Vollen-hover Kanaal with a thumb-shaped chunk of wild(ish) moorland behind. The town boasts dozens of restored seventeenth-century houses, but its pride and joy is the **Grote Kerk**, which, with its splendid wooden pulpit and ceiling, was one of the country's first Protestant churches. Blokzijl also makes a good base for exploring the **National Park De Weerribben**, a chunk of protected canal and marshland starting about 3km to the north of town. The VVV can suggest cycle routes through the park and has details of the summer boat trips that leave Blokzijl to explore its waterways.

Buses to Blokzijl drop passengers on the north edge of town, a five-minute walk from the harbour, where the **VVV**, at Kerkstraat 9a (May–June & early Sept Mon–Fri 10am–12.30pm & 1.30–4pm, Sat 10am–2pm; July & Aug Mon–Sat 9am–5.30pm, Sun 10am–3.30pm; ℡0900/567 4637, ⓦwww.kopvanoverijssel .nl), has a small supply of private rooms (❶). There are three **hotels** here, the pick of which is *Kaatjes Résidence*, a smart, four-star place in a substantial old house not far from the harbour at Zuiderstraat 1 (℡0527/208 580, ⓦwww.kaatjesresidence .nl; ❹).

The town is stuffed with **restaurants**, including the *Kaatje bij de Sluis*, close to the harbour at Brouwerstraat 20 (closed Sun, Sept–April also closed Mon; ℡0527/291 833), where they serve outstanding French cuisine with mains from €25.

Deventer and Zutphen

South of Zwolle, the River IJssel marks the provincial boundary between Over-ijssel and Gelderland as it twists its way through flat, fertile farmland. For two

Cycling along the IJssel

Beginning at the Wilhelminabrug in Deventer, a signposted **cycleway** follows the banks of the IJssel 20km south to Zutphen. It's a gentle ride through farmland and along quiet, winding lanes. There are plenty of places to stop for a picnic, there are some fine views of the river and the weeping willows that thrive along its banks. Once in Zutphen, the return journey can either be made on the opposite shore, bringing the total distance to around 45km, or direct by train. You can **rent bikes** for the day from both Deventer and Zutphen train stations.

hundred years the towns of the lower IJssel, **Deventer** and **Zutphen**, shared with Zwolle and Kampen a period of tremendous prosperity at the junction of trade routes from Germany, the Baltic and Amsterdam. Both towns suffered grievously during the wars with Spain, but the real reasons for their subsequent decline were economic: they could do little to stop the movement of trade to the west and could not compete with the emerging cities of Noord- and Zuid-Holland. By the eighteenth century, they had slipped into provincial insignificance – and this remains the case today, though both, especially Zutphen, have a clutch of handsome old buildings and an amenable small town air.

Deventer

Glued to the east bank of the IJssel, **DEVENTER**, some 30km from Zwolle, is an intriguing and – in tourist terms – rather neglected town, whose origins can be traced back to the missionary work of the eighth-century Saxon monk, Lebuinus. An influential centre of medieval learning, it was here in the late fourteenth century that Gerrit Groot founded the **Brotherhood of the Common Life**, a semi-monastic collective that espoused tolerance and humanism within a philosophy known as *Moderne Devotie* ("modern devotion"). This progressive creed attracted some of the great minds of the time, and Thomas à Kempis and Erasmus both studied here.

The Town

Enclosed by the river and the remains of a moat, Deventer's busy, broadly circular centre has kept its medieval street plan, which zeroes in on the **Brink**, a surprisingly large, cobbled marketplace that runs roughly north to south. At the square's southern end is the **Waag**, a late-Gothic redbrick structure of 1528, whose good-looking medley of towers and turrets is fronted by a grand stone portico that was added a century later. Oddly enough, there's a large **pan** nailed to the outside of the Waag's western wall, which must once have served as a warning: when the city council learnt that the mint master was debasing the town's coins, he was promptly put in the pan and boiled alive. The bullet holes weren't, an attempt to prolong the agony, however, but the work of idle French soldiers garrisoned here, who were taking, quite literally, "pot shots".

From the Waag, it's a short walk south then west along Polstraat to the **Lebuinuskerk** (Mon–Sat 1pm–5pm; free), a vast Gothic edifice built during Deventer's fifteenth-century pomp. Inside, the church's soaring, three-aisled nave, with its high-arched windows and slender pillars, rises to a vaulted ceiling adorned by intricate tracery. Look out also for the medieval murals on the walls of the nave – they may be faded, but enough remains to see the skill of their original execution. Back outside, the large square flanking the church, the **Grote Kerkhof**, is a good deal prettier than the Brink and here, attached to

The Dutch Golden Age

Ever wondered about those grim-faced portraits of black-hatted Dutch burghers who stare at us out of the gloom? The Dutch Golden Age of the seventeenth century was an amazing phenomenon: the Netherlands was the dominant economic force of Europe, and its people, for a brief period at least, grew richer than they could have ever imagined. This prosperity was matched by an unparalleled progressive and tolerant attitude to religion, the poor and the elderly, and an explosion of creativity in art that has left us with a magnificent record of the time – its values, its achievements and its people.

The history

▲ Huis Bartolotti, Amsterdam

After the death of Philip II, Spain was more or less forced to accept the independence of the United Provinces in 1609. The country was then formally recognized with the **Peace of Westphalia** in 1648, which also enforced the closure of the Scheldt river to sea traffic – a key factor in the decline of Antwerp as a sea port and the rise of Amsterdam, to which the upturn in trade brought extraordinary wealth. This was a **bourgeois revolution**, a triumph of the nouveau riche. The people who benefited most weren't aristocrats, and it was taking place in a country that had spent the past fifty years getting rid of the Catholic Church. Amsterdam's burghers didn't build churches and fill them with art glorifying God, and their architecture was domestic rather than monumental in scale. Though certain families became very rich, and displayed their success at every opportunity, there was also a subtlety and relative humility to their efforts. A collective attitude also underlied the aims of the authorities – such as with the extension of Amsterdam's canals – that in some ways make seventeenth-century Holland the world's first example of a modern welfare state.

▲ Leiden University

Despite – or maybe because of – the country being a product of the religious conflicts of the Reformation, **Calvinist Holland** was an unusually tolerant place. With the Inquisition dispatched, Catholic worship was tolerated, as long it was conducted behind closed doors, and the Jews and other religious refugees were welcomed. Partly as a result of this, the population of Amsterdam quadrupled in the first half of the seventeenth century, with a knock-on effect in the other towns of Holland, as well as the ports of the Zuider Zee – Hoorn and Enkhuizen – which benefited from the flourishing Baltic trade. Other Dutch institutions date back to this time, not least the university at **Leiden**, which was founded in 1575 as a reward to the people of the city for withstanding a famous siege by the Spanish (see p.165). Its motto, Presidium Libertatis, or "Bastion of Liberty", deliberately reflected its founding principles of freedom and tolerance, particularly when it came to religion.

The organization that kept the country's coffers full during the Golden Age was the **East India Company**.

Formed in 1602, it enjoyed a trading monopoly with the territories of the East, and effectively became the governing power in the countries the Dutch controlled – Malaysia, Sri Lanka and Indonesia. In 1632 the West India Company was formed, and had the same function, extending Dutch dominion over parts of South America and the Caribbean (and even New York at one point), to bring back the goods that oiled the wheels of the Dutch economic miracle.

The art

The first half of the seventeenth century in Holland, particularly in Amsterdam and around, was, like the Renaissance in Florence, or the Counter-Reformation in Rome, a time of extraordinary creative output, with the arts benefiting from – and mirroring perfectly – the society that was its sponsor. But here works of art weren't commissioned by the church; instead the patrons were the businesspeople who had grown rich on the back of the success of the Dutch republic, and they either wanted something to promote their own importance, or something to decorate their home. Paintings were designed to hang in smaller spaces, and portraiture flourished, as did so-called "genre" painting – basically scenes of everyday domestic life – and landscapes.

Portraits were intended to dignify the sitters' roles and glorify their achievements, either in stiff formal pose, as in **Jan Lievens'** depiction of the politician Constantijn Huygens, in Amsterdam's Rijksmuseum, or with their wives, as in **Frans Hals'** twin portraits of Jacon Olycan and his wife-to-be Aletta Hanemmanns, in the Mauritshuis in Den Haag; or, more informally, as in the same painter's marriage portrait of the self-satisfied Isaac Massa, also in the Rijksmuseum. Groups were painted together, for example in the so-called Civic Guard portraits of ex-military luncheon clubs, of which **Rembrandt's** *Night Watch*

▼ *The Mill at Wijk-bij-Duurstede*, Jacob van Ruisdael

For more on the history and art of the Dutch Golden Age see Contexts p.364 and p.374.

is just the best-known example. It was also common for the groups that ran the country's almshouses and orphanages to have their portraits captured for posterity, for example Frans Hals' two late great paintings of the Regents of the Haarlem almshouse where he died and where they are still displayed today, in the marvellous Frans Hals Museum.

Among genre painters, **Gerrit Dou**, an early pupil of Rembrandt, **Gerard ter Borch**, of Zwolle, and **Jan Steen** stand out – the latter for his raucous scenes of workaday Dutch life – as does **Jan Vermeer** of Delft, whose small output belies the massive popularity of his peaceful and quietly meaningful domestic scenes. And most people know the bucolic landscapes of **Jacob van Ruisdael** even if they couldn't name the painter. He, and his namesake **Salomon van Ruisdael**, and **Jan van Goyen**, among others, capture perfectly the huge skies and large expanses of water that characterize the in-part man-made Dutch landscape of the time – and perhaps the innate national pride in it as another of their own achievements. All of these painters are well represented in the Rijksmuseum in Amsterdam, but you should find examples of their work, except perhaps that of Vermeer, in most of the big city Dutch galleries.

Tulipmania

Nothing exemplifies the economic bubble of seventeenth-century Holland more than the arrival of the tulip. As a relatively exotic flower, a native of Turkey, it had already captured the imagination of other parts of Europe and its arrival in Holland, coinciding as it did with an abrupt rise in personal domestic wealth, led to it becoming the bloom of choice

for the discerning collector and horticulturalist. New varieties were developed voraciously and the trade in tulip bulbs boomed in the 1630s, with prices spiralling out of control and culminating at its height in three rare bulbs changing hands for the equivalent of the price of a house. By this time it was less about flowers, and more about speculation, with tulips being seen as a way of getting rich quick. However, such speculation couldn't be sustained, and the bottom fell out of the tulip market in 1637, when within three months prices collapsed to around ten percent of their previous value, and thousands lost everything they had. Today tulips and other blooms still define the Dutch landscape, especially in the polderlands of North and South Holland. Getting up close is easiest at the Keukenhof gardens (see p.169), if you're here at the right time of year, or just indulge yourself at Amsterdam's wonderful Bloemenmarkt (see p.80) – tulips are still as popular as ever, but a lot cheaper!

the south end of the Lebuinuskerk, are the bruised remains of the fourteenth-century **Oude Mariakerk**. Services haven't been held here since 1591 and the town council considered demolishing the church as early as 1600, but in the event it survived as the town's arsenal and now houses a smart restaurant – the *Arsenal* (see below).

Doubling back to the Brink, take Rijkmanstraat from the square's east side – from just behind the Waag – and you're in the **Bergkwartier**, an area of old housing that was tastefully refurbished during the 1960s in one of the region's first urban renewal projects. Proceeding up Rijkmanstraat, turn hard left onto **Kerksteeg**, at the end of which is **Bergkerk**, fronted by two tall towers, which dates from the thirteenth century, the differences in the colouring of the brick indicating the stages of construction.

From the church, Roggestraat leads to the east side of Brink and on the way, at no.3, you'll pass the **Etty Hillesum Centrum** (Wed, Sat & Sun 1–4pm; ⓦ www.ettyhillesumcentrum.nl), which celebrates the life of the eponymous Jewish woman who perished in Auschwitz in 1943; Hillesum lived in Deventer from 1924 to 1932. Moving on, Roggestraat arrives at the Brink opposite the **Penninckshuis**, whose florid Renaissance frontage is decorated with statuettes of six virtues. The inscription *Alst Godt behaget beter benyt als beclaget* is smug indeed: "If it pleases God it is better to be envied than to be pitied".

Practicalities

Deventer's **bus** and **train stations** are on the north side of the town centre, a five- to ten-minute walk from the Brink: turn left out of the train station and take the first right, straight down Keizerstraat. On the way, you'll pass the **VVV**, at Keizerstraat 22 (Mon–Fri 9.30am–6pm & Sat 9.30am–5pm; ☏0900/353 5355, ⓦ www.vvvdeventer.nl), which is strong on local information.

Hotels are thin on the ground, but there is the excellent ⚜ *Gilde Hotel*, Nieuwstraat 41 (☏0570/641 846, ⓦ www.gildehotel.nl; ❸), which occupies an intelligently revamped, nineteenth-century convent hospital with an attractive arcaded courtyard. The cheapest rooms here are a tad spartan, but others have their own little balconies. The hotel is located a five- to ten-minute walk west of the Brink – take Kleine Overstraat and keep straight ahead.

Deventer does well for **cafés** and **restaurants**. Among a score of places lining up along the Brink, one good choice is *De Sjampetter*, a popular eetcafé at no.82, or you could pop into one of the region's oldest cake shops, Jacob Bussink's Koekwinkel, at no.84, to try the local speciality, *Deventer koek*, spiced gingerbread biscuit. Moving up the food chain, *Restaurant 't Arsenal*, at the back of Lebuinuskerk on Grote Kerkhof (Tues–Sat 5.30–10pm; ☏0570/616 495), is a smart little place offering a wide, modern menu with mains averaging €25; and *Chez Antoinette*, just east off the Brink at Roggestraat 10 (Tues–Sun from 5pm; ☏0570/616 630), is a cosy Portuguese place with a first-rate wine cellar; main courses average €18. Finally, don't leave Deventer without popping into ⚜ De Leeuw, an old-fashioned, but incredibly cutesy sweet shop and café at Nieuwstraat 27.

Zutphen

ZUTPHEN, 11km south of Deventer, is everything you might hope for in a Dutch country town: there's no crass development, and the centre musters up dozens of old buildings set amid a medieval street plan that revolves around three long and very appealing piazzas – Groenmarkt, Houtmarkt and Zaad-markt. Much of the centre is pedestrianized and, without a supermarket in sight, the town's old-fashioned shops still flourish, as do its cafés and, in a quiet sort of way, its bars.

Zutphen was founded in the eleventh century as a fortified settlement at the confluence of the Berkel and IJssel rivers. It took a hundred years for the town to become an important trading post, but thereafter its very success brought torrid times. Habsburg armies sacked Zutphen on several occasions, but the worst came in 1572, when Spanish troops massacred its citizens, an outrage that became part of Protestant folklore, strengthening their resolve against Catholic absolutism right across Europe. It was also here in Zutphen that **Sir Philip Sidney**, the English poet, soldier and courtier, met his end while fighting against the Spanish in 1586. Every inch the Renaissance man, Sidney even managed to die with some measure of style: mortally wounded in the thigh – after having loaned his leg-armour to a friend – he offered his last cup of water to a wounded chum, protesting "thy need is greater than mine".

The Town

From the train station, it's a couple of minutes' walk south along Stationsstraat to the narrow passageway that leads through the old city wall to reach the town centre. Here, at the junction of Groenmarkt and Houtmarkt, is the **Wijnhuis**, a conspicuous if somewhat disjointed clock tower, whose assorted pillars and platforms date from the seventeenth century. Keep straight ahead from here, along Lange Hofstraat, and you soon reach **St Walburgiskerk** (June Tues–Sat 1.30–4.30pm; July to early Sept Mon 1.30–4.30pm, Tues–Sat 10.30am–4.30pm; €1.20, €3 with library), an immense, Gothic church whose massive, square tower rises high above the town. Inside, the most impressive features are an extravagant brass baptismal font and a remarkable medieval **library**, sited in the sixteenth-century chapterhouse. The library boasts a beautiful low-vaulted ceiling that twists around in a confusion of sharp-edged arches above the original wooden reading desks. It has all the feel of a medieval monastery, but it was in fact one of the first Dutch libraries to be built for the general public, a conscious effort by the Protestant authorities to dispel ignorance and superstition. The library owns over 700 items, ranging from early illuminated manuscripts to sixteenth-century books, a selection of which are still chained to the lecterns on which they were once read. Curiously, the tiles on one side of the floor are dotted with paw marks, which some contemporaries attributed to the work of the Devil.

Across from St Walburgiskerk is the **Stadhuis**, an elegant Neoclassical building whose main facade is decorated with military carvings in the style of ancient Rome. Proceeding south from here, you cross the old town **moat** to reach Martinetsingel, which curves east offering exquisite views over the town centre on its way to the **Drogenapstoren**, one of the old city gates – and a fine example of a brick rampart tower – that takes its name from the time when the town trumpeter, one Thomas Drogenap, lived here.

The Drogenapstoren is a few metres from **Zaadmarkt**, a wide and especially handsome street that leads back towards the Wijnhuis. Zaadmarkt is also home to the **Museum Henriette Polak**, at no.88 (Tues–Sun 11am–5pm; €4.50), which features temporary displays of modern, usually Dutch art. The house itself looks nineteenth century, but in fact it is much older as evidenced by the tiny chapel on the top floor. When the Protestants took control of the Netherlands in the sixteenth century, Catholics were allowed to hold services in any private building providing that the exterior revealed no sign of their activities – hence the development of clandestine churches (*schuilkerken*) all over the country, of which this is one of the few to have survived.

△ Zutphen street scene

Practicalities

Zutphen's **train** and **bus stations** are on the north side of the town centre; the **VVV** is nearby, at Stationsplein 39 (Mon 10am–5.30pm, Tues–Fri 9am–5.30pm, Sat 10am–4pm; ☎0900/269 2888, ⓦwww.vvvzutphen.nl). There are two good **hotels**, both handily located in the centre: *Eden Hotel Zutphen* is a comfortable, four-star hotel in a fine old mansion across from St Walburgiskerk at 's Gravenhof 6 (☎0575/596 868, ⓦwww.edenhotelzutphen.com; ❹); and the much more low-key, distinctly cosy, three-star ⌁ *Berkhotel*, in a pleasant, two-storey, late nineteenth-century building at Marschpoortstraat 19 (☎0575/511 135, ⓦwww.berkhotel.nl; ❶), a short walk west of the Wijnhuis via Groenmarkt.

For **food**, the *Berkhotel* has a very competent vegetarian café called *De Kloostertuin* (Tues–Sun 5–9pm); and there's also the *Gastenhuys de Klok* (Tues–Sun noon–9pm; ☎0575/517 035), which serves up tasty French and Dutch dishes (from €15) in antique, wood-panelled premises at Pelikaanstraat 6 – at the foot of Zaadmarkt. *Camelot*, a dark bar with a wide range of beers at Groenmarkt 34, is a good place for a **drink**; or, even better, try *De Korenbeurs*, a little, old-fashioned place complete with a splendid wooden stairway at Houtmarkt 84.

Around Zutphen: the Achterhoek

Extending some 30km southeast from Zutphen to the German border, the **Achterhoek** ("Back Corner") is aptly named, a dozy rural backwater whose towns and villages have little to hold your attention. The easy hills have made it a popular spot for cyclists, however, and the area is compact enough to tour from Zutphen. There are no really noteworthy monuments, with the possible exception of the old frontier settlement of **'s-Heerenberg**, whose modern centre edges the medieval town hall, church and castle that once belonged to the counts Van de Bergh. Of the three, it's the castle – the Huis Bergh – that dominates, its impressive red-brick walls rising abruptly above the moat, bedecked with shutters. Its present appearance dates from 1912 when an Enschede industrialist, J.H. van Heek, bought the place and had it restored. Guided tours (May–Oct Tues–Sun 12.30–4.30pm; Nov–Dec Sun 12.30–4.30pm; outside season call ℡0314/661 281; €7; ⓦwww.huisbergh.nl) whisk you round an interior littered with sundry late medieval paintings, statues, prayer books and other paraphernalia installed by van Heek. The quickest way to reach 's-Heerenberg is to take bus #24 from Doetinchem train station.

Twente

Southeast of Zwolle, the flat landscapes of the west give way to the lightly undulating, wooded countryside of **Twente**, an industrial region within the province of Overijssel whose principal towns – Almelo, Hengelo and Enschede – were once dependent on the textile industry. Hit hard by cheap Asian imports, all three have been forced to diversify their industrial base with mixed success: the largest town, **Enschede**, still has a serious unemployment problem, but it's the only one you're likely to visit on account of its excellent train connections and first-rate museum, the **Rijksmuseum Twente**.

Enschede

The university town of **ENSCHEDE**, some 50km east of Zutphen and 65km from Zwolle, may have a desultory modern centre, but it's a lively place and it hosts regular festivals, events and exhibitions. As ever, the obvious place to start a visit is the main square, the **Markt**, which is home to both the nineteenth-century **Grote Kerk** and the rather more interesting **St Jacobuskerk**, which was completed in 1933 in a sort of neo-Byzantine-meets-Art Deco style with angular copper-green roofs, huge circular windows and an inconclusively lumpy main tower. The **Stadhuis**, a couple of minutes away down Langestraat, was finished in the same year and is also something of an architectural landmark, its brown brick tower topped by four eye-catching blue and gold clocks.

Rijksmuseum Twente

Housed in an Art Deco mansion of 1930, the **Rijksmuseum Twente**, at Lasondersingel 129 (Tues–Sun 11am–5pm; €4; ⓦwww.rijksmuseum-twenthe .nl), possesses an outstanding collection of fine art gifted to the city by a wealthy mill-owning family, the Van Heeks. The museum contains two key sections – fifteenth- to nineteenth-century art and modern and contemporary art, primarily Dutch with the emphasis on Expressionism – and is located a fifteen-minute walk north of the centre: go over the train tracks at the crossing beside the station, take the first right, second left and follow the road to the end.

Among a fine sample of early religious art, three particular highlights are a set of brilliant blue and gold fragments from a French hand-illuminated missal; a primitive twelfth-century wood carving of Christ on Palm Sunday, and a delightful cartoon strip of contemporary life entitled *De Zeven Werken van Barmhartigheid* ("The Seven Acts of Charity"). Of later canvases, Hans Holbein's *Portrait of Richard Mabott* is typical of his work, the stark black of the subject's gown offset by the white cross on his chest and the face so finely observed it's possible to make out the line of his stubble. Pieter Brueghel the Younger's *Winter Landscape* is also fastidiously drawn, down to the last twig, and contrasts with the more loosely contoured figures and threatening clouds of his brother Jan's *Landscape*. Moving on, Jan Steen's *The Alchemist* is all scurrilous satire, from the skull on the chimneypiece to the lizard suspended from the ceiling and the ogre's whispered advice. Steen also mocks sex, most memorably here in his *Lute Player*, which features a woman with bulging breasts and flushed countenance in the foreground, while on the wall behind is the vague outline of tussling lovers.

High points of the modern and contemporary section include Monet's volatile *Falaises près de Pourville*; a characteristically unsettling canvas by Carel Willink, *The Actress Ank van der Moer*; and examples of the work of less well-known Dutch modernists like Theo Kuypers, Jan Roeland and Emo Verkerk.

Practicalities

Enschede **train** and **bus stations** are on the northwest edge of the town centre, about 600m from the Markt – just follow the signs. The **VVV** is bang in the middle of town at Oude Markt 31 (Mon 1–5.30pm, Tues–Fri 10am–5.30pm, Sat 9am–4pm; ☏053/432 3200, ⓦwww.vvvenschede.nl). They have a small supply of **private rooms** (❶) and the town also has a couple of central **hotels**, the more promising of which is the three-star *Amadeus*, in an older, two-storey block at Oldenzaalsestraat 103 (☏053/435 7486, ⓦwww.amadeushotel.nl; ❸); Oldenzaalsestraat is on the east side of the town centre.

For something to **eat**, head for the *Twentse Schouwburg*, just off the Markt on Langestraat, where they have a particularly good café and bar; this is also the town's principal venue for the performing arts.

Through the Veluwe

Extending west of the River IJssel, the **Veluwe** (literally "Bad Land") of the province of Gelderland is an expanse of heath, woodland and dune edged by **Apeldoorn** and Amersfoort to the east and west and the Veluwemeer and Arnhem to the north and south. For centuries these infertile lands lay almost deserted, but today they make up the country's busiest holiday centre, a profusion of campsites, bungalow parks and second homes that extends down to the Hoge Veluwe National Park (see p.295), a protected zone in the southeast corner that is much the prettiest part and the best place to experience the area – though, unless you're camping, it's more sensibly reached from Arnhem (see p.287).

Apeldoorn

The administrative capital of the Veluwe, **APELDOORN** was no more than a village a century ago, but it's grown rapidly to become an extensive garden city, a rather characterless modern place that spreads languidly into the surrounding countryside. However, as one-time home of the Dutch royal family, Apeldoorn is a major tourist centre in its own right, popular with those Dutch senior citizens who like an atmosphere of comfortable privilege.

Apeldoorn is most famous for the **Paleis Het Loo** (Tues–Sun 10am–5pm; €9; ⓦwww.paleishetloo.nl), situated on the northern edge of town and reachable by half-hourly bus #5, #96 or #102 from the station. Looking something like an imposing military academy, it was designed in 1685 by Daniel Marot for William III and his queen, Mary, shortly before he acceded to the throne of England and Scotland. Later the palace was the favourite residence of Queen Wilhelmina, who lived here until her death in 1962. No longer used by the Dutch royal family – they moved out in 1975 – it was opened as a national museum in the early 1980s to illustrate three hundred years of the history of the House of Orange-Nassau. Years of repair work have restored an apparently endless series of bedrooms,

△ Paleis Het Loo

ballrooms, living rooms and reception halls to their former glory. A self-guided tour, with information in English, leads you along a warren of passageways from one room to the next, packed with displays of all things royal, from lavish costumes and silk hangings to documents and medals, via roomfuls of austere portraits and curly antlers. It's a fascinating and infinitely detailed snapshot of royal life, and you can view the rooms of William and Mary, including their colourful individual bedchambers, as well as the much later study of Queen Wilhelmina.

After immersing yourself in a bygone era, the formal **gardens** (both William and Mary were apparently keen gardeners) make for a relaxing place to wander. A maze of miniature hedgerows and a series of precise and neatly bordered flowerbeds are accessible by long walkways ornamented in the Dutch Baroque style, with tiered fountains, urns, statuettes and portals. The other part of the palace, the **Royal Stables** of 1906, has displays of some of the old cars and carriages of past monarchs, including a baby carriage that's rigged up against gas attack.

The town's second draw is the **Apenheul** monkey reserve (April–Oct daily 9.30am–5pm; July & Aug until 6pm; €15; ⓦwww.apenheul.nl), just west of town on bus #3. The highlight is the gorillas – among the world's largest colonies of the creatures – living on wooded islands that isolate them from the visitors and from the dozen or so species of monkey that roam around the rest of the park. It's best to go early to catch the young gorillas fooling around and antagonizing the elders; as the day warms up they all get a bit more slothful. The park is well designed, with a reasonable amount of freedom for most of the animals (at times it's not obvious who is watching who), and you'll see other wildlife including otters, deer and capybara.

If you're staying here in August, it's worth catching the **film festival** at the Natuurpark Berg & Bos, featuring international films but with only Dutch subtitles; details are available from the VVV. Finally, in July and August an old **steam train** is put back into service between Apeldoorn and Dieren (a 75-minute ride), facilitating a pleasant half-day journey.

The Apeldoorn **VVV**, Deventerstraat 18 (Mon–Fri 9am–5.30pm, Sat 9am–5pm; ☎055/526 0200, ⓦwww.vvvapeldoorn.nl), stocks maps of the town and the surrounding area and lists of **rooms** – in season it's advisable to ask them to ring ahead to confirm vacancies. The most reasonably priced **hotel** near the centre, with only twelve rooms, is the *Abbekerk*, Canadalaan 26, a ten-minute walk north (☎055/522 2433, ⓦwww.hotelabbekerk.nl; ❶–❷): head up Stationstraat and Canadalaan is the fourth left turn after the Marktplein. There's also an **HI hostel**, 4km west at Asselsestraat 330 (☎055/355 3118, ⓦwww.stayokay.com; €27 for a dorm bed), which is open year-round and reachable with bus #6 (Mandala stop) or #7 (Chamavenlaan stop). The nearest **campsite** is *De Parelhoeve*, Zwolseweg 540 (☎055/312 1332, ⓦwww.deparelhoeve.nl), in the village of Wenum Wiesel some 5km north of Apeldoorn centre (bus #96 from the train station). The VVV also has a list of nearby mini-campsites.

Don't expect a lot of night-time excitement. The main hive of evening activity is the **Caterplein**, where Hoofdstraat meets Nieuwstraat. *Tipico*, an excellent Italian place with **food** for all budgets, is nearby at Kapelstraat 11, while *Eetcafé 't Pakhuys*, Beekpark 9, has reasonable Dutch food; there are also plenty of cheap kebab joints nearby. Further south on Hoofdstraat, Raadhuisplein has several good **café-bars**, and the *Blues Café* on Nieuwstraat has occasional live music.

An easy way to see the countryside around town is by **bike**. Details of suggested routes are available from the VVV and bikes can be rented from the station (€5.50/day, or €6.50 for a three-geared bike). The VVV can also provide details of walking trails in the forests around the Paleis Het Loo.

Arnhem

Around 20km south of Apeldoorn, on the far side of the heathy Hoge Veluwe National Park, **ARNHEM** was once a wealthy resort, a watering hole to which the merchants of Amsterdam and Rotterdam would flock to idle away their fortunes. Last century it became better known as the place where thousands of British and Polish troops died in the failed Allied airborne operation of September 1944, codenamed Operation Market Garden (see box on p.290). The town is most famous for its bridge, a key objective in Field Marshal Montgomery's audacious attempt to shorten the war by dropping parachute battalions behind enemy lines to secure a string of advance positions across the rivers of southeast Gelderland. Much of the city was destroyed as a result of the operation, and most of what you see today is a postwar reconstruction. Arnhem is now something of a place of pilgrimage for English visitors, who flock here every summer to pay their respects to the soldiers who died and visit the crucial sites of the battle. However, it's also a lively town that makes a good centre for seeing the numerous attractions scattered around its forested outskirts – the war museums and memorials near **Oosterbeek**, the **Nederlands Openluchtmuseum**, the **Burgers' Zoo** and one of the highlights of the area, the **Hoge Veluwe National Park** itself, incorporating a superb collection of modern art at the **Kröller-Müller Museum**.

Arrival, information and accommodation

Arnhem is a major transport junction with the town's **train** and **bus stations** only a few minutes' walk from the centre. The **Arnhem Tourist Info**, Velperbuitensingel 25 (April–Sept Mon–Fri 9.30am–5.30pm, Sat 9.30am–5pm;

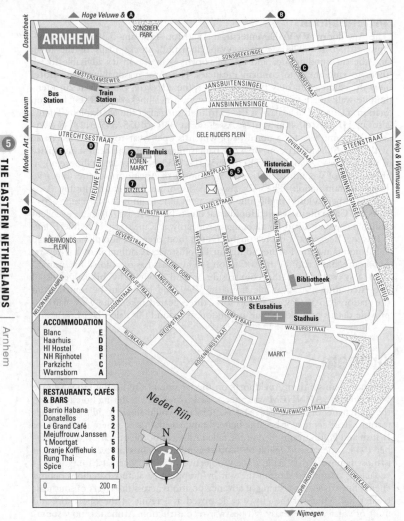

ARNHEM

SONSBEEK PARK

Bus Station

Train Station

ℹ

ACCOMMODATION
Blanc	E
Haarhuis	D
HI Hostel	B
NH Rijnhotel	F
Parkzicht	C
Warnsborn	A

RESTAURANTS, CAFÉS & BARS
Barrio Habana	4
Donatellos	3
Le Grand Café	2
Mejuffrouw Janssen	7
't Moortgat	5
Oranje Koffiehuis	8
Rung Thai	6
Spice	1

Neder Rijn

N

0   200 m

Filmhuis

KOREN-MARKT

DUIZELST.

Historical Museum

Bibliotheek

St Eusabius

Stadhuis

MARKT

RÖERMONDS PLEIN

GELE RIJDERS PLEIN

Hoge Veluwe & A

Oosterbeek

Museum

Modern Art

Velp & Wijnmuseum

Nijmegen

Oct–March Tues–Sat 9.30am–5pm; ☎0900/112 2344, ⓦwww.vvvarnhem
.nl), has a good selection of Dutch maps, books on Operation Market Garden,
brochures and up-to-date cultural information. **Walking** is the best way to get
around the centre, although to see any of the outlying attractions and for some
of the accommodation you'll need at some point to use a trolley **bus**. Arnhem
has a rather odd system of trolley buses which follow a figure-of-eight route
round town. This means there'll often be two buses at the station with the same
number and different destinations, so it's important to get the direction as well
as the number right. The VVV operates an **accommodation-booking** service – useful in July and August when Arnhem's handful of reasonably priced
pensions and hotels can fill up early. The nearest **campsite** is *Camping Warnsborn*, 6km northwest of the centre at Bakenbergseweg 257 (☎026/442 3469,

ⓦwww.campingwarnsborn.nl; bus #2, direction Schaarsbergen), attractively situated on a large estate and hemmed in by beech and oak trees. You can **rent bikes** here for the lovely cycle ride through the trees to the Hoge Veluwe National Park, 5km further north. There are many other campsites around the edge of the park, including one by the Hoenderloo entrance in the park itself (ⓣ055/378 2232; April–Oct) – an ideal spot for a quiet night's camping.

Hotels

Blanc Coehoornstraat 4 ⓣ026/442 8072, ⓦwww .hotel-blanc.nl. This small hotel has only 22 rooms, a few with balconies, located in one old and one more modern building, and with a café which has recently been revamped. ➋

Haarhuis Stationsplein 1 ⓣ026/442 7441, ⓦwww.hotelhaarhuis.nl. The reassuringly comfortable *Haarhuis* is conveniently located opposite the train station. Breakfast can be somewhat of a letdown though. ➍

NH Rijnhotel Onderlangs 10 ⓣ026/443 4642, ⓦwww.nh-hotels.com. Located just ten minutes' walk from the train station in the direction of Oosterbeek, this four-star hotel offers luxury with great views over the river Rhine. Don't be put off by its concrete facade; the interior is stylish with a Spanish twist. ➌–➍

Parkzicht Apeldoornsestraat 16 ⓣ026/442 0698, ⓦwww.parkzichthotel.nl. Friendly, family-run hotel with only four rooms, all in traditional style. ➊

Rozenhoek Rozendaalselaan 60 ⓣ026/364 7290, ⓕ361 7588. If you have problems finding a room, this is a good alternative outside the city in the leafy suburb of Velp. *Rozenhoek* is located in an old villa, just five minutes from the Rosendael castle. Untouched by the war, parts of Velp are still much as they were a century ago – comfortable country mansions and landscaped streets and gardens. ➋

🎿 **Warnsborn** Schelmseweg 1 ⓣ026/442 5994, ⓦwww.pensionwarnsborn.nl. By far the cheapest option is located near all Arnhem's main attractions and the Hoge Veluwe National Park, just north of the centre of town. This family run B&B in an eighteenth-century house has spacious rooms, some with private balconies. ➊

Hostels

HI hostel Diepenbrocklaan 27 ⓣ026/442 0114, ⓦwww.stayokay.com. Some 5km north of town in the woods and within walking distance to Burgers' Zoo and the Nederlands Openluchtmuseum. Facilities included a pool table, Internet access and a restaurant. Take bus #3, direction Altaveer, to the Rijnstaete hospital stop. €27 for a dorm bed.

The Town

Predictably, post-war rebuilding has left Arnhem a patchy place with the usual agglomerations of concrete and glass; however, five minutes' walk southeast from the train station is the **Korenmarkt**, a small square that escaped much of the destruction. The streets leading off it are choc-a-block with restaurants and bars, while the **Filmhuis**, at Korenmarkt 42, has an excellent programme of international films and late-night showings, and a small gallery on the ground floor.

Arnhem deteriorates as you walk southeast from the Korenmarkt and into the area most badly damaged by the fighting. Here stands the "Bridge too Far", the **John Frostbrug**, named after the commander of the battalion that defended it for four days. It's a plain modern bridge, but it remains a symbol of people's remembrance of the battle, Dutch and British alike. Around its north end you can see the results of the rebuilding: wide boulevards intersect broad open spaces edged by haphazardly placed tower blocks and car parks. Overlooking this rather desolate spot, at the end of the characterless **Markt**, is the church of **St Eusebius** (April–Oct Tues–Sat 10am–5pm, Sun noon–5pm; Nov–March Tues–Sat 11am–4pm, Sun noon–4pm; free), with the dainty fifteenth-century **Stadhuis** tucked in behind. The church is a fifteenth- to sixteenth-century structure surmounted by a valiantly attempted but rather obvious replacement tower which was extensively renovated for the fiftieth anniversary of Operation Market Garden in 1994; you can take a lift to the top (€2.50) for fine views around the surrounding area.

From outside the train station, it's a fifteen-minute walk west along Utrecht-sestraat (or take bus #1 direction Oosterbeek) to the **Museum voor Moderne Kunst**, Utrechtseweg 87 (Modern Art Museum; Tues–Fri 10am–5pm, Sat & Sun 11am–5pm; €5.75; ⓦ www.mmkarnhem.nl), whose speciality is exhibitions of modern Dutch art. The nucleus of the permanent collection is the work of the Magic Realists, particularly Carel Willink and Pyke Koch, whose *Vrouwen in de Straat* is a typically disconcerting canvas, the women's eyes looking out of the picture in a medley of contrasting emotions. The paintings of Reinier Lucassen, for example *The Kiss* of 1976, establish the stylistic link between the Magic Realism of the 1930s and Dutch contemporary art, the familiar once again given a disturbing and alienating slant.

The more centrally located **Historisch Museum** (Historical Museum; Tues–Fri 10am–5pm, Sat & Sun 11am–5pm; €3.65; ⓦ www.hmarnhem.nl) is in an old orphanage at Bovenbeekstraat 21. The collection includes a display of Chinese, Japanese and Delft ceramics from the seventeenth and eighteenth centuries; Dutch silver, notably several guild beakers, whose size and degree of decoration indicated the status of the owner; and a modest selection of paintings from the sixteenth to the nineteenth centuries, with the emphasis on views of the landscape, villages and towns of Gelderland.

Operation Market Garden

By September 1944 most of France and much of Belgium had been liberated from Nazi occupation. Fearing that an orthodox campaign would take many months and cost many lives, Field Marshal Montgomery decided that a pencil thrust north through the Netherlands and subsequently east into the Ruhr, around the back of the Siegfried line, offered a good chance of ending the war early. To speed the advance of his land armies, Montgomery needed to cross several major rivers and canals in a corridor of territory stretching from Eindhoven, a few kilometres north of the front, to Arnhem. The plan, codenamed **Operation Market Garden**, was to parachute three Airborne Divisions behind enemy lines, each responsible for taking and holding particular bridgeheads until the army could force their way north to join them. On Sunday, September 17, the 1st British Airborne Division parachuted into the fields around Oosterbeek, their objective to seize the bridges over the Rhine at Arnhem. Meanwhile, the 101st American Airborne Division was dropped in the area of Veghel to secure the Wilhelmina and Zuid-Willemsvaart canals, and the 82nd was dropped around Grave and Nijmegen, for the crossings over the Maas and the Waal.

The American paratroopers were successful, and by the night of September 20, sections of the main British army, 30 Corps, had reached the American bridgehead across the River Waal at Nijmegen. However, the landings around Arnhem ran into serious problems: Allied Command had estimated that opposition was unlikely to exceed three thousand troops, but, as it turned out, the entire 2nd SS Panzer Corps was refitting near Arnhem just when the 1st Division landed. Taking the enemy by surprise, 2nd Parachute Battalion, under Lieutenant-Colonel John Frost, did manage to capture the north end of the road bridge across the Rhine, but it proved impossible to capture the southern end. Surrounded, out-gunned and out-manned, the 2nd Battalion held their position from September 17th to the morning of the 21st, a feat of extraordinary heroism. Meanwhile, other Polish and British battalions had concentrated around the bridgehead at Oosterbeek, which they held at tremendous cost under the command of General Urquhart. By the morning of the 25th it was apparent that reinforcements in sufficient numbers would not be able to get through in support, so under cover of darkness, a dramatic withdrawal saved 2163 soldiers out of an original force of 10,005.

Wine lovers will enjoy the **Nederlands Wijnmuseum**, Velperweg 23 (Dutch Wine Museum; Tues–Fri 2–5pm, Sat 11am–5pm; €3; wine tastings on Saturday 11am–3pm; €7.50; ⓦ www.wijnmuseum.nl), towards Velp, where the entire process from grape to bottle is explained. On Saturday you can visit their immense wine cellars below the museum where thousands of litres of wine are kept in barrels, waiting to be drunk. Ask for their English guide book.

Eating, drinking and nightlife

Although Arnhem doesn't have a rich culinary tradition, there are plenty of decent places for reasonably priced **food** and a range of good **bars**. Most people head for the pavement cafés of **Korenmarkt** with lively terraces in summer for their drinking. Cheap food can be found around the **Jansplein**, while there are some more stylish places along **Pauwstraat**. There's often **live music** at one or other of the bars; get hold of a copy of the listings magazine *Uit Loper* for details of what's on.

Barrio Habana Pauwstraat 3. Gigantic restaurant and bar, with a deliberately run-down Cuban feel. Don't mind Che looking over your shoulder while you enjoy large tapas or one of their cocktails.

Donatellos Jansplein 50. Cheap Italian chain restaurant, frequented by students on a tight budget. All pizzas and pastas are under €6 and a three-course meal is the amazingly low price of €10.

Le Grand Café Korenmarkt 16. Probably the most popular spot for drinking on Korenmarkt, complete with fake palm trees and tacky lamp-shades. If it's too crowded there are a dozen other places around here to choose from.

Mejuffrouw Janssen Duizelsteeg 7. Just south of Korenmarkt, this restaurant offers excellent value for money with a three-course meal for €12.95; choices include tuna steak, shrimp skewer and steak. The only down side is that it can take a while between courses.

't Moortgat Ruiterstraat 35. This brown-style café, with beer memorabilia on the walls and over 120 beers to choose from, caters to an older crowd. There's also a billiards table to pass the time on a rainy day.

Oranje Koffiehuis Arke Noachstraat 7. Tiny café with Art Deco interior that, despite its name (coffeehouse), also serves stronger drinks. One nice detail is the miniature glass of liquor that they serve with their coffee. Live music three times a week.

Rung Thai Ruiterstraat 43. Trendy Thai place with bright pink walls and a wicked *Tom Yam Kai*. Main dishes around €14. Also does take-away.

Spice Jansplein 49. Cheap restaurant with a varied menu, serving everything from curry to spareribs. Starters never exceed €5 and mains are around €10.

Around Arnhem

Most people who visit Arnhem do so for the attractions outside the city: you could certainly spend several days here visiting the wartime sites of Operation Market Garden around **Oosterbeek**, taking in the countryside of the **Hoge Veluwe** park, and its superb modern art collection, the **Kröller-Müller Museum**, not to mention the **Nederlands Openluchtmuseum**, the country's largest open-air museum of Dutch vernacular architecture, and **Burgers' Zoo**, which has a sizeable menagerie of animals housed in sensitively re-created and attractive habitats, plus a **castle** or two.

Two castles: Doorwerth and Rosendael

For the most part the banks of the River Rhine near Arnhem are rather dull, though there's an appealing stretch to the west, where you'll find the massive, moated thirteenth-century **Kasteel Doorwerth** (Tues–Fri 10am–5pm, Sat 1–5pm, Sun 11am–5pm, last entry 4pm; €6), carefully reconstructed after

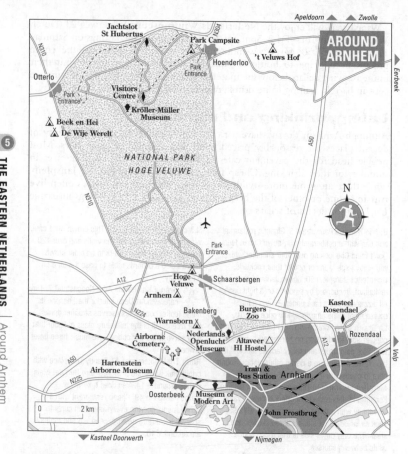

war damage. To get there, take bus #50 from the station in the direction of Wageningen and ask to be dropped at the Dunolaan stop, from where it's a thirty-minute walk down to the riverbanks. There are no great thrills inside the castle, which contains a collection of stuffed carcasses and old weapons in the Hunting Museum.

On the opposite side of Arnhem, lying on the edge of the suburbs of Velp, is the **Kasteel Rosendael** (mid-April to Oct Tues–Sun 10am–5pm; €5.50; bus #31 direction Velp Zuid) – an attractive mixture of medieval and eighteenth-century architecture, set in its own parkland. Not far away, on the west side of Velp, the **Museum Bronbeek**, Velperweg 147 (Tues–Sun 10am–5pm; €2.30; bus #3 direction Velp), occupies a building donated to ex-soldiers by William III in 1859. The collection has all sorts of curious relics left over from the Dutch occupation of Surinam and Indonesia.

Oosterbeek's World War II memorials

The area around Arnhem is scattered with the graveyards of thousands of soldiers who died during Operation Market Garden (see box on p.290). Arnhem VVV sells specialist books on the campaign for devotees of battlegrounds and battle plans, and provides details of organized tours (minimum 20 people). Otherwise, the easiest way to get some idea of the conflict and its effect on this part of the Netherlands is to visit **OOSTERBEEK**, once a small village and now a prosperous suburb of Arnhem (train or bus #1).

Following the signs from beside Oosterbeek train station, it's a five-minute walk east to the **Airborne Cemetery**, a neat, symmetrical tribute to nearly two thousand paratroopers, mostly British and Polish, whose bodies were brought here from the surrounding fields. It's a quiet, secluded spot; the

△ War memorial in Oosterbeek

personal inscriptions on the gravestones are especially poignant. Ten minutes' walk (or bus #1) south of the station down Stationsweg, the village proper has spruced lawns and walls dotted with details of the battle – who held out where and for how long – as the Allied forces were pinned back within a tighter and tighter perimeter.

The **Airborne Museum**, Utrechtseweg 232 (April–Oct Mon–Sat 10am–5pm, Sun noon–5pm; Nov–March Mon–Sat 11am–5pm, Sun noon–5pm; €5.80; ⓦwww.airbornemuseum.nl), is just to the west of the village centre along Utrechtseweg, reachable direct from Arnhem on bus #1 or #86, housed in the former Hotel Hartenstein, where the British forces were besieged by the Germans for a week before retreating across the river. With the use of an English commentary, photographs, dioramas and original military artefacts – from rifles and light artillery to uniforms and personal memorabilia – the museum gives an excellent outline of the battle and, to a lesser extent, aspects of World War II as it affected the country as a whole. The Army Film and Photographic Unit landed with the British forces, and it's their photographs that stick in the memory: grimly cheerful soldiers hauling in their parachutes; tense, tired faces during the fighting; and shattered Dutch villages.

The Nederlands Openluchtmuseum and Burgers' Zoo

Immediately north of Arnhem, the **Nederlands Openluchtmuseum**, Schelmseweg 89 (Dutch Open-Air Museum; daily: April–Oct 10am–5pm; Nov & mid-Jan to March 11am–4.30pm; Dec to mid-Jan noon–8pm; €12.90; ⓦwww.openluchtmuseum.nl), reachable by bus #3 direction Alteveer (every 20min), or direct by special bus #13 (July & Aug only; every 20min), is a huge collection of Dutch buildings open to public view. One of the first of its type, the museum was founded in 1912 in order to "present a picture of the daily life of ordinary people in this country as it was in the past and has developed in the course of time". Over the years, original buildings have been taken from all over the country and assembled here in a large area of the Veluwe forest. Where possible, buildings have been placed in groups that represent the different regions of the Netherlands – from the farmsteads of Friesland to the farming communities of Zuid-Holland and the peat colonies of Drenthe. There are about 80 buildings in all, including examples of every type of Dutch windmill, most sorts of farmhouse, a variety of bridges and several working craftshops, demonstrating the traditional skills of papermaking, milling, baking, brewing and bleaching. More controversial aspects of the Netherlands' past are also covered with a Mollucan barrack giving a realistic view on how the KNIL (Royal Netherlands East Indian Army) soldiers who fled from the former colony of the East Indies in 1951 had to live in dire circumstances once they had left.

Other parts of the museum incorporate one of the most extensive regional costume exhibitions in the country and a modest herb garden. The giant snail building houses *Hollandrama*, which shows visual footage of typical Dutch scenes through the ages. All in all, it's an imaginative attempt to re-create the rural Dutch way of life over the past two centuries.

Near the Nederlands Openluchtmuseum is another of Arnhem's major attractions. **Burgers' Zoo**, Antoon van Hooffplein 1 (April–Oct 9am–7pm; Nov–March 9am–5pm; €16; ⓦwww.burgerszoo.nl), was started in 1913 with a small private collection and has since grown to become one of the largest zoos in the Netherlands. Artificial ecosystems like Burgers' Ocean, Safari and Desert copy the animals' habitats as accurately as possible to show their natural behaviour.

The Hoge Veluwe National Park

Spreading north from the Open-Air Museum is the **Hoge Veluwe National Park** (ⓦwww.hogeveluwe.nl), an area of sandy heath and thick woodland. Just ninety minutes by train from Amsterdam, the impressive **Kröller-Müller Museum** and Europe's largest sculpture garden lie at the heart of 5500 hectares of national park. Cycle paths wind through this beautiful nature reserve, home to wild game and inland sand dunes as well as over a thousand free white bicycles which can be used to explore it all. Today, the park is one of the region's most popular day-trip destinations, with its perfect blend of nature and art.

The park was formerly the private estate of Anton and Helene Kröller-Müller. Born near Essen in 1869, Helene Müller came from a wealthy family whose money was made in the blast-furnace business. She married Anton Kröller of Rotterdam, whose brother ran the Dutch side of their trading interests, and the couple's fortunes were secured when the death of her father and his brother's poor health placed Anton at the head of the company at the age of 27. Apart from extending their business empire and supporting the Boers in South Africa, they had a passionate desire to leave a grand bequest to the nation, a mixture of nature and culture which would, she felt, "be an important lesson when showing the inherent refinement of a merchant's family living at the beginning of the century". She collected the art, he the land, and in the 1930s ownership of both was transferred to the nation on the condition that a museum was built in the park. The museum opened in 1938 and Helene acted as manager until her death in 1939.

Park practicalities

The park has three entrances: one near the village of **Otterlo** on the northwest perimeter, another near **Hoenderloo** on the northeast edge, and a third to the south at Rijzenburg, near the village of **Schaarsbergen**, only 7km from Arnhem. It has long **opening hours** (daily: April 8am–8pm; May & Aug 8am–9pm; June & July 8am–10pm; Sept 9am–8pm; Oct 9am–7pm; Nov–March 9am–6pm). **Admission** is €6 (park only) or €12 (park and Kröller-Müller museum); cars cost an extra €6. During the deer rutting season in September and early October, certain areas of the park are off-limits.

As there are very few roads in the national park, the best way to explore is on one of the 1700 **white bicycles** which lie in wait at each of the park's three entrances and are free to use. These famous white bikes come in all shapes and sizes for the whole family, and several have children's seats at the front and rear. There are also trikes, tandems and wheelchair bikes available from next to the **Bezoekerscentrum** (Visitors' Centre; April–Oct daily 9.30am–6pm; Nov–March 9.30am–5pm), located in the middle of the park near the museum.

There are a number of ways to get to De Hoge Veluwe by **bus**. From Arnhem, bus #107 runs hourly to Otterlo; here, you can change to bus #106, which runs 4km east to the Kröller-Müller Museum or you can walk to the park entrance (5min) and pick up a free white bike. On its full trip, bus #110 runs hourly on a handy route between Ede-Wageningen and Apeldoorn, stopping midway at the Otterlo entrance, the Bezoekerscentrum and the Hoenderloo entrance.

Alternatively, you can **rent a bike** at Arnhem train station and cycle yourself; the round trip from Arnhem station to the Kröller-Müller museum and back is a total of about 28km.

Around the park

At Eikenzoom 12 in Otterlo village, ten minutes' walk from the park entrance and across from the VVV, is the small **Tegel Museum** (Tile Museum; Tues–Fri

10am–5pm, Sat & Sun 1–5pm; €4; ⓦ www.nederlandstegelmuseum.nl), which is worth an hour of your time. Displays trace the development of the Dutch tile from the sixteenth to the twentieth century, and include themes such as biblical scenes, shipping and sea monsters. Slideshows and guided tours in English are available on request.

Cycle paths wind through the park's heathland, woodland, sand dunes and lakes, with some themed routes such as the 14km "Images in the Landscape" taking in the best of the open-air art (map available from the Bezoekerscentrum; €1). Or you can just make it up as you pedal along – you won't get lost thanks to the mushroom-like kilometre stones with directions and distances at every twist and turn.

While Helene collected art, her husband, Anton Kröller, imported animals such as moufflons (wild sheep from Corsica) and bought up land. The parkland is now carefully managed for its unusual ecosystems, such as wandering inland dunes, which form unexpected desert vistas, and the endangered species that survive in them. Hides are dotted throughout the park, from where you can observe bigger game such as red deer, roe deer and wild boar. To understand the environment you're cycling through, don't miss the **Museonder** (same hours; free), beneath the Bezoekerscentrum (see p.295). This engrossing subterranean museum brings to life the unusual ecosystems of the park through an array of interactive presentations – great for children, and adults will find themselves morbidly fascinated too. Look out for the giant beetle-mites, a rabbit morgue and a 23m-long beech tree banister.

Apart from the Kröller-Müller Museum, point your handlebars towards the **Jachtslot St Hubertus** (open only for guided tours, book at the Bezoekerscentrum; €2), some 3km north of the Visitors' Centre, a hunting lodge and country home built in 1920 for the Kröller-Müllers by the modernist Dutch architect H.P. Berlage. Dedicated to the patron saint of hunters, it's an impressive Art Deco monument, with lots of plays on the hunting theme. The floor plan – in the shape of branching antlers – is representative of the stag bearing a crucifix that appeared to St Hubert, the adopted patron of hunters, while he was hunting, and each room of the sumptuous interior symbolizes an episode in the saint's life: all in all, a somewhat unusual commission for a committed socialist who wrote so caustically about the haute bourgeoisie.

The Kröller-Müller Museum

Most people who visit the Hoge Veluwe Park come for the **Kröller-Müller Museum** (Tues–Sun 10am–5pm; €12 with park admission included; ⓦ www .kmm.nl), made up of the private art collection of the Kröller-Müllers. It's one of the country's finest museums, a wide cross-section of modern European art from Impressionism to Cubism and beyond, housed in a low-slung building that was built for the collection in 1938 by the Belgian architect Van de Velde. In the 1970s a new transparent wing by the Dutch architect Wim Quist was added.

The bulk of the collection is in one long wing, starting with the most recent painters and working backward. There's a good set of paintings, in particular some revealing self-portraits by Charley Toorop, one of the most skilled and sensitive of twentieth-century Dutch artists. Her father, Jan, also gets a good showing throughout the museum, from his pointillist studies to later, turn-of-the-century works more reminiscent of Aubrey Beardsley and the Art Nouveau movement. Piet Mondrian is well represented, too, his 1909 *Beach near Domburg* a good example of his more stylized approach to landscape painting, a development from his earlier sombre-coloured scenes in the Dutch tradition. In 1909 Mondrian moved to Paris, and his contact with Cubism transformed his work, as illustrated by his *Composition* of 1917: simple flat rectangles of colour with the elimination of the object complete, the epitome of the De Stijl approach. Much admired by Mondrian, Fernand Léger was one of the most influential of the Cubists, and his *Soldiers Playing Cards* is typical of his bold, clear lines and tendency toward the monumental. One surprise is an early Picasso, *Portrait of a Woman*, from 1901, a classic post-Impressionist canvas very dissimilar from his more famous works.

The building as a whole gravitates toward the works of **Vincent van Gogh**, with one of the most complete collections of his work in the world, housed in a large room around a central courtyard and placed in context by accompanying contemporary pictures. The museum owns no fewer than 278 Van Gogh pieces (both paintings and drawings), and exhibits are rotated, with the exception of his most important paintings. Of earlier canvases, *The Potato Eaters* and *Head of a Peasant with a Pipe* are outstanding: rough, unsentimental paintings of labourers from around his parents' home in Brabant. His penetrating *Self-portrait* from 1887 is a superb example of his work during his years in Paris, the eyes fixed on the observer, the head and background a swirl of grainy colour and streaky brush-strokes. One of his famous sunflower paintings also dates from this period, an extraordinary work of alternately thick and thin paintwork in dazzlingly sharp detail and colour.

The joyful *Haystacks in Provence* and *Bridge at Arles*, with its rickety bridge and disturbed circles of water spreading from the washerwomen on the river bank, are from his months in Arles in 1888, one of the high points of his troubled life. In stark contrast his *Prisoners Exercising* of 1890 is a powerful, sombre painting full of the sadness and despair of his last years: heads bent, the prisoners walk around in a pointless circle as the walls around them seem to close in.

Finally, outside the museum, behind the main building, there's a **Sculpture Garden** (Tues–Sun 10am–4.30pm; free entrance with museum ticket), recently doubled in size and now the largest in Europe. Some frankly bizarre creations reside within its 25 hectares, as well as works by Auguste Rodin, Jacob Epstein and Barbara Hepworth. In contrast to the carefully conserved paintings of the museum, the sculptures are exposed to the weather and you can even clamber all over Jean Dubuffet's *Jardin d'email*, one of his larger and more elaborate jokes.

Nijmegen

The oldest town in the Netherlands, **NIJMEGEN**, some 20km south of Arnhem, was built on the site of the Roman frontier fortress of *Novio Magus*, from which it derives its name. Situated on the southern bank of the Waal, just to the west of its junction with the Rhine, the town's location has long been strategically important. The Romans used Nijmegen as a buffer against the unruly tribes to the east; Charlemagne, Holy Roman Emperor from 800 to 814, made the town one of the principal seats of his administration, building the **Valkhof Palace**, an enormous complex of chapels and secular buildings completed in the eighth century. Rebuilt in 1155 by another emperor, Frederick Barbarossa, the complex dominated Nijmegen right up until 1769, when the palace was demolished and the stonework sold; what was left suffered further demolition when the French occupied the town in 1796. In September 1944, the town's bridges were a key objective of Operation Market Garden (see box on p.290) and although these were captured by the Americans, the disaster at Arnhem put the town on the front line for the rest of the war. The results are clear to see: the old town was largely destroyed and has been replaced by a centre reconstructed to a new plan.

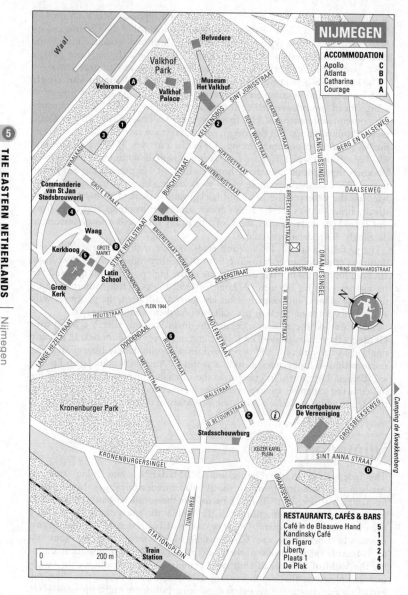

Arrival, information and accommodation

Nijmegen's **train** and **bus stations** are a good fifteen-minute trudge south-west of the town centre; if you can't face the walk, take any bus from the station. The **VVV** is housed in the **Stadsschouwburg** at Keizer Karelplein 32/H, five minutes' walk from the station (Mon–Fri 9.30am–5.30pm, Sat

10am–5pm; ☎0900/112 2344, ⓦwww.vvvnijmegen.nl). During July and August, a variety of **boat trips** operate on the Waal. Prices vary according to the itinerary: an hour's river tour is €3, or you can sail all the way to Rotterdam for €35.

  Accommodation is pretty thin on the ground in Nijmegen, so it's a good idea to book in advance. The **pension** *Catharina* at St Annastraat 64 (☎024/323 1251, ⓦwww.hotelcatharina.nl; ❶–❷), not far east of the train station, offers simple rooms in an old mansion. **Hotels** are a little more expensive but tend to be more convenient: the *Apollo* is on the street running east off Keizer Karelplein, at Bisschop Hamerstraat 14 (☎024/322 3594, ⓦwww.apollo-hotel-nijmegen. nl; ❷). If you're stuck, try the *Atlanta*, right in the centre at Grote Markt 38 (☎024/360 3000, ⓦwww.atlanta-hotel.nl; ❷), which is reasonably priced for its central location, although it can be rather noisy. Overlooking the river Waal, the new *Courage*, Waalkade 108 (☎024/360 4970, ⓦwww.hotelcourage.nl, ❷), is a classy alternative, right next to the Velorama. Most **campsites** are around Groesbeek, including *De Oude Molen*, Wylerbaan 2 (☎024/397 1715, ⓦwww .oudemolen.nl; April–Oct), a few kilometres southeast of town, reachable from the station by bus #5, direction Groesbeek.

The Town

The town centre is **Grote Markt**, a good fifteen-minute walk from the train station, or five minutes by any bus from immediately outside. Much of the Grote Markt survived the wartime shelling and is surprisingly well preserved, in stark contrast to the modern shops across the road. The **Waag**, with its traditional stepped gables and shuttered windows, stands beside a vaulted passage, the Kerkboog, which leads through to the peaceful precincts of the much-renovated Gothic **Grote Kerk** (Easter–Oct Mon 10.30am–1.30pm, Tues, Thurs, Fri & Sun 1–4pm, Wed & Sat 10.30am–4.30pm). The church, dedicated to St Stephen, is entered around the back to the left, past the attractively carved facade of the old Latin School; inside there's some fine Renaissance woodwork. The **tower**, with its vaguely oriental spire, offers a commanding vista over the surrounding countryside (June–Aug Mon–Fri 3pm; only opened for groups of five or more; €2). The view over the streets beside and behind the church isn't what it used to be: the huddle of medieval houses that sloped down to the Waal was almost totally destroyed during World War II and has been replaced by a hopeful but rather sterile residential imitation.

  A few metres away, down toward the river, the **Commanderie van St Jan** is more authentic-looking, a reconstruction of a seventeenth-century building that now houses the **Stadsbrouwerij De Hemel**, Franse Plaats 1 (Tues–Sun noon–8pm; free; guided tours €6 with a drink included; ⓦwww.brouwerijdehemel.nl), which features a brewery museum, tasting room and even a small B&B (❷) with only two rooms and self-service breakfast.

  From the Grote Markt, Burchtstraat heads east roughly parallel to the river, past the dull reddish-brown brick of the **Stadhuis**, a square, rather severe edifice with an onion-domed tower, another reconstruction after extensive war damage.

  Bike enthusiasts shouldn't miss the **Velorama Nationaal Fietsmuseum**, just a few minutes' walk north at Waalkade 107 (National Bicycle Museum; Mon–Sat 10am–5pm, Sun 11am–5pm; €4.60; ⓦwww.velorama .nl), with the largest collection of bicycles and other human-powered vehicles in western Europe. The museum devotes three floors to over 200 contraptions dating from the early nineteenth century to the present day. There are bicycles delicately carved from wood, a bicycle for five people, penny-farthings, recumbents and quadricycles – anything and everything that has helped shape bicycle design in the last few centuries, all lovingly restored and beautifully displayed – the perfect museum to visit in a country where the bicycle rules.

The Valkhof

In a park beside the east end of Burchtstraat lie the scanty remains of the **Valkhof Palace** – a ruined fragment of the Romanesque choir of the twelfth-century palace chapel and, just to the west, a sixteen-sided chapel built around 1045, in a similar style to the palatinate church at Charlemagne's capital, Aachen. These bits and pieces are connected by a footbridge to a **belvedere**, which was originally a seventeenth-century tower built into the city walls; today it's a restaurant and a lookout platform with excellent views over the river.

The modern-looking **Museum Het Valkhof**, Kelfkensbos 59 (Tues–Fri 10am–5pm, Sat & Sun noon–5pm; €6; ⓦ www.museumhetvalkhof.nl), houses a variety of exhibits with a local flavour, including innumerable paintings of Nijmegen and its environs – none particularly distinguished except for Jan van Goyen's *Valkhof Nijmegen*, which used to hang in the town hall. Painted in 1641, it's a large, sombre-toned picture – pastel variations on green and brown – where the Valkhof shimmers above the Waal, almost engulfed by sky and river. Also contained in the museum is the collection of the eminent archeologist G.M. Kam, who died in 1922. Alongside his Roman discoveries are other more recent artefacts; together they form a comprehensive picture of the first Roman settlements in the area and elsewhere in the Netherlands.

Nearby museums

Southeast of Nijmegen on the road to Groesbeek, the **Bijbels Openluchtmuseum**, Profetenlaan 2 (Biblical Open-Air Museum; Easter–Oct daily 10am–5pm; €9.50; ⓦ www.bijbelsopenluchtmuseum.nl), is accessible by bus #5 and #25 (destination Groesbeek) from beside the train station. Here you'll

The Four Day Marches

Every year on the third Tuesday of July, Nijmegen is flooded with walking fanatics taking part in the **Nijmeegse Vierdaagse**, the world's largest walking event attracting more than 40,000 participants (ⓦ www.4daagse.nl), who go for the 30-, 40- or 50-kilometre route depending on age and gender, all receiving the much-coveted Four Day Marches Cross at the end. The event dates back to 1909 when "four days" was a popular theme, with events like four days' cycling, rowing and horseback riding. It was not until 1928 that The Four Day Marches became international, with delegations from Germany, France, Norway and the United Kingdom taking part. Even after the war, which destroyed much of Nijmegen, the marches carried on, thanks to many volunteers and fundraisers. Nowadays over 60 countries are represented in the exhausting walking event, with everyone from children to grandparents taking part, making this a real family occasion. The image of the marches was damaged in 2006 when two people died on the first day because of extreme heat. The march was cancelled amid debates about whether the authorities could have prevented it, though the traditional parties that happen around the event continued (ⓦ www .vierdaagsefeesten.nl), with live performances all over town. If you're planning to visit during it, make sure you book your accommodation ahead.

find a series of reconstructions of the ancient Holy Land, including a Galilean fishing village, a complete Palestinian hamlet, a town street lined with Egyptian, Greek, Roman and Jewish houses and, strangely enough, "Bedouin tents of goats' hair as inhabited by the patriarchs". An experience not to be missed on any account.

There's another unusual museum 2km east of here, along Meerwijkselaan – the **Afrika Museum** at Postweg 6, Berg en Dal (April–Oct Mon–Fri 10am–5pm, Sat & Sun 11am–5pm; Nov–March Tues–Fri 10am–5pm, Sat & Sun 1–5pm; €7.50; Ⓦ www.afrikamuseum.nl), where there's a purpose-built West African village, a small animal park and a museum full of totems, carved figurines and musical instruments. You can get here on bus #8 (destination Berg en Dal), though from the bus stop it's still a twenty-minute walk to the museum.

Eating, drinking and nightlife

As you'd expect in a student town, Nijmegen has a wide range of places to eat and drink at sensible prices. Kelfkensbos is a good area for **restaurants**: *Liberty* at no. 21 has an eclectic mix of European, Asian and South American food with mains around €17, while *Appels & Peren* at no. 30 is a little less expensive but almost as adventurous. Cheap and mainly organic food can be found at *De Plak*, Bloemerstraat 90, with a large selection of vegetarian dishes. A must in summer is *Plaats 1*, located in the Commanderie van St Jan, with a terrace under the trees and all courses around €8. For **drinking**, head down Grote Straat to the waterfront; *Kandinsky Café* at Waalkade 65 is usually a lively spot, or you could go for *Le Figaro* at Waalkade 47. If you want to be indoors, try *Café in de Blaauwe Hand* – a cosy little bar behind the Grote Kerk and, supposedly, the oldest bar in town.

Every inch a fashionable town, Nijmegen attracts some top-name rock **bands**, especially during the academic year. Most perform at the Concertgebouw De Vereeniging, Keizer Karelplein 2/D or the Stadsschouwburg, Keizer Karelplein 32/H; for latest information about what's on, check with the VVV. For **films**, the Lux, Marienburg 38–39, has a good international programme of independent films and some late-night shows.

Travel details

Trains

Apeldoorn to: Amersfoort (every 30min; 25min); Deventer (every 30min; 10min); Zutphen (every 30min; 15min).
Arnhem to: Amsterdam CS (every 20min; 1hr 10min); Nijmegen (every 10min; 15min); Roosendaal (every 30min; 1hr 45min–2hr 10min); Velp (every 30min; 10min).
Enschede to: Amsterdam CS (every 30min; 2hr); Deventer (every 30min; 45min).
Lelystad to: Amsterdam CS (every 20min; 40min).
Zutphen to: Arnhem (every 30min; 25min); Deventer (every 30min; 15min).
Zwolle to: Amersfoort (every 30min; 35–50min); Amsterdam CS (every 30min; 1hr 10min–1hr

35min); Arnhem (every 30min; 1hr); Deventer (every 30min; 20min); Emmen (every 30min; 55min); Groningen (3 hourly; 1hr–1hr 15min); Kampen (every 30min, Sun hourly; 10min); Leeuwarden (every 30min; 55min–1hr 5min); Nijmegen (every 30min; 1hr 15min); Schiphol airport (3 hourly; 1hr 20min–1hr 45min); Steenwijk (every 30min; 15min); Zutphen (every 30min; 35min).

Buses

Doetinchem to: 's-Heerenberg (Mon–Fri every 30min, Sat & Sun hourly; 20min).
Kampen to: Lelystad (Mon–Sat every 30min, Sun hourly; 1hr).
Lelystad to: Enkhuizen (hourly; 35min); Kampen (Mon–Sat every 30min, Sun hourly; 55min).

Steenwijk to: Blokzijl (Mon–Fri hourly; 20min); Giethoorn (Mon–Fri hourly; 10min); Zwartsluis (Mon–Fri hourly; 30min); Zwolle (Mon–Fri hourly; 1hr 10min).

Zwartsluis to: Vollenhove (Mon–Sat every 30min, Sun hourly; 20min).

Zwolle to: Elburg (Mon–Sat every 30min, Sun hourly; 35min); Ens (Mon–Fri every 30min, Sat & Sun hourly; 50min); Giethoorn (Mon–Fri hourly; 1hr); Steenwijk (Mon–Fri hourly; 1hr 10min); Urk (Mon–Fri every 30min, Sat hourly; 1hr 30min); Vollenhove (Mon–Sat every 30min, Sun hourly; 50min); Zwartsluis (Mon–Sat every 30min, Sun hourly; 30min).

Ferries

Urk to: Enkhuizen (late June to Aug Mon–Sat 3 daily; 1hr 30min).

The south and Zeeland

N

GERMANY

BELGIUM

6

THE SOUTH AND ZEELAND

CHAPTER 6

Highlights

✳ **Middelburg** Pleasant maritime town, capital of the watery province of Zeeland. See p.308

✳ **The Walcheren coast** Zeeland's windswept coast has some dramatic footpaths and cycle routes. See p.312

✳ **Delta Expo** The Delta Project – a monumental engineering project to protect the Netherlands from flooding – is commemorated in this outstanding exhibition. See p.319

✳ **Carnival at Bergen-op-Zoom** If you're around in February, don't miss the country's most exuberant carnival. See p.323

✳ **Breda** Pretty little town with a stunning Gothic cathedral. See p.323

✳ **'s Hertongenbosch** This lively market town has a picturesque old quarter of alleys and little bridges. See p.328

✳ **Roermond** A popular holiday spot, Roermond makes a good base for exploring the nearby lakes on the Maasplassen and woods of the National Park De Meinweg. See p.337

✳ **Maastricht** Alluringly cosmopolitan city in the far south, squashed between the Belgian and German borders. See p.341

✳ **South Limburg** The region around Maastricht has some scenic cycle routes amid the gentle hills. See p.349

△ Limburg landscape

The south and Zeeland

Three widely disparate provinces make up the southern Netherlands. **Zeeland** is a scattering of villages and towns whose wealth, survival and sometimes destruction have long depended on the vagaries of the sea. Secured only in 1986, when the dykes and sea walls of the **Delta Project** were finally completed, many settlements seem held in suspended animation from a richer past, like the regional market centre of **Middelburg** and the small wool settlement of **Veere**.

As you head across the arc of towns of **Noord-Brabant** the landscape slowly fills out, rolling into a rougher countryside of farmland and forests, unlike the precise rectangles of neighbouring provinces. Though the change is subtle, there's a difference in the people here, too – less formal and for the most part Catholic, a fact manifest in the magnificent churches of **Breda** and **'s-Hertogenbosch**. But it's in solidly Catholic Limburg that a difference in character is really felt.

Continental rather than Dutch, **Limburg** has only been part of the Netherlands since the 1830s, but way before then the presence of Charlemagne's court at neighbouring Aachen greatly influenced the identity of the region. As Frankish emperor, Charlemagne had a profound effect on early medieval Europe, revitalizing Roman traditions and looking to the south for inspiration in art and architecture. Some of these great buildings remain, like **Maastricht**'s St Servaas. Indeed, the city is far and away the highlight of the province, with its unique blend of Catholic history and modern day cosmopolitan panache. As Belgium and Germany press closer, the landscape steepens sharply and you're within sight of the Netherlands' first and only hills.

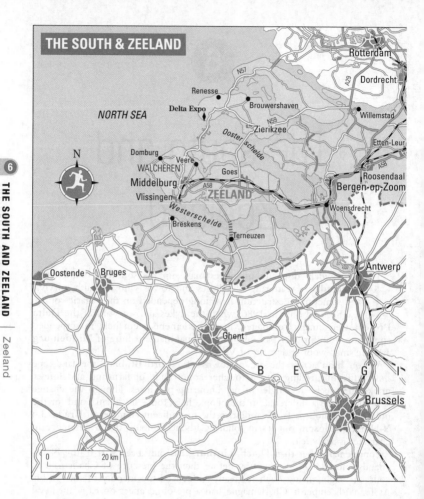

Zeeland

Luctor et Emergo, reads **Zeeland**'s slogan: "I struggle and I emerge", a reference to the eternal battle waged with the sea. As its name suggests, the southwestern corner of the Netherlands is bound as much by water as by land. Comprising three main peninsulas submerged by the delta of the Rijn (Rhine), the Schelde and the Maas, each consists of a cluster of islands and semi-islands linked by kilometres of dykes. This concrete web not only gives protection from flooding but also forms the main lines of communication between each slither of land. The northernmost landmass, **Goeree-Overflakkee**, a little

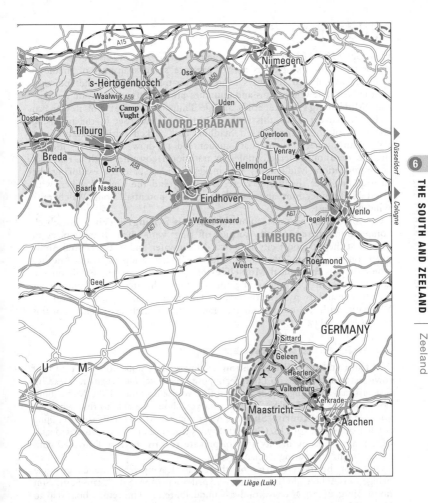

▲ Düsseldorf

▲ Cologne

▼ Liège (Luik)

south of Rotterdam, is connected by two dams to **Schouwen-Duiveland**, while further south are Noord and Zuid **Beveland**, the western tip of which, site of Middelburg and traversed by a narrow canal, is **Walcheren**. Furthest south of all is **Zeeuws Vlaanderen**, lying across the blustery waters of the Westerschelde on the Belgian mainland.

Before the Delta Project (see p.318) secured the area, silting up and fear of the sea's encroachment had prevented any large towns developing; Zeeland remains a condensed area of low dunes and nature reserves, popular with holidaymakers escaping the cramped conurbations nearby. The province also has more sun than anywhere else in the Netherlands: the winds blow the clouds away, with spectacular sunsets guaranteed, beams of sunlight puncturing fast-moving clouds. Getting around is easy, with bus services making up for the lack of north–south train connections, though undoubtedly the best way to see these islands is to **cycle**, using **Middelburg** as a base and venturing out to the surrounding smaller towns.

Middelburg

Compact **MIDDELBURG**, the largest town in Zeeland, is by any reckoning the most likeable. Its streets preserve some snapshots of medieval Holland, its cobbled alleyways echo the sea-trading days of the sixteenth century, and a few museums and churches provide targets for your wanderings. Middelburg's centre holds a large Thursday **market** and if you can only make it for a day, this is the best time to visit. Set to the imposing backdrop of the reconstructed Stadhuis and packed with local produce, it's an atmospheric event that's guaranteed to draw a crowd – including, on occasion, elderly couples in traditional costume. With a range of accommodation, Middelburg also makes an ideal base for exploring the surrounding area, including Veere, Domburg and the Delta Project, with good bus connections and excellent cycling potential along Walcheren's windswept coast.

One of the town's most colourful **festivals** is **Ringrijderij**, a horseback competition where riders try to pick off rings with lances. It takes place in August at the Koepoort city gate near Molenwater, and in the central Abdijplein on one day in July. Check with the Tourist Shop for dates. Another major draw is the annual **Mosselfeesten** (ⓦwww.mosselfeesten.nl) on the last weekend in July, celebrating the arrival of the fresh black mussels, of which Zeeland is particularly proud. The festival takes place around the Vlasmarkt with live music and restaurants offering their own version of this regional speciality.

Arrival and information

The **train station** and **bus station** are just a short walk from the centre of town, across the bridge on Loskade, opposite the hotel *Du Commerce*. Head up Segeersstraat and Lange Delft and you find yourself on the Markt. Middelburg does not have an official VVV office, but you should be able to find whatever you need at the **Tourist Shop** at Markt 65/C (Mon–Fri 9.30am–5.30pm, Sat 9.30am–5pm; ☎0118/674 300, ⓦwww.touristshop.nl), which has details of summer events in the city, a list of **private rooms** and is well stocked with cycling maps for touring Zeeland's coast.

Open-top **boats** offer trips on the canals, leaving from the Lange Viele bridge on Achter de Houttuinen (April–Oct Mon–Sat 11am–5pm, Sun noon–5pm; €5.50; ⓦwww.rondvaartmiddelburg.nl). The return boat trip to Veere (May–Sept daily 10.15am & 2pm; €11.80) leaves from near the train station. The Tourist Shop has a **guided walking tour** (April–Oct daily except Fri 1.30pm; €4.50), which leaves from their office and lasts an hour and a half, taking in the city's main landmarks. **Horse-drawn carriage rides** operate from Nieuwe Burg 38–40 (June–Sept Mon–Sat 11.30am–5pm, Sun 1–5pm; €3; 20min).

Accommodation

Most of Middelburg's **hotels** and **pensions** are just minutes from the Markt. There is not an awful lot to choose from, so it's wise to book in advance, especially in summer.

The nearest **campsite**, *Camping Middelburg*, Koninginnelaan 55 (☎0118/625 395, ⓦwww.campingmiddelburg.nl; April–Oct), is about 2km out of town: head down Zandstraat and Langeviele Weg, or take bus #53 of #55 (every 30min) from the station.

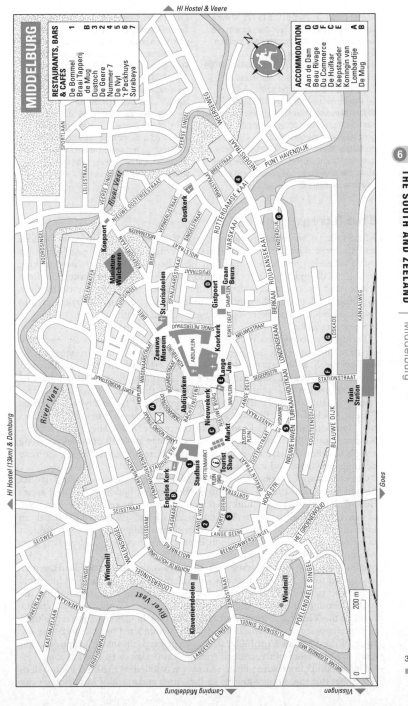

MIDDELBURG

RESTAURANTS, BARS & CAFÉS

De Bommel	1
Braai Tapperij de Mug	B
Dustoch	3
De Geere	2
Nummer 7	4
De Nyl	5
't Packhuys	6
Surabaya	7

ACCOMMODATION

Aan de Dam	D
Beau Rivage	G
Du Commerce	F
De Huifkar	C
Kaepstander	E
Koningin van Lombardije	A
De Mug	B

HI Hostel & Veere

HI Hostel (13km) & Domburg

Camping Middelburg

Vlissingen

Goes

Train Station

200 m

309

Aan de Dam Dam 31 ☎0118/643 773, ⓦwww
.aandedamhotel.nl. A well-kept treasure with only
seven suites, all in different styles, and a garden
that's a real oasis in summer. ❷

Beau Rivage Loskade 19 ☎0118/638 060, ⓕ629
673. This small hotel has only nine rooms, all
furnished with old Chesterfields. ❸

Du Commerce Loskade 1 ☎0118/636 051,
ⓦwww.hotelducommerce.nl. You really can't miss
this hotel, right in front of the train station, with
great views over the canal. ❹

De Huifkar Markt 19 ☎0118/612 998, ⓦwww
.hoteldehuifkar.nl. Located above the cafés of the
Markt, this hotel can be noisy. Book ahead as they
only have six rooms. ❷

Kaepstander Koorkerkhof 10 ☎0018/640 767,
ⓦwww.kaepstander.nl. Small rooms, but with
great views of the Abbey Churches and a relaxing
café downstairs. Breakfast is very simple. ❶

Koningin van Lombardije Blindehoek 12 ☎ &
ⓕ0118/637 099. The cheapest option in town is
the friendly *Koningin van Lombardije*, which also
boasts a gargantuan breakfast. ❶

De Mug Vlasmarkt 54–56 ☎0118/614 851,
ⓦwww.demug.nl. Four spacious rooms
are located in a completely renovated building,
also housing a restaurant, bar and shop with local
specialities, and with friendly owners who'll make
you feel immediately at home. ❸

The Town

Middelburg is an appealing town to explore, small enough to cover on foot
and scattered with architectural clues to its rich, sea-trading past. The town
owed its early growth to its position on a bend in the River Arne, making
it easy to defend. The slight elevation gave the settlement protection from
the sea and its streets slope down to the harbour, protecting the centre from
flooding. Look out for the surviving stone blocks at the end of Brakstraat, into
which wooden planks were slotted then bolstered with sand banks, acting as
a temporary dyke.

Though its **abbey** was founded in 1120, Middelburg's isolation restricted
its development until the late Middle Ages, when, being at the western
end of the Scheldt estuary, it began to get rich off the back of Antwerp,
Bruges and Ghent. Conducting its own trade in wool and cloth, it became
both the market and administrative centre of the region. The town's street
names – Houtkaai ("Timber Dock"), Korendijk ("Grain Dyke"), Bierkaai
("Beer Dock") – reveal how diverse its trade became, while house names
like "London" and "Samarkand" tell of the routes Middelburg's traders plied.
Kuiperspoort ("Barrelmaker's Port") is an alleyway off Rouaansekaai along
which warehouses have been impressively restored, many of which are now
occupied by artists and musicians.

Once a town of wood and thatch, Middelburg's newly acquired wealth
bought bricks and tiles to clothe its timber-framed buildings. In "de Laurier
Boom", Rouaansekaai 2, chunky wooden rafters can be seen on the first floor,
as can exposed oak beams at Spanjaardstraat 3a and 49. Indeed, with oak an
increasingly scarce and valued material for shipbuilding – supplies were sought
out from as far as the Baltic – inhabitants even recycled hulls and rigging,
salvaged from old or damaged ships, to build their homes.

Most interesting buildings date from this period, though the **Stadhuis**, generally agreed to be Zeeland's finest, is a wonderfully eclectic mix of architectural
styles. The towering Gothic facade is especially magnificent, dating from the
mid-fifteenth century and designed by the Keldermans family from Mechelen.
Inside is the **Vleeshal**, a former meat hall that now houses changing exhibitions
of contemporary art, which can be visited on conducted tours. A forty-minute
tour of the Stadhuis (April–Oct daily except Fri 11.30am & 3.15pm; €3.95)
takes in the mayor's office, council chambers and various reception rooms.

The Stadhuis's impressive pinnacled tower was added in 1520, but it's as well to
remember that this, along with the Stadhuis itself and much of Middelburg's city

△ Middelburg's Stadhuis and market

centre, is only a reconstruction of the original. On May 17, 1940, the city was all but flattened by German bombing in the same series of raids that destroyed Rotterdam. In 1944, in an attempt to isolate German artillery in Vlissingen, Walcheren's sea defences were breached, which resulted in severe flood damage to Middelburg's already treacherous streets. Restoration was a long and difficult process, but so successful that you can only occasionally tell that the city's buildings have been patched up. Bricks were made locally from sea clays, which when fired in the kiln, salts form a natural glaze of reds, greens or yellows; these hues can be seen on the corner of Nieuwstraat and Korte Delft, glinting in the sun.

The Abdijkerken and around

Middelburg's most distinctive tower, that of the **Abdijkerken** ("Abbey Churches") on Onderdentoren, collapsed under German bombing, destroying the churches below. Today the abbey complex – really three churches in one (April–Oct Mon–Fri 10.30am–5pm; May–Aug also Sat & Sun 1.30–5pm; free) – is quite bare inside, considering it's been around since the twelfth century. There's a reason for this: Middelburg was an early convert to Protestantism following the uprising against the Spanish, and in 1574 William the Silent's troops threw out the Premonstratensian monks and converted the abbey to secular use. Occupied by various unlikely syndicates, including a gun manufacturer and a mint, the abbey's three churches were then adapted back to Protestant worship.

The **Nieuwe Kerk** has an organ case of 1692, and the **Wandel Kerk** the outrageously triumphalistic tomb of admirals Jan and Cornelis Evertsen, brothers killed fighting in a naval battle against the English in 1666. The **Koor Kerk**, on the eastern side of the tower, retains the oldest decoration, including a Nicolai organ of 1478. Best of all is climbing the 207 steps of the **tower** (April–June & Sept–Oct Mon–Sat 11am–4pm; July & Aug daily 11am–5pm; €3.50), known locally as *Lange Jan* (Long John). In clear weather, the view from its 91-metre summit across over Walcheren and as far as the Zeelandbrug

Cycling around the Walcheren

Countless cycling options are available to make the most of the Walcheren's stunning coastline, with plenty of refreshments en route. With limited transport for bikes, most routes are best completed as loops. As a rule of thumb, red cycleway signs indicate utility paths, often parallel to a main road, while the green signs favour more scenic alternatives.

Possible day-trips include cycling west to **Domburg**, picking up signs to the Domburg HI hostel and continuing through the woods to **Breezand**. A cycleway follows the polder to **Veere**, from where you can ride alongside the Walcheren canal, cutting back to Middelburg. Alternatively, pick up the same canal out of town to **Vlissingen**, joining the cycleway that runs between dune and woodland to **Zoutelande** and **Westkapelle**: there's a fabulous stretch of dyke to cycle along, in the direction of Domburg, with spectacular sunsets out to sea and a photogenic lighthouse. A red-signposted cycle path leads directly back to Middelburg.

If Zeeland's well-founded reputation for blustery winds is putting you off, pay a visit to one of Middelburg's more unusual factories. **M5**, at Nieuwe Kleverskerkseweg 23 (℡0118/628 759, ⓦwww.m5-ligfietsen.com), is a company at the cutting edge of bicycle technology: it specializes in **recumbents**, or *ligfietsen* in Dutch. With their low-slung riding position, recumbents are not only fun and comfortable to ride but will also slice through Zeeland's fiercest headwinds – though it might take a few minutes to learn to ride one. You can rent from M5 for around €20 a day (plus €150 deposit), with significant discounts if renting for a week or more. Otherwise, you can **rent bikes** from the train station. Alternatively, head for Delta Cycles at Zusterplein 8 (down the alleyway next to the ING bank on Marktplein; ℡0118/639 245), which is part of a project that places people with mental disabilities in employment. Single-speed bikes are €5 per day.

and the eastern Scheldt gives a good sense of how vulnerable the province is to the sea. The **carillon** of *Lange Jan* plays every quarter-hour, with additional concerts year-round.

At the rear of the abbey, housed in what were once the monks' dormitories, the **Zeeuws Museum** (closed for renovation at time of writing; check with Tourist Shop; ⓦwww.zeeuwsmuseum.nl) holds a mixed bag of collections and finds from the Zeeland area. The museum has a tiny but choice collection of twentieth-century paintings by Mesdag, Jan and Charley Toorop and other local artists. There are also some lively tapestries, commissioned by the local authorities between 1591 and 1604 to celebrate the naval battles against the Spanish, and a comprehensive display of local costumes.

The **Roosevelt Study Centre**, Abdij 8 (Mon–Fri 9.30am–12.30pm & 1.30–4.30pm; ⓦwww.roosevelt.nl), a centre for the study of twentieth-century American history (one of the largest in Europe), has a permanent exhibition on presidents Theodore and Franklin Delano Roosevelt and the latter's remarkable wife Eleanor.

East of the abbey, **Damplein** was restored to its original breadth by the demolition of a couple of rows of houses. It forms a quieter focus for bars than the Markt and is the site of the **Graanbeurs**, a grain exchange rebuilt in the nineteenth century and today containing some intriguing and humorous stone plaques by international artists – a project known as "Podio del Mondo per l'Arte".

Directly north of Damplein on Molenwater, **Miniature Walcheren** (April–Oct daily 10am–6pm; July & Aug till 7pm; €8; ⓦwww.miniatuurwalcheren .nl) has scaled-down models of Walcheren island's best buildings that might entertain kids for an hour or so. Further east, the distinctive profile of the domed, octagonal **Oostkerk** (May–Oct Thurs 10am–4pm; free) stands high above the surrounding suburbs, near the main road to Veere; built in 1647 to designs by Pieter Post and others, it was one of the first churches in the Netherlands expressly for Protestant use. What's more, its construction was financed by taxes raised on beer, a profitable commodity to tax: in seventeenth-century Middelburg, water was so dirty that the whole population, children included, drank light beer instead.

Kloveniersdoelen

While the streets around the Abdijkerken and Stadhuis are the most atmospheric, it's worth walking to the western edge of town to reach the landmark of the **Kloveniersdoelen** at the end of Langeviele. Built in 1607 in exuberant Flemish Renaissance style, this was the home of the city's civic guard, the Arquebusiers, until the end of the eighteenth century, later becoming the local headquarters of the East India Company, and later still a military hospital. Restored in 1969 (as you might guess if you spot the weather vane), it's now a recital hall and is renowned for presenting new and experimental music. A short walk to the north and south of the Kloveniersdoelen, by the edge of Middelburg's old star-shaped defensive canal, are a couple of eighteenth-century **windmills**: De Hoop mill to the south was once a barley peeling mill; De Seismolen to the north a cereal mill, though it's not possible to enter either today.

Eating and drinking

Vlasmarkt, running northwest of Markt, has Middelburg's widest selection of **restaurants**. Most other restaurants are situated on or around Markt and many are tourist-orientated and pricey for what you get. **Bars** and **cafés** are also concentrated on or near the Markt.

On Thursdays the **market** stalls supply limitless cheap and tasty snacks, especially fresh fish and seafood. Look out for *bolus,* a circular sweetbread brought to Middleburg by Portuguese Jews, best served hot with butter and a cup of coffee.

De Bommel Markt 85. This is the pick of the bars along here, although there's not much to choose between them at the weekends; it's open seven days a week and is convenient for a quick bite.

Braai Tapperij De Mug Vlasmarkt 56. Good Dutch–French cooking (mussels in season) at moderate prices, an excellent array of beers, and occasional live jazz, all in an old-fashioned setting decorated with old cognac barrels.

Dustoch Korte Geere 16. This colourful and cheap café is part of a project placing people with mental disabilities in jobs (as with Delta Cycles; see box on p.312), and includes a children's menu.

De Geere Lange Viele 55. Daily specialities for €8.50, and cheap beer, are what's on offer at this centrally located café with red-brick walls and smart chandeliers.

Nummer 7 Rotterdamsekai 7. This cosy restaurant with only a few tables serves a three-course meal for €23.75, including dishes like red snapper and monkfish combined with fresh seasonal products.

De Nyl St Janstraat 45. Don't expect a romantic dinner, but if your budget is tight try *De Nyl,* which serves decent *shwarma,* pizza and chicken in an unappetizing atmosphere.

't Packhuys Kinderdijk 82. Located in an old warehouse with a great waterfront terrace, this maritime-themed restaurant serves fabulous food like lobster soup, salads and lambs racks. Mains around €19.

Surabaya Stationstraat 20. A slightly run-down Indonesian restaurant, specializing in Javan food, with reasonably priced *rijsttafels,* and an €18 evening buffet.

Listings

Bookshop De Drukkerij, Markt 51, has a wide selection of books, Internet access and a popular café centred around a communal table.

Markets General market on the Markt is on Thursday (8.30am–4pm); there's also a book and curio market on Monday (April–Oct, same hours). Vismarkt has a flea market on the first Sat

of the month (except Jan) 9am–4pm, and an art and antique market in summer (June–Aug Thurs 9am–4pm).

Police Achter de Houttuinen 10 ☎0118/688 000.

Post office Lange Noordstraat 48 (Mon 10am–5.30pm, Tues–Fri 9am–5.30pm, Sat 9am–5pm).

Taxi Taxicentrale ☎0118/612 600 or 601 100.

Vlissingen

VLISSINGEN (Flushing), 5km south of Middleburg, was previously an important ferry terminus, but its role as a hub for transport to Belgium has been reduced by the completion of the tunnel between Ellewoutsdijk and Terneuzen a little upstream to the east. There's not an awful lot to see in the town, although a new maritime museum warrants a couple of hours of exploration, and the shipping trade that plies the choppy Westerschelde estuary has an appeal of its own.

The town centre itself is less attractive, with the unremarkable **St Jacobskerk** on Oude Markt (hours vary; free; ⓦ www.sintjacobskerk.nl) and the improbably named **Cornelia Quackhofje**, an eighteenth-century almshouse for sailors just north of the Lange Zelke shopping precinct.

For more atmosphere, head for the **harbour**. Popular with Dutch and German tourists in the summer and school holidays, it's awash with pavement cafés and fresh fish and chip stalls. The **Zeeuws Maritiem "Muzeeum"** at Nieuwendijk 11 (Mon–Fri 10am–5pm, Sat & Sun 1–5pm; €7; ⓦ www.muzeeum.nl) is the place to gen up on Zeeland's rich maritime tradition. The museum is divided into four themes – the sea, trade, glory and adventure. Multimedia presentations (in Dutch) explain the sea's crucial role in shaping Zeeland's livelihood, while excellent audiovisuals reconstruct scenes of naval battles to dramatic effect.

Displays include wares shipped along the trading routes of the Dutch East Indies – nutmeg, ginger, salt, tea, silver, porcelain and even bricks. A thriving port in the Golden Age, Vlissingen was the hometown of Admiral Michiel de Ruyters, famous throughout the Netherlands – his face even appears on Pilsner bottles – though the town was renowned too for spawning its fair share of marauding pirates. Not that some ships needed pillaging: so overloaded was the Asia-bound *'t Vliegent Hart* in 1735, it didn't even make it further than the Westerschelde; most of its cargo was retrieved in 1982 and is now on display in the museum.

Families will enjoy **Het Arsenaal**, on Arsenaalplein (July & Aug daily 10am–8pm; hours vary outside season; last admission 2hr before closing; €11; Ⓦwww.arsenaal.com), a theme park where you can go on a simulated sea voyage, climb an observation tower and walk on a mocked-up sea bed among tanks of sharks.

The blustery **walk** along the Nieuwendijk offers views of the enormous vessels that sail the Westerschelde. Keeping to a narrow, often tortuous path, these enormous container ships must negotiate the shallow waters and shifting sandbanks that frequently reveal centuries-old wrecks. Further round the harbour, the promenade has a pleasant seaside feel, with a beach at the end. Alternatively, you can rent a bike from the train station next to the ferry terminal – it has a wide selection, including recumbents – and continue past the promenade on the green-signposted cycle path to Dishoek and Zouteland; along the way there are plenty of opportunities to lock your bike and hike up and over the dunes, emerging onto a beach that runs for miles.

Practicalities

The **VVV** is at Oude Markt 3 (July & Aug Mon 11am–5.30pm, Tues–Fri 10am–5.30pm, Sat 10am–5pm; Sept–June Mon 1–5pm, Tues–Sat 10am–5pm; closed lunch; ☎0118/422 190, Ⓦwww.vvvvlissingen.nl). It has a list of **pensions**, including the nearby *Pension Marijke*, Coosje Buskenstraat 88 (☎0118/415 062, Ⓦwww.pensionmarijke.nl; ❶), with simple rooms, and *Belgische Loodsen Societeit*, on the seafront near the end of Nieuwendijk at Boulevard de Ruyter 4 (☎0118/413 608, Ⓦwww.bsoos.nl; ❶–❷), with a fabulous view of ships passing by; the VVV also has information on local cycling routes.

The West Zeeland coast

The coastline west of Middelburg offers some of the Netherlands' finest beaches and makes for excellent walking and cycling country, although on

Vlissingen to Breskens by ferry

The 6.6km **tunnel** beneath the Westerschelde, linking Ellewoutsdijk and Terneuzen, is open 24 hours a day; the toll for cars is €4.40. The **ferry** across the Westerschelde between Vlissingen and Breskens (takes 20min) carries foot passengers and bicycles. Buses #56, #57 and #58 from Vlissingen town centre, via the train station, run to the port. Ferry departures from Vlissingen are daily (every 30min 5.50am–9.50pm), and there are buses on the other side from Breskens to the Belgian town of Bruges. In the opposite direction, the ferry departs Breskens daily (every thirty minutes 6.20am–10.20pm). Tickets are €2.45 per person single way, with an 80c surcharge for bicycles. Check Ⓦwww.bba.nl for up-to-date information.

midsummer weekends parts of it virtually disappear beneath the crowds of Dutch and German holidaymakers. Bus #53 from Middelburg station (hourly) runs through **OOSTKAPELLE**, notable for its striking church tower, before passing the thirteenth-century **Kasteel Westhove**, now home to the fine Domburg **HI hostel** (☎0118/581 254, ⓦwww.stayokay.com; dorms €26.75) – complete with moat and set amid a nature reserve. You can rent bikes from here (€5/day). Next door at Duinvlietweg 6, the **Zeeuws Biologisch Museum** (May–Oct daily 10am–5pm; Nov-April Wed–Sun noon–5pm; €4 in summer, €5 in winter; ⓦwww.zbm-westhove.nl) has an aquarium and displays on local flora and fauna. Oostkapelle's **VVV** is at Lantsheerstraat 1 (hours vary but usually Mon–Sat 9.30am–4.30pm; closed lunch; ☎0118/582 910, ⓦwww.vvvzeeland.nl).

A couple of kilometres further on, **DOMBURG**, 14km northwest of Middelburg, is the area's principal resort, a favourite haunt for artists since early last century when Jan Toorop gathered together a group of like-minded painters (including, for a while, Piet Mondrian), inspired by the peaceful scenery and the fine quality of the light. Toorop built a pavilion to exhibit the paintings and the building has been recreated as the **Marie Tak van Poortvliet Museum Domburg**, Ooststraat 10a (April–Nov 1–5pm; €2.50; ⓦwww.marietakvanpoortvlietmuseumdomburg.nl), where exhibitions display works by members of the group. Parts of the Domburg church, including the tower, date from the thirteenth century, although it's off limits to visitors most of the time. On the whole, though, you'd come here to walk on the dunes and through the woods or to cycle the coast path. An easy ride 7km west of Domburg is **Westkapelle**, a quieter beach resort with a picturesque lighthouse and a critical spot where the dyke was breached during the 1953 flood.

Domburg's **VVV** is at Schuitvlotstraat 32 (April–June, Sept & Oct Mon–Sat 9.30am–12.30pm & 1–5pm; July & Aug Mon–Sat 9.30am–6pm, Sun noon–4pm; Nov–March Mon–Fri 9.30am–12.30pm & 1–4.30pm; ☎0118/581 342, ⓦwww.vvvzeeland.nl); ask the bus driver to drop you nearby. They'll help with accommodation and provide you with a map of the village. Staff can recommend dozens of **pensions** – *Duinlust* is a safe bet at Badhuisweg 28 (☎ & ⓕ0118/582 943, ⓦwww.hotelduinlust.nl; ❶), walking distance from the beach. There are several **campsites**, the nearest being *Hof Domburg* at Schelpweg 7 (☎0118/588 200, ⓕ583 668), a few minutes' walk west of town. Domburg has plenty of simple **cafés**: try the great pizzas at *Pizzeria Milano* on 't Groentje 11. *Tramzicht*, on Stationstraat 8, is the best bar with themed parties attracting a young crowd. The other resorts also have plenty of pensions and campsites, although you may need to book rooms through one of the VVVs at busy times.

Veere

Some 8km northeast of Middelburg, **VEERE** is a picturesque little town by the banks of the Veerse that makes an ideal day-trip. Today it's a centre for all things maritime, its small harbour jammed with yachts and its cafés packed with weekend admirals, but a handful of buildings and a large church point to a time when Veere was rich and quite independent of other, similar towns in Zeeland. To reach Veere from Middelburg, catch bus #54, which runs hourly, or rent a bike from Middelburg train station (€7.50) and take either the cycle path beside the main road or the circuitous but more picturesque route from the north of the town.

Veere made its wealth through a fortuitous Scottish connection: in 1444 Wolfert VI van Borssele, the lord of Veere, married Mary, daughter of James I of Scotland. As part of the dowry, van Borssele was granted a monopoly on trade with Scottish wool merchants; in return, Scottish merchants living in Veere were granted special privileges. A number of their houses still stand, best of which are those on the dock facing the harbour: *Het Lammetje* (The Lamb) and *De Struys* (The Ostrich), dating from the mid-sixteenth century, were combined offices, homes and warehouses for the merchants; they now house the **Museum Schotse Huizen** (April–Oct daily 1–5pm; €4; Ⓦwww.schotsehuizen.nl), a rather lifeless collection of local costumes, old books, atlases and furniture, along with an exhibit devoted to fishing. Elsewhere there are plenty of Gothic buildings, whose rich decoration leaves you in no doubt that the Scottish wool trade earned a bundle for the sixteenth- and seventeenth-century burghers of Veere: many of the buildings (which are usually step-gabled with distinctive green and white shutters) are embellished with whimsical details that play on the owners' names or their particular line of business. The **Stadhuis** at Markt 5 (open by arrangement; ℡0118/583 615) is similarly opulent, dating from the 1470s, with an out-of-scale Renaissance tower added a century later. Its facade is decorated with statues of the lords of Veere and their wives (Wolfert VI is third from the left) and, inside, a small museum occupies what was formerly the courtroom, pride of place going to a goblet that once belonged to Maximilian of Burgundy.

Of all Veere's buildings the **Grote Kerk** (May–Sept daily 11am–5pm; €2.50) seems to have suffered most: finished in 1560, it was badly damaged by fire a century later and restoration removed much of its decoration. In 1808 invading British troops used the church as a hospital and three years later Napoleon's army converted it into barracks and stables, destroying the stained glass, bricking up the windows and adding five floors in the nave. Despite all this damage, the church's blunt 42-metre **tower** (same hours and ticket; last admission 4.30pm) adds a glowering presence to the landscape, especially when seen across the misty polder fields. According to the original design, the tower was to have been three times higher, but even as it stands there's a great view from the top, back to the pinnacled skyline of Middelburg and out across the breezy Veerse Meer.

Veere fell from importance with the decline of the wool trade. The opening of the Walcheren canal in the nineteenth century, linking the town to Middelburg and Vlissingen, gave it a stay of execution, but the construction of the Veersegatdam and Zandkreekdam in the 1950s finally sealed the port to seagoing vessels, and simultaneously created a freshwater lake ideal for watersports.

Practicalities

The **VVV**, Oudestraat 28 (April, May & Oct Mon, Fri & Sat 1.30–4.30pm; June & Sept daily noon–4pm; July & Aug daily 10am–12.30pm & 1–4.30pm; ℡0118/501 365, Ⓦwww.vvvzeeland.nl), can advise on the rental of all types of watercraft and has details of **private rooms**. The cheaper of Veere's two **hotels** is *'t Waepen van Veere*, Markt 23–27 (℡0118/501 231, Ⓦwww.waepenvanveere.nl; ❶–❷), with a pricy restaurant, while the *De Campveerse Toren*, Kade 2, is beautifully situated overlooking the water (℡0118/501 291, Ⓦwww.campveersetoren .nl; ❸). There are a few **cafés** around the Markt including the *Suster Anna Pannekoekhuis* at Markt 8, which serves pancakes, sandwiches and cakes.

The Delta Project

On February 1, 1953, a combination of an exceptionally high spring tide and powerful northwesterly winds drove the North Sea over the dykes to **flood** much of Zeeland. The results were catastrophic: 1855 people drowned, 47,000 homes and 500km of dykes were destroyed and some of the country's most fertile agricultural land was ruined by salt water. Towns as far as Bergen-op-Zoom and Dordrecht were flooded and Zeeland's road and rail network was wrecked. The government's response was immediate and on a massive scale. After patching up the breached dykes, work was begun on the **Delta Project**, one of the largest engineering schemes the world has ever seen and one of phenomenal complexity and expense.

The plan was to ensure the safety of Zeeland by radically shortening and strengthening its coastline. The major estuaries and inlets would be dammed, thus preventing unusually high tides surging inland to breach the thousands of kilometres of small dykes. Where it was impractical to build a dam – such as across the Westerschelde or Nieuwe Waterweg, which would have closed the seaports of Antwerp and Rotterdam respectively – secondary dykes were to be reinforced. New roads across the top of the dams would improve communications to Zeeland and Zuid-Holland and the freshwater lakes that formed behind the dams would enable precise control of the water table of the Zeeland islands.

It took thirty years for the Delta Project to be completed. The smaller, secondary dams – the **Veersegat**, **Haringvliet** and **Brouwershaven** – were built first to provide protection from high tides as quickly as possible, a process that also enabled engineers to learn as they went along. In 1968, work began on the largest dam, intended to close the Oosterschelde estuary that forms the outlet of the Maas, Waal and Rijn rivers. It soon ran into intense opposition from environmental groups, who pointed out that the mud flats were an important breeding ground for birds, while the estuary itself was a nursery for plaice, sole and other North Sea fish. Local fishermen, too, saw their livelihoods in danger: if the Oosterschelde were closed the oyster, mussel and lobster beds would be destroyed, representing a huge loss to the region's economy.

Schouwen-Duiveland

The Storm Surge Barrier spans the mouth of the Oosterschelde estuary over to **SCHOUWEN-DUIVELAND**. Most of the Dutch and German tourists who come here head directly to the western corner for the acres of beach, pine forest and dune between **Burgh-Haamstede** and **Renesse**, two villages situated 6km apart. In the summer, this western flank of the island is packed with families and predominantly young holidaymakers, making the most of its waterborne activities. **Zierikzee** further east is a more traditional affair, a miniature Middelburg that makes an appealing base for exploring the island, with some fine trips through the countryside and one of Europe's longest (and perhaps windiest) bridges nearby.

If you're coming for peace and quiet, you should steer clear of the school holidays. Travel over the season's bookends in June and September and you'll find you have much of the long, pristine beaches to yourself, though the weather can be varied: facilities dwindle with the approach of autumn, and storms blot the sky.

Renesse and around

En route to Renesse, the village of **BURGH-HAAMSTEDE** is well placed to explore the Beschermd Natuur-Monument around Westerschouwen, a large

The environmental and fishing lobbies argued that strengthening the estuary dykes would provide adequate protection; the water board and agricultural groups raised the emotive spectre of the 1953 flood. In the end a compromise was reached, and in 1976 work began on the **Stormvloedkering** ("Storm Surge Barrier"), a gate that would stay open under normal tidal conditions, allowing water to flow in and out of the estuary, but close ahead of potentially destructive high tides.

Delta Expo

It's on the Stormvloedkering, completed in 1986, that the fascinating **Delta Expo** (April–Oct daily 10am–5.30pm; €16; Nov–March Wed–Sun 10am–5pm; €10.50; ⓦwww.neeltjejans.nl), signposted as Waterland Neeltje Jans, is housed. Only once you're inside the Expo, though, do you get an idea of the scale of the project. It's best to start with the half-hour video presentation before taking in the exhibition, which is divided into three areas: the historical background of the Netherlands' water management problems; the technological developments that enabled the country to protect itself; the environmental consequences of applying the technologies and the solutions that followed. The Surge Barrier (and the Delta Project as a whole) has been a triumphant success: computer simulations predict most high tides, but if an unpredicted rise does occur, the sluice gates close automatically in a matter of minutes.

Transport to the Delta Expo is easy: from Middelburg take bus #133 (twice hourly in summer) from Langevieleweg on the west side of town, or you can easily cycle there (it takes 1hr 30min), following national cycleway LF16 (noord), alongside open beaches and dunes, past wind turbines and onto the storm barrier itself; there are ample opportunities to peer into the sluice gates and appreciate the full scale of the project. Allow for blustery winds on the way back. From Rotterdam, take the metro to Zuidplein and then bus #133; tell the driver you want the Waterland stop.

expanse of forest and dune run by the Staatsbosbeheer. With a network of bicycle tracks and walking trails, it's a lovely spot to get lost in for a couple of hours – which is probably what will happen, as the signposting is pretty confusing. You can rent a geared bike for €6.70 a day from Fietswereld Bouwman, Noordstraat 17.

△ The Delta Project

About 6km north, **RENESSE** is a modern sprawl of bungalows, set just a kilometre from the beach, that makes a more appealing base. Popular with the surfing and windsurfing crowd, its sixteen-kilometre beach is divided in summer into sectors, catering for families, surfers, kite-flyers and naturists. A free open-top electric **bus** (9am–7pm) plies the length of the beach, linking hotels, campsites and the "Transferium" – the modern bus station on the edge of town that offers changing rooms, showers and bike rental, in an attempt to encourage holidaymakers to abandon their cars at the free car park alongside. Parking at the beach is limited to two hours. **Surfboards** cost €35 a day from Windsurfing Renesse, De Zoom 15 (ⓦwww.windsurfingrenesse.nl); they'll also provide lessons. Windsurfs can be rented too, but the best spot for windsurfing is at the Brouwersdam, 8km away. Jonker Funsports, Zeeanemoonweg 8 (ⓦwww.jonkerfunsports.nl), rents out blades and protective gear. These shops are often only open on the weekends in winter.

The area is teeming with hotels, campsites and holiday homes, many of which run B&Bs. If you're planning on visiting over the summer, you should book accommodation well in advance. One **hotel** option, situated walking distance from both town and beach, is *Hotel de Logerij*, Laône 15 (ⓉⒺ0111/462 570, ⓦwww.delogerij.nl; ❷), with simple but clean rooms. The **VVV**, Zeeanemoonweg 4a (Mon–Sat 9am–5pm; hours vary out of season; Ⓣ0900/2020 233, ⓦwww.vvvschouwenduiveland.nl), has a list of available accommodation or try the English website ⓦwww.renesse.nl, which includes lists of accommodation and services. Travel with a tent and you're more likely to find a plot of grass to squeeze onto. The VVV sells an excellent map detailing beach allotment, as well as walking and cycling trails on the island (€3) and has a free booklet, *Toegankelijk Schouwen-Duiveland*, on areas suitable for the disabled or those in wheelchairs.

Surfcentrum

The **Surfcentrum**, at Ossenhoek 1, Kabbellaarsbank (Ⓣ0111/671 480, ⓦwww.brouwersdam.nl), is an invigorating detour from Renesse, with views across the Grevelingenmeer inlet. Reached by bus #104 (ask the driver for the Port Zélande stop), it's situated halfway along the Brouwersdam, linking Schouwen-Duiveland to Goeree-Overflakkee. The centre offers excellent windsurfing on one side, and one of Europe's cleanest beaches on the other – renting a board and wetsuit costs €60 a day, or €90 for a weekend. Tuition, small sailboats and four-bed dorms (€55 per room) are also available.

Zierikzee and around

Schouwen-Duiveland's most interesting town lies to the south. **ZIERIKZEE**'s position at the intersection of shipping routes between England, Flanders and Holland led to it becoming an important port in the late Middle Ages as it traded with the towns of the Hanseatic League. It was also famed for its salt and madder – a root that, when dried and ground, produces a brilliant red dye. Nowadays, it's a picturesque town of narrow cobbled streets and traditional gabled facades, an ideal base for exploring the area.

Encircled by a defensive canal and best entered by one of two sixteenth-century watergates, Zierikzee's centre is small and easily explored, easier still if you arm yourself with a map from the **VVV** at Nieuwe Haven 7 (Mon–Sat 10am–4pm; Ⓣ0111/412 450, ⓦwww.vvvschouwenduiveland.nl). A few minutes' walk from the office, the Gothic **'s Gravensteen** building, Mol 25 (April–Oct Mon–Sat 10am–5pm, Sun noon–5pm; €2), was once the jail and is today home to a maritime museum, although the building is more interesting than the exhibits: the removal of plaster walls from the old prison cells in 1969 uncovered graffiti and drawings by the prisoners, and the basements contain torture chambers and iron cage cells built to contain two prisoners. Zierikzee's **Stadhuis** is easy enough to find – just head for the tall spire on Meelstraat 6. Inside, the **Stadhuismuseum** (May–Oct Mon–Sat 10am–5pm, Sun noon–5pm; €2) has collections of silver, costumes and a regional history exhibition. Also worth seeing is the **Monstertoren** (March–Oct daily 11am–4pm; €2), a tower designed by the Keldermans family on which work was stopped when it reached 97 of its planned 167 metres.

The VVV has details of **private rooms**, including a lovely self-contained apartment at Minderbroederstraat 36–38 (☎0111/416 759; ❶). Other options include the *Pension Klaas Vaak*, Nieuwe Bogerdstraat (☎0111/414 204, ⓦwww .pensionklaasvaak.nl; ❶), with simple rooms but a lovely garden, and the *Hotel Van Oppen China Garden*, Verrenieuwstraat 11 (☎0111/412 288, ⓦwww .hotel-van-oppen.nl; ❷), which offers a bit more luxury. Book early during the summer; like the rest of the island Zierikzee is a magnet for Dutch, German and Belgian tourists. **Bus** #132 shuttles between Goes and Zierikzee in half an hour; it's an hour and a quarter to Rotterdam on twice-hourly bus #133.

Around Zierikzee

If you have your own transport – or rent a bike from Bike Totaal, Weststraat 5 – you have plenty of scope for discovering the surrounding countryside and coastline. **Dreischor**, 8km northeast, makes a pleasant half-day ride. There, the fourteenth-century St Adriaanskirche lies surrounded by a moat and plush green lawns, encircled by a ring of attractive houses. Complete with waddling geese and a restored *travalje* (livery stable), it's an idyllic setting – although busy on weekends. A wander round the Ring will reveal several appealing **B&Bs**, such as the one at Ring 5 (☎0111/406 006; ❶).

Six kilometres out of Zierikzee in the opposite direction, the simple but atmospheric **Watersnoodmuseum**, Weg van de Buitenlandse Pers 5 in Ouwerkerk (Tues–Sun: April–June, Sept & Oct 1–5pm; July & Aug 11am–5pm; €3; ⓦwww.watersnoodmuseum.nl), commemorates the great floods of 1953 (see box on p.318), the catalyst for the massive Delta Project. Atmospherically set in a desolate *caisson*, one of the original concrete bunkers manoeuvred into plugging a break in the dyke, it houses construction machinery used in the 1950s, scale models showing the extent of the damage, old photographs and original newsreel footage beamed onto the wall.

Finally, to put colour in your cheeks you could follow the bike lane over the wind tunnel-like **Zeelandbrug**, a graceful bridge that spans the Oosterschelde south of Zierikzee. Refreshments are available in **Colijnsplaat** on the other side, where you can rest up, having cycled one of the longest bridges in Europe, at 5022m. Prevailing winds will be against you on the way out; expect the journey back to take half the time.

Noord-Brabant

Noord-Brabant, the Netherlands' largest province, stretches from the North Sea to the German border. Woodland and heath form most of the natural scenery, the gently undulating arable land a welcome change from the watery polders of the west. While it's unlikely to form the focus of an itinerary, the instantly likeable provincial capital of **Den Bosch** is well worth a lingering visit. Along with **Breda**, its cobbled and car-free centre enjoys a lively market, pulling crowds that spill into the adjoining streets. In contrast, **Eindhoven** lacks the historic interest of these towns, as hardly anything was spared during the war. It is, however, renowned for its modern architecture and design and has a fairly vibrant nightlife. North of **Tilburg** is the province's other highlight, for kids at least – **Efteling** theme park, which is beautifully set in the woods.

Originally part of the independent Duchy of Brabant, Noord-Brabant was taken over by the Spanish, and eventually split in two when its northern towns joined the revolt against Spain. This northern part was ceded to the United Provinces in 1648; the southern half formed what today are the Belgian provinces of Brabant and Antwerp. As a result, a Catholic influence is still strong here: the region takes its religious festivals seriously and if you're here in February and March, the boozy **carnivals** (especially in **Bergen-op-Zoom** and Den Bosch) are must-sees – indeed, it's difficult to miss them. Towns even change their names for the occasion; Den Bosch becomes Oeteldonk, Eindhoven is Lampegat and people in Bergen-op-Zoom live in Krabbegat during the festivities.

Bergen-op-Zoom

BERGEN-OP-ZOOM, only 30km north of Antwerp, is an untidy town, a jumble of buildings old and new that are the consequence of being shunted between various European powers from the sixteenth century onwards. In 1576 Bergen-op-Zoom sided with the United Provinces against the Spanish and as a result was under near-continuous siege until 1622. This war-ravaged theme continued: the French bombarded the city in 1747 and took it again in 1795, though it managed to withstand a British attack in 1814. Unless you're coming for the town's famous February carnival, there's little reason for more than a passing visit.

Walk straight out of the train station and you'll soon find yourself on the **Grote Markt**, most cheerful during summer when it's decked out with open-air cafés and the like. The **Stadhuis**, on the north side of the square (May–Oct Tues–Sun 1–4.30pm), is Bergen's most attractive building, spruced up in recent years and comprising three separate houses: to the left of the gateway an alderman's house of 1397, to the right a merchant's house of 1480 and on the far right a building known as "De Olifant" whose facade dates from 1611. All of this is a lot more appealing than the blunt ugliness of the **Grote Kerk**, a uniquely unlucky building that's been destroyed by siege, fire and neglect innumerable times over the past four hundred years.

Left of the Stadhuis, Fortuinstraat leads to the **Markiezenhof Museum**, Steenbergsestraat 8 (Tues–Sun 11am–5pm; €5; ⓦ www.markiezenhof.nl), a first-rate presentation of a collection that has a little of everything: domestic utensils and samplers from the sixteenth century onward, sumptuous period rooms, architectural drawings, pottery and galleries of modern art. All this is housed in a palace built by Anthonis Keldermans between 1485 and 1522 to a late-Gothic style that gives it the feel of an Oxford college. Of the rest of old Bergen-op-Zoom, little remains: at the end of Lievevrouwestraat, near the entrance to the Markiezenhof, the **Gevangenpoort** is practically all that remains of the old city defences, a solid-looking fourteenth-century gatehouse that was later converted to a prison.

In February each year Bergen-op-Zoom hosts one of the southern Netherlands' most vibrant **carnivals**, with virtually every inhabitant – as well as revellers from all over Europe – joining in the Tuesday procession. It's a great time to be in the town if you can manage it, although you shouldn't expect to find any accommodation – the whole place gets packed; just do as the locals do and party all night. Contact the Tourist Information for the exact dates.

Practicalities

The **Tourist Information**, at Grote Markt 1 (Mon 1–5pm, Tues–Sat 10am–5pm; May–Oct also Sun noon–4pm; ☎0164/277 482, ⓦwww.bergenopzoom .com), has details of **private rooms**, along with a map of the centre. The cheapest **hotel** is *De Lantaarn*, Bredasestraat 8 (☎0164/236 488, ⓕ246 879; ❶), while the **HI hostel** (☎0164/233 261, ⓦwww.stayokay.com; dorms €25) is 4km out of town at Boslustweg 1; take bus #21 or #22 from the station and it's a five-hundred-metre walk from the Lievensberg stop.

There's a variety of **restaurants** grouped around the Grote Markt and, while the town's drinking scene is not exactly buzzing, *Kunst-en Proeflokaal de Hemel* is a lively spot at Moeregrebstraat 35, just off Steenbergsestraat.

Breda

BREDA, one of the prettier towns of Noord-Brabant, is a pleasant, easygoing place to while away a day. The centre is compact, largely pedestrianized and eminently strollable. A magnificent Gothic cathedral looms above the three-storey buildings that front its stone-paved square, crammed with stallholders and shoppers on market days. There's a range of well-priced accommodation, inexpensive restaurants and lively bars, though ultimately it's less appealing than Den Bosch as a base for exploring central Noord-Brabant.

While there's little evidence of it today, Breda developed as a strategic fortress town and was badly damaged following its capture by the Spanish in 1581. The local counts were scions of the House of Nassau, which in the early sixteenth century married into the House of Orange. The first prince of the Orange-Nassau line was **William the Silent**, who spent much of his life in the town and would probably have been buried here, had Breda not been in the hands of the Spanish at the time of his assassination in Delft. In 1566 William was among the group of Netherlandish nobles who issued the **Compromise of Breda** – an early declaration against Spanish domination of the Low Countries. The town later fell to the Spanish, was retaken by Maurice, William's son, captured once more by the Spanish, but finally ceded to the United Provinces in 1648.

King Charles II of England lived in the town for a while (it was here that he issued his **Declaration of Breda** in 1660, the terms by which he was prepared to accept the throne), as did – though less reliable historically – Oliver Cromwell and Daniel Defoe. Breda was last fought over in 1793, when it was captured by the French, who hung on to it until 1813.

As well as the carnival, which is exuberantly celebrated, the annual **jazz festival** (ⓦwww.bredajazzfestival.nl) is a great time to be in town. Some twenty stages are scattered around the centre during this four-day festival, traditionally starting on Ascension Day.

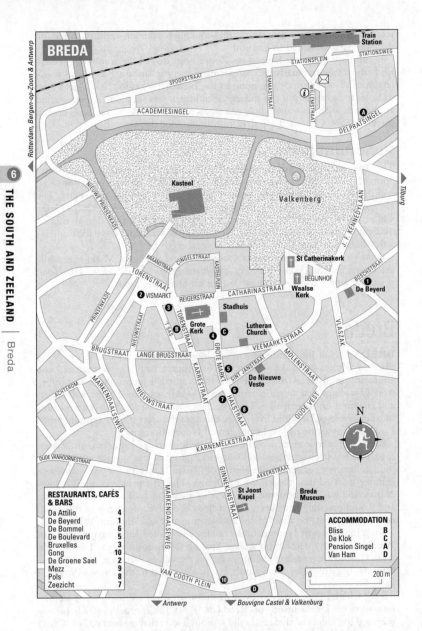

BREDA

Train Station

STATIONSPLEIN · STATIONSWEG

SPOORSTRAAT

ACADEMIESINGEL

STATIONSWEG

WILLEMSTRAAT

EMMASTRAAT

DELPRATSINGEL

A

Rotterdam, Bergen-op-Zoom & Antwerp

Kasteel

Valkenberg

J. F. KENNEDYLAAN

Tilburg

NIEUWE PRINSENKADE

KRAANSTRAAT · CINGELSTRAAT

KASTEELEIN

St Catharinakerk

BOSCHSTRAAT

TORENSTRAAT

BEGIJNHOF

2 VISMARKT

REIGERSTRAAT

CATHARINASTRAAT

Waalse Kerk

1 De Beyerd

PRINSENKADE

3

NIEUWSTRAAT

'T SAS

TORENSTRAAT

Stadhuis

VLASZAK

Grote Kerk

C

Lutheran Church

BRUGSTRAAT

LANGE BRUGSTRAAT

GROTE MARKT

4

VEEMARKTSTRAAT

ACHTEROM

MARKENDAALSEWEG

NIEUWSTRAAT

KARRESTRAAT

5

SINT JANSTRAAT

De Nieuwe Veste

MOLENSTRAAT

6

7

HALSTRAAT

8

OUDE VEST

OUDE VANHOORNESTRAAT

KARNEMELKSTRAAT

N

AKKERSTRAAT

GINNEKENSTRAAT

St Joost Kapel

Breda Museum

MARKENDAALSEWEG

VAN COOTH PLEIN

10

9

D

RESTAURANTS, CAFÉS & BARS

Da Attilio	4
De Beyerd	1
De Bommel	6
De Boulevard	5
Bruxelles	3
Gong	10
De Groene Sael	2
Mezz	9
Pols	8
Zeezicht	7

ACCOMMODATION

Bliss	B
De Klok	C
Pension Singel	A
Van Ham	D

0   200 m

▼ *Antwerp*   ▼ *Bouvigne Castel & Valkenburg*

Arrival, information and accommodation

The **VVV** office, Willemstraat 17–19 (Mon 1–6pm, Tues–Fri 9am–6pm, Sat 9am–5pm; ☏0900/522 2444, ⓦwww.vvvbreda.nl), is straight outside the **train station**, about five minutes' walk from the Grote Markt and the town centre. It sells the handy *Strolling through Breda* (€2.50).

Hotels and **pensions** include the old-fashioned *Pension Singel,* Delprats-ingel 14 (☎076/521 6271; ❶), walking distance from the train station, and the surprisingly cheap and conveniently located *De Klok* at Grote Markt 26–28 (☎076/521 4082, ⓦwww.hotel-de-klok.nl; ❶), though it fills quickly in summer. The *Van Ham,* Van Coothplein 23 (☎076/521 5229; ❶), is another option although they don't have private facilities. If you're not on a tight budget, the *Bliss* hotel, Torenstraat 9 (☎076/ 533 5980, ⓦwww.blisshotel.nl; ❼), is a must, with nine exclusive suites, located in the chic shopping area in the centre of town.

The nearest **campsite,** *Liesbos* (☎076/514 3514, ⓦwww.camping-liesbos .nl; April–Sept), is 8km out of town on the route of bus #111. The nearest **HI hostel** is 15km away at Chaam, Putvenweg 1 (☎0161/491 323, ⓦwww .stayokay.com; dorms €23.75) – take bus #132 and it's a 3km walk further.

The Town

From the train station and VVV, head down Willemstraat and cross the park for the town centre. The **Grote Markt** is the focus of life, site of a general **market** every Tuesday and Friday morning and a secondhand market every Wednesday morning, when stalls loaded with books, bric-a-brac, clothes and small furniture pieces push up against the pocket-Gothic **Grote Kerk** (Mon–Sat 10am–5pm, Sun 1–5pm; €3, tower only; €4.50; ⓦwww.grotekerkbreda.nl), whose intimate interior generates a sense of awe you don't usually associate with so small a building, the short nave and high, spacious crossing adding to the illusion of space. Like the majority of Dutch churches, the Grote Kerk had its decorations either removed or obscured after the Reformation, but a few murals have been uncovered and reveal just how colourful the church once was. At the end of the south aisle there's a huge *St Christopher* and other decorations in the south transept embellish the walls and roof bosses. The Grote Kerk's most remark-able feature is the **Mausoleum of Count Engelbrecht II**, a Stadholder and Captain-General of the Netherlands who died in 1504 of tuberculosis – vividly apparent in the drawn features of his intensely realistic face. Four kneeling figures (Caesar, Regulus, Hannibal and Philip of Macedonia) support a canopy that carries his armour, so skilfully sculpted that their shoulders seem to sag slightly under the weight. It's believed that the mausoleum was the work of Tomaso Vincidor of Bologna, but whoever created it imbued the mausoleum with grandeur without resorting to flamboyance; the result is both eerily real-istic and oddly moving. During the French occupation the choir was used as a stable, but fortunately the sixteenth-century misericords, showing rustic every-day scenes, survived. A couple of the carvings are modern replacements – as you'll guess from their subject matter.

At the top of Kasteelplein sits the **Kasteel** – too formal to be forbidding and considerably rebuilt since the Compromise of Breda was signed here in 1566. Twenty-five years later the Spanish captured Breda, but it was regained in 1590 thanks to a neat trick by Maurice of Nassau's troops: the Spanish garrison was regularly supplied by barge with peat, so, using the Trojan Horse strategy, seventy troops under Maurice's command hid beneath the peat on the barge and were towed into the castle, jumping out to surprise the Spanish and regain the town. The Spanjaardsgat, an early sixteenth-century watergate with twin defensive bastions that's just west of the Kasteel, is usually (but inac-curately) identified as the spot where this happened. Today the Kasteel is a military academy and there's no admission to its grounds, unless you join one of the VVV tours.

To the east of Kasteelplein on Catherinastraat, the **Begijnhof**, built in 1531, was until quite recently the only *hofje* in the Netherlands still occupied by Beguines. Today it has been given over to elderly women, some of whom look after the dainty nineteenth-century chapel at the rear, the St Catherinakerk, and tend the herb garden that was laid out several hundred years ago. To the right of the Begijnhof entrance, incidentally, is the **Waalse Kerk** (Walloon Church), where Peter Stuyvesant, governor of New York during the 1600s when that city was a Dutch colony, was married.

To the south, at St Janstraat 18, **De Nieuwe Veste** (☎076/529 9600, ⓦwww .nieuweveste.nl) is a lively cultural centre; the converted building dates from 1534 and offers regular theatre and concerts, as well as a chance to catch some local art in progress during the day. Check their website for information. The **Breda Museum**, at Parade 12 near Oude Vest (Tues–Sun 10am–5pm; €3.50; ⓦwww.bredamuseum.nl), holds a forgettable collection of exhibits concerning the town's history.

Finally, 5km out of town, the village of **ULVENHOUT** is the start of some stunning cycling, along narrow cycleways that twist and turn through dense forest. Bikes can be rented at Breda train station; follow LF13b in the direction of Alphen, a national cycleway that eventually leads to the Rhine.

Eating and drinking

Breda has a decent range of places to **eat**, many of them located around the Grote Markt and the streets running of it. Kebab joints and Turkish pizzas are plentiful at Havermarkt, a square packed with hole-in-the-wall eateries for late-night snacks. This is also the best place for **drinking** with plenty of bars that stay open late into the night.

De Beyerd Boschstraat 26. The place to be for connoisseurs of Low Countries' beer, just outside the centre.

De Bommel Halstraat 3. A large and lively café-bar frequented by a mix of customers with occasional live music and DJs on weekends.

De Boulevard St Janstraat 3. Located in an old theatre, this eetcafé mainly attracts large families and people on a tight budget with its extremely cheap three-course meals and a wide variety of dishes – anything from French to Mexican.

Bruxelles Havermarkt 5. This is a great place for Low Countries' beer and cheap daily specialities; also popular for after work drinks.

Da Attilio Grote Markt 35. A decent pizzeria right on the market square, with the classic wine bottles hanging from the ceiling and paintings depicting typical Italian scenes on the walls; there's also a pleasant terrace in summer.

Gong Van Coothplein 24. If you're looking for something trendy, stylishly decorated *Gong* is your best bet; Asian food for around €17.

De Groene Sael Havermarkt 8. For down-to-earth drinking, try this unpretentious bar with a small dance floor at the back.

Mezz Keizerstraat 1. This concert hall is the best place in town for live music and the occasional DJ on weekends.

Pols Halstraat 15. A small and excellent eetcafé with an intimate garden and four courses for €24.50.

Zeezicht Halstraat 2a. This upmarket café is good for its large choice of beers, which makes up for their overprized snacks. Live music on Fridays.

Tilburg and around

Tilburg, 20km east of Breda, is a faceless industrial town, its streets a maze of nineteenth-century houses and anonymous modern shopping precincts. The main reason you might find yourself passing through is to change transport on your way to the action-packed **De Efteling** theme park (see opposite). However, four decent museums within easy walking distance of the train station provide a worthwhile detour. There's no need to explore further – if that's as far as you get, you haven't missed much.

The Town

TILBURG developed as a textile town, though today most of its mills have closed in the face of cheap competition from India and southeast Asia. The **Nederlands Textielmuseum** is housed in an old mill at Goirkestraat 96 (out of the station, walk west along Spoorlaan, turn right along Gasthuisring and Goirkestraat is the fourth turn on the right; Tues–Fri 10am–5pm, Sat & Sun noon–5pm; €6; ⓦ www.textielmuseum.nl), and displays aspects of the industry relating to design and textile arts. It houses a collection of textile designs by Dutch artists, and a range of looms and weaving machines from around the world, and puts on demonstrations of weaving and spinning. The **Scryption**, Spoorlaan 434a (Tues–Fri 10am–5pm, Sat & Sun 1–5pm; €4.50; ⓦ www.scryption.nl), is a fancy name for a collection of writing implements – everything from lumps of chalk to word processors. Particularly interesting are the old, intricate typewriters, some of which you can operate yourself. Next door, the **Noordbrabants Natuurmuseum** (Tues–Fri 10am–5pm, Sat & Sun 1–5pm; €5.50; ⓦ www.natuurmuseumbrabant.nl) is basically a load of dead animals and (live) creepy crawlies. The **De Pont** modern art museum in a converted woolspinning mill (Tues–Sun 11am–5pm; €6; ⓦ www.depont.nl), a ten-minute walk behind the station at Wilheminapark 1, has both a permanent international collection and annual exhibitions; its main gallery space is complemented by more intimate side rooms, previously used for wool storage.

Worth a detour is **Koningshoeven** monastery (April–Oct Tues–Sat 11am–6pm, Sun noon–6pm; guided tours Tues–Sat at 1.30pm & 3pm; €6.50, beer included; ⓦ www.latrappe.nl), home to the brewery of **La Trappe** beer, the only Dutch *Trappisten* beer. *Trappist* does not refer to the type of beer, but to the fact that it has been brewed by monks; worldwide there are only seven monasteries that brew this beer. Take bus #141 in the direction of Eindhoven and ask to be dropped at the Trappistenklooster.

Thrill seekers shouldn't miss the largest **funfair** in the Benelux (ⓦ www.tilburgsekermis.nl), a ten-day event held annually at the end of July. Surprisingly, Monday is the busiest day of the fair as it was declared Pink Monday about a decade ago, attracting thousands of gays and lesbians from all over the country.

Practicalities

The **VVV** office is at Spoorlaan 364 (Mon 1–6pm, Tues–Fri 9am–6pm, Sat 10am–4pm; ☎0900/202 0815, ⓦ www.vvvtilburg.nl), a few minutes' walk from the station – cross the main road and head left. There's little reason to **stay** in Tilburg, but, for the record, the least expensive room in town is at the *Het Wapen van Tilburg* hotel, next to the VVV at Spoorlaan 362 (☎013/542 2692, ⓦ www.hetwapenvantilburg.nl; ❷), with a decent restaurant. There are several good **cafés** around Korte Heuvel.

De Efteling

Hidden in the woods fifteen minutes' drive north of Tilburg, the prize-winning **De Efteling** theme park (April–Oct daily 10am–6pm, €26; mid-July to late-Aug until 9pm, €28; check website for opening hours in winter; ⓦ www.efteling.nl) is one of the country's principal attractions. It's an excellent day out, and not just for children. The setting is superbly landscaped, especially in spring when the tulips are out. And while it's not Disney, it's certainly vast enough to swallow up the crowds.

Of the rides, *Python* is the most hair-raising, a rollercoaster twister with great views of the park before plunging down the track; *De Bob*, a bobsleigh run, is almost as exhilarating although over far too quickly, especially if you've queued for ages. *Piranha* takes you through some gentle whitewater rapids (expect to get wet). Of the quieter moments, *Villa Volta* is a slightly unsettling room that revolves around you, after a rather lengthy introduction in Dutch. For kids, the *Fairy-Tale Wood*, where the park began – a hop from Gingerbread House to Troll King to Cinderella Castle – is popular. *Vogel Rok* and *Droomvlucht* are the best of the rides, and there are afternoon shows in the Efteling Theatre. In addition, there are a number of fairground attractions, canoes and paddle-boats, and a great view over the whole shebang and the surrounding woods from the *Pagoda*. A sedate way to check whether you've missed anything is to take the steam train around the park. Prepare yourself for long queues on summer weekends; if you're not up to doing it all, skip the disappointing *Haunted Castle* and the *Carnaval Festival*.

Bus #136 and #137 run to De Efteling every half-hour from Tilburg (15min), and from Den Bosch (40min); in summer, the direct services #169 from Tilburg and #168 from Den Bosch are slightly faster. The park is well signposted just off the A261 between Tilburg and Waalwijk; parking costs €7. Though there's little need to **stay**, if you're eager for another day's fun, the *Efteling Hotel* is right by the park (℡0416/287 111, ⓦwww.efteling.nl; ❸). There are plenty of **maps** posted around the complex, and snack bars and refreshment stops at every turn.

's-Hertogenbosch (Den Bosch) and around

Capital of Noord-Brabant, **'s-HERTOGENBOSCH** is a lively town, particularly on Wednesdays and Saturdays, when its medieval Markt fills with traders from all over the province. Better known as **Den Bosch** (pronounced "bos"), it merits exploration over a day or two. The town's full name – "the Count's Woods" – dates from the time when Henry I, Duke of Brabant, established a hunting lodge here in the twelfth century. Beneath the graceful town houses of the old city flows the Binnendieze, its gloomy depths spanned by small wooden bridges. Staggered crossroads, winding streets and the twelfth-century town walls are vestiges of conflict with Holland, Gelderland and the far north and south of today's Netherlands. The town's history is written into its street and house names: "Corn Bridge", "The Gun Barrel", "Painters' Street" and more, while its most famous son is the fifteenth-century artist **Hieronymous Bosch**, whose statue now stands, palette in hand, in the middle of the Markt.

Arrival, information and accommodation

Den Bosch's centre is fifteen minutes' walk east of the **train station**. Stop by the **VVV** office, housed in De Moriaan, the oldest brick-building in town, at Markt 77 (Mon 1–6pm, Tues–Fri 9.30am–6pm, Sat 9am–5pm; ℡073/613 9629, ⓦwww.vvvs-hertogenbosch.nl), to pick up the useful Tourist Information Guide (€1.50) and *Walking tour 's-Hertogenbosch* (€1.90), which unearths all kinds of historical and architectural nuggets.

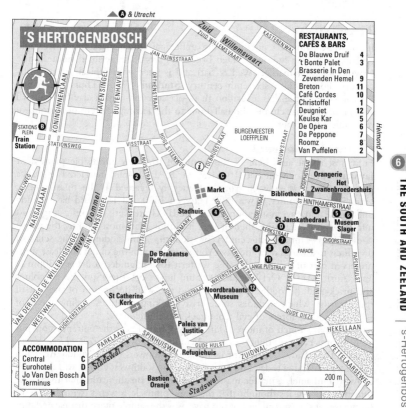

'S HERTOGENBOSCH

N

RESTAURANTS, CAFÉS & BARS

De Blauwe Druif	4
't Bonte Palet	3
Brasserie In Den Zevenden Hemel	9
Breton	11
Café Cordes	10
Christoffel	1
Deugniet	12
Keulse Kar	5
De Opera	6
Da Peppone	7
Roomz	8
Van Puffelen	2

STATIONS PLEIN **B**
Train Station

Markt

Stadhuis

De Brabantse Poffer

St Catherine Kerk

Noordbrabants Museum

Paleis van Justitie

Refugiehuis

Bastion Oranje

Orangerie

Het Zwanenbroedershuis

Bibliotheek

St Janskathedraal

Museum Slager

ACCOMMODATION

Central	C
Eurohotel	D
Jo Van Den Bosch	A
Terminus	B

0 — 200 m

One good way to see a lot of the town is on a **boat trip**. Traditional open boats depart from Molenstraat 15a, next to *Café van Puffelen* (mid-April to Oct Mon 2–5.40pm, Tues–Sun 10am–5.40pm; every 20min; €5; reserve on ☎0900/202 0178, ⓦwww.kringvriendenvanshertogenbosch.nl). Closed boats depart from St Janssingel near the Wilhelmina bridge, and tours taken in the River Aa, Dommel and the Oude Dieze (May–Sept Tues–Sun 11am, 12.30pm, 2pm & 3.30pm; €6.50). *Rederij Wolthuis*, Leunweg 17 (☎073/631 2048, ⓦwww.rederijwolthuis.nl), has information and reservations for closed-boat tours

For **hotels** in the centre of town there is the family-run *Eurohotel*, at Kerkstraat 56 (☎073/613 7777, ⓦwww.eurohotel-denbosch.com; ❷), with well-equipped rooms, a recently renovated front entrance and a lively terrace, and *Central*, Burgemeester Loeffplein 98, near the Markt with spacious rooms and occasional live jazz in one of their bars. Breakfast is served in a fourteenth-century vault (☎073/692 6926, ⓦwww.hotel-central.nl; ❺). There are two hotels to the west of town by the train station: more convenient of the two is *Terminus*, Boschveldweg 15 (☎073/613 0666, ⓦwww.hotel-terminus.nl; ❶), above a folk pub of the same name and with shared facilities. The *Jo van de Bosch*, Boschdijkstraat 39a (☎073/613 8205, ⓦwww.jovandenbosch.nl; ❷), is further out and a notch up in price but does have an authentic Spanish tapas restaurant.

The Town

If you were to draw a picture of the archetypal Dutch marketplace, it would probably look like the one in Den Bosch. It's broad and cobbled, home to the province's largest market (Wed & Sat) and is lined with typical seventeenth-century houses. The sixteenth-century **Stadhuis** (Mon–Thurs 8am–5pm, Fri 8am–noon; free) has a carillon that's played every Wednesday between 10 and 11am and that chimes the half-hour to the accompaniment of a group of mechanical horsemen.

St Janskathedraal

From just about anywhere in the centre of town it's impossible to miss **St Janskathedraal** (Mon–Sat 10–11.30am & 1.30–4pm; restricted entrance during services; Ⓦwww.sint-jan.nl). Generally regarded as the finest Gothic church in the country, it was built between 1330 and 1530 and has recently undergone a massive restoration. But if Breda's Grote Kerk is Gothic at its most intimate and exhilarating, then St Jan's is Gothic at its most gloomy, the garish stained glass – nineteenth-century or modern – only adding to the sense of dreariness that hangs over the nave. You enter beneath the oldest and least well-preserved part of the cathedral, the western **tower** (guided tours at 1.30pm & 3pm: April, May & Oct Wed, Sat & Sun; June–Sept Tues–Sun; €3.50): blunt and brick-clad, it's oddly prominent amid the wild decoration of the rest of the exterior, which includes some nasty-looking creatures scaling the roof – symbols of the forces of evil that attack the church.

Inside, there's much of interest. The **Lady Chapel** near the entrance contains a thirteenth-century figure of the Madonna known as *Zoete Lieve Vrouw* ("Sweet Dear Lady"), famed for its miraculous powers in the Middle Ages and still much venerated today. The brass **font** in the southwest corner was the work of Alard Duhamel, a master mason who worked on the cathedral in the late fifteenth century. It's thought that the stone pinnacle, a weird twisted piece of Gothicism at the eastern end of the nave, was the sample piece that earned him the title of master mason.

Almost filling the west wall of the cathedral is an extravagant **organ case**, assembled in 1602. It was described by a Victorian authority as "certainly the finest in Holland and probably the finest in Europe… it would be difficult to conceive a more stately or magnificent design". Equally elaborate, though on a much smaller scale, the south transept holds the **Altar of the Passion**, a retable (a piece placed behind and above the altar to act as a kind of screen) made in Antwerp in around 1500. In the centre is a carved Crucifixion scene, flanked by Christ bearing the Cross on one side and a Lamentation on the other. Though rather difficult to make out, a series of carved scenes of the life of Christ run across the retable, made all the more charming by their attention to period (medieval) costume detail.

Though a few painted sections of the cathedral remain to show how it would have been decorated before the Reformation, most of its paintings were destroyed in the iconoclastic fury of 1566. These included several by the late Gothic painter **Hieronymus Bosch**, who lived in the town all his life: his fantastically vivid and tormented religious paintings won him the epithet "The master of the monstrous… the discoverer of the unconscious" from Carl Jung. However, only two works by Bosch remain in the cathedral (in the north transept) and even their authenticity is doubtful. What is more certain is that Bosch belonged to the town's Brotherhood of Our Lady, a society devoted to the veneration of the Virgin, and that as a working artist he would have been

△ St Janskathedraal, 's-Hertogenbosch

expected to help adorn the cathedral. None of his major works remain in Den Bosch today, but there's a collection of his prints in the town's Noordbrabants Museum.

The rest of the town

Opposite the cathedral at Hinthamerstraat 94, the **Zwanenbroedershuis** (Tues & Thurs 1.30–4.30pm; €5; Ⓦwww.zwanenbroedershuis.nl) has an intriguing collection of artefacts, liturgical songbooks and music scores that belonged to the Brotherhood of which Bosch was a member. Founded in 1318, there's nothing sinister about the Brotherhood: membership is open to all and its aim is to promote and popularize religious art and music.

South and east of the cathedral, the **Museum Slager**, Choorstraat 16 (Tues–Sun 2–5pm; €3; ⓦwww.museum-slager.nl), contains the works of three generations of the Slager family who lived in Den Bosch. The paintings of the family's doyen, P.M. Slager (1841–1912), such as *Veterans of Waterloo*, have the most authority, but some of the other works are competent, encompassing the major trends in European art as they came and went. Over the decades, the Slager family seems to have spent most of its time painting either Den Bosch or their own relatives.

A few minutes' walk southwest of the cathedral, the **Noordbrabants Museum**, Verwersstraat 41 (Tues–Fri 10am–5pm, Sat & Sun noon–5pm; €7; ⓦwww.noordbrabantsmuseum.nl), is housed in an eighteenth-century building that was once the seat of the provincial commissioner and has been enlarged with two new wings and complemented by a sculpture garden. The good-looking collection of local art and artefacts from prehistory to the present is uniformly excellent and interesting, and the downstairs galleries often hold superb temporary exhibitions of modern art. The permanent collection includes drawings and prints by Hieronymus Bosch, works by other medieval painters and assorted early torture equipment.

Just down the road from the museum, St Jorisstraat leads down to the site of the old city walls, which still marks the southern limit of Den Bosch. The **Bastion Oranje** once defended the southern section of the city walls, but, like the walls themselves, it has long gone. Still remaining is a large cannon, **De Boze Griet** ("The Devil's Woman"), cast in 1511 in Cologne and bearing in German the inscription "Brute force I am called, Den Bosch I watch over". The only action she sees now is from the cows, chewing serenely in the watermeadows below.

For the rest, the backstreets of Den Bosch are a mass of intriguing buildings and facades. Particularly pleasant is the **Uilenburg** quarter, with pint-size houses squashed up against each other; look out for the restored farmhouse opposite Molenstraat 29, and the picturesque Uilenburgstraatje bridge. Finally, the **Stedelijk Museum 's-Hertogenbosch**, at Magistratenlaan 100 (Tues & Thurs 1–9pm, Wed & Fri–Sun 1–5pm; €4; ⓦwww.sm-s.nl), is the museum for contemporary art and design with varied exhibitions.

Eating and drinking

You can find anything from cheap eetcafés to pricey restaurants in Den Bosch, some better value for money than others. Make sure to try the "Bossche Bol", a local speciality with chocolate and whipped cream; an absolute calorie bomb. **Nightlife** isn't particularly exiting but it's easy enough to wander up and down Hinthamerstraat or the streets that radiate from the Markt and find somewhere convivial to drink.

De Blauwe Druif Markt 13. At the corner of Markt and Kolperstraat, this big and boozy pub takes off on market days.

't Bonte Palet Hinthamerstaat 97. A tiny, popular bar with a cornucopia of kitsch hanging from the ceiling and occasional live music.

Brasserie in den Zevenden Hemel Korte Putstraat 13–17. Located on the cosiest street for a romantic dinner, this restaurant uses seasonal products with an international twist.

Breton Korte Putstraat 26. Soberly decorated restaurant with an intimate terrace. The menu consists of numerous starter-sized dishes inspired by the French, Italian and Japanese cuisine.

Café Cordes Parade 4. Up a few notches on the trendiness scale, this aluminium-clad café-bar brings in Den Bosch's bright young things.

Christoffel Korenbrugstraat 11. Just round the corner from *Van Puffelen* this is a great place to taste the original "Bossche Bol" while overlooking the canal.

Da Peppone Kerkstraat 77. A little more chic than your standard kitschy pizzeria, *Da Peppone* serves tasty pastas and risottos for around €18.

Deugniet Verwersstraat 55. A deftly decorated bar near the Noordbrabants Museum, specializing in beer, with tastings available on request.

Keulse Kar Hinthamerstraat 101. This fairly traditional bar near the cathedral is as good a starting point as any for an evening's drinking along Hinthamerstraat.

De Opera Hinthamerstraat 115–17. This small restaurant offers a range of wonderful Dutch–French cooking in a relaxed setting: well worth a splurge.

Roomz Korte Putstraat 10. Nightlife is slow in Den Bosch, but if you're lucky you might catch one of the better-known Dutch DJs in *Roomz*, which has a great inner courtyard overlooking the bishop's private chapel.

Van Puffelen Molenstraat 4. A fairly short distance from the centre of town, this is an attractive eetcafé above the canal, with affordable *dagschotels* (daily specialities).

Camp Vught

Camp Vught was the only official SS concentration camp in the occupied northwest Europe, modelled after the camps in Germany. It was a transport camp, from where many Jews first went to Westerbork (see p.259) before being transported to the death camps in the east. Still, many people died here due to lack of food and hygiene, or they were murdered in the nearby execution area in the woods. Although it's a reconstruction, and only a fraction the size it used to be, Camp Vught (Tues–Fri 10am–5pm, Sat & Sun noon–5pm; free; ⓦwww .nmkampvught.nl) still provides a vivid impression of the imprisonment of many Jews and members of the resistance during World War II. Next to the old camp fences the walls of a high security prison arise, giving this location quite an eerie feel. All information is in Dutch, but an English guide is available for €3.50. From Den Bosch take bus #203 (hourly) and get off at the Lunettenlaan stop.

Eindhoven

You might wonder why a town the size of **EINDHOVEN** merits only a page in a guidebook; half an hour there, and a few statistics, will tell you why. In 1900 Eindhoven's population was approximately 4700. A century later it had passed 200,000. What happened in between was **Philips**, the multinational electrical firm: the town is home to Philips' research centre (the manufacturing plant had such trouble recruiting here, it relocated to the more popular Amsterdam), and the name of Eindhoven's benevolent dictator is everywhere – on bus stops, parks, even the stadium of the famous local football team, PSV Eindhoven. The town even moved the main train station (in the shape of a Philips transistor radio) to make sure all the company's employees could get to work sooner.

The centre of town was badly damaged during the war, leaving no trace of the fact that Eindhoven is one of the oldest cities in the Netherlands. But being modern does have its advantages, with a leading modern design academy and many high-tech multinationals. The internationally renowned **Dutch Design Week** draws almost 50,000 visitors, and the city even had the honour of being European Design Capital in 2006. The technical university draws in many international students making nightlife vibrant with many bars and clubs to choose from.

If you do find yourself in Eindhoven, it's worth visiting the **Van Abbe Museum**, Vonderweg 1 (Tues–Sun 11am–5pm; €8.50; ⓦwww.vanabbemuseum

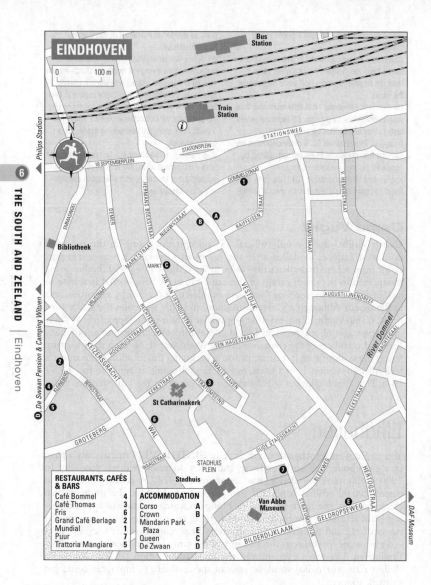

EINDHOVEN

0   100 m

RESTAURANTS, CAFÉS
& BARS
Café Bommel   4
Café Thomas   3
Fris   6
Grand Café Berlage   2
Mundial   1
Puur   7
Trattoria Mangiare   5

ACCOMMODATION
Corso   A
Crown   B
Mandarin Park
  Plaza   E
Queen   C
De Zwaan   D

.nl), with its superb collection of modern paintings that includes works by Picasso, Klein, Chagall, Kandinsky and Bacon. The museum, built in 1936 by architect Kropholler and expanded with a new wing designed by Cahen, is an attraction itself with a very pleasant café overlooking the Dommel river. The **DAF Museum**, at Tongelresetraat 27 (Tues–Sun 10am–5pm; €6; Ⓦwww .daf-museum.nl), is another of Eindhoven's highlights, devoted to the history of the only Dutch truck manufacturer, at least for anyone with an interest in cars and trucks.

Practicalities

Eindhoven's **VVV** (Mon 10am–5.30pm, Tues–Thurs 9am–5.30pm, Fri 9am–6.30pm, Sat 10am–5pm; ☏0900/112 2363, ⓦwww.vvveindhoven.nl), outside the train station, is where guided city walks start every Saturday (11am) and Wednesday (2pm; €4.50). They can also provide a handy brochure on the city and a list of **pensions**. Of these, *De Zwaan*, above Broodje Smits, Wilhelminaplein 4 (☏040/244 8992, ⓦwww.budgethotel.nl; ❶), is cheap and near several good restaurants. The **hotels** are even better placed: *Corso*, Vestdijk 17 (☏040/244 9131, Ⓕ245 7399; ❶), is the cheapest; the *Crown*, opposite at nos. 14–16 (☏040/844 4000, ⓦwww.crownhotel.nl; ❹), caters to a mostly corporate clientele; and the *Queen* is above a pleasant café at Markt 7 (☏040/245 2480, ⓦwww.queeneindhoven.nl; ❸). Near the Van Abbe Museum and the main bar area, the *Mandarin Park Plaza*, at Geldropseweg 17 (☏040/214 6500, ⓦwww.parkplaza.com; ❺), offers a high level of comfort and great Chinese and Japanese cuisine. Many hotels have weekend deals all year round, offering discounts of up to twenty percent. There's a **campsite**, *Witven* (☏040/230 0043, ⓦwww.witven.nl; April–Oct), 5km southwest of the city at Witvenseweg 6 in Veldhoven; bus #150 runs from the station.

Eindhoven comes alive at night with the Kleine Berg being the best place for **eating**, the restaurants along there offering a diverse range of international food. For spaghetti and risottos, try the trendy *Trattoria Mangiare,* which has a beautiful inner courtyard. The *Grand Café Berlage* at no. 16 is as slick as anything you'll find in Amsterdam, serving a three-course meal for €22.50; while *Café Bommel*, a little further down, is a more old-fashioned traditional bar, and good for a quiet drink. Worth a detour, *Fris*, at Wal 9, serves cactus soup, shrimps and mussels – all in a kitsch interior.

Eindhoven's main strip for **drinking** is the Stratumseind, which starts just south of Cuypers' gloomy neo-Gothic St Catherinakerk. This street has the honour of being the longest bar street in the Netherlands, with much of the action at *Café Thomas* and *Puur*, although you could go with any of them. A little less crowded is the Dommelstraat, with a good range of restaurants and trendy bars such as *Mundial* at no. 13.

Limburg

Pressed between Belgium and Germany, the Netherlands' southernmost province, **Limburg**, is shaped like an hourglass and only eight miles across at its narrowest. By Dutch standards, this is a geographically varied province: the north is a familiarly flat landscape of farmland and woods until the town of **Roermond**, where the River Maas loops and curls its way across the map; in the south, and seemingly out of nowhere, rise rolling hills studded with vineyards and châteaux. The people of Limburg are as distinct from the rest of the Netherlands as their landscape – their dialects incomprehensible to "Hollanders", their outlook more closely forged by Belgium and Germany than the distant Randstad. Nowhere is this international flavour more apparent than in the main city, **Maastricht**, an energetic and cosmopolitan blend of the very old (Imperial Rome) and very new (European Union). **South Limburg**'s distinctive, and notably un-Dutch, atmosphere makes it popular with tourists from the rest of the Netherlands, who head to its many caves and scenic cycle routes, and in summertime tourist resorts like **Valkenburg** are jam-packed with young people and families. The North and central Limburg are less colourful but still have some places that are well worth visiting. **Venlo**, with its stunning Stadhuis, is a good starting point for heading on to the **National War and Resistance Museum**, and **Roermond** makes a good base to explore the **National Park De Meinweg**.

Venlo and around

Just a few kilometres from the German border, **VENLO** has been repeatedly destroyed and recaptured throughout its history, particularly during the last war, when most of its ancient buildings were knocked down during the Allied invasion of Europe. As a result the town is short of sights, but makes a good base for the National War and Resistance Museum at Overloon.

The cramped streets of Venlo's centre wind medievally around the town's architectural highlight, the fancily turreted and onion-domed **Stadhuis**, a much-modified building dating from the sixteenth century. Nearby, along Grote Kerkstraat, is the imposing pile of **St Martinus Kerk** (Mon & Sun 2–4pm, Tues–Fri 10.30am–12.30pm & 2–4pm, Sat 10am–4pm; free), rebuilt after bombing in 1944, but still holding a brilliant golden seventeenth-century reredos. Near the station is the **Limburgs Museum**, Keulsepoort 5 (Tues–Sun 11am–5pm; €5.50; ⓦ www.limburgsmuseum.nl), which houses the city's historical collection. Best exhibit is the nineteenth-century kitchenware, the largest such assortment in western Europe. Venlo's other museum, the **Van Bommel Van Dam**, Deken van Oppensingel 8 (Tues–Sun 11am–5pm; €2; ⓦ www.vanbommelvandam.nl), shows temporary exhibitions of the work of contemporary, mostly local artists; from the train station, take the third right off the roundabout.

From beside the train station, bus #83 makes the 10km trip north along the Maas to the village of Arcen, home to the **Kasteeltuinen** (April & Oct 10am–5pm; May–Sept 10am–6pm; €12.50; ⓦ www.kasteeltuinen.nl), a trim seventeenth-century moated castle surrounded by a fine series of formal gardens set beside narrow canals and a string of tiny lakes.

Practicalities

Venlo's **VVV**, Koninginneplein 2 (Mon noon–6pm, Tues–Fri 9.30am–6pm, Sat 9.30am–5pm; ☏ 077/354 3800, ⓦ www.lekker-genieten.nl), is located opposite the train station, about 800m south of the market square. They have details of **boat trips** and can help find **accommodation**. The trendiest hotel in town is 🏛 *Puur,* Parade 7 (☎077/351 5790, 🌐www.hotelpuur.nl; ❷), a hospitable place with basic but stylish rooms and a breakfast area with an industrial feel.

Flanking the train station are *Hotel Wilhelmina*, Kaldenkerkerweg 1 (☎077/351 6251, 🌐www.hotel-wilhelmina.nl; ❷), with spacious rooms and a decent restaurant, and the cheaper *American*, Keulsepoort 14 (☎077/351 5454, 🌐www.hotelamerican.nl; ❶), which boasts a big terrace.

Try the *D'n Dorstigen Haen*, Markt 26, for **snacks** and a few samples of their huge range of **beers**. Several cafés around the Stadhuis and the Parade are other options for cheap light lunches.

National War and Resistance Museum

The cosy residential town of Venray, a few minutes north of Venlo by train, is a stepping-stone to **OVERLOON**, in Noord-Brabant, site of the **Nationaal Oorlogs- en Verzetsmuseum** (National War and Resistance Museum). To reach the museum from Venray, take the *treintaxi* (see Basics p.33; €4.20 each way). Alternatively, you could rent a bike from Venlo and follow route LF33, turning off at Venray to cycle the last 6km through fields of wheat to Overloon. This affluent little town was rebuilt following its destruction in World War II during a fierce battle in October 1944 in which 2400 men died. The final stages took place in the woods to the east, where hand-to-hand fighting was needed to secure the area, and it's on this site that the **museum** (daily: July–Aug 10am–6pm; Sept–June 10am–5pm; €9.50; 🌐www.oorlogsmuseum-overloon .nl) now stands, founded with the military hardware that was left behind after the battle. Its purpose is openly didactic: "Not merely a monument for remembrance, it is intended as an admonition and warning, a denouncement of war and violence". In showing the machinery of war, including tanks, rocket launchers, armoured cars, a Bailey bridge and a V1 flying bomb, the museum powerfully achieves this, making it a moving experience and a poignant prelude to its excellent collection of documents and posters. Touring the whole museum takes a couple of hours.

Roermond and around

ROERMOND, the focal point of central Limburg, is something of an oddity. While not especially exciting, it does have a rich Catholic heritage, as numerous shrines to the Virgin suggest – a legacy of 250 years of Habsburg rule that ended only in 1839 with the unification of the Netherlands. Indeed it was here that the architect P.J.H. Cuypers, who crowded the country with Gothic-revival Catholic churches, lived and worked. Today, the town's greatest asset is its position: Roermond lies on the banks of the River Maas, at the point where it meanders into the small, artificial lakes of the **Maasplassen**. Come summertime, these lakes fill with small boats, windsurfs and water-skis as holidaymakers take to the water or fish under the town's skyline. For those less aquatically inclined, it's only 9km to **De Meinweg**, the Netherlands' largest national park, with forests and fens that extend to the German border. Roermond is also useful as a base for visiting nearby **Thorn**, and a handy stopover on the way to Maastricht and the south, or Aachen, Düsseldorf and Cologne in Germany.

Though it looks straightforward enough on the map, Roermond is a confusing place to walk around, its series of wide streets and broad squares all too

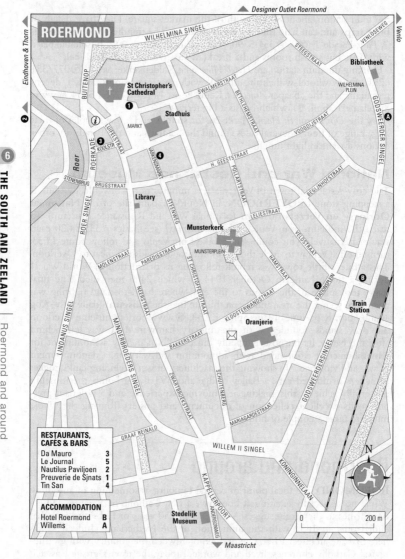

**RESTAURANTS,
CAFÉS & BARS**

Da Mauro	3
Le Journal	5
Nautilus Paviljoen	2
Preuverie de Sjnats	1
Tin San	4

ACCOMMODATION

Hotel Roermond	B
Willems	A

similar to the unacquainted. Use the Munsterkerk and river as landmarks and
you shouldn't get lost for too long.

The Town

Walk into town from the train station and you'll come to the **Munsterkerk**
(April–Oct daily 2–5pm; Sat closes 4pm; Nov–March Sat 2–4pm; free), on
Munsterplein, built in Romanesque style in the thirteenth century, but much
altered and gothicized by Cuypers in the nineteenth century. Inside, the chief
thing to see is the polychrome thirteenth-century tomb of Gerhard III and his

wife Margaret of Brabant. From here it's a short walk to the large sloping square of the **Markt**, on the eastern side of which is the early eighteenth-century **Stadhuis**, a dull building that's easily overlooked. More noticeable (though not more interesting), **St Christopher's Cathedral** (April–Oct daily 2–5pm; free) was rebuilt following damage in World War II.

Making your way down the larger streets leading south from the Markt – Marktstraat, Neerstraat and Minderbroeders Singel – you'll come across some later and much more attractive architecture. Wherever you are in town, it's worth keeping an eye open for Roermond's alluring twentieth-century **facades**: the majority are Art Nouveau, often strongly coloured with heavily moulded vegetal patterns and designs, sometimes with stylized animal heads and grotesque characters. Some examples can be found at Neerstraat 38 and 10.

Roermond's principal architectural claim to fame is celebrated at the **Stedelijk Museum**, Andersonweg 2–8 (Tues–Fri 11am–5pm, Sat & Sun 2–5pm; €2). P.J.H. Cuypers (1827–1921) was the Netherlands' foremost ecclesiastical architect in the nineteenth century, his work paralleling that of the British Gothic revivalist, Augustus Pugin. Almost every large city in the country has a Catholic church by him – those in Eindhoven, Leeuwarden and Hilversum are notable – though his two most famous buildings are secular: the Rijksmuseum and Centraal Station in Amsterdam. Roermond's museum is the building in which Cuypers lived and worked for much of his life and preserves a small private chapel as well as a large extension in which masses of decorative panels, mouldings and fixtures were produced. Other exhibits show his plans and paintings, along with a collection of works by other local artists, chiefly Hendrik Luyten.

Practicalities

The **VVV** office, Kraanpoort 1, behind Markt (Nov–March Mon–Fri 9.30am–5pm; April–Oct Mon–Fri 9.30am–6pm, Sat 9.30am–4pm; ℡0475/335 847, ⓦwww.lekker-genieten.nl), is a fair walk from the train station. They can provide details (and licences if necessary) for **fishing** and **boat trips** along the River Maas (April–Sept). If you want to rent a boat, visit Watersportschool Frissen, Hatenboer 75 (℡0475/327 873), where a five-person boat costs €50 a day.

Roermond has a good range of **hotels**, including *Willems*, above a café of the same name on Godsweerdersingel 58 (℡0475/333 021; ❶), and the more expensive *Hotel Roermond*, Stationsplein 9 & 13 (℡0475/332 325, ⓦwww .hotelroermond.nl; ❷), which has modern rooms, an inviting terrace and three restaurants to choose from.

The three main areas to **eat** and **drink** are around the Markt, the Munsterkerk and the train station. On Stationsplein, *Le Journal*, at no. 17, is an inexpensive café-bar that stays open till late at weekends. The restaurant of the *Hotel Roermond*, although a bit pricey for dinner, is worth checking out for some night-time excitement on Saturday when a DJ takes over after dinner. *Tin San* is the best of several Chinese places, just south of the Markt at Varkensmarkt 1, while *Da Mauro* (closed Weds), Koolstraat 8, is an Italian restaurant that serves a three-course meal for €22.50. In summertime, the *Nautilus Paviljoen* at Maasboulevard 2 is a popular café overlooking the yachts moored up in the marina. Roermond lacks first-rate watering holes, though the cafés at Stationsplein are often the liveliest nightspots; otherwise try *Preuverie de Sjnats,* Markt 24, for a good range of beers. For a more artistic night out, check out the *Orangerie* (ⓦwww.oranjerieroermond.nl), at Kloosterwandplein 12–16, which is a hotel and a theatre, showing musicals, ballet and cabaret. Check their website for up-to-date information.

Shopping fanatics have yet another reason for visiting Roermond: the **Designer Outlet**, Stadsweide 2 (Ⓦ www.designeroutletroermond.nl), which has over a hundred outlet stores and attracts a huge number of Dutch and German visitors looking for a bargain.

National Park De Meinweg

Roermond makes a good base for exploring the nearby **National Park De Meinweg**, an excellent region for walking and cycling right by the German border. It comprises 1600 hectares of oak, birch and pine trees, dotted with small lakes and heather, and home to adders and shy wild boars. If you get really lost, you'll either find yourself in Germany or on the private estate of the Maharishi Mahesh Yogi, famous as the Beatles' guru in the 1960s. Entrance to De Meinweg is free (open daily, unlimited access), and the **Bezoekerscentrum** (visitors' centre; April–Oct daily 10am–5pm), just before the park entrance, sells maps with routes and starting points for walkers and cyclists, and has a small nature museum.

To get to the park, you're best off using your own **transport** as bus connections aren't great – rent a bike from the Rijwielshop at Roermond station (€7/day for a three-geared bike) and cycle the 9km, following signs to the village of Herkenbosch, or drive. From Herkenbosch, follow Keulsebaan, then turn left down Meinweg to reach the Bezoekerscentrum and entrance to the park. In Herkenbosch, Manege de Venhof, Venhof 2 (☎0475/531 495), can arrange group **horse-riding** in the park.

Thorn

The village of **THORN** makes for an enjoyable half-day outing from Roermond. Regular buses link the two, but it's more fun to rent a bike from the train station and cycle alongside the River Maas, following LF Route 5b (Roermond to Thorn). Take a map though (available at the Roermond VVV), as the signposting can be patchy. To return, follow the 5a signs; a round trip is roughly 30km.

Once you get here, it's easy to see why Thorn is a favourite for travel agents' posters, and something of a tourist honeypot. Its houses and farms are all painted white, a tradition for which no one seems to have a credible explanation, but has a photogenic effect. The farms intrude right into the village itself, giving Thorn a barnyard friendliness that's enhanced by its cobblestone streets, the closed-shuttered propriety of its houses and, at the centre, the **Abdijkerk** (March–Oct daily 10am–5pm; Nov–Feb Sat & Sun noon–5pm; €2). The abbey was founded at the end of the tenth century by a powerful count, Ansfried, and his wife Hilsondis, as a sort of religious retirement home after Ansfried had finished his tenure as bishop of Utrecht. Under his control the abbey and the land around it was granted the status of an independent principality under the auspices of the Holy Roman Empire and it was in the environs of the abbey that the village developed.

The abbey was unusual in having a double cloister that housed both men and women (usually from local noble families), a situation that carried on right up until the French invasion of 1797, after which the principality of Thorn was dissolved, the monks and nuns dispersed and all the abbey buildings save the church destroyed. Most of what can be seen of the church today dates from the fifteenth century, with some tidying up by P.J.H. Cuypers in the nineteenth.

The interior decoration, though, is congenially restrained Baroque of the seventeenth century, with some good memorials and side chapels. If you're into the macabre, aim for the crypt under the chancel, which has a couple of glass coffins containing conclusively dead members of the abbey from the eighteenth century: this and other highlights are described in the notes that you can pick up on entry (in English) for a self-guided walking tour.

Thorn has one small museum, the **Museum Land of Thorn**, in the historic heart of the village at Wijngaard 14 (April–Oct Mon noon–5pm, Tues–Sun 10am–5pm; Nov–March Tues–Sun 11am–4pm; €2; ⓦwww.museumhetlandvanthorn.nl), which details the history of Thorn, hosts temporary exhibitions of art and houses a three-dimensional painting of the village.

Practicalities

The **VVV**, at the entrance to the museum at Wijngaard 14 (April–Oct Mon noon–5pm, Tues–Sun 10am–5pm; Nov–March Tues–Sun 11am–4pm; ⓣ0475/562 761), can help with regional information. The cheaper of the towns two **hotels** is the *Crasborn*, Hoogstraat 6 (ⓣ0475/561 281, ⓦwww.stadsherberg-crasborn.nl; ❷), though the atmospheric *Hostellerie La Ville Blanche*, Hoogstraat 2 (ⓣ0475/562 341, ⓦwww.villeblanche.nl; ❸), offers surprisingly affordable luxury. There's also a private **campsite**, *Vijverbroek*, Kessenicherweg 20 (ⓣ0475/561 914, ⓕ565 565; April–Oct), reached by turning right halfway down Hofstraat.

Maastricht

MAASTRICHT made world headlines in 1992, when the signing of the Maastricht Treaty created the European Union. With its cobbled streets and fashionable boutiques in the old town, contemporary architecture in the Céramique district, a fantastic art fair and excellent cuisine, Maastricht is one of the most vibrant cities in the Netherlands. Add in its continental feel, the multilingual population and close proximity to Belgium and Germany and it's no wonder why the Eurocrats signed the treaty here: Maastricht epitomizes the most positive aspects of European union.

Keen to promote itself as the oldest town in the Netherlands (a title mildly contested by Nijmegen), Maastricht was first settled by the **Romans**, who took one look at the River Maas and dubbed the town *Mosae Trajectum* or "Crossing of the Maas". An important stop-off on the trading route between Cologne and the North Sea, the town boasted a Temple of Jupiter; that and other relics are now on view in a hotel basement. A millennium later, **Charlemagne**'s legacy is two churches – some of the best surviving examples of the Romanesque in the Low Countries. Politically, the landscape around Maastricht has always consisted of small states ruled by powers as remote as Austria and Spain in the eighteenth century. Once dependent on its natural resources, the closure of the last coal mines in the 1960s sent Maastricht into a sharp decline and unemployment was rife. A massive **regeneration** scheme turned the city around, and generous subsidies and aid programmes attracted foreign investors and businesses. Now Maastricht has become something of a call-centre capital, hosting the likes of Mercedes Benz and DHL. Redevelopment continues apace today with the "City Centre in Motion" scheme, whose most recent contribution is **'t Bassin**, a spruced up inland harbour north of the Markt, with restaurants, cafés, shops and galleries.

To the Dutch, Maastricht and the province of Limburg have an almost foreign flavour: being twice as far away from Amsterdam as from Brussels, and in the centre of a constellation of Liège, Cologne and Düsseldorf, the attitude here is breezily cosmopolitan. In fact, it's a popular day-trip destination not only for the Dutch but also for Belgians and Germans, who hop over the borders to fill the all-year pavement cafés for which Maastricht is renowned. The town is also a temporary home to students and professionals from around the world, studying at over forty international institutes, including the European Journalism Centre and the University of the United Nations, all of which boosts the vivacity of the place no end.

Arrival, information and tours

The centre of Maastricht is on the west bank of the river and most of the town spreads out from here toward the Belgian border. You're likely to arrive, however, on the east bank, in the district known as **Wyck**, a sort of extension to the centre that's home to the **train** and **bus stations** and many of the city's hotels. The train station itself is about ten minutes' walk from the St Servaas bridge, which takes you across the river into the centre. All local buses connect with Markt from the station, but if you have no heavy luggage, it's easy enough to walk. You only really need to use **city buses** to get from the station out to St Pietersberg. Maastricht **airport** is 12km north of the city at Beek; from here it's a twenty-minute ride on bus #61 (bus #51 on Sun) to Markt and the train station; a taxi costs about €25. Arriving by **car**, follow signs for Q-Parking; there's no free parking in the town centre. The VVV has a detailed "Parking in Maastricht" leaflet.

The main **VVV** (May–Oct Mon–Sat 9am–6pm, Sun 11am–3pm; Nov–April Mon–Fri 9am–6pm, Sat 9am–5pm; ☏043/325 2121, ⓦ www.vvvmaastricht .nl) is housed just across the river in the Dinghuis, a tall, late-fifteenth-century building at Kleine Staat 1, at one end of the main shopping street. As well as information on the city and on film, theatre and music events around town, they have decent maps and good walking guides. In July and August they organize **walking tours** (in English) which leave from the office daily at 12.30pm (€3.95) and last about an hour and a half. From March until November, City Tour Maastricht offers a ride through the historical centre of town by **horse carriage**, departing from the Onze Lieve Vrouweplein (daily from noon; 45 min; €10).

Between mid-May and September, Stiphout runs hourly **cruises** from the bottom of Graanmarkt down the Maas (Mon–Sat 10am–5pm, Sun 1–5pm; 50min; €6; ☏043/351 5300, ⓦ www.stiphout.nl), and offers trips taking in the St Pietersberg caves (3hr; €9.95) or even as far as Liège (day-trip €18.95). Since not all cruises are available every day, phone to confirm, or ask at the VVV.

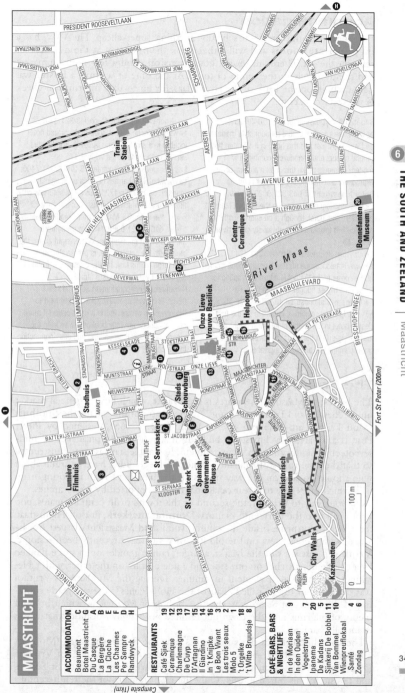

MAASTRICHT

ACCOMMODATION

Beaumont	C
Botel Maastricht	G
Du Casque	A
La Bergère	B
La Cloche	E
Les Charmes	F
Per Sempre	D
Randwyck	H

RESTAURANTS

Café Sjiek	19
Ceramique	12
Charlemagne	13
De Cuyp	17
D'Artagnan	15
Il Giardino	14
In 't Knijpke	16
Le Bon Vivant	3
Les trois seaux	2
Molo 5	1
't Orgelke	18
't Witte Bruudsje	8

CAFÉ-BARS, BARS & NIGHTLIFE

In de Moriaan	9
In den Ouden Vogelstruys	7
Ipanema	20
De Kadans	5
Sjinkerij De Bobbel	11
Van Bommel	10
Wienpreuflokaal Santé	4
Zondag	6

PRESIDENT ROOSEVELTLAAN

Train Station

Centre Ceramique

Bonnefanten Museum

River Maas

Onze Lieve Vrouwe Basiliek

Helpoort

Stadhuis

St Servaaskerk

Stads Schouwburg

Spanish Government House

St Janskerk

Lumière Filmhuis

Natuurhistorisch Museum

City Walls

Kazematten

Fort St Peter (200m)

Campsite (1km)

N

0   100 m

Accommodation

For **accommodation**, there's hardly anything super-cheap. The VVV has a list of **private rooms** and will either book them for you at the usual fee or sell you the list. There are several good **pensions**, and a few more upmarket and trendy hotels in the centre of town. At the time of writing, a **hostel** was being rebuilt on the bank of the river Maas; for up-to-date information check ⓦ www.stayokay.com.

Beaumont Wyckerbrugstraat 2 ☎043/325 4433, ⓦ www.beaumont.nl. Grab a random style magazine and you might just find this hotel in it. Wooden floors, natural colours and chandeliers combined with modern elements make this hotel a picture-perfect example of a contemporary designer hotel. ❺

Botel Maastricht ☎043/321 9023, ⓦ www .botelmaastricht.nl. Moored on the river at Maas-boulevard this botel, though a bit spartan, offers an excellent breakfast and obviously great river views. ❶

Du Casque Helmstraat 14 ☎043/321 4343, ⓦ www.hotelducasque.nl. This four-star hotel located at the corner of the Vrijthof is a luxurious option for those on a higher budget. No restaurant. ❺

La Bergère Stationsstraat 40 ☎043/328 2525, ⓦ www.la-bergere.com. It claims to be the first design hotel in the Netherlands, with bright colours and daring art on the walls (all for sale), and a great champagne breakfast available as well. ❹

La Cloche Bredestraat 41 ☎043/321 2407, ⓦ www.lacloche.com. A soberly decorated hotel located in a small historic building. Breakfast is served in the café at the Vrijthof. ❷

Les Charmes Lenculenstraat 18 ☎043/321 7400, ⓦ www.hotellescharmes.nl. Located in an old mansion dating from 1725, this small hotel has only fifteen rooms, which are stylish, but still cosy. ❹–❺

🏃 **Per Sempre** Maastrichter Smedenstraat 28 ☎043/321 9969, ⓦ www.persempre .nl. This smart guesthouse, located right above the store with the same name, is great value for money with large rooms (ask for the ones in the front) and a friendly owner. No private facilities. ❶

Randwyck Endepolsdomein 30 ☎043/361 6835, ⓦ www.hotelrandwyck.nl. Right next to the congress centre, this is a good option if more central options are fully booked, away from the inner-city bustle. Free parking and easy connection to the centre. ❷

The Town

The busiest of Maastricht's squares is the **Markt**, which hosts a general market on Wednesday and Friday mornings. At the centre of the square, the **Stadhuis** (Mon–Fri 8.30am–12.30pm & 2–5.30pm; free) of 1664, designed by Pieter Post, is a square, grey limestone building that is a fairly typical slice of mid-seventeenth-century Dutch civic grandeur. Its double staircase was constructed so that the rival rulers of Brabant and nearby Liège didn't have to argue about who should go first on the way in. Inside, the building has an imposing main hall, which gives way to a rear octagonal dome supported by heavy arches.

On your way to Vrijthof, the second of the town's main central squares, pop your head into the thirteenth-century **Dominicanerkerk**, just off Helmstraat, for a bit of a surprise. Inside the church you'll find Maastricht's largest **bookstore**, with a great view on the old frescos which have recently been restored. **Vrijthof** is just west of the Markt, a larger, rather grander open space flanked by a couple of churches on one side and a line of cafés on the other, with tables taking over the wide pavement in summer. During the Middle Ages, Vrijthof was the scene of the so-called "Fair of the Holy Relics", a seven-yearly show-ing of the bones of St Servaas, the first bishop of Maastricht, which brought plenty of pilgrims into the town but resulted in such civil disorder that it was eventually banned.

The church that holds the saint's relics now, the **St Servaaskerk** (Mon–Sat 10am–5pm, Sun 12.30–5pm; €3.50), dominates the west side of Vrijthof. Dating from 950, it's on the site of an earlier shrine dedicated to St Servaas and the site of his burial in 384. Only the crypt remains of the tenth-century

△ Onze Lieve Vrouwe Basiliek, Maastricht

church, containing the tomb of the saint himself, and the rest is mostly of medieval or later construction. You enter on the north side of the church, where a fifteenth-century Gothic cloister leads into the **treasury**, which holds a large collection of reliquaries, goblets and liturgical accessories, including a bust reliquary of St Servaas, decorated with reliefs telling the saint's story, which is carried through the town in Easter processions. There's also a coffin-reliquary of the saint, the so-called "Noodkist", dating from 1160 and bristling with saints, stones and ornate copperwork, as well as a jewelled crucifix from 890 and a twelfth-century Crucifixion in ivory. Beyond the treasury is the entrance to the rich and imposing interior, the round-arched nave supporting freshly painted Gothic vaulting. Don't miss the mid-thirteenth-century **Bergportaal** on the south side of the church, the usual entrance during services.

The second most prominent building on the square, next door, is Maastricht's main Protestant church, the fourteenth-century **St Janskerk** (April–Oct Mon–Sat 11am–4pm), the baptistery of the church of St Servaas when it was a cathedral and nowadays competing for attention with its high and faded, delicate red fifteenth-century Gothic tower. The church has some medieval murals, but a climb up the tower (€1.25) is the church's main appeal. On the south side of the square, the sixteenth-century **Spanish Government House** (Wed–Sun 1–5pm; €3) has an attractive Renaissance arcade and a number of period rooms furnished in Dutch, French and the more local Liège–Maastricht style. Among various exhibits are statues and figurines, porcelain and applied arts and a handful of seventeenth-century paintings.

Another prominent Maastricht church, the **Onze Lieve Vrouwe Basiliek**, is a short walk south of Vrijthof, down Bredestraat, in a small, shady square crammed with café tables in summer. It's unusual for its fortified west front, with barely more than one or two slits for windows. First built around the year 1000, it's a solid, dark and eerily devotional place after the bright Protestant churches of the north – or even the relative sterility of the St Servaaskerk. The Gothic vaulting of the nave springs from a Romanesque base, while the galleried choir is a masterpiece of proportion, raised under a high half-dome, with a series of capitals exquisitely decorated with Old Testament scenes. Off the north aisle, the **treasury** (Easter to mid-Oct Mon–Sat 11am–5pm, Sun 1–5pm; €3) holds the usual array of reliquaries and ecclesiastical garments, most notably the dalmatic of St Lambert – the evangelical bishop of Maastricht who was murdered at Liège in 705, allegedly by a local noble whom he had rebuked for adultery. Entrance to the church is through a side chapel on the Onze Lieve Vrouweplein, which houses the statue of Stella Mare, an object of pilgrimage for centuries and which attracts as many devotees as the church itself.

Stokstraat Kwartier and the city walls

Around the corner from the Onze Lieve Vrouweplein is a district of narrow streets known as the **Stokstraat Kwartier** after its main gallery- and boutique-lined spine, Stokstraat. This quarter has an intimate feel, with its vermilion town houses, scattered sculptures and Maasland-Renaissance style houses in warm Namur stone. On Plankstraat, the **Museumkelder Derlon** (Sun noon–4pm; free), in the basement of the hotel of the same name, contains one of the few remnants of Roman Maastricht – the remains of a temple to Jupiter, a well and several layers of pavement, discovered before the building of the present hotel in the mid-1980s.

On the other side of Onze Lieve Vrouweplein lies another of Maastricht's most appealing quarters, narrow streets winding out to the remains of the town battlements alongside the fast-flowing River Jeker, which weaves in and out of the various houses and ancient mills. The best surviving part of the walls is the **Helpoort** of 1229, close to a stretch overlooking the river at the end of St Bernadusstraat; and from here you can walk along the top of the walls almost as far as the **Natuurhistorisch Museum** at De Bosquetplein 6–7 (Mon–Fri 10am–5pm, Sat & Sun 2–5pm; €3.50), where there's a small collection on the geology, flora and fauna of the surrounding area, along with a small, lush garden display.

A little way southwest of here, the **Kazematten** (Casemates) in the Waldeck Park (tours July & Aug daily at 2pm; outside these months, check with the VVV; €3.95) are further evidence of Maastricht's once-impressive fortifications, a system of galleries created through mining between 1575 and 1825 that were used in times of siege for surprise attacks on the enemy. There used to be many more casemates around the town, but only these survive, and they make a fairly draughty way to spend an hour. Tours take you through a small selection of the 10km or so of damp passages. Trivia buffs might be interested to know that the famous fourth "musketeer", d'Artagnan, was killed here, struck down while engaged in an attack on the town as part of forces allied to Louis XIV in 1673.

The east bank

Ten minutes' walk south of the St Servaas bridge, the **Bonnefanten Museum**, Avenue Céramique 250 (Tues–Sun 11am–5pm; €7; ⓦ www.bonnefanten.nl), is one of Maastricht's highlights. Named after the Bonnefanten monastery where it used to be housed, the museum now inhabits an impressive modern building, designed by Aldo Rossi, on the banks of the Maas. Its space rocket-style cupola is instantly recognizable, zooming skywards. Inside is a permanent collection of old masters and contemporary fine art, including works from the Minimal Art and Arte Povera movements. The rest of the museum is given over to various temporary exhibitions, superbly displayed: you could find anything from giant spider installations to Titians. Don't miss the cupola space, which is usually given over to a single piece of art.

Not far from the Bonnefanten Museum on Plein 1992, with its low horizons and euro symbols studded into the paving stones, is the **Centre Céramique**, Avenue Céramique 50 (Mon–Fri 10.30am–5pm, Tues & Thurs until 8.30pm, Sat 10am–3pm, Sun 1–5pm; ⓦ www.centreceramique.nl). This huge modern building is home to the European Journalism Centre, the city archives and the library (which has free Internet access).

Outside the centre: St Pietersberg

There are more dank passageways to explore fifteen minutes' walk from the casemates on the southern outskirts of Maastricht, where the flat-topped hill of **St Pietersberg** rises to a height of about 110m – a popular picnic spot on warm summer weekends. Again these aren't so much caves as galleries created by quarrying, hollowed out of the soft sandstone, or marl, that makes up the hill – an activity that has been going on here since Roman times. There are more than 20,000 passages, but nowadays only 8000 of them are accessible. The caves used to claim the lives of people (usually children) who never found their way out, but these days it's almost impossible to enter the caves without guidance. Of the two cave systems, the **Zonneberg** is probably the better, situated on the far side of the St Pietersberg hill at Casino Slavante (guided tours in English July & Aug daily 1.55pm; €3.95). These caves were intended to be used as air-raid shelters during World War II and were equipped accordingly, though they were in fact only used during the last few days before Maastricht's liberation. There is some evidence of wartime occupation, plus what everyone claims is Napoleon's signature on a graffiti-ridden wall. Also on the walls are recent charcoal drawings, usually illustrating a local story and acting as visual aids for the guides, not to mention the ten varieties of bat that inhabit the dark (and cold) corridors.

The other, more northerly system of caves, the **Grotten Noord** (€3.95) is easier to reach (15min walk from the centre of town). The entrance is at Chalet Bergrust on the near side of St Pietersberg close by **Fort St Pieter**, and has

Maastricht is often known as the culinary capital of the Netherlands, and never more so than during **Preuvenemint**, an annual four-day culinary event held on the last full weekend in August (ⓦwww.preuvenemint.nl). Vrijthof square is filled with over thirty stands functioning as restaurants. "Preuvenemint" is a contraction of the Maastricht words "*preuve*" (to taste) and "*evenemint*" (event), and it's a great way to explore the richness of Dutch flavours. The main attraction, though, has to be the crowd the event attracts. Posh Maastricht comes out to show off their latest purchases, but also to contribute to a good cause, since all the proceeds go to charity.

panoramic views over the town and surrounding countryside. This fort is a low brick structure, pentagonal in shape and built in 1702 (tours July & Aug daily at 12.30pm and 2pm; outside these months, check with the VVV; €3.95).

Eating, drinking and nightlife

Maastricht has some of the best cooking in the Netherlands, so options abound for good **eating** and **drinking**, including some Michelin-starred restaurants. Regional delicacies include asparagus, cave mushrooms, "Limburgse Vlaai" (fruit tart) and Rommedou cheese. Limburg is also the only wine-producing province in the Netherlands although not everyone will be charmed by the slightly sour taste of the produce.

For drinking, the **bars** on the east side of the Vrijthof have most pulling-power, particularly in summer when the pavement cafés are packed. A more intimate environment can be found around the Onze Lieve Vrouweplein, while heavy night-time entertainment is concentrated around the Platielstraat.

Lumière Filmhuis, Bogaardenstraat 40b (ⓣ043/321 4080), regularly shows interesting, often English-language, **movies**.

Restaurants

Café Sjiek Sint Pieterstraat 13, ⓣ043/321 0158. Anyone from a carpenter to a top lawyer feels at home in this pleasant eetcafé, which serves a wide selection of regional dishes at affordable prices. Make sure you book ahead in summer as the terrace is one of the most popular places in the city. Their cheese platter is a must for connoisseurs.

Ceramique Rechtstraat 78 ⓣ043/325 2097. Located in the Wyck, an upcoming area with many restaurants, this eetcafé serves no-nonsense food, with mains like salmon, steak and sea bass for around €18.

Charlemagne Onze Lieve Vrouweplein 24 ⓣ043/321 9373. Cosy café with reasonably priced steaks, salads and a wide variety of beers. Great terrace in summer and attentive staff.

De Cuyp Tongersestraat 30 ⓣ043/321 8382. Located in the university district, a few minutes from the centre, this restaurant serves Dutch–French dishes (around €17.50) and

seasonal specialities. There's also a tiny terrace which is shared with the neighbours across the street.

D'Artagnan Graanmarkt 3 ⓣ043/325 5164. Despite the slightly posh looking terrace this is a traditional brown-café-style place that serves a great range of daily specialities with a better than average wine list. Main dishes around €15.

Il Giardino Onze Lieve Vrouweplein 15 ⓣ043/325 6229. Colourful Italian restaurant with good pizzas and pastas from €10. Daily fresh products and pleasant Italian chaos make this a great place for a lively night out.

In 't Knijpke St Bernardusstraat 13 ⓣ043/321 6525. The onion soup and cheese platter are the specialities at this restaurant located in a former jail, made a little cosier by the welcoming fireplace and medieval decor. There's also a tiny cinema here showing non-commercial movies every night.

Le Bon Vivant Capucijnenstraat 91 ⓣ043/321 0816. Pure French cuisine such as *fois gras*, scallops, pigeon and fish soup. A three-course meal in this seventeenth-century vault starts at €34.

Les trois seaux Markt 41 ☎043/321 2038. Just off the crowded Markt, this fish restaurant offers fresh lobster, oysters and seasonal products in a maritime setting. Mains around €20.

Molo 5 Bassinkade 5 ☎043/327 0033. There are a few good restaurants and art galleries situated in this inland harbour; *Molo 5* serves Italian food starting from €10 for a pasta dish and €18 for a main course.

't Orgelke Tongersestraat 40 ☎043/321 6982. This restaurant is famous for its *sateh* (pork skewers) and stews but they also serve a wide variety of fish and meat dishes for around €15. If you beat the record holder in skewer eating, your name will be added to the list of fame.

't Witte Bruudsje Platielstraat 12. Late-night snack attacks can be assuaged here from their choice of baguettes, salads and hot staples such as chilli con carne and fish and chips. Open until 2am (Fri & Sat 3am).

Café-bars, bars and nightlife

In de Moriaan Stokstraat 12. Possibly the smallest bar in the country with a cosy terrace in summer.

In den Ouden Vogelstruys Vrijthof 15. One of the nicest bars on the otherwise touristy Vrijthof, just on the corner of Platielstraat.

Ipanema Avenue Ceramique 250. Located in a wing of the Bonnefanten Museum, this trendy bar occasionally turns into a club in weekends.

De Kadans Kesselskade 62. Bar, restaurant and club in one with weekly salsa and merengue nights.

Sjinkerij De Bobbel Wolfstraat 32. Just off Onze Lieve Vrouweplein, this is a bare-boards place, which is lively in the early evening.

Van Bommel Platielstraat 13–15. While the neighbouring bars mainly attract students, *Van Bommel* aims at an older crowd. Open till late.

Wienpreuflokaal Santé Kesselskade 56. Tiny wine bar, great for tasting Dutch wines.

Zondag Wijckerbrugstraat 42. The place to go for a coffee and grandma's apple pie, but it also has live DJs at weekends.

Listings

Bike rental Aon de Stasie, Stationsplein ☎043/321 1100. Mon–Fri 5.15am–1.15am, Sat 6am–1am, Sun 7.15am–1.15am; from €7/day with a €50 deposit.

Books There's a branch of De Slegte at Grote Straat 53, good for second-hand English-language paperbacks and much else besides. Try also Bergmans, located in the Dominicanerkerk, which has a good selection of new English-language titles.

Bureau de change There's a GWK office at the train station, open daily.

Car rental Europcar, Sibemaweg 1 ☎043/361 2310, ☏408 4337. The major companies also have desks at the airport.

Markets General market on Markt (Wed & Fri 8am–1pm). Antique and curiosities market on Stationsstraat (Sat 8am–4pm).

Post office Keizer Karelplein, just off the northwest corner of Vrijthof.

Taxis Crals, Posthoornstraat 75 ☎043/362 2222.

South Limburg

South Limburg boasts the Netherlands' only true **hills** and as such is a popular holiday area for the Dutch, many of the villages crammed in summer with walkers from the north taking in the scenery. Several long-distance **walking routes** converge on Maastricht, including the popular and scenic Grand Randonné 5 "Traject der Ardennen", the Pieterpad (from St Pietersberg to Groningen's Pieterburen), and the Krijtlandpad, which winds its way to the German border. The countryside is green and rolling, studded with castles (many of which have been converted to hotels), seamed with river valleys and dotted with the crooked timber-framed houses that are unique to the area. Everywhere is within easy reach of Maastricht, although since public transport connections are patchy it makes more sense to take a **car**. This puts you in easy reach of Liège in Belgium (Luik in Dutch) and Aachen in Germany, and just an hour away from the cities of Brussels, Düsseldorf and Cologne – or the wild river valleys and peaks of Belgium's Ardennes.

Valkenburg is South Limburg's main resort, perhaps the easiest place to visit as it's on the main train line from Maastricht to Aachen, though it does get packed throughout the summer. Further east down the train line, **Heerlen** and **Kerkrade** are also easily reached, though neither is any great shakes. To the south of the train line, toward the Belgian border, the countryside is wilder and more impressive, with expansive views all around.

East of Maastricht

Some 5km east of Maastricht, the first stop on the #54 bus route – which eventually goes to Vaals on the German border – **CADIER-EN-KEER** is a small suburb best known for its **Africa Centre** (Tues–Sun 1.30–5pm; €5; Ⓦwww .afrikacentrum.nl), ten minutes' walk off to the left of the main road (follow the signs). Housed in the headquarters of the African Missionaries Society, this contains a small museum of mainly West African artefacts, masks, jewellery and statuary arranged by tribe and dating back as far as the thirteenth century – as well as giving details on the contemporary way of life of African peoples.

Bus #54 continues to **MARGRATEN**, where just before the town proper there's an **American War Cemetery** (daily sunrise–sunset), a peaceful and moving memorial to over eight thousand American servicemen who died in the Dutch and Belgian campaigns of late 1944 and 1945. Buses stop right outside. The centrepiece is a stone quadrangle recording the names of the soldiers, together with a small visitors' room and a pictorial representation and narrative describing the events in this area leading up to the German surrender, while beyond the quadrangle, the white marble crosses that mark the burial places of the soldiers cover a depressingly huge area.

There's not much else to Margraten, nor is there to **GULPEN**, a few kilometres beyond, a nondescript place with good bus connections to all over South Limburg. The town is known for its Gulpener beer, the name of which you see all over the province and indeed the rest of the country, though that aside the only thing that distinguishes Gulpen is the 161m-high Gulpenberg, which rises roundly behind the town and is home to a campsite. At the end of the #54 route, the small town of **VAALS** is perched on a hillside whose peak is the highest point in the Netherlands, at a lofty 321m. Just a few metres further on are three flags in a graffiti-covered concrete block symbolizing the "**Drieland-enpunt**", where the borders of Belgium, Germany and the Netherlands meet. A nearby labyrinth (April–Oct 10am–6pm; €3; Ⓦwww.drielandenpunt.nl), an observation tower (€3), car parks and fast-food outlets contrive to make this a truly underwhelming experience.

South of Gulpen, the countryside makes for a pretty route back to Maastricht, either driving or via the #57 bus route from Gulpen's bus station, taking in the scenically sited villages of **Mechelen**, **Epen** and **Slenaken**.

Valkenburg

Set in the gently wooded valley of the River Geul, **VALKENBURG**, ten minutes east of Maastricht by train, is southern Limburg's major tourist resort. A medieval castle, its ruins starkly silhouetted on crags above the town, surveys the fake castle train station, garish centre and bus loads of tourists throughout the summer heading for its innumerable hotels, restaurants and casino. While you probably wouldn't want to stay here, it's certainly a change from the rest of the Netherlands, with a feel more akin to a Swiss or Austrian alpine resort. Valkenburg is famed for its Christmas-season markets, held in Fluwelengrot and Gemeentegrot, with all manner of special foodstuffs, decorations and

On a leisurely cycle route from Maastricht east to Vaals, right on the border on the edge of Aachen, scenic villages nestle among vineyards and orchards, linked by quiet lanes dotted with shrines. The pace of life is slow – the pony and trap is still a common sight – and cycling is a perfect way to appreciate this peaceful landscape and its un-Dutch hills. Allow a day for this seventy-kilometre round-trip ride, and carry a Limburg province map from the VVV.

From Maastricht train station, follow the river south to **Gronsveld**, picking up signs to the eleventh-century village of St Geertruid. The black and white half-timbered farmsteads in these villages are known as *vakwerkhuisjes*, built from clay, wood and dried dung. The road snakes over hills draped with vineyards before swooping into the villages **Mheer**, **Norbeek** and **Slenaken** – all highly picturesque and popular with walkers throughout the year. Each can conjure up accommodation, should you decide to spend longer in the area. At Slenaken, the road develops some hairpin tendencies as it climbs the valley side above, overlooked by grazing sheep. Continue through **Eperheide** and **Epen**, with sweeping views across to the rolling valleys of Belgium on the right. Between Epen and **Vaals**, there's a gradual eight-kilometre climb on narrow roads, winding between woods of red oaks, with glimpses of bright green farmland below. For a six-kilometre round-trip to the highest point in the Netherlands, follow the signs to the **Drielandenpunt** (see opposite) from Vaals – the monument celebrating 321m of altitude is just in front of the concrete observation tower. Otherwise, follow the main road out of Vaals (there's a dedicated cycle lane), turning left to **Vijlen** where ploughed fields and potatoes take up as much space on the main street as the houses. Surrounding you is a panoramic view over Belgium, Germany and the Netherlands, beautiful on a clear day, presided over by the wind turbines in the distance. From eleventh-century **Mechelen** and **Gulpen**, you're in striking distance of **Valkenburg** to the north, approached through the old town. Climb the steep but brief Cauberg hill to return to Maastricht, enjoying a speedy descent between orchards and farmland with the city locked in your sights. Once on the outskirts, follow the cycle route signs to bring you back to the station.

An alternative (and shorter) return route is to continue from Gulpen to Maastricht on a straight route via **Margraten** and **Cadier-en-Keer**.

street entertainment, and it is also where the **Amstel Gold Race** (Ⓦwww .amstelgoldrace.nl) finishes, a classic cycling event held in April with many world-renowned cyclists.

Theodoor Dorrenplein, five minutes' walk from the train station, is the centre of town, fringed with cafés and home to the VVV. From here the main Grote Straat leads up through the pedestrianized old centre through the old **Grendelpoort** arch to **Grendelplein**, which provides a second focus, with streets leading off to Valkenburg's main attractions. A great many of these are aimed at children – things like bobsleigh runs, a fairytale wood, a hopeful reconstruction of Rome's catacombs – and even those that aren't are still the kind of things kids enjoy.

It's worth a walk up to the **castle** (entrance off Grendelplein; daily: April–June 10am–5.30pm; July–Sept 10am–6pm; Oct–Dec 10am–4.30pm; hours vary outside season; €3.10; joint ticket with Fluwelengrot €6.30; Ⓦwww .kasteelvalkenburg.nl). The edifice was blown up in 1672 on the orders of William III, after he had recaptured it from its French occupiers. Repair and restoration began in 1921 and continue still, uncovering a series of underground passages that served as an escape route in times of siege. These form part of the **Fluwelengrot** (guided tours only: Jan–March Mon–Fri 11am & 1pm, Sat & Sun 11am–3pm on the hour; April–June daily 11am–4pm on the hour; July & Aug daily 10.30am–5pm every half-hour and at 8pm; Sept & Oct daily 11am–4pm on the hour; closed Nov & Dec for Christmas market; extra tours during school and public holidays; €4.75, joint ticket with castle €6.30); further up the road on the left are a series of caves that were formed – like those of St Pietersberg in Maastricht – by the quarrying of marl, which has been used for much of the building in this area over the years. On the whole they're a damp, cold way to spend an hour, the most interesting features being the signatures and silhouettes of American soldiers who wintered here from 1944 to 1945 and a clandestine chapel that was used during the late eighteenth-century French occupation.

There are several other caves you can visit in the area, including ones you can cycle through – **Grotbiken** (cave biking; ℡043/ 6040 675, Ⓦwww.aspadventure.nl) – which is becoming increasingly popular, and the **Gemeentegrot** (check website for hours; €4.50; Ⓦwww.gemeentegrot.nl), which does the trip to an underground lake by train.

If the idea of trudging around dank underground passages doesn't appeal to you, you can ascend to the top of the hill above the castle by way of a **cable car** (April & Sept Mon–Fri on request, Sat & Sun 11am–5pm; May–June Mon–Fri noon–5pm, Sat & Sun 11am–5pm; July–Aug daily 10.30am–6pm; hours vary outside season; €3.50 return; Ⓦwww.kabelbaan.nl), five minutes' walk down Berkelstraat from the top of Grote Straat – or you can cut through the passage between the castle and the Fluwelengrot. This, a fairly primitive structure of the kind used for ski lifts, with two-person open cars, takes you up to the **Wilhemina Toren**, where you can enjoy the view from the terrace of the inevitable bar-restaurant.

Practicalities

The **VVV**, Theodoor Dorrenplein 5 (April–Oct Mon–Fri 9am–5.30pm, Sat 9am–5pm, Sun 10am–3pm; Nov–March Mon–Fri 9am–5.30pm, Sat 9am–1pm; ℡043/609 8600, Ⓦwww.vvvzuidlimburg.nl), has maps and information on all Valkenburg's attractions, as well as lists of the dozens of **hotels** and **pensions**.

Among the cheapest hotels is *La Casa* at Grotestraat 25–27 (℡043/601 2180, Ⓦwww.la-casa.nl; ❶), with sixteen soberly decorated rooms and a kitsch Spanish/Italian restaurant. Slightly upmarket are the family run *Hostellerie Valckenborgh*, Hovetstraat 3 (℡043/601 2484, Ⓦwww.valckenborgh.nl; ❷), and *Gaudi*, Grendelplein 14 (℡043/601 5333, Ⓦwww.hotelgaudi.nl; ❷), inspired by the Spanish architect, centrally located with only fifteen rooms. The nearest **campsite** is *Den Driesch*, a short walk up Dahlemerweg from Grendelplein on the left (℡043/601 2025, Ⓦwww.campingdendriesch.nl; April to mid-Dec), which attracts a young crowd. Virtually every second building in Valkenburg is a **restaurant**, though they're all very touristy and fairly cheap, and nowhere stands out.

For a break from sightseeing, head to **Thermae 2000** spa, located up a steep hill on Cauberg 27 (daily 9am–11pm; €16.50 for 2hr, €28 for whole day; Ⓦwww.thermae2000.nl). It has a sauna complex, eucalyptus steam rooms, indoor and outdoor pools (with views over the Limburg countryside), plus relaxation and yoga rooms, and a range of face and body treatments. The adjoining hotel, *Thermaete* (℡043/609 2001, Ⓦwww.thermae2000.nl; ❼), has free use of all these facilities.

Heerlen and Kerkrade

HEERLEN, ten minutes northeast of Valkenburg by train, is quite different, an ugly modern town that sprawls gracelessly over the rolling countryside. But it has one definite attraction in the excellent **Thermen Museum**, Coriovallumstraat 9 (Tues–Fri 10am–5pm, Sat & Sun noon-5pm, Ⓦ www.thermenmuseum .nl; €4), which incorporates the excavations of a bath complex from the Roman city of Coriovallum here – a key settlement on the Cologne–Boulogne trade route. These have been enclosed in a gleaming, purpose-built hi-tech structure, with walkways leading across the ruins and tapes (in English) explaining what's what. An adjacent room displays finds and artefacts from the site, including glasswork from Cologne, shards of pottery, tombstones and coins, all neatly labelled. To get to the museum, follow Saroleastraat from the station as far as Raadhuisplein and turn right.

Fifteen minutes on from Heerlen by train lies **KERKRADE** by the German border, again an unappealing place, but worthy of a visit for its **Abdij van Rolduc** complex (opening hours vary, call ☎045/546 6888), situated on the far side of town, about a twenty-minute walk from the station. Originally founded by one Ailbert, a young priest who came here in 1104, this is now almost entirely sixteenth century, used as a seminary and conference centre, but it does preserve a fine twelfth-century church, a model of simplicity and elegance, with contemporary frescoes and a marvellous mosaic floor. The clover-leaf-shaped crypt, dark and mysterious after the church and with pillar capitals carved by Italian craftsmen, contains the relics of Ailbert, brought here from Germany where he died.

Kerkrade also has, beside the train station, the **Industrion** (Tues–Sun 10am–5pm; July & Aug also Mon; €7; Ⓦ www.industrion.nl), an interesting museum that traces the nation's industrial development, with a focus on paper, graphics, ceramics and coal-mining, and the recently opened **Gaia Zoo**, Dentgenbachweg 105 (daily: March, Oct & Nov 10am–5pm; April–Sept 10am–6pm; Dec–Feb 10am–4pm; €15; Ⓦ www.gaiapark.nl), with more than eighty species living in a natural and modern environment.

Travel details

Trains

Breda to: Dordrecht (every 20min; 20min); 's Hertogenbosch (every 30min; 30min); Maastricht (every 30min; 1hr 50min). Middelburg (every 30min; 1hr 15min);
Eindhoven to: Roermond (every 30min; 30min); Venlo (every 30min; 35min).
's Hertogenbosch to: Eindhoven (every 10min; 25min).
Maastricht to: Amsterdam (every 30min; 2hr 35min); Den Haag/The Hague (every 30min; 2hr 45min); Roermond (every 30min; 40min).
Middelburg to: Bergen-op-Zoom (every 30min; 40min); Goes (every 30min; 13min); Roosendaal (every 30min; 50min).
Roermond to: Venlo (every 30min; 24min).

Roosendaal to: Breda (every 30min; 17min); Dordrecht (every 20min; 25min).
Tilburg to: Eindhoven (every 20min; 35min); 's Hertogenbosch (every 30min; 15min).
Vlissingen to: Middelburg (every 30min; 8min).

Buses

Middelburg to: Delta Expo (Mon–Fri twice hourly, Sat hourly, Sun every 2 hours; 30min); Renesse (hourly; 45min); Veere (Mon–Sat hourly; 12min).
Renesse to: Brouwershaven (hourly; 30min).
Zierikzee to: Goes (every 30min; 30min).

Ferries

Vlissingen to: Breskens (hourly; 30min).

Contexts

Contexts

The historical framework

T
he country now known as the **Netherlands** didn't reach its present delimitations until 1830. Until then the borders of the entire region, formerly known as the **Low Countries** and including present-day Belgium and Luxembourg, were continually being redrawn following battles, treaties and alliances. Inevitably, then, what follows is, in its early parts at least, an outline of the history of the whole region, rather than a straightforward history of the Netherlands as such. Please note, incidentally, that the term "Holland" refers to the province – not the country – throughout.

Beginnings

Little is known of the **prehistoric** settlers of the Low Countries, their visible remains largely confined to the far north of the Netherlands, where mounds known as *terpen* were built to keep the sea at bay in Friesland and Groningen. There are also megalithic tombs, *hunebeds*, among the hills near Emmen in the northeast corner of the Netherlands, but quite how these tie in with the Iron Age culture that had established itself across the region by the fifth century BC is impossible to say.

Clearer details of the region begin to emerge at the time of Julius Caesar's conquest of Gaul (broadly France) in 57 to 50 BC. He found three tribal groupings living in the region: the mainly Celtic **Belgae** (hence the nineteenth-century term "Belgium") settled by the Rhine, Maas and Waal to the south; the Germanic **Frisians** living on the marshy coastal strip north of the Scheldt; and the **Batavi**, another Germanic people, inhabiting the swampy river banks of what is now the southern Netherlands. The Belgae were conquered and their lands incorporated into the imperial province of **Gallia Belgica**, but the territory of the Batavi and Frisians was not considered worthy of colonization. These tribes were granted the status of allies, a source of recruitment for the Roman legions and curiosity for imperial travellers. In 50 AD **Pliny** observed: "Here a wretched race is found, inhabiting either the more elevated spots or artificial mounds... When the waves cover the surrounding area they are like so many mariners on board a ship, and when again the tide recedes their condition is that of so many shipwrecked men."

The Roman occupation of Gallia Belgica continued for 500 years until the legions were pulled back to protect the heartlands of the crumbling empire. As the empire collapsed in chaos and confusion, the Germanic **Franks**, who had been settling within Gallia Belgica from the third century, filled the power vacuum, establishing a **Merovingian** kingdom around their capital Tournai (in modern Belgium) with their allies the Belgae. A great swathe of forest extending from the Scheldt to the Ardennes separated this Frankish kingdom from the more confused situation to the north and east, where other tribes of Franks settled along the Scheldt and Leie, Saxons occupied parts of Overijssel and Gelderland, and the Frisians clung to the seashore.

Towards the end of the fifth century, the Merovingian king Clovis was converted to **Christianity** and the faith slowly filtered north, spread by energetic missionaries like St Willibrord, first bishop of Utrecht, from about 710, and St Boniface, who was killed by the Frisians in 754 in a final act of pagan resistance before they too were converted. Meanwhile, after the death of the last distinguished Merovingian king, Dagobert, in 638, power passed increasingly to the so-called "mayors of the palace", a hereditary position whose most outstanding occupant was **Charles**

Martel (c.690–741). Martel inherited a large, but all-too-obviously shambolic, kingdom whose military weakness he determined to remedy. Traditionally, the Merovingian (Frankish) army was comprised of a body of infantry led by a small group of cavalry. Martel replaced this with a mounted force of highly trained knights, who bore their own military expenses in return for land – the beginnings of the **feudal system**. These reforms came just in time to save Christendom: in 711 an extraordinary Arab advance, which had begun early in the seventh century in modern-day Saudi Arabia, reached the Pyrenees and a massive Muslim army occupied southern France in preparation for further conquests. In the event, Martel defeated the invaders outside Tours in 732, one of Europe's most crucial engagements and one that saved France from Arab conquest for good. Ten years after Martel's death, his son, Pepin the Short, formally usurped the Merovingian throne with the blessing of the pope, becoming the first of the **Carolingian** dynasty, whose most famous member was **Charlemagne**, son of Pepin and king of the west Franks from 768. In a dazzling series of campaigns, Charlemagne extended his empire south into Italy, west to the Pyrenees, north to Denmark and east to the Oder. His secular authority was bolstered by his coronation as the first **Holy Roman Emperor** in 800, a title bestowed on him by the pope in order to legitimize his claim as the successor to the emperors of Imperial Rome.

The strength and stability of Charlemagne's court at Aachen spread to the Low Countries, bringing a building boom that created a string of superb Romanesque churches like Maastricht's St Servaas, and a trading bonanza along the region's principal rivers. However, unlike his Roman predecessors, Charlemagne was subject to the divisive inheritance laws of the Salian tribe of Franks, and after his death in 814, his kingdom was divided between his grandsons into three roughly parallel strips of territory, the precursors of France, the Low Countries and Germany.

The growth of the towns

The tripartite division of Charlemagne's empire placed the **Low Countries** between the emergent French- and German-speaking nations, a dangerous location, which was subsequently to decide much of its history. Amid the cobweb of local alliances that made up **early feudal western Europe** in the ninth and tenth centuries, however, this was not apparent. During this period, French kings and German emperors exercised a general authority over the region, but power was effectively in the hands of local lords who, remote from central control, brought a degree of local stability. From the twelfth century, feudalism slipped into a gradual decline, the intricate pattern of localized allegiances undermined by the increasing strength of certain lords, whose power and wealth often exceeded that of their nominal sovereign. Preoccupied by territorial squabbles, this streamlined nobility was usually willing to assist the growth of towns by granting charters that permitted a certain amount of **autonomy** in exchange for tax revenues, and military and labour services. The first major cities were the cloth towns of Flanders – Bruges, Ieper (Ypres) and Ghent. Meanwhile, their smaller northern neighbours concentrated on trade, exploiting their strategic position at the junction of the region's main waterways – Amsterdam being a case in point.

Burgundian rule and the Habsburgs

By the late fourteenth century the political situation in the Low Countries was fairly clear: five lords controlled most of the region, paying only nominal homage to their French or German overlords. In 1419 **Philip the Good** of Burgundy succeeded to the countship of Flanders and by a series of adroit political moves gained control over Holland, Zeeland, Brabant and Limburg to the north, and Antwerp, Namur and Luxembourg to the south. He consolidated his power by establishing a strong central administration in Bruges and restricting the privileges granted in the towns' charters. During his reign Bruges became a showcase for the Hanseatic League, a mainly German association of towns who acted as a trading group and protected their interests by an exclusive system of trading tariffs. Philip died in 1467 to be succeeded by his son, **Charles the Bold**, who was killed in battle ten years later, plunging his father's carefully crafted domain into turmoil. The French seized the opportunity to take back Arras and Burgundy and before the people of Flanders would agree to fight the French they kidnapped Charles's daughter, Mary, and forced her to sign a charter that restored the civic privileges removed by her grandfather Philip.

After her release, Mary married the **Habsburg** Maximilian of Austria, who assumed sole authority when Mary was killed in a riding accident in 1482. **Maximilian** continued to implement the centralizing policies of Philip the Good, but in 1494, when he became Holy Roman Emperor, he transferred control of the Low Countries to his son, Philip the Handsome. The latter died in 1506 and his territories were passed on to Maximilian's grandson **Charles V**, who also became King of Spain and Holy Roman Emperor in 1516 and 1519, respectively. Charles was suspicious of the turbulent burghers of Flanders and, following in Maximilian's footsteps, favoured Antwerp at their expense; it soon became the greatest port in the empire, part of a general movement of trade and prosperity away from Flanders to the cities to the north.

Through sheer force of will and military might, Charles bent the merchant cities of the Low Countries to his will, but regardless of this display of force, a spiritual trend was emerging that would soon question not only the rights of the Emperor but also rock the power of the Catholic Church itself.

Stirrings of the Reformation

An alliance of Church and State had dominated the medieval world: pope and bishops, kings and counts were supposedly the representatives of God on earth, and they combined to crush religious dissent wherever it appeared. Much of their authority depended on the ignorance of the population, who were entirely dependent on their priests for the interpretation of the scriptures, their view of the world carefully controlled.

There were many complex reasons for the **Reformation**, the stirring of religious revolt that stood sixteenth-century Europe on its head, but certainly the **development of typography** was key. For the first time, printers were able to produce relatively cheap bibles in quantity, and the religious texts were no longer the exclusive property of the Church. Consequently, as the populace snaffled up the bibles, so a welter of debate spread across much of western Europe under the auspices of theologians like **Erasmus of Rotterdam** (1465–1536), who wished to cleanse the Catholic Church of its corruptions, superstitions and extravagant ceremony; only later did many of these same thinkers – principally **Martin Luther** (1483–1546) – decide to support a breakaway church. In 1517, Luther produced his 95 theses against indulgences, rejecting – among other things – Christ's presence in the Eucharist and denying the Church's monopoly on the interpretation of the Bible. There was no way back, and when Luther's works were disseminated his ideas gained a European following among reforming groups that were soon branded **Lutheran** by the Church. Luther asserted that the Church's political power was subservient to that of the state, whereas the supporters of another great reforming thinker, **John Calvin** (1509–64), emphasized the importance of individual conscience and the need for redemption through the grace of Christ rather than the confessional.

These seeds of **Protestantism** fell on fertile ground among the Low Countries' merchants, whose wealth and independence could not easily be accommodated within a rigid caste society. Similarly, their employees, the guildsmen and their apprentices, had a long history of opposing arbitrary authority, and were soon convinced of the need to reform an autocratic, venal church. In 1555, **Charles V abdicated**, transferring his German lands to his brother Ferdinand, and his Italian, Spanish and Low Countries territories to his son, the fanatically Catholic **Philip II**. In the short term, the scene was set for a bitter confrontation, while the dynastic ramifications of the division of the Habsburg Empire were to complicate European affairs for centuries.

The revolt of the Netherlands

After his father's abdication, Philip decided to teach his heretical subjects a lesson they wouldn't forget. He garrisoned the towns of the Low Countries with Spanish mercenaries, imported the Inquisition and passed a series of anti-Protestant edicts. However, other pressures on the Habsburg Empire forced him into a tactical withdrawal and he transferred control to his sister, **Margaret of Parma**, in 1559. Based in Brussels, the equally resolute Margaret implemented the policies of her brother with gusto. In 1561 she reorganized the Church and created fourteen new bishoprics, a move that was construed as a wresting of power from civil authority, and an attempt to destroy the local aristocracy's powers of religious patronage. Protestantism – and Protestant sympathies – now spread to the nobility, who formed the "League of the Nobility" to counter Habsburg policy. The League petitioned Philip for moderation, but was dismissed out of hand by one of Margaret's Walloon advisers, who called them *ces geux* ("those beggars"), an epithet that was to be enthusiastically adopted by the rebels. In 1565 a harvest failure caused a winter famine among the workers, and, after years of repression, they struck back: a Protestant sermon in the tiny Flemish textile town of Steenvoorde incited the congregation to purge the local church of its "papist idolatry". The crowd smashed up the church's reliquaries and shrines, broke the stained-glass windows and terrorized the priests, thereby launching the **Iconoclastic Fury**, which spread like wild fire: within ten days churches had been ransacked from one end of the Low Countries to the other, nowhere more so than in Antwerp.

The ferocity of this outbreak shocked the upper classes into renewed support for Spain, and Margaret regained the allegiance of most nobles – with the principal exception of the country's greatest landowner, Prince William of Orange-Nassau, known as **William the Silent** (though William the Taciturn is a better translation of the Dutch moniker). Of Germanic descent, he was raised a Catholic but the excesses and rigidity of Philip had caused him to side with the Protestant movement. A firm believer in individual freedom and religious tolerance, William became a symbol of liberty, but after the Fury had revitalized the pro-Spanish party, he prudently slipped away to his estates in Germany.

Philip II was encouraged by the increase in support for Margaret and so, in 1567, he sent the **Duke of Alva**, with an army of 10,000 men, to the Low Countries to suppress his religious opponents absolutely. Margaret was, however, not at all pleased by Philip's decision and, when Alva arrived in Brussels, she resigned in a huff, thereby abandoning the Low Countries to military rule. One of Alva's first acts was to set up the Commission of Civil Unrest, which was soon nicknamed the "**Council of Blood**", after its habit of executing those it examined: no fewer than 12,000 citizens were polished off by the Commission, mostly for participating in the Fury. Initially the repression worked: in 1568, when William attempted an invasion from Germany, the towns, garrisoned by the Spanish, offered no support. William waited and considered other means of defeating Alva. In April 1572, a band of privateers entered Brielle on the Maas and captured it from the Spanish. This was one of several commando-style attacks by the so-called **Waterguezen**, or sea-beggars, who were at first obliged to operate from England, although it was soon possible for them to secure bases in the Netherlands, whose citizens had grown to loathe Alva and his Spaniards.

After the success at Brielle, the revolt spread rapidly: by June the rebels controlled most of the province of Holland and William was able to take command of his troops in Delft. Alva and his son Frederick fought back, taking Gelderland, Overijssel and the towns of Zutphen and Naarden, and in June 1573 Haarlem, massacring the Calvinist ministers and most of the defenders. But the Protestants retaliated: utilizing their superior naval power, the dykes were cut and the Spanish forces, unpaid and threatened with destruction, were forced to withdraw. Frustrated, Philip replaced Alva with **Luis de Resquesens**, who initially had some success in the south, where the Catholic majority was more willing to compromise with Spanish rule than their northern neighbours.

William's triumphant relief of Leiden in 1574 increased the confidence of the rebel forces, and when de Resquesens died in 1576, his unpaid garrison in Antwerp mutinied and attacked the town, slaughtering some eight thousand of its people in what was known as the **Spanish Fury**. Though Spain still held several towns, the massacre alienated the south and pushed its inhabitants into the arms of William, whose troops now swept into Brussels, the heart of imperial power. Momentarily, it seemed possible for the whole region to unite behind William, and all signed the **Union of Brussels**, which demanded the departure of foreign troops as a condition for accepting a diluted Habsburg sovereignty. This was followed, in 1576, by the **Pacification of Ghent**, a regional agreement that guaranteed freedom of religious belief, a necessary precondition for any union between the largely Protestant north (the Netherlands) and Catholic south (Belgium and Luxembourg).

Philip was, however, not inclined to compromise, especially when he realized that William's Calvinist sympathies were giving his newly found Walloon and Flemish allies the jitters. The king bided his time until 1578, when, with his enemies still arguing among themselves, he sent another army from Spain to the Low Countries under the command of Alessandro Farnese, the **Duke of Parma**. Events played into Parma's hands. In 1579, tired of all the wrangling, seven northern provinces (Holland, Zeeland, Utrecht, Groningen, Friesland, Overijssel and Gelderland) broke with their southerly neighbours to sign the **Union of Utrecht**, an alliance against Spain that was to be the first unification of the Netherlands as an identifiable country – the so-called **United Provinces**. The agreement stipulated freedom of belief within the provinces, an important step since the struggle against Spain wasn't simply a religious one: many Catholics disliked the Spanish occupation and William did not wish to alienate this possible source of support. This liberalism did not, however, extend to freedom of worship, although to all intents and purposes a blind eye was turned to the celebration of Mass if it was done privately and inconspicuously – giving rise to the "hidden churches" found throughout the Netherlands today. Meanwhile, in the south – and also in 1579 – representatives of the southern

△ Engraving of William the Silent

provinces signed the **Union of Arras**, a Catholic-led agreement that declared loyalty to Philip II in counter-balance to the Union of Utrecht in the north. Parma used this area as a base to recapture all of Flanders and Antwerp, which fell after a long and cruel siege in 1585. But Parma was unable to advance any further north and the Low Countries were, de facto, divided into two – the Spanish Netherlands and the United Provinces – beginning a separation that would lead, after many changes, to the creation of three modern countries – Belgium, Luxembourg and the Netherlands.

The United Provinces 1579–1713

To follow the developments of the sixteenth and seventeenth centuries in the **United Provinces**, it's necessary to have an idea of its organization. Throughout the period, Holland, today comprising Noord- and Zuid-Holland, was by far the dominant province economically and politically, and although the provinces maintained a degree of decentralized independence, as far as the United Provinces as a whole were concerned, what Holland said pretty much went.

The assembly of these United Provinces was known as the **States General** and it met at Den Haag (The Hague); it had no domestic legislative authority, and could only carry out foreign policy by unanimous decision, a formula designed to make potential waverers feel more secure. The role of **Stadholder** was the most important in each province, roughly equivalent to that of governor, though the same person could occupy this position in any number of provinces – and mostly did, with the Orange-Nassaus characteristically picking up five or six provinces at any one time. The **Council Pensionary** was another major post. The man who held either title in Holland was a centre of political power. Pieter Geyl, in his seminal *Revolt of the Netherlands*, defined the end result as the estab-lishment of a republic which was "oligarchic, erastian (and) decentralized".

In 1584, a Catholic fanatic assassinated William the Silent at his residence in Delft. It was a grievous blow to the provinces and, as William's son **Maurice** was only 17, power passed to **Johan van Oldenbarneveldt**, the country's leading statesman and Council Pensionary of Rotterdam and ultimately Hol-land. Things were going badly in the war against the Spanish: Nijmegen had fallen and Henry III of France refused to help even though the States General had made him tentative offers of sovereignty. In desperation, Oldenbarneveldt turned to **Elizabeth I** of England, who suggested the Earl of Leicester as gov-ernor general. Leicester was accepted, but completely mishandled the military situation, alienating the Dutch into the bargain. Short of options, Oldenbarn-eveldt and Maurice then stepped into the breach and, somewhat to their sur-prise, drove the Spanish back. International events then played into their hands: in 1588, the English defeated the Spanish Armada and the following year the powerful and ambitious king Henry III of France died. Most important of all, Philip II of Spain, the scourge of the Low Countries, died in 1598, a necessary preamble to the **Twelve Year Truce** (1609–21) signed between the Habsburgs and the United Provinces, which grudgingly accepted the independence of the new republic.

The early seventeenth century

In the breathing space created by the truce, the **rivalry** between Maurice and Oldenbarneveldt intensified and an obscure argument within the Cal-vinist church on predestination proved the catalyst for Oldenbarneveldt's downfall. The quarrel, between two Leiden theologians, began in 1612: one of them, Armenius, argued that God gave man the choice of accepting or rejecting faith; Gomarus, his opponent, that predestination was absolute – to the degree that God chooses who will be saved and who damned with man powerless in the decision. This row between the two groups (known respec-tively as Remonstrants and Counter-Remonstrants) soon became attached to the political divisions within the republic. When a synod was arranged at Dordrecht to resolve the doctrinal matter, the province of Holland, led by Oldenbarneveldt, refused to attend, insisting on Holland's right to decide its own religious orthodoxies. At heart, he and his fellow deputies supported the provincial independence favoured by Remonstrant sympathizers, whereas Maurice sided with the Counter-Remonstrants, who favoured a strong central authority. The Counter-Remonstrants won at Dordrecht and Maurice, with his troops behind him, quickly overcame his opponents and had Oldenbarn-eveldt arrested. In May 1619 Oldenbarneveldt was **executed** in Den Haag "for having conspired to dismember the states of the Netherlands and greatly troubled God's church".

With the end of the Twelve Year Truce in 1621, fighting with Spain broke out once again, this time part of the more general **Thirty Years' War** (1618–48), a largely religious-based conflict between Catholic and Protestant countries that involved most of western Europe. In the Low Countries, the Spanish were initially successful, but they were weakened by war with France and by the fresh attacks of Maurice's successor, his brother **Frederick Henry**. From 1625, the Spaniards suffered a series of defeats on land and sea that forced them out of what is today the southern part of the Netherlands, and in 1648 they were compelled to accept the humiliating **Peace of Westphalia**, the general treaty that ended the Thirty Years' War. Under its terms, the independence of the United Provinces was formally recognized and the Dutch were even able to insist that the Scheldt estuary be closed to shipping, an action designed to destroy the trade and prosperity of Antwerp, which – along with the rest of modern-day Belgium – remained part of the Habsburg empire. By this act, the commercial expansion and pre-eminence of Amsterdam was assured, and the Golden Age began.

The Golden Age

The brilliance of **Amsterdam**'s explosion onto the European scene is as difficult to underestimate as it is to detail. The size of the city's merchant fleet carrying Baltic grain into Europe had long been considerable and even during the long war with Spain it had continued to expand. Indeed, not only were the Spaniards unable to undermine it, but they were, on occasion, even obliged to use Dutch ships to supply their own troops – part of a burgeoning cargo trade that was another key ingredient of Amsterdam's economic success.

It was, however, the emasculation of Antwerp by the Treaty of Westphalia that launched a period of extraordinarily dynamic growth – the so-called **Golden Age** – and Amsterdam quickly became the emporium for the products of north and south Europe and the new colonies in the East and West Indies. Dutch banking and investment brought further prosperity, and by the mid-seventeenth century Amsterdam's wealth was spectacular. The Calvinist bourgeoisie indulged themselves in fine canal houses, and commissioned images of themselves in group portraits. Civic pride knew no bounds: great monuments to self-aggrandizement, such as Amsterdam's new town hall, were hastily erected, and, if some went hungry, few starved, as the poor were cared for in municipal almshouses. The arts flourished and religious tolerance extended even to the traditional scapegoats, the Jews, and in particular the Sephardic Jews, who had been hounded from Spain by the Inquisition but were guaranteed freedom from religious persecution under the terms of the Union of Utrecht of 1579. By the end of the eighteenth century, Jews accounted for ten percent of the city's inhabitants. Guilds and craft associations thrived, and in the first half of the seventeenth century the city's population quadrupled. Furthermore, although Amsterdam was the centre of this boom, economic ripples spread across much of the United Provinces. Dutch farmers were, for instance, able to sell all they could produce in the expanding city and a string of Zuider Zee ports cashed in on the flourishing Baltic trade.

Throughout the Golden Age, one organization that kept the country's coffers brimming was the **East India Company**. Formed in 1602, this Amsterdam-controlled enterprise sent ships to Asia, Indonesia, and as far as China to bring back spices, woods and other assorted valuables. The States General granted the company a trading monopoly in all lands east of the Cape of Good Hope and, for good measure, threw in unlimited military powers over the lands it controlled. As a consequence, the company became a colonial power in its own right, governing, at one time or another, Malaya, Sri Lanka and parts of modern-day

Indonesia. In 1621, the **West India Company** was inaugurated to protect Dutch interests in the Americas and Africa. However, this second company never achieved the success of its sister, expending most of its energies in waging war on Spanish and Portuguese colonies from its base in Surinam. The company was dismantled in 1674, ten years after its nascent colony of New Amsterdam had been captured by the British and renamed **New York**. Elsewhere, the Netherlands held on to its colonies for as long as possible: Java and Sumatra remained under Dutch control until 1949.

Although the economics of the Golden Age were dazzling, the **politics** were dismal. The United Provinces were dogged by interminable wrangling between those who hankered for a central, unified government under the pre-eminent **House of Orange-Nassau** and those who championed provincial autonomy. Frederick Henry died in 1647 and his successor, William II, lasted just three years before his death from smallpox. A week after William's death, his wife bore the son who would become William III of England, but in the meantime the leaders of the province of Holland seized their opportunity. They forced measures through the States General abolishing the position of Stadholder, thereby reducing the powers of the Orangists and increasing those of the provinces, chiefly Holland itself. Holland's foremost figure in these years was **Johan de Witt**, Council Pensionary to the States General. He guided the country through wars with England and Sweden, concluding a triple alliance between the two countries and the United Provinces in 1678. This didn't last, however, and when France and England marched on the Provinces two years later, the republic was in deep trouble – previous victories had been at sea– and the army, weak and disorganized, could not withstand an attack. In panic, the country turned to **William III of Orange** for leadership and Johan de Witt was brutally murdered by a mob of Orangist sympathizers in Den Haag. By 1678, William had defeated the French and made peace with the English – and was rewarded (along with his wife Mary) with the English crown ten years later.

The United Provinces in the eighteenth century

Though King William had defeated the French, Louis XIV retained designs on the United Provinces and the pot was kept boiling in a long series of dynastic wars that ranged across northern Europe. In 1700, Charles II of Spain, the last of the Spanish Habsburgs, died childless, bequeathing the Spanish throne and control of the Spanish Netherlands to Philip of Anjou, Louis' grandson. Louis promptly forced Philip to cede the latter to France, which was, with every justification, construed as a threat to the balance of power by France's neighbours. The **War of the Spanish Succession** ensued, with the United Provinces, England and Austria forming the Triple Alliance to thwart the French king. The war itself was a haphazard, long-winded affair distinguished by the spectacular victories of the Duke of Marlborough at Blenheim, Ramillies and Malplaquet. It dragged on until the **Treaty of Utrecht** of 1713 in which France finally abandoned its claim to the Spanish Netherlands.

All this fighting had, however, drained the United Provinces' reserves and its slow economic and political decline began, accelerated by an ossification of its ruling class. This reflected the development of an increasingly socially static society, with power and wealth concentrated within a small, immovable elite. Furthermore, with the threat of foreign conquest effectively removed, the Dutch ruling class divided into two main camps – the **Orangists** and the pro-French "**Patriots**" – whose interminable squabbling soon brought political life to a virtual standstill. The situation deteriorated even further in the latter half of the century and the last few years of the United Provinces present a sorry state of affairs.

French occupation and the United Kingdom of the Netherlands

In 1795 the French, aided by the Patriots, invaded, setting up the **Batavian Republic** and dissolving the United Provinces – and much of the hegemony of the rich Dutch merchants. Effectively part of the Napoleonic empire, the Netherlands were obliged to wage unenthusiastic war with England, and in 1806 Napoleon appointed his brother **Louis** as their king in an attempt to create a dynastic gulf between the country and England. Louis, however, wasn't willing to allow the Netherlands to become a simple satellite of France; he ignored Napoleon's directives and after just four years of rule was forced to abdicate. The country was then formally incorporated into the French Empire, and for three gloomy years suffered occupation and heavy taxation to finance French military adventures.

Following Napoleon's disastrous retreat from Moscow, the Orangist faction surfaced to exploit weakening French control. In 1813, Frederick William, son of the exiled William V, returned to the country and eight months later, under the terms of the **Congress of Vienna**, was crowned King William I of the **United Kingdom of the Netherlands**, incorporating both the old United Provinces and the Spanish (Austrian) Netherlands. A strong-willed man, he spent much of the latter part of his life trying to control his disparate kingdom, but he failed primarily because the Catholic south did not trust him or his advisors. The southern provinces revolted against his rule and in 1830 the independent Kingdom of Belgium was proclaimed.

From 1830 to the early twentieth century

In 1839, a final fling of the military dice gave William most of Limburg, and all but ended centuries of territorial change within the Low Countries. The Netherlands benefited from this new stability both economically and politically, emerging as a unitary state with a burgeoning industrial and entrepot economy. The outstanding political figure of the times, **Jan Rudolph Thorbecke**, formed three ruling cabinets (1849–53, 1862–66 and 1872, in the year of his death) and steered the Netherlands through these changes. The political parties of the late eighteenth century had wished to resurrect the power and prestige of the seventeenth-century Netherlands; Thorbecke and his allies resigned themselves to the country's reduced status and eulogized the advantages of being a small power. For the first time, from about 1850, liberty was seen as a luxury made possible by the country's very lack of power, and the malaise that had long disturbed public life gave way to a positive appreciation of the very narrowness of its national existence. One of the results of Thorbecke's liberalism was a gradual extension of the franchise, culminating in the **Act of Universal Suffrage** of 1917.

The war years

The Netherlands remained neutral in **World War I** and although it suffered privations from the Allied blockade of German war materials, this was offset by the profits accrued by continuing to trade with both sides. But similar attempts to remain neutral in **World War II** failed: the Germans invaded on May 10, 1940, destroying Rotterdam four days later, a salutary lesson that

△ The Dutch Bicycle Regiment in April 1940

made prolonged resistance inconceivable. The Dutch army was quickly overwhelmed, Queen Wilhelmina fled to London to set up a government-in-exile, and members of the **NSB**, the Dutch fascist party, which had welcomed the invaders, were rewarded with positions of authority. Nevertheless, in the early stages of the occupation, life for the average Netherlander went on pretty much as usual, which is just what the Germans wanted – they were determined to transform the country by degrees. Even when the first roundups of the **Jews** began in late 1940, many managed to turn a blind eye, though the newly outlawed Dutch Communist Party did organize a widely supported strike to protest, a gesture perhaps, but an important one all the same.

As the war progressed, so the German grip got tighter and the Dutch **Resistance** stronger, its activities focused on destroying German supplies and munitions as well as the forgery of identity papers, a real Dutch speciality. The Resistance also trumpeted its efforts in a battery of underground newspapers, most notably *Het Parool* (The Pasword), which survives in good form today. Inevitably, the Resistance paid a heavy price with some 23,000 of its fighters and sympathizers losing their lives, but Amsterdam's Jews took the worst punishment: in 1940, Amsterdam's Jewish population, swollen by refugees from Hitler's Germany, was around 140,000, but by the end of the war there were only a few thousand left, rendering the Jodenhoek deserted and derelict.

Liberation began from the south in the autumn of 1944. To speed the process, the British determined on **Operation Market Garden**, an ambitious plan to finish the war quickly by creating an Allied corridor stretching from Eindhoven to Arnhem. If it had been successful, the Allies would have secured control of the country's three main rivers and been able to drive on into Germany, thereby isolating the occupying forces in the western Netherlands. On September 17, 1944, the 1st Airborne Division parachuted into the countryside around Oosterbeek, a small village near the most northerly target of the operation, the **bridge at Arnhem**. However German opposition was, much stronger than expected and after heavy fighting the paratroopers could only take the northern end of the bridge. The advancing British army was unable to break through fast enough, and after four days the decimated battalion defending the bridge was forced to withdraw.

With the failure of Operation Market Garden, the Allies were obliged to resort to more orthodox military tactics. In their push towards Germany, they slowly cleared the east and south of the country in the winter and spring of 1944–45, leaving the coastal provinces pretty much untouched, though here lack of food and fuel created desperate conditions, with hundreds starving to death. Finally, on **April 5, 1945**, the remains of the German army in the Netherlands surrendered to the Canadians at Wageningen.

Reconstruction – 1945 to 1960

The **postwar years** were spent patching up the damage of occupation and liberation: Rotterdam was rebuilt in double quick time, the dykes blown during the war were speedily repaired, and the canals and waterways were soon cleared of their accumulated debris. At the same time, the country began a vast construction programme, with modern suburbs mushrooming around every major city, especially Amsterdam, where almost all the land projected for use by the year 2000 was in fact used by 1970.

However, an ill-advised foreign adventure was to mar the late 1940s and early 1950s: the former **Dutch colonies** of Java and Sumatra had been occupied by the Japanese at the outbreak of the war and they were now ruled by a nationalist Republican government that refused to recognize Dutch sovereignty. Following the failure of talks between Den Haag and the islanders in 1947, the Dutch dispatched the army in a colonial enterprise that soon became a bloody debacle. International opposition was intense and, after much condemnation, the Dutch reluctantly surrendered their most important Asian colonies, which were incorporated as **Indonesia**, in 1950.

Back home, **tragedy** struck on February 1, 1953, when an unusually high tide was pushed over Zeeland's sea defences by a westerly wind, flooding 40,000 acres of land and drowning over 1800 people. The response was to secure the area's future with the **Delta Project**, closing off the western part of the Scheldt and Maas estuaries with massive sea dykes. A brilliant and graceful piece of engineering, the main storm surge barrier on the Oosterschelde was finally completed in 1986. Amsterdam itself had already been secured by the completion of the **Afsluitdijk** between Noord-Holland and Friesland in 1932. This dyke separated the North Sea from the former Zuider Zee, which now became the freshwater **IJsselmeer**, and in 1976 a second dyke was added, calving the **Markermeer** from the IJsselmeer. For more on the Netherlands' sea defences see *The Battle with the Sea* colour section.

1960 to the early 1980s

The radical and youthful mass movements that swept across the West in the 1960s transformed Amsterdam from a middling, rather conservative city into a turbo-charged hotbed of hippy action – and where Amsterdam led, all the big cities of the Randstad followed. Initially, it was the Provos (see box opposite) who led the counter-cultural charge, but in 1967 they dissolved themselves and many of their supporters moved on to the **squatter movement**, which opposed the wholesale destruction of low-cost (often old) urban housing as envisaged by many municipal councils. For many squatters, it seemed as if local councils were neglecting the needs of their poorer citizens in favour of business interests, and in Amsterdam, the epicentre of the movement, there were regular confrontations between the police and the protestors at a handful of symbolic squats. The first major incident came in Amsterdam in March

In 1963, one-time window cleaner and magician extraordinaire **Jasper Grootveld** won celebrity status by painting "K" – for *kanker* ("cancer") – on cigarette billboards throughout Amsterdam. Two years later, he proclaimed the statue of the *Lieverdje* ("Loveable Rascal") on the Spui (see p.80) the symbol of "tomorrow's addicted consumer" – since it had been donated to the city by a cigarette manufacturer – and organized large-scale gatherings there once a week. His actions enthused others, most notably **Roel van Duyn**, a philosophy student at Amsterdam University, who assembled a left-wing-cum-anarchist movement known as the **Provos** – short for *provocatie* ("provocation"). The Provos participated in Grootveld's meetings and then proceeded to organize their own street "**happenings**", which proved to be fantastically popular among young Amsterdammers. The number of Provos never exceeded about thirty and the group had no coherent structure, but they did have one clear aim – to bring points of political or social conflict to public attention by spectacular means. More than anything they were masters of publicity, and pursued their "games" with a spirit of fun rather than grim political fanaticism. The reaction of the Amsterdam police, however, was aggressive: the first two issues of the Provos' magazine were confiscated and, in July 1965, they intervened at a Saturday night "happening", setting a pattern for future confrontations. The magazine itself contained the Provos' manifesto, a set of policies which later appeared under the title "**The White Plans**". These included the famously popular **white bicycle plan**, which proposed that the council ban all cars in the city centre and supply 20,000 bicycles (painted white) for general public use.

There were regular police–Provo confrontations throughout 1965, but it was the **wedding of Princess Beatrix** to Claus von Amsberg on March 10, 1966, that provoked the most serious unrest. Amsberg had served in the German army during World War II and many Netherlanders were deeply offended by the marriage. Consequently, when hundreds took to the streets to protest, pelting the wedding procession with smoke bombs, a huge swath of Dutch opinion supported them – to some degree or another. Amsberg himself got no more than he deserved when he was jeered with the refrain "Give us back the bicycles", a reference to the commandeering of hundreds of bikes by the retreating German army in 1945. The wedding over, the next crisis came in June when, much to the horror of the authorities, it appeared that students, workers and Provos were about to combine. In panic, the Hague government ordered the dismissal of Amsterdam's police chief, but in the event the Provos had peaked and the workers proved far from revolutionary, settling for arbitration on their various complaints instead.

The final twist in the Provos' tale was the formation of a splinter group called the **Kabouters**, named after a helpful gnome in Dutch folklore. Their manifesto described their form of socialism as "not of the clenched fist, but of the intertwined fingers, the erect penis, the escaping butterfly…" – appealing perhaps, but never massively popular.

1980 when several hundred police evicted squatters from premises on **Vondelstraat**. Afterwards, there was widespread rioting, but this was small beer in comparison with the protests of April 30, 1980 – the **coronation day of Queen Beatrix** – when a mixed bag of squatters and leftists vigorously protested both the lavishness of the proceedings and the expense of refurbishing Beatrix's palace in Den Haag. Once again there was widespread rioting and this time it spread to other Dutch cities, though the unrest was short-lived.

Now at its peak, Amsterdam's squatter movement boasted around ten thousand activists, many of whom were involved in two more major confrontations with the police – the first at the Lucky Luyk squat, on Jan Luykenstraat, the second at the Wyers building, when, in February 1984, the squatters were forcibly cleared to make way for a hotel. Thereafter, the movement faded away, at least partly because of its repeated failure to stop the developers, who could now claim, with some justification, to be more sensitive to community needs.

The 1980s to the present

The street protests and squats of the country's recent past now seem a distant memory, but some of the old ideas – and ideals – have been carried forward by the **Greens**, who attract a small but significant following in every national election. The much larger Labour Party – the Pvda – has picked up on some of these issues too, though it has a problem with **Schiphol airport**, which needs to be expanded, but is an environmental minefield. Politically, one of the main problems is that the country's finely balanced system of **proportional representation** brings little rapid change and often mires in interminable compromise and debate, altogether a bland if necessary business conducted between the three main parties, the **Protestant–Catholic CDA** coalition, the **Liberal VVD** and the **Socialist Pvda**. However, the entire political class received a jolt in the national elections of May 2002 when a brand-new Rightist grouping – **Leefbaar Neederlands** (Liveable Netherlands) – led by Rotterdam's **Pim Fortuyn** swept to second place behind the CDA, securing seventeen percent of the national vote. Stylish and witty, openly gay and a former Marxist, Fortuyn managed to cover several popular bases at the same time, from the need for law and order through to tighter immigration controls. Most crucially, he also attacked the liberal establishment's espousal of multiculturalism even when the representatives of minority groups were deeply reactionary, anti-gay and sexist. Politically, it worked a treat, but a year later Fortuyn was assassinated and his party rapidly unravelled, losing most of its seats in the general election of January 2003. One of the reasons for Fortuyn's electoral success reflected the other shock to the Dutch system, which came with the publication of a damning report on the failure of the Dutch army to protect the Bosnian Muslims ensconced in the UN safe-haven of **Srebrenica** in 1995, published in April 2002. In a country that prides itself on its internationalism, the report was an especially hard blow and the whole of the Pvda-led government, under **Wim Kok**, resigned in April 2002 – in the same year as the Netherlands dropped the guilder in favour of the euro.

The general election of 2003 was a close run thing, and there was certainly a revival in Pvda fortunes, but a **Rightist alliance** – consisting of the VVD, the CDA and the Lijst Pim Fortuyn (formerly Leefbaar Neederlands) – still managed to cobble together an administration under the leadership of Jan Peter Balkenende. In the event, this coalition proved most unstable and at time of writing Balkenende has teamed up with different partners to remain at the head of a minority government that will stay in office until the next general election. Superficially, therefore, and with the Fortuyn representatives reduced to a rump, it seems that normal political service has been resumed, but although the CDA, the Pvda and the VVD are once again the largest parties, there is an uneasy undertow. In truth, Fortuyn's popularity pushed certain sorts of social debate, particularly on **immigration**, to the right and the situation got much worse – and race relations much tenser – when, in late 2004, the filmmaker **Theo van Gogh** was shot dead on an Amsterdam street by a Moroccan who objected to a film Van Gogh had made – *Submission* – about Islamic violence against women. Shown on Dutch TV, the film was scripted by an MP, **Ayaan**

Hirsi Ali, a Somali refugee and current Dutch citizen, whose pronouncements on this same subject have been hard-hitting and headline-grabbing in equal measure: "But tell me", she was reported to have said in a *Telegraph* interview in December 2004, "why any Muslim man would want Islamic women to be educated and emancipated? Would a Roman voluntarily have given up his slaves?" Unfortunately for Ali, she was engulfed by controversy of a different kind in 2006 when it turned out that her application for asylum had not been entirely truthful – and the ensuing furore created parliamentary panic. More generally, with polls indicating that many Dutch feel apprehensive if not actually hostile to the Muslims in their midst, it will take all of Balkenende's skills to keep the lid on the inter-communal pot; other Netherlanders are voting with their feet: in 2005, 121,000 mostly middle-class Dutch citizens emigrated, the largest number ever.

Dutch art

D esigned to serve only as a quick reference, the following **outline** is the very briefest of introductions to a subject that has rightly filled volumes. Inevitably, it covers artists that lived and worked in both the Netherlands and Belgium, as these two countries have – along with Luxembourg – been bound together as the "Low Countries" for most of their history. For in-depth and academic studies, see the recommendations in "Books" on p.384.

Beginnings: the Flemish Primitives

Throughout the medieval period, **Flanders**, in modern-day Belgium, was one of the most artistically productive parts of Europe and it was here that the solid realist base of later Dutch painting developed. Today the works of these early Flemish painters, the **Flemish Primitives**, are highly prized and although examples are fairly sparse in the Netherlands, all the leading museums – especially Amsterdam's Rijksmuseum and Den Haag's Mauritshuis – have a healthy sample.

Jan van Eyck (1385–1441) is generally regarded as the first of the Flemish Primitives, and has even been credited with the invention of oil painting – though it seems more likely that he simply perfected a new technique by thinning his paint with (the newly discovered) turpentine, thus making it more flexible. His most famous work, the *Adoration of the Mystic Lamb*, displayed in Ghent cathedral in Belgium, was revolutionary in its realism, for the first time using elements of native landscape in depicting Biblical themes, and Van Eyck's style and technique were to influence several generations of Low Countries artists.

Firmly in the Eyckian tradition were the **Master of Flemalle** (1387–1444) and **Rogier van der Weyden** (1400–64), one-time official painter to the city of Brussels. The Flemalle master is a shadowy figure: some believe he was the teacher of Van der Weyden, others that the two artists were in fact the same person. There are differences between the two, however: the Flemalle master's paintings are close to Van Eyck's, whereas Van der Weyden shows a greater degree of emotional intensity in his religious works. Van der Weyden also produced serene portraits of the bigwigs of his day that were much admired across a large swath of western Europe. His style influenced many painters with one of the most talented of these being **Dieric Bouts** (1415–75). Born in Haarlem but active in Leuven, Bouts is recognizable by his stiff, rather elongated figures and horrific subject matter, all set against carefully drawn landscapes. **Hugo van der Goes** (d.1482) was the next Ghent master after Van Eyck, most famous for the Portinari altarpiece in Florence's Uffizi gallery. Goes died insane and his later works have strong hints of his impending madness in their subversive use of space and implicit acceptance of the viewer's presence.

Few doubt that **Hans Memling** (1440–94) was a pupil of Van der Weyden: active in Bruges throughout his life, he is best remembered for the pastoral charm of his landscapes and the quality of his portraiture, much of which survives on the rescued side panels of triptychs. **Gerard David** (1460–1523) was a native of Oudewater, near Gouda, but he moved to Bruges in 1484, becoming the last of the great painters to work in that city before it was outstripped by Antwerp, producing formal religious works of traditional bent. Strikingly different, but broadly contemporaneous, was **Hieronymus Bosch** (1450–1516), who lived for most of his life in Holland, though his style is linked to that of his Flemish contemporaries. His frequently reprinted religious allegories are filled with macabre visions of tortured people and grotesque beasts, and appear at first faintly unhinged, though it's now thought that these are visual representations of contemporary sayings, idioms and parables. While their interpretation is far from resolved, Bosch's paintings draw strongly on subconscious fears and archetypes, giving them a lasting, haunting fascination.

The sixteenth century

At the end of the fifteenth century, Flanders was in economic and political decline and the leading artists of the day migrated to the booming port of Antwerp. The artists who worked here soon began to integrate the finely observed detail that characterized the Flemish tradition with the style of the Italian painters of the Renaissance. **Quentin Matsys** (1464–1530) introduced florid classical architectural details and intricate landscapes to his works, influenced perhaps by the work of Leonardo da Vinci. As well as religious works, he painted portraits and genre scenes, all of which have recognizably Italian facets – and paved the way for the Dutch genre painters of later years. **Jan Gossart** (1478–1532) made the pilgrimage to Italy, too, and his dynamic works are packed with detail, especially finely drawn classical architectural backdrops. He was the first Low Countries artist to introduce the subjects of classical mythology into his works, part of a steady trend towards secular subject matter, which can also be seen in the work of **Joachim Patenier** (d.1524), who painted small landscapes of fantastical scenery.

The middle of the sixteenth century was dominated by the work of **Pieter Bruegel the Elder** (c.1525–69), whose gruesome allegories and innovative interpretations of religious subjects are firmly placed in Low Countries settings. Pieter also painted finely observed peasant scenes, though he himself was well connected in court circles in Antwerp and, later, Brussels. **Pieter Aertsen** (1508–75) also worked in the peasant genre, adding aspects of still life; his paintings often show a detailed kitchen scene in the foreground, with a religious episode going on behind. Bruegel's two sons, **Pieter Bruegel the Younger** (1564–1638) and **Jan Bruegel** (1568–1625), were lesser painters: the former produced fairly insipid copies of his father's work, while Jan developed a style of his own – delicately rendered flower paintings and genre pieces that earned him the nickname "Velvet". Towards the latter half of the sixteenth century highly stylized Italianate portraiture became the dominant fashion, **Frans Pourbus the Younger** (1569–1622) being the leading practitioner. Frans hobnobbed across Europe, working for the likes of the Habsburgs and the Medicis.

Meanwhile, there were artistic rumblings in Holland. Leading the painterly charge was **Geertgen tot Sint Jans** (Little Gerard of the Brotherhood of St John; d.1490), who worked in Haarlem, initiating – in a strangely naive style – an artistic vision that would come to dominate the seventeenth century. There was a tender melancholy in his work very different from the stylized paintings produced in Flanders and, most importantly, a new sensitivity to light – and lighting. **Jan Mostaert** (1475–1555) took over after Geertgen's death, developing similar themes, but the first painter to effect real changes in northern painting was **Lucas van Leyden** (1489–1533). Born in Leiden, Van Leyden's bright colours and narrative technique were refreshingly novel, and he introduced a new dynamism into what had become a rigidly formal treatment of devotional subjects. There was rivalry, of course. Eager to publicize Haarlem as the artistic capital of the northern Netherlands, **Karel van Mander** (see p.374) claimed **Jan**

van Scorel (1495–1562) as the better painter, complaining, too, of Van Leyden's dandyish ways. Certainly Van Scorel's influence should not be underestimated. Like many of his contemporaries, Van Scorel hotfooted it to Italy to view the works of the Renaissance, but in Rome his career went into overdrive when he found favour with Pope Hadrian VI, one-time bishop of Utrecht, who installed him as court painter in 1520. Van Scorel stayed in Rome for four years and when he returned to Utrecht, armed with all that papal prestige, he combined the ideas he had picked up in Italy with those underpinning Haarlem realism, thereby modifying what had previously been an independent artistic tradition once and for all. Among his several students, probably the most talented was **Maerten van Heemskerck** (1498–1574), who duly went off to Italy himself in 1532, staying there five years before doubling back to Haarlem.

The Golden Age

The seventeenth century begins with **Karel van Mander**, Haarlem painter, art impresario and one of the few contemporary chroniclers of the art of the Low Countries. His *Schilderboek* of 1604 put Flemish and Dutch traditions into context for the first time, and in addition specified the rules of fine painting. Examples of his own work are rare – though Haarlem's Frans Hals Museum weighs in with a couple – but his followers were many. Among them was **Cornelius Cornelisz van Haarlem** (1562–1638), who produced elegant renditions of biblical and mythical themes; and **Hendrik Goltzius** (1558–1616), who was a skilled engraver and an integral member of Van Mander's Haarlem academy. These painters' enthusiasm for Italian art, combined with the influence of a late revival of Gothicism, resulted in works that combined Mannerist and Classical elements. An interest in realism was also felt, and, for them, the subject became less important than the way in which it was depicted: biblical stories became merely a vehicle whereby artists could apply their skills in painting the human body, landscapes, or copious displays of food. All of this served to break religion's stranglehold on art, and make legitimate a whole range of everyday subjects for the painter.

In Holland – and this was where the north and south finally diverged – this break with tradition was compounded by the **Reformation**: the austere Calvinism that had replaced the Catholic faith in the United (that is northern) Provinces had no use for images or symbols of devotion in its churches. Instead, painters catered to the burgeoning middle class, and no longer visited Italy to learn their craft. Indeed, the real giants of the seventeenth century – Hals, Rembrandt, Vermeer – stayed in the Netherlands all their lives. A further innovation was that painting split into more distinct categories, such as genre, portrait and landscape, and artists tended (with notable exceptions) to confine themselves to one field throughout their careers. So began the **Golden Age** of Dutch art; for more on this period see *The Dutch Golden Age* colour section.

Historical and religious painting

The artistic influence of Renaissance Italy may have been in decline, but Italian painters still had clout with the Dutch, most notably Caravaggio (1571–1610), who was much admired for his new realism. Taking Caravaggio's cue, many artists – Rembrandt for one – continued to portray classical subjects, but in a way that was totally at odds with the Mannerists' stylish flights of imagination. The Utrecht artist **Abraham Bloemaert** (1564–1651), though a solid Mannerist throughout his career, encouraged these new ideas, and his students – **Gerard van Honthorst** (1590–1656), **Hendrik Terbrugghen** (1588–1629) and **Dirck van Baburen** (1590–1624) – formed the nucleus of the influential **Utrecht School**, which followed Caravaggio almost to the point of slavishness. Honthorst was perhaps the leading figure, learning his craft from Bloemaert and travelling to Rome, where he was nicknamed "Gerardo delle Notti" for his ingenious handling of light and shade. In his later paintings, however, this was to become more routine technique than inspired invention, and though a supremely competent artist, Honthorst is somewhat discredited among critics today. Terbrugghen's reputation seems to have aged rather better: he soon forgot Caravaggio and developed a more individual style, his later, lighter work having a great influence on the young Vermeer. After a jaunt to Rome, Baburen shared a studio with Terbrugghen and produced some fairly original work – work that also had some influence on Vermeer – but today he is the least studied member of the group and few of his paintings survive.

Above all others, **Rembrandt van Rijn** (1606–69) was the most original historical artist of the seventeenth century, also chipping in with a slew of religious paintings. In the 1630s, the poet and statesman Constantijn Huygens procured for him his greatest commission – a series of five paintings of the Passion, beautifully composed and uncompromisingly realistic. Later, however, Rembrandt received fewer commissions, perhaps because his treatment of biblical and historical subjects was far less dramatic than that of his contemporaries and he ignored their smooth brushwork, preferring a rougher, darker and more disjointed style. It's significant that while the more conventional Jordaens, Honthorst and Van Everdingen were busy decorating the Huis ten Bosch near Den Haag for the Stadholder Frederick Henry, Rembrandt was having his monumental *Conspiracy of Julius Civilis* – painted for the new Amsterdam town hall – thrown out. The reasons for this ejection have been hotly debated, but it seems probable that Rembrandt's rendition was thought too pagan an interpretation of what was an important event in Dutch history: Julius had organized a revolt against the Romans, which had obvious resonance in a country just freed from the Habsburgs. Even worse, perhaps, Rembrandt had shown Julius to be blind in one eye, which was historically accurate but not at all what the city's burghers had in mind for a Dutch hero.

Finally, **Aert van Gelder** (1645–1727), Rembrandt's last pupil and probably the only one to concentrate on historical painting, followed the style of his master closely, producing shimmering biblical scenes well into the eighteenth century.

Genre painting

Often misunderstood, the term **genre painting** was initially applied to everything from animal paintings and still lifes through to historical works and landscapes, but later – from around the middle of the seventeenth century – came to be applied only to scenes of everyday life. Its target market was the region's burgeoning middle class, who had a penchant for non-idealized portrayals of common scenes, both with and without symbols – or subtly disguised details – making one moral point or another. One of its early practitioners was Antwerp's **Frans Snijders** (1579–1657), who took up still-life painting where Aertsen (see p.373) left off, amplifying his subject – food and drink – to even larger, more sumptuous canvases. Snijders also doubled up as a member of the Rubens art machine (see p.379), painting animals and still-life sections for the master's works. In the north, in Utrecht, Hendrik Terbrugghen and Gerard Honthorst adapted the realism and strong chiaroscuro learned from Caravaggio to a number of tableaux of everyday life, though they were more concerned with religious works, whilst Haarlem's Frans Hals dabbled in genre too, but is better known as a portraitist. The opposite is true of one of Hals' pupils, **Adriaen Brouwer** (1605–38), whose riotous tavern scenes were well received in their day and collected by, among others, Rubens and Rembrandt. Brouwer spent only a couple of years in Haarlem under Hals before returning to his native Flanders, where he influenced the inventive **David Teniers the Younger** (1610–90), who worked in Antwerp, and later in Brussels. Teniers' early paintings are Brouwer-like peasant scenes, although his later work is more delicate and diverse, including *kortegaardje* – guardroom scenes that show soldiers carousing. **Adriaen van Ostade** (1610–85), on the other hand, stayed in Haarlem most of his life, skilfully painting groups of peasants and tavern brawls, though his later acceptance by the establishment led him to water down the realism he had learnt from Brouwer. He was teacher to his brother **Isaak van Ostade** (1621–49), who produced a large number of open-air peasant scenes, subtle combinations of genre and landscape work.

The English critic E.V. Lucas dubbed Teniers, Brouwer and Ostade "coarse and boorish" compared with **Jan Steen** (1625–79), who, along with Vermeer, is probably the most admired Dutch genre painter. You can see what he had in mind: Steen's paintings offer the same Rabelaisian peasantry in full fling, but they go their debauched ways in broad daylight, and nowhere do you see the filthy rogues in shadowy hovels favoured by Brouwer and van Ostade. Steen offers more humour, too, as well as more moralizing, identifying with the hedonistic mob and reproaching them at the same time. Indeed, many of his pictures were illustrations of well-known proverbs – popular epithets on the evils of drink or the transience of human existence that were supposed to teach as well as entertain.

Leiden's **Gerrit Dou** (1613–75) was one of Rembrandt's first pupils. It's difficult to detect any trace of the master's influence in his work, however, as Dou initiated a style of his own: tiny, minutely realized and beautifully finished views of a kind of ordinary life that was decidedly more genteel than Brouwer's, or even Steen's. He was admired, above all, for his painstaking attention to detail: he would, it's said, sit in his studio for hours waiting for the dust to settle before starting work. Among his students, **Frans van Mieris** (1635–81) continued the highly finished portrayals of the Dutch bourgeoisie, as did **Gabriel Metsu** (1629–67) – perhaps Dou's most talented pupil – whose pictures often convey an overtly moral message. Another pupil of Rembrandt's, though a much later one, was **Nicholaes Maes** (1629–93), whose early works were almost entirely genre paintings, sensitively executed and again with an obvious didacticism. His later paintings show the influence of a more refined style of portrait, which he had picked up in France.

As a native of Zwolle, **Gerard ter Borch** (1619–81) found himself far from all these Leiden/Rembrandt connections; despite trips abroad to most of the artistic capitals of Europe, he remained very much a provincial painter. He depicted Holland's merchant class at play and became renowned for his curious doll-like figures and his ability to capture the textures of different types of cloth. His domestic scenes were not unlike those of **Pieter de Hooch** (1629–84), whose simple depictions of everyday life are deliberately unsentimental, and have little or no moral commentary. De Hooch's favourite trick was to paint darkened rooms with an open door leading through to a sunlit courtyard, a practice that, along with his trademark rusty red colour, makes his work easy to identify and, at its best, exquisite. That said, his later pictures reflect the cultural decline of the Dutch Republic: the rooms are more richly decorated, the arrangements more contrived and the subjects far less homely.

It was, however, **Jan Vermeer** (1632–75) who brought the most sophisticated methods to painting interiors, depicting the play of natural light on indoor surfaces with superlative skill – and the tranquil intimacy for which he is now famous the world over. Another recorder of the better-heeled Dutch household and, like De Hooch, without a moral tone, he is regarded (with Hals and Rembrandt) as one of the big three Dutch painters, though he was, it seems, a slow worker. Fewer than forty paintings can be attributed to him with any certainty. Living all his life in Delft, Vermeer is perhaps the epitome of the seventeenth-century Dutch painter – rejecting the pomp and ostentation of the High Renaissance to record quietly his contemporaries at home, painting for a public that demanded no more than that: bourgeois art at its most complete.

Portraits – and Rembrandt

Predictably enough, the ruling bourgeoisie of Holland's flourishing mercantile society wanted to record and celebrate their success, and consequently portraiture was a reliable way for a young painter to make a living. **Michiel Jansz Miereveld** (1567–1641), court painter to Frederick Henry in Den Haag, was the first real portraitist of the Dutch Republic, but it wasn't long before his stiff and rather conservative figures were superseded by the more spontaneous renderings of **Frans Hals** (1585–1666). Hals is perhaps best-known for his militia paintings – group portraits of the Dutch civil guard regiments that were formed to defend the country from the Habsburgs, but subsequently became social clubs for the well heeled. These large group pieces demanded superlative technique, since the painter had to create a collection of individual portraits while retaining a sense of the group, and accord prominence based on the relative importance of the sitters and the size of the payment each had made. Hals was particularly good at this, using innovative lighting effects, arranging his sitters subtly, and putting all the elements together in a fluid and dynamic composition. He also painted many individual portraits, making the ability to capture fleeting and telling expressions his trademark; his pictures of children are particularly sensitive. Later in life, however, his work became darker and more akin to Rembrandt's, spurred – it's conjectured – by his penury.

Jan Cornelisz Verspronck (1597–1662) and **Bartholomeus van der Helst** (1613–70) were the other great Haarlem portraitists after Frans Hals – Verspronck recognizable by the smooth, shiny glow he always gave to his sitters' faces, Van der Helst by a competent but unadventurous style. Of the two, Van der Helst was the more popular, influencing a number of later painters and leaving Haarlem as a young man to begin a solidly successful career as portrait painter to Amsterdam's burghers.

The reputation of **Rembrandt van Rijn** (1606–69) is still relatively recent – nineteenth-century connoisseurs preferred Gerard Dou – but he is now justly regarded as one of the greatest and most versatile painters of all time. Born in Leiden, the son of a miller, he was a boy apprentice to Jacob van Swanenburgh, a then quite important, though singularly uninventive, local artist. Rembrandt shared a studio with Jan Lievens, a promising painter and something of a rival, though now all but forgotten, before venturing forth to Amsterdam to study under the fashionable Pieter Lastman. Soon he was painting commissions for the city elite and became an accepted member of their circle. The poet and statesman Constantijn Huygens acted as his agent, pulling strings to obtain all of Rembrandt's more lucrative jobs, and in 1634 the artist married Saskia van Ulenborch, daughter of the burgomaster of Leeuwarden and quite a catch for a relatively humble artist. His self-portraits from this period show the confident face of security – he is on top of things and quite sure where he's going.

Rembrandt would not always be the darling of the Amsterdam burghers, but his fall from grace was still some way off when he painted *The Night Watch*, a group portrait often – but inaccurately – associated with the artist's decline in popularity. Indeed, although Rembrandt's fluent arrangement of his subjects was totally original, there's no evidence that the military company who commissioned the painting was anything but pleased with the result. More likely culprits are the artist's later pieces, whose obscure lighting and psychological insights took the conservative Amsterdam merchants by surprise. His patrons were certainly not sufficiently enthusiastic about his work to support his taste for art collecting and his expensive house on Jodenbreestraat, and in 1656 he was declared bankrupt. Rembrandt died thirteen years later a broken and embittered old man, as his last self-portraits indicate. Throughout his career he maintained a large studio, and his influence pervaded the next generation of Dutch painters. Some – Dou and Maes – more famous for their genre work have already been mentioned, but others turned to portraiture.

Govert Flinck (1615–60) was perhaps Rembrandt's most faithful follower, and he was, ironically enough, given the job of decorating Amsterdam's new Stadhuis (town hall) after his teacher had been passed over. Unluckily for him, Flinck died before he could execute his designs and Rembrandt took over, but although the latter's *Conspiracy of Julius Civilis* was installed in 1662, it was discarded a year later. The early work of **Ferdinand Bol** (1616–80) was so heavily influenced by Rembrandt that for centuries art historians couldn't tell the two apart, though his later paintings are readily distinguishable, blandly elegant portraits, which proved very popular with the wealthy. At the age of 53, Bol married a rich widow and promptly stopped painting – perhaps because he knew how emotionally tacky his work had become. Most of the pitifully slim extant work of **Carel Fabritius** (1622–54) is portraiture, but he too died young, before he could properly realize his promise as perhaps the most gifted of all Rembrandt's students. Generally regarded as the teacher of Vermeer, he forms a link between the two masters, combining Rembrandt's technique with his own practice of painting figures against a dark background, prefiguring the lighting and colouring of Vermeer.

Landscapes

Aside from Pieter Bruegel the Elder (see p.373), whose depictions of his native surroundings make him the first true Low Countries landscape painter, **Gillis van Coninxloo** (1544–1607) stands out as the earliest Dutch landscapist. He imbued his native scenery with elements of fantasy, painting the richly wooded views he had seen on his travels around Europe as backdrops to biblical scenes. In the early seventeenth century, **Hercules Seghers** (1590–1638), apprenticed to Coninxloo, carried on his mentor's style of depicting forested and mountainous landscapes, some real, others not: his work is scarce but is believed to have had considerable influence on the landscape work of Rembrandt. **Esaias van der Velde**'s (1591–1632) quaint and unpretentious scenes show the first real affinity with the Dutch countryside, but while his influence was likewise considerable, he was soon overshadowed by his pupil **Jan van Goyen** (1596–1656). A remarkable painter, who belongs to the so-called "tonal phase" of Dutch landscape painting, Van Goyen's early pictures were highly coloured and close to those of his teacher, but it didn't take him long to develop a marked touch of his own, using tones of green, brown and grey to lend everything a characteristic translucent haze. His paintings are, above all, of nature, and if he included figures it was just for the sake of scale.

A long neglected artist, Van Goyen only received recognition with the arrival of the Impressionists, when his fluid and rapid brushwork was at last fully appreciated.

Another "tonal" painter, Haarlem's **Salomon van Ruisdael** (1600–70) was also directly affected by Esaias van der Velde, and his simple and atmospheric landscapes were for a long time consistently confused with those of Van Goyen. More esteemed is his nephew, **Jacob van Ruysdael** (1628–82), generally considered the greatest of all Dutch landscapists, whose fastidiously observed views of quiet flatlands dominated by stormy skies were to influence European landscapists right up to the nineteenth century. Constable, certainly, acknowledged a debt to him. Ruysdael's foremost pupil was **Meindert Hobbema** (1638–1709), who followed the master faithfully, sometimes even painting the same views (his *Avenue at Middelharnis* may be familiar).

Nicholas Berchem (1620–83) and **Jan Both** (1618–52) were the "Italianizers" of Dutch landscapes. They studied in Rome, taking back to Holland rich, golden views of the world, full of steep gorges and hills, picturesque ruins and wandering shepherds. **Allart van Everdingen** (1621–75) had a similar approach, but his subject matter stemmed from his travels in Norway, which, after his return to the Netherlands, he reproduced in all its mountainous glory. **Aelbert Cuyp** (1620–91), on the other hand, stayed in Dordrecht all his life, painting what was probably the favourite city skyline of Dutch landscapists. He inherited the warm tones of the Italianizers, and his pictures are always suffused with a deep, golden glow.

Of a number of specialist seventeenth-century painters who can be included here, **Paulus Potter** (1625–54) is rated as the best painter of domestic animals. He produced a surprisingly large number of paintings in his short life, the most reputed being his lovingly executed pictures of cows and horses. The accurate rendering of architectural features also became a specialized field, in which **Pieter Saenredam** (1597–1665), with his finely realized paintings of Dutch church interiors, is the most widely known exponent. **Emanuel de Witte** (1616–92) continued in the same vein, though his churches lack the spartan crispness of Saenredam's. **Gerrit Berckheyde** (1638–98) worked in Haarlem soon after, but he limited his views to the outside of buildings, producing variations on the same scenes around town. Nautical scenes in praise of the Dutch navy were, on the other hand, the speciality of **Willem van der Velde II** (1633–1707), whose melodramatic canvases, complete with their churning seas and chasing skies, are displayed to greatest advantage in the Nederlands Scheepvaartsmuseum in Amsterdam.

A further thriving category of seventeenth-century painting was the still life, in which objects were gathered together to remind the viewer of the transience of human life and the meaninglessness of worldly pursuits – with, for example, a skull shown alongside a book, pipe or goblet, and some half-eaten food. Two Haarlem painters dominated this field: **Pieter Claesz** (1598–1660) and **Willem Heda** (1594–1680), who confined themselves almost entirely to this area of work.

Rubens and his followers

Back down in the south, in Antwerp, **Pieter Paul Rubens** (1577–1640) was easily the most important exponent of the Baroque in northern Europe. Born in Siegen, Westphalia, he was raised in Antwerp, where he entered the painters' guild in 1598. He became court painter to the Duke of Mantua in 1600 and travelled extensively in Italy, absorbing the art of the High Renaissance and classical architecture. By the time of his return to Antwerp in 1608 he had acquired an enormous artistic vocabulary and, like his Dutch contemporaries, the paintings of Caravaggio were to influence his work profoundly. His first major success was *The Raising of the Cross*, painted in 1610 and displayed today in Antwerp cathedral. A large, dynamic work, it caused a sensation at the time, establishing Rubens' reputation and leading to a string of commissions that enabled him to set up his own studio.

The division of labour in Rubens' studio, and the talent of the artists working there (who included Anthony van Dyck and Jacob Jordaens) ensured an extraordinary output of excellent work. The degree to which Rubens personally worked on a canvas would vary, and would determine its price. From the early 1620s onwards he turned his hand to a plethora of themes and subjects – religious works, portraits, tapestry designs, landscapes, mythological scenes, ceiling paintings – each of which was handled with supreme vitality and virtuosity. From his Flemish antecedents he inherited an acute sense of light, and used it not to dramatize his subjects (a technique favoured by Caravaggio and other Italian artists), but in association with colour and form. The drama in his works comes from the vigorous animation of his characters. His large-scale allegorical works, especially, are packed with heaving, writhing figures that appear to tumble out from the canvas.

The energy of Rubens' paintings was reflected in his private life. In addition to his career as an artist, he also undertook diplomatic missions to Spain and England, and used these opportunities to study the works of other artists and – as in the case of Velázquez – to meet them personally. In the 1630s, gout began to hamper his activities, and from this time his painting became more domestic and meditative. Hélène Fourment, his second wife, was the subject of many portraits and served as a model for characters in his allegorical paintings, her figure epitomizing the buxom, well-rounded women found throughout his work.

Rubens' influence on the artists of the period was enormous. The huge output of his studio meant that his works were universally seen and also widely disseminated by the engravers he employed to copy his work. Chief among his followers was the portraitist **Anthony van Dyck** (1599–1641), who worked in Rubens' studio from 1618, often taking on the depiction of religious figures in his master's works that required particular sensitivity and pathos. Like Rubens, Van Dyck was born in Antwerp and travelled widely in Italy, though his initial work was influenced by Rubens rather than the Italians. Eventually van Dyck developed his own distinct style and technique, establishing himself as court painter to Charles I in England, and creating portraits of a nervous elegance that would influence the genre there for the next hundred and fifty years. **Jacob Jordaens** (1593–1678) was also an Antwerp native who studied under Rubens. Although he was commissioned to complete several works left unfinished by Rubens at the time of his death, his robustly naturalistic works have an earthy – and sensuous – realism that is quite distinct in style and technique.

The eighteenth and nineteenth centuries

Accompanying Holland's economic decline was a gradual deterioration in the quality and originality of Dutch painting. The subtle delicacies of the seventeenth century were replaced by finicky still lifes and minute studies of flowers, or finely finished portraiture and religious scenes, as in the work of **Adrian van der Werff** (1659–1722). Of the era's big names, **Gerard de Lairesse**

(1640–1711) spent most of his time decorating a rash of brand new civic halls and mansions, but, like the buildings he worked on, his style and influences were French. **Jacob de Wit** (1695–1754) continued where Lairesse left off, painting ceiling after ceiling in a flashy, Italianate style. Wit also benefited from a relaxation in the laws against Catholics, decorating several of their (newly legal) churches. The period's only painter of any true renown was **Cornelis Troost** (1697–1750) who, although he didn't produce anything really original, painted competent portraits and some neat, faintly satirical pieces that have since earned him the title of "the Dutch Hogarth". Cosy interiors also continued to prove popular and the Haarlem painter **Wybrand Hendriks** (1744–1831) satisfied the demand with numerous proficient examples.

Johann Barthold Jongkind (1819–91) was the first important artist to emerge in the nineteenth century, painting landscapes and seascapes that were to influence Monet and the early Impressionists. He spent most of his life in France and his work was exhibited in Paris with the Barbizon painters, though he owed less to them than to Van Goyen and the seventeenth-century "tonal" artists. Jongkind's work was a logical precursor to the art of the **Hague School**. Based in and around Den Haag between 1870 and 1900, this prolific group of painters tried to re-establish a characteristically Dutch national school of painting. They produced atmospheric studies of the dunes and polders around Den Haag, nature pictures that are characterized by grey, rain-filled skies, windswept seas, and silvery, flat beaches – pictures that, for some, verge on the sentimental. **J.H. Weissenbruch** (1824–1903) was a founding member, a specialist in low, flat beach scenes dotted with stranded boats. The banker-turned-artist **H.W. Mesdag** (1831–1915) did the same but with more skill than imagination, while **Jacob Maris** (1837–99), one of three artist brothers, was perhaps the most lyrical with his rural and sea scenes heavily covered by grey, chasing skies. His brother **Matthijs Maris** (1839–1917) was less predictable, ultimately tiring of his colleagues' interest in straight observation and going to London to design windows, while the youngest brother **Willem Maris** (1844–1910) is best-known for his small, unpretentious studies of nature.

Anton Mauve (1838–88) is better-known, an exponent of soft, pastel landscapes and an early teacher of Van Gogh. Profoundly influenced by the French Barbizon painters – Corot, Millet, et al – he went to Hilversum in 1885 to set up his own group, which became known as the "**Dutch Barbizon**". **Jozef Israëls** (1826–1911) has often been likened to Millet, though it's generally agreed that he had more in common with the Impressionists, and his best pictures are his melancholy portraits and interiors. Lastly, **Johan Bosboom**'s (1817–91) church interiors may be said to sum up the romanticized nostalgia of the Hague School: shadowy and populated by figures in seventeenth-century dress, they seem to yearn for Holland's Golden Age.

Vincent van Gogh (1853–90), on the other hand, was one of the least "Dutch" of Dutch artists, and he lived out most of his relatively short painting career in France. After countless studies of peasant life in his native Noord-Brabant – studies that culminated in the sombre *Potato Eaters* – he went to live in Paris with his art-dealer brother Theo. There, under the influence of the Impressionists, he lightened his palette, following the pointillist work of Seurat and "trying to render intense colour and not a grey harmony". Two years later he went south to Arles, the "land of blue tones and gay colours", and, struck by the brilliance of Mediterranean light, his characteristic style began to develop. A disastrous attempt to live with Gauguin, and the much-publicized episode when he cut off part of his ear and presented it to a local prostitute led eventually to his committal in an asylum at St-Rémy. Here he produced some of his most famous, and most expressionistic, canvases – strongly coloured and with the paint thickly, almost frantically, applied. Now one of the world's most popular, and popularized, painters, Van Gogh has his own museum in Amsterdam.

Like Van Gogh, **Jan Toorop** (1858–1928) went through multiple artistic changes, though he did not need to travel to do so; he radically adapted his technique from a fairly conventional pointillism through a tired Expressionism to Symbolism with an Art Nouveau feel. Roughly contemporary, **George Hendrik Breitner** (1857–1923) was a better painter, and one who refined his style rather than changed it. His snapshot-like impressions of his beloved Amsterdam figure among his best work and offered a promising start to the new century.

The twentieth century

Each of the major modern art movements has had its followers in the Netherlands and each has been diluted or altered according to local taste. Of many lesser names, **Jan Sluyters** (1881–1957) stands out as the Dutch pioneer of Cubism, but this is small beer when compared with the one specifically Dutch movement – **De Stijl** (The Style). **Piet Mondrian** (1872–1944) was De Stijl's leading figure, developing the realism he had learned from the Hague School painters – via Cubism, which he criticized for being too cowardly to depart totally from representation – into a complete abstraction of form which he called Neo-Plasticism. He was something of a mystic, and this was to some extent responsible for the direction that De Stijl, and his paintings, took: canvases painted with grids of lines and blocks made up of the three primary colours and white, black and grey. Mondrian believed this freed the work of art from the vagaries of personal perception, making it possible to obtain what he called "a true vision of reality".

De Stijl took other forms, too: there was a magazine of the same name, and the movement introduced new concepts into every aspect of design, from painting to interior design and architecture. But in all these media, lines were kept simple, colours bold and clear. **Theo van Doesburg** (1883–1931) was a De Stijl cofounder and major theorist. His work is similar to Mondrian's except for the noticeable absence of thick, black borders and the diagonals that he introduced into his work, calling his paintings "contra-compositions" – which, he said, were both more dynamic and more in touch with twentieth-century life. **Bart van der Leck** (1876–1958) was the third member of the circle, identifiable by white canvases covered by seemingly randomly placed interlocking coloured triangles. Mondrian split with De Stijl in 1925, going on to attain new artistic extremes of clarity and soberness before moving to New York in the 1940s and producing atypically exuberant works such as *Victory Boogie Woogie* – named for the artist's love of jazz and now exhibited at Den Haag's Gemeentemuseum.

During and after De Stijl, a number of other movements flourished, though their impact was not so great and their influence largely confined to the Netherlands. The Expressionist **Bergen School** was probably the most localized, its best-known exponent **Charley Toorop** (1891–1955), daughter of Jan, developing a distinctively glaring but strangely sensitive realism. **De Ploeg** (The Plough), centred in Groningen, was headed by **Jan Wiegers** (1893–1959) and influenced by Kirchner and the German Expressionists; the group's artists set out to capture the uninviting landscapes around their native town, and produced violently coloured canvases that hark back to Van Gogh. Another group, known as the **Magic Realists**, surfaced in the 1930s, painting quasi-Surrealistic scenes that, according to their leading light, **Carel Willink** (1900–83), revealed "a world stranger and more dreadful in its haughty impenetrability than the most terrifying nightmare".

Postwar Dutch art began with **CoBrA**: a loose grouping of like-minded painters from Denmark, Belgium and the Netherlands, whose name derives from the initial letters of their respective capital cities. Their first exhibition at Amsterdam's Stedelijk Museum in 1949 provoked a huge uproar, at the centre of which was **Karel Appel** (1921–2006), whose brutal Abstract Expressionism, his pieces plastered with paint inches thick, was, he maintained, necessary for the era – indeed, inevitable reflections of it: "I paint like a barbarian in a barbarous age," he claimed. In the graphic arts the most famous twentieth-century Dutch figure was **Maurits Cornelis Escher** (1898–1972), whose Surrealistic illusions and allusions were underpinned by his fascination with mathematics, and were deemed popular enough for him to have his own museum in Den Haag.

As for today, there's as vibrant an art scene as there ever was, with all the major cities possessing at least a couple of art galleries that feature regular exhibitions of contemporary art. Among contemporary Dutch artists, look out for the abstract work of **Edgar Fernhout** (1912–74) and **Ad Dekkers** (1938–74), the reliefs of **Jan Schoonhoven** (1914–94), the multimedia productions of **Jan Dibbets** (b.1941), the glowering realism of **Marlene Dumas** (b.1953), the imprecisely coloured geometric designs of **Rob van Koningsbruggen** (b.1948), the smeary expressionism of **Toon Verhoef** (b.1946), and the exuberant figures of **Rene Daniels** (b.1950) – to name just a few of the more important figures.

Books

Most of the following books should be readily available in bookshops or online, though you may have a little more difficulty tracking down those few titles we mention which are currently out of print, signified o/p. Titles marked with the ✱ symbol are especially recommended.

Travel and general

A. Burton et al *Smokers Guide to Amsterdam*. Exactly what it says – a dope-smoker's guide to the city with no leaf unturned. There's an associated website too – ⓦwww .smokersguide.com.

✱ **Han van der Horst** *The Low Sky: Understanding the Dutch*. Thoughtful, thorough attempt to explain the Dutch mentality to the outside world, from the peripheral – herring eating and gardening – to weightier sections on attitudes to egalitarianism and conspicuous consumption. The best book of its type on the market.

Simon Kuper *Ajax, the Dutch, the War: Football in Europe in the Second World War*. Great idea, with some intriguing details, but a tad cumbersome in its execution.

Sir William Temple *Observations upon the United Provinces of The Netherlands*. An entertaining and evocative account of the country written by a seventeenth-century English diplomat. o/p.

Tim Webb *Good Beer Guide to Belgium & Holland*. Detailed and enthusiastic guide to the best bars, beers and breweries, including a strong

showing for Amsterdam. A good read, and extremely well informed to boot, though it's beginning to show its age – it was published in 2002. Nonetheless, it's the best book on its subject on the market.

David Winner *Brilliant Orange – The Neurotic Genius of Dutch Football*. Great title, great cover and great idea – zeroing in on the fine Dutch footballers of the 1960s and 1970s, including super-talented Johan Cruyff, and the way they – and their style of play – reflect Dutch culture and history. The problem is that sometimes the inferences and conclusions seem too obtuse, or at least unconvincing.

✱ **Manfred Wolf** (ed.) *Amsterdam: A Traveler's Literary Companion*. Published by, Whereabout Press, an independent American press, these anthologies aim to get to the heart of the modern cities they cover, and this well-chosen mixture of travel pieces, short fiction and reportage does exactly that, uncovering a low-life aspect to the city of Amsterdam that exists beyond the tourist brochures. A high-quality and evocative selection, and often the only chance you'll get to read some of this material in translation.

History and politics

Leo Akveld et al *The Colourful World of the VOC*. Beautifully illustrated, coffee-table-sized book on the VOC – the East India Company. The subject is dealt with in a series

of intriguing essays on subjects such as the uses of Eastern spices, Indonesian fashion and furniture, rituals and beliefs. Hard to get hold of outside Amsterdam.

J.C.H. Blom (ed.) *History of the Low Countries*. Books on the totality of Dutch history are thin on the ground, so this heavyweight volume fills a few gaps, though it's hardly sun-lounge reading. A series of historians weigh in with their specialities, from Roman times onwards. Taken as a whole, its forte is in picking out those cultural, political and economic themes that give the region its distinctive character.

Mike Dash *Tulipomania*. An examination of the introduction of the tulip into the Low Countries at the height of the Golden Age – and the extraordinarily inflated and speculative market that ensued. There's a lot of padding and scene-setting, but it's an engaging enough read, and has nice detail on seventeenth-century Amsterdam, Leiden and Haarlem.

Pieter Geyl *The Revolt of The Netherlands 1555–1609* and *The Netherlands in the Seventeenth Century 1609–1648*. Geyl presents a detailed account of the Netherlands during its formative years, chronicling the uprising against the Spanish and the formation of the United Provinces. First published in 1932, it has long been regarded as the classic text on the subject, though it's a hard and ponderous read.

Christopher Hibbert *Cities and Civilisation*. Includes a diverting chapter on Amsterdam in the age of Rembrandt. Hibbert, one of the UK's best historians, is always a pleasure to read.

🏃 **Lisa Jardine** *The Awful End of Prince William the Silent*. Great title for an intriguing book on the premature demise of one of the country's most acclaimed heroes, who was assassinated in Delft in 1584 (see p.189). At just 160 pages, the tale is told succinctly, but – unless you have a particular interest in early firearms – there is a bit too much information on guns.

🏃 **Carol Ann Lee** *Roses from The Earth: The Biography of Anne Frank*. Among a spate of recent publications trawling through and over the life of the young Jewish diarist, this is probably the best, written in a straightforward and insightful manner without sentimentality. Working the same mine is the same author's *The Hidden Life of Otto Frank* – clear, lucid and equally interesting.

🏃 **Geert Mak** *Amsterdam: A Brief Life of the City*. First published in 1995, this infinitely readable trawl through the city's past is a simply wonderful book – amusing and perceptive, alternately tart and indulgent. It's more a social history than anything else so – for example – it's here you'll find out quite why Rembrandt lived in the Jewish Quarter and why the city's merchant elite ossified in the eighteenth century. It's light and accessible enough to read from cover to cover, but its index of places makes it easy to dip into. Highly recommended.

🏃 **Geoffrey Parker** *The Dutch Revolt*. Compelling account of the struggle between the Netherlands and Spain. Quite the best thing you can read on the period. Also *The Army of Flanders and the Spanish Road 1567–1659*; the title may sound academic, but this book gives a fascinating insight into the Habsburg army that occupied the Low Countries for well over a hundred years – how it functioned, was fed and moved from Spain to the Low Countries along the so-called Spanish Road.

Simon Schama *The Embarrassment of Riches: An Interpretation of Dutch Culture in the Golden Age*. Long before his reinvention on British TV, Schama had a reputation as a specialist in Dutch history and this chunky volume draws on a huge variety of archive sources. Also by Schama, *Patriots and Liberators: Revolution in the Netherlands 1780–1813* focuses on one of the less familiar periods of Dutch history and is particularly good on the Batavian Republic set-up in the Netherlands under French auspices. Both are heavyweight tomes and leftists might well find Schama too reactionary by half. See also Schama's *Rembrandt's Eyes* (see below).

Art and architecture

Svetlana Alpers *Rembrandt's Enterprise*. Intriguing 1988 study of Rembrandt, positing the theory – in line with findings of the Leiden-based Rembrandt Research Project – that many previously accepted Rembrandt paintings are not his at all, but merely the products of his studio. Bad news if you own one.

Anthony Bailey *A View of Delft*. Concise, startlingly well-researched book on Vermeer complete with an accurate and well-considered exploration of his milieu.

R. H. Fuchs *Dutch Painting*. As complete an introduction to the subject – from Flemish origins to the present day – as you could wish for, in just a couple of hundred pages. First published in the 1970s.

Walter S. Gibson *Hieronymus Bosch* and *Bruegel*. Two wonderfully illustrated titles on these two exquisite allegorical painters. The former contains everything you wanted to know about Hieronymus Bosch, his paintings and his late fifteenth-century milieu, while the latter takes a detailed look at Pieter Bruegel the Elder's art, with nine well-argued chapters investigating its various components.

H.L.C. Jaffe *De Stijl: Visions of Utopia*. A good, informed introduction to the twentieth-century movement and its philosophical and social influences. Well illustrated too. o/p

Andrew Wheatcroft *The Habsburgs*. Excellent and well-researched trawl through the family's history, from eleventh-century beginnings to its eclipse at the end of World War I. Enjoyable background reading.

Melissa McQuillan *Van Gogh*. Extensive, in-depth look at Vincent's paintings, as well as his life and times. Superbly researched and illustrated.

Simon Schama *Rembrandt's Eyes*. Published in 1999, this erudite work received good reviews, but it's very, very long – and often very long-winded.

Irving Stone *Lust for Life: The Life of Vincent Van Gogh*. Everything you ever wanted to know about Van Gogh in a genius-is-pain biography.

Dirk de Vos *Rogier van der Weyden*. One of the most talented and influential of the Flemish Primitives, Weyden was the official city painter to Brussels in the middle of the fifteenth century. This 400-page volume (o/p) details everything known about him and carries illustrations of all his works – but there again no more than you would expect from such an expensive tome. Similarly detailed in the same author's *Hans Memling: The Complete Works* and the rather more manageable, 200-page *The Flemish Primitives: The Masterpieces*.

Mariet Westerman *The Art of the Dutch Republic 1585–1718*. This excellently written, immaculately illustrated and enthralling book tackles its subject thematically, from the marketing of works to an exploration of Dutch ideologies. Highly recommended. Also by Westerman is an all-you-could-ever-want-to-know book about *Rembrandt* (o/p).

Christopher White *Rembrandt.*
White is something of a Rembrandt
specialist, writing a series of books
on the man and his times. Most of
these books are expensive and aimed
at the specialist art market, but this
particular title, published in 1984
in the "World of Art" series, is perfect for the general reader, with a
wonderfully incisive and extremely
detailed commentary.

Literature

Tracey Chevalier *Girl with a Pearl
Earring.* Chevalier's novel is a fanciful piece of fiction, building a story
around the subject of one of Vermeer's most enigmatic paintings. It's
an absorbing read, which has proved
very popular, if a tad too detailed
and slow-moving for some tastes,
and it paints a convincing picture of
seventeenth-century Delft and Holland, exploring its social structures
and values.

Rudi van Dantzig *For a Lost Soldier.* Honest and convincing tale,
largely autobiographical, that gives an
insight into the confusion and lone-
liness of the approximately 50,000
Dutch children evacuated to foster
families during World War II. The
novel's leading character is Jeroen,
an 11-year-old boy from Amsterdam who is sent away to live with
a family in Friesland. During the
Liberation celebrations, he meets an
American soldier, Walt, with whom
he has a brief sexual encounter; Walt
disappears a few days later. One of
the Netherlands' most famous chore-
ographers, Van Dantzig was the artistic director of the Dutch National
Ballet until 1991; this was his debut
novel. o/p.

Anne Frank *The Diary of a
Young Girl.* Lucid and moving,
the most revealing book you can
read on the plight of Amsterdam's
Jews during the German occupation.
An international best seller since its
original publication in 1947.

Nicolas Freeling *Love in
Amsterdam*; *Dwarf Kingdom*; *A
Long Silence*; *A City Solitary* (o/p);
Strike Out Where Not Applicable
(o/p). Freeling writes detective
novels, and his most famous creation is the rebel cop Van der Valk.
These are light, carefully crafted
tales, with just the right amount of
twists to make them classic cops 'n'
robbers reading – and with good
Amsterdam (and Dutch) locations.
London-born, Freeling still evokes
Amsterdam (and Amsterdammers)
as well as any writer ever has, subtly
and unsentimentally using the city
and its people as a vivid backdrop to
his fast-moving action.

Etty Hillesum *An Interrupted
Life: The Diaries and Letters of Etty
Hillesum, 1941–43.* The Germans
transported Hillesum, a young
Jewish woman, from her home in
Amsterdam to Auschwitz, where she
died. As with Anne Frank's more
famous journal, penetratingly written – though on the whole a little
less readable.

Richard Huijing (ed & trans) *The
Dedalus Book of Dutch Fantasy.* A fun
and artfully selected collection of
stories that contains contributions
from some of the greats of Dutch
literature, including a number
whose work does not, as yet, appear
in translation anywhere else. o/p.

Arthur Japin *The Two Hearts of
Kwasi Boachi.* Inventive re-creation
of a true story in which the eponymous Ashanti prince was dispatched
to the court of King William of the
Netherlands in 1837. Kwasi and his
companion Kwame were ostensibly
sent to Den Haag to further their
education, but there was a strong

colonial sub-text. Superb descriptions of Ashanti-land in its pre-colonial pomp. Japin's *Lucia's Eyes* is an imaginative extrapolation of a casual anecdote found in Casanova's memoirs and set for the most part in eighteenth-century Amsterdam.

Sylvie Matton *Rembrandt's Whore*. Taking its cue from Chevalier's *Girl with a Pearl Earring* (see p.387), this slim novel tries hard to conjure Rembrandt's life and times with some (limited) success. Matton certainly knows Rembrandt – she worked for two years on a film of his life.

Marga Minco *The Fall*; *An Empty House*; *The Glass Bridge*; *Bitter Herbs: Vivid Memories of a Fugitive Jewish girl in Nazi-occupied Holland*. One of the best-known of Amsterdam's modern writers, the prolific Marga Minco has written widely and well about the city's Jewish community, particularly during the German occupation. She herself was a Holocaust survivor, spending several years in hiding – unlike the rest of her family, who were dispatched to concentration camps where they all died. One of Minco's favourite hideaways was Kloveniersburgwal 49, which served as a safe house for various Dutch artists and later as the inspiration for *An Empty House*. Published in 1989, *Bitter Herbs* is her testament.

Deborah Moggach *Tulip Fever*. At first Deborah Moggach's novel seems no more than an attempt to build a story out of her favourite domestic Dutch interiors, genre scenes and still life paintings. But ultimately the story is a basic one – of lust, greed, mistaken identity and tragedy. The Golden Age Amsterdam backdrop is well realized, but almost incidental.

Marcel Moring *In Babylon*. Popular Dutch author with an intense style and thought-provoking, philosophical content. *In Babylon* has an older Jewish man and his niece trapped in a cabin in the eastern Netherlands and here they ruminate on their family's history. Moring's *Dream Room* is also gracefully nostalgic in its concentration on the family of Boris and his son, David, while Moring's latest novel, *Dis*, is set in the town of Assen, again in the east of the country, during the annual Dutch TT motorbike races.

Harry Mulisch *The Assault*. Set part in Haarlem, part in Amsterdam, this novel traces the story of a young boy who loses his family in a reprisal raid by the Nazis. A powerful tale, made into an excellent and effective film. Also by Mulisch: *The Discovery of Heaven*, a gripping yarn of adventure and happenstance; *The Procedure*, featuring a modern-day Dutch scientist investigating strange goings-on in sixteenth-century Prague; and 2004's offering, *Siegfried: A Black Idyll*, whose central question is whether a work of imagination can help to understand the nature of evil in general and Hitler in particular.

Multatuli *Max Havelaar: Or, The Coffee Auctions of the Dutch Trading Company*. Classic nineteenth-century Dutch satire of colonial life in the East Indies. Eloquent and intermittently amusing. If you have Dutch friends, they should be impressed (dumbstruck) if you have actually read it, not least since it's 352 pages long.

Cees Nooteboom *Rituals*. Cees Nooteboom is one of the country's best-known writers. He published his first novel in 1955, but only really came to public attention after the publication of his third novel, *Rituals*, in 1980. The central theme of all his work is the phenomenon of time: *Rituals* in particular is about the passing of time and the different ways of controlling the process. Inni Wintrop, the main character, is an outsider, a well-heeled, antique-dabbling "dilettante" as he describes himself. The book is almost entirely set in Amsterdam, and although it describes the inner life of Inni himself, it also paints a strong picture of the city. Bleak but absorbing. Born in Den Haag in 1933, Nooteboom lives by turn in Germany, Spain and the Netherlands.

David Veronese *Jana*. A hip thriller set in the druggy underworld of Amsterdam and London.

Janwillem van de Wetering *Tumbleweed*; *Hard Rain*; *Corpse on the Dyke*; *Outsider in Amsterdam*. Off-beat detective tales set in Amsterdam and the provinces. Humane, quirky and humorous, Wetering's novels have inventive plots and feature unusual characters in interesting locations, though the prose itself can be somewhat indigestible.

Jan Wolkers *Turkish Delight*. Wolkers is one of the Netherlands' best-known artists and writers, and this is one of his early novels, a close examination of the relationship between a bitter, working-class sculptor and his young, middle-class wife. A compelling work, at times misogynistic and even offensive, by a writer who seeks reaction above all. If you like it, try Wolkers' *Horrible Tango*. Both o/p.

CONTEXTS

Language

Language

Dutch

n the Netherlands, the native language is **Dutch**. Most Dutch-speakers, however, particularly in the bigger towns and the tourist industry, speak English to
varying degrees of excellence. The Dutch have a seemingly innate talent for
languages, and your attempts at speaking theirs may be met with some bewil-
derment – though this can have as much to do with your pronunciation (Dutch
is very difficult to get right) as their surprise that you're making an effort.

Dutch is a Germanic language – the word itself is a corruption of "Deutsche",
a label inaccurately given by English sailors in the seventeenth century and
indeed, although the Dutch are at pains to stress the differences between the
two languages, if you know any German you'll spot many similarities. As noted
above, English is very widely spoken, but in smaller towns and in the countryside, where things aren't quite as cosmopolitan, the following words and phrases
should be the most you'll need to get by. We've also included a basic food and
drink glossary, though **menus** are nearly always multilingual and where they
aren't, ask and one will almost invariably appear.

As for **phrasebooks**, the *Rough Guide to Dutch* is pocket-sized, and has a
good dictionary section (English–Dutch and Dutch–English) as well as a menu
reader; it also provides a useful introduction to grammar and pronunciation.

Pronunciation

Dutch is **pronounced** much the same as English. However, there are a few
Dutch sounds that don't exist in English, which can be difficult to get right
without practice.

Consonants

Double-consonant combinations generally keep their separate sounds in Flemish: **kn**, for example, is never like the English "knight". Note also the following
consonants and consonant combinations:

j is an English y

ch and **g** indicate a throaty sound, as at the
end of the Scottish word loch. The Dutch
word for canal – *gracht* – is especially
tricky, since it has two of these sounds
– it comes out along the lines of *khrakht*.

A common word for hello is *Dag!* – pronounced like *daakh*

ng as in bring

nj as in onion

y is not a consonant, but another way of writing **ij**

Vowels and diphthongs

A good rule of thumb is that doubling the letter lengthens the vowel sound.

a is l-ike the English apple

aa like cart

e like let

ee like late

393

▬

o as in pop

oo in pope

u is like the French tu if preceded by a consonant; it's like wood if followed by a consonant

uu is the French tu

au and ou like how

ei and ij as in fine, though this varies strongly

from region to region; sometimes it can
sound more like lane

oe as in soon

eu is like the diphthong in the French leur

ui is the hardest Dutch diphthong of all, pronounced like how but much further forward in
the mouth, with lips pursed (as if to say "oo").

Words and phrases

The basics

ja	yes
nee	no
alstublieft	please
dank u or bedankt	thank you
hallo or dag	hello
goedemorgen	good morning
goedemiddag	good afternoon
goedenavond	good evening
tot ziens	goodbye
tot straks	see you later
Spreekt u Engels?	Do you speak English?

Ik begrijp het niet	I don't understand
vrouwen/mannen	women/men
kinderen	children
heren/dames	men's/women's toilets
Ik wil…	I want…
Ik wil niet…	(+verb) I don't want to…
Ik wil geen…	(+noun) I don't want any…
Wat kost…?	How much is…?

Travel and shopping

postkantoor	post office
postzegel(s)	stamp(s)
geldwisselkantoor	money exchange
kassa	cash desk
Hoe kom ik in…?	How do I get to…?
Waar is…?	Where is…?
Hoe ver is het naar…?	How far is it to…?
Wanneer?	When?
ver/dichtbij	far/near
links/rechts	left/right
rechtdoor	straight ahead

spoor or perron	railway platform
loket	ticket office
hier/daar	here/there
goed/slecht	good/bad
groot/klein	big/small
open/gesloten	open/closed
duwen/trekken	push/pull
nieuw/oud	new/old
goedkoop/duur	cheap/expensive
heet or warm/koud	hot/cold
met/zonder	with/without

Useful cycling terms

band	tyre
lek	puncture
rem	brake
ketting	chain
wiel	wheel

trapper	pedal
pomp	pump
stuur	handlebars
kapot	broken

Numbers

nul	0	negentien	19
een	1	twintig	20
twee	2	een en twintig	21
drie	3	twee en twintig	22
vier	4	dertig	30
vijf	5	veertig	40
zes	6	vijftig	50
zeven	7	zestig	60
acht	8	zeventig	70
negen	9	tachtig	80
tien	10	negentig	90
elf	11	honderd	100
twaalf	12	honderd een	101
dertien	13	twee honderd	200
veertien	14	twee honderd een	201
vijftien	15	vijf honderd	500
zestien	16	vijf honderd vijf en twintig	525
zeventien	17		
achttien	18	duizend	1000

Days and times

zondag	Sunday	Het is…	It's…
maandag	Monday	drie uur	3.00
dinsdag	Tuesday	vijf over drie	3.05
woensdag	Wednesday	tien over drie	3.10
donderdag	Thursday	kwart over drie	3.15
vrijdag	Friday	tien voor half vier	3.20
zaterdag	Saturday	vijf voor half vier	3.25
gisteren	yesterday	half vier	3.30
vandaag	today	vijf over half vier	3.35
morgen	tomorrow	tien over half vier	3.40
morgenochtend	tomorrow morning	kwart voor vier	3.45
jaar	year	tien voor vier	3.50
maand	month	vijf voor vier	3.55
week	week	acht uur 's ochtends	8am
dag	day	een uur 's middags	1pm
uur	hour	acht uur 's avonds	8pm
minuut	minute	een uur 's nachts	1am
Hoe laat is het?	What time is it?		

A Dutch menu reader

Basic terms

boter	butter	peper	pepper
boterham/broodje	sandwich/roll	pindakaas	peanut butter
brood	bread	sla/salade	salad
dranken	drinks	smeerkaas	cheese spread
eieren	eggs	stokbrood	french bread
gerst	barley	suiker	sugar
groenten	vegetables	vis	fish
honing	honey	vlees	meat
hoofdgerechten	main courses	voorgerechten	starters/hors d'oeuvres
kaas	cheese	vruchten	fruit
koud	cold	warm	hot
nagerechten	desserts	zout	salt

Starters and snacks

erwtensoep/snert	thick pea soup with bacon or sausage	patat/friet	chips/french fries
		soep	soup
huzarensalade	potato salad with pickles	uitsmijter	ham or cheese with eggs on bread
koffietafel	light midday meal of cold meats, cheese, bread, and perhaps soup		

Meat and poultry

biefstuk (duitse)	hamburger	kip	chicken
biefstuk (hollandse)	steak	kroket	spiced veal or beef in hash, coated in breadcrumbs
eend	duck		
fricandeau	roast pork		
fricandel	frankfurter-like sausage	lamsvlees	lamb
		lever	liver
gehakt	minced meat	ossenhaas	tenderloin beef
ham	ham	rookvlees	smoked beef
kalfsvlees	veal	spek	bacon
kalkoen	turkey	worst	sausages
karbonade	a chop		

Fish

forel	trout	oesters	oysters
garnalen	prawns	paling	eel
haring	herring	schelvis	haddock
haringsalade	herring salad	schol	plaice
kabeljauw	cod	tong	sole
makreel	mackerel	zalm	salmon
mosselen	mussels		

Cooking terms

belegd belegde broodjes	filled or topped, as in (bread rolls topped with cheese, etc)	gekookt	boiled
		geraspt	grated
		gerookt	smoked
doorbakken	well-done	gestoofd	stewed
gebakken	fried or baked	half doorbakken	medium-done
gebraden	roast	Hollandse saus	hollandaise sauce
gegrild	grilled	rood	rare

Vegetables

aardappelen	potatoes	rijst	rice
bloemkool	cauliflower	sla	salad, lettuce
bonen	beans	stampot andijvie	mashed potato and endive
champignons	mushrooms		
erwten	peas	stampot boerenkool	mashed potato and cabbage
hutspot	mashed potatoes and carrots		
		uien	onions
knoflook	garlic	wortelen	carrots
komkommer	cucumber	zuurkool	sauerkraut
prei	leek		

Indonesian dishes and terms

ajam	chicken	nasi goreng	fried rice with meat/chicken and vegetables
bami	noodles with meat/chicken and vegetables		
		nasi rames	a rijsttafel on a single plate
daging	beef		
gado gado	vegetables in peanut sauce	pedis	hot and spicy
		pisang	banana
goreng	fried	rijsttafel	collection of different spicy dishes served with plain rice
ikan	fish		
katjang	peanut		
kroepoek	prawn crackers	sambal	hot chilli-based sauce
loempia	spring rolls	sateh	meat on a skewer
nasi	rice		

satesaus	peanut sauce to accompany meat grilled on skewers

seroendeng	spicy shredded and fried coconut
tauge	beansprouts

Sweets and desserts

appelgebak	apple tart or cake
drop	Dutch liquorice, available in zoet (sweet) or zout (salted) varieties – the latter an acquired taste
gebak	pastry
ijs	ice cream
koekjes	biscuits
oliebollen	traditional sweet sold at New Year – something like a doughnut

pannenkoeken	pancakes
pepernoten	Dutch ginger nuts
poffertjes	small pancakes, fritters
(slag)room	(whipped) cream
speculaas	spice and cinnamon-flavoured biscuit
stroopwafels	waffles
taai-taai	spicy Dutch cake
vla	custard

Fruits and nuts

aardbei	strawberry
amandel	almond
appel	apple
appelmoes	apple purée
citroen	lemon
druiven	grape
framboos	raspberry

hazelnoot	hazelnut
kers	cherry
kokosnoot	coconut
peer	pear
perzik	peach
pinda	peanut
pruim	plum/prune

Drinks

anijsmelk	aniseed-flavoured warm milk
appelsap	apple juice
bessenjenever	blackcurrant gin
chocomel	chocolate milk
citroenjenever	lemon gin
droog	dry
frisdranken	soft drinks
jenever	Dutch gin
karnemelk	buttermilk
koffie	coffee
koffie verkeerd	coffee with warm milk
kopstoot	beer with a jenever chaser

melk	milk
met ijs	with ice
met slagroom	with whipped cream
pils	Dutch beer
proost!	cheers!
sinaasappelsap	orange juice
thee	tea
tomatensap	tomato juice
vruchtensap	fruit juice
wijn	wine
(wit/rood/rosé)	(white/red/rosé)
vieux	Dutch brandy
zoet	sweet

Glossary

Dutch terms

Abdij Abbey

Amsterdammertje Phallic-shaped bollard placed in rows alongside many Amsterdam streets to keep drivers off pavements and out of the canals

A.U.B. *Alstublieft* – "please" (also shown as **S.V.P.**, from French)

BG *Begane grond* – "ground floor" ("basement" is **K** for *kelder*)

Begijnhof Similar to a *hofje* but occupied by Catholic women (*begijns*) who led semi-religious lives without taking full vows

Beiaard Carillon chimes

Belfort Belfry

Beurs Stock exchange

Botermarkt Butter market

Brug Bridge

B.T.W. *Belasting Toegevoegde Waarde* – VAT (sales tax)

Burgher Member of the upper or mercantile classes of a town, usually with certain civic powers

Fietspad Bicycle path

Gasthuis Hospice for the sick or infirm

Geen toegang No entry

Gemeente Municipal, as in *Gemeentehuis* (town hall)

Gerechtshof Law Courts

Gesloten Closed

Gevel Gable: decoration on narrow-fronted canal houses

Gezellig A hard term to translate – something like "cosy", "comfortable" and "inviting" in one – which is often said to lie at the heart of the Dutch psyche. A long, relaxed meal in a favourite restaurant with friends is *gezellig*; grabbing a quick snack is not. The best brown cafés ooze *gezelligheid;* a shopping mall on a Saturday afternoon definitely doesn't

Gilde Guild

Gracht Canal

Groentenmarkt Vegetable market

Grote Kerk Literally "big church" – the main church of a town or village

Hal Hall

Hijsbalk Pulley beam, often decorated, fixed to the top of a gable to lift goods and furniture. Essential in canal houses whose staircases were narrow and steep; *hijsbalken* are still very much in use today

Hof Courtyard

Hofje Almshouse, usually for elderly women who could look after themselves but needed small charities such as food and fuel; usually a number of buildings centred around a small, enclosed courtyard

Huis House

Ingang Entrance

Jeugdherberg Youth hostel

Kasteel Castle

Kerk Church

Koning King

Koningin Queen

Koninklijk Royal

Kunst Art

Lakenhal Cloth hall: the building in medieval weaving towns where cloth would be weighed, graded and sold

Let Op! Attention!

Luchthaven Airport

Markt Central town square and the heart of most Dutch communities, normally still the site of weekly markets

Mokum A Yiddish word meaning "city", originally used by the Jewish community to indicate Amsterdam; now in general usage as a nickname for the city

Molen Windmill

Nederland The Netherlands

Nederlands Dutch

Noord North

Ommegang Procession

Oost East

Paleis Palace

Plein A square or open space

Polder An area of land reclaimed from the sea

Poort Gate

Postbus Post office box

Raadhuis Town hall

Randstad Literally "rim-town", this refers to the urban conurbation that makes up much of Noord- and Zuid-Holland, stretching from Amsterdam in the north to Rotterdam and Dordrecht in the south

Rijk State

Schepenzaal Alderman's Hall

Schone kunsten Fine arts

Schouwburg Theatre

Sierkunst Decorative arts

Spionnetje Small mirror on a canal house enabling the occupant to see who is at the door without descending the stairs

Spoor Train station platform

Stadhuis The most common word for a town hall

Stedelijk Civic, municipal

Steeg Alley

Steen Stone

Stichting Institute or foundation

Straat Street

T/M *Tot en met* – "up to and including"

Toegang Entrance

Toren Tower

Tuin Garden

Uitgang Exit

V.A. *Vanaf* – "from"

V.S. *Verenigde Staten* – "United States"

Vleeshuis Meat market

Volkskunde Folklore

VVV Tourist information office

Waag Old public weighing-house, a common feature of most towns

Weg Way

West West

Wijk District (of a city)

Z.O.Z. Please turn over (page, leaflet, etc)

Zuid South

Architectural terms

Ambulatory Covered passage around the outer edge of the choir of a church.

Apse Semi-circular protrusion (usually) at the east end of a church.

Art Deco Geometrical style of art and architecture popular in the 1930s.

Art Nouveau Style of art, architecture and design based on highly stylized vegetal forms. Especially popular in the early part of the twentieth century.

Baroque The art and architecture of the Counter-Reformation, dating from around 1600 onwards. Distinguished by extreme ornateness, exuberance and by the complex but harmonious spatial arrangement of interiors.

Carillon A set of tuned church bells, either operated by an automatic mechanism or played by a keyboard.

Carolingian Dynasty founded by Charlemagne; mid-eighth to early tenth century. Also refers to art of the period.

Caryatid A sculptured female figure used as a column.

Chancel The eastern part of a church, often separated from the nave by a screen (see "rood screen". Contains the choir and ambulatory.

Classical Architectural style incorporating Greek and Roman elements – pillars, domes, colonnades etc – at its height in the seventeenth century and revived, as Neoclassical, in the nineteenth century.

Clerestory Upper story of a church with windows.

Diptych Carved or painted work on two panels. Often used as an altarpiece – both static and, more occasionally, portable.

Expressionism Artistic style popular at the beginning of the twentieth century, characterized by the exaggeration of shape or colour; often accompanied by the extensive use of symbolism.

Flamboyant Florid form of Gothic.

Fresco Wall painting – durable through application to wet plaster.

Gable The triangular upper portion of a wall – decorative or supporting a roof – which is a feature of many Amsterdam canal houses. Initially fairly simple, they became more ostentatious in the late seventeenth century, before turning to a more restrained Classicism in the eighteenth and nineteenth centuries.

Genre painting In the seventeenth century the term "genre painting" applied to everything from animal paintings and still lifes through to historical works and landscapes. In the eighteenth century, the term came only to be applied to scenes of everyday life.

Gothic Architectural style of the thirteenth to sixteenth centuries, characterized by pointed arches, rib vaulting, flying buttresses and a general emphasis on verticality.

Merovingian Dynasty ruling France and parts of the Low Countries from the sixth to the middle of the eighth century. Refers also to art, etc, of the period.

Misericord Ledge on choir stall on which the occupant can be supported while standing; often carved with secular subjects (bottoms were not thought worthy of religious subjects).

Nave Main body of a church.

Neoclassical A style of Classical architecture revived in the nineteenth century, popular in the Low Countries during and after French rule in the early nineteenth century.

Neo-Gothic Revived Gothic style of architecture popular between the late eighteenth and nineteenth centuries.

Renaissance The period of European history marking the end of the medieval period and the rise of the modern world. Defined, amongst many criteria, by an increase in classical scholarship, geographical discovery, the rise of secular values and the growth of individualism. Began in Italy in the fourteenth century. Also refers to the art and architecture of the period.

Retable Altarpiece

Rococo Highly florid, light and intricate eighteenth-century style of architecture, painting and interior design, forming the last phase of Baroque.

Romanesque Early medieval architecture distinguished by squat, heavy forms, rounded arches and naive sculpture.

Rood screen Decorative screen separating the nave from the chancel. A rood loft is the gallery (or space) on top of it.

Stucco Marble-based plaster used to embellish ceilings, etc.

Transept Arms of a cross-shaped church, placed at ninety degrees to nave and chancel.

Triptych Carved or painted work on three panels. Often used as an altarpiece.

Tympanum Sculpted, usually recessed, panel above a door.

Vauban Seventeenth-century military architect, whose fortresses still stand all over Europe – including the Low Countries; hence the adjective Vaubanesque.

Vault An arched ceiling or roof.

LANGUAGE | Glossary

Travel store

www.roughguides.com

nformation on over 25,000 destinations around the world

- **Read** Rough Guides' trusted travel info
- **Access** exclusive articles from Rough Guides authors
- **Update** yourself on new books, maps, CDs and other products
- **Enter** our competitions and win travel prizes
- **Share** ideas, journals, photos & travel advice with other users
- **Earn** points every time you contribute to the Rough Guide
  community and get rewards

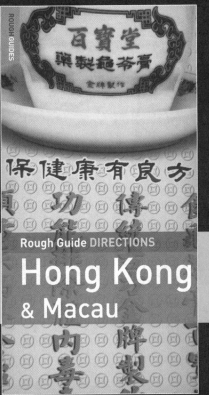

Avoid Guilt Trips

Buy fair trade coffee + bananas ✓

Save energy - use low energy bulbs ✓
    - don't leave tv on standby ✓

Offset carbon emissions from flight to Madrid ✓

Send goat to Africa ✓

Join Tourism Concern today ✓

Slowly, the world is changing.
Together we can, and will, make a difference.

Tourism Concern is the only UK registered charity fighting exploitation in one of the largest industries on earth: people forced from their homes in order that holiday resorts can be built, sweatshop labour conditions in hotels and destruction of the environment are just some of the issues that we tackle.

Sending people on a guilt trip is not something we do. We know as well as anyone that holidays are precious. But you can help us to ensure that tourism always benefits the local communities involved.

Call 020 7133 3330
or visit **tourismconcern.org.uk** to find out how.

A year's membership of Tourism Concern costs just £20 (£12 unwaged) - that's 38 pence a week, less than the cost of a pint of milk, organic of course.

Fighting
Exploitation
in Tourism

TourismConcern

Small print and
Index

A Rough Guide to Rough Guides

Published in 1982, the first Rough Guide – to Greece – was a student scheme that became a publishing phenomenon. Mark Ellingham, a recent graduate in English from Bristol University, had been travelling in Greece the previous summer and couldn't find the right guidebook. With a small group of friends he wrote his own guide, combining a highly contemporary, journalistic style with a thoroughly practical approach to travellers' needs.

The immediate success of the book spawned a series that rapidly covered dozens of destinations. And, in addition to impecunious backpackers, Rough Guides soon acquired a much broader and older readership that relished the guides' wit and inquisitiveness as much as their enthusiastic, critical approach and value-for-money ethos.

SMALL PRINT

These days, Rough Guides include recommendations from shoestring to luxury and cover more than 200 destinations around the globe, including almost every country in the Americas and Europe, more than half of Africa and most of Asia and Australasia. Our ever-growing team of authors and photographers is spread all over the world, particularly in Europe, the USA and Australia.

In the early 1990s, Rough Guides branched out of travel, with the publication of Rough Guides to World Music, Classical Music and the Internet. All three have become benchmark titles in their fields, spearheading the publication of a wide range of books under the Rough Guide name.

Including the travel series, Rough Guides now number more than 350 titles, covering: phrasebooks, waterproof maps, music guides from Opera to Heavy Metal, reference works as diverse as Conspiracy Theories and Shakespeare, and popular culture books from iPods to Poker. Rough Guides also produce a series of more than 120 World Music CDs in partnership with World Music Network.

Visit www.roughguides.com to see our latest publications.

Rough Guide travel images are available for commercial licensing at www.roughguidespictures.com

Rough Guide credits

Text editor: Alice Park
Layout: Ankur Guha
Cartography: Animesh Pathak
Picture editor: Mark Thomas
Production: Aimee Hampson
Proofreader: Susannah Wight
Cover design: Chloë Roberts
Photographer: Tim Draper and Mark Thomas
Editorial: London Kate Berens, Claire Saunders, Joanna Kirby, Ruth Blackmore, Polly Thomas, Richard Lim, Alison Murchie, Karoline Densley, Andy Turner, Keith Drew, Edward Aves, Nikki Birrell, Sarah Eno, Lucy White, David Paul, James Smart, Sam Cook, Joe Staines, Duncan Clark, Peter Buckley, Matthew Milton, Tracy Hopkins, Ruth Tidball; **New York** Andrew Rosenberg, Steven Horak, April Isaacs, AnneLise Sorensen, Amy Hegarty, Ella Steim, Anna Owens, Joseph Petta, Sean Mahoney
Design & Pictures: London Scott Stickland, Dan May, Diana Jarvis, Jj Luck, Harriet Mills, Nicole Newman; **Delhi** Madhavi Singh, Umesh Aggarwal, Ajay Verma, Jessica Subramanian, Pradeep Thapliyal, Sachin Tanwar, Anita Singh
Production: Lauren Britton, Katherine Owers
Cartography: London Maxine Repath, Ed Wright, Katie Lloyd-Jones; **Delhi** Jai Prakash Mishra, Rajesh Chhibber, Ashutosh Bharti, Rajesh Mishra, Jasbir Sandhu, Karobi Gogoi, Amod Singh, Alakananda Bhattacharya, Athokpam Jotinkumar
Online: New York Jennifer Gold, Kristin Mingrone; **Delhi** Manik Chauhan, Narender Kumar, Rakesh Kumar, Amit Verma, Amit Kumar, Rahul Kumar, Ganesh Sharma, Debojit Borah
Marketing & Publicity: London Niki Hanmer, Louise Maher, Anna Paynton, Jess Carter, Libby Jellie; **New York** Geoff Colquitt, Megan Kennedy, Katy Ball; **Delhi** Reem Khokhar
Special projects editor: Philippa Hopkins
Manager India: Punita Singh
Series editor: Mark Ellingham
Reference Director: Andrew Lockett
Publishing coordinator: Megan McIntyre
Publishing Director: Martin Dunford

Publishing information

This fourth edition published March 2007 by
Rough Guides Ltd,
80 Strand, London WC2R 0RL;
345 Hudson St, 4th Floor,
New York, NY 10014, USA;
14 Local Shopping Centre, Panchsheel Park,
New Delhi 110017, India
Distributed by the Penguin Group
Penguin Books Ltd,
80 Strand, London WC2R 0RL
Penguin Putnam, Inc.
375 Hudson St, NY 10014, USA
Penguin Group (Australia)
250 Camberwell Rd, Camberwell,
Victoria 3124, Australia
Penguin Books Canada Ltd,
10 Alcorn Ave, Toronto, Ontario,
Canada M4V 1E4
Penguin Group (NZ)
67 Apollo Drive, Mairangi Bay, Auckland 1310,
New Zealand
Cover concept by Peter Dyer.

Typeset in Bembo and Helvetica to an original design by Henry Iles.

Printed and bound in Singapore by SNP Security Printing Pte Ltd

© Martin Dunford, Phil Lee and Rough Guides

No part of this book may be reproduced in any form without permission from the publisher except for the quotation of brief passages in reviews.

424pp includes index

A catalogue record for this book is available from the British Library

ISBN 10: 1-84353-804-0

ISBN 13: 9-78184-353-804-2

The publishers and authors have done their best to ensure the accuracy and currency of all the information in **The Rough Guide to The Netherlands**, however, they can accept no responsibility for any loss, injury, or inconvenience sustained by any traveller as a result of information or advice contained in the guide.

3   5   7   9   8   6   4

Help us update

We've gone to a lot of effort to ensure that the fourth edition of **The Rough Guide to The Netherlands** is accurate and up-to-date. However, things change – places get "discovered", opening hours are notoriously fickle, restaurants and rooms raise prices or lower standards. If you feel we've got it wrong or left something out, we'd like to know, and if you can remember the address, the price, the time, the phone number, so much the better. We'll credit all contributions, and send a copy of the next edition (or any other Rough Guide if you prefer) for the best letters. Everyone who writes to us and isn't already a subscriber will receive a copy of our full-colour thrice-yearly newsletter. Please mark letters: "**Rough Guide The Netherlands Update**" and send to: Rough Guides, 80 Strand, London WC2R 0RL, or Rough Guides, 4th Floor, 345 Hudson St, New York, NY 10014. Or send an email to **mail@roughguides.com**
Have your questions answered and tell others about your trip at
www.roughguides.atinfopop.com

Acknowledgements

Martin Dunford would like to thank Alice Park for her patience and attention to detail – and as ever Daisy and Caroline.

Phil Lee would like to thank his editor, Alice Park, for her patience, humour and thoroughness during the preparation of this new edition of the Netherlands. Special thanks also to Suzanne Kuijer of the Netherlands Board of Tourism; my co-authors, Martin Dunford and Suzanne Morton Taylor; and to the ever helpful Els Wamsteeker of the ATCB.

Suzanne Morton Taylor would like to thank Catharina Jansen of Fryslan Marketing, Mirjam Schuiling and Annemiek Woldring of Groningen Marketing and Ine Creemers of the Maastricht tourist board. Special thanks to my mother for lending me her car almost every weekend and my boyfriend for being an excellent driver and assistant.

Readers' letters

Thanks to all the readers who have taken the time to write in with comments and suggestions (and apologies if we've inadvertently omitted anyone's name):

Joachim Allgaier; Caroline Baurdoux; Maarten Bax; Christel de Boer; Diederik von Bonninghausen; Chris Booth; Bram Bos; Howard Bourne; Anna Broisma; Dick Butler; Sarah Clayton; Brian Clapp; Lyndsey Daley; Natalie Delorme; Julian Dorling; Francine van de Duin; Annette Eenkhoorn; Michael Farr; Eep Francken; Steve Graham; Francis Groves; Karin Grunewald; Lesley Hall; Annmarie Hanlon; Graham Heaney; Maartje Heerkens; Dominic Herrington; Frederik Hemmes; Dominic Herrington; Jeff Hobbs; Lynn Horton; Diana den Houdijker; Chris Jackson; Gerlag Jeroen; Peter de Koning; Suzanne Kuijker; Natali Lekka; Richard Lim; Riana Ligthart; Marit Lokhorst; Jonas Ludvigsson; Malijn Maat; Betty Anne McCall; Craig MacDonald; Caroline McElwee; Edward Mayor; Jenny McCubbin; Caroline McElwee; Lera Miles; Norman Miller; Alison Morley; John Morton; Bernadette and Michael Mossley; Boris de Munnick; Jay Nemes; Judith Orford; Jill Pearson; Bill Paton; Nick Reeves; Fiona Rempt; Lesa Rollo; Bobby Russell; Nigel Sandford; Toby Screech; Johanna Sleeswijk; K Tan; Matthew Teller; Anna Jim Vander Putten; Vidou; Clare Webster; Susan Webster; Christel van Weezep; Paul Weston; B. White; J Wood; Karen Woods; Alison Young; Liz Young.

SMALL PRINT

ROUGH GUIDES

Photo credits

All photography by Tim Draper and Mark Thomas © Rough Guides except the following:

Introduction
The Milkmaid by Jan Vermeer (1658–60)
  © Bridgman Art Library/Getty Images

Things not to miss
05 The Elfstedentocht © Mike King/Corbis
08 Anne Frank House © The Anne Frank House
18 Tulips in Keukenhof Gardens © George D. Lepp/Corbis
23 *Self portrait* by Vincent Van Gogh, 1889 © Gianni Dagli Orti/Corbis
24 Wadlopen © Reyer Boxem/Hollandse Hoogte

The Dutch Golden Age colour section
The Managers of the Haarlem Orphanage by Jan de Bray, 1663 © The Bridgeman Art Library
The Night Watch by Rembrandt van Rijn, 1642 © Archivo Iconografico, S.A./Corbis

The Mill at Wijk-bij-Duurstede by Jacob van Ruisdael © The Rijksmuseum, Amsterdam
Tulips: from "Verzameling van Bloemen naar deNatuur getekend" (Collection of flowers drawn from nature) c.1630; by Dutch School, (17th century); Lindley Library, RHS, London, UK © The Bridgeman Art Library

Black and whites
p.362 Engraving of William the Silent © Mary Evans Picture Library/Alamy
p.367 The famous Dutch bicycle regiment at attention, ready to speed toward the German frontier should danger from the Nazis threaten Queen Wilhelmina's kingdom © Corbis

SMALL PRINT

Index

Map entries are in colour.

Map symbols

maps are listed in the full index using coloured text

– – –	Chapter division boundary
▬ ▬ ▬	International boundary
— ··	Provincial boundary
══	Motorway
══	Main road
—	Minor road
- - - -	Tunnel
▬▬	Pedestrianized street
- - - - -	Footpath
▬▪▬	Railway
▨▨▨	River/canal
— —	Ferry route
) (	Bridge
✦	Point of interest
♟	Museum
⊙	Statue
⍓	Gardens
▪ ▪ ▪	Wall
⚠	Campsite
△	Hostel
✈	Airport
Ⓜ	Metro station
✡	Synagogue
♱	Cemetery
⊠	Post office
ⓘ	Tourist information (VVV)
⊞	Hospital
⊠	Gate
▮	Building
→|	Church
▦	Park
▦	Beach/dune